ISAIAH 1–39

VOLUME 19

THE ANCHOR BIBLE is a fresh approach to the world's greatest classic. Its object is to make the Bible accessible to the modern reader; its method is to arrive at the meaning of biblical literature through exact translation and extended exposition, and to reconstruct the ancient setting of the biblical story, as well as the circumstances of its transcription and the characteristics of its transcribers.

THE ANCHOR BIBLE is a project of international and interfaith scope: Protestant, Catholic, and Jewish scholars from many countries contribute individual volumes. The project is not sponsored by any ecclesiastical organization and is not intended to reflect any particular theological doctrine. Prepared under our joint supervision, THE ANCHOR BIBLE is an effort to make available all the significant historical and linguistic knowledge which bears on the interpretation of the biblical record.

THE ANCHOR BIBLE is aimed at the general reader with no special formal training in biblical studies; yet it is written with the most exacting standards of scholarship, reflecting the highest technical accomplishment.

This project marks the beginning of a new era of cooperation among scholars in biblical research, thus forming a common body of knowledge to be shared by all.

William Foxwell Albright
David Noel Freedman
GENERAL EDITORS

THE ANCHOR BIBLE

ISAIAH 1–39

◆

A New Translation
with Introduction and Commentary

JOSEPH BLENKINSOPP

THE ANCHOR BIBLE
Doubleday
New York   London   Toronto   Sydney   Auckland

THE ANCHOR BIBLE
PUBLISHED BY DOUBLEDAY
a division of Random House, Inc.
1540 Broadway, New York, New York 10036

THE ANCHOR BIBLE DOUBLEDAY, and the portrayal of an
anchor with the letters A and B are trademarks of
Doubleday, a division of Random House, Inc.

Library of Congress Cataloging-in-Publication Data

Bible. O.T. Isaiah I–XXXIX. English. Blenkinsopp. 2000.
    Isaiah 1–39: a new translation with introduction and commentary /
By Joseph Blenkinsopp. — 1st ed.
        p. cm. — (The Anchor Bible; vol. 19)
    Includes bibliographical references and indexes.
    ISBN 0-385-49716-4 (v. 1 : alk. paper)
      1. Bible. O.T. Isaiah I–XXXIX—Commentaries. I. Title: Isaiah one-
thirty-nine. II. Blenkinsopp, Joseph, 1927– III. Title. IV. Bible. English.
Anchor Bible. 1964; v. 19.

    BS192.2.A1 1964 .G3
    [BS1515.3]
    224′. 1077—dc21

                                                    00–021326
                                                    CIP

First Edition

10 9 8 7 6 5 4 3 2 1

for Jean
with gratitude

CONTENTS

◆

PREFACE

◆

In his annotated edition of the Authorised Version of Isaiah, published in 1883, Matthew Arnold lamented that "the apparatus to Isaiah is so immense that the student who has to handle it is in danger of not living long enough to come ever to enjoy the performance of Isaiah himself" (Matthew Arnold, *Isaiah of Jerusalem in the Authorised English Version with an Introduction, Corrections and Notes* [London: Macmillan, 1883], 10). His lament echoed that of Jerome, who found writing a commentary on the same book "a great and wearisome undertaking . . . one which has challenged the skill and stamina of our predecessors" (*PL* 24.18– 21). One of these predecessors, the great biblical scholar Origen, nevertheless produced a commentary on the entire book in thirty volumes, a work no longer extant. While there is no question of attempting to emulate Origen, I can sympathize with Jerome's complaint. In the course of working on this commentary on Isaiah, I have learned to appreciate how easy it is to lose sight of the forest for the textual, linguistic, and exegetical trees, thickly overgrown as they are with hapax legomena, scribal emendations, and various other inconcinnities.

In writing this first of three volumes of the commentary, I have made my way through the forest as circumspectly as I could without attempting to be encyclopedic, a goal in any case impossible of attainment. The bibliographies are extensive but by no means comprehensive and are confined for the most part to works in English, German, and French published during the last century. The time is perhaps ripe for a comprehensive, annotated bibliography of Isaiah studies, as a prelude to a history of the interpretation of the book, but such a history would best be done by a team of scholars and might well eventuate in the publication of almost as many volumes as Origen's commentary. In the introduction I have had to limit myself to the earliest stages in the interpretation of the book and have consulted the classic commentaries (Jerome, Ibn Ezra, Calvin, and others) where it seemed appropriate to do so; but I am aware, as *a fortiori* the reader will be, that this has left many gaps unfilled and many names unmentioned. Constraints of space and time have also obliged me to reduce the textual notes to what I hope will be an acceptable minimum. It is fortunate that they can now be supplemented by consulting the first volume in the Hebrew University Bible Project, edited by the late Prof. Goshen-Gottstein. All this is to say that a commentary of this kind has to mediate between the expectations of colleagues in biblical studies, especially the growing number drawn to the study of Isaiah in recent years, and the expectations of educated but nonspecialist readers whom the General Editors of the Anchor Bible had in view in inaugurating the series some forty years ago.

In view of current widespread unease with the conventional tripartite division of the book, the decision to extend the first volume of the commentary to ch. 39 will inevitably raise questions. Breaking off after ch. 33, the mid-point according to chapters just as 33:20 is the Masoretic mid-point according to verses, might have been convenient in practical terms, but I see no justification for doing so in terms of the structure of the book. The commentary will present arguments for the view that chs. 34–35 belong together as an apt conclusion to the many sayings about judgment and forgiveness in the preceding chapters and are not an integral part of chs. 40–55. The contrary opinion was defended by C. C. Torrey (1928, 53, 279), and his arguments, or at least his conclusions, have been repeated many times since his book appeared. Furthermore, we cannot simply ignore the place and function in the book of chs. 36–39, which are integral to the 35 chapters preceding and have nothing in common with those following, though thematically connected to them by the prediction of exile in 39:5–7. The three-line gap in 1QIsa^a between chs. 33 and 34 has been cited in support of a composition with two equal and thematically related parts (e.g. by Brownlee 1964, 247–59), but it may simply be the case that the two scribes who shared the work of transcription agreed to do half each.

A word of thanks is due to the University of Notre Dame for granting me a leave of absence during the academic year 1997–1998, to my colleague Gene Ulrich, who kindly put the unpublished Isaiah fragments at my disposal, to my gifted assistant Angela Kim, who helped with research and solved many problems with a recalcitrant computer, to colleagues in the Faculty of Divinity at the University of Oxford and the members of the Old Testament Seminar for their hospitality, and to the staff of the library at Via Pilotta 48, Rome, for their gracious assistance during my time there as a Visiting Professor in 1998. I must also express my appreciation for the many conversations about Isaian matters with friends and colleagues in the Society for Old Testament Studies (United Kingdom). My thanks also go to the staff at Doubleday, especially to Dr. Mark Fretz and Prof. David Noel Freedman who encouraged me to go ahead with the commentary. Professor Freedman's editorial skills and his attention to detail need no advertising, and I have profited by his comments even when unable to agree with them. Finally, I wish to thank my wife, Jean, to whom the commentary is dedicated, for her love, support, and stimulating conversation.

LIST OF TABLES

◆

LIST OF ABBREVIATIONS

◆

AASOR — *Annual of the American Schools of Oriental Research*

AB — Anchor Bible

ABD — *Anchor Bible Dictionary.* Edited by D. N. Freedman. 6 vols. New York: Doubleday, 1992

'Abod. Zar. — *'Abodah Zarah* (a tractate of the Talmud)

Ag.Ap. — *Against Apion.* Josephus

AJSL — *Americal Journal of Semitic Languages and Literature*

AJT — *American Journal of Theology*

Akk. — Akkadian

ANEP — *The Ancient Near East in Pictures.* Edited by J. B. Pritchard. Princeton: Princeton University Press, 1954

ANET — *Ancient Near Eastern Texts Relating to the Old Testament.* Edited by J. B. Pritchard. 2d ed. Princeton: Princeton University Press, 1955

Ant. — *Jewish Antiquities.* Josephus

AcOr — *Acta Orientalia*

Arab. — Arabic

ARAB — *Ancient Records of Assyria and Babylonia.* Edited by D. D. Luckenbill. 2 vols. Chicago: University of Chicago Press, 1926–1927

Aram. — Aramaic

ArOr — *Archiv Orientální*

ARW — Archiv für Religionswissenschaft

ASTI — *Annual of the Swedish Theological Institute*

ATD — Das Alte Testament Deutsch

ATR — *Anglican Theological Review*

AUSS — *Andrews University Seminary Studies*

b. — Babylonian Talmud

BA — *Biblical Archaeologist*

BAR — *Biblical Archaeology Review*

BASOR — *Bulletin of the American Schools of Oriental Research*

BAT — Die Botschaft des Alten Testaments

B.Bat. — *Baba Batra* (The Last Gate)

BDB — Brown, F., S. R. Driver, and C. A. Briggs. *A Hebrew and English Lexicon of the Old Testament.* Oxford: Oxford University Press, 1907

BHK — *Biblia Hebraica.* Edited by R. Kittel. Stuttgart: 1905–1906

BHS — *Biblia Hebraica Stuttgartensia.* Edited by K. Elliger and

	W. Rudolph. Stuttgart: Deutsche Bibelgesellschaft, 1983.
Bib	*Biblica*
BIOSCS	*Bulletin of the International Organization for Septuagint and Cognate Studies*
BJRL	*Bulletin of the John Rylands University Library*
BKAT	Biblischer Kommentar: Altes Testament
BN	*Biblische Notizen*
BO	*Bibbia e Oriente*
BR	*Biblical Research*
BSac	*Bibliotheca Sacra*
BT	*The Bible Translator*
BTB	*Biblical Theology Bulletin*
BWANT	Beiträge zur Wissenschaft vom Alten und Neuen Testament
BZ	*Biblische Zeitschrift*
BZAW	Beihefte zur Zeitschrift für die alttestamentliche Wissenschaft
CAD	*The Assyrian Dictionary of the Oriental Institute of the University of Chicago.* Edited by I. J. Gelb et al. Chicago: Oriental Institute, 1956–
CAH	Cambridge Ancient History. Edited by I. E. S. Edwards et al.
CB	The Cambridge Bible
CBQ	*Catholic Biblical Quarterly*
CTA	*Corpus des tablettes en cunéiformes alphabétiques découvertes à Ras Shamra–Ugarit de 1929 à 1939.* Edited by A. Herdner. Mission de Ras Shamra 10. Paris, 1963
CTR	*Criswell Theological Review*
DBSup	*Dictionnaire de la Bible: Supplément.* Edited by L. Pirot and A. Robert. Paris, 1928–
DCH	*Dictionary of Classical Hebrew.* Edited by D. J. A. Clines. Sheffield: Sheffield Academic Press, 1993–
DJD	Discoveries in the Judaean Desert
ʿEd.	ʿEduyyot (Testimonies)
En.	Enoch
EncJud	*Encyclopaedia Judaica.* 16 vols. Jerusalem: Keter, 1972
EstBib	*Estudios bíblicos*
Eth.	Ethiopic
ETL	*Ephemerides Theologicae Lovanienses*
ETR	*Études théologiques et religieuses*
EvQ	*Evangelical Quarterly*
EvT	*Evangelische Theologie*
ExpTim	*Expository Times*
Esd	Esdras
FO	*Folia Orientalia*
FRLANT	Forschungen zur Religion und Literatur des Alten und Neuen Testaments
Gen. Rab.	*Genesis Rabbah*
GKC	*Gesenius' Hebrew Grammar.* Edited by. E. Kautzsch. Translated by A. E. Cowley. 2d ed. Oxford: Oxford University Press, 1910
HAR	*Hebrew Annual Review*
HAT	Handbuch zum Alten Testament
HeyJ	*Heythrop Journal*

HKAT	Handkommentar zum Alten Testament	JSS	*Journal of Semitic Studies*
HS	*Hebrew Studies*	JTS	*Journal of Theological Studies*
HTR	*Harvard Theological Review*	Jub.	*Jubilees*
HUCA	*Hebrew Union College Annual*	J.W.	*Jewish War.* Josephus
IB	*Interpreter's Bible*	KAT	Kommentar zum Alten Testament
ICC	International Critical Commentary	KHC	Kurzer Hand-Commentar zum Alten Testament
IDB	*Interpreter's Dictionary of the Bible.* Edited by G. A. Buttrick. 4 vols. Nashville: Abingdon, 1962	Lev. Rab.	*Leviticus Rabba*
		LXX	The Septuagint
		m.	Mishnah
		MH	Mishnaic Hebrew
IDBSup	*Interpreter's Dictionary of the Bible: Supplementary Volume.* Edited by K. Crim. Nashville: Abingdon, 1962.	MT	Masoretic Text
		Meg.	*Megillah* (the Esther Scroll)
		Menaḥ.	*Menaḥot* (tractate of the Talmud)
IEJ	*Israel Exploration Journal*	MS(S)	Manuscript(s)
		Mus	*Muséon*
Int	*Interpretation*	NAB	New American Bible
JAOS	*Journal of the American Oriental Society*	NCB	New Century Bible
		NEB	New English Bible
JBL	*Journal of Biblical Literature*	NICOT	New International Commentary on the Old Testament
JCS	*Journal of Cuneiform Studies*	NRSV	New Revised Standard Version
JETS	*Journal of the Evangelical Theological Society*	NRTh	*Nouvelle revue théologique*
		NT	New Testament
JJS	*Journal of Jewish Studies*	NTT	*Norsk Teologisk Tidsskrift*
JNES	*Journal of Near Eastern Studies*	OBO	Orbis Biblicus et Orientalis
JNSL	*Journal of Northwest Semitic Languages*	OG	Old Greek Version
		Or	*Orientalia*
JPOS	*Journal of the Palestine Oriental Society*	OTE	*Old Testament Essays*
		OTL	Old Testament Library
JQR	*Jewish Quarterly Review*	OtSt	*Oudtestamentische Studiën*
JSOT	*Journal for the Study of the Old Testament*		
		OTWSA	*Ou-Testamentiese Werkgemeenskap van Suid-Afrika*
JSOTSup	Journal for the Study of the Old Testament: Supplement Series		
		PEQ	*Palestine Exploration Quarterly*

PIBA	Proceedings of the Irish Biblical Association	TBT	The Bible Today
PL	Patrologia Latina. Edited by J. P. Migne. 217 vols. Paris, 1844–64.	TDOT	Theological Dictionary of the Old Testament. Edited by G. J. Botterweck and H. Ringgren. Translated by J. T. Willis, G. W. Bromiley, and D. E. Green. Grand Rapids: Eerdmans, 1974–
PRSt	Perspectives in Religious Studies		
Qere Or	Qere Orientale		
RB	Revue biblique		
RevQ	Revue de Qumran	Tg.	Targum
RHPR	Revue d'histoire et de philosophie religieuses	THAT	Theologisches Handwörterbuch zum Alten Testament. Edited by E. Jenni and C. Westermann. 2 vols. Munich: Chr. Kaiser Verlag, 1971–1976
RHR	Revue de l'histoire des religions		
RivB	Rivista biblica		
RSR	Recherche de science religieuse		
RSV	Revised Standard Version	Theod.	Theodotion
RTL	Revue théologique de Louvain	TLZ	Theologische Literaturzeitung
RTP	Revue de théologie et de philosophie	TRu	Theologische Rundschau
Sanh.	Sanhedrin (tractate of Babylonian Talmud)	TS	Theological Studies
		TTZ	Trierer theologische Zeitschrift
SB	Sources bibliques	TynBul	Tyndale Bulletin
SBLSP	Society of Biblical Literature Seminar Papers	TZ	Theologische Zeitschrift
		UF	Ugarit-Forschungen
		Ug.	Ugaritic
SBS	Stuttgarter Bibelstudien	VD	Verbum Domini
SBT	Studies in Biblical Theology	VT	Vetus Testamentum
		VTSup	Vetus Testamentum Supplements
Scr	Scripture		
SEÅ	Svensk exegetisk årsbok	Vulg.	Editio Vulgata
Sir	Ben Sira	WBC	Word Biblical Commentary
SJOT	Scandinavian Journal of the Old Testament	WC	Westminster Commentary
SJT	Scottish Journal of Theology	WMANT	Wissenschaftliche Monographien zum Alten und Neuen Testament
ST	Studia Theologica		
Symm.	Symmachus		
Syr.	Vetus Testamentum Syriace (The Peshitta Version)	WO	Welt des Orients
		WTJ	Westminster Theological Journal
Šabb.	Šabbat (a tractate of the Talmud)	Yebam.	Yebamot (tractate of Babylonian Talmud)
TB	Theologische Bücherei		

ZAW	*Zeitschrift für die alttes-tamentliche Wissen-schaft*	ZKT	*Zeitschrift für katholische Theologie*
ZDMG	*Zeitschrift der deutschen morgenländischen Gesellschaft*	ZRGG	*Zeitschrift für Reli-gions- und Geistes-geschichte*
ZDPV	*Zeitschrift des deutschen Palästina-Vereins*	ZTK	*Zeitschrift für Theologie und Kirche*

ISAIAH 1–39
A TRANSLATION

◆

TITLE (1:1)

1 ¹The vision of Isaiah ben Amoz which he saw concerning Judah and Jerusalem in the days of Uzziah, Jotham, Ahaz and Hezekiah, kings of Judah.

THE GREAT ARRAIGNMENT (1:2–31)

i

1 ²Hear, heaven, earth, give heed,
for Yahveh speaks!
"Children I have raised and reared,
but they have rebelled against me.
³An ox will recognize its owner,
a donkey its master's stall;
Israel has no such knowledge,
my people no comprehension."

ii

⁴Woe, sinful nation,
people burdened with crime,
wicked offspring,
depraved children!
They have abandoned Yahveh,
despising the Holy One of Israel.
[They have fallen away.]

iii

⁵Why be forever beaten,
rebelling time out of mind?
The whole head is sick,
the whole heart faint.
⁶From the sole of the foot to the head
there is no soundness in him—
bruises, sores, and open wounds,
not drained, not bandaged, not treated with oil.

iv

⁷Your land is a desolation,
your cities burned to the ground;
before your very eyes
foreigners devour your land.
[A desolation as if overthrown by foreigners]

[8]Daughter Zion is left
like a lean-to in a vineyard,
like a shack in a cucumber patch,
like a city besieged.
[9]Had not Yahveh of the hosts
left us a few survivors,
we would have shared Sodom's fate,
resembled Gomorrah.

v

[10]Hear the word of Yahveh,
you rulers of Sodom!
Give heed to the teaching of our God,
you people of Gomorrah!
[11]"What are your many sacrifices to me?"
[It is Yahveh who speaks]
"I have had enough of burnt offerings of rams,
and the suet of fatted animals;
I take no pleasure in the blood of bulls,
or of lambs and goats.
[12]When you come to appear in my presence,
who is asking this of you,
this trampling of my precincts?
[13]Bring no more useless offerings,
incense disgusts me.
New moon, sabbath, holy convocation—
I cannot stand wickedness combined with solemn assembly.
[14]I hate your new moons and festivals,
they have become a burden to me,
I am tired of putting up with them.
[15]When you stretch out your hands in prayer
I will hide my eyes from you;
even though you keep on praying,
I will not be listening;
you have blood all over your hands.
[16]Wash yourselves, make yourselves clean;
remove the evil you are doing from my sight;
stop doing evil,
[17]learn to do good;
seek after justice, rescue the oppressed;
defend the rights of the orphan,
plead the widow's cause."

vi

18 "Come now, let us reason together,"
[It is Yahveh who speaks.]
"If your sins are colored scarlet,
can they become white like snow?
If dyed crimson red,
can they become like pure wool?
19 If you are willing to obey,
you shall feed off the goodness of the land;
20 but if you refuse and rebel,
you shall be consumed by the sword."
The mouth of Yahveh has spoken.

vii

21 See how the town once loyal
has become like a whore!
Once she was full of justice,
righteousness lodged in her
[but now assassins].
22 Your silver has turned into slag,
your beer is watered down;
23 your princes are rebels,
associates of thieves;
each one of them loves a bribe,
runs after gifts.
They do not defend the orphan,
the widow's cause does not reach them.
24 "Therefore"—oracle of Yahveh, Lord of hosts,
Strong One of Israel:
"I will assuage my anger on my foes,
I will be avenged on my enemies;
25 I will turn my hand against you,
burn off your dregs in the furnace,
removing all your dross.
26 I will restore your judges as of yore,
your counselors as at the beginning;
then your name will be City of Righteousness,
Loyal Town."

viii

27 Zion will be saved in the judgment,
her penitents in the retribution,
28 but rebels and sinners will be destroyed together,
those forsaking Yahveh will be consumed.

²⁹You will feel shame for the terebinths
in which you took delight,
you will blush for the gardens
that you chose for yourselves;
³⁰you will be like a terebinth
whose foliage is withered,
or like a garden
without any water.
³¹The strong will become like tow,
and his deeds like a spark;
both will be burned together,
with no one to put out the fire.

TITLE (2:1)

2 ¹The word that Isaiah ben Amoz saw in vision concerning Judah and Jerusalem.

THE PILGRIMAGE OF THE NATIONS TO ZION (2:2–5)

2 ²It will come to pass in days to come
that the mountain, Yahveh's house, shall be established
at the top of the mountains,
raised high over the hills.
Then all nations shall stream towards it,
³many peoples shall come and say,
"Up, let us go to Yahveh's mountain,
to the house of Jacob's God,
that he may instruct us in his ways
that we may walk in his paths."
For from Zion instruction will proceed,
the word of Yahveh from Jerusalem.
⁴He will adjudicate among nations,
arbitrate for many peoples.
They shall beat their swords into plowshares,
their spears into pruning hooks.
No nation shall take up the sword against another,
no more shall they learn to make war.
⁵O household of Jacob, come, let us walk in the light of Yahveh!

THE FINAL JUDGMENT (2:6–22)

2 ⁶For you have rejected your people,
the household of Jacob,
for they are full (of sorcerers) from the east
and soothsayers like the Philistines.
They teem with the children of foreigners.
⁷Their land is full of silver and gold,
and there is no end to their treasures;
their land is full of horses,
and there is no end to their chariots;
⁸their land is full of idols,
(and there is no end to their idolatry).
To the work of their hands they bow down,
to that which their fingers have made.

⁹*Humanity is humbled, all people are brought low;*
Do not forgive them!
¹⁰Go into the rock,
hide in the dusty earth
from the terror of Yahveh,
from the splendor of his majesty!

¹¹The proud regard of humanity is brought low,
the pride of all people shall be humbled,
and Yahveh alone shall be exalted
on that day.

¹²For Yahveh of the hosts has a day
against all that is haughty and high,
all that is lifted up and lofty,
¹³against all the cedars of Lebanon [high and lofty],
all the oaks of Bashan,
¹⁴against all the high mountains,
all the lofty hills,
¹⁵against every high tower,
every impregnable wall,
¹⁶against all the Tarshish ships,
all the splendid vessels.
¹⁷The pride of humanity will be humbled,
the haughtiness of the people will be brought low,
and Yahveh alone shall be exalted
on that day.
¹⁸[The idols will utterly pass away.]

¹⁹They will go into caves in the rock,
into caverns in the dusty earth,
from the terror of Yahveh,
from the splendor of his majesty,
when he begins to strike fear on the earth.
²⁰*On that day people will throw out their silver and gold idols that they made as their own objects of worship to the shrews and the bats.*
²¹To go into the crevices of the rocks,
the clefts of the cliffs,
from the terror of Yahveh,
from the splendor of his majesty,
when he begins to strike fear on the earth.
²²*Leave the rest of humanity alone; doomed to perish as they are, of what value are they?*

SOCIAL AND MORAL CHAOS (3:1–15)

3 ¹For now the sovereign Lord of hosts
will remove from Jerusalem and Judah
every kind of support,
all supply of food,
all supply of water;
²mercenary and warrior,
magistrate and prophet,
diviner and elder,
³captain of fifty,
nobleman and counselor,
skilled magician and expert in charms.
⁴"I will make striplings their princes;
infants will rule over them.
⁵The people will oppress one another,
each one his fellow;
the young will be insolent to the old,
the one of mean estate to the honorable."

⁶If a man were to grab hold of his kinsman in his paternal household and say to him, "You are the one with the cloak, so you shall be our leader, you must take control of this heap of ruins," ⁷he would answer on that day, "I will not be in charge; there is neither food nor clothing in my house; you shall not appoint me leader of the people." ⁸Ah, Jerusalem has stumbled,
Judah has fallen
for in word and in deed they oppose Yahveh,
defying his majestic presence.

⁹Their very looks testify against them,
they vaunt their sin openly like Sodom,
they do not conceal it.
Woe to them!
They have brought evil on themselves.
¹⁰A blessing on the righteous, for it will go well with them,
they will eat the fruit of their labors;
¹¹A woe on the wicked, it will go badly with them,
what they have done will be done to them.
¹²As for my people, their oppressors plunder them,
usurers lord it over them;
O my people, your leaders mislead you,
confusing the course you should take.

¹³Yahveh takes his stand to argue his case;
he rises to judge the peoples;
¹⁴Yahveh enters into judgment
with the elders of his people and their princes:
"It is you who have ravaged the vineyard,
the plunder of the poor is in your houses.
¹⁵How dare you crush my people,
and stamp on the face of the poor?"
—An oracle of the sovereign Lord of hosts.

THE FATE OF THE COURT LADIES (3:16–4:1)

3 ¹⁶Yahveh declares:
"Because the daughters of Zion have become so proud,
going around with necks thrust out,
and with ogling eyes,
walking with mincing gait,
making a tinkling noise with their feet . . ."
¹⁷The Sovereign Lord will uncover the heads of the daughters of Zion,
he will lay bare their private parts . . .
¹⁸On that day Yahveh will remove the finery of anklets, headbands and crescents; ¹⁹earrings, bracelets and veils; ²⁰head-dresses, armlets, sashes, talismans and amulets; ²¹ (Yahveh will remove) signet rings and nose rings; ²²gowns, wraps, shawls and handbags; ²³mirrors, linen garments, head scarves and capes.
²⁴Then, instead of perfume there shall be rot,
instead of a sash, a rope,
a shaved head instead of hair well groomed,
a loincloth of burlap instead of expensive robes,
yes, shame where beauty once was.

²⁵Zion's men shall fall by the sword,
her warrior class in battle;
²⁶her gates shall lament and mourn,
ravaged, she shall sit on the ground.

4   ¹Seven women will grab hold of one man on that day. They will say, "We will eat our own food and wear our own clothing; just let us take your name; please take away our shame."

AFTER JUDGMENT,
PEACE AND SECURITY (4:2–6)

4   ²On that day, the shoot that Yahveh has planted will be an object of magnificence and glory, and the fruit of the land an object of pride and splendor for the survivors of Israel.
   ³Those who are left in Zion and who remain in Jerusalem will be called holy, all those who are recorded for life in Jerusalem.
   ⁴Once the sovereign Lord has washed away the filth of the daughters of Zion and cleansed the bloodstains from Jerusalem with a fiery wind in the judgment, ⁵Yahveh will create over the entire site of Mount Zion and over its liturgical assemblies a cloud by day and smoke together with a brightly burning fire by night. Yes, over all the glorious scene there will be a canopy, ⁶and a booth will serve as a shade from the heat by day, and a shelter and refuge from the rainstorm.

THE VINEYARD SONG (5:1–7)

5   ¹Let me sing for my friend
my love song about his vineyard.
My friend had a vineyard
on a hillside rich in soil;
²he dug it up, cleared it of stones,
and planted it with choicest vines;
he built a watchtower inside it,
hewed out a wine vat in it;
then he looked for it to yield good grapes
but the grapes it produced were rotten.
³So now, you who live in Jerusalem,
and you, people of Judah:
judge between me and my vineyard!
⁴What more could be done for my vineyard
that I have failed to do?

Why did I look for it to yield good grapes,
when the grapes it produced were rotten?

5So now, I give you notice
as to what I will do with my vineyard:
deprived of its hedge, it will be open for grazing,
its fence breached and broken, it will be trampled down;
6I will turn it into a wasteland,
it will be neither pruned nor hoed,
thorns and weeds will spring up,
I will give command to the clouds
to send down no rain upon it.

7For the vineyard of Yahveh of hosts
is the house of Israel,
and the people of Judah
the plantation in which he delighted.
He looked for justice,
and instead there was bloodshed,
for righteousness,
and instead a cry of distress.

A SERIES OF WOES (10:1–4; 5:8–24)

i

10   1Woe to those who issue wicked decrees,
who draft oppressive regulations,
2to turn away the needy from judgment,
to rob of their rights the poor of my people,
that widows may be their prey,
that they may plunder the fatherless.
3What will you do on the day of punishment,
in the disaster that comes from afar?
To whom will you flee for help?
Where will you leave your belongings?
4Nothing to do but cower among the prisoners,
down among those already killed. . . .
Yet his anger did not abate,
still is his hand stretched out.

ii

5   8Woe to those who add house to house,
who join one plot of land to another,
until there is no space left
for any but you to be settled on the land!

⁹Yahveh of the hosts has sworn in my hearing:
"many houses will be turned into ruins,
houses splendid and spacious left without occupants;
¹⁰a vineyard of ten hectares will yield but one barrel of wine,
a homer of seed will produce but one bushel.

iii

¹¹Woe to them who rise early in the morning
in pursuit of strong drink,
who stay up late in the evening
that wine may inflame them;
¹²Lyre and harp, timbrel and flute,
and wine are not lacking at their feasts.
They pay no heed to the work of Yahveh,
they regard not the operation of his hands.
¹³Therefore:
bereft of understanding, my people is exiled,
their nobles are famished,
their commoners parched with thirst.
¹⁴Therefore:
Sheol stretches wide its gullet,
its mouth opens wide beyond measure,
down go her nobles and commoners,
her throng in the midst of their revels.
¹⁵*Humanity is humbled, all people are brought low,*
the haughty looks are humbled,
¹⁶*Yahveh of the hosts shall be exalted in the judgment,*
in the vindication the Holy God will reveal himself as holy.
¹⁷Lambs will graze in their pasture,
sheep will feed among the ruins.

iv

¹⁸Woe to those who drag along iniquity like a sheep with cords,
and sin like a heifer with ropes!
¹⁹Who are saying, "Let Yahveh make haste,
let him speed his work that we may see it,
let the plan of Israel's Holy One soon come to pass
that we may acknowledge it!

v

²⁰Woe to those who call evil good
and good evil,
who put darkness in the place of light,
light in the place of darkness,
who make the bitter sweet and the sweet bitter!

vi

²¹Woe to those who are wise in their own eyes,
shrewd in their own understanding!

vii

²²Woe to those heroic guzzlers of wine,
those redoubtable mixers of strong drink!
²³who acquit the guilty on payment of a bribe,
while depriving the innocent of their rights.
Therefore:
²⁴As the tongue of fire consumes the stubble,
and chaff shrivels up in the flame,
their root will be all rottenness,
their flower disappear like dust;
for they have rejected the instruction of Yahveh of the hosts
and despised the word of Israel's Holy God.

A POEM ABOUT THE ANGRY GOD
(9:7–20 [9:8–21] + 5:25)

i

9 ⁷The Lord sent a message against Jacob,
and it will fall on Israel;
⁸the entire people will experience it
—Ephraim and the people of Samaria.
In pride and highmindedness they said,
⁹"so the bricks have collapsed,
we will rebuild with dressed stone;
so the sycamores have been cut down,
we will replace them with cedars."
¹⁰But Yahveh supported their adversaries,
and incited their enemies against them:
¹¹Arameans from the east, Philistines from their rear,
they devoured Israel with mouth open wide.
Yet his anger did not abate,
still was his hand outstretched.

ii

¹²The people did not return to the one who struck them,
they did not seek out Yahveh of the hosts,
¹³so Yahveh cut off from Israel both head and tail.
¹⁴[Elder and dignitary are the head;
the prophet, the teacher of falsehood, the tail.]

[15] Those who led the people led them astray,
those who were led were left in disarray,
[16] so the Sovereign Lord had no mercy on their youths,
no compassion on their orphans and widows,
for they are all ungodly and wicked,
every mouth utters impiety.
Yet his anger did not abate,
still was his hand outstretched.

iii

[17] Wickedness burns like a fire,
consuming thorns and weeds,
it has kindled the thickets of the forest,
they go up in the swirling smoke.
[18] Through the fury of Yahveh of the hosts
the land is shaken,
the people are fuel for the fire.
No one spares a companion,
all eat the flesh of their children.
[19] Here one gorges and is still famished,
there one devours and is not sated.
[20] Manasseh devours Ephraim and Ephraim Manasseh,
and both of them together against Judah.
Yet his anger did not abate,
still was his hand outstretched.

iv

5   [25] So the anger of Yahveh was roused against his people;
he stretched out his hand against them and struck them down.
The mountains quaked, their corpses lay like refuse in the streets.
Yet his anger did not abate,
still was his hand outstretched.

ASSYRIA IS SUMMONED
TO THE ATTACK (5:26–30)

5   [26] He will raise an ensign for a nation from afar,
and whistle for it from the ends of the earth.
Swiftly, speedily, it comes!
[27] None among them grows weary, none of them stumbles,
they neither drowse nor sleep;
no belt is unloosed round the waist,
no sandal laces untied;

²⁸their arrows are sharpened,
all their bows are strung and taut;
the hooves of their horses are reckoned like flint,
their chariot wheels like the whirlwind;
²⁹their roaring is like a lion,
they roar like lion cubs;
snarling, they seize their prey;
when they carry it off, none can rescue it.
³⁰*He will growl over it on that day like the growling of the sea,*
If one looks to the earth there is only darkness and distress,
the light is obscured by the clouds.

THE THRONE ROOM VISION (6:1–13)

6   ¹In the year King Uzziah died I saw the Sovereign Lord seated on a throne raised up on high, with his train filling the palace. ²Seraphs were stationed round about him, each with six wings. With two they covered their faces, with two their bodies, and with two they hovered. ³Each cried out to the other saying, "Holy, holy, holy is Yahveh of the heavenly hosts; all the earth is full of his glory." ⁴As each cried out the uprights attached to the threshhold shook and the house began to fill with smoke. ⁵"Alas, I am lost," I cried, "for I am a man of unclean lips living among a people with unclean lips. My eyes have looked on the king, Yahveh of the hosts!" ⁶One of the seraphs flew to me with a hot coal in his hand he had taken from the altar with a pair of tongs. ⁷ He touched me on the mouth with it, saying, "Now this has touched your lips your iniquity has been removed, your sin purged away."

⁸I then heard the voice of the Sovereign Lord saying, "Whom shall I send, and who will go for us?" I replied, "Here I am, send me!" ⁹"Go then to this people," he said, "and say to them, 'Keep on hearing without understanding, keep on seeing without perceiving.' ¹⁰Make this people dull of perception, hard of hearing, sight impaired, lest they see with their eyes, hear with their ears, and grasp with their mind, and then change their ways and be healed." ¹¹Then I asked, "How long, O Lord?" He replied, "Until cities lie deserted without inhabitants, houses without occupants, and the land left a desolation." ¹²[Yahveh will carry off the people to a distant place, and desolation will be great in the land.] ¹³If but a tenth of the land is left it will revert to pasture. It will be like the oak and the terebinth which, when felled, have only a stump left. [Its stump is the holy seed.]

ISAIAH'S FIRST INTERVENTION IN JUDEAN POLITICS (734 B.C.E.) (7:1–17)

7 ¹In the days of Ahaz son of Jotham son of Uzziah, king of Judah, Rezin, king of Syria, and Pekah son of Remaliah, king of Israel, went up to fight against Jerusalem but were unable to win a decisive victory against it. ²When the house of David was told that Syria had prevailed on Ephraim to join them, its resolve, and the resolve of its people, was shaken as the trees of the forest shake in the wind. ³Then Yahveh said to Isaiah: "Go out to meet Ahaz together with Shear-yashub your son at the end of the conduit of the Upper Pool on the way to Bleacher's Meadow. ⁴Say to him, 'See that you remain calm; don't be afraid or fainthearted on account of these two stumps of smoldering firebrands and the fury of Rezin, Syria, and the son of Remaliah. ⁵Together with Ephraim and the son of Remaliah, Syria has planned to do you harm. ⁶"Let us invade Judah," they are saying, "and terrify it; let us conquer it for ourselves. We will then put the son of Tabeel on the throne of Judah."'"

⁷Thus says the Lord Yahveh:
"It shall not hold up, it shall not continue to be
⁸that Damascus is the head of Syria,
and Rezin the head of Damascus;
⁹that Samaria is the head of Ephraim,
and the son of Remaliah the head of Samaria.
[In sixty-five years' time Ephraim will be broken to pieces and will no
     longer be a nation.]
If you do not hold fast in faith
you will surely fail to stand firm."

¹⁰Yahveh spoke once again to Ahaz: ¹¹"Ask for a sign from Yahveh your God, from as deep as Sheol or as high as the sky," ¹²but Ahaz replied, "I will not put Yahveh to the test by asking for a sign." ¹³Then Isaiah said, "Listen, you house of David: not content with testing the patience of people, will you also test the patience of my God? ¹⁴Wherefore, the Lord God himself will give you a sign: See, the young woman is pregnant and about to give birth to a son; she will give him the name Immanuel. ¹⁵By the time he knows how to reject what is bad and choose what is good he will be feeding on buttermilk and honey. ¹⁶For before the child knows how to reject what is bad and choose what is good, the land whose two kings now fill you with fear will be deserted. ¹⁷Yahveh will bring on you, your people, and your ancestral house a time such has not been witnessed since Ephraim broke away from Judah [namely, the king of Assyria]."

DISASTERS OF WAR: FOUR CAMEOS (7:18–25)

7 [18]On that day Yahveh will whistle for the flies along the edges of Egypt's streams and for the bees in the land of Assyria, [19]and they will all come and settle in the steep wadis and the clefts of the cliffs, on all the thornbushes and watering holes.

[20]On that day the Sovereign Lord will shave with a razor borrowed from the king of Assyria across the Euphrates the head and the pubic hair, and he will sweep away the beard as well.

[21]On that day a person will raise a young cow and a couple of sheep, [22]and they will give so much milk that the owner will feed on buttermilk; for everyone left in the land will feed on buttermilk and honey.

[23]On that day every place where there are a thousand vines worth a thousand shekels of silver will be turned into a place of thorns and weeds. [24]People will come there with bow and arrows, for the entire land will be turned into a place of thorns and weeds. [25]For fear of thorns and weeds you will not venture on to any of the hills that used to be worked with the hoe. There oxen will roam free and sheep and goats wander about.

THE CHILD WITH THE NAME OF ILL OMEN (8:1–4)

8 [1]Yahveh said to me, "take a large tablet; write on it with a common stylus 'belonging to Maher-shalal-hash-baz.'" [2]So I had it notarized by reliable witnesses, Uriah the priest and Zechariah son of Jeberechiah. [3]I then approached the prophetess; she became pregnant and gave birth to a son. "Call him Maher-shalal-hash-baz," Yahveh said to me, [4]"for before the child is able to say 'my father' or 'my mother', the wealth of Damascus and the spoil of Samaria will be brought into the presence of the king of Assyria."

JUDAH WILL BE SUBMERGED (8:5–10)

8 [5]Once again Yahveh addressed me, [6]"Since this people has rejected the waters of Shiloah that flow so softly, rejoicing with Rezin and the son of Remaliah, [7]therefore the Sovereign Lord is about to bring up against them the waters of the River, mighty and abundant [the king of Assyria in all his splendor]. It will crest over all its channels and overflow all its banks, [8]sweeping on into Judah in a flood, reaching up to the neck. Its branches will be spread far and wide, filling the breadth of your land, Immanuel.

⁹Acknowledge it, you peoples, and be dismayed,
Give heed, remote places of the earth,
Gird yourselves for war and be shattered!
Gird yourselves for war and be shattered!
¹⁰Propose a plan—it shall be thwarted,
devise a scheme—it shall not take place,
for God is with us.

ISAIAH AND HIS CO-CONSPIRATORS (8:11–15)

8 ¹¹For thus Yahveh addressed me, with his hand strong upon me, warning me against following the lead of this people.¹²"Do not call conspiracy whatever this people calls conspiracy," he said, "neither fear what they fear nor be terrified. ¹³But Yahveh of the hosts, with him you shall conspire, he shall be the one you fear and hold in dread. ¹⁴He will be your co-conspirator, a stone, a rock on which both houses of Israel will strike their feet and stumble, a trap and snare for the inhabitants of Jerusalem. ¹⁵Many among them shall stumble, fall, and be broken; they shall be snared and taken captive."

A CLOSING REFLECTION (8:16–22)

8 ¹⁶Secure the message, seal the instruction among my disciples. ¹⁷I will wait for Yahveh who is hiding his face from the house of Jacob. I will wait in hope for him.¹⁸Here I am with the children Yahveh has given me as signs and portents in Israel. All this is from Yahveh of the hosts who dwells on Mount Zion.
¹⁹They will surely say to you, "Consult the spirits of the dead and the ghosts that chirp and mutter, for should not a people consult their divine ancestors, the dead, ²⁰for instruction and a message on behalf of the living?" They will assuredly speak in this way, but what they say will have no magical power. ²¹They will pass on into the underworld, wretched and hungry; and when they are famished they will be enraged and will curse their king and their gods. ²²And if they turn upwards or look down into the underworld all they will see is distress and darkness, gloom and misery; then they themselves will be thrust down into deep darkness.

NEW RULER, NEW AGE (8:23–9:6 [9:1–7])

8 ^{23[9:1]}There is no gloom for her who is oppressed. At that time the earlier ruler treated with contempt the territory of Zebulon and Naphthali, and the later one oppressed the way of the sea, the land across the Jordan, Galilee of the nations.

9   [1][2]The people that walk in the dark
have seen a great light,
on the dwellers in the land of gloom
light has shone forth.
[2][3]You have increased their joy,
and brought them great gladness;
they are glad in your presence
with a gladness like that of the harvest,
as those rejoice who divide the spoil.
[3][4]For the yoke with which they were burdened,
the bar across their shoulders,
the rod of their oppressors,
you have smashed as on the day of Midian.
[4][5]Every boot of troops on the march,
every garment caked in blood
is destined to be burned, to be fuel for the fire.
[5][6]For a child has been born for us,
a son has been given to us,
the emblems of sovereignty rest on his shoulders.
His titles will be: Marvelous Counselor,
Hero Warrior, Eternal Father,
Prince of Peace.
[6][7]Sovereignty will be great, peace will be endless
for David's throne and his kingdom,
to establish and sustain it
in justice and righteousness
from this time forth and ever more.
[The zeal of Yahveh of the hosts will accomplish this.]

"ASSYRIA, ROD OF MY ANGER" (10:5–14)

10   [5]Woe to Assyria, rod of my anger,
the stick in their hands is my fury!
[6]Against an impious nation I send him,
against a people that stir me to wrath I commission him
to seize spoil, to pillage and plunder,
to trample them down like mud in the streets.
[7]But he did not reckon it so,
his mind did not see it that way,
destroying was all he intended,
cutting off nation after nation.
[8]He thinks: "Are not my commanders kings every one?
[9]Did Calno fare better than Carchemish?
Did Hamath fare better than Arpad?
Did not Samaria share the fate of Damascus?

¹⁰Since my hand has grasped worthless kingdoms,
with more images than those of Jerusalem and Samaria,
¹¹what I have done to Samaria and its idols
shall I not do to Jerusalem and its images?"
¹²*When the Sovereign Lord will have completed all that he will do on Mount
Zion and in Jerusalem, he will bring punishment on the high-minded arrogance
of the king of Assyria, on the splendor of his lofty regard.*
¹³He thought: "It is by the strength of my own hand I have done it,
by my wisdom, for I have understanding.
I have swept away the boundaries of peoples,
I have plundered their riches,
like a bull I have laid low their inhabitants;
¹⁴my hand has plundered the wealth of the nations like a nest,
I have scooped up all the earth
as one scoops up abandoned birds' eggs;
no one moved a wing,
or opened his mouth to let out a single chirp.

PROPHETIC RESPONSE TO ASSYRIAN HUBRIS (10:15–19)

10 ¹⁵Should the axe vaunt itself over the one wielding it?
Should the saw flaunt itself over the one handling it?
As if a rod should brandish the one wielding it!
As if a wooden stick should wield one not made of wood!
¹⁶Therefore the Sovereign Lord, Yahveh of the hosts,
will send wasting disease among the most prosperous of his people,
under his most distinguished folk a fire will be kindled,
¹⁷The Light of Israel will become a fire,
The Holy One of Israel will become a flame;
it will burn up and consume in a single day
his land choked with thorns and weeds.
¹⁸The best of his woodlands and orchards will be destroyed root and
    branch
as a sick person faints and falls;
¹⁹the remnant of the trees of his forest will be so few
that a child can count them and write them down.

THREE EDITORIAL COMMENTS (10:20–27A)

10 ²⁰On that day the residue of Israel and the survivors of the household of
Jacob will no longer rely on the one who struck them, but they will rely in truth

on Yahveh the Holy One of Israel. [21]A residue will return, the residue of Jacob, to the God of Might, [22]for even if your people Israel were as numerous as the sand of the sea, only a residue of them will return. Destruction is decreed, with vindication abounding; [23]for the Sovereign Lord, Yahveh of the hosts, will bring about the destruction that is decreed in the midst of the earth.

[24]Therefore, thus says the Sovereign Lord, Yahveh of the hosts: "O my people who dwell in Zion, do not be afraid of the Assyrians when they beat you with a rod and wield their stick over you as the Egyptians did. [25]In a very short while the time of wrath will be over and my anger will be directed at their destruction. [26]Yahveh of the hosts will wield a whip against them as when he struck Midian at the rock of Oreb. His staff will be extended [over the sea,] and he will wield it as the Egyptians did.

[27]On that day his burden will be removed from your shoulder, and his yoke broken off from your neck."

THE ENEMY APPROACHES (10:27B–34)

10   [27b]They have gone up from . . .
[28]they have come upon Ayyath,
passed by Migron,
left their baggage at Michmash;
[29]they have crossed the ravine,
bivouacked at Geba.
Ramah is racked with fear,
Gibeah of Saul has fled;
[30]cry aloud, Bath-Gallim,
hear it, Laish!
answer her, Anathoth!
[31]Madmenah is in flight,
the people of Gebim take cover.
[32]This very day they halt at Nob,
they shake their fist at the mount of the daughter of Zion,
the hill of Jerusalem.

[33]See, the Sovereign Lord, Yahveh of the hosts,
will lop off the branches with frightening force,
the tallest of them will be hewn down,
the lofty ones laid low;
[34]the thickets of the forest will be cut down with an axe,
Lebanon in its majesty will fall.

THE PEACEFUL KINGDOM (11:1–9)

11   ¹A branch will grow from Jesse's stock,
a shoot will spring from its roots.
²Yahveh's spirit will rest on him,
a spirit of wisdom and understanding,
a spirit of counsel and strength,
a spirit of knowledge and the fear of Yahveh.
³[His delight will be in the fear of Yahveh.]
He will not judge by appearances,
he will not decide by hearsay,
⁴but with righteous judgment he will judge the poor,
and with equity defend the lowly of the earth.
He will strike the violent with the rod of his mouth,
with the breath of his lips he will kill the wicked.
⁵Justice will be the belt around his waist,
Truth will be the band around his middle.
⁶The wolf will share its lodging with the lamb,
the leopard will lie down beside the goat,
the calf and the lion cub will feed together,
even a small child will lead them;
⁷the cow and the bear will share their pasture,
their young lying down side by side,
the lion will eat hay like the ox,
⁸the infant will play at the cobra's hole,
the child barely weaned will put its hand over the viper's lair.
⁹No longer will they hurt or destroy
in all my holy mountain;
for the earth will be full of the knowledge of Yahveh
as the waters cover the sea.

A REUNITED PEOPLE (11:10–16)

11   ¹⁰On that day the root of Jesse will stand as a signal for the peoples of the world; him will the nations seek out; glory will rest on him.
¹¹On that day the Sovereign Lord will raise his hand to recover the residue of his people that is left from Assyria, from Egypt, from Pathros, Nubia, Elam, Shinar, Hamath, and the islands of the sea.
¹²He will raise a signal for the nations,
and gather the dispersed men of Israel;
he will assemble the scattered women of Judah
from the four corners of the earth.
¹³Ephraim's jealousy will cease,
Judah's opponents will be destroyed;

Ephraim will not be jealous of Judah,
Judah will not be hostile to Ephraim.
[14]They will swoop on the flank of the Philistines to the west,
together they will plunder peoples to the east;
Edom and Moab will be in their power,
Ammonites will be subject to them.
[15]Yahveh will dry up the tongue of the Egyptian sea,
will wave his hand over the Euphrates River
together with a violent wind.
He will split it into seven channels
so that it may be crossed dry-shod.
[16]There will be a highway for the residue of his people,
those left over from Assyria,
just as there was for Israel
at the time they went up from the land of Egypt.

CONCLUDING HYMN
OF THANKSGIVING (12:1–6)

12 [1]You will say on that day:
Yahveh, I thank you,
for though you were angry with me
your anger has abated,
and you have consoled me.
[2]See, God is my salvation,
I will trust and feel no dread
for Yahveh is my strength and my power,
God has been my salvation.

[3]You will draw water with joy
from the wells of salvation.

[4]You will say on that day:
Give thanks to Yahveh, call on his name,
make known his deeds among the peoples,
proclaim that his name is exalted.
[5]Sing hymns to Yahveh for he has wrought splendidly,
let this be known over all the earth;
[6]Shout aloud, exult, you who dwell in Zion,
for great in your midst is the Holy One of Israel.

THE FALL OF BABYLON PRESAGES
UNIVERSAL JUDGMENT (13:1–22)

13   ¹An oracle about Babylon that Isaiah ben Amoz saw in vision.

i

²On a bare hill raise the standard,
shout aloud to them,
wave your hand for them to enter
the princely gates.
³I have issued the command to those sworn to my service;
I have summoned my warriors eager and proud,
to serve as instruments of my anger.
⁴The sound of a rumbling on the mountains
as of a vast horde;
the sound of the clamor of kingdoms,
of nations assembled for battle.
It is Yahveh of the hosts who musters
an army for war.
⁵They come from a distant land,
from the far horizon,
Yahveh and the weapons of his wrath
to destroy all the earth.

ii

⁶Lament, for the day of Yahveh is near,
it approaches like destruction from Shaddai!
All hands will then fall limp,
all hearts dissolve in fear,
⁸[they will be terrified].
Convulsions and pains will seize them,
they will writhe like a woman in labor,
they will look aghast at each other,
their faces aflame.

iii

⁹Yes, the day of Yahveh approaches,
cruel, with unbridled fury,
to reduce the earth to rubble,
rooting out its sinners from its midst.
¹⁰For the stars and constellations in the sky
will no longer give their light,
the sun will be dark at sunrise,
the moon will not shed its light.

¹¹I will visit disaster on the world
and punish the wicked for their crimes,
put an end to the pride of the insolent,
lay low the arrogance of tyrants.
¹²I will make mortals more scarce than pure gold,
human beings than gold of Ophir.
¹³Then will I rattle the heavens,
the earth will be shaken from its base
at the fury of Yahveh of the hosts,
on the day of his burning anger.
¹⁴Then, like hunted gazelles,
like sheep with no one to herd them,
all will turn back to their kin,
flee to their native land;
¹⁵any found lagging will be skewered,
any that are caught will fall by the sword;
¹⁶their infants dashed to death in their sight,
their houses plundered, their wives ravished.

iv

¹⁷Observe, I am inciting the Medes against them,
they have no regard for silver,
no great desire for gold,
¹⁸[bows will dismember young men]
no pity for the fruit of the womb,
their eye will not spare the children.
¹⁹Babylon, most glorious of kingdoms,
the proud splendor of the Chaldeans
will be like Sodom and Gomorrah
when overthrown by God.
²⁰Never will it be inhabited
nor settled for ages to come,
no Arab will bivouac there,
no shepherd tend his flock,
²¹but wildcats will have their lairs there,
owls make their nests in the houses;
ostriches will live there,
there satyrs will dance;
²²hyenas will howl in its forts,
jackals in its pleasant palaces.
Its appointed time is close at hand
with not many days to wait.

AN EDITORIAL COMMENT (14:1–2)

14   [1]But Yahveh will take pity on Jacob and will once again choose Israel. He will settle them on their own land, and proselytes will attach themselves to them and will be incorporated into the household of Jacob. [2]The nations will take them and bring them to their place, and the household of Israel will possess the nations as male and female slaves. They will make captives of those who had captured them and lord it over those who had oppressed them.

THE KING OF BABYLON IN THE UNDERWORLD (14:3–23)

14   [3]After Yahveh has given you respite from your pain and turmoil, and the hard labor laid on you, [4a]you will intone this oracular poem about the king of Babylon. This is what you will say:

i

[4b]See how the tyrant has come to nothing,
how the persecutor has come to an end!
[5]Yahveh has broken the staff of the reprobate,
the scepter of dominion;
[6]he who in his fury struck down peoples,
striking again and again,
he who in his rage lorded it over nations
relentlessly hunting them down.
[7]But now the whole earth rests and relaxes,
breaks out into joyful song;
[8]the cypress too rejoices over you,
and the cedar of Lebanon:
"since you were laid low," they say,
"none comes to cut us down."
Sheol below is astir,
preparing to greet your arrival,
[9]rousing the shades to meet you,
all the princes of the earth;
raising up from their thrones
all that were rulers of nations.
[10]All will address you, saying,
"You too have become weak as we are,
you have become like us.
[11]Your pride is brought down to Sheol
together with the throng of your dead,
maggots are the bed you lie on,
worms will be your blanket."

ii

¹²How you have fallen from the sky,
Star of the dawning day!
how felled and fallen to the ground,
you who laid low all the nations.
¹³You thought in your heart:
"I will ascend to the sky,
I will set up my throne
higher than the highest stars,
I will take my seat on the Mount of Assembly,
in the furthest reaches of the north.
¹⁴I will ascend on the highest clouds,
become like the Most High God."
¹⁵Yet here you are, brought down to Sheol,
to the furthest reaches of the Pit.
¹⁶Those who see you will stare at you,
they will ponder over you, saying:
"Is this the man who shook the earth,
who caused kingdoms to quake with fear?
¹⁷who turned the whole world into a wilderness,
destroying its cities?
who would not set his prisoners free
to go back to their homes?"
¹⁸All the rulers of the nations
are one and all laid to rest with honor,
each in his resting place,
¹⁹but you have been cast out of your grave
like loathsome carrion.
Like a corpse trampled underfoot,
covered over by the slain, those pierced by the sword,
gone down to the foundations of the Pit.
²⁰You will not be united with them in burial,
for you ruined your land
and slew your own people.
Never more will the name be recalled
of such evil seed.
²¹So get ready the slaughterhouse for his sons
to be butchered for their father's guilt,
let them not undertake to possess the earth,
covering the world's surface with cities.

²²I will rise up against them (a saying of Yahveh of the hosts) to cut off
Babylon's name and remnant, offspring and progeny (a saying of Yahveh). ²³I
will turn Babylon into the haunt of bitterns, a watery wasteland, and I will
sweep it with the broom of destruction (a saying of Yahveh of the hosts).

THE END OF IMPERIAL ASSYRIA (14:24–27)

14   [24]Yahveh of the hosts has sworn an oath:
Surely as I have purposed, so will it be,
as I have planned, so will it come to pass:
[25]to shatter the Assyrians in my land,
to trample them down on my mountains;
their yoke will be removed from the people,
their burden lifted from their shoulder.
[26]This is the plan devised for the whole earth,
this is the hand outstretched over all the nations;
[27]for Yahveh of the hosts has planned, who will frustrate it?
it is his hand that is outstretched, who will turn it back?

AN ORACULAR PRONOUNCEMENT ABOUT THE PHILISTINES (14:28–32)

14   [28]In the year King Ahaz died there came this oracle:
[29]Do not rejoice, you people of Philistia,
that the rod that struck you is broken;
for from a serpent's root an adder will come forth,
its offspring will be a flying serpent.
[30]The poor will graze their flocks in my pastures,
the needy will lie down and rest securely,
but your seed he will kill by starvation,
he will slay your remnant.
[31]Wail, O gate, cry aloud, O city!
dissolve in fear, all you people of Philistia,
for the smoke of an army comes from the north,
no one of them strays from his station.
[32]What answer will one give the envoys of the nation?
"Yahweh has established Zion,
the afflicted among his people will find refuge there."

ORACLES AND PRONOUNCEMENTS ABOUT MOAB (15:1–16:14)

15   [1]An oracle about Moab

i

Destroyed in the nighttime,
Ar Moab is silenced;

destroyed in the nighttime,
Kir Moab is silenced.
²The people of Dibon go up to the temple,
to the hill-shrines to weep.
Over Nebo and over Medeba
Moab is wailing;
the hair of all heads is cut back,
all beards are shaved off;
³in their streets they put on sackcloth,
on the roofs of her houses,
in her open spaces everyone is wailing,
the tears rolling down.
⁴Heshbon and Elealah cry out,
their clamor is heard as far as Jahaz,
Moab's warriors cry out,
each one trembling with fear.
⁵My heart cries out for Moab,
for those who have fled as far as Zoar.
[Eglath, Shelishiyah].
By the Ascent of Luhith
they go up weeping,
on the road to Horonaim
there are cries of "disaster!"
⁶The waters of Nimrim
are a place of desolation,
the grass dried up, the vegetation withered,
no green in sight.
⁷They carry their possessions, whatever they can salvage,
over the Wadi Arabim.
⁸The cry echoes around the borders of Moab,
her wailing as far as Eglaim,
her wailing as far as Beer-elim.
⁹The waters of Dibon run with blood,
yet for Dibon I have worse news in store,
a vision for Moab's survivors,
for the remnant of the land.

ii

16   ¹The ruler of the land has sent lambs
from Sela in the wilderness
to the mount of the daughter of Zion.
²[Like fluttering birds thrown out of the nest
are the Moabite women at the Arnon fords.]
³Take counsel, decide in our favor,
Make your protecting shadow like night in the noonday;

shelter the outcast,
do not hand over the fugitive,
[4]let the Moabite refugees settle among you,
conceal them against the one who would destroy them.

iii

When the oppression has come to an end,
when destruction has ceased
and marauders have been cleared from the land,
[5]a throne will be established in loyalty in David's tent;
on it will sit one who judges rightly,
who seeks justice and is swift to do right.

iv

[6]We have heard tell of the pride of Moab,
so very proud!
its haughtiness, pride, and arrogance,
its talk that is full of lies.
[7]For this Moab will wail,
the whole country will wail for Moab,
utterly stricken, they will mourn
for the raisin-cakes of Kir-hareseth.
[8]The fields of Heshbon languish,
the vineyards of Sibmah,
though their red grapes used to lay low
the lords of foreign lands,
though they spread out as far as Jazer,
ranging out into the wilderness,
though their cuttings were spread abroad,
and crossed the sea.
[9]Therefore I join with the weeping at Jazer,
weeping for the vineyards of Sibmah;
I drown you in my tears,
Heshbon and Elealeh,
for the glad shouts at harvesting
of summer fruit and grain have ceased.
[10]Gladness and rejoicing are banished from the fertile land,
no singing or shouting in the vineyards,
no one treads grapes in the wine press,
I have silenced your shouts of joy.
[11]My innards throb like a harp for Moab,
my very being for Kir-heres.

v

[12]When Moab wears himself out presenting himself at the hill-shrine,
when he comes to his sanctuary to pray, he will not succeed.

vi

[13]This is the saying Yahveh addressed to Moab a long time ago, [14]but now Yahveh says: "Within three years, the length of employment for a hired laborer, the pomp of Moab will be humbled in spite of its great population. Those who are left will be few indeed and of no account."

ONCE AGAIN, THE FATE OF SYRIA AND ISRAEL (17:1–11)

17   [1]An oracle about Damascus

i

See, Damascus has ceased to be a city,
it has become a heap of ruins;
[2]the cities of Aroer are deserted,
they will serve as pasture for herds
that will lie there undisturbed.
[3]There will be no more fortified cities in Ephraim,
nor sovereignty in Damascus;
what remains of Aram will resemble
what the glory of Israel has become.
A word of Yahveh of the hosts.

ii

[4]On that day
 Jacob's weight will diminish,
the fat waste away from his body;
[5]It will be as when a reaper gathers in the standing corn,
harvesting the ears in armfuls;
as when one gleans the ears of corn
in the Valley of Rephaim;
[6]as when one beats an olive tree
and only gleanings are left in it—
two or three berries at the top of a bough,
four or five on the branches of the fruit tree.
This is the word of Yahveh, God of Israel.

iii

[7]On that day:
People will look to their Maker, their eyes will turn towards the Holy One of Israel. [8]They will not look to the altars, the work of their hands; they will not turn their gaze to that which their fingers have made [the Asherah steles and the incense altars].

iv

⁹On that day:
Their fortified cities will be like the deserted sites of the Hivites and Amorites which they abandoned when attacked by the Israelites. There will be a scene of desolation.

v

¹⁰You have forgotten your God who saves,
the Rock, your fortress, you have not kept in mind;
therefore plant your shoots of Adonis,
sow the slip of an alien god.
¹¹Even if you got them to sprout the day you planted them,
or got them to blossom the morning you sowed them,
the crop will be gone when disease comes along with incurable pain.

A SUDDEN END TO POLITICAL
OPPRESSION (17:12–14)

17   ¹²Hear the thunder of many peoples,
they thunder like the thunder of the sea!
Hear the roaring of the nations,
they roar like the roaring of mighty waters!
¹³[the nations roar like the roaring of many waters].
When he rebukes them they flee far away,
blown away by the wind like chaff on the hills,
like specks of dust by the whirlwind.
¹⁴As night approaches there is terror,
but before the day dawns they are no more.
This is the fate of those who despoil us,
the lot of those who plunder us.

AGAINST AN ALLIANCE
WITH EGYPT (18:1–7)

18   ¹Woe to a land full of buzzing insect wings
beyond the rivers of Kush,
which sends its envoys by sea,
in reed vessels over the water!
²Go, swift messengers,
to a nation tall and smooth-skinned,
to a people feared far and near,

a nation strong and conquering
whose land rivers divide.

³All you denizens of the world,
you who live on the earth,
when the signal is raised in the hills you will see it,
when the trumpet sounds you will hear it.
⁴This is what Yahveh said to me:
"I will calmly look down from my dwelling
while the heat is bright in the sunlight,
while the dew covers the ground at the time of the vintage."
⁵For before the vintage, when the blossoms are gone,
and the seed-berry is ripening into a grape,
he will cut off the shoots with pruning shears,
lop off and remove the branches.
⁶They will all be abandoned to birds of prey on the hills
and to the beasts of the earth.
Birds of prey will live off them in the summer,
all the beasts of the earth in the winter.

⁷At that time:
Tribute will be brought to Yahveh of the hosts from a people tall and smooth-skinned, a people feared far and near, a nation strong and conquering, whose land is divided by rivers. Their tribute will be brought to Mount Zion, the place where the name of Yahveh of the hosts is invoked.

THE FATE OF EGYPT (19:1–15)

19 ¹An oracle about Egypt

i

See how Yahveh comes riding on a swift cloud,
on his way to Egypt.
The idols of Egypt tremble at his approach,
the hearts of the Egyptians melt within them.
²"I will incite Egyptians against Egyptians,
kin will contend against kin, neighbor against neighbor,
city against city, kingdom against kingdom.
³Egypt's spirit will be poured out and voided,
I will confound their plans.
They will consult the idols, the spirits of the dead,
the shades and the ghosts,

⁴but I will hand Egypt over to a hard taskmaster,
a powerful king will lord it over them."
This is a saying of the Sovereign Lord, Yahveh of the hosts.

ii

⁵The water will be dried up from the Nile,
the river will be parched and run dry,
⁶the canals will be foul,
Egypt's watercourses drained and dried up,
the rushes and reeds will wither,
⁷the plants by the Nile, at the edge of the Nile,
with all that is sown beside the Nile
will wither, blow away, and be no more.
⁸Fishermen also will lament,
all who cast hook in the Nile will mourn,
those who spread nets over the water will pine away.
⁹The workers in flax will be troubled,
carders and weavers grow pale,
¹⁰the weavers of Egypt will be crushed,
all the brewers sad at heart.

iii

¹¹The princes of Zoan are nothing but fools,
Pharaoh's counselors have counseled him folly.
How can you say to Pharaoh,
"I am descended from a line of sages,
from kings of ancient times?"
¹²Where then are your sages
to tell you and make it known
what Yahveh of the hosts has planned for Egypt?
¹³The princes of Zoan have become fools,
the princes of Noph are deluded,
her tribal leaders have led Egypt astray;
¹⁴Yahveh has poured into them a spirit of confusion,
they have led Egypt astray in all its operations
like a drunkard reeling in his own vomit.
¹⁵There will be nothing anyone can do for Egypt,
neither head nor tail, palm branch nor reed.

"BLESSED BE MY PEOPLE EGYPT" (19:16–25)

i

19   ¹⁶On that day the Egyptians will be as weak as women. They will tremble
with fear on account of the raised hand of Yahveh of the hosts when he raises

his hand to strike them. [17]The land of Judah will strike terror into Egypt. Anyone who so much as hears it mentioned will be filled with fear on account of the plan of Yahveh of the hosts which he has devised against Egypt.

ii

[18]On that day there will be five cities in the land of Egypt speaking the language of Canaan and swearing their oaths in the name of Yahveh of the hosts. One of them will be called the City of the Sun.

iii

[19]On that day there will be an altar to Yahveh in the middle of the land of Egypt and a monument dedicated to him at its frontier. [20]It will serve as a sign and testimony to Yahveh of the hosts in the land of Egypt. When they appeal to Yahveh on account of those who are oppressing them he will send them a savior who will come to their defense and rescue them. [21]Yahveh will make himself known to the Egyptians, and the Egyptians will acknowledge him on that day and will worship him with animal sacrifice and cereal offering. They will make vows to Yahveh and perform them. [22]Yahveh will strike Egypt, but with a blow that heals; then they will turn to Yahveh, he will hear their prayers and heal them.

iv

[23]On that day there will be a highway from Egypt to Assyria. Assyrians will come to Egypt and Egyptians to Assyria. Egyptians will worship together with Assyrians.

v

[24]On that day Israel will make up one-third of a whole together with Egypt and Assyria, a blessing in the middle of the world. [25]Yahveh of the hosts will pronounce this blessing over them: "Blessed be my people Egypt, Assyria the work of my hands, Israel my possession."

AN OMINOUS SIGN-ACT (20:1–6)

20 [1]In the course of the year during which the commander in chief, having been dispatched by Sargon king of Assyria, came to Ashdod, fought against it and took it— [2]at that time Yahveh sent this message to Isaiah ben Amoz: "Go, untie the sackcloth from around your waist and take your sandals off your feet." He did so and went around naked and barefoot. [3]Yahveh then said, "Just as my servant Isaiah walked around over a period of three years naked and barefoot as a sign of ill omen to Egypt and Ethiopia, [4]so shall the king of Assyria lead away Egyptians into captivity and Ethiopians into exile, both young and old, naked, barefoot, their buttocks exposed [the nakedness of Egypt]. [5]They will be aggrieved and ashamed on account of Ethiopia the source of their confidence

and Egypt the source of their pride. [6]At that time, the inhabitants of this coastal region will think, 'So that is what happened to those to whom we looked for help and to whom we fled looking for assistance and rescue from the king of Assyria. How then shall we escape?'"

"FALLEN, FALLEN IS BABYLON" (21:1–10)

21   [1]The oracle "the wasteland by the sea"

As whirlwinds in the Negev advance,
coming from the wilderness, from a land of terror,
[2]a grim vision is announced to me:
"The treacherous one is betrayed,
the despoiler is despoiled.
Attack, then, Elam!
Lay siege, Media!
I have brought all sighing to an end."

[3]At this my loins are filled with anguish,
pangs have seized me
like the pangs of a woman in labor;
I am so bent double I cannot hear,
I am so dumbfounded I cannot see.
[4]My mind reels,
Shuddering, I am filled with dread;
the cool of the evening I longed for
has been turned for me into trembling.

[5]Set the table,
lay its covering,
eat and drink!
Then arise, you princes,
rub your shields with oil,
[6]for thus the Lord has addressed me:
"Go, post a lookout,
let him announce what he sees;
[7]when he sees chariots drawn by two horses,
riders on donkeys, riders on camels,
let him listen hard, very hard."

[8]Then the seer cried out,
"On the watchtower, O Lord, I stand
all the day long;

at my post I take my station
night after night."
⁹Now, look, there approaches
a man riding in a chariot drawn by two horses,
when addressed, he replies,
"Fallen, fallen is Babylon,
and all the statues of her gods
lie smashed on the ground!"

¹⁰O my people, once threshed and winnowed,
what I have heard from Yahveh of the hosts,
from the God of Israel, I have announced to you.

ORACLES ABOUT ARAB PEOPLES (21:11–17)

i

21   ¹¹An oracle about Dumah

Someone is calling me from Seir,
"Sentinel, how much of the night is left?
Sentinel, how much of the night is left?"
¹²The sentinel replied,
"the morning is coming, though it is still nighttime;
if you wish to ask you may do so,
come back once again."

ii

¹³"In Arabia": an oracle

In the scrubland, in Arabia where you lodge,
you caravans of Dedan,
¹⁴go to meet the thirsty, bring them water;
you dwellers in the land of Tema,
meet the refugees with the food they need;
¹⁵for they are fleeing from the sword,
from the drawn sword,
from the bent bow and the stress of battle.

iii

¹⁶This is what Yahveh said to me:
"Within three years, the length of employment for a hired laborer, all the pomp
of Kedar will come to an end, ¹⁷and the remaining archers among the Kedarite
warriors will be few in number, for Yahveh, Israel's God, has spoken."

THE VALLEY OF VISION (22:1–14)

22   [1]"The Valley of Vision": an oracle

What is wrong with you that you go up,
all of you, to the rooftops,
[2]inhabitants of a city in tumult, full of clamor,
of a town in an uproar?
Your slain were not slain by the sword,
they did not perish in battle;
[3]your leaders have fled, one and all,
withdrawn out of range of the bow;
your strongest warriors
have fled far away.

[4]Therefore I said: "Turn your gaze away from me,
leave me to weep bitter tears,
do not attempt to console me
for the ruin of the daughter of my people!"

[5]The Sovereign Lord Yahveh of the hosts has a day of tumult, trampling,
and turmoil in the Valley of Vision, with crying out for help to his holy place
on the mountain.

[6]Elam has picked up the quiver,
with chariots of Aram and horsemen;
Kir has uncovered the shield.
[7]The best of your valleys teemed with chariots;
horsemen were stationed at the city gate,
[8]leaving Judah naked and defenseless.

You looked [on that day] to the weapons stored in the "House of the Forest."
[9]You observed that there were many breaches in the defenses of the City of
David, and you brought together the waters of the Lower Cistern. [10]You made
a census of the houses in Jerusalem, and demolished some houses to
strengthen the city wall. [11]You made a reservoir between the two walls for the
water of the Old Cistern, but you did not look to the One who made it all, or
take account of the One who fashioned it ages ago.

[12]The Sovereign Lord Yahveh of the hosts called [on that day] for weeping
and mourning,
for heads shaved bare and the wearing of sackcloth;
[13]but instead there was gladness and joy,
killing of oxen, slaughtering of sheep,

eating meat, drinking wine.
"Eat and drink," you said, "for tomorrow we die."

[14]This message has been revealed in my hearing
[Yahveh of the hosts]:
"Such iniquity will not be pardoned you until you die."
[This is the message of the Sovereign Lord Yahveh of the hosts.]

PALACE OFFICIALS CONDEMNED (22:15–25)

22 [15]About Shebna superintendent of the palace:

This is what the Sovereign Lord Yahveh of the hosts said: "Go, then, to this official and say to him: [16]'What business have you here, and whom do you have here to authorize you to hew out a tomb for yourself, hewing out a tomb on the high ground and carving out a resting place for yourself in the rock? [17]Yahveh will knock you to the ground with great force, my fine fellow, he will grab hold of you firmly, [18]and fling you like a ball into a broad and spacious land. There you will die, and there will your splendid chariots be. You are a disgrace to your master's household.

[19]I will dismiss you from your office,
and banish you from your post.

[20]On that day:
I will summon my servant Eliakim ben Hilkiah; [21]I will invest him with your robe, bind your sash on him, and hand over your authority to him. He will be a father to the inhabitants of Jerusalem and to the household of Judah. [22]I will place on his shoulder the key of the house of David. When he opens no one will close, and when he closes no one will open. [23]I will fasten him firmly in place like a peg. He will be like a throne of honor to his paternal household.

[24]They will hang on him all the weight of his household, their offspring and their issue, all the smallest utensils, from beakers to every kind of bowl.

[25]On that day:
[Oracle of Yahveh of the hosts] The peg fastened firmly in place will give way. It will be cut down and fall, and the load that was on it will be destroyed'"; for Yahveh has spoken.

ABOUT PHOENICIA (23:1–18)

23 ¹An oracle about Tyre

Wail, Tarshish ships,
for your harbor is destroyed!
When they came from Cyprus
they found it out.
²Lament, dwellers on the seacoast,
merchants of Sidon,
whose agents traverse the great waters,
³whose harvest is the grain of Sihor,
whose revenue is the commerce of nations.
⁴Be ashamed and cry out,
Sidon, harbor by the sea,
"I am not in labor,
I do not give birth,
I neither rear young men
nor bring up young women."
⁵[As soon as the Egyptians hear it
they sway in anguish at the news about Tyre.]
⁶Cross over to Tarshish,
wail, dwellers on the seacoast!
⁷Is this your bustling city
whose origin was so long ago,
whose people took off and voyaged
to settle in far distant lands?
⁸Who has devised this thing
against Tyre, bestower of crowns,
whose merchants were princes,
whose traders were the most honored in the world?
⁹Yahveh of the hosts has devised it
to puncture all pride and splendor,
to bring the world's most honored into contempt.
¹⁰Till your land, for there is no longer a harbor
for the Tarshish ships.
¹¹He has stretched out his hand over the sea,
he has shaken kingdoms.
Yahveh has given the command
to destroy the harbors of Canaan.
¹²You will no more exult,
oppressed virgin daughter of Sidon.
By all means cross over to Cyprus,
even there you will have no respite.

¹³[This is the land of the Chaldeans, this is the people . . .it was not . . .]
There the Assyrians established it for their fleet, they erected their siege towers
and destroyed their palaces, turning the place into a ruin.
   ¹⁴So, wail ships of Tarshish
for your harbor is destroyed!

   ¹⁵On that day:
Tyre will be forgotten for seventy years, one king's lifetime. At the end of seventy years Tyre will experience what the song says about the harlot:
   ¹⁶Take up a harp,
go around the town,
poor, forgotten harlot!
Play a sweet tune,
play song after song,
so they may remember you!
   ¹⁷At the end of seventy years Yahveh will be mindful of Tyre. She will engage once more in commerce, and she will play the harlot with all the kingdoms of the world on the face of the earth. ¹⁸Her trade and commerce will be dedicated to Yahveh. Her merchandise will not be put in storage; it will not be hoarded but will serve to feed to satiety and clothe in rich attire those who dwell in the presence of Yahveh.

A CURSE ON THE EARTH AND
ITS INHABITANTS (24:1–13)

i

24   ¹Observe, Yahveh is about to lay waste the earth and split it open,
contort its surface and disperse its inhabitants.
   ²Then it will be the same for priest as for people,
for master as for slave,
for mistress as for female slave,
for the one who sells as for the one who buys,
for the lender as for the borrower,
for the creditor as for the debtor.
   ³The earth will be utterly laid waste,
utterly despoiled;
for Yahveh has spoken this word.

ii

   ⁴The earth dries up and withers away,
the whole world languishes and withers away,
the highest heaven languishes with the earth.
   ⁵The earth lies polluted beneath those who dwell on it,
for they have transgressed laws,

disobeyed statutes,
violated the perpetual covenant.
[6]Therefore a curse has consumed the earth,
its inhabitants suffer for their guilt.
Therefore the dwellers on earth dwindle,
leaving but a few people.
[7]The new wine dries up,
the vine languishes,
all the revellers moan.
[8]The joyful beat of the tabor is stilled,
the shouting of the merrymakers hushed,
the joyful sound of the harp is stilled.
[9]No longer do they drink wine as they sing;
strong drink now tastes bitter to those who drink it.
[10]Chaos Town is broken down,
all its houses closed so that no one can enter.
[11]They cry out for wine in the streets,
all joy has reached its eventide,
gladness is banished from the earth.
[12]The city is left a shambles,
the gate lies broken in pieces.
[13]This is how it will be in all the earth,
among all the peoples—
as when an olive tree is beaten,
and gleanings are left when the harvest is over.

DIES IRAE, DIES ILLA (24:14–23)

i

24   [14]They lift up their voices,
singing joyfully of Yahveh's majesty;
they exult more loudly than the sea!
[15]Therefore give glory to Yahveh in the east,
in the western isles to Yahveh's name,
Yahveh, Israel's God!
[16]From the ends of the earth we hear the refrain
"Glory to the Conquering One!"
But meanwhile I thought,
"I have my secret, I have my secret!
Woe to the unfaithful ones who deal faithlessly,
who deal with an utter lack of faith!"

ii

¹⁷Terror, the trap, the deep pit
await you who dwell on the earth!
¹⁸If you flee from the sound of the terror
you will fall into the pit;
and if you get out of the pit,
you will be caught in the trap;
for the sluicegates of the sky are opened
and the earth's foundations quake;
¹⁹the earth is utterly shattered,
the earth is tossed about,
the earth shudders and shakes;
²⁰the earth reels like a drunkard,
swaying like a shelter in the wind;
its sins lie heavy upon it,
it falls, to rise no more.

iii

²¹On that day:
Yahveh will punish the hosts of the high heavens in the sky and the kings of the
earth on the earth. ²²They will be herded together like prisoners in a deep pit
and confined in prison. Then, after a long interval, they will be punished.
²³The moon will be put to shame and the sun abashed, when Yahveh of the
hosts inaugurates his reign on Mount Zion and in Jerusalem, revealing his
glory in the presence of his elders.

THE ESCHATOLOGICAL BANQUET (25:6–8)

25 ⁶Yahveh of the hosts will prepare
for all peoples on this mountain
a banquet of rich food,
a banquet of wine well aged,
of food rich in marrow,
of well-aged wine strained clear.
⁷Yahveh will destroy on this mountain
the mantle in which all peoples are wrapped,
the covering cast over all the nations;
⁸he will swallow up death for ever.
Then will the Sovereign Lord Yahveh wipe away tears from every face,
and remove the reproach of his people from all the earth;
for Yahveh has spoken.

THREE THANKSGIVING PSALMS
(25:1–5, 9–12; 26:1–6)

i

25 ¹Yahveh, you are my God.
I exalt you, I praise your name,
for you have carried out your wonderful counsels
firm and sure, formed ages since.
²You have reduced the city to a heap of rubble,
turned the fortified town into a ruin,
the citadel of the insolent is destroyed,
never will it be rebuilt;
³for this will cruel peoples respect you,
ruthless nations fear you.
⁴Truly you have been a refuge to the poor,
a refuge to the needy in their distress,
shelter from the rainstorm, shade from the heat.
⁵[for the blast of the ruthless is like a winter rainstorm,
like heat in a time of drought.]
You suppress the clamor of the insolent,
[heat in the shadow of a cloud]
the singing of the ruthless is silenced.

ii

⁹You will say on that day:
"See, this is our God,
we have waited for him to save us
[this is Yahveh, we have waited for him].
Let us be glad and rejoice in his salvation."

¹⁰ᵃfor Yahveh's hand will rest on this mountain.

¹⁰ᵇMoab will be trampled in its place
as straw is trampled down in a cesspool.
¹¹Moab spreads out his arms in the cesspool
as a swimmer spreads them out to swim,
but his pride will sink with each stroke that he takes.

¹²The lofty defense of your walls he has brought low;
he has thrown it down, brought it down to the ground,
down into the dust.

iii

26 ¹On that day
this song will be sung in the land of Judah:
"A strong city is ours!
He has set up its walls and ramparts as our salvation.
²Throw open the gates that a righteous people may enter,
a people that keeps faith!
³Those of trustful mind you keep in peace,
in peace, since in you they trust.
⁴Trust in Yahveh for ever,
for Yahveh is the rock of ages!
⁵He has brought low the dwellers on the height,
the lofty town he throws down,
throws it down to the ground,
lays it in the dust.
⁶It will be trodden underfoot, by the feet of the oppressed
and the tread of the poor.

AN ESCHATOLOGICAL PSALM (26:7–27:1)

26 ⁷For the righteous the path goes straight;
you smooth out the course of the upright;
⁸Yahveh, we look to you
for your just decrees to be manifest.
To invoke your name is the soul's desire.
⁹My soul yearns for you in the nighttime;
my spirit within me seeks you eagerly,
for when your judgments are manifest on the earth
the inhabitants of the world learn righteousness.

¹⁰But if mercy is shown to the wicked
they do not learn righteousness;
disregarding the majesty of Yahveh,
they pervert what is straight on the earth.
¹¹Yahveh, your hand is raised,
but they do not see it;
may they be ashamed when they see your zeal for your people,
may the fire consume them that is destined for your enemies.
¹²Yahveh, decree well-being for us,
for all that we achieve is your doing.
¹³Yahveh our God,
masters other than you have ruled over us,
yet your name, yours alone, we invoke.

¹⁴The dead will not live,
the shades will not rise from the dead;
to this end you punished and destroyed them,
obliterating their memory entirely.
¹⁵Yahveh, you enlarged the nation,
you enlarged the nation, won honor for yourself,
extending wide the boundaries of the land.
¹⁶Yahveh, in distress we sought you,
your chastening has been a burden for us.
¹⁷As a pregnant woman, when her time is at hand,
writhes and cries out in pain,
so, Yahveh, were we in your presence;
¹⁸we were with child, we were in labor,
but brought forth nothing but wind;
we do nothing to redeem the earth,
no one is born to people the world.

¹⁹Your dead will live,
their corpses will rise from the dead;
you that lie in the dust, awake and sing for joy!
For your dew is a radiant dew,
and earth will bring forth the shades of the dead.

²⁰Come, my people, enter your rooms,
shut tight the doors behind you,
take cover for a little while
till the wrath has passed;
²¹for Yahveh will proceed from his place
to punish those who dwell on the earth
for their iniquity.
The earth will disclose the blood shed on it;
no longer will it cover up its slain.

27   ¹On that day:
Yahweh will punish with his sword
grim, mighty, and strong,
Leviathan the pursuing serpent,
Leviathan the twisting serpent,
and he will slay the dragon in the primeval sea.

THE VINEYARD REVISITED (27:2–6)

27 [2]On that day:
A lovely vineyard, sing about it!
[3]I, Yahveh, am its guardian,
I water it all the time
lest any harm come to it;
[4]I hold no grudge against it.
If it gives me thorns and weeds,
I will wage war against it,
burn it all up;
[5]so let it cling to me for protection,
let it make peace with me,
let it make peace with me.

[6]In days to come
Jacob will take root,
Israel will bud forth and blossom,
filling the whole world with fruit.

ONCE AGAIN, AND FINALLY, THE DESTINY OF THE CITY AND OF GOD'S PEOPLE (27:7–13)

27 [7]Did God strike Israel like those that struck him?
or is Israel slain, as those that slew him lie slain?
[8]By driving her out, by sending her away,
 God contended with her,
removing her with a fierce blast, as when the east wind blows.
[9]By this, then, is Jacob's iniquity purged,
this it is that removes his sin, and all that comes of it:
when he shall have treated all the stones of his altars
like limestone blocks that have been crushed to powder,
with no Asherah pillar or incense altar left standing.
[10]The fortified city is solitary,
an abode now abandoned, deserted like the wilderness;
there calves will graze,
there they will lie down and strip off the branches;
[11]when the boughs dry out they are broken off;
women come by and light their fires with them.
For this is a people deprived of understanding;
therefore the One who made them will show them no mercy,
the One who formed them will not regard them with favor.

¹²On that day:
Yahveh will thresh out the grain from the basin of the Euphrates to the Wadi of Egypt; and you, people of Israel, will be gathered in one by one.

¹³And on that day:
A great ram's horn will be blown; those who were lost in the land of Assyria, and those dispersed in the land of Egypt will come and worship Yahveh on the holy mountain, in Jerusalem.

THE FATE OF SAMARIA AND ITS LEADERS (28:1–13)

i

28 ¹Woe, proud coronet of the drunkards of Ephraim,
a flower doomed to fade is its splendid beauty
at the head of a fertile valley
[overcome with wine].
²Observe, the Sovereign Lord is holding in reserve one who is strong and
     powerful;
Yahveh will bring him down on the land with violence,
like a hailstorm, a destructive tempest,
a downpour of mighty water overflowing.
³Then the proud coronet of the drunkards of Ephraim
will be trampled underfoot,
⁴and the flower of its spendid beauty doomed to fade
at the head of a fertile valley
will be like figs that ripen before the summer;
those who see them will swallow them
as soon as they have them in their hand.

ii

⁵On that day:
Yahveh will be a splendid coronet, a beautiful diadem
for the remnant of his people,
⁶a spirit of justice for the one who sits in judgment,
and strength for those who turn back the fighting from the gate.

iii

⁷These too stagger with wine,
lurch about with strong drink;
priest and prophet stagger with strong drink;
they are befuddled with wine;
they lurch about with strong drink,

stagger as they see visions,
go astray in giving judgment;
[8]all tables are covered in vomit,
no place free of filth.

iv

[9]"To whom would he impart knowledge?
To whom would he expound what has been heard?
Those newly weaned from milk?
Those just taken from the breast?
[10]For it is *ṣav lāṣāv, ṣav lāṣāv,*
qav lāqāv, qav lāqāv,
here a little, there a little!"

[11]It will be with stammering speech
and in another language
that God will speak to this people.
[12]To them God once said,
"This is true rest, let them give rest to the weary,
this is true repose"—but they would not listen.
[13]So to them the word of Yahveh will be:
"*ṣav lāṣāv, ṣav lāṣāv,*
qav lāqav, qav lāqāv,
here a little, there a little,"
so that when they walk
they will stumble and fall backwards,
injured, trapped, and taken.

THE DEAL WITH DEATH UNDONE (28:14–22)

28   [14]Therefore, hear the word of Yahveh, you scoffers
who rule this people in Jerusalem:
[15]You have declared:
"We have cut a deal with Death,
with Sheol we have made a pact,
that when the raging flood passes through
it will not touch us;
for we have made a lie our shelter,
in falsehood we have taken refuge."
[16]Wherefore, thus says the sovereign lord Yahveh:
"I will lay in Zion a stone, a foundation stone for a tower,
a precious cornerstone set firmly in place;
the one who is trustful will not act hastily.

¹⁷I will make justice the measuring line,
righteousness the plummet;
hail will sweep away the shelter of lies,
water will overwhelm the refuge;
¹⁸then your deal with Death will be annulled,
your pact with Sheol will not stand;
when the raging flood passes through
you will be battered down by it."
¹⁹[Whenever it passes through it will reach you,
it will pass through morning after morning,
by day and by night;
grasping the message will bring nothing but panic]
²⁰for the bed is too short to stretch out on,
the blanket too skimpy for a covering.
²¹Yahveh will arise as he arose on Mount Perazim;
he will rage as in the Valley of Gibeon,
to do his deed—strange is his deed!
to perform his work—uncanny is his work!
²²And now, do not go on scoffing
or your bonds will be tightened even more,
for I have heard destruction decreed
by the sovereign lord Yahveh of the hosts
over all the earth.

THE PARABLE OF THE GOOD
FARMER (28:23–29)

i

28   ²³Listen with attention to my voice.
Take note and hear what I say:
²⁴Does the plowman plow all day long [for the sowing],
breaking up his soil and harrowing it?
²⁵Or rather, when he has leveled its surface,
will he not scatter fennel and sow cummin,
plant wheat in fair measure, barley in its proper place,
and spelt as a border?
²⁶He deals with it in just measure; his God provides the rain.

ii

²⁷Fennel is not crushed with a threshing-sledge,
a cartwheel is not rolled over cummin,
but fennel is beaten with a stick,
cummin with a rod.

²⁸Grain for bread is pounded,
but the thresher doesn't thresh it forever;
he drives the cartwheel over it,
he spreads it out but doesn't crush it.
²⁹This too is a lesson that comes from Yahveh of the hosts;
wonderful is his counsel,
great is his wisdom.

ARIEL'S REVERSAL OF FORTUNE (29:1–8)

i

29 ¹Alas for Ariel, Ariel,
town where David encamped!
Let one year follow another,
let the festivals follow their course.
²I will still bring distress on Ariel.
There will be moaning and mourning;
she will be an Ariel indeed for me!
³I will encamp [like David] against you,
besiege you with a siege tower,
erect ramparts against you;
⁴you will be brought down, you will speak from the underworld,
from the dust your words will issue,
your voice will sound like a ghost from the underworld,
your words like a whisper from the dust.

ii

⁵But then the horde of your foes will become like fine dust,
the horde of oppressors like chaff blowing by;
then suddenly, in an instant,
⁶punishment will come from Yahveh of the hosts,
with thunder, earthquake, and a fearsome noise,
whirlwind, tempest, a flame of devouring fire.
⁷Then the horde of all the nations that war against Ariel,
all who build siegeworks against her,
all who oppress her,
will fade like a dream, like a vision of the night;
⁸like one who is famished and dreams he is eating,
and wakes up as hungry as before,
or like one who is thirsty and dreams he is drinking,
but wakes up as thirsty and parched as before.
So shall be the horde of all nations
that war against Zion.

THE BLIND AND THE OBTUSE (29:9–14)

i

29   ^{9}Be in a daze, be in a stupor,
        close your eyes fast, be blind,
        be drunk, but not with wine,
        stagger, but not with strong drink!
   ^{10}For Yahveh has poured out upon you
        a spirit of deepest slumber;
        he has closed your eyes [the prophets]
        he has covered your heads [the seers].

ii

^{11}The vision of all these things has become for you like the words of a sealed book. When they hand it to one who knows how to read saying, "Read this," he replies, "I can't, for it is sealed." ^{12}When they hand the book to one who cannot read saying, "Read this," he replies, "I don't know how to read."

iii

^{13}The Lord says:
Because this people approach me with their mouths
and honor me with their lips
while their hearts are far from me,
and their reverence for me is a human commandment learnt by rote,
^{14}I will perform yet more strange and wonderful things with this people;
the wisdom of their sages shall vanish,
the discernment of their knowing ones shall disappear.

THE LIMITATIONS OF POLITICAL
KNOW-HOW (29:15–24)

i

29   ^{15}Woe to those who would hide their plans
        too deep for Yahveh to see,
        and think, since their deeds are done in the dark,
        "Who sees us? Who knows what we are about?"
   ^{16}You have things the wrong way round!
        As if the potter were no different from the clay,
        or as if what is made were to say of its maker,
        "He did not make me,"
        or the product made of clay of the one who fashioned it,
        "He has no skill."

ii

¹⁷In just a little while
will not Lebanon be turned into a fertile land
and fertile land be as common as scrubland?
¹⁸On that day the deaf will hear the words of a book,
and free of all gloom and darkness
the eyes of the sightless will see;
¹⁹the lowly will once more have joy in Yahveh,
the needy will rejoice in the Holy One of Israel;
²⁰for the violent will be no more,
the arrogant will cease to be;
all those who are prompt to do evil,
²¹who frustrate those seeking redress,
who entrap those bringing a case to judgment,
who pervert by falsehood the cause of the innocent
—all these will be extirpated.

iii

²²Therefore, thus says Yahveh, the God of the household of Jacob, who redeemed Abraham:
This is no time for Jacob to be ashamed,
no time for his face to grow pale;
²³when his children see what I do in their midst
they will hallow my name,
they will hallow the Holy One of Jacob,
stand in awe of the God of Israel;
²⁴those who err in their thinking will acquire understanding,
the obstinate will accept instruction.

THE FOLLY OF AN ALLIANCE
WITH EGYPT (30:1–5)

30   ¹Woe to the rebellious children
[an oracle of Yahveh]
making plans but not derived from me,
seeking security but not inspired by me,
piling sin upon sin.
²They set out on the journey to Egypt
but without consulting me,
to take refuge under Pharaoh's protection,
to shelter in Egypt's shadow;
³but Pharaoh's protection will bring you shame,
sheltering in Egypt's shadow will end in humiliation,

⁴for though his nobles are at Zoan,
and his envoys have reached Hanes,
⁵all remain disillusioned
on account of that profitless people;
for them they can offer no help, no advantage,
only shame and disgrace.

ANIMALS OF THE NEGEV: AN ORACLE (30:6–7)

30 ⁶Animals of the Negev: an oracle:

Through a land of dire distress,
the haunt of lioness and roaring lion,
poisonous snake and flying serpent,
they carry their goods on the backs of donkeys,
their treasures on the humps of camels
to a profitless people.
⁷Vain and worthless is Egypt's help;
therefore, I name it:
"Rahab reduced to silence."

WRITE IT FOR POSTERITY (30:8–14)

i

30 ⁸Now come, write it on a tablet,
inscribe it in a book in their presence
that it may be there in time to come
as a witness forever;
⁹for they are a rebellious people,
deceitful children,
children unwilling to obey
Yahveh's instructions;
¹⁰who say to the seers, "do not see,"
to the visionaries "do not envision what is right for us,
tell us smooth and soft things,
see seductive visions,
¹¹turn aside from the way,
leave the right path,
stop talking to us about the Holy One of Israel!"

ii

¹²So, this is what the Holy One of Israel says:
"Since you reject this saying,

trusting in a perverse oppressor
and placing your confidence in him,
¹³this iniquitous act will be for you
like a fault in a lofty wall
bulging out and ready to fall;
its collapse will come suddenly, in an instant,
¹⁴it will come apart like the breaking of a potter's vessel
that is smashed without mercy;
among its fragments no sherd will be found
for carrying fire from the hearth
or scooping water from the cistern."

IGNOMINIOUS DEFEAT
AWAITS YOU (30:15–17)

30   ¹⁵This is what the Sovereign Lord Yahveh, the Holy One of Israel, has said:
"In turning back and staying still you will be safe,
in quiet confidence your strength will lie"
—but you did not want it.
¹⁶"No," you said, "we can always flee on horseback."
"All right, then, flee you shall!"
"Swiftly will we ride."
"Then those who pursue you will swiftly follow.
¹⁷[A thousand will flee when threatened by one.]
You will flee when threatened by five,
until you are left
like a flagpole on top of a mountain,
like a lookout post on a hill."

MERCY WILL EMBRACE YOU
ON EVERY SIDE (30:18–26)

i

30   ¹⁸Therefore Yahveh waits to show you favor,
therefore he bestirs himself to have compassion on you;
for Yahveh is a God of justice,
blessed are all those who wait for him!

ii

¹⁹You people in Zion, you who dwell in Jerusalem, you shall weep no
more. He will surely show you favor when you cry for help, and he will answer
you when he hears you. ²⁰The Sovereign Lord may give you the bread of

adversity and the water of affliction, yet your teacher will no longer remain hidden. Your eyes will see your teacher, [21]and whenever you turn aside either to the right or the left your ears will hear a word spoken behind you: "This is the way, keep to it."

[22]Then you will reject as unclean your silver-coated images and your molten idols plated with gold. You will refer to them as filth and throw them out like a thing unclean.

iii

[23]Yahveh will give rain for the seed with which you sow the soil and grain for bread, the produce of the soil, will be rich and abundant. On that day your cattle will graze in broad pastures, [24]and the oxen and donkeys that work the land will feed on rich fodder winnowed with shovel and pitchfork. [25]On every high mountain and on every lofty hill there will flow channels of running water—on a day of great slaughter when the towers come crashing down. [26]Moonlight will be as bright as sunlight, and sunlight will be seven times brighter than now [like the light of seven days]. All this on the day Yahveh binds up the broken limbs of his people and heals the wounds caused by the blows inflicted on them.

ASSYRIA—THE FINAL PHASE (30:27–33)

i

30 [27]Observe: the name of Yahveh comes from afar
blazing in anger,
heavy with a sense of doom;
his lips are charged with wrath,
his tongue is a consuming fire,
[28]his breath is like an overflowing torrent
that reaches up to the neck;
he will place on the nations a yoke that spells their ruin,
a bit on the jaws of the peoples to lead them where they would not go.

ii

[29]But for you there will be singing as on a night of sacred pilgrimage; heartfelt rejoicing as when one sets out to the sound of the flute to go to Yahveh's mountain, the rock of Israel. [30]Yahveh will make his glorious voice heard and reveal his arm sweeping down in furious anger, together with a flame of devouring fire, with cloudburst, torrents of rain, and hailstones. [31]At the sound of Yahveh's voice Assyria will be seized with terror as Yahveh plies the rod. [32]Every stroke of the stick that Yahveh lays on them in punishment will be to the sound of tabors, harps, and dancing. [His brandishing arm fights for him.] [33]For his tophet was set up long ago; [it was also prepared for Molek]; his pyre Yahveh has made deep and wide, with fire and wood in abundance. Yahveh's breath inside it will keep it burning like a stream of sulphur.

THE ALLIANCE WITH EGYPT
IS DOOMED (31:1–10)

i

31   ¹Woe to those who go down to Egypt for help,
who rely on horses,
who put their trust in chariots on account of their size
and in horsemen on account of their great strength,
but do not look to the Holy One of Israel
nor seek guidance from Yahveh.
²But he too is wise and can bring about disaster;
he does not renege on what he says
but will rise up against a household of evildoers,
against those who help others do wrong.
³Egypt is human, it is not superhuman,
its horses are flesh and not spirit;
when Yahveh puts forth his hand
the helper will stumble, the one helped will fall,
and both will perish together.

ii

⁴This is what Yahveh said to me:
As the lion or the lion cub growls over its prey
when a band of shepherds is called out against it,
and is not frightened off by their shouting
nor cowed by their clamor,
so Yahveh of the hosts will descend to do battle
on Mount Zion and on its summit.
⁵Like birds hovering overhead
so will Yahveh of the hosts protect Jerusalem;
he will protect and deliver,
he will spare and rescue.

iii

⁶Return, O Israel, to the One whom you have so profoundly offended, ⁷for
on that day all of you will reject your gods of silver and gods of gold that your
sinful hands made for yourselves.

iv

⁸Assyria will fall by no human sword,
and no mortal sword will consume him;
before that sword he will flee,
his youths will be put to forced labor,
⁹his leaders will pass away from terror,
his officers shrink in terror from the enemy's standard.

¹⁰This is a saying of Yahveh, whose light burns in Zion, whose furnace is in Jerusalem.

THE RIGHTEOUS KINGDOM (32:1–8)

32   ¹When a king reigns with righteousness,
and princes govern with justice,
²each of them will be like a refuge from the wind,
a shelter from the tempest;
or like streams of water on the parched soil,
like the shade of a great rock in an arid land.

³Then the eyes that can see will no longer be closed,
the ears that can hear will listen,
⁴the minds of the rash will understand and know,
the tongues of stammerers will speak freely,
⁵a fool will no longer be called noble,
nor a villain reckoned of high estate;
⁶for fools speak only what is foolish,
their minds devise only what is worthless,
they act in an impious fashion
speaking deviously even to Yahveh.
They do not satisfy the appetite of the hungry;
they leave the thirst of the thirsty unquenched.
⁷The ways of the villain are evil;
he devises infamous plans
to destroy the poor with false discourse,
and the cause of the needy with their speech;
⁸but those who are noble devise only what is noble,
taking their stand on honor.

MOURNING, BUT NOT FOREVER (32:9–20)

32   ⁹You women at ease, hear my voice;
complacent young women, attend to what I say:
¹⁰Though now without a care, within a year at most
you will be trembling with fear;
the vintage will be lost, the harvest will fail.

¹¹So shake with fear, you women at ease;
tremble, you complacent ones;
strip yourselves bare,
put a cloth around your waists,

¹²beat your breasts
for the fields once pleasant, the vine once fruitful.
¹³On the soil of my people
you bring up thorns and briars,
in every happy home
and in the bustling town.
¹⁴For the palace is abandoned,
the city once crowded deserted,
the citadel and the watchtower have become open fields forever,
the joy of wild donkeys
pastureland for flocks . . .

¹⁵ . . . until a spirit from on high is poured out on us,
then the wilderness will be turned into fertile land,
and fertile land will be reckoned as common as forest;
¹⁶justice will make a home in the wilderness,
righteousness will dwell in the fertile land,
¹⁷peace will be the outcome of righteousness,
justice will bring about tranquillity and trust forevermore;
¹⁸my people will reside in a peaceful abode,
in secure dwellings where they can rest at ease.
¹⁹It will hail when the forest goes down,
and in the lowlands the city will be laid low.
²⁰Happy will you be as you sow beside every waterway,
leaving ox and ass to roam free.

A TYRANT CONDEMNED (33:1)

33 ¹Woe to you, destroyer, not yourself destroyed,
treacherous one, who has not been betrayed!
When you have finished your destroying you yourself will be destroyed;
when you have finished acting treacherously you will be dealt with
    treacherously.

A PSALM OF PETITION AND PRAISE (33:2–6)

33 ²Yahveh, show us your favor,
in you we place our trust;
be our support every morning,
our salvation in the time of trouble.
³At the sound of a tumult peoples take to flight,
when you rise up in majesty nations are scattered;

⁴then spoil is gathered as the locust gathers it,
like swarming locusts they settle upon it.
⁵Yahveh is exalted, for he dwells on high,
he has filled Zion with justice and righteousness;
⁶he will be the stability of her times;
wisdom and knowledge are riches that lead to salvation;
her treasure is the fear of Yahveh.

A SCENE OF SOCIAL AND PHYSICAL DISASTER (33:7–13)

i

33 ⁷Hark, Ariel's people cry for help in the streets,
Salem's messengers are weeping bitterly.
⁸The highways are destroyed,
there are no more wayfarers;
he has broken the agreement, despised the witnesses;
people have no thought for others.
⁹The land is mourning, pining;
Lebanon, ashamed, is withering away;
Sharon has become a desert;
Bashan and Carmel are stripped bare.

ii

¹⁰Now, Yahveh declares, "I will rise up,
now I will exalt myself,
now I will raise myself up.
¹¹You conceive chaff, you bring forth stubble;
a fiery wind will consume you;
¹²nations will be turned into heaps of burnt-out ash,
like thorns cut down and set on fire.
¹³Hear, you who are far away, what I have done,
acknowledge my power, you who are close at hand."

A MORAL CATECHISM (33:14–16)

i

33 ¹⁴Sinners shake with fear in Zion;
trembling has seized the impious.
Which of us can abide this devouring fire?
Which of us can abide this everlasting burning?

ii

¹⁵Those whose conduct is righteous,
whose speech is honest,
who scorn what is gained by oppression,
who shake their hands free of a bribe,
who stop their ears from hearing murderous plans
and close their eyes so as not to look on evil.
¹⁶These are the ones who dwell on the heights,
whose refuge is a fortress among the rocks,
whose bread is at hand, whose supply of water is secure.

A FUTURE WITHOUT FEAR (33:17–24)

33 ¹⁷Your eyes will behold a king in his beauty;
they will look on a land stretching far and wide;
¹⁸your mind will dwell on what you once dreaded:
"Where is the one who took the census?
Where is the one who assessed the tribute?
Where is the one who counted the towers?"
¹⁹You will no longer see an insolent people,
a people whose speech is too obscure to understand,
stammering in a language you cannot comprehend.
²⁰Look on Zion, city of our festivals;
let your eyes look on Jerusalem,
a secure place to live, a tent that will not be moved,
whose pegs will never be pulled out,
and none of its ropes untied.
²¹There the glorious name of Yahveh will be ours.
[It will be a place of broad rivers and streams,
but there no galley can sail,
no stately ship can pass.]
²²Yahveh is our ruler, Yahveh is our leader,
Yahveh is our king, he will save us!
²³[Your rigging is slack,
it cannot hold steady the mast
nor can they spread the sail.]
Then even the blind will have their share of abundant spoil;
even the lame will take part in the pillage.
²⁴None of the inhabitants will say, "I am sick";
the people that live there will be quit of all guilt.

A SWORD OVER EDOM (34:1–17)

i

34 ¹Approach, you nations to listen;
you peoples, give heed!
Let the earth and what fills it hear,
the world and all its issue!
²Yahveh is incensed with all the nations,
his fury is directed against all their hosts,
he has doomed them and destined them for slaughter;
³their slain will be cast out,
the stench of their corpses will arise,
the mountains will flow with their blood;
⁴all the hosts of heaven will rot,
the sky will be rolled up like a scroll;
all its hosts shall wither away
like the leaf that withers from the vine,
like the fruit that withers from the fig tree.

ii

⁵When my sword is seen in the sky
then it will descend upon Edom,
on a people I have destined for judgment.
⁶Yahveh has a sword, it is covered in blood,
it is dripping with fat,
with the blood of lambs and goats,
with the fat from the kidneys of rams;
for Yahveh has a sacrifice in Bozrah,
a great slaughtering in the land of Edom;
⁷wild oxen will be felled with the people,
bulls alongside of their strongest;
their land will drink deep of blood,
their soil will be soaked in fat.

iii

⁸Yahveh has a day of vengeance,
a year of reckoning for Zion's complaint;
⁹the wadis of Edom will be turned into pitch,
her soil into brimstone,
her land will be burning pitch;
¹⁰night and day it will burn unquenched,
its smoke will go up for ever.
From age to age the land will lie waste,
to all eternity no people will pass through it.

¹¹The hawk and the hedgehog will claim it as their own,
owl and raven will make it their home;
Yahveh has stretched over it the measuring line of chaos,
and the stones of turmoil.
¹²Her nobles . . .
They shall acclaim no monarchy there;
all her princes will be of no account.
¹³Thorns will spring up in her palaces,
nettles and thistles in her forts;
it will become the haunt of jackals,
the abode of ostriches;
¹⁴wildcats will gather with hyenas,
the satyr will call to his mate,
there too will Lilith alight
and there find a spot for herself;
¹⁵there the owl will nest,
lay her eggs, hatch them, and give them shelter;
there too the kites will gather,
not one without its mate.

iv

¹⁶Consult the book of Yahveh, read it:
none of these will be missing,
[not one of them without its mate]
for from his own mouth came the command,
and with his own breath he has assembled them;
¹⁷it is he who has allotted them their place,
his hand has assigned it with the measuring line;
they will claim it as their own forever,
they will dwell there for all ages to come.

THE FINAL RESTORATION OF JUDAH (35:1–10)

i

35   ¹Let the desert and parched land be glad,
the wilderness rejoice and blossom;
²let it burst into blossom like the asphodel,
rejoicing and shouting for joy.
The glory of Lebanon will be given to it,
the splendor of Carmel and Sharon;
they will witness the glory of Yahveh,
the splendor of our God.

ii

³Strengthen the hands that are weak,
steady the knees that are feeble,
⁴say to the fearful of heart,
"Courage, don't be afraid;
Behold your God!
Vengeance is at hand,
fearsome retribution;
it is he who comes to save you."

iii

⁵Then the eyes of the blind will be opened,
the ears of the deaf unstopped;
⁶then the cripple will leap like the deer,
and the tongue of the dumb shout for joy.
Yes, water will burst forth in the desert,
wadis flow in the wilderness;
⁷the mirage will turn into a pool,
the parched land into gushing streams;
the haunt where jackals crouched
will be a place of reeds and rushes.
⁸There will be a highway there;
it will be called The Way of Holiness;
the unclean will not pass by that way,
it will be for the use of pilgrims,
fools will not wander along it.
⁹There will be no lions there,
no savage beasts will come up on it,
none shall be found there.
The redeemed shall walk there,
¹⁰those ransomed by Yahveh shall return;
shouting for joy, they shall enter Zion
crowned with joy everlasting;
gladness and joy will be theirs,
sorrow and sighing will depart.

JERUSALEM THREATENED AND RESCUED (36:1–37:38)

First Version

36 ¹In the fourteenth year of King Hezekiah, Sennacherib king of Assyria attacked and captured all the fortified cities of Judah. ²The king of Assyria then sent the Rabshakeh from Lachish to Jerusalem to King Hezekiah together with

a large force, and the Rabshakeh stationed himself at the conduit of the Upper Pool on the way to Bleacher's Meadow. [3]There went out to him Eliakim ben Hilkiah superintendent of the palace, Shebna the first minister, and Joah ben Asaph the herald.

[4]The Rabshakeh addressed them: "Give Hezekiah this message: Thus says the great king, the king of Assyria, 'What makes you so confident? [5]Do you think mouthing mere words amounts to a plan for waging war and the means to do it? On whom, then, are you relying that you have rebelled against me? [6]So you are relying on Egypt, a support no better than a splintered reed that will pierce and gouge the hand of the one who leans on it. Such is Pharaoh king of Egypt for all those who rely on him. [7]And if you tell me you are relying on Yahveh your God, was it not he whose high places and altars Hezekiah removed, instructing Judah and Jerusalem that they were to worship before this altar? [8]Come now, make a wager with my master the king of Assyria: I will give you two thousand horses if you can put riders on them. [9]How then can you, relying as you do on Egypt for chariots and cavalry, repulse a single one among the least of my master's servants? [10]Furthermore, was it without the consent of Yahveh that I attacked this land to destroy it? No; Yahveh himself told me, "Attack this land and destroy it." ' "

[11]Eliakim [Shebna and Joah] made this reply to the Rabshakeh: "Please address your servants in Aramaic, since we understand it; do not address us in Hebrew in the hearing of the people who are on the wall." [12]But the Rabshakeh replied: "Did my master send me to deliver this message to you and your master and not also to these people sitting on the wall who together with you are doomed to eat their own shit and drink their own piss?" [13]So the Rabshakeh stood up and shouted out loud in Hebrew: "Hear the message of the great king, the king of Assyria! [14]These are the king's words: Do not let Hezekiah deceive you; he is unable to rescue you. [15]Do not let Hezekiah con you into relying on Yahveh with the message, 'Yahveh will surely rescue us; this city will not be handed over to the king of Assyria.' [16]Do not listen to Hezekiah. This is the message of the king of Assyria: Make your peace with me; come out to me; then each one of you may eat the fruit of his own vine and fig tree and drink the water from his own well, [17]until such time as I take you to a land like your own, a land rich in wheat and wine, grain and vineyards. [18]Do not let Hezekiah mislead you with his claim, 'Yahveh will rescue us.' Did any of the gods of the other nations rescue his land from the king of Assyria? [19]Where now are the gods of Hamath and Arpad? Where are the gods of Sepharvaim? Where are the gods of the land of Samaria? Did they rescue Samaria from me? [20]Did any of the gods of these lands rescue their lands from me? How then will Yahveh rescue Jerusalem from me?"

[21]They remained silent, answering him not a word, for the king had ordered them not to answer him. [22]So Eliakim ben Hilkiah superintendent of the palace, Shebna the first minister, and Joah ben Asaph the herald went back to Hezekiah with their clothes torn and reported to him what the Rabshakeh had said. 37 [1]When King Hezekiah heard it, he tore his clothes, put on

sackcloth, and went to the house of Yahveh. [2]He sent Eliakim superintendent of the palace, Shebna the first minister, and the senior priests clothed in sackcloth to the prophet Isaiah ben Amoz. [3]They said to him, "This is Hezekiah's message: Today is a day of trouble, reproach and contempt. We are like women who do not have the strength to bring forth their children as they are about to be born. [4]It may be that Yahveh your God will pay heed to the words of the Rabshakeh whom his master the king of Assyria sent to insult the living God and will refute what Yahveh your God heard said. Offer a prayer, then, for the remnant that is left here."

[5]King Hezekiah's officials then came to Isaiah, [6]and Isaiah told them, "This is what you must say to your master: this is the message of Yahveh: 'Do not be alarmed at what you have heard said when the king of Assyria's officials reviled me. [7]I am about to put a spirit in him; he will hear a rumor, return to his own country, and I will cause him to fall by the sword in his own land.'"

[8]Having heard that the king of Assyria had moved on from Lachish, the Rabshakeh returned to find him attacking Libnah.

Second Version

[9]When the king heard that Tirhakah the Nubian king had set out to wage war against him, he [once again] sent envoys to Hezekiah with this message: [10]"This is what you are to say to Hezekiah king of Judah: 'Do not let your God in whom you trust deceive you with the promise that Jerusalem will not be handed over to the king of Assyria. [11]You must have heard what the kings of Assyria did to all the countries, destroying them completely, and you expect to escape? [12]Did the gods of the lands that my ancestors destroyed rescue them—the gods of Gozan, Haran, Reseph, and the people of Eden living in Telassar? [13]Where now is the king of Hamath, the king of Arpad, the king of the city of Sepharvaim or of Hena or of Ivvah?'"

[14]Hezekiah took the letter from the envoys and read it. He then went up into the house of Yahveh and opened it out in the presence of Yahveh. [15]Hezekiah offered this prayer to Yahveh:

[16]Yahveh of hosts, God of Israel enthroned on the cherubim, you alone are God of all the kingdoms of the earth. It is you who made the heavens and the earth. [17]Yahveh, incline your ear and listen; Yahveh, open your eyes and see; hear all the words that Sennacherib has sent to insult the living God. [18]It is true, O Yahveh, that the kings of Assyria have devastated every land [19]and have consigned the gods of these lands to the fire, for they are no gods but rather objects of wood and stone, the work of human hands, and so they were destroyed. [20]But now, Yahveh our God, rescue us from his grasp, so that all the kingdoms of the earth may acknowledge that you alone, Yahveh, are God.

[21]Isaiah ben Amoz then sent the following message to Hezekiah: This is what Yahveh God of Israel says: Since you have prayed to me concerning Sennacherib king of Assyria, [22]this is the word that Yahveh has spoken concerning him:

The virgin daughter of Zion despises you, she scorns you;
the daughter of Jerusalem tosses her head as you withdraw.
[23] Whom have you mocked and abused?
Against whom have you raised your voice?
You have looked down on the Holy One of Israel!
[24] Through your servants you have mocked the Sovereign Lord;
you have declared: "With my many chariots
I have gone up the highest mountains,
to the inner recesses of Lebanon;
I have felled its tallest cedars,
its finest cypresses;
I have reached its highest point,
the forest of its pasture land;
[25] I have dug wells,
I have drunk the water of foreigners;
with the sole of my foot I have dried up
all the streams of Egypt."

[26] Have you not heard
how I devised it a long time ago,
devised it from days of old?
And now I have brought it about
that fortified cities are turned into heaps of rubble,
[27] their inhabitants devoid of strength,
dismayed, ashamed.
They have become like wild plants,
like green grass,
like grass on the housetops, blighted by the east wind.
[28] I know your rising up and your sitting down,
your coming and your going;
[29] your fury directed at me and your arrogance
have come to my hearing.
I will put my hook in your nose,
my bit through your lips,
and I will lead you back by the way you came.

[30] This shall be the sign for you: This year eat aftergrowth, in the second year what grows naturally, but in the third year sow and reap, plant vineyards and eat their fruit. [31] The remaining survivors of the household of Judah shall once again take root below and bring forth fruit above; [32] for from Jerusalem a remnant shall go forth, survivors from Mount Zion. The zeal of Yahveh of hosts shall bring this about.

[33] This, therefore, is the word of Yahveh concerning the king of Assyria:
He shall not enter this city,
he shall shoot no arrow there,

he shall not advance on it with shield
nor cast up a siege ramp against it.
[34]By the way he came he will return,
but this city he shall not enter!
An oracle of Yahveh.
[35]I will defend this city to rescue it,
for my own sake and for the sake of my servant David.

[36]The angel of Yahveh went out and struck down one hundred and eighty-
five thousand people in the Assyrian camp; when morning came they were all
lying dead. [37]Then Sennacherib king of Assyria broke camp and left. He returned to Nineveh and stayed there. [38]While he was worshiping in the temple
of Nisroch his god, Adrammelek and Sarezer his sons killed him with the sword
and escaped to the land of Ararat. Esarhaddon his son reigned in his place.

Hezekiah's Sickness and
Recovery (38:1–22)

38   [1]At that time Hezekiah fell sick and was close to death. The prophet Isaiah
ben Amoz came and said to him, "This is what Yahveh has said: 'Put the affairs
of your household in order for you are going to die; you will not recover.'"
[2]Hezekiah turned his face to the wall and prayed to Yahveh: [3]"Remember,
Yahveh, I beseech you, how I have conducted myself in your presence faithfully and wholeheartedly, and how I have done what pleases you." And Hezekiah wept copious tears.

[4]Then the word of Yahveh came to Isaiah: [5]"Go and tell Hezekiah: 'This
is what Yahveh, God of David your ancestor, has said: I have heard your prayer,
I have seen your tears. I will add fifteen years to your life span. [6]I will also rescue you and this city from the grasp of the king of Assyria, and I will defend this
city.'" [7]This is the sign for you from Yahveh that Yahveh will bring about what
he has promised. [8]When the sun sets on the stairway to the upper room of Ahaz,
I will turn backwards a distance of ten steps the shadow on the stairs. The light
from the setting sun went back ten steps on the stairway.

[9]A composition of Hezekiah king of Judah written after he had recovered
from his sickness.
[10]I thought, in the prime of life
I must depart,
consigned to the gates of Sheol
for the rest of my days.
[11]I thought, Yahveh no longer will I behold
in the land of the living,

no longer look on mortals
with the people who inhabit the world.
[12]My dwelling is plucked up, removed from over my head
like a shepherd's tent;
I have gathered up my life like a weaver;
he cuts me off from the loom.
All day long, all night long, you consume me,
[13]I cry for help until the morning.
Like a lion he breaks all my bones,
[14]like a swallow or a thrush I chirp,
I moan like a dove,
my eyes are worn out from looking upwards;
O Lord, take up my cause, be my surety!
[15]What can I say? for he has addressed me,
it is he who did it.
I toss to and fro all the time I am sleeping
because of the bitterness of my soul.
[16]Lord, those to whom you give life will live,
all these have the spirit of life;
restore me, let me live!

[17]Bitterness was my lot instead of peace,
but now in love you have preserved my life
from the pit of destruction;
for you have cast all my sins
behind your back.
[18]Sheol cannot thank you,
death cannot praise you;
those who go down to the abyss
cannot hope for your faithfulness.
[19]It is the living, the living that will thank you
as I do this day.
The father makes known to the children
how faithful you are.
[20]Yahveh is here to save us,
let us make music with psalms of praise
all the days of our life in the house of Yahveh.

[21]Then Isaiah said, "Let them take a cake of figs and apply it to the boil.
[They did so] and he recovered.

[22]Said Hezekiah, "What is the sign assuring me that I will go up to the
house of Yahveh?"

A BABYLONIAN DELEGATION
VISITS HEZEKIAH (39:1–8)

39 ¹At that time Merodach-Baladan son of Baladan king of Babylon sent envoys with a gift to Hezekiah, for he had heard that he had recovered from his illness. ²Hezekiah made them welcome. He showed them all his treasury, silver and gold, spices and precious oil, his armory and everything in his storerooms. There was nothing in his palace and in all his realm that Hezekiah did not show them.

³Then the prophet Isaiah approached Hezekiah and asked him, "What did these people say, and where did they come from to you?" "They came to me from a distant land, from Babylon," replied Hezekiah. ⁴Then Isaiah asked, "And what did they see in your palace?" "They saw everything in my palace," replied Hezekiah, "There was nothing in my store rooms that I did not show them." ⁵Isaiah then said to Hezekiah: "Hear the word of Yahveh of the hosts: ⁶The time is coming, says Yahveh, when everything in your palace and everything that has been accumulated by your forebears down to the present will be carried off to Babylon. Not a thing will be left. ⁷They will also take some of your male descendants who will issue from you, whom you will beget, and they will be made eunuchs in the palace of the king of Babylon." ⁸Hezekiah said to Isaiah, "The word of Yahveh that you have spoken is positive." He was thinking: "So long as there is peace and security in my lifetime."

INTRODUCTION

◆

INTRODUCTION TO THE BOOK OF ISAIAH

◆

FOREWORD

Writing a commentary on Isa 1–39 in the middle of a paradigm shift has not been easy. In Isaiah studies, as in the study of the Pentateuch, we observe over the last quarter of a century or so a growing dissatisfaction with the received wisdom on the formation of the book and a more insistent probing for a new paradigm. In biblical studies, major paradigms seem to have a life-span of about a century: Wellhausen's *Prolegomena*, which set the agenda for the critical study of the Pentateuch, appeared in 1883, and Duhm's *Das Buch Jesaja*, a landmark publication in Isian studies, in 1892. By the 1970s, the inadequacies of both the classic Wellhausenian documentary hypothesis and the standard divisioning of the book by Duhm were becoming increasingly apparent. As a heterogeneous literary compilation, First Isaiah (chs. 1–39) was beginning to look more like the Book of the Twelve and less like Jeremiah or Ezekiel, and it was beginning to appear that Isaiah could be considered the author of the book only in something of the same way that traditionally the authorship of the Pentateuch was assigned to Moses, the Psalms to David, and the didactic compositions to Solomon. The disparate character of the material in Isa 1–39 also came into clearer focus the more the cohesion and unity of chs. 40–55 were emphasized.

The tendency among many critical scholars in recent decades is to assume that both the Pentateuch and the book of Isaiah are essentially Second Temple compilations, literary constructs put together by the intellectual and religious elite during the Persian period (sixth to the fourth centuries B.C.E.) or even later. It is therefore not surprising that interest in the person and personality of an historical Isaiah has receded, for some commentators to the vanishing point. Few critical scholars today would feel justified in emulating Samuel Rolles Driver by writing on "Isaiah, His Life and Times," and many would be uncomfortable with George Buchanan Gray's contention that it is the task of the commentator "to disengage the work of the prophet from the accretions which it has received" (1912, xi). It may be readily admitted that Isaiah's authorship of the sayings is weakly attested on any showing, resting as it does on three titles (1:1; 2:1; 13:1), all acknowledged to be of late date and one of which, introducing an anti-Babylonian poem (13:1), is impossible to put back into the time of the prophet. There is also considerable intertexual overlap between Isaiah and the Book of the Twelve, to the extent of suggesting to us that the editors of the prophetic material allowed themselves considerable fluidity and license in attributing prophetic sayings to specific authors, or even that the book of Isaiah served as a kind of deposit for miscellaneous prophecies dealing with the destiny of Jerusalem and Judah. The prose narratives in chs. 7, 20, and 36–39 further complicate the issue, since they present a prophetic figure, a "man of God," significantly different from the putative author of the sayings. In the commentary I believe that I give these considerations due weight, and I recognize the contrasting profiles in the sayings and in the narrative as a major issue in the interpretation of the book. But I see no reason to disallow a significant eighth century B.C.E. Isaian substratum, especially in view of the rather clear indications of affinity with Amos and Micah, however overlaid it may be by the literary deposit of subsequent rereadings before and after the disasters of the early sixth century B.C.E. I will also hold out for a degree of consistency of language, subject matter, and theme throughout Isa 1–39 that allows us to speak of an Isaian tradition carried forward by means of a cumulative process of reinterpretation and reapplication. Such a solution will probably satisfy neither traditional readers nor those of a more radical frame of mind, but this is the position that seems to me suggested by a careful reading of the texts.

1. THE BOOK OF ISAIAH WITHIN THE LATTER PROPHETS AND THE CANON OF THE HEBREW BIBLE/OLD TESTAMENT

Almost all Hebrew manuscripts have the book of Isaiah in the first position among the Latter Prophets (*nĕbî'îm 'aḥărōnîm*), though the Talmudic list of biblical books and authors in *b.B.Bat.*14b–15a places it after Ezekiel. The book of Isaiah is part of a well-thought-out and well-structured arrangement: the four historical books or Former Prophets (Joshua, Judges, Samuel, Kings) followed by the four prophetic compilations (Isaiah, Jeremiah, Ezekiel, the Twelve), of which Jeremiah is the longest (22,000 words) and the Twelve the shortest (14,000), with Isaiah in between (17,000). That all eight books are classified as prophetic is due to the belief that emerged in the late Second Temple period that the writing of history was a prophetic activity. This idea is already in evidence in the way the author of Chronicles attributes the sources for his history to prophetic authors (1 Chr 29:29; 2 Chr 9:29; 12:15; 20:34; 33:19), including Isaiah (2 Chr 26:22; 32:32). It is even clearer in Josephus, who affirms—not without a thought to his own claims to prophetic inspiration and his own profession as historian—that "the prophets alone had this privilege [i.e. writing history], obtaining their knowledge of the most remote and ancient history through the inspiration that they owed to God, and committing to writing an account of the events of their own time just as they occurred" (*Ag. Ap.* 1.37). The Talmudic attestation referred to earlier turns this tradition on its head by attributing the authorship of Isaiah, in addition to Proverbs, Song of Songs, and Ecclesiastes (Qoheleth), to Hezekiah (*b.B.Bat.* 14b–15a). There seems to have been a tradition of scribal activity during Hezekiah's reign (e.g. Prov 25:1), and he is closely associated with Isaiah in the prophetic legends in chs. 36–39, in which he is said to have authored a psalm (38:9). In any case, the allusion in *Baba Batra* is probably to copying rather than authoring.

Apart from these later conceptualizations, the book of Isaiah does in fact have connections with Former Prophets (the historical books) since chs. 36–39 are roughly equivalent to 2 Kgs 18:13, 17–20:19, and 7:1 parallels 2 Kgs 16:5. Moreover, Isa 20:1–6 (Isaiah dramatizing the fate of Egyptian and Nubian captives by parading naked) belongs to the same class of prophetic stories as occur frequently in the Deuteronomistic History (hereafter the History) and reproduces the style and idiom of the Historian even in details (see the commentary on Isa 20). Herein lies one of the major problems of the book still awaiting a satisfactory solution, namely, the relation between the Isaiah of the judgment sayings and the very different personality and prophetic role performance attested in the narrative material. The issue will be addressed in due course; at this point it will suffice to note that it is not simply a matter of historical narrative excerpted by the editors of Isaiah from the History, since the material common to 2 Kgs 18–20 and Isa 36–39 draws on anti-Assyrian and anti-Egyptian diatribe in the first part of Isaiah. This, at any rate, will be argued at the appropriate point in the commentary. Somewhat less obvious are the intertextual links between Isaiah and the Twelve. It has long been suspected that Isa 1–35 and Micah have much in common with respect to their transmission and the traditions they represent. The clearest instance is Mic 4:1–5, practically identical as it is with Isa 2:2–5, but a close reading will reveal other connections (e.g. Mic 5:9–14[10–15] cf. Isa 2:6–22; Mic 1:8 cf. Isa 20:1–6). Linguistic and thematic parallels between denunciations of Nineveh in Nahum and anti-Assyrian diatribe in Isaiah would also repay investigation. Moreover, Nah 2:1a[1:15a] ("See, on the mountains the feet of one who brings good news, who announces well-being") is clearly related in some way to Isa 40:9 and 52:7, and the name Nahum in the title of this short book is reminiscent of Isa 40:1 (*naḥămû naḥămû ʿammî* . . .). To take a final example: the unfulfilled vision of Habakkuk, and the way in which the reception of the visionary experience is described (Hab 2:1–3) have much in common with the vision of the fall of Babylon in Isa 21:1–10 and may even be directly related to it (see commentary on 21:1–10). This issue of the distribution of prophetic material among books, the titles of which were assigned only at a late period, awaits further exploration.

The section called the Latter Prophets is therefore a literary construct put together at a relatively late date. That the arrangement (3 + 12) called for some manipulation of the material available at that time is also apparent, at least from the inclusion of Malachi (a fictitious name taken from Mal 3:1) and the attribution of two distinct sections beginning *maśśāʾ* . . . *dĕbar YHVH* ("an oracle . . . the word of Yahveh") to Zechariah (Zech 9:1; 12:1). In view of the allusion to the eschatological restoration and re-integration of Israel by prophetic agency in the final paragraph (Mal 3:23–24[4:5–6]), the *dodekapropheton* (Book of the Twelve) was probably meant to correspond symbolically to twelve-tribal Israel, and the 3 + 12 arrangement therefore could be taken to correspond to the three ancestors and the twelve sons of Jacob = Israel. If this is so, it would provide us with important clues to the perspective from which the prophetic books were intended to be read—namely, the eschatological restoration and reintegration of the household of Israel.

The order of books in MSS of the Septuagint (LXX) or Old Greek version (OG) is quite different from that of the Masoretic Bible (MT). In LXX the prophetic books follow the histories and didactic compositions, the sequence perhaps representing time past, present, and future, and therefore emphasizing the eschatological content of the prophetic books. Isaiah, Jeremiah, and Ezekiel, placed in chronological sequence, follow the *dodekapropheton*, the twelve so-called "minor prophets" (a misnomer), rather than preceding them, as they do in MT.

Attention to the canonical shaping of the book is frequently recommended in recent Isaian studies. The canonical approach is to be welcomed as a contribution to the theological understanding of the book as in some sense a unity, but it cannot by itself resolve critical issues having to do with the formation of the book. We cannot, for example, simply assume that chs. 40–55 were deliberately added to chs. 1–39 as a word of promise after judgment pronounced by the eighth century prophet. It is clearly not the case that in order to attach his discourses to chs. 1–39 the author of chs. 40–55 suppressed the historical context of the time of writing, since Cyrus is mentioned, his campaigns fairly clearly alluded to, and the fall of Babylon anticipated in chs. 40–48. Theological reflection on the book as a whole should follow critical study of its formation not substitute for it.

2. THE TEXT OF ISAIAH AND
THE ANCIENT VERSIONS

Most of the difficulties with the Hebrew text arise from the language itself, including the high incidence of hapax legomena, but there are also numerous textual problems. We are fortunate that the medieval text prepared by the Masoretes (MT) can now be compared with the one entire scroll of Isaiah, another partially preserved scroll, and many fragments of text discovered in the Judean Wilderness, most of which antedate the earliest previously known manuscripts of Isaiah—the Aleppo Codex (early tenth century) and the Petersburg Codex of the Latter Prophets, copied by Moses ben Asher in 895—by more than a thousand years. Next to Psalms and Deuteronomy, Isaiah is the best represented biblical text from Qumran, with at least twenty-one copies, though not all were produced there. The complete scroll of Isaiah from the first cave at Qumran (1QIsaª), the second-longest of the Qumran scrolls (54 columns and

7.34 m in length), is generally dated between 150 and 120 B.C.E. It appears to have been copied by two scribes, their assignments being marked off by a gap of three lines in the middle of the book, at the bottom of column 27 and the end of ch. 33. While in good part identical with MT, it has its own orthographic conventions, especially a generous use of vowel letters. The more significant variants, some of them dictated by a distinctive and perhaps sectarian point of view, will be pointed out in the notes as we work our way through the book.

The second, imperfectly preserved, scroll from the first Qumran cave (1QIsa[b]) was copied from a text closer to MT than 1QIsa[a]. It is of Herodian origin and covers parts of some forty-six chapters beginning at 7:22 and including most of chs. 38–66. There are few variants of any great significance (they are listed in Roberts 1959, 134–40) with the exception of 53:11, where the word *ʾôr*, "light," is added, as it is also in 1QIsa[a], 4QIsa[d], and LXX ("out of his anguish he [the Servant] shall see *light*"). In addition, fragments of eighteen MSS have been recovered from Cave 4, some (4QIsa[b] and 4QIsa[c]) quite substantial, two from Cave 1, and a small fragment from Cave 5 containing a few words from ch. 40. A fragment of a copy was also discovered in Wadi Murabbaʿat. This material can be dated approximately to the period from the early first century B.C.E. to the mid–first century C.E. and shows little significant divergence from MT. Less useful but not to be neglected are citations and references occurring here and there in the non-biblical scrolls from Qumran and citations in the Isaiah *pešārîm* (3QpIsa and 4QpIsa[a–e]).

Among the ancient versions translated directly from the Hebrew the most important is the LXX (OG), generally dated to around the middle of the second century B.C.E. Since this version is very free, paraphrastic, and interpretative, some scholars have suspected a *Vorlage* significantly different from MT, but the tendency today is to explain variants as the result of a conscious process of contemporizing and actualizing by the translator. The fact that LXX has few readings in common with 1QIsa[a] against MT points in the same direction. Comparison with MT shows a few minuses (2:22; 38:15; 40:7; 56:12) and even fewer pluses; it is quite different therefore from LXX Jeremiah, which is roughly one-eighth shorter than MT Jeremiah. At several points the translator shows an interest in bringing the text to bear on current issues and situations, a tendency characteristic of the Targum. Isaiah 8:11–15, for example, has been worded to make MT's mention of "this people" refer to the Hellenized leadership in Jerusalem under Seleucid rule (van der Kooij 1997, 519–28). Allusions to creation in the second section of the book have been brought into line with Hellenistic and especially Stoic philosophical ideas, as in the use of the verb *deiknumi*, "show forth," for *bārāʾ*, "create" in 40:26, with reference to the created world as a panorama displayed before the gods (Koenig 1982, 173–93). In this respect the translator is simply taking further the process of reapplication, reinterpretation, and *relecture* that was going on during the long period of the formation of the original Hebrew text.

There appears to be general agreement that Targum Pseudo-Jonathan comprises a Tannaitic strand composed before the Second Revolt (132–135 C.E.), in which the messianic potential of the text is maximized, and an Amoraic re-working in which it is de-emphasized. The Targum is based on a text quite close to MT. The same can be said of the Peshitta version of Isaiah, to which Syriac-speaking Christians made additions in keeping with their own messianic ideas (e.g. 7:14; 9:5; 25:6–8). *Vetus Latina*, an important secondary witness to LXX, was superseded by Jerome's *editio Vulgata*, which seldom diverges from the Masoretic-type text that became dominant in the first century of the era. Where occasion offers, Jerome will, however, choose a form of expression designed to hint at a christological-messianic sense. No doubt the most familiar example is the choice of *virgo* for ʿ*almâ* in 7:14 (*ecce virgo concipiet et pariet filium*) in preference to other possibilities (*puella, adulescentia, iuvencula*). Quotations from other early Christian authors (Ignatius, Justin Martyr, Clement of Alexandria, Eusebius, Origen), some doubtless cited from memory, are too late to be of much use. (They are conveniently collected in James 1959, 271–397.)

The earliest Arabic translation was made by the philosopher and exegete Saadia Gaon (882–942), who also produced a more popular and free translation known as the *tafsir* ("commentary"). Other secondary versions—Aquila, Symmachus, Theodotion—and the translations into Ethiopic and Armenian have had little impact on the study of the text of Isaiah. Text critics and Isaian scholars are fortunate that the first volume of the Hebrew University Bible Project to appear is *The Book of Isaiah*, edited by the late Prof. Moshe H. Goshen-Gottstein (1995). The textual basis is the Ben Asher Aleppo Codex, the earliest extant codex of the entire Bible, together with its *masora parva* and *masora magna*. The text is provided with a very rich critical apparatus covering the ancient versions, the scrolls and fragments from the Judean Wilderness, rabbinic quotations, and medieval manuscripts, including fragments from the Cairo Geniza. A separate apparatus is dedicated to variants of spelling, vowels and accents.

3. LITERARY AND STRUCTURAL CHARACTERISTICS OF THE BOOK

In the NRSV about thirty percent of chs. 1–39 and five percent of chs. 40–66 of Isaiah are typeset in prose and the rest in verse. Though probably unavoidable, and therefore maintained in the present translation with some modifications, the practice of setting out the text in this way is artificial and to some extent misleading, since it is often impossible to distinguish between rhythmic prose and prosodically irregular verse. Take as an example a few lines from Isaiah's vision (Isa 6:2), which is set out as prose in BHS and in modern English translations but which could as easily be set out in verse (the tonic accent is marked ´):

śĕrāpîm ʿōmdîm mimmaʿal lô
šēš kĕnāpáyîm šēš kĕnāpáyîm lĕʾeḥād
bištáyîm yĕkasséh pānáv
ûbištáyîm yĕkasséh ragláv
ûbištáyîm yĕʿôpēp

Seraphs were stationed round about him, each with six wings. With two they covered their faces, with two their bodies, and with two they hovered.

Parallelism has been identified as the basic characteristic of Hebrew verse since Robert Lowth's *De Sacra Poesi Hebraeorum Praelectiones* (1753). This peculiar modality was well expressed by Matthew Arnold in contrasting Isaiah with Homer and Dante. His point was that the effect of both of these great poets is achieved largely through meter and rhyme, while "Isaiah's is a poetry of parallelism; it depends not on metre and rhyme, but on a balance of thought conveyed by a corresponding balance of sentence; and the effect of this can be transferred to another language" (Arnold 1883, 4). But the phenomenon of parallelism is found in cadenced prose as well as in verse, so that for much of the material in Isaiah it can be said that "there are not two modes of utterance, but many different elements which elevate style and provide for formality and strictness of organization" (Kugel 1981, 85). Genres or literary types characteristically set in either prose or verse can, of course, be identified in the book. There is some straightforward narrative and annalistic prose (chs. 6–8; 20; 36–39) and there are numerous notes or addenda in prose, many of them introduced with the future-looking or eschatological incipit "on that day" (*bayyôm hahûʾ*). Most of these would be more at home in a commentary on the book than as part of the text. Familiar genre designations or labels also occur, though what they introduce is not always what the label leads us to expect. This is the case with the song (*šîr* 23:16; 26:1) and especially the love song of the vineyard (if "love song" is the correct translation of *šîrat dôd* 5:1), which does not look anything like a love song. Perhaps also Hezekiah's psalm, if we may read *miktām* (a type of psalm) for MT *miktāb*, a more generic term for a literary composition, in 38:9; in any case, it found its way into *The Penguin Book of Hebrew Verse* (ed. T. Carmi, 1981). There are also psalm-like passages that are not identified as such (12:1–6; 25:1–5; 33:2–6; 42:10–13; 63:7–64:12) and the limping or echoing rhythm used for the dirge (*qînâ* e.g. 1:21). The composition describing the arrival of the king of Babylonia in the underworld (14:4–21) is presented as a *māšāl*, usually translated "proverb" or "proverbial saying," but in this case evidently meaning a spoof or satire. Other designations associated with specific forms or *Gattungen* occur — "vision" (*ḥāzôn* 1:1), "utterance" (*dābār* 2:1 etc.), "oracle" (*maśśāʾ* 13:1 etc.), "woe-saying" (*hôy* 5:8 etc.) — though rarely corresponding to a *fixed* literary structure.

In view of these uncertainties of classification, I propose the term *recitative* for the bulk of the longer discourses in all sections of the book, the kind usually laid out in verse. This term has the advantage of allowing for variations in rhythmic regularity and cadence, given that any kind of public utterance in high rhetorical style will tend to fall into patterns of bicola or tricola, the major prosodic units in Hebrew verse structure. This type of discourse is characteristically prophetic and may be taken to correspond to the role of the prophet as public speaker or preacher (in Hebrew *maṭṭîp*, cf. Amos 7:16; Mic 2:6, 11; Ezek 21:2, 7; later *daršān*), at least in the view of the tradents and editors to whom we owe the present state of the text. The degree of prosodic regularity and consistency usually increases with the intensity of the emotional charge with which the words are uttered or endowed, a characteristic that supports the ultimately *oral* origin of this kind of diction, whatever the actual original circumstances of composition may have been. Prophetic discourse is therefore predominantly *vocative* (Alter 1985, 139) and is characterized, inter alia, by frequent calls for attention (1:2, 18–20), the use of forensic language and themes (3:13–15), brief and vivid illustrative "cameos" (3:6–7; 4:1; 7:20; 29:11–12 cf. Amos 3:12; 6:9–10), putting words into the mouths of opponents in order to condemn them (e.g. 10:8–14), rhetorical questions (e.g. 1:5; 5:4), and diatribe sometimes of an extremely violent and intemperate nature (e.g. 25:10–12; 34:5–17; 57:1–21). When we follow the use of this rhetorical high utterance along a chronological trajectory, we see emerging a strongly homiletic style, especially in the second major section of the book (e.g. 44:9–20, an expository and somewhat prosaic homily on idolatry; 58:1–14, a more high-energy sermon on fasting)—in other words, the beginnings of what might be called ecclesiastical literature. This was not entirely an innovation, since the activity of preaching had always been carried out by prophets rather than by priests.

While no critical reader will suppose that recurring stylistic, rhetorical, and thematic features in the book must be traced to one author or even one "school," several commentators (e.g. Clements) have detected features of this kind and have seen their recurrence as indicating a cumulative and self-consistent editorial process and therefore a unifying element that allows us to speak of an Isaian literary tradition. Along this line of inquiry recent scholarship has moved beyond the conventional breakdown into First, Second, and Third Isaiah. Some of these motifs—light and darkness, vision and sightlessness, judgment by fire, together with frequently recurring metaphors associated with agriculture and warfare—have been frequently noted and will be pointed out in the commentary. Others are less obvious. It is remarkable, for example, how often the theme of ecological degradation and the passage from cityscape to landscape, the return of cities to nature, a wilderness inhabited only by wild animals, occurs in chs. 1–39 (13:20–22; 17:2; 19:5–10; 24:4–9, 19–20; 27:10–11; 32:14; 34:9–17), perhaps indicative of a certain utopian and anti-urban proclivity, similar, therefore, in this respect to Hosea.

Much work still remains to be done on the many ways in which the Isaian poets exploit the resources—especially the sound patterns—of the Hebrew language by means of paronomasia, anaphora, onomatopoeia, etc. (see Alonso-Schökel 1963; 1987). One or two small-scale examples may be given here; others will be noted throughout the commentary:

šim'û šāmayîm
hear, heaven! (1:2)

giddaltî věrômamtî
I have raised and reared (1:2)

hôy gôy ḥōṭē'
woe, sinful nation! (1:4)

maš'ēn ûmaš'ēnâ
every kind of support (3:1)

vayěqav lěmišpāṭ věhinnēh miśpāḥ
liṣdāqâ věhinnēh ṣě'āqâ
He looked for justice, and instead there was bloodshed,
for righteousness, and instead a cry of distress (5:7)

'im lō' ta'ămînû kî lō' tē'āmēnû
If you do not hold fast in faith
you will surely fail to stand firm. (7:9)

bōgědîm bāgādû ûbeged bôgědîm hāgādû
Unfaithful ones who deal faithlessly,
who deal with an utter lack of faith. (24:16)

paḥad vāpaḥat vāpāḥ
Terror, the pit, and the trap (24:17).

While there is much to admire from the literary point of view in Isaiah, for the modern reader the book may seem to lack the note of interiority heard occasionally in Jeremiah—though to what extent the Jeremian "confessions" are spontaneous lyrical irruptions may be questioned. Isaiah also contains, especially in the later phases of composition, much that is, from the literary point of view, mediocre at best, and it was popular at one time to distinguish between the contribution of Isaiah and that of the Isaian *epigoni* on the basis of literary quality. The frequent editorializing, especially in the first 39 chapters, also distracts the reader looking for a consistent thread of meaning. Nonetheless, the power and moral passion of the work can come through for the reader willing to make the effort to read closely and project the imagination back into that distant epoch full of violence and danger, to look out on the world and see things through these other eyes.

The most recent phase of scholarship on the book has, in any case, concentrated much more on the structuring and organization of the material, its internal interconnections and intertextual links, than on the more traditional subject matter of literary criticism (poetics, imagery, etc.). If we are to speak of structure it is inevitable that we begin with the conventional threefold division of the book (chs. 1–39, 40–55, 56–66). While the authorial unity of the book is still stubbornly defended in traditionalist circles (e.g. Allis 1950), critical scholars acknowledge that it is a compilation put together over a long period of time rather than the production of a single individual active in the eighth century B.C.E. The critical consensus that chs. 40–66, which refer near the beginning to the career of Cyrus founder of the Persian Empire (559–530 B.C.E.), form a distinct unit composed no earlier than the sixth century B.C.E. was anticipated by the medieval Jewish commentator Abraham Ibn Ezra (1089–1164), first expounded by J. C. Döderlein in 1775, and widely accepted following publication of Wilhelm Gesenius's three-volume commentary on the book in 1821. The further step of identifying chs. 56–66 as a distinct and later composition authored by "Third Isaiah" was taken (but not argued at any length) by Bernhard Duhm in his commentary of 1892. At the same time, it was understood that much of the material in chs. 1–39 could not have been authored by Isaiah ben Amoz whose name is on the title page, that in fact this first major section is much more diverse in style, content, origin and date than chs. 40–66 and is itself a collection of compilations (typically divided into chs. 1–12, 13–23, 24–27, 28–35, 36–39), each with its own distinctive history.

For the majority of critical scholars this view of the matter is not, as conservative polemicists argue, dictated by a disposition to rule out the possibility of predictive prophecy. Critical commentators for whom this is still an issue would probably want to ask why inspiration should be denied to *anonymous* biblical authors. And in the most debated case, the authorship of chs. 40–66, predictive prophecy would mean, for example, that Isaiah, active in the eighth century B.C.E., was comforting his people in view of a disaster—the fall of Jerusalem and deportation—that was still a century and a half in the future, a not very plausible scenario.

We have seen that Isaian scholarship over the last two or three decades has been exercised to move beyond this critical orthodoxy either by attempting to demonstrate a deliberately unifying theological intent (Childs) or by identifying structural, thematic, and lexical clues to an underlying unity at the redactional rather than the authorial level (Ackroyd, Clements, Rendtorff). This involved looking for correspondences and parallels that cross over the conventional tripartite division, for example, between the first and last chapters of the book, or between ch. 6, the visionary experience, and what (questionably in my opinion) is taken to be a prophetic call narrative in ch. 40. The divisions themselves were in any case never hard and fast. The historical narrative featuring Hezekiah and Isaiah in chs. 36–39, more or less identical with 2 Kgs 18:13–20:19, breaks the connection between ch. 40 and the end of ch. 35, both of which speak of a highway for the return from exile (35:8–10; 40:3–5), but in so doing it creates a new link by concluding with a prediction of exile in Babylon (39:5–8). The link is not merely mechanical and external, however, for the fulfillment of the predictions of doom pronounced in the first part of the book, inescapably brought home to all in the destruction of Jerusalem, provides the basis for the assurance expressed in chs. 40–48 that the new predictions of restoration will also be fulfilled.

It is this somewhat curious argument from prophecy that drives the polemic in Isa 40–48. Working backwards from this point, the contrasting descriptions of the devastation of Edom and the future restoration of Judah and Jerusalem in chs. 34 and 35, respectively, form a kind of diptich and make for an appropriate finale to the first part of the book (chs. 1–33). They do this by recapitulating its core message in the form of judgment on a real and symbolic Edom and ultimate restoration for Judah.

Chapters 40–48, the centerpiece of which is the Cyrus oracle (44:24–45:13), deal with issues quite different from those of chs. 49–55, namely, the victorious career of Cyrus, the anticipated fall of Babylon, and anti-Babylonian polemic, and end with a call to return from Babylon to the homeland (48:20–22), thus forming an inclusio with 40:1–5. The fact that the final statement of ch. 48, "there is no peace for the wicked," is repeated in 57:21 might also indicate an alternative divisioning of the material introduced at some point in the editorial history of the book.

The extent of the next section of the book is also far from settled. To some commentators the reference to "the servants of Yahveh" (54:17) reads as a conclusion to the preceding chapters and an anticipation of a major theme in the chapters following. A division into chs. 49–54 and 55–66 also finds some support in the statement about an everlasting sign or name that shall not be cut off repeated at the end of successive paragraphs in chs. 55–56 (55:13; 56:5).

We will have more to say about these somewhat confusing structural features at appropriate points in the second volume of the commentary. We will also have to bear in mind that the book has undergone *successive* restructurings and rearrangements in the course of a long editorial history, and that consequently no single hypothesis will account adequately and exhaustively for the present order.

4. THE FORMATION OF THE BOOK

It is obviously possible, though perhaps not easy, to read the book of Isaiah as a rhetorical and structural unity and appreciate it aesthetically as well as theologically while disregarding the process by which it reached its present shape. Readers have been doing just that for centuries. It is nevertheless not difficult to justify a diachronic or historical approach to the text, however tentative it may turn out to be. Reading the text in this way provides at least potential source material for the religious history of Israel over several centuries. Read critically, it can open windows on debates and conflicts prior to the disaster (the pivotal date is 586 B.C.E.) on essential issues such as divisions and conflicts within Israelite society and political alliances, and in the later period on such matters as the return of the dispersed Jews to the homeland, qualifications for membership in the community, and the struggle between integrationist and universalist tendencies in Second Temple Judaism. In other words, it can provide points of entry into the world or the successive worlds that generated the texts and in doing so can enlarge our understanding of the text itself and conceivably also of the world we ourselves inhabit. We do not need to apologize for reading Isaiah as a potential source of information on the history of the kingdoms and the nascent Judaism of the Second Temple period. On the assumption that the book did not reach its present shape as the result of a haphazard process of accumulation, an inquiry into how it came to be what it is also introduces us to a developing textual and interpretative religious tradition of great significance for Second Temple Judaism inclusive of the early Christian movement.

Since it is impossible to provide a thorough review of opinion on the formation of the book without greatly increasing the length of the commentary, thereby testing the patience of the reader, in the present section I offer a brief outline of one way of reconstructing its editorial history. As are all other attempts, this one will necessarily be hypothetical. We have no transcripts of what was said and no eyewitness reports of what was done. As in other works from antiquity, the discourses are either condensations of previous reports or versions of what the scribe thought the speaker might have said or ought to have said. That the situation becomes more obscure the further back we go in time is not surprising, nor is it surprising that opinions differ as widely as they do on the contribution of Isaiah himself. Prophetic literature is not self-referential in general and, apart from titles, certainly inserted at a late date (1:1; 2:1; 13:1), the name *Isaiah* occurs only in annalistic passages deriving from a Deuteronomistic author or from a source closely related to the History (7:3; 20:2–3; 37–39). Furthermore, the fact that no critical scholar attributes the passage introduced by the last of the three above-mentioned titles to Isaiah may serve to illustrate the problematic nature of prophetic attribution in general.

The Greek translation and the Qumran copies oblige us to conclude that the editorial process had ended by about 150 B.C.E. at the latest, with the possible exception of some minor addenda. Writing about 180 B.C.E., Ben Sira was familiar at least with chs. 36–39 and part of chs. 40–66 (Sir 48:22–25), and his allusion to the bones of the Twelve (49:10) suggests that the compilation of the prophetic collection as a whole was far advanced by that time. Writing probably in the second half of the fourth century B.C.E., the author of Chronicles refers to a composition of Isaiah with the title *ḥāzôn* ("vision"), identical with the title of the book of Isaiah (1:1), dealing with the achievements and meritorious deeds of Hezekiah (2 Chr 32:32) but saying nothing about the relation between the prophet and Ahaz. In working back beyond this point we must rely exclusively on indications in the book itself. In doing so it seems advisable to proceed upstream from the external witnesses just mentioned rather than following what is still for many the standard approach by trying to sort out the genuine sayings of the Isaiah of the eighth century B.C.E. and then peeling away successive editorial layers or strata of "secondary" material.

The last chapter of the book would be the logical place to look for clues to the final stages of editorial activity. This last chapter ends with three paragraphs of unequal length, each concluding with the phrase "oracle of Yahveh" (*ně'ūm YHVH*, 66:17, 18–21, 22–23). They are rounded off with a finale (24) so dark and threatening that it was stipulated to be read in synagogue *before* the preceding verses. This final verse is linked with the preceding passage (22–23) through the repetition of the phrase "all flesh" (*kol-bāśār*), the occurrence of which in Isaiah is restricted to the second half of the book (40:5, 6; 49:26; 66:16, 23, 24), and the linkage is meant to imply that those who go out of the city to gloat over the corpses of the reprobates are the worshipers who come to Jerusalem to celebrate new moon and sabbath. The scenario is similar to, and perhaps draws on, Zech 14:12–15 which speaks of rotting corpses and people coming to Jerusalem to worship, but it also echoes language in the first chapter that condemns those who rebel against Yahveh (1:2, 28; verbal stem *pš'*) and speaks of a fire that will not be extinguished (1:31). But verbal and thematic parallels with the first chapter also occur in the three preceding passages, including the celebration of new moon and sabbath (1:13 cf. 66:23) and transgressive cults carried out in gardens (1:29 cf. 66:17). (Other parallels are listed by Liebreich 1995, 276–77). This attempt to impose a kind of unity on the entire book by means of the literary technique of inclusio was the last of many efforts at giving the vast amount of heterogeneous material in the book some semblance of coherence and unity. The inclusio makes the point that this is a single work with a definite beginning and end and one attributed to a single author named in the superscription. The procedure can be seen in the context of book production in the Hellenistic period, when there emerged for the first time the idea of a *book* in something like the modern sense of the term.

The final paragraph (66:24) contrasting the fate of the elect with that of the reprobate in the most extreme and intransigent terms, eternal torment no less, strongly suggests a sectarian perspective, and the suspicion is confirmed by the fact that the term translated "abhorrence" (*dērā'ôn*) occurs elsewhere only in Daniel (12:2). But the passage immediately preceding the three sayings in 66:17–23 (that is, 66:12–16) also ends with the apocalyptic scenario of a dread *parousia*, judgment by fire, and the corpses of the wicked openly displayed, and its affinity with 66:24 is highlighted by the occurrence of the phrase "all flesh" (*kol-bāśār*) in both. Perhaps, then, this last chapter ends with a conflation of *two* conclusions: the first (66:12–16) rounding off the third section of the book, chs. 55–66 or 56–66; the second (66:17–24) serving as the conclusion to the entire book in a way somewhat similar to the two conclusions to the book of Job (38:1–40:5; 40:6–42:6). Like 54:11–17 (for some commentators the conclusion to Second Isaiah), 66:12–16, the first of the two conclusions, ends with the vindication of the "servants of Yahveh," a central theme of Third Isaiah. It is also significant that the metaphor of a river for the condition of peace or well-being occurs only in 66:12–16 (*kěnāhār šālôm* 66:12) and in the final paragraph of chs. 40–48 (*kannāhār šělômekā*, 48:18), providing therefore another clue to structure. That each of the sections 40–48, 49–54, and 55–66 concludes by referring to the redemption or vindication of Yahveh's servants (48:21; 54:17; 66:14) may be taken to indicate a way of structuring the material at a late stage of the editorial process and to indicate an important theme binding all of these sections together.

While it is sometimes possible to arrange Isaian texts in chronological sequence they can rarely if at all be assigned an absolute date. In this respect Isaiah is less helpful than Jeremiah with its relative abundance of historical information or Ezekiel with its system of precise dating. In Isa 40–66 only one individual known to history is mentioned (Cyrus 44:28; 45:1), and no historical events are directly alluded to, though the conquests of Cyrus and the anticipated fall of Babylon (539 B.C.E.) are hinted at (47:1–15), and we hear that Jerusalem and its temple have been destroyed (63:18; 64:10–11). At best, then, we can trace broad developments or trajectories; for example, from the euphoria of chs. 40–48 occasioned by the conquests of Cyrus and the projected collapse of the Babylonian Empire to the disillusionment and disorientation reflected in chs. 49–54 and even more so in chs. 55–66. Along the same line we note frequent recourse to apocalyptic language and imagery of the kind that comes to full expression in the final chapter (e.g. judgment by fire 66:15–16, 24; new heaven, new earth 66:22 cf. 65:17) but that we also encounter throughout the book. While it is becoming clearer in recent years that sectarianism, with which the apocalyptic mind-set is closely associated, can be traced back beyond the emergence of Hasidim, Essenes, and Pharisees to the early Second Temple period, some of the sayings dealing with the diaspora, a mission to the Gentile world, and the final intervention of God in human affairs must be considerably later. We know too little about the Second Temple community between the conquests of Alexander (332 B.C.E.) and the persecution launched by Antiochus IV (167 B.C.E.) to make any precise correlations, but there are indications that the book passed through its final compositional phase during this obscure period, at the hands of a pietistic or "hasidic" group with a well-developed apocalyptic world view. These indications create difficulties for Sweeney's contention that the book, which he believes reached its final form in the fifth century B.C.E., was intended to promote the religious reforms of Ezra and Nehemiah (Sweeney 1996, 51–55, 60–62). This issue will be discussed more fully in the commentary to the last eleven or twelve chapters of the book.

References to writing in 8:16–18 and 30:8 suggest that committing prophecies to writing was a reaction to attempts to control the activity of the prophet as a public speaker or the result of the prophet's failure to convince by means of oral communication. A parallel instance is Jeremiah writing his prophecies—delivered over a period of more than two decades—after being barred from speaking in the temple precincts (Jer 36:1–8). At neither point in Isaiah's career are we told exactly what he wrote (the issue is discussed at the relevant points in the commentary), but these self-referential allusions to the production of a prophetic text are of obvious interest for the formation of the book as we have it. At another point we come across what reads like a scribal comment on the reception or non-reception of the book of Isaiah as it existed at the time of writing:

> The vision of all these things has become for you like the words of a sealed book. When they hand it to one who knows how to read saying, "Read this," he replies, "I cannot, for it is sealed." When they hand the book to one who can't read saying, "Read this," he replies, "I don't know how to read." (29:11–12)

The scroll is here described as a vision (*ḥāzût*), similar to the title (*ḥāzôn*, 1:1), and one that is sealed, as in the first reference to Isaiah's writing (8:16). I take it as recording in figurative language a disingenuous refusal to make the effort to break the seal, that is, crack the code or grasp the point of the prophecies now committed to writing, or a simple failure to get the point (see the commentary on 29:11–12).

In our attempt to get inside the editorial history of the book we have one firm point of reference in chs. 40–55 or 40–54 usually known as Second or Deutero-Isaiah (I continue to use this terminology for convenience). These chapters comprise the most stable and homogeneous section of the book with relatively little evidence of editorial additions. According to several contemporary scholars, even the so-called "servant songs" (42:1–4; 49:1–6; 50:4–11; 52:13–53:12) belong to the original text. These chapters (40–55) can be dated with a reasonable degree of assurance to the closing years of the Neo-Babylonian Empire under Nabonidus (556–539) and the successful campaigns of Cyrus II, founder of the Persian Empire during the period 547 to 539. Given this Archimedean point in the redactional history of the book, a key question arises concerning the relation between Second Isaiah and Isa 1–39. We would like to know whether these two large sections of the book developed independently and why and under what circumstances one of them was attached to the other. The assumption that it was purely a practical issue of making use of the empty space on the First Isaiah scroll is possible but should be adopted only if a more satisfactory explanation is not at hand, while the supposition that it was because the author of chs. 40–55 was also called Isaiah is too desperate to contemplate. The traditio-historical explanation in terms of an uninterrupted succession of disciples, a prophetic-Isaian *diadochē* or school tradition as proposed by Mowinckel and taken up more recently by Jones and Eaton, is unsupported by evidence and runs up against the problem that—as we shall see—the links between Second Isaiah and First Isaiah are too few and sporadic to justify it. We are also in the dark about when the linkage was effected, the majority opinion favoring a later rather than earlier date. Following up on the mention of Isaiah in Ben Sira (48:22–25), Gray for example (1912, lvi) put it shortly before 180 B.C.E.

The solution least open to objection is that Second Isaiah's concern for the reconstruction and repopulation of Jerusalem (44:26–28; 49:16–21; 51:3) was seen to make a good fit with the single-minded concentration on the fate of the city throughout the first 39 chapters of the book. It was this connection that suggested the "argument from prophecy" that Second Isaiah pitted against the advocates of political "realism" in the unpropitious circumstances of that time. The point would be that this author's frequent allusion to "the former things" (hāri'šōnôt, 41:22; 42:9; 43:9, 18; 46:9; 48:3) refers back to prophecies of judgment uttered by First Isaiah, in the first place against Jerusalem, the evident fulfillment of which served to confirm the truth of Second Isaiah's own very different predictions made in the name of the same deity.

If this explanation is accepted, it need not imply more than that the Second Isaiah was familiar with a collection of Isaian prophecies, in whatever state they lay before the author at the time of speaking or writing, and that the author took the fulfillment of these earlier predictions of disaster as the starting point for a very different message in the post-destruction period. That Second Isaiah contains the only reference in the entire book to a name (Cyrus) and events (his conquests) known to history after the lifetime of Isaiah ben Amoz practically rules out the possibility that these chapters were connected with chs. 1–39 from the beginning. This view of the matter would not exclude the possibility that some of the later, post-Isaian material in chs. 1–39 may have been influenced by Second Isaiah (e.g. tribute brought to Jerusalem by Nubians: 45:14 cf. 18:7), but the evidence for such borrowings is not overwhelming.

This minimalist conclusion about the relation between First and Second Isaiah has been challenged recently by Hugh Williamson (1994). Williamson argues that Second Isaiah was deeply influenced by the message of the First Isaiah and that its author felt called upon to proclaim that the time had arrived to unseal Isaiah's prophecy (with reference to 8:16 and 30:8–9), and announce the advent of salvation. He maintains further that it was Second Isaiah who edited and expanded the material in chs. 1–35 and attached it to his own work, so that there never existed a First Isaiah published independently of Second Isaiah. Both parts were therefore meant from the beginning to be read in tandem, and Isaiah of Jerusalem is even referred to—albeit obliquely as Yahveh's servant—in Second Isaiah ("who confirms the word of his servant," 44:26).

While this is not the place for the thorough critique that Williamson's arguments merit, some remarks are in order, leaving more detailed consideration to the relevant sections of the commentary. It would be prudent to note first of all that there is no allusion anywhere in chs. 40–55 to the unsealing of sealed prophecies, prophecies that had in any case already been fulfilled in the fall of Jerusalem, the extinction of the Judean state, and the subsequent deportations. It also seems unlikely that 44:26 refers to the original Isaiah, since the context makes it clear that the prophecies to be fulfilled concern not judgment on Israel but the rebuilding of the cities of Judah and the repopulation of Jerusalem, which rules out First Isaiah. (The text reads: "who confirms his servant's prophecies and fulfils his messengers' plans; who says of Jerusalem, it will be inhabited, of the towns of Judah, they will be rebuilt."). Williamson agrees with the recent commentators who read 40:1–8 as the call of Second Isaiah, based on the original Isaiah's call in Isa 6:1–13 (Williamson 1994, 30–56). This is one of those conclusions often repeated and more or less taken for granted that nevertheless call for careful scrutiny. It will suffice to note at this point that the commands (seven imperatives) in these verses are addressed to a *plurality*, and the designated tasks—to console Israel, to announce good news to Jerusalem and prepare the route for the return from exile—are indeed suggestive of prophets but do not amount to a call to the prophetic office. This is confirmed by later allusions to a plurality of "messengers" (*mal'ākîm* 44:26), "sentinels" (*ṣōpîm* 56:10) and "watchmen" (*šōmĕrîm* 62:6), all in the context of specifically prophetic responsibilities. In this and other test cases Williamson relies heavily on identifying similar elements of vocabulary and theme in both major sections of the book, but the net result is unconvincing, not least when he claims that Second Isaiah authored such key passages in First Isaiah as 11:11–16; 12:1–6; and 14:1–4*a*.

The position taken here is that, while it is entirely probable that the author of chs. 40–55 was familiar with Isaian sayings circulating at that time and may well have been to some degree influenced by them, this section is quite strikingly different from First Isaiah in the type of discourse it contains, its rhetorical expressions, and its themes. In addition to titulary already familiar from chs. 1–39 (the Holy One of Israel and Yahveh of the hosts, neither of which is confined to the book of Isaiah), we encounter several titles that are absent from chs. 1–39, including "Creator" (*bôrē'*), "Redeemer" (*gô'ēl*), "Savior" (*môšia'*), "the First and the Last" (*hari'šôn vĕ'aḥărôn*). Or again, when we compare the treatment of major themes in both sections of the book we find more often than not that they have little in common. The anti-Babylonian poems in the first section (13:1–22; 14:3–23; 21:1–10) are quite different in language and theme from the anti-Babylonian diatribe in 47:1–15. They also assume that the city has already fallen, an event that in Second Isaiah still seems to lie in the future (14:12–21; 21:9 cf. 47:11). Or again, both sections condemn the worship of idols but in entirely different ways. The terminology is different, and the monotonous harping on the manufacture of idols in Second Isaiah by way of dismissing idolatry as stupid (40:19–20; 41:16–17; 44:9–20; 46:5–7) is absent from First Isaiah. A final example: the term "servant" (*'ebed*) used in a religiously significant way occurs thirty-two times in chs. 40–66 and only twice in chs. 1–39, with reference to Isaiah himself (20:3) and to David (37:35)—this last, and perhaps both, derived from the History.

The identification of the original author of the core Isaian material depends on the solution to the problem alluded to above, namely, the relation between the Isaiah to whom sayings are attributed and the Isaiah of the narrative sections. If Isaiah is one of the most elusive of prophets compared with, for instance, Jeremiah or Ezekiel, it is also because so much has been added to the original core of his sayings over such a long period of time. The literary evidence supports the view that in chs. 1–39 this accumulation came about not through a succession of disciples but as the result of an incremental exegetical process. We might say that the eighth century B.C.E. prophet has been buried under an exegetical mountain, which at least testifies to the esteem in which his prophecies were held. In some instances this cumulative and incremental process is quite clear and easily detectable. After a saying denouncing Moab we read, "This is the saying Yahveh addressed to Moab a long time ago, but now Yahveh says . . . ," and another prophetic saying follows (16:13–14). We find a similar addendum at the end of the oracle about Tyre (23:17–18). In numerous instances these exegetical expansions are introduced with the formula "on that day" (e.g. the series of addenda dealing with the Egyptian diaspora, 19:18–25).

The situation is complicated by cross-references between Isaiah and other prophetic books. One example: the prediction of a surviving group on Mount Zion and in Jerusalem in Joel 3:5[2:32] is supported by an earlier prophecy ("as Yahveh has said") and is couched in language suggestive of Isa 4:2–3. The same process can be seen in transformational shifts and subtle changes in the reapplication of earlier turns of phrase; for example, 'ēl gibbôr refers to the once and future ruler in 10:21 and to Yahveh in 9:5 (Carroll 1978). It is not always, indeed not generally, possible to determine the historical setting and time of these exegetical expansions. Since the entire process is attributed to Isaiah, it is understandable that, in marked contrast to Second Isaiah, the scholiasts and learned seers and scribes of a later day would find ways to efface themselves and give their sayings the semblance of antiquity or anonymity. It has been suggested, for example, that in some clearly late texts "Assyria" could be a coded allusion to the Seleucids and "Egypt" to the Ptolemies (e.g. in 27:12–13).

One of the rare points of agreement among commentators is that the fall of Jerusalem and the extinction of the Judean state marked a decisive stage in the process we have been describing and therefore in the formation of this and other prophetic books. In the first major section (chs. 1–12) the judgment of doom pronounced on the two kingdoms is countered at each step by the prospect of the survival of a remnant, return from exile, and well-being for Jerusalem (2:1–5; 4:2–6; 10:20–27; 11:10–16).

This must have been the only way for those who preserved the old prophecies to make sense of them theologically in the post-destruction situation, and a similar process is detectable throughout the book and in other preexilic prophetic books (e.g. Amos 9:11–15). The historical epilogue (chs. 36–39) is set in parallelism to chs. 1–12 with a view to contrasting the behavior of Ahaz with the behavior of Hezekiah and the correspondingly different roles played by the prophet. (Note, for example, that the fateful encounter between Isaiah and Ahaz and between Hezekiah's emissaries and the Assyrian generalissimo takes place at the same location; 7:3 and 36:2.). Chapter 39 ends with a prediction of exile in Babylon in a not-too-distant future; the word of judgment pronounced by the prophet against Jerusalem and the dynasty is therefore postponed from the Assyrian to the Babylonian period but is still valid. The same point is made more obliquely by locating the Babylonian poems (13–14; 21:1–10) together with the other "oracles" against foreign peoples in chs. 13–27 between the two Assyrian sections (chs. 1–12 and 28–31—the last allusion to Assyria is 31:8). What is implied in this arrangement is that the theopolitical agenda of the prophet during the period of Assyrian ascendancy provides the essential clues for interpreting international events after the Babylonians had taken the place of the Assyrians on the stage of world affairs. Even after the Babylonians themselves had disappeared from the scene, and deep into the Second Temple period, this authoritative Isaian corpus continued to be read, interpreted, expanded, and applied to the changing situation of the province of Judah and its inhabitants until the point was reached when the results of this activity could no longer find their place in the text but had to be incorporated in a commentary.

Returning now to the starting point of this long and complex development: Isaiah makes his first appearance on the political scene in an attempt to persuade Ahaz of Judah to remain calm faced with the Syrian-Israelite axis opposing the forward advance of the Assyrians under Tiglath-pileser III (744–727). This event and its outcome (734–732 B.C.E.) are described in some detail in first (6:1–13; 8:1–22) and third person (7:1–17) accounts. After a further and more curious intervention or demonstration in 711 B.C.E. during a revolt of the Philistine city of Ashdod against Sargon II (722–705; parading naked to simulate the fate of prisoners of war 20:1–6), the next crisis in which Isaiah played a part was the punitive campaign of Sennacherib (704–681) against Hezekiah in 701 (chs. 36–37). Except for obvious glosses (e.g. 6:13b; 7:8b) and "on that day" additions (7:18–25; 10:20–23), these accounts give the appearance of having been composed close to the events described. While this is not impossible, it was inevitable that the earlier event would be interpreted and construed in the light of what happened about three decades later and that the interpretation and construction would become part of the text.

If this process of serial interpretation had been done as we would do it today, in the form of commentary distinct from the text or at least as footnotes or endnotes, the task of the interpreter would have been greatly simplified. But since the results were incorporated into the text itself—comments, additions, perhaps also omissions—it is often difficult and sometimes impossible to make the necessary distinctions. Hence the wide range of opinion in the commentaries on the origin and date of, for example, the first chapter (1:2–31) or the additions to the narrative in the seventh chapter (7:18–25).

Within about two generations of Sennacherib's punitive expedition in southern Palestine the Assyrian Empire was in irreversible decline, and Judah took the opportunity to assert its independence after a century of vassalage to one of the most oppressive imperial powers of antiquity. Although of relatively brief duration, we would expect the resulting euphoria, during the reign of Josiah, to leave its imprint on the first part of the book. The hypothesis of an Assyrian redaction (*Assur-Redaktion*, Barth) or a "Josianic Redaction" (Clements), i.e., the addition of a further layer of edited text in the latter part of the reign of Josiah (640–609), therefore, makes good sense but is no easier to identify precisely than the earlier Hezekian redaction. In fact, Barth and Clements differ significantly in assigning passages to this stage of the editorial history. (The passages on which they agree are 8:9–10; 10:16–19; 14:24–27; 17:12–14; 28:23–29; 29:8; 30:27–33; 31:5, 8–9; 32:1–5, 15–20.)

Since this hypothesis has justifiably received much attention, most of it benign, in recent scholarship on the book one or two additional remarks may be permitted:

(1) Whether the religious reforms of Josiah are dated to 622 (following 2 Kgs 22:3) or 628 (following 2 Chr 34:3), or whether they happened at all as described, it is unlikely that a serious drive for independence could have been mounted before the accession of Nabopolassar of Babylon in 625, and by 612 at the latest Assyria was no longer a threat. People could have anticipated the fall of Assyria some years before it happened, but this still leaves a rather narrow window of opportunity for this stage of editorial activity. Moreover, the biblical narrative of Josiah's reign can give us a misleading impression of the mood in the country at that time; the account does, after all, contain two predictions of the destruction of Jerusalem (2 Kgs 22:14–20; 23:27), and the death of Josiah in 609 was followed immediately by political and religious debacle.

(2) Several of the designated passages are either too unspecific to be dated at all (10:4b, 33–34; 17:12–14; 28:23–29) or too negative to fit the upbeat mood allegedly characteristic of this redactional stage (5:30; 7:20–25).

(3) We should allow for the possibility that some passages could simply have been reapplied to Josiah (rather than Hezekiah) and to the situation in his (rather than Hezekiah's) reign without significant change or addition—a simple case of *relecture* or tacit referential shift, leaving no trace in the text. Examples would be allusions to Immanuel (8:9–10) and the "messianic" poem (8:23b–9:6). But if the latter celebrates the birth rather than the accession of a royal heir, as argued in the commentary, the poem could not have been written about Josiah during his reign.

5. Isaiah Interpreted in Judaism and Early Christianity

To write the history of the interpretation of the book of Isaiah would be an immense undertaking, calling for the collaboration of experts in different fields and epochs over a considerable period of time. Even to familiarize oneself with the major expositors in the premodern period (some, such as Calvin's multi-volume commentary, important religious classics) would be a task for a lifetime. It occurred to me, therefore, that the only practical solution was to say something about the earliest stages in the interpretation of the book as a religious text read in very different ways by Jews and Christians and to refer selectively to the later "classics" (Rashi, Ibn Ezra, Kimchi, the Victorines, Calvin, and others) in the commentary itself, as the occasion offered and limitations of space permitted.

The first chapter in the history of the interpretation of Isaiah, or any prophetic book, has to be recovered from a critical reading of the book itself. This much is clear from what has been said about the formation of the book and will be illustrated at numerous points in the commentary. However, it is interesting that in the earliest stages of the development of what we will call the Isaian tradition attention was focused not on the sayings but on biographical or hagiographical aspects. It seems that this development can be traced back to the Deuteronomists, whose contribution to the biographical element in Isaiah and Jeremiah is generally acknowledged, and who in the History pointedly omit mention of prophets who passed judgment on the people.

To judge by the Deuteronomistic portraits of Moses and Jeremiah, prophetic biography seems to have entered a new phase in the post-destruction period in the process of development from simple prophetic *legenda* (e.g. miracle stories about Elisha) to the complex and more or less fixed pattern in which the life of the prophet or holy person came to be presented (Steck 1967; Baltzer 1975). With respect to Isaiah the following stages may be noted. Much about the biographical material in the book is still uncertain, and it will be sufficient for the moment to point to its evident links with the prophetic *legenda* incorporated in the History. 2 Kings 16:5 is reproduced in Isa 7:1 and 2 Kgs 18:13, 17–20:19 in Isa 36–39, but the brief account of Isaiah's sign-act in 20:1–6 is equally reminiscent of the Deuteronomists. Its Deuteronomic origin is betrayed by the historical introduction (cf. 2 Kgs 12:18; 15:29; 16:5; 18:13), the designation "my servant Isaiah" (*ʿabdî yešaʿyāhû* cf. Deut 34:5; 2 Kgs 17:13) and the prophet as a "sign and portent" (*ʾôt ûmôpēt* cf. Deut 34:11). Other indications will be noted in the commentary on this brief narrative.

In the account of the reign of Ahaz in 2 Chr 28 a prophet Oded brings about a cessation of hostilities between Israel and Judah, but there is no mention of Isaiah's political activity. In 2 Chr 32, the account of Sennacherib's invasion, Jerusalem is saved by the combined prayer of Hezekiah and Isaiah (32:20), and *Isaiah's Vision* (*ḥăzôn yešaʿyāhû*) is cited as a source for the reign (32:32), but this is all we hear about Isaiah. The king is healed in answer to his own prayer and not as a result of Isaiah's intervention, a sign is mentioned but not described, and there is no prediction of exile. There is therefore no clear indication in any of this that the author was familiar with the book of Isaiah as we have it but, if he was, he selected from it only what suited his purposes. Isaiah is named only as historian and as a prophet who intercedes for city and people alongside the pious king; again, therefore, no mention of the Isaiah of the many threats and predictions of disaster.

The *res gestae* of Isaiah on which the Chronicler is silent are, however, mentioned in Ben Sira's brief notice about the prophet, whom he describes as "great and trustworthy in his visions" (Sir 48:22). He delivered his people and is even represented as striking down the Assyrians (Sir 48:21a), though the subject of the verb (*vayyak*) could be YHVH or the Destroying Angel, as in

2 Kgs 19:35. He revealed hidden things before they happened, saw in vision or ecstasy the last things, and comforted the mourners in Zion (Sir 48:23–25). This last point seems to reflect an acquaintance with both Isa 40:1 and 61:3, which, as noted above, would suggest that the second large section of the book was in circulation by that time (early second century B.C.E.).

Continuing along a predictable trajectory, *The Lives of the Prophets* (perhaps early first century C.E.) represents Isaiah as saint and martyr whose tomb, located near the pool of Siloam, was the object of veneration. The martyrdom of Isaiah was also known to *4 Baruch* (9:21–22), Justin (*Dialogue with Trypho*, 120:5), the author of Hebrews (Heb 11:37) and other Christian writers of the apostolic and subapostolic periods, and is described in appropriately gruesome detail in *The Martyrdom of Isaiah*, reminiscent of the martyrdoms in 2 Maccabees (6:18–7:42) and perhaps originating in either written or oral form in the same period. The martyrdom tradition seems to have had some influence on early Christian presentations of Jesus as a martyred prophet, especially in Luke's gospel (11:50–51; 13:33; 22:37). Both the *Martyrdom of Isaiah* text and the gospels introduce the figure of the Suffering Servant (Isa 52–53), both the Isaiah of this text and the Jesus of the gospels are accused of blasphemy, Isaiah claims to be greater than Moses and Jesus claims to be greater than Abraham, Satan is involved in the events leading up to the death of both, and both are mocked as they are being put to death. Both, finally, instruct their disciples to leave the city, and both meet their death and are buried in or near Jerusalem.

Rabbinic traditions about Isaiah speak of his royal lineage, since his father Amoz was King Amaziah's brother (*b. Meg.* 10b; *Lev. Rab.* 6:6), and add their own baroque embellishments to the martyrdom tradition, the point of departure of which was a single scriptural verse: Manasseh shed much innocent blood in Jerusalem (2 Kgs 21:16). Accused of false prophesying, Isaiah fled and took refuge in the trunk of a cedar or carob tree (or, alternatively, was swallowed by it); Satan, however, detained him so that his cloak or *ṣiṣit* stuck out and gave him away; Manasseh then ordered the tree to be cut down and Isaiah was sawn in two (*b. Yebam.* 49b; *b. Sanh.* 103b etc.). It is interesting to note that several of the rabbis did not take kindly to Isaiah's harsh judgments on his people. He is taken to task for his unsympathetic personality evidenced by his calling Jerusalem Sodom (*Pesiq. Rab Kah.* 14:4), he claimed to have seen God, in defiance of Moses' statement that no one can see God and live (Isa 6:1; Exod 33:20), and was guilty of impiety in pronouncing the ineffable divine name before dying (*b. Yebam.* 49b).

In the early days of Qumran research David Flusser argued that *The Martyrdom of Isaiah* originated in the Qumran community and contained a coded history of the community featuring the Teacher of Righteousness (Isaiah), the Wicked Priest (Manasseh), and the Teacher of the Lie (Belkira). This ingenious hypothesis was accepted with modifications by one or two scholars but seems now to be out of favor. Though Isaiah is among the best-represented texts deposited at Qumran, to date no reference to the death of the prophet has come to light there. The two or more Isaiah *pĕšārîm* reconstructed from several fragments (4QpIsa^{a-e} and 3QpIsa = 4Q161–65 and 3Q4) interpret the biblical text eschatologically and connect events and personalities mentioned in it to the contemporaneous situation, as with the other Qumran *pěšārîm*. Isaiah 5:11–14, for example, is taken to refer to the Congregation of the Scoffers in Jerusalem, probably meaning the followers of the Wicked Priest (4Q162), and the Assyrian advance on Jerusalem in Isa 10:28–32 is reapplied to the anticipated eschatological war, though the fragment has not preserved the name of the enemy (4Q161).

In his paraphrase of biblical history Josephus states that Isaiah wrote his prophecies in books (*biblois*, *Ant.* 10.35) and emphasizes the prophet's activity in association with Hezekiah but not with Ahaz. (The books in question would be Isaiah as it existed at the time of Josephus and the putative history authored by Isaiah according to 2 Chr 32:32). Josephus also speaks of him as predicting the conquests of Cyrus, the rebuilding of the Jerusalem temple, and the building of a temple by Onias in Egypt (*Ant.* 9.243–57, 276; 10.12–16, 27–35; 11.5–7; 13.62–73). It need not surprise us that Josephus gives less attention to Isaiah than to other prophets. Opposition to imperial rule, advocated by the prophet, would have gone against the grain for Josephus who urged his fellow-Jews to accept Roman rule, and the criticism of the temple cult occurring here and there throughout the book (Isa 1:10–17; 43:34; 66:1–4) would not have been to his liking. Josephus's evident attachment to the temple and its cult could also explain his silence on Isaiah's relations with Ahaz, since this ruler introduced unacceptable innovations into the temple liturgy (2 Kgs 16:10–18). The royalist and messianic emphasis in Isaiah would also not have suited Josephus' purposes in composing his histories.

Unlike the Qumran community, early Christian churches did not produce biblical commentaries, perhaps because early Christians did not constitute learned, textual communities of the Qumran type. The closest approach in the New Testament to the Qumran *pěšārîm* would be the formulaic presentation of the prophetic fulfillment of events in the life of Jesus in Matthew's gospel (event + fulfillment formula + text). Most of these prophetic texts are from Isaiah (Matt 1:23 → Isa 7:14; Matt 2:23 → Isa 11:1; Matt 3:3 → Isa 40:3; Matt 4:14–16 → Isa 9:1–2; Matt 8:17 → Isa 53:4; Matt 12:17–21 → Isa 42:1–4; Matt 13:14–15 → Isa 6:9–10; Matt 21:4–5 → Isa 62:11 combined with Zech 9:9).

For the first sustained treatment of Isaian themes we have to wait for Origen (184–253) who, as Jerome reports, wrote a thirty-volume commentary on Isaiah now lost. The nine surviving homilies of Origen on Isaian texts concentrate heavily on the vision of the heavenly throne. Here as elsewhere the approach is allegorical. That the vision is dated to the year of the death of Uzziah (Isa 6:1), afflicted with a deadly skin disease because of his impiety, renders the spiritual meaning that we are fit to see the vision of God only when sin no longer reigns over us. The seraphic acclamation proclaims the mystery of the Trinity, and the two seraphs themselves represent Christ and the Holy Spirit. Likewise, the seven women who take hold of one man (4:1) stand for the seven gifts of the

Holy Spirit, and the house of David addressed by Isaiah (7:14) is the church of Christ.

The spiritual sense obtained by the allegorical method perfected in the Alexandrian schools also featured prominently in the first extant commentaries on the book, those of Jerome and Cyril of Alexandria from the early fifth century. To what extent the Christian reality was viewed and interpreted through a reading of Isaiah may be seen in the prologue to Jerome's commentary, in which he claims that the book "contains the totality of the mysteries of the Lord: Immanuel born of a virgin, worker of famous deeds and signs, his death, burial, and resurrection from the lower regions, together with the proclamation of the Savior to all the nations" (*PL* 24.18–21). Augustine, Jerome's great contemporary, was introduced to Isaiah by Ambrose but tells us that at first he found the book too difficult (*Confessions* 9.5, 13). A key Isaian text for Augustine, one to which he returned many times, was Isa 7:9b in the *Vetus Latina* (*Afra*) version: *nisi credideritis, non intellegetis* ("unless you believe, you will not understand").

For both Qumran sectarians and early Christians a sense of identity, purpose, and destiny as communities living through the last age, the culmination of a prophetic history, was channeled to a great extent through a reading of Isaiah. The point is made in the earliest gospel, which begins with a conflation of Isa 40:3 and Mal 3:1 (Mark 1:1–3). The first words spoken by the Markan Jesus take up the announcement of the good news or gospel in Isa 52:7, the essence of which is the coming rule of God in human affairs (*basileia tou theou*, an abstract formulation of the phrase "your God reigns" in Isa 52:7). The idea of a gospel, and of Jesus as the one announcing it (the *měbaśśēr* or "gospeller"), derives from certain well-known passages in the second part of Isaiah (40:9; 41:27; 52:7; 60:6; 61:1). In his sermon in the Nazareth synagogue, the Jesus of Luke's gospel identifies himself explicitly as the prophet anointed with the Spirit who is sent to announce good news to the poor and downtrodden (Luke 4:14–21 cf. Isa 61:1–2). The call for "repentance" (*metanoia, těšûbâ*), the first necessary step in accepting the gospel, is also frequently heard in the later chapters of Isaiah (44:22; 46:8; 55:7; 59:20), and the healing of the blind, deaf, and lame as signs of the eruption of the new age, is also typically Isaian (Matt 11:4–5 = Luke 17:18–23 Q cf. Isa 35:5–7). We conclude that the reading of Isaiah in early Christian liturgy must have been as prominent as it is in the synagogue *haftarot*.

The reading and interpretation of Isaiah have from the beginning been a major factor in the formation of Christian beliefs, liturgies and devotional practices (e.g. the cult of Mary mother of Jesus and the virgin birth following Matt 1:23 LXX, the Advent liturgy, devotions inspired by the sufferings and death of Jesus, projections of the end time). They have also, unfortunately, been taken out of context and used to corroborate anti-Jewish animus, for example, by a prejudicial reading of the song of the vineyard (Isa 5:1–7 cf. Matt 21:33) and the reference to obduracy and spiritual blindness in the vision report (Isa 6:9–10 applied to the Jewish people, cf. the many representations of the synagogue as a blindfolded woman). It is beyond the scope of this commentary to cover this vast subject even in outline (on which see Sawyer) or to take account of the influence of Isaiah on early Christian writings in any detail, an influence exerted for the most part indirectly by way of the extremely paraphrastic LXX version. The interesting issue of intertextual links and parallels between gospels and targums must also with regret be left aside (see Chilton, Evans).

One important and somewhat neglected aspect should, however, be briefly noted. Historically considered, the early Christian movement may be viewed as a late Second Temple Palestinian Jewish sect that understood and modeled itself on the Scriptures, particularly on the prophetic Scriptures, and among these principally Isaiah. As described in the synoptic gospels, the Jesus discipleship looks like a composite image modeled on Isaian texts, especially the texts that speak of prophetic figures and their followers. The profile of Jesus himself owes much to the Isaian Servant (*'ebed*) seen through the eyes of *his* disciples (e.g. Matt 8:17; Mark 9:12; 10:45; 14:24; Luke 22:37). The language used in the gospels to characterize the early disciples also reflects the kind of language occurring often in the last section of Isaiah. The point may be made by comparing the Beatitudes (Matt 5:1–12 = Luke 6:20–26) with the declaration towards the end of the book of Isaiah on behalf of "the servants of Yahveh," perhaps disciples of *the* Servant spoken of earlier:

> See, my servants will eat, while you go hungry;
> my servants will drink, while you go thirsty;
> my servants will rejoice, while you are put to shame;
> my servants will exult in gladness of heart,
> while you cry out with heartache, wailing in anguish of spirit.
>   (Isa 65:13–16)

This language of eschatological reversal is a response to ostracism and persecution in both Isaiah and the gospels (Isa 66:5; Matt 10:16–25; Mark 13:9–13; note the phrase "for my name's sake" Mark 13:13 cf. Isa 66:5 *lĕmaʿan šĕmî*). The beliefs of the earliest Christian community as described in the gospels also owe a great, indeed decisive, debt to Isaiah. This is most obviously true of the belief in an imminent divine intervention in human affairs, a theophany or *parousia*, accompanied by cosmic upheaval (e.g. Matt 24:29 cf. Isa 13:10, 13; 34:4), when the elect will be gathered in (Matt 24:31 cf. Isa 27:12–13), and the reprobate consigned to the flames (Matt 25:41 cf. Isa 66:24). Of particular interest is the conviction that a mission to the Gentiles must precede this final event (Matt 24:14 cf. Isa 42:6; 49:6; 56:8; 66:18–19, 21). In this respect the early Christian group moved in a different direction from the Qumran community, with its strong insistence on ritual segregation. Interest in the world of the Gentiles was, however, by no means an early Christian innovation. On the contrary, both tendencies are represented in the editorial history of the book of Isaiah and form an important aspect of the religious history of the Second Temple period from the very earliest years.

A final observation: at an early stage of the growth of Christianity it seems that Christians came to refer to themselves collectively as "the Way" (*hodos* Acts 9:2, 9, 23; 22:4; 24:14, 22). While other explanations are possible, it may be suggested that this too derives from Isaiah. Following an interesting development, the way in the wilderness destined for the return of dispersed Israelites (35:8; 40:3; 43:19) comes to be interpreted metaphorically within the Isaian tradition as the way to survival and salvation in the coming judgment (57:14; 62:10). Reference may also be made to that mysterious allusion to a teacher whose disciples feel his presence and hear his comforting and guiding voice *from behind* (*mē'aḥărêkā*)—meaning, perhaps, posthumously: "this is the way; walk in it" (see the commentary on 30:20–21).

6. THE HISTORICAL CONTEXT

THE NEO-ASSYRIAN CONTEXT

As the narrative sections of the book tell it, Isaiah was involved in Judean politics at three critical junctures between 734 and 701 B.C.E. during the reigns of Ahaz and Hezekiah and the reigns of three Assyrian kings. The first was his intervention in the crisis of Ahaz's reign in 734–732 while Tiglath-pileser III ruled in Assyria; then, after more than two decades, under Hezekiah during Sargon II's Philistia campaign in 713–711; finally, in direct association with Hezekiah during Sennacherib's campaign in southern Palestine to suppress the revolt inspired by the death of Sargon (705–701). Assyrian annals, fairly abundant for all three reigns, and the information in the biblical sources (2 Kgs 15–20; 2 Chr 27–32; Isa 7–8; 36–39), permit a tentative reconstruction of the historical context of these interventions. We must allow for the obvious self-aggrandizing intent of the Assyrian inscriptions and the less obviously problematic arrangement of the information, which is not always in chronological sequence. The strongly moralizing intent of the biblical Historian, who alternates good and bad kings, results in a villainous Ahaz and an idealized Hezekiah, and the contrast is highlighted even further in Chronicles. It seems likely, however, that Ahaz did not pay the Assyrians to save him from the aggression of Syria and Israel but simply paid tribute during the Palestinian campaign of 734, as he is reported to have done together with other western rulers in Tiglath-pileser's annals (Tadmor 1994, 277; *ANET*, 282 where his name is given as *iauhazi* corresponding to Jehoahaz). On the other hand, it was the imprudence of the pious Hezekiah in joining a rebellion after the death of Sargon that led to the devastation of his country and the prudence of the wicked Manasseh, his son and successor, in staying clear of rebellion, that gave Judah another century of quasi independence.

The stage on which the events were enacted was the Syro-Palestinian corridor comprising the Syrian and Phoenician city-states, the Philistine cities along the southern Mediterranean littoral, and the two Israelite kingdoms together with the adjacent Transjordanian region from Gilead in the north to Edom in the south, contiguous with the Arabian tribal federations farther east. This entire area was then, as always, under the shadow of the riverine powers in Mesopotamia and Egypt. The Egyptian connection looms quite large in Isaiah (7:18–19; 18:1–2; 19:1–17; 20:1–6; 30:1–7; 31:1–3; 36:6), but for most of the period in question the twenty-fifth (Nubian) dynasty, ruling from distant Napata beyond the third cataract of the Nile, was too occupied in establishing control over Lower Egypt to look beyond its borders. Egyptian neutrality vis-à-vis Assyria was broken only by Osorkon IV's ill-advised support of the Gaza revolt in 720 and Shebitku's unsuccessful involvement with the Palestinian states in the revolt against Sennacherib in 702–701. The Rabshakeh's assessment of Egypt as a broken reed was therefore not far off the mark (Isa 36:6).

Our starting point, the death of Uzziah or Azariah (6:1), is uncertain, but a date somewhere between 736 and 734 seems likely. Before leprosy (Hansen's disease) obliged him to hand over power to his son Jotham, Uzziah had fought successfully against the Syrians and had won back from either Syrian or Edomite control the Persian Gulf port of Elat, crucial for trade with Arabia and the Horn of Africa and the incense trade in particular.

During the late ninth and early eighth centuries the dominant fact of political life in Syria–Palestine was the almost incessant state of war between Syria (Aram, Damascus) and Israel (Samaria, Ephraim) in which Judah was sporadically involved. About a century before the death of Azariah, Syria attained a position of dominance under Hazael with the conquest of much of the Transjordanian region and control of the trade routes east of the Jordan Valley and along the Mediterranean littoral. After Hazael's death, however, this state of affairs was reversed by the military successes of the Israelite kings Jehoash and Jeroboam II. After the accession of Tiglath-pileser III in 744, however, Assyrian pressure brought the warring states together, as it had more than once previously. Syria was obliged to pay tribute to Assyria in 738 together with Tyre and other western states. While Tiglath-pileser's armies were occupied in Urartu and Persia during the next three years, Syria put together another anti-Assyrian coalition, again involving Tyre and Israel, which Ahaz of Judah prudently decided not to join. But in 733 the Assyrians were back again in strength in the west, Damascus was taken in the following year, and Syria formed into another province of the Assyrian Empire.

While these events were building towards a climax during Uzziah's long lifetime, Judah was overshadowed by the more powerful, prosperous, and populous Kingdom of Samaria to the north. It may even have been a Samarian vassal after a crushing defeat at the hands of Samaria during the previous reign (2 Kgs 14:8–14; 2 Chr 25:17–24). Jeroboam II of Samaria (ca. 788–748) continued the successful military activity of his father Jehoash in Syrian territory and the Transjordanian region (2 Kgs 13:24–25; 14:22; Amos 6:13–14), but the dynasty of Jehu to which he belonged, roundly condemned by Amos (7:9, 11) and Hosea (1:4–5), came to an end within six months of his death, with the assassination of his successor, Zechariah (2 Kgs 15:8–12). Shallum, murderer of Zechariah, was himself dispatched almost immediately in another coup, and from that point until the liquidation of the state in 722 political events were determined by the struggle between the forces of appeasement and those of opposition to the imperial designs of the Assyrians. Menahem bought off the Assyrians with a huge indemnity, and his name appears as a tributary, together with names of Syrian and Phoenician rulers, in the annals of Tiglath-pileser III (Tadmor 1994, 69, 107; ANET, 283 cf. 2 Kgs 15:17–22). His successor Pekahiah lost his life in another coup engineered by the anti-Assyrian Pekah, who in his turn was displaced and dispatched by Hoshea, last of the line (732–722). After submitting to Tiglath-pileser, Hoshea refused to pay tribute to his successor, Shalmaneser V, thus sealing his country's doom and bringing to an end the two-centuries-long existence of the Northern Kingdom.

The decisive event that determined the course of history in the Syro-Palestinian region was therefore the accession of the usurper Tiglath-pileser III (also known as Pulu or Pul, 2 Kgs 15:19; 1 Chr 5:26) to the Assyrian throne in 744, following a period of instability and internal troubles. The chronicles for the reign are abundant, but the sequence of events is often uncertain due to the secondary use of the inscriptions in Sennacherib's palace. But it is clear that Tiglath-pileser set out on a deliberate project of restoring Assyrian prestige, securing his frontiers contiguous with Urartu to the north and Babylon to the south, subduing the western states as far as the Mediterranean, and setting up a tightly controlled system of provinces and client kingdoms. During the early years of his reign he was occupied in Babylon, Iran, and Urartu, then in 738 he campaigned in Syria, securing the submission of Hamath, Damascus, Byblos, Tyre, and Samaria. After a further hiatus he was back in the west seizing control of the Mediterranean coastal route and subduing Gaza under its king, Hanun (Hanno), in 734. It was probably immediately after the Assyrian army withdrew that Rezin (Radyan?) of Damascus and Pekah of Samaria launched their attack on Jerusalem (2 Kgs 16:5). The purpose of the assault, which also had Philistine and Edomite support (2 Kgs 16:6; 2 Chr 28:18), was to replace Ahaz with a ruler in favor of revolt, a son of Tabeel, of uncertain origin (Isa 7:6). The biblical historian's account of the reign of Ahaz assumes that Tiglath-pileser returned the following year to attack Damascus in response to the plea of the Judean king, but Assyrian plans were not contingent on any decisions made in Jerusalem, and we have seen that it is far from established that Ahaz did request assistance from the Assyrians at the price of vassal status. At any rate, 733 witnessed another western campaign and more last-minute submissions. The Assyrians broke off the siege of Damascus but returned the following year to finish off the city. Hoshea saved Israel from extinction by assassinating the anti-Assyrian Pekah and occupying the throne, with Assyrian backing. The regions of Megiddo, Dor, and Gilead were made over into the Assyrian provinces of Magidu, Duru, and Galazu, respectively, and Hoshea's client kingdom, reduced to the city of Samaria and surrounding region, preserved its quasi independence for another decade.

Tiglath-pileser was succeeded by Shalmaneser V (726–722), who was deposed by Sargon II (722–705), on the probably spurious claim of legitimacy as another son of Tiglath-pileser. Sargon II also claimed in his inscriptions to have conquered Samaria, but the three-year siege (recorded in 2 Kgs 17:1–6; 18:9–10) was almost certainly conducted by Shalmaneser, from whose brief reign, unfortunately, no records have survived. Sargon no doubt organized the deportations consequent on the fall of the city and put down a rebellion of Syrian states in 720, in which apparently people from Samaria were in some way involved. Sargon continued the expansionist policies of Tiglath-pileser, engaging in a continuous series of campaigns in Asia Minor, the Caucasus, Syria, and Palestine. One of his most persistent opponents was the Chaldean Marduk-apla-iddina, the biblical Merodach-baladan (Isa 39:1), whose control of Babylon was broken only in the last years of the reign when Sargon, like Tiglath-pileser before him, ruled Babylonia directly. During the period 713–711 Sargon had to deal with rebellion in the Philistine city of Ashdod, whose client-king Aziru was plotting rebellion with the anticipated assistance of Egypt and neighboring states including Judah, Edom, and Moab. Aziru was deposed in favor of his brother Akhimetu, but Akhimetu was rejected by his subjects and replaced by Yamani, apparently a Greek, who refused tribute and pressed on with building up an anti-Assyrian coalition. Egypt was not at that point interested in getting involved in hostilities with Assyria, and in fact Yamani, who had fled to Egypt after the occupation of the city, was handed over to the Assyrians in irons by Pharaoh Shabako. It was at an early stage of these disturbances that Isaiah is said to have simulated, perhaps together with supporters, the anticipated outcome of Egyptian and Ethiopian participation in the Philistine revolt by parading, presumably in Jerusalem, in the guise of a prisoner of war (Isa 20).

We come now to the third, climactic intervention of Isaiah in the politics of the Judean court. The chronology of Hezekiah's reign is disputed and in the absence of new information is likely to remain so. The one fixed point is Sennacherib's Palestinian campaign in 701, and if this took place in the fourteenth year of Hezekiah (2 Kgs 18:13) the reign would have begun in 715, therefore after the fall of Samaria. The biblical portrait of the king is idealized, as we have seen, the account of the Assyrian failure to take Jerusalem exhibits elements of religious ideology and folklore (e.g. the role of the Destroying Angel), and the historical perspective has been drastically foreshortened (e.g. Sennacherib was assassinated twenty years later, not immediately after returning to Nineveh, Isa 37:36–38 = 2 Kgs 19:36–37). The genesis of the campaign can be traced to the death of Sargon in 705, which was the signal for revolt in many parts of the Assyrian Empire, from Anatolia to the Philistine cities. Hezekiah seems to have taken an active role in planning rebellion in the west together with Sidon, the Tranjordanian states, and several of the Philistine city-states, the plotting perhaps deliberately synchronized with renewed efforts by Marduk-aplu-idinna to drive the Assyrians out of Babylonia. The fact that Padi, the pro-Assyrian ruler of Ekron, was forced out by his own people and handed over to Hezekiah suggests that the latter played a prominent part in planning the revolt, and in fact Hezekiah was the last western ruler to hold out after the arrival of the Assyrian army in the west. Sidon and its dependencies submitted; Ammon, Moab, and Edom followed; Sidqia, ruler of Ashkelon, was deposed and deported; and Padi was reinstated in Ekron as an Assyrian puppet. Sennacherib's army devastated Judah, capturing or destroying 46 towns (including Lachish, whose fate is graphically portrayed in the Nineveh wall plaques now in the British Museum), and driving out 200,150 of their inhabitants. (Either the figures are greatly exaggerated or there is a scribal error for 2,150.)

Up to this point the record is fairly clear, but the biblical account in 2 Kgs 18:13–19:37 (omitting for the moment 18:14–16) and Isa 36–37 of how the campaign ended is far from straightforward. These parallel and practically identical versions concentrate on the Assyrian attempt to intimidate the population of Jerusalem to surrender, curiously similar in some respects to a letter sent to Tiglath-pileser III reporting how two Assyrian officials under the walls of besieged Babylon tried to persuade the citizens to surrender (H. W. F. Saggs 1963, *Iraq* 25:70–73). The narrative in the History and in Isa 36–37 is itself a conflation of two versions: one (2 Kgs 18:17–19:9a = Isa 36:1–37:9a + 37:37–38) ends with the assassination of Sennacherib in Nineveh, the other (2 Kgs 19:9b–35 = Isa 37:9b–36) with the annihilation of the Assyrian army by the *mašḥît* ("Destroying Angel") outside the walls of Jerusalem. The much briefer and more annalistic account in 2 Kgs 18:14–16 records the submission of Hezekiah at Lachish and payment to Sennacherib of a huge indemnity. Since this version of what happened is in essential agreement with the detailed account in Sennacherib's royal annals we must accept it as closer to the events. It seems that what persuaded Hezekiah to submit at the last minute was the brutal treatment of Lachish rather than the Rabshakeh's oratory before the walls of his capital, a clever and persuasive literary creation, and we can easily imagine that the salvation of Jerusalem, even at terrible cost, would have been celebrated as an act of supernatural deliverance.

Table 1. Judah in the Neo-Assyrian Period

Assyria	Egypt	Judah	
Tiglath-Pileser III— (744–727)	Py (Piankhi); (ca. 747–716)	742	**Regency of Jotham**
738 Campaign against Hamath, Damascus, Tyre, Byblos, Samaria	Founding of XXV (Nubian) dynasty		
		736/734	Death of Uzziah
734 Campaign against Tyre, Gaza (Hanun); Syrian-Samarian attack on Judah		734	Syro-Ephraimite war

Assyria	Egypt	Judah
733 Campaign against Tyre, Damascus (Rezin), Israel (Pekah)		
732 Damascus (Hazael) captured; Israel loses Gilead, Galilee, Dor		732–722 Hoshea, last king of Israel
	730 Py subjugates the Delta princes	
729 Second Babylonian campaign		
Shalmaneser V (726–722)		
		724–722 Siege and capture of Samaria
722 Fall of Samaria		
Sargon II (721–705)		
720 Revolt of Syrian states, Samaria, Gaza suppressed; defeat of Egyptians at Raphia	**Shabako (ca. 716–702)** Final subjection of Lower Egypt to the Nubian ruler	
713–711 Suppression of rebellion in Ashdod (Aziru)		713–711 Rebellion of Ashdod; possible Judean involvement
710 Capture of Babylon (Merodach-baladan II		
		704–701 Preparations for revolt in Judah; negotiations with Egypt
Sennacherib (704–681)		
703 Revolt of Merodach-baladan supported by Medes, Egypt, Judah	**Shebitku (ca. 702–690)**	
701 Campaign against Judah	**Taharqa (690–664)** Defeat of Egyptians at Eltekeh	701 Sennacherib's campaign in Judah
689 Capture and destruction of Babylon by Assyrians		687 Accession of Manasseh; Judean recovery

Assyria	*Egypt*	*Judah*
Esarhaddon (680–669)		
677 Sidonian revolt crushed		
676 Western states, including Judah, pay tribute		
671 Revolt of Tyre and Ashkelon suppressed	Egypt under Assyrian rule	
671 Conquest of Egypt		
669 Second Egyptian campaign		
Ashurbanipal (668–627)		
667 Memphis recaptured		
662 Siege of Tyre		
652 War with Babylon (Shamash-shum-ukin, Ashurbanipal's brother)		
648 Campaign against Elam; destruction of Susa		640 The boy Josiah put on the throne by "the people of the land"
Assyria: the final chapter (627–604)		
625 Nabopolasser king of Babylon		622? Cult reforms including restoration of temple fabric
612 Fall of Nineveh		
		609 Death of Josiah at Megiddo
604 Accession of Nebuchadrezzar II	605 Defeat of Egyptians at Carchemish	604 Judah falls under Babylonian control

Table 2. Chronology of Judean Rulers
During the Neo-Assyrian Period

The chronology of rulers of the Judean kingdom is beset by many problems, some of them not susceptible of definitive solutions in the present state of our knowledge. Presented here for the convenience of the reader are the principal options available in English-language scholarship. Supporting arguments can be reviewed in: W. F. Albright, "The Chronology of the Divided Monarchy of Israel," *BASOR* 100 (1945) 16–22; E. R. Thiele, *The Mysterious Numbers of the Hebrew Kings: A Reconstruction of the Chronology of the Kingdoms of Israel and Judah* (3d ed.; Grand Rapids: Zondervan, 1984); J. H. Hayes and P. K. Hooker, *A New Chronology for the Kings of Israel and Judah* (Atlanta: John Knox, 1988). In the commentary I have generally but not invariably followed the Albright system.

	Albright	*Thiele*	*Hayes/Hooker*
Uzziah (Azariah)	783–742	767–740	785–760
Jotham	742–735	740–735	759–744
Ahaz (Jehoahaz I)	735–715	735–715	743–728
Hezekiah	715–687	715–686	727–699
Manasseh	687–642	686–642	698–644
Amon	642–640	642–640	643–642
Josiah	640–609	640–609	641–610

7. ASPECTS OF ISAIAN THEOLOGY

In the early years of the twentieth century it was not uncommon for monographs or introductions to commentaries to be entitled "Isaiah, His Life and Times" (S. R. Driver) or "Isaiah as Prophet and Teacher" (George Buchanan Gray). Critical scholars are, by and large, less confident today of their ability to identify Isaiah's own contribution, but the problem will appear less severe if we can speak of an Isaian tradition, meaning a broad continuity in religious thinking in most if not all the successive stages of the formation of the book. The title of the present section is meant to acknowledge the critical problems involved in identifying the *ipsissima verba* of Isaiah spoken or written in the eighth century B.C.E. without denying the role of an extraordinary individual prophetic figure as originator of this tradition.

To take one example, the prophetic critique of the Assyrian Empire provides the basis for a critical assessment of its imperial successors, beginning with the Babylonians, and eventually of the exercise of arbitrary political power in general (chs. 13–27). This is a central issue, since there is a great deal of commentary on political events and situations in the book. In his chapter on "The Prophet" in *Economy and Society*, Max Weber argued that the primary concern of Israelite prophets was with foreign politics, since international affairs constituted the theater of their God's activity. A reading of the first major sections of Isaiah supports this contention. We hear much about Yahveh's "plan" or "agenda" (*ʿēṣâ*, 5:19; 28:29; 30:1) and his "work" (*maʿaśeh*, 5:12, 19; 28:21; *ʿăbôdâ*, 28:21), always in the sphere of politics and often of a kind going directly against the grain of ordinary political common sense and expectations (29:13–14).

Foreign nations, Assyria in the first place (10:5) but also lesser powers such as Syria and the Philistine cities (9:10–11[11–12]), are the instruments by which Yahveh's plan for his own people is being implemented. He summons these nations to punish Israel (5:26–30; 7:18–20; 8:7–8; 10:6) and turns against them when they exceed their commission (10:16–19, 24–27). The implication is that Yahveh's reach encompasses the whole earth, just as in Isaiah's vision we hear that his glory fills it (6:3b), a broader claim, therefore, than that of Amos, which is confined to the nations forming part of a putative "Greater Israel" under the early monarchy (Amos 1:3–2:3 and 9:11–12).

The way Yahveh acts towards Israel in benevolence or anger, as set out in Isaiah, is rooted in the common theology of the ancient Near East, which attributed success to the benevolence and disaster to the anger of the native deity. In his famous stele, Mesha king of Moab records that Omri of Israel had humbled Moab for many years because Chemosh was angry with his land— why, we are not told (*ANET*, 320). It is a more difficult matter to state more precisely what the plan entailed for Judah, faced with military threat from Assyria and its neighbors, which is to say enemies.

On the face of it, the recommendation seems to be to let events take their course while trusting in Yahveh's ability and willingness to take care of his own. In his encounter with Ahaz, the prophet has nothing to say explicitly about policy vis-à-vis Assyria, but it soon becomes clear that there were to be no alliances either with Assyria or against it; no joining any of the numerous coalitions formed among the western states with a view to throwing off the Assyrian yoke (see especially 30:1–5; 31:1–3). This policy is not political quietism, and certainly not pacifism; witness the relentless opposition to Assyrian imperial ambitions and predictions of their eventual undoing. But in the meantime a policy of nonalignment is advocated, an option that must have seemed dangerously unrealistic to many of the seer's contemporaries (e.g. 5:19; 30:1).

A distinctive feature of prophetic preaching by Isaiah and his near-contemporaries is that the cause of political success or failure was to be found in the moral condition of Israelite society. Its prominence in the earlier material in the book places Isaiah firmly in the first wave of political and social protest in eighth century B.C.E. Israel and Judah. The connections are not made explicitly since unfortunately these early dissidents (Amos, Hosea, Micah, Isaiah) never refer to one another by name, though at one point Isaiah may be alluding obliquely to Amos ("Yahveh sent a message against Jacob, and it will fall on Israel," 9:7[8]). Isaiah's debt to Amos is nevertheless not difficult to detect. It can be seen in his criticism of the state cult (Isa 1:10–17 cf. Amos 5:21–24) and the popular but misguided enthusiasm for it (Isa 29:13 cf. Amos 4:5), his denunciation of members of the socioeconomic and political elite and their wives (Isa 3:16–4:1 cf. Amos 4:1–3), and even more clearly when he denounces the exploitation of the poor, needy, and disinherited, widows, orphans, and other *personae miserae* by the ruling class (Isa 5:8–13 cf. Amos 6:1–7). In this respect neither Amos nor Isaiah is content with moral generalizations. They target (for example) the manipulation and corruption of the judicial system and the acceptance of bribes (Isa 1:23; 5:23; 10:1–2; 33:15; Amos 2:7–8; 5:10), "joining house to house, field to field" (Isa 5:8)—in other words, the sequestration and enclosure of peasant holdings and the formation of latifundia exploited by absentee owners living in Samaria and Jerusalem (cf. Amos 5:11; 7:1; Mic 2:2). In these and similar respects the relevant sections of Isaiah read like an application to Judah of Amos's threats directed at the sister-kingdom to the north.

Echoes of Hosea in Isaiah are not as strong but have been picked up in the reference to unfaithful sons (1:2–3), the harlot city (1:21–26), and Israel the vineyard (5:1–7 cf. Hos 10:1). Both also make use of the title "the Holy One of Israel" (1:4; 5:24 etc.; Hos 11:9; 12:1). We saw above a few of the associations between Isaiah and Micah. Isaiah 2:2–5 and Mic 4:1–5 are variants, Micah has an attitude towards the state cult similar to Isaiah's (Mic 6:6–8), and Micah's reference to going stripped and naked (1:8) recalls Isaiah's sign-act during the Philistine rebellion against Sargon II (20:1–6). Isaiah's accusation of devouring the vineyard, confiscating the goods of the poor, and grinding their faces into the ground (Isa 3:13–15) could have come straight out of Micah (cf. Mic 2:8–9).

These common features point to a gradually coalescing tradition of protest, both conservative and radical, originating with these "demagogues and pamphleteers" (Max Weber) in the eighth century B.C.E. and conducted on behalf of the casualties of an encroaching state system—dispossessed and impoverished peasants, widows, orphans, day laborers, and the like. This facet of social ethics provides some counterbalance to the view that the book of Isaiah is essentially a Second Temple text. The insistence on social justice and righteousness and the violent diatribe against the ruling class seem at first sight so distinct from Isaiah's interventions in Judean politics in support of Ahaz and Hezekiah and his single-minded preoccupation with the Assyrian imperial power, as described in the narrative sections, that one might suspect a conflation of two quite different figures. There are, however, links between the two apparently distinct roles. The Isaiah to whom sayings are attributed condemns the ruling class, including judges and elders, as scoundrels and murderers (1:21, 23, 26; 3:14; 5:13–14; 28:14) but, unlike Hosea and Amos, he never attacks the monarch in the same direct and uncompromising way.

In the biographical parts of the book Isaiah is represented as being in close and generally sympathetic collaboration with Ahaz and Hezekiah. More importantly, the nation's fate in the arena of international politics is seen from the prophetic angle to be dependent on its striving towards a just society within its own boundaries. It is this causal connection, not empirically demonstrable, that provides the key to interpreting international relations from a prophetic-theological perspective. That it was vulnerable to falsification by historical experience is obvious from later contributors to the book and other compositions from the post-destruction period. At that point other avenues and other explanations would have to be pursued.

The key terms in this critique of society are "justice" and "righteousness" (*mišpāṭ, ṣĕdāqâ*), whether employed singly, in parallelism, or together as a hendiadys. Used by itself, *mišpāṭ* can refer to a divine attribute (30:18), a legal stipulation, a specific act of judgment (3:14; 26:8–10; 34:5), or a judicial system in general (10:2). When used in tandem with *ṣĕdāqâ*, the basic connotation is of a society in which the rights of all, including the most marginalized—the destitute, orphans, and widows (1:17, 21–23; 11:4–5)—are respected. For this to come about the proper functioning of the judicial system is absolutely essential (10:2). Few acts are therefore denounced with as much vehemence as the offering and accepting of bribes (1:23; 5:23; 33:15 cf. Mic 3:11). With the passing of time both terms come to be used of a final condition of vindication, the overcoming of evil, deliverance, salvation (e.g. 1:27; 46:12; 49:4; 50:8; 56:1). This is overwhelmingly the case with chs. 40–55, thus providing another indication of the distinctive character of this section of the book vis-à-vis chs. 1–39.

In contrast to other prophetic books deemed to be pre-exilic, and here too in particularly stark contrast to Isa 40–55, Isa 1–12 and 28–33 have very little to say about normative Israelite tradition either historical or legal. The fate of the Cities of the Plain (Isa 1:9–10; 13:19; also Amos 4:22; Jer 49:18; 50:40) is exceptional since it was widely known and circulated independently of its present context in the ancestral narrative series. Isaiah 28:21 mentions David's defeat of the Philistines at Baal-perazim (2 Sam 5:17–21) and Joshua's victory at Gibeon (Josh 10:10–14), neither of which is a particularly prominent component of the historical tradition. Another passage, certainly of later date (see commentary), refers to the victory at the Papyrus Sea and the defeat of Midian at the rock of Oreb (Isa 10:26). Apart from these few instances, allusion to past history is couched in general terms of ingratitude for benefits received (1:2–3; 5:1–7). As von Rad (1965, 147–75) and many others have noted, Isaiah and his continuators seem to have drawn on Jerusalemite and dynastic traditions rather than on the interventions of the native deity on Israel's behalf in Egypt, in the wilderness, and the conquest of Canaan—the latter deemed to be more at home among the tribes of Ephraim and Manasseh than in Judah and Jerusalem.

In the tradition on which Isaiah is drawing Yahveh is inseparable from Jerusalem–Zion. The divine appellative "Yahveh of the hosts" (*YHVH ṣĕbā'ôt*), of such frequent occurrence in chs. 1–39 (more than seventy times compared with six times in chs. 40–66), is associated with the ark (*'ărôn*) which, according to tradition, was brought to Jerusalem by David and deposited in the sanctuary by Solomon as the visible symbol of the divine presence. Only slightly less frequent is the incidence of the title "the Holy One of Israel" (*qĕdôš yiśrā'ēl*) also associated with the sanctuary and the "holy city." It is there that Yahveh rules as king (6:4; 24:23; 33:22) enthroned above the cherubim (37:16). He is addressed as "the Strong One of Israel" (*'ăbîr yiśrā'ēl* 1:24), a title the only liturgical occurrence of which is in the psalm celebrating the transfer of the ark to Jerusalem (Ps 132:2, 5).

As for the legal traditions, though things forbidden in laws in the Pentateuch are often condemned in these chapters (1–12, 28–33), there are no explicit references either to specific laws or to the law as a known and acknowledged basis for conduct. On the contrary, the familiar terms for legal enactments are either absent or, if present, carry a different meaning. Wherever it appears in these chapters, the word *tôrâ* connotes prophetic teaching (1:10; 2:3; 5:24; 8:16, 20; 30:9); *miṣvâ* means either a royal decree (36:21) or conventional religious behavior, like going to synagogue on Saturday or church on Sunday (29:13); *mišpāṭ* occurs frequently but never with the meaning "statute" or "ordinance," as in the so-called Book of the Covenant (Exod 21:1); "decrees" (*ḥūqqîm*), finally, are mentioned only in the context of the abuse of legislative power (10:1). This does not oblige us to conclude that no written legal compilation was in existence in the eighth century B.C.E., but it does suggest that Isaiah and other dissidents of that time authorized their categorical ethical demands and their teaching with reference to a traditional consensual social ethic rather than to specific legal enactments.

Prophetic engagement with and critique of the great empires has left a deep impress on language about God used in Jewish and Christian theology and worship. The metaphors of *imperium* and royalty feature prominently in religious language long before the eighth century prophets; compare, for example, the language in which the Pharaoh is addressed by the rulers of Syrian and Palestinian city-states in the Amarna Letters from the early second millennium B.C.E. with the language in which Yahveh is addressed in the biblical psalms. Isaiah is admitted into the throne room of Yahveh in vision and sets out from it as a royal messenger. The "glory of Yahveh" (*kĕbôd YHVH*) can be compared with the "radiance" (*melammu*) or the "splendor of royalty" (*melam šarruti*) of the Assyrian imperial deity Ashur, a manifestation that in both cases inspires awe, fear, and terror in those who behold it (e.g. 2:10, 19, 21). To speak of Yahveh as king is to dwell on his absolute and even arbitrary power and his attributes as warrior (Yahveh of the heavenly armies) and judge (e.g. 2:4; 3:13–15).

In Isaiah the metaphor also entails recurring images of the violent exercise of power—the hand raised to strike, blows raining down on the obdurate, Moab drowned in a cesspool (25:10–12), Assyria flogged mercilessly to musical accompaniment (30:29–33), Edom slaughtered or pounded to a pulp in the winepress (34:5–17; 63:1–6). These texts therefore profile a personality of overpowering will and strong emotion. Alternative metaphors do occur, of course— Yahveh as *paterfamilias* (1:2–3; 30:9), teacher (2:3), farmer (5:1–7; 27:2–5; 28:23–29); Yahveh as bridegroom (61:10; 62:4–5), husband (54:5–8), father (63:16; 64:8); even Yahveh as mother and midwife (49:15; 66:7–13)—but the image of supreme kingly power predominates and leaves the most lasting and

the most disturbing impression. The offense to the modern reader may be miti-
gated if not entirely removed by other aspects, in particular the fact that power
is also exercised on behalf of the poor and needy and in the struggle for a social
order based on justice and righteousness (25:4; 28:17; 33:5). There is also
movement within the tradition from the regal figure to "the God of the sufferers" (Buber); from the deployment of power towards a future in which violence
and injustice will be overcome (11:1–9), when even the traditional enemies,
Egypt and Assyria, will receive blessing (19:24–25), when the God of heaven
will dry all tears, and fear can finally be set aside (25:6–8).

Much of prophetic teaching about the future course of events and the pros-
pects for the people of Israel is encapsulated in the concept of a "surviving
remnant" (šĕ'ērît, šĕ'ār, pĕlēṭâ). This way of speaking originated in the context
of warfare, defeat, and the consequent attempt to escape an unpleasant death
(e.g. Deut 2:34; 3:3). It is not confined to Israel, since other nations could be
and were faced at one time or another with the prospect of only a small residue's surviving annihilation (Babylon 14:22; Philistia 14:30; Moab 15:9; 16:14;
Syria 17:3; the Kedarite Arabs 21:17). It seems likely that Isaiah took over the
idea from Amos, but there is a long-standing discussion concerning whether
Amos held out any prospect for the survival of Israel at all. The figure in Amos
of a (literally) decimated city (5:3) might suggest an affirmative answer, but
elsewhere in the book none of the ten people living in the plague-stricken or
earthquake-stricken house survive (6:9–10). The "seek" passages (5:4–7, 14–15)
presuppose the possibility of repentance, "turning," and therefore survival, but
their language is so close to that of the Deuteronomists that attribution to
Amos must be doubted.

On the other hand, the cameo of the shepherd's rescuing a few mangled
remnants of a sheep from the jaws of the lion (3:12) is not a hopeful image—
no more than the lament over the dead virgin Israel (5:2). The statement towards the end of the book that Yahveh will destroy the sinful kingdom from the
face of the ground (9:8a) seems perspicuous and definitive and may have
prompted a rebuttal in the annals of the reign of Jeroboam II—"Yahveh had
not said that he would blot out the name of Israel from under heaven" (2 Kgs
14:27). Who at that time had said this if not Amos? It also prompted an editor
of Amos to add a modifying clause—"except that I will not utterly wipe out the
house of Jacob" (Amos 9:8b), since it was at least clear that Judah survived after
the fall of the Kingdom of Samaria.

This is the point at which the idea of a remnant transits from Amos to Isaiah.
The question would have arisen a decade or so before the fall of Samaria when
Ahaz, threatened by the Syrian-Samarian axis, was confronted by Isaiah and his
son, bearing for the occasion the name Shear-yashub ("a remnant will return"
7:3). The much greater threat from Sennacherib thirty-three years later once
again raised the prospect of annihilation and with it the possibility of a surviving remnant (37:4 cf. 1:9).

With the liquidation of the Kingdom of Judah in 586 B.C.E. and the attempt
to found a new commonwealth in the province of Judah (Yehud) we can see

that this topos of a remnant is also used to trace the transition from nation to religious community. Shear-yashub now represents the faithful minority who will accept repentance or conversion; "returning" is now "turning" (*těšûbâ*, "repentance," 10:20–22 cf. the *šābîm*, "penitents," of 1:27). The purified community of survivors in Jerusalem will be holy (4:2–6), an oracular statement taken up, as it seems, by other Jerusalemite seers, as was noted above ("On Mount Zion and in Jerusalem there will be a surviving remnant *as Yahveh has said*," Joel 3:5[2:32]). A Second Temple glossator makes the same point in identifying the stump of the felled tree as the "holy seed" (*zera' qodeš* 6:13). It is therefore not just a matter of survival, as important as it is to survive, but of the transitory and inessential nature of political and military power and the possibility of envisaging quite different forms of social life.

BIBLIOGRAPHY

◆

THE BOOK OF ISAIAH

◆

TEXTS AND VERSIONS

Barthélemy, D.
    1986   *Critique textuelle de l'Ancien Testament, 2: Isaïe, Jérémie, Lamentations.*
            Göttingen: Vandenhoeck & Ruprecht.
    1987   *Isaiah. Vol. 3/1 of Vetus Testamentum Syriace.* Edited by S. P. Brock.
            Leiden: Brill.
Ben-Shammai, H.
    1990–91   Saadia Gaon's Introduction to Isaiah: Arabic Text and Hebrew Transla-
            tion. *Tarbiz* 60:371–404.
Brownlee, W. H.
    1964   *The Meaning of the Qumrân Scrolls for the Bible: With Special Attention
            to the Book of Isaiah.* New York: Oxford University Press.
Burrows, M.
    1948–49   Variant Readings in the Isaiah Manuscript. *BASOR* 111:16–24; 113:24–32.
Chilton, B.
    1982   *The Glory of Israel: The Theology and Provenience of the Isaiah Targum.*
            Sheffield: JSOT Press.
    1987   *The Isaiah Targum: Introduction, Translation, Apparatus and Notes.*
            Wilmington: Michael Glazier.
Flint, P. W.
    1997   The Isaiah Scrolls from the Judean Desert. Pages 481–90 in vol. 2 of
            Writing and Reading the Scroll of Isaiah. Edited by C. C. Broyles and
            C. A. Evans. 2 vols. Leiden: Brill.
Flint, P. W., E. Ulrich, and M. G. Abegg
    1999   *Edition of the Cave One Isaiah Scrolls.* DJD 37. Oxford: Clarendon.
García Martínez, F.
    1987   Le Livre d'Isaïe à Qumrân: Les textes. L'influence. *Le Monde de la Bible*
            49:43–45.
Gelston, A.
    1997   Was the Peshitta of Isaiah of Christian Origin? Pages 563–82 in vol. 2 of
            Writing and Reading the Scroll of Isaiah. Edited by C. C. Broyles and
            C. A. Evans. 2 vols. Leiden: Brill.
Gonçalves, F. J.
    1992   Isaiah Scroll. Pages 470–72 in vol. 3 of *ABD.* Edited by D. N. Freedman.
            6 vols. New York: Doubleday.
Goshen-Gottstein, M.
    1954   Die Jesajah-Rolle und das Problem der hebräischen Bibelhandschriften.
            Bib 35:429–42.
    1995   *The Book of Isaiah* (The Hebrew University Bible). Jerusalem: Magnes.

James, F. D.
1959   A *Critical Examination of the Text of Isaiah*. Ph.D. dissertation, Boston University.

Koenig, J.
1982   *L'herméneutique analogique du Judaïsm antique d'après les témoins textuels d'Isaïe*. Leiden: Brill.

Kooij, A. van der
1981   *Die alten Textzeugen des Jesajabuches*. Freiburg: Universitätsverlag/Göttingen: Vandenhoeck & Ruprecht.
1989   The Septuagint of Isaiah: Translation and Interpretation. Pages 127–33 in *The Book of Isaiah—Le Livre d'Isaïe: Les oracles et leur relecture. Unité et complexité de l'ouvrage*. Edited by J. Vermeylen. Leuven: Peeters and Leuven University Press.
1992   The Old Greek of Isaiah in Relation to the Qumran Texts of Isaiah: Some General Comments. Pages 195–213 in *Septuagint, Scrolls and Cognate Writings*. Edited by G. J. Brooke and B. Lindars. Atlanta: Scholars Press.

Kutscher, E. Y.
1974   *The Language and Linguistic Background of the Isaiah Scroll (1QIsaᵃ)*. Leiden: Brill.

Olley, J. W.
1993   Hear the Word of YHWH: The Structure of the Book of Isaiah in 1QIsaᵃ. *VT* 43:19–49.

Porter, S. E., and B. W. R. Pearson
1997   Isaiah through Greek Eyes: The Septuagint of Isaiah. Pages 531–46 in vol. 2 of *Writing and Reading the Scroll of Isaiah: Studies of an Interpretive Tradition*. Edited by C. C. Broyles and C. A. Evans. 2 vols. Leiden: Brill.

Roberts, B. J.
1959   The Second Isaiah Scroll from Qumrân (1QIsᵇ). *BJRL* 42/1:132–44.

Rubinstein, A.
1955   The Theological Aspect of Some Variant Readings in the Isaiah Scroll. *JJS* 6:187–200.

Seeligmann, I. L.
1948   *The Septuagint Version of Isaiah*. Leiden: Brill.

Skehan, P. W.
1955   The Text of Isaias at Qumrân. *CBQ* 17:158–63.

Talmon, S.
1989   Observations on Variant Readings in the Isaiah Scroll (1QIsaᵃ). Pages 117–30 in *The World of Qumran from Within: Collected Studies*. Jerusalem: Magnes/Leiden: Brill.

Tov, E.
1997   The Text of Isaiah at Qumran. Pages 491–511 in vol. 2 of *Writing and Reading the Scroll of Isaiah*. Edited by C. C. Broyles and C. A. Evans. 2 vols. Leiden: Brill.

Troxel, R. L.
1993   Exegesis and Theology in the LXX: Isaiah V 26–30. *VT* 43:102–11.

Ulrich, E.
1997   An Index to the Contents of the Isaiah Manuscripts from the Judean
            Desert. Pages 477–80 in vol. 2 of *Writing and Reading the Scroll of
            Isaiah.* Edited by C. C. Broyles and C. A. Evans. 2 vols. Leiden: Brill.
Ulrich, E., et al.
1997   *Qumran Cave 4, X: The Prophets.* DJD 15. Oxford: Clarendon.
Ziegler, J.
1939   *Isaias.* Septuaginta 14. Göttingen: Vandenhoeck & Ruprecht.
1959   Die Vorlage der Isaias-Septuaginta (LXX) und die erste Isaias-Rolle von
            Qumran (1QIsaᵃ). *JBL* 78:34–59.

COMMENTARIES
(in chronological order)

Gesenius, W.
1821   *Philologisch-kritischer und historiker Commentar über den Jesaia.* 3 vols.
            Leipzig: Vogel.
Cheyne, T. K.
1880   *The Book of the Prophet Isaiah.* New York: Dodd, Mead. 5th ed., 1904.
Smith, G. A.
1889   *The Book of Isaiah.* Expositor's Bible. London: Hodder & Staunton.
Duhm, B.
1892   *Das Buch Jesaja.* Göttingen: Vandenhoeck & Ruprecht. 4th edition,
            1922.
Dillmann, A.
1896   *Der Prophet Jesaja.* HAT. Leipzig: Hirzel.
Marti, K.
1900   *Das Buch Jesaja.* BKAT. Tübingen: Mohr/Siebeck.
Condamin, A.
1905   *Le Livre d'Isaïe.* Paris: Lecoffre.
Whitehouse, O. C.
1905   *Isaiah I–XXXIX.* CB. Edinburgh: T. & T. Clark.
Box, G. H.
1908   *The Book of Isaiah.* London: Pitman.
Wade, G. W.
1911   *The Book of the Prophet Isaiah.* London: Methuen.
Gray, G. Buchanan
1912   *A Critical and Exegetical Commentary on the Book of Isaiah I–XXVII.*
            ICC. Edinburgh: T. & T. Clark.
Skinner, J.
1915   *The Book of the Prophet Isaiah: Chapters I–XXXIX.* 2d ed. Cambridge:
            Cambridge University Press.
Feldman, E.
1925   *Das Buch Isaias.* Münster: Aschendorff.
König, E.
1926   *Das Buch Jesaja.* Gütersloh: Bertelsmann.

Torrey, C. C.
1928   *The Second Isaiah: A New Interpretation.* Edinburgh: T. & T. Clark.
Wade, G. W.
1929   *The Book of the Prophet Isaiah with Introduction and Notes.* 2d ed. WC. London: Methuen.
Procksch, O.
1930   *Jesaja I: Kapitel 1–39 übersetzt und erklärt.* KAT. Leipzig: Deichert.
Fischer, J.
1937   *Das Buch Isaias.* Bonn: Hanstein.
Kissane, E. J.
1941–43 *The Book of Isaiah.* 2 vols. Dublin: Browne & Nolan. 2d ed., 1960.
Bentzen, A.
1944   *Jesaja I: Jes. 1–39.* Copenhagen: G. E. C. Gads.
Ziegler, J.
1948   *Isaias.* Echter Bibel. Würzburg: Echter Verlag.
Slotki, I. W.
1949   *Isaiah.* London: Soncino.
Bewer, J. A.
1950   *The Book of Isaiah.* 2 vols. New York: Harper.
Hertzberg, H. W.
1952   *Der Erste Jesaja.* Kassel: Oncken.
Herntrich, V.
1954   *Der Prophet Jesaja: Kapitel 1–12.* ATD. Göttingen: Vandenhoeck & Ruprecht.
Scott, R. B. Y.
1956   The Book of Isaiah. Pages 149–381 in *IB* 5. New York/Nashville: Abingdon.
Ziegler, J.
1958   *Das Buch Isaias.* Würzburg: Echter.
Penna, A.
1958   *Isaia.* SB. Turin/Rome: Marietti. 2d ed., 1964.
Eichrodt, W.
1960   *Der Heilige in Israel: Jesaja 1–12.* BAT. Stuttgart: Calwer.
1967   *Der Herr der Geschichte: Jesaja 13–23, 28–39.* BAT. Stuttgart: Calwer.
Bright, J.
1962   "Isaiah I." In *Peake's Commentary on the Bible.* London/New York: Nelson.
Mauchline, J.
1962   *Isaiah 1–39.* Torch Bible Commentaries. New York: Macmillan.
Leslie, E. A.
1963   *Isaiah.* New York/Nashville: Abingdon.
Wright, G. E.
1964   *Isaiah.* Richmond: John Knox.
Young, E. J.
1965–72 *The Book of Isaiah.* 3 vols. Grand Rapids: Eerdmans.
Fohrer, G.
1966   *Das Buch Jesaja, I: Kap. 1–23.* Zürcher Bibelkommentare. Zurich/Stuttgart: Zwingli Verlag.

1967a   *Das Buch Jesaja, II: Kap. 24–39*. Zürcher Bibelkommentare. Zurich/ Stuttgart: Zwingli Verlag.

Becker, J.
1968   *Isaias: Der Prophet und sein Buch*. SBS. Stuttgart: Calwer.

Ackroyd, P. R.
1971   "Isaiah." In *Interpreter's One-Volume Commentary on the Bible*. Nashville: Abingdon.

Auvray, P.
1972   *Isaïe 1–39*. SB. Paris: Gabalda.

Schoors, A.
1972   *Jesaja 1*. Roermond: Romen en Zonen.

Kaiser, O.
1972   *Isaiah 1–12*. OTL. Philadelphia: Westminster. 2d ed., 1983.
1974   *Isaiah 13–39*. OTL. Philadelphia: Westminster. 2d ed., 1980.

Herbert, A. S.
1973   *The Book of the Prophet Isaiah: 1–39*. Cambridge: Cambridge University Press.

Vermeylen, J.
1977–78   *Du Prophète Isaïe à l'Apocalyptique: Isaïe I–XXXV*. 2 vols. Paris: Gabalda.

Wildberger, H.
1978   *Jesaja 2: Jesaja 13–27*. BKAT. Neukirchen-Vluyn: Neukirchener Verlag. (Eng. tr. 1997 *Isaiah 13–27*. Minneapolis: Fortress).
1980   *Jesaja 1: Jesaja 1–12*. BKAT. Neukirchen-Vluyn: Neukirchener Verlag.
1982   *Jesaja 3: Jesaja 28–39*. BKAT. Neukirchen-Vluyn: Neukirchener Verlag.
1991   *Isaiah 1–12: A Commentary*. Continental Commentary. Minneapolis: Fortress. [English translation of 1980]

Clements, R. E.
1980a   *Isaiah 1–39*. NCB. Grand Rapids: Eerdmans.

Watts, J. D. W.
1985   *Isaiah 1–33*. WBC. Waco, Texas: Word.
1987   *Isaiah 34–66*. WBC. Waco, Texas: Word.

Oswalt, J. N.
1986   *The Book of Isaiah: Chapters 1–39*. NICOT. Grand Rapids: Eerdmans.

Kilian, R.
1986   *Jesaja I: Kap. 1–12*. Neue Echter Bibel. Würzburg: Echter Verlag.
1994   *Jesaja II: Kap. 13–39*. Neue Echter Bibel. Würzburg: Echter Verlag.

Jacob, E.
1987   *Esaïe 1–12*. Geneva: Labor et Fides.

Sheppard, G. T.
1988   "Isaiah 1–39." In *Harper's Bible Commentary*. San Francisco: Harper & Row.

Jensen, J., and W. H. Irwin
1990   "Isaiah 1–39." In *The New Jerome Biblical Commentary*. Englewood Cliffs. N.J.: Prentice-Hall.

Seitz, C. R.
1993   *Isaiah 1–39*. Interpretation. Louisville: John Knox.

Sweeney, M. A.
1996   *Isaiah 1–39 with an Introduction to the Prophetic Literature*. The Forms of Old Testament Literature. Grand Rapids: Eerdmans.

Monographs, Articles, Special Studies

Allis, O. T.
1950   *The Unity of Isaiah: A Study in Prophecy.* Philadelphia: Presbyterian & Reformed.
Alonso-Schökel, L.
1963   *Estudios de poética hebrea.* Barcelona: Juan Flores.
1987   Isaiah. Pages 165–83 in *The Literary Guide to the Bible.* Edited by R. Alter and F. Kermode. Cambridge, Mass: Belknap Press of Harvard University Press.
Alter, R.
1985   *The Art of Biblical Poetry.* New York: Basic Books.
Anderson, B. W.
1988   The Apocalyptic Rendering of the Isaian Tradition. Pages 45–63 in *The Social World of Formative Christianity and Judaism.* Edited by J. Neusner et al. Philadelphia: Fortress.
Auld, A. G.
1980   Poetry, Prophecy, Hermeneutic: Recent Studies in Isaiah. *SJT* 33:567–81.
Baltzer, K.
1975   *Die Biographie der Propheten.* Neukirchen-Vluyn: Neukirchener Verlag.
Barth, H.
1977   *Die Jesaja-Worte in der Josiazeit: Israel und Asshur also Thema einer produktiven Neuinterpretation der Jesajaüberlieferung.* Neukirchen-Vluyn: Neukirchener Verlag.
Barthel, J.
1997   *Prophetenwort und Geschichte.* Tübingen: Mohr Siebeck.
Barton, J.
1981   Ethics in Isaiah of Jerusalem. *JTS* 32:1–18.
Becker, J.
1968   *Isaias: Der Prophet und sein Buch.* Stuttgart: Katholisches Bibelwerk.
Blank, S.
1958   *Prophetic Faith in Isaiah.* New York: Harper.
Bosshard-Nepustil, E.
1997   *Rezeptionen von Jesaja 1–39 im Zwölfprophetenbuch.* Freiburg: Universitätsverlag/Göttingen: Vandenhoeck & Ruprecht.
Bovati, P.
1989   Le langage juridique du prophète Isaïe. Pages 177–96 in *The Book of Isaiah — Le Livre d'Isaïe: Les oracles et leur relecture. Unité et complexité de l'ouvrage.* Edited by J. Vermeylen. Leuven: Leuven University Press.
Brooke, G. J.
1997   Isaiah in the Pesharim and Other Qumran Texts. Pages 609–32 in *Writing and Reading the Scroll of Isaiah.* Edited by C. C. Broyles and C. A. Evans. 2 vols. Leiden: Brill.
Broyles, C. C., and C. A. Evans, eds.
1997   *Writing and Reading the Scroll of Isaiah.* 2 vols. Leiden: Brill.
Brueggemann, W.
1984   Unity and Dynamic in the Isaiah Tradition. *JSOT* 29:89–107.

Carr, D. M.
1993   Reaching for Unity in Isaiah. *JSOT* 57:61–80.
Carroll, R. P.
1979   *When Prophecy Failed: Cognitive Dissonance in the Prophetic Traditions of the Old Testament.* New York: Seabury.
Childs, B. S.
1979   Pages 305–38 in *Introduction to the Old Testament as Scripture.* Philadelphia: Fortress.
Clements, R. E.
1980b   *Isaiah and the Deliverance of Jerusalem: A Study of the Interpretation of Prophecy in the Old Testament.* Sheffield: JSOT Press.
1980c   The Prophecies of Isaiah and the Fall of Jerusalem. *VT* 30:421–36.
1982   The Unity of the Book of Isaiah. *Int* 36:117–29.
1985   Beyond Tradition-History: Deutero-Isaianic Development of First Isaiah's Themes. *JSOT* 31:95–113.
Conrad, E. W.
1991   *Reading Isaiah.* Minneapolis: Fortress.
Dietrich, W.
1976   *Jesaja und die Politik.* Munich: Kaiser.
Donner, H.
1964   *Israel unter den Völken.* Leiden: Brill.
Driver, G. R.
1968   Isaiah I–XXXIX: Textual and Linguistic Problems. *JSS* 13:36–57.
Driver, S. R.
1897   *Isaiah: His Life and Times.* 2d ed. New York: Fleming & Revell.
Dumbrell, W. J.
1985   The Purpose of the Book of Isaiah. *TynBul* 36:111–28.
Eaton, J. H.
1959   The Origin of the Book of Isaiah. *VT* 9: 138–57.
1982   The Isaiah Tradition. Pages 58–76 in *Israel's Prophetic Heritage: Essays in Honour of Peter Ackroyd.* Edited by R. J. Coggins et al. Cambridge: Cambridge University Press.
Eichrodt, W.
1970   Prophet and Covenant: Observations on the Exegesis of Isaiah. Pages 167–88 in *Proclamation and Presence.* Edited by J. I. Durham and J. I Porter. London: SCM.
Evans, C. A.
1986   On Isaiah's Use of Israel's Sacred Traditions. *BZ* 30:92–99.
1988   On the Unity and Parallel Structure of Isaiah. *VT* 38:129–47.
Feldman, L. H.
1997   Josephus' Portrait of Isaiah. Pages 583–608 in vol. 2 of *Writing and Reading the Scroll of Isaiah.* Edited by C. C. Broyles and C. A. Evans. 2 vols. Leiden: Brill.
Feuillet, A.
1947   Isaïe (Le Livre de). Pages 647–729 in vol. 4 of *DBSup.*
Fey, R.
1963   *Amos und Jesaja: Abhängigkeit und Eigenständichkeit des Jesaja.* Neukirchen-Vluyn: Neukirchener Verlag.

Fichtner, J.
  1951   JHWHs Plan in der Botschaft des Jesaja. ZAW 63:16–33.
Fohrer, G.
  1967   Entstehung, Komposition und Überlieferung von Jesaja 1–39. Pages
            113–47 in *Studien zur alttestamentlichen Prophetie*. Berlin: de Gruyter.
Ginsberg, H. L.
  n.d.   Isaiah: First Isaiah. Pages 44–60 in vol. 9 of *EncJud*. 9.
Gitay, Y.
  1991   *Isaiah and His Audience*. Assen: Van Gorcum.
Hardmeier, C.
  1986   Jesajaforschung im Umbruch. *Verkundigüng und Forschung* 31:3–31.
Hayes, J., and S. Irvine
  1987   *Isaiah the Eighth-Century Prophet: His Times and His Preaching*. Nash-
            ville: Abingdon.
Høgenhaven, J.
  1988   *Gott und Volk bei Jesaja: Eine Untersuchung zur biblischen Theologie*.
            Leiden: Brill.
Hoffmann, H. W.
  1974   *Die Intention der Verkündigung Jesajas*. Berlin/New York: de Gruyter.
Holladay, W. L.
  1978   *Isaiah: Scroll of a Prophetic Heritage*. Grand Rapids: Eerdmans.
Huber, F.
  1976   *JHWH, Juda und die anderen Völker beim Propheten Jesaja*. Berlin/New
            York: de Gruyter.
Jensen, J.
  1973   *The Use of tôrâ by Isaiah: His Debate with the Wisdom Tradition*. Wash-
            ington: Catholic Biblical Association.
  1986   Yahweh's Plan in Isaiah and in the Rest of the Old Testament. *CBQ*
            48:443–55.
Jones, D.
  1955   The Traditio of the Oracles of Isaiah of Jerusalem. *ZAW* 67:226–46.
Kaiser, O.
  1989   Literaturkritik und Tendenzkritik: Überlegungen zur Methode des Jesaja-
            exegese. Pages 55–71 in *The Book of Isaiah — Le Livre d'Isaïe: Les oracles
            et leur relecture, Unité et complexité de l'ouvrage*. Edited by J. Vermey-
            len. Leuven: Leuven University Press.
Knibb, M. A.
  1997   Isaianic Traditions in the Apocrypha and Pseudepigrapha. Pages 633–50
            in vol. 2 of *Writing and Reading the Scroll of Isaiah*. Edited by C. C.
            Broyles and C. A. Evans. 2 vols. Leiden: Brill.
Kugel, J. L.
  1981   *The Idea of Biblical Poetry*. New Haven/London: Yale University Press.
Lack, R.
  1973   *La Symbolique du Livre d'Isaïe*. Rome: Pontifical Biblical Institute.
Liebreich, L. J.
  1955–56   The Compilation of the Book of Isaiah. *JQR* n.s. 46:259–77; 47:114–38.
Loretz, O.
  1960   Der Glaube des Propheten Isaias an das Gottesreich. *ZKT* 82:40–73,
            159–81.

Martin-Achard, R.
1960   Sagesse de Dieu et sagesse humaine chez Esaïe. Pages 137–44 in *La Branche d'Amandier: Fst. W. Vischer.* Montpellier: Causse, Graille, Catelnau.
1967   Isaïe et Jérémie aux prises avec les problèmes politiques. *RHPR* 47:208–24.
Melugin, R. F., and M. A. Sweeney, eds.
1996   *New Visions of Isaiah.* Sheffield: JSOT Press.
Mowinckel, S.
1933   Die Komposition des Jesajabuches Kap. 1–39. *AcOr* 11:267–92.
1946   *Prophecy and Tradition.* Oslo: J. Dybwad.
Napier, B. D.
1966   Isaiah and the Isaian. Pages 240–51 in *Volume du Congrès International pour l'étude de l'Ancien Testament: Genève, 1965.* VTSup 15. Leiden: Brill.
Niehr, H.
1984   Bedeutung und Funktion kanaanäischer Traditions-elements in der Sozialkritik Jesajas. *BZ* 28:69–81.
Nielsen, K.
1989   *There Is Hope for a Tree: The Tree as Metaphor in Isaiah.* Sheffield: JSOT Press.
North, C. R.
1962   Isaiah. Pages 731–44 in vol. 2 of *IDB.*
Olley, W.
1993   "Hear the Word of YHWH": The Structure of the Book of Isaiah in 1QIsa[a]. *VT* 43:19–49.
Pelletier, A.-M.
1990   Le livre d'Isaïe et le temps de l'histoire. *NRTh* 112:30–43.
Porton, G.
1997   Isaiah and the Kings: The Rabbis on the Prophet Isaiah. Pages 693–716 in vol. 2 of *Writing and Reading the Scroll of Isaiah.* Edited by C. C. Broyles and C. A. Evans. 2 vols. Leiden: Brill.
Rad, Gerhard von
1965   Volume 2 of *Old Testament Theology.* New York: Harper & Row.
Rendtorff, R.
1984   Zur Komposition des Buches Jesaja. *VT* 34:295–320.
1993   The Composition of the Book of Isaiah. Pages 146–69 in *Canon and Theology: Overtures to an Old Testament Theology.* Minneapolis: Fortress.
Roberts, J. J. M.
1982   Isaiah in Old Testament Theology. *Int* 36:130–43.
Sawyer, J. F. A.
1996   *The Fifth Gospel: Isaiah in the History of Christianity.* Cambridge: Cambridge University Press.
Schmidt, W. H.
1977   Die Einheit der Verkündigung Jesajas: Versuch einer Zusammenschau. *EvT* 37:260–72.
Scott, R. B. Y.
1950   The Literary Structure of Isaiah's Oracles. Pages 175–86 in *Studies in Old Testament Prophecy presented to T. H. Robinson.* Edited by H. H. Rowley. Edinburgh: T. & T. Clark.

Seitz, C. R.
  1991   Zion's Final Destiny: The Development of the Book of Isaiah. Minneapolis: Fortress.
  1992   Isaiah, Book of. Pages 472–88 in vol. 3 of ABD.
Sheppard, G. T.
  1985   The Anti-Assyrian Redaction and the Canonical Context of Isaiah 1–39. JBL 104:193–216.
Skehan, P.
  1940   Isaias and the Teaching of the Book of Wisdom. CBQ 2:289–99.
Stegemann, U.
  1969   Der Restgedanke bei Isaias. BZ 13:161–86.
Sweeney, M. A.
  1993   The Book of Isaiah in Recent Research. Currents in Research: Biblical Studies 1:141–62.
Tadmor, H.
  1994   The Inscriptions of Tiglath-pileser III King of Assyria. Jerusalem: The Israel Academy of Sciences and Humanities.
Van Ruiten, J., and M. Vervenne, eds.
  1997   Studies in the Book of Isaiah: Festschrift Willem A. M. Beuken. Leuven: University of Leuven Press.
Vermeylen, J.
  1989   L'Unité du Livre d'Isaïe. Pages 11–53 in The Book of Isaiah—Le Livre d'Isaïe: Les oracles et leur relecture. Unité et complexité de l'ouvrage. Edited by J. Vermeylen. Leuven: Peeters/Leuven University Press.
Vermeylen, J., ed.
  1989   The Book of Isaiah—Le Livre d'Isaïe: Les oracles et leur relecture. Unité et complexité de l'ouvrage. Leuven: Peeters/Leuven University Press.
Vriezen, T. C.
  1962   Essentials of the Theology of Isaiah. Pages 128–46 in Israel's Prophetic Heritage. Edited by B. W. Anderson and W. Harrelson. London: SCM.
Ward, J. M.
  1969   Amos and Isaiah: Prophets of the Word of God. Nashville/New York: Abingdon.
Werner, W.
  1982   Eschatologische Texte in Jesaja 1–39: Messias, Heiliger Rest, Völker. Würzburg: Echter Verlag.
Whedbee, J. W.
  1971   Isaiah and Wisdom. Nashville: Abingdon.
Wildberger, H.
  1963   Jesajas Verständnis der Geschichte. Pages 83–117 in Congress Volume: Bonn, 1962. VTSup 9. Leiden: Brill.
Williamson, H. G. M.
  1994   The Book Called Isaiah: Deutero-Isaiah's Role in Composition and Redaction. Oxford: Clarendon.
Zimmerli, W.
  1974   Verkündigung und Sprache der Botschaft Jesajas. Pages 73–87 in Gesammelte Aufsätze, Vol 2: Studien zur alttestamentlichen Theologie und Prophetie. Munich: Kaiser.

ISAIAH 1–12

◆

Abramski, S.
1958   "Slag" and "Tin" in the First Chapter of Isaiah. *Eretz-Israel* 5 (Mazar Volume):105–7.

Ackroyd, P. R.
1963   A Note on Isaiah 2.1. *ZAW* 75:320–21.
1978   Isaiah I–XII: Presentation of a Prophet. Pages 16–48 in *Congress Volume: Göttingen, 1977*. VTSup 29. Leiden: Brill. (= Pages 79–104 in *Studies in the Religious Tradition of the Old Testament*. London: SCM, 1987.)
1984   The Biblical Interpretation of the Reigns of Ahaz and Hezekiah. Pages 247–59 in *In The Shelter of Elyon*. Fst. G. W. Ahlström. Edited by W. B. Barrick and J. R. Spencer. Sheffield: JSOT Press (= Pages 181–92 in *Studies in the Religious Tradition of the Old Testament*. London: SCM, 1987.)

Aharoni, Y.
1979   *The Land of the Bible: A Historical Geography*. Philadelphia: Westminster.

Ahlström, G. W.
1974   Isaiah VI.13. *JSS* 19:169–72.

Albright, W. F.
1924   The Assyrian March on Jerusalem, Isa X 28–32. *AASOR* 4:134–40.
1955   The Son of Tabeel (Isaiah 7:6). *BASOR* 140:34–35.

Alonso-Schökel, L.
1956   De duabus methodis pericopam explicandi. *VD* 34:154–60.

Alt, A.
1964a   Hosea 5,8–6,6: Ein Krieg und seine Folgen in prophetischer Beleuchtung. Pages 163–87 in vol. 2 of *Kleine Schriften zur Geschichte des Volkes Israel*. 3d ed. Munich: Beck. [1st ed, 1919.]
1964b   Jesaja 8,23–9,6: Befreiungsnacht und Krönungstag. Pages 206–25 in vol. 2 of *Kleine Schriften zur Geschichte des Volkes Israel*. 3d ed. Munich: Beck. [1st ed., 1919.]

Anderson, R. T.
1960   Was Isaiah a Scribe? *JBL* 79:57–58.

Arnold, P. M.
1990   *Gibeah: The Search for a Biblical City*. Sheffield: JSOT Press.

Auret, A.
1990   Another look at *wmśwś* in Isaiah 8:6. *OTE* 3:107–14.

Avigad, N.
1963   The Seal of Yeshaʿyahu. *IEJ* 13:324.

Bahar, S.
1993   Two Forms of the Root NWP in Isaiah x 32. *VT* 43:403–5.

Baker, D. W.
1992   Tarshish (Place). Pages 331–33 in vol. 6 of *ABD*.

Baldwin, J. G.
1964   *Semah* as a Technical Term in the Prophets. *VT* 14:93–97.
Baltzer, K.
1968   Considerations Regarding the Office and Calling of the Prophet. *HTR* 61:567–81.
Bardtke, H.
1971   Die Latifundien in Juda während der zweiten Hälfte des achten Jahrhunderts v.Chr. Pages 235–54 in *Festschrift A. Dupont-Sommer*. Paris: Adrian-Maisonneuve.
Bartelmus, R.
1984   Jesaja 7,1–17 und das Stilprinzip des Kontrastes Syntaktisch-stylistische und traditionsgeschichtliche Anmerkungen zur "Immanuel-Perikope." *ZAW* 96:50–66.
Barth, H.
1977   *Die Jesaja-Worte in der Josiazeit: Israel und Asshur also Thema einer produktiven Neuinterpretation der Jesajaüberlieferung.* Neukirchen-Vluyn: Neukirchener Verlag.
Beale, G. K.
1991   Isaiah vi 9–13: A Retributive Taunt Against Idolatry. *VT* 41:257–78.
Ben Zvi, E.
1991   Isaiah 1,4–9: Isaiah and the Events of 701 in Judah. *SJOT* 1:95–111.
Berg, W.
1980   Die Identität der "junger Frau" in Jes 7,14,16. *BN* 13:7–13.
Bickert, R.
1987   König Ahas und der Prophet Jesaja: Ein Beitrag zum Problem des Syrisch-ephraimitischen Krieges. *ZAW* 99:361–84.
Bjørndalen, A. J.
1982   Zur Frage der Echtheit von Jesaja 1,2–3, 1,4–7 und 5,1–7. *NTT* 83:89–100.
Blenkinsopp, J.
1971   The Prophetic Reproach. *JBL* 90: 267–78.
1981   Fragments of Ancient Exegesis in an Isaian Poem (Jes 2 6–22). *ZAW* 93: 51–62.
1995   Pages 150–54 in *Sage, Priest, Prophet: Religious and Intellectual Leadership in Ancient Israel*. Louisville: Westminster/John Knox Press.
Blum, E.
1992–93   Jesaja und der DBR des Amos: Unzeitgemässe Uberlegungen zu Jes 5,25; 9,7–20; 10,1–4. *Dielheimer Blätter zum Alten Testament* 28:75–95.
1997   Jesajas prophetisches Testament: Beobachtungen zu Jes 1–11. *ZAW* 108: 547–68; 109:12–29.
Brandscheidt, R.
1996   Ein grosses Licht (Jes 9,1–6): Standortbestimmung zur Stärkung des Glaubens. *TTZ* 105:21–38.
Brekelmans, C. H. W.
1989   Deuteronomistic Influence in Isaiah 1–12. Pages 167–76 in *The Book of Isaiah—Le Livre d'Isaïe: Les oracles et leur relecture. Unité et complexité de l'ouvrage*. Edited by J. Vermeylen. Leuven: Peeters/Leuven University Press.

Brown, W. P.
    1990   The So-Called Refrain in Isaiah 5:25–30 and 9:7–10:4. *CBQ* 52:432–43.
Buda, J.
    1939   *Semah* Jahweh. *Bib* 20:10–26.
Budde, K.
    1926   Jesaja 8,6b. ZAW 44:65–67.
    1927   Verfasser und Stelle von Mi. 4,1–4 (Jes. 2,2–4). ZDMG 81:152–58.
    1928   *Jesajas Erleben: Eine gemeinverständliche Auslegung der Denkschrift des Propheten (Kap. 6,1–9,6)*. Gotha: L. Klotz.
    1930   Zu Jesaja 8:19–20. *JBL* 49:423–28.
    1931   Zu Jesaja 1–5. ZAW 49:16–40, 182–211; 50:38–72.
    1933   Das Immanuelzeichen und die Ahaz-Begegnung Jesaja 7. *JBL* 52:22–54.
Cannawurf, E.
    1963   The Authenticity of Micah 4.1–4. *VT* 13:26–33.
Carlson, R. A.
    1974   The Anti-Assyrian Character of the Oracle in Is. IX 1–6. *VT* 24:130–35.
Carroll, R. P.
    1978   Inner Tradition Shifts in Isa 1–11. *ExpTim* 89:301–4.
    1980   Translation and Attribution in Isaiah 8.19f. *BT* 31:126–34.
Cathcart, K. J.
    1992   Day of Yahweh. Pages 84–85 in vol. 2 of *ABD*.
Cazelles, H.
    1975   La Vocation d'Isaïe (ch. 6) et les rites royaux. Pages 89–108 in *Homenaje a Juan Prado*. Edited by L. Alvarez Verdes and E. J. Alonso Hernandez. Madrid: Consejo Superior de Investigaciones Cientificos.
    1980   Qui aurait visé, à l'origine, Isaïe II 2–5. *VT* 30:409–20.
    1982   Quelques questions de critique textuelle et littéraire en Is. 4,2–6. *Eretz-Israel* 16 (Orlinsky Volume):17*–25*.
Childs, B. S.
    1959   The Enemy from the North and the Chaos Tradition. *JBL* 78:187–98.
    1967   *Isaiah and the Assyrian Crisis*. London: S.C.M.
Chisholm, R. B.
    1986   Structure, Style, and the Prophetic Message: An Analysis of Isaiah 5:8–30. *BSac* 143:46–60.
Christensen, D. L.
    1976   The March of Conquest in Isaiah X 27c–34. *VT* 26:395–99.
Claassen, W. T.
    1974   Linguistic Arguments and the Dating of Isaiah 1:4–9. *JNSL* 3:1–18.
Clements, R. E.
    1985   Beyond Tradition History: Deutero-Isaianic Development of First Isaiah's Themes. *JSOT* 31:95–113.
    1990   The Immanuel Prophecy of Isa. 7:10–17 and its Messianic Interpretation. Pages 225–40 in *Die hebräische Bibel und ihre zweifache Nachgeschichte: Fst. R. Rendtorff*. Edited by E. Blum et al. Neukirchen-Vluyn: Neukirchener Verlag.
    1996   Pages 78–82 in *Old Testament Prophecy: From Oracles to Canon*. Louisville: Westminster/John Knox.

Clifford, R.
1972   *The Cosmic Mountain in Canaan and the Old Testament*. Cambridge:
            Harvard University Press.
Cogan, M.
1974   *Imperialism and Religion: Assyria, Judah and Israel in the Eighth and
            Seventh Centuries* B.C.E. Missoula, Montana: Scholars Press.
Cole, D. P.
1994   Archaeology and the Messiah Oracles of Isaiah 9 and 11. Pages 53–69 in
            Scripture and Other Artifacts: Essays in Honor of Philip J. King. Edited by
            M. D. Coogan. Louisville: Westminster/John Knox.
Compston, H. F. B.
1926–27   Ladies' Finery in Isaiah III 18–23. *Church Quarterly Review* 103:316–30.
Conrad, E. W.
1988   The Royal Narratives and the Structure of the Book of Isaiah. *JSOT* 41:
            67–81.
1991   Pages 83–116 in *Reading Isaiah*. Minneapolis: Fortress.
Coppens, J.
1952   La prophétie de l'*Almah*. *ETL* 28:648–78.
Crenshaw, J. L.
1970   A Liturgy of Wasted Opportunity (Am 4,6–12; Isa 9,7–10,4; 5,25–29).
            Semitics 1:27–37.
Crook, M. B.
1949   A Suggested Occasion for Isaiah 9,2–7 and 11,1–9. *JBL* 68:213–24.
Crüsemann, F.
1969   *Studien zur Formgeschichte von Hymnus und Danklied in Israel*. Neu-
            kirchen-Vluyn: Neukirchener Verlag.
Culver, R. D.
1969   Is 1:18: Declaration, Exclamation or Interrogation? *JETS* 12:133–41.
Davidson, R.
1966   The Interpretation of Isaiah II 6ff. *VT* 16:1–7.
Day, J.
1981   Shear-Jashub (Isaiah VII 3) and "The Remnant of Wrath" (Psalm LXXVI
            11). *VT* 31:76–78.
Dearman, J. A.
1996   The Son of Tabeel (Isaiah 7.6). Pages 33–47 in *Prophets and Paradigms:
            Essays in Honor of Gene M. Tucker*. Edited by S. Breck Reid. Sheffield:
            JSOT Press.
Deist, F.
1973   Jes 11,3a: Eine Glosse? *ZAW* 85:351–55.
Dequeker, L.
1962   Isaïe vii 14. *VT* 12:331–35.
Dietrich, W.
1976   *Jesaja und die Politik*. Munich: Kaiser.
Diringer, D.
1934   *Le Iscrizioni Antico-Ebraiche Palestinesi*. Florence.
Donner, H.
1964   *Israel unter den Völken*. Leiden: Brill.
1968   Der Feind aus dem Norden: Topographische und archäologische Erwä-
            gungen zu Jes. 10:27b–34. *ZDPV* 84:46–54.

Driver, G. R.
1933   Studies in the Vocabulary of the Old Testament VI. *JTS* 34:375–85 (377).
1937   Isaiah i–xxxix, Linguistic and Textual Problems. *JTS* 38:36–50.
1940   Hebrew Notes on Prophets and Proverbs. *JTS* 41:162–75.
1955   Two Misunderstood Passages of the Old Testament. *JTS* n.s. 6:82–84.
1971   His Train Filled the Temple. Pages 87–96 in *Near Eastern Studies in Honor of William Foxwell Albright*. Edited by H. Goedicke. Baltimore: Johns Hopkins University.

Edwards, D. R.
1992   Dress and Ornamentation. Pages 232–38 in vol. 2 of *ABD*.

Emerton, J. A.
1967   The Textual Problems of Isaiah V 14. *VT* 17:135–42.
1969   Some Linguistic and Historical Problems in Isaiah VIII.23. *JSS* 14:151–75.
1982   The Translation and Interpretation of Isaiah vi.13. Pages 85–118 in *Interpreting the Hebrew Bible: Essays in Honour of E. I. J. Rosenthal*. Edited J. A. Emerton and S. C. Reif. Cambridge: Cambridge University Press.
1992   The Translation of Isaiah 5,1. Pages 18–30 in *The Scriptures and the Scrolls: Studies in Honour of A. S. van der Woude on the Occasion of His 65th Birthday*. Edited by F. García Martínez and C. J. Labuschagne. VTSup 49. Leiden: Brill.
1993   The Historical Background of Isaiah 1:4–9. *Eretz-Israel* 24 (Malamat Volume):34–40.

Engnell, I.
1949   *The Call of Isaiah*. Uppsala: Lundeqvistska/Leipzig: Harrassowitz.

Eshel, H.
1990   Isaiah viii 23: An Historical-Geographical Analogy. *VT* 40:104–9.

Evans, C. A.
1982   The Text of Isaiah 6:9–10. *ZAW* 94:415–18.
1985   An Interpretation of Isa.8,11–15 Unemended. *ZAW* 97:112–13.
1989   *To See and Not Perceive: Isaiah 6.9–10 in Early Jewish and Christian Interpretation*. Sheffield: JSOT Press.

Everson, A. J.
1976   Day of the Lord. Pages 209–10 in *IDBSup*.

Fensham, F. C.
1987   A Fresh Look at Isaiah 7:7–9. Pages 11–17 in *Perspectives on Language and Text: Essays and Poems in Honor of Francis I. Andersen's Sixtieth Birthday, July 28, 1985*. Edited by E. W. Conrad and E. G. Newing. Winona Lake, Indiana: Eisenbrauns.

Fey, R.
1963   *Amos und Jesaja: Abhängigkeit und Eigenständigkeit des Jesaja*. Neukirchen-Vluyn: Neukirchener Verlag.

Fichtner, J.
1949   Jesaja unter den Weisen. *TLZ* 74:cols. 75–80.
1951   Jahwes Plan in der Botschaft des Jesaja. *ZAW* 63:16–33.

Fohrer, G.
1962   Jesaja 1 als Zusammenfassung der Verkündigung Jesajas. *ZAW* 74:251–68.

Fullerton, K.
1917–18   The Problem of Isaiah, Chapter 10. *AJSL* 34:170–84.
1924   The Interpretation of Isaiah 8,5–10. *JBL* 43:253–89.
Gelin, R.
1993   L'enigma dei 65 anni in Is. 7,8b. *Lateranum* 59:49–70.
Gerstenberger, E.
1962   The Woe-Oracles of the Prophets. *JBL* 81:249–63.
Gevaryahu, H. M. I.
1975   Biblical Colophons: A Source for the "Biography" of Authors, Texts and
           Books. Pages 42–59 in *Congress Volume: Edinburgh, 1974.* VTSup 28.
           Leiden: Brill.

Gitay, Y.
1983   Reflections on the Study of Prophetic Discourse: The Question of Isaiah
           I 2–20. *VT* 33:207–21.

Görg, M.
1978   Die Funktion der Serafen bei Jesaja. *BN* 5:28–39.
1983   Hiskija als Immanuel: Plädoyer für eine typologische Identifikation. *BN*
           22:107–25.
Gosse, B.
1991   Isaïe 52,13–53,12 et Isaïe 6. *RB* 98:537–43.
1992a   Isaïe vi et la tradition isaïenne. *VT* 42:340–49.
1992b   Isaïe 1 dans la rédaction du livre d'Isaïe. *ZAW* 104:52–66.
1996   Isaiah 8:23b and the Three Great Parts of the Book of Isaiah. *JSOT*
           70:57–62.
Gottwald, N. K.
1958   Immanuel as the Prophet's Son. *VT* 8:36–47.
Graffy, A.
1979   The Literary Genre of Isaiah 5,1–7. *Bib* 60:400–409.
Grayson, A. K.
1991   Pages 71–161 in *The Assyrian and Babylonian Empires and Other States
           of the Near East, from the Eighth to the Sixth Centuries* B.C. Vol. 3, part 2
           in CAH. 2d ed. Cambridge: Cambridge University Press.
Grelot, P.
1981   L'interprétation messianique d'Isaïe 9,5 dans le Targoum des prophètes.
           Pages 535–43 in *De la Torah au Messie: Mélanges H. Cazelles.* Edited by
           J. Doré et al. Paris: Desclée.
1983   Le Targoum d'Isaïe X, 32–34 dans ses diverses recensions. *RB* 90:202–28.
Haag, E.
1991   Das Immanuelzeichen in Jesaja 7. *TTZ* 100:3–22.
Habel, N.
1965   The Form and Significance of the Call Narratives. *ZAW* 77:297–323.
Hammershaimb, E.
1966   *Some Aspects of Old Testament Prophecy from Isaiah to Malachi.* Copen-
           hagen: Rosenkilde & Bagger.
Hardmeier, C.
1981   Jesajas Verkündigungsabsicht und Jahwes Verstockungsauftrag in Jes 6.
           Pages 235–51 in *Die Botschaft und die Boten: Fst. H. W. Wolff.* Edited by
           J. Jeremias and L. Perlitt. Neukirchen: Neukirchener Verlag.

Harvey, J.
1967   *Le playdoyer prophétique contre Israël après la rupture de l'alliance.*
          Bruges and Montreal.

Hayes, J. H., and P. K. Hooker
1988   Pages 50–80 in A *New Chronology for the Kings of Israel and Judah.*
          Atlanta: John Knox.

Hermisson, H.-J.
1973   Zukunftserwartung und Gegenwartskritik in der Verkündigung Jesajas.
          EvT 33:54–77.

Herrmann, W.
1974   Das Buch des Lebens. *Das Altertum* 20:3–10.

Hesse, F.
1955   *Das Verstockungsproblem im Alten Testament.* BZAW 74. Berlin: de
          Gruyter.

Hillers, D. R.
1983   *Hôy* and *Hôy*-Oracles: A Neglected Syntactic Aspect. Pages 185–88 in
          *The Word of the Lord Shall Go Forth: Essays in Honor of David Noel
          Freedman in Celebration of his Sixtieth Birthday,* eds. C. L. Meyers and
          M. O'Connor. Winona Lake, Indiana: Eisenbrauns.

Höffken, P.
1980   Notizen zum Textcharacter von Jesaja 7,1–17. *TZ* 36:321–27.
1982   Probleme in Jesaja 5,1–7. ZTK 79:392–410.
1989   Grundfragen zu Jesaja 7,1–17 im Spiegel neuerer Literatur. *BZ* n.s.
          33:25–42.

Høgenhaven, J.
1987   On the Structure and Meaning of Isaiah viii 23b. *VT* 37:218–21.
1990   The Prophet Isaiah and Judean Foreign Policy under Ahaz and Heze-
          kiah. *JNES* 49:351–54.

Hoffner, H. A.
1974   'ôbh. Pages 130–34 in vol. 1 of *TDOT.*

Holladay, W. L.
1968   Isa. III 10–11: An Archaic Wisdom Passage. *VT* 18:481–87.
1983   A New Suggestion for the Crux in Isaiah I 4B. *VT* 33:235–37.

Honeyman, A. M.
1951   An Unnoticed Euphemism in Isaiah IX 19–20? *VT* 1:221–23.

Horst, P. W. van der
1978   A Classical Parallel to Isaiah 5[8]. *ExpTim* 89:119–20.

Huber, F.
1976   *Jahwe, Juda und die anderer Völker beim Propheten Jesaja.* Berlin and
          New York: de Gruyter.

Huffmon, H. B.
1959   The Covenant Lawsuit in the Prophets. *JBL* 78:285–95.

Humbert, P.
1932   Maher Šalal Haš Baz. ZAW 50:90–92.

Hurowitz, V. A.
1989   Isaiah's Impure Lips and Their Purification in Light of Mouth Purifica-
          tion in Akkadian Sources. *HUCA* 60:39–89.

Irsigler, H.
1985   Zeichen und Bezeichneter in Jes 7,1–17: Notizen zum Immanueltext.
            BN 29:75–114.
Irvine, S. A.
1990   Isaiah, Ahaz, and the Syro-Ephraimite Crisis. Atlanta: Scholars Press.
1992   The Isaianic Denkschrift: Reconsidering an Old Hypothesis. ZAW
            104:216–31.
1993   Isaiah's She'ar-Yashub and the Davidic House. BZ 37:78–88.
Jamieson-Drake, D. W.
1991   Scribes and Schools in Monarchic Judah. JSOTSup 109. Sheffield:
            Almond.
Janzen, W.
1972   Mourning Cry and Woe Oracle. BZAW 125. Berlin and New York: de
            Gruyter.
Jenni, E.
1962   Day of the Lord. Pages 784–85 in vol. 1 of IDB.
Jensen, J.
1973   The Use of tôrâ by Isaiah: His Debate with the Wisdom Tradition. Wash-
            ington: Catholic Biblical Association.
1979   The Age of Immanuel. CBQ 41:220–39.
Jeppesen, K.
1982   Call and Frustration: A New Understanding of Isaiah VIII 21–22. VT 32:
            145–57.
Jepsen, A.
1960   Die Nebiah in Jes 8,3. ZAW 72:267–68.
Jepsen, K.
1982   Call and Frustration: A New Understanding of Isaiah VIII 21–22. VT 32:
            145–57.
Joines, K. R.
1967   Winged Serpents in Isaiah's Inaugural Vision. JBL 86:410–15.
Jones, B. C.
1993   Isaiah 8.11 and Isaiah's Vision of Yahweh. Pages 145–59 in History and
            Interpretation: Essays in Honour of John H. Hayes. Edited by M. P. Gra-
            ham et al. Sheffield: JSOT Press.
Jones, D. R.
1964   Exposition of Isaiah Chapter One Verses One to Nine. SJT 17:463–77.
1965–66   Exposition of Isaiah 1:10–17. SJT 18:457–71; 19:319–27.
Junker, H.
1959   Die literarische Art von Is. 5.1–7. Bib 40:259–66.
Kaiser, O.
1959   Die mythische Bedeutung des Meeres in Agypten, Ugarit und Israel.
            BZAW 78. Berlin: de Gruyter.
Kamesar, A.
1990   The Virgin of Isaiah 7:14: The Philological Argument from the Second
            to the Fifth Century. JTS 41:51–75.
Kellermann, D.
1987   Frevelstricke und Wagenseil: Bemerkungen zu Jesaja V 18. VT 37:90–97.
Kennett, R. H.
1906   The Prophecy in Isaiah IX 1–7. JTS 7:321–42.

Kilian, R.
1968   *Die Verheissung Immanuels Jes 7,14.* Stuttgart: Katholisches Bibelwerk.
Klein, H.
1980   Freude an Rezin: Ein Versuch mit dem Text Jes. viii 6 ohne Kenjektur auszukommen. *VT* 30:229–34.
Knierim, R.
1968   The Vocation of Isaiah. *VT* 18:47–68.
1977   "I Will Not Cause It to Return" in Amos 1 and 2. Pages 163–75 in *Canon and Authority.* Edited by G. W. Coats and B. O. Long. Philadelphia: Fortress.
Korpel, M. C. A.
1996   Structural Analysis as a Tool for Redactional Criticism: The Example of Isaiah 5 and 10.1–6. *JSOT* 69:53–71.
Kruger, P. A.
1989   Another Look at Isaiah 9:7–20. *JNSL* 15:127–41.
Kselman, J. S.
1975   A Note on Isaiah II 2. *VT* 25:225–27.
Laato, A.
1988   *Who Is Immanuel?* Åbo, Finland: Åbo Akademis Förlag.
Lescow, T.
1967   Das Geburtsmotif in den messianischen Weissagungen bei Jesaja und Micha. *ZAW* 79:172–207.
Lewis, T. J.
1989   Pages 128–32 in *Cults of the Dead in Ancient Israel and Ugarit.* Atlanta: Scholars Press.
L'Heureux, C. E.
1984   The Redactional History of Isaiah 5:1–10:4. Pages 99–119 in *In the Shelter of Elyon: Essays on Ancient Palestinian Life and Literature in Honor of G. W. Ahlström.* Edited by W. B. Barrick and J. R. Spencer. Sheffield: JSOT Press.
Liebreich, L. J.
1954   The Position of Chapter Six in the Book of Isaiah. *HUCA* 25:37–40.
Lind, M. C.
1997   Political Implications of Isaiah 6. Pages 317–38 in vol. 1 of *Writing and Reading the Scroll of Isaiah.* Edited by C. C. Broyles and C. A. Evans. 2 vols. Leiden: Brill.
Lindblom, J.
1958   *A Study on the Immanuel Section in Isaiah (Is 7:1–9:6).* Lund: Gleerup.
Lipiński, E.
1970   *B'hrjt hjmjm* dans les textes préexiliques. *VT* 20:445–50.
Loewenclau, I. von
1966   Zur Auslegung von Jesaja 1,2–3. *EvT* 26:294–308.
Loewenstamm, S. E.
1972   Is I 31. *VT* 22:246–48.
Lohfink, N.
1963   Isaias 8,12–14. *BZ* n.s. 7:98–104.
Long, B. O.
1976   Reports of Visions among the Prophets. *JBL* 95:353–65.

Loretz, O.
1975   Weinberglied und prophetische Deutung im Protest-Song Jes. 5:1–7. *UF* 7:573–76.
1984   Pages 63–83 in *Der Prolog des Jesaja-Buches (1,1–2,5)*. Altenberge: Akademische Bibliothek.

Luria, B. Z.
1981   The Prophecy in Isaiah 11:11–16 on the Gathering of the Exiles. *Beth Mikra* 26:108–14.

Lust, J.
1974   On Wizards and Prophets. Pages 133–42 in *Studies on Prophecy: A Collection of Twelve Papers*. VTSup 26. Leiden: Brill.

Machinist, P.
1983   Assyria and its Image in the First Isaiah. *JAOS* 103:719–37.

Magonet, J.
1991   Isaiah's Mountain or The Shape of Things to Come. *Prooftexts* 11:175–81.

Marshall, R. J.
1962   The Structure of Isaiah 1–12. *BR* 7:19–32.

Marx, A.
1990   Esaïe II 20: Une Signature Karaïte? *VT* 40:232–37.

Mattioli, A.
1966   Due schemi letterari negli oracoli d'introduzione al libro d'Isaia: Is. 1,1–31. *RivB* 14:345–64.

May, H. G.
1954   Some Cosmic Connotations of *Mayim Rabbîm*, 'Many Waters'. *JBL* 74:9–29.

Mazar, B.
1957   The Tobiads. *IEJ* 7:236–37.

McKane, W.
1965   *Prophets and Wise Men*. London: S.C.M.
1967   The Interpretation of Isaiah VII 14–25. *VT* 17:208–19.

McLaughlin, J. L.
1994   Their Hearts Were Hardened: The Use of Isaiah 6:9–10 in the Book of Isaiah. *Bib* 75:1–25.

Metzger, W.
1981   Der Horizont der Gnade in der Berufungsvision Jesajas. *ZAW* 93:281–84.

Milgrom, J.
1964   Did Isaiah Prophesy during the Reign of Uzziah? *VT* 14:164–82.
1991   *Leviticus 1–16*. AB 3. New York: Doubleday.

Mitchell, T. C.
1991   Israel and Judah from the Coming of Assyrian Domination until the Fall of Samaria, and the Struggle for Independence in Judah (c. 750–700 B.C.). Pages 323–73 in *The Assyrian and Babylonian Empires and Other States of the Near East, from the Eighth to the Sixth Centuries* B.C. Vol. 3, part 2 in CAH. Cambridge: Cambridge University Press.

Mittmann, S.
1989   "Wehe! Assur, Stab meines Zorns" (Jes 10,5–9.13ab–15). Pages 111–32 in *Prophet und Prophetenbuch: Fst. Otto Kaiser*. Edited by V. Fritz et al. Berlin: de Gruyter.

Morenz, S.
    1949   Eilebeute. *TLZ* 74:697–99.
Mowinckel, S.
    1946   *Prophecy and Tradition.* Oslo: Jakob Dybwad.
    1959   *He That Cometh.* Oxford: Blackwell.
Müller, H.-P.
    1961   Uns ist ein Kind geboren. . . . *EvT* 21:408–19.
Myers, J. M.
    1962   Dress and Ornaments. Pages 869–71 in vol. 1 of *IDB.*
Niditch, S.
    1980   The Composition of Isaiah 1. *Bib* 61:509–29.
Niehr, H.
    1983   Zur Intention von Jes 6,1–9. *BN* 21:59–65.
    1986   Zur Gattung von Jes 5,1–7. *BZ* 30:99–104.
Nielsen, K.
    1979   Das Bild des Gerichts (Rîb Pattern) in Jes i–xii. *VT* 29:309–24.
    1986   Is 6:1–8:18 as Dramatic Writing. *ST* 40:1–16.
Nobile, M.
    1989   Jes 6 und Ez 1,1–3,15: Vergleich und Funktion im Jeweiligen Redaktionellen Kontext. Pages 211–16 in *The Book of Isaiah—Le Livre d'Isaïe: Les oracles et leur relecture. Unité et complexité de l'ouvrage.* Edited by J. Vermeylen. Leuven: Peeters/Leuven University Press.
Oded, B.
    1972   The Historical Background of the Syro-Ephraimite War Reconsidered. *CBQ* 34:153–65.
    1979   *Mass Deportations and Deportees in the Neo-Assyrian Empire.* Wiesbaden: Reichert.
Olivier, J. P. J.
    1996   Rendering YDYD as Benevolent Patron in Isaiah 5:1. *JNSL* 22:59–65.
Oswalt, J. H.
    1993   The Significance of the ʿAlmah Prophecy in the Context of Isaiah 7–12. *CTR* 6:223–35.
Parpola, S., and K. Watanabe
    1988   *Neo-Assyrian Treaties and Loyalty Oaths.* Helsinki: Helsinki University Press.
Pitard, W. T.
    1987   Aram-Damascus from the Rise of Hazael to the Fall of the City in 732 B.C.E. Pages 145–89 in *Ancient Damascus: A Historical Study of the Syrian City-State from Earliest Times until its Fall to the Assyrians in 732 B.C.E.* Winona Lake, Indiana: Eisenbrauns.
Platt, E. E.
    1979   Jewelry of Bible Times and the Catalogue of Isa. 3:18–23. *AUSS* 17:71–84.
Premnath, D. N.
    1988   Latifundialization and Isaiah 5.8–10. *JSOT* 40:49–60.
Prinsloo, W. S.
    1992   Isaiah 12: One, Two, or Three Songs? Pages 25–33 in *Goldene Äpfel in silbernen Schalen.* Edited by K.-D. Schunck and M. Augustin. Frankfurt am Main: Peter Lang.

Rad, G. von
1958   Das judäische Königsritual. Pages 205–13 in *Gesammelte Studien zum Alten Testament*. Munich: Kaiser. Eng. translation, pages 222–31 in *The Problem of the Hexateuch and Other Essays*. Edinburgh: Oliver & Boyd, 1966.
1966   The City on the Hill. Pages 232–42 in *The Problem of the Hexateuch and Other Essays*. Edinburgh and London: Oliver & Boyd. [English translation of Die Stadt auf dem Berg. *EvT* 8 (1948–1949) 439–47.]

Reider, J.
1952   Etymological Studies in Biblical Hebrew. *VT* 2:115–17.

Renaud, B.
1985   La Forme Poetique d'Is 9,1–6. Pages 331–48 in *Mélanges bibliques et orientaux en l'honneur de M. Mathias Delcor*. Edited by A. Caquot et al. Kevelaer: Butzon & Bercker/Neukirchen-Vluyn: Neukirchener Verlag.

Rendtorff, R.
1989   Jesaja 6 im Rahmen der Komposition des Jesajabuches. Pages 73–83 in *The Book of Isaiah — Le Livre d'Isaïe: Les oracles et leur relecture. Unité et complexité de l'ouvrage*. Edited by J. Vermeylen. Leuven: Peeters/Leuven University Press.

Reventlow, H. Graf
1971   A Syncretistic Enthronement Hymn in Is. 9,1–6. *UF* 3:321–25.
1987   Das Ende der sog. "Denkschrift" Jesajas. *BN* 38–39:62–67.

Rice, G.
1977   The Interpretation of Isaiah 7:15–17. *JBL* 96:363–69.
1978   A Neglected Interpretation of the Immanuel Prophecy. *ZAW* 90:220–27.

Rignell, L. G.
1957a   Das Orakel "Maher-salal Hash-bas." Jesaja 8. *ST* 10:40–52.
1957b   Isaiah Chapter 1: Some Exegetical Remarks with Special Reference to the Relationship between the Text and the Book of Deuteronomy. *ST* 11:140–58.

Ringgren, H.
1956   Pages 30–33 in *The Messiah in the Old Testament*. London: SCM Press.

Roberts, J. J. M.
1973   The Davidic Origin of the Zion Tradition. *JBL* 92:329–44.
1985a   Isaiah 2 and the Prophet's Message. *JQR* 75:290–308.
1985b   Isaiah and His Children. Pages 193–203 in *Biblical and Related Studies Presented to Samuel Iwry*. Edited by A. Kort and S. Morschauser. Winona Lake, Indiana: Eisenbrauns.

Robertson, E.
1934   Isaiah Chapter I. *ZAW* 52:140–58.

Ross, J. F.
1962a   Vine, Vineyard. Pages 784–86 in vol. 4 of *IDB*.
1962b   Wine. Pages 849–52 in vol. 4 of *IDB*.

Ruiten, G. M. van
1992   The Intertextual Relationship between Isaiah 65,25 and Isaiah 11,6–9. Pages 31–42 in *The Scriptures and the Scrolls: Fst. A. S. van der Woude*. Edited by F. García Martínez et al. VTSup 49. Leiden: Brill.

Saebø, M.
1960   Formgeschichtliche Erwägungen zu Jes. 7,3–9. *ST* 14:54–69.

1964   Zur Traditionsgeschichte von Jesaia 8,9–10. *ZAW* 76:132–44.
Sanmartin-Ascaso, J.
1978   *dôdh*. Pages 143–46 in vol. 3 of *TDOT*.
Savignac, J. de
1972   Les "Seraphim." *VT* 22:320–25.
Sawyer, J. F. A.
1964   The Qumran Reading of Isaiah 6.13. *ASTI* 3:111–13.
1996   *The Fifth Gospel. Isaiah in the History of Christianity.* Cambridge: Cambridge University Press.
Schmidt, B. B.
1994   Pages 147–54 in *Israel's Beneficent Dead: Ancestor Cult and Necromancy in Ancient Israelite Religion and Tradition.* Tübingen: Mohr. Repr., Winona Lake, Indiana: Eisenbrauns, 1996.
Schmidt, J. M.
1978   Gedanken zum Verstockungauftrag Jesajas (Is. VI). *VT* 21:68–90.
Schoneveld, J.
1963   Jesaja I 18–20. *VT* 13:342–44.
Schoors, A.
1977   Isaiah, the Minister of Royal Appointment. *OtSt* 20:85–107.
Schottroff, W.
1970   Das Weinberglied Jesajas (Jes 5.1–7): Ein Beitrag zur Geschichte des Parabel. *ZAW* 82:68–91.
Schulz, H.
1973   Page 118 in *Das Buch Nahum*. Berlin: de Gruyter.
Schunck, K.-D.
1973   Der fünfte Thronname des Messias (Jes. 9,5–6). *VT* 23:108–10.
Schwartz, G.
1965   ". . . Das Licht Israels?" *ZAW* 77:329–32.
Scullion, J. J.
1968   An Approach to the Understanding of Isa 7:10–17. *JBL* 87:288–300.
Seitz, C. R.
1990   The Divine Council: Temporal Transition and New Prophecy in the Book of Isaiah. *JBL* 109:229–47.
Sheppard, G.
1982   More on Isaiah 5:1–7 as a Juridical Parable. *CBQ* 44:45–47.
Soggin, J. A.
1970   Das Erdbeben von Amos 1:1 und die Chronologie der Könige Ussia und Jotham von Juda. *ZAW* 82:117–21.
1971   Tablitam in Isaiah 10:25b. *BO* 13:232.
Sonnet, J.-P.
1992   Le Motif de l'endurcissement (Is 6,9–10) et la lecture d'"Isaïe." *Bib* 73:208–39.
Speier, S.
1965   Zu drei Jesajastellen Jes. 1,7; 5,24; 10,7. *TZ* 21:310–13.
Stamm, J. J.
1960   Die Immanuel-Weissagung und die Eschatologie des Jesaja. *TZ* 16:439–55.
1974   Die Immanuel-Perikope: Eine Nachlese. *TZ* 30:11–22.

Staub, J. J.
1979   A Review of the History of the Interpretation of Isaiah 8:11–9:6. Pages 89–107 in vol. 1 of *Jewish Civilization: Essays and Studies*. Edited by R. A. Brauner. Philadelphia: Reconstructionist Rabbinical College.

Steck, O. H.
1967   *Israel und das gewaltsame Geschick der Propheten*. Neukirchen-Vluyn: Neukirchener Verlag.
1972   Bemerkungen zu Jesaja 6. *BZ* 16:188–206.
1973   Beiträge zum Verständnis von Jesaja 7,10–17 und 8,1–4. *TZ* 29:161–78.
1982   *Wahrnehmungen Gottes im Alten Testament. Gesammelte Studien.* Munich: Kaiser.
1992   "... ein kleiner Knabe kann sie leiten": Beobachtungen zum Tierfrieden in Jesaja 11,6–8 und 65,25. Pages 104–13 in *Alttestamentliche Glaube und biblische Theologie: Fst. für H. D. Preuss zum 65. Geburtstag.* Edited by J. Hausman and H.-J. Zobel. Stuttgart: Kohlhammer.

Sweeney, M. A.
1988   *Isaiah 1–4 and the Post-exilic Understanding of the Isaianic Tradition.* Berlin: de Gruyter.
1993   On ûm^esôs in Isaiah 8:6. Pages 42–54 in *Among the Prophets: Language, Image and Structure in the Prophetic Writings.* Edited by P. R. Davies and D. J. A. Clines. Sheffield: JSOT Press.
1994a   A Philological and Form-Critical Reevaluation of Isaiah 8:16–9:6. *HAR* 14:215–31.
1994b   Sargon's Threat against Jerusalem in Isaiah 10,27–32. *Bib* 75:457–70.
1996   Jesse's New Shoot in Isaiah 11: A Josianic Reading of the Prophet Isaiah. Pages 103–18 in *A Gift of God in Due Season: Essays on Scripture and Community in Honor of James A. Sanders.* Edited by R. D. Weis and D. M. Carr. Sheffield: Sheffield Academic Press.

Tadmor, H.
1958   The Campaigns of Sargon II of Assur: A Chronological-Historical Study. *JCS* 12:22–40, 77–100.
1994   *The Inscriptions of Tiglath-pileser III King of Assyria.* Jerusalem: The Israel Academy of Sciences and Humanities.

Talmage, F.
1967   HRT 'NWŠ in Isaiah 8:1. *HTR* 60:465–68.

Thompson, M. E. W.
1982   Israel's Ideal King. *JSOT* 24:79–88.
1983   Isaiah's Sign of Immanuel. *ExpTim* 95:67–71.

Tomasino, A. J.
1993   Isaiah 1.1–2.4 and 63–66 and the Composition of the Isaianic Corpus. *JSOT* 57:81–98.

Troxel, R. L.
1993   Exegesis and Theology in the LXX: Isaiah V 26–30. *VT* 43:102–11.

Tsevat, M.
1969   Isaiah I 31. *VT* 19:261–63.

Tucker, G. M.
1977   Prophetic Superscriptions and the Growth of a Canon. Pages 56–70 in *Canon and Authority: Essays in OT Religion and Theology.* Edited by G. W. Coats and B. O. Long. Philadelphia: Fortress.

Uchelen, A. van.
1981   Isaiah I 9: Text and Context. *OtSt* 21:153–63.
Vanel, A.
1974   Tabe'el en Is. VII 6 et le roi Tubail de Tyr. Pages 17–24 in *Studies on Prophecy: A Collection of Twelve Papers.* VTSup 26. Leiden: Brill.
Vermeylen, J.
1977   Volume 1 of *Du Prophète Isaïe à l'Apocalyptique.* Paris: Gabalda.
Vieweger, D.
1992   "Das Volk das durch das Dunkel zieht . . ." Neue Uberlegungen zu Jes (8,23aβb) 9,1–6. *BZ* 36:77–86.
Vollmer, J.
1968   Zur Sprache von Jesaja (9:1–6). *ZAW* 80:343–50.
Wallenstein, M.
1952   An Unnoticed Euphemism in Isaiah IX 19–20? *VT* 2:179–80.
Wegner, P.
1991   Another Look at Isaiah viii 23b. *VT* 41:481–84.
1992a   *An Examination of Kingship and Messianic Expectation in Isaiah 1–35.* Lewiston, N.Y.: Mellen.
1992b   A Re-examination of Isaiah ix 1–6. *VT* 42:103–12.
Weil, H. M.
1940   Exégèse d'Isaïe III, 1–15. *RB* 49:76–85.
Weinfeld, M.
1986   The Protest against Imperialism in Ancient Israelite Prophecy. Pages 169–82 in *The Origins and Diversity of Axial Age Civilizations.* Edited by S. N. Eisenstadt. New York: State University of New York Press.
Werlitz, J.
1992   *Studien zur literarkritischen Methode: Gericht und Heil in Jesaja 7,1–17 und 29,1–8.* BZAW 204. Berlin: de Gruyter.
Whitley, C. F.
1959   The Call and Mission of Isaiah. *JNES* 18:38–48.
1978   The Language and Exegesis of Isaiah 8:16–23. *ZAW* 90:28–43.
Widengren, G.
1984   Yahweh's Gathering of the Dispersed. Pages 227–45 in *In the Shelter of Elyon: Essays on Ancient Palestinian Life and Literature in Honor of G. W. Ahlström.* Edited by W. B. Barrick and J. R. Spencer. Sheffield: JSOT Press.
Wildberger, H.
1957   Die Völkerwallfahrt zum Zion, Jes 2,1–5. *VT* 7:62–81.
1960   Die Thronnamen des Messias, Jes. 9:5b. *TZ* 16:314–32.
Williams, G. R.
1985   Frustrated Expectations in Isaiah V 1–7: A Literary Interpretation. *VT* 35:459–65.
Williamson, H. G. M.
1993   Isaiah 1.11 and the Septuagint of Isaiah. Pages 401–12 in *Understanding Poets and Prophets: Essays in Honour of George Wishart Anderson.* Edited by A. G. Auld. Sheffield: JSOT Press.
1994   Pages 30–56, 97–103, and 118–43 in *The Book Called Isaiah: Deutero-Isaiah's Role in Composition and Redaction.* Oxford: Clarendon.

1995   Isaiah XI 11–16 and the Redaction of Isaiah I-XII. Pages 343–47 in *Congress Volume: Paris, 1992*. Edited by J. A. Emerton. VTSup 61. Leiden: Brill.

1997   Relocating Isaiah 1:2–9. Pages 263–77 in vol. 1 of *Writing and Reading the Scroll of Isaiah: Studies of an Interpretive Tradition*. 2 vols. Edited by C. C. Broyles and C. A. Evans. Leiden: Brill.

Willis, J. T.
1977   The Genre of Isaiah 5:1–7. *JBL* 96:337–62.
1983   On the Interpretation of Isaiah 1:18. *JSOT* 25:35–54.
1984   The First Pericope in the Book of Isaiah. *VT* 34:63–77.
1985   An Important Passage for Determining the Historical Setting of a Prophetic Oracle: Isaiah 1.7–8. *ST* 39:151–69.
1986   Lament Reversed: Isaiah 1,21ff. *ZAW* 98:236–48.
1997   Isaiah 2:2–5 and the Psalms of Zion. Pages 295–316 in vol. 1 of *Writing and Reading the Scroll of Isaiah: Studies of an Interpretive Tradition*. 2 vols. Edited by C. C. Broyles and C. A. Evans. Leiden: Brill.

Wolf, H. M.
1972   A Solution to the Immanuel Prophecy in Isa 7:14–8:22. *JBL* 91:449–56.

Wolff, H. W.
1962   *Frieden ohne Ende: Jesaja 7,1–17 und 9,1–6 ausgelegt*. Neukirchen-Vluyn: Neukirchener Verlag.
1984   Schwerter zu Pflugscharen: Missbrauch eines Prophetenwortes? Praktische Fragen und exegetische Klärungen zu Joël 4,9–12, Jes 2,25 und Mic 4,1–5. *EvT* 44:280–92.

Wright, C. J. H.
1990   *God's People in God's Land*. Grand Rapids: Eerdmans.

Würthwein, E.
1970   Jesaja 7:1–9 — Ein Beitrag zu dem Thema: Prophetie und Politik. Pages 127–43 in *Wort und Existenz: Studien zum Alten Testament*. Göttingen: Vandenhoeck & Ruprecht.

Yadin, Y.
1960   Pages 24–26, 36–37 in *Hazor II: An Account of the Second Season of Excavations, 1956*. Jerusalem: Magnes.

Yee, G. A.
1981   The Form Critical Study of Isaiah 5:1–7 as a Song and a Juridical Parable. *CBQ* 43:30–40.

Zeron, A.
1981   Das Wort NIQPĀ, Zum Sturz der Zionstöchter (Is III 24). *VT* 41:95–97.

Zobel, H.-J.
1978   *hôy*. Pages 359–64 in vol. 3 of *TDOT*.
1986   *yadîd*. Pages 444–48 in vol. 5 of *TDOT*.

ISAIAH 13–27

◆

Ackroyd, P. R.
1958   The Seventy Years' Period. *JNES* 17:23–27.
1968   *Exile and Restoration*. Philadelphia: Westminster.
Aharoni, Y.
1963   *PEQ* 95
Albright, W. F.
1932   The Seal of Eljakim and the Latest Preexilic History of Judah, with Some Observations on Ezekiel. *JBL* 51:77–106.
Alonso-Schökel, L.
1960   La canción de la viña: Is. 27,2–5. *Estudios Ecclesiasticus* 34:767–74.
Amiram, R.
1976   The Water Supply of Israelite Jerusalem. Pages 75–78 in *Jerusalem Revealed: Archaeology of the Holy City, 1968–1974*. Edited by Y. Yadin. Jerusalem: Israel Exploration Society.
Amsler, S.
1989   Des visions de Zacharie à l'apocalypse d'Esaïe 24–27. Pages 263–73 in *The Book of Isaiah—Le Livre de Isaïe: Les oracles et leurs relecture. Unité et complexité de l'ouvrage*. Edited by J. Vermeylen. Leuven: Peeters/Leuven University Press.
Anderson, B. W.
1994   The Slaying of the Fleeing, Twisting Serpent: Isaiah 27:1 in Context. Pages 3–15 in *Uncovering Ancient Stones: Essays in Memory of H. Neil Richardson*. Edited by L. M. Hopfe. Winona Lake, Indiana: Eisenbrauns.
Anderson, G. A.
1991   *A Time to Mourn, A Time to Dance*. University Park: Pennsylvania State University Press.
Anderson, G. W.
1963   Isaiah XXIV–XXVII Reconsidered. Pages 118–26 in *Congress Volume: Bonn, 1962*. VTSup 9. Leiden: Brill.
Auret, A.
1993   A Different Background for Isaiah 22:15–25 Presents an Alternative Paradigm: Disposing of Political and Religious Opposition? *OTE* 6:46–56.
Avigad, N.
1953   The Epitaph of a Royal Steward from Siloam Village. *IEJ* 3:137–52.
1983   *Discovering Jerusalem*. Nashville: Nelson.
1986   *Hebrew Bullae from the Time of Jeremiah*. Jerusalem: Israel Exploration Society.
Bach, R.
1962   *Die Aufforderung zur Flucht und zum Kampf im alttestamentlichen Prophetenspruch*. Neukirchen-Vluyn: Neukirchener Verlag.

Bailey, L. R.
    1982   Isaiah 14:24–27. *Int* 36:171–76.
Baker, D. W.
    1992   Tarshish (Place). Pages 331–33 in vol. 6 of *ABD*.
Barnes, W. E.
    1900   A Fresh Interpretation of Isaiah XXI 1–10. *JTS* 1:583–92.
Barrick, W. B.
    1991   The Bamoth of Moab. *Maʿarav* 7:67–89.
Barth, H.
    1977   *Die Jesaja-Worte in der Josiazeit: Israel und Asshur also Thema einer
                produktiven Neuinterpretation der Jesajaüberlieferung.* Neukirchen-Vluyn:
                Neukirchener Verlag.
Bartlett, J. R.
    1973   The Moabites and Edomites. Pages 229–44 in *Peoples of Old Testament
                Times.* Edited by D. Wiseman. Oxford: Clarendon.
    1979   From Edomites to Nabataeans: A Study in Continuity. *PEQ* 111:53–66.
    1992   Edom. Pages 287–95 in vol. 2 of *ABD*.
Beek, M. A.
    1949   Ein Erdbeben wird zum prophetischen Erleben (Jesaja 24–27). *ArOr* 17,
                no. 1:31–40.
Begg, C. T.
    1989   Babylon in the Book of Isaiah. Pages 121–25 in *The Book of Isaiah—Le
                Livre de Isaïe: Les oracles et leurs relecture. Unité et complexité de l'ou-
                vrage.* Edited by J. Vermeylen. Leuven: Peeters/Leuven University Press.
Begrich, J.
    1932   Jesaja 14,28–32: Ein Beitrag zur Chronologie der israelitisch-jüdischen
                Königszeit. *ZDMG* 86:66–79.
Ben-David, Y.
    1980   Ugaritic Parallels to Isa 24:18–19. *Lešonénu* 45:56–59 [Heb.].
Bentzen, A.
    1950   The Ritual Background of Amos 1,2–2,16. *OtSt* 8:85–89.
Biddle, M. E.
    1995   The City of Chaos and the New Jerusalem: Isaiah 24–27 in Context.
                PRSt 22:5–12.
Birkeland, H.
    1950–51   The Belief in Resurrection of the Dead in the Old Testament. *ST* 3:60–
                78.
Blenkinsopp, J.
    1988   Second Isaiah: Prophet of Universalism? *JSOT* 41:83–103.
Boer, P. A. H. de
    1948   An Inquiry into the Meaning of the Term *mśʾ*. *OtSt* 5:197–214.
Bonnet, C.
    1987   Échos d'un rituel de type Adonidien dans l'oracle contre Moab d'Isaïe
                (Isaïe 15). *Studi epigrafici e linguistici* 4:101–19.
Bosshard-Nepustil, E.
    1997   *Rezeptionen von Jesaia 1–39 im Zwölfprophetenbuch.* Freiburg: Univer-
                sitätsverlag.
Bost, H.
    1984   Le Chant sur la chute d'un tyran en Esaïe 14. *ETR* 59:3–14.

Bourke, J.
    1959   Le Jour de Yahwe dans Joël. *RB* 66:5–31, 191–212.
Brinkman, J. A.
    1964   Merodach-baladan II. Pages 6–53 in *Studies Presented to A. Leo Oppen-heim, June 7, 1964.* Edited by R. M. Adams. Chicago: The Oriental Institute.
Broshi, M.
    1974   The Expansion of Jerusalem in the Reigns of Hezekiah and Manasseh. *IEJ* 24:21–26.
Brueggemann, W.
    1997   Planned People/Planned Book? Pages 19–37 in vol. 1 of *Writing and Reading the Scroll of Isaiah.* Edited by C. C. Broyles and C. A. Evans. 2 vols. Leiden: Brill.
Budde, K.
    1918   Jesaja 13. Pages 55–70 in *Abhandlungen zur semitischen Religionskunde und Sprachwissenschaft: Fst. Von Baudissin.* Giessen: Alfred Töpelmann.
Burney, C. F.
    1910   The Three Serpents of Isaiah xxvii 1. *JTS* 11:443–47.
Burns, J. B.
    1989   *Holēš ʿal* in Isaiah 14:12: A Newal. *ZAW* 2:199–204.
Carroll, R. P.
    1986   *Jeremiah. A Commentary.* Philadelphia: Westminster.
Causse, A.
    1927   Les origines de la diaspora juive. *RHPR* 7:97–128.
Cheyne, T. K.
    1893   The Nineteenth Chapter of Isaiah. *ZAW* 13:125–28.
Childs, B. S.
    1967   *Isaiah and the Assyrian Crisis.* London: SCM.
Chilton, B. D.
    1987   *The Isaiah Targum: Introduction, Translation, Apparatus and Notes.* Collegeville, Minnesota: Liturgical Press.
Chisolm, R. B.
    1993   "The Everlasting Covenant" and the "City of Chaos": Intentional Ambiguity and Irony in Isaiah 24. *CTR* 6:237–53.
Christensen, D. L.
    1975   *Transformations of the War Oracle in Old Testament Prophecy.* Missoula, Montana: Scholars Press.
Clements, R. E.
    1980b   *Isaiah and the Deliverance of Jerusalem: A Study of the Interpretation of Prophecy in the Old Testament.* Sheffield: JSOT Press.
    1989   Isaiah 14:22–27: A Central Passage Reconsidered. Pages 253–62 in *The Book of Isaiah—Le Livre de Isaïe: Les oracles et leurs relecture. Unité et complexité de l'ouvrage.* Edited by J. Vermeylen. Leuven: Peeters/Leuven University Press.
Clifford, R.J.
    1972   *The Cosmic Mountain in Canaan and the Old Testament.* Cambridge: Harvard University Press.
Cobb, W. H.
    1898   Isaiah XXI 1–10 Reexamined. *JBL* 17:40–61.

Cogan, M.
1974   *Imperialism and Religion: Assyria, Israel and Judah in the Eighth and Seventh Centuries* B.C.E. Missoula, Montana: Scholars Press.

Coggins, R. J.
1979   The Problem of Isaiah 24–27. *ExpTim* 90:328–33.

Coste, J.
1954   Le texte grec d'Isaïe XXV 1–5. *RB* 61:67–86.

Couroyer, B.
1984   Le NES biblique: Signal ou enseigne? *RB* 91:5–21.

Cowley, A.
1967   *Aramaic Papyri of the Fifth Century* B.C. Osnabruck: Otto Zeller. 1st ed., 1923.

Craigie, P. C.
1973   Helel, Athtar and Phaethon (Jes 14:12–15). *ZAW* 85:223–25.

Daiches, S.
1915–16   An Explanation of Isaiah 27,8. *JQR* 6:399–404.

Davies, G. I
1989   The Destiny of the Nations in the Book of Isaiah. Pages 93–120 in *The Book of Isaiah—Le Livre de Isaïe: Les oracles et leurs relecture. Unité et complexité de l'ouvrage*. Edited by J. Vermeylen. Leuven: Peeters/Leuven University Press.

Day, J.
1978   TL ʿWRT in Isaiah 26:19. *ZAW* 90:265–69.
1980   A Case of Inner-Scriptural Interpretation: The Dependence of Isaiah xxvi.13–xxvii.11 on Hosea xiii.4–xiv.10 (Eng. 9) and Its Relevance to Some Theories of the Redaction of the "Isaiah Apocalypse." *JTS* 31:301–19.
1992   Asherah. Pages 483–87 in vol. 1 of *ABD*.

Delcor, M.
1968   Le Temple d'Onias en Egypte. *RB* 75:188–205.
1977   Le problème des jardins d'Adonis dans Isaïe 17,9–11. *Syria* 54:371–94.
1979   Le festin d'immortalité sur la montagne de Sion à l'ère eschatologique en Is. 25,6–9 à la lumière de la littérature ugaritique. Pp. 122–31 in *Études bibliques et orientales de religions comparées*. Edited by M. Delcor. Leiden: Brill.

Dhorme, P.
1922   Le desert de la mer (Isaïe XXI). *RB* 31:403–6.

Diakonoff, I. M.
1985   Media. Pages 142–48 in vol. 2 of *The Cambridge History of Iran*. Cambridge: Cambridge University Press.

Dietrich, W.
1976   *Jesaja und die Politik*. Munich: Kaiser.

Donner, H.
1964   *Israel unter den Völken: Die Stellung der klassischen Prophetie des 8. Jh.v.Chr. zur Aussenpolitik der Könige von Israel und Juda*. Leiden: Brill.

Doyle, B.
1997   A Literary Analysis of Isaiah 25:10a. Pages 173–93 in *Studies in the Book of Isaiah: Fst. W. A. M. Beuken*. Edited by J. van Ruiten and M. Vervenne. Leuven: Leuven University Press.

Driver, G. R.
1937   Isaiah i–xxxix, Linguistic and Textual Problems. *JTS* 38:36–50.
1956   Mythical Monsters in the Old Testament. Pages 234–49 in vol. 1 of *Studi orientalistici in Honore di G. L. della Vida.*
1958a   BZAW 77. Berlin: de Gruyter.
1958b   On *ḥēmāh* 'hot anger, fury' and also 'fiery wine'. *TZ* 14:133–35.
1968   Isaiah 1–39: Textual and Linguistic Problems. *JSS* 13:36–57.

Dupont-Sommer, A.
1948   Note exégetique sur Isaïe 14:16–21. *RHR* 134:72–80.

Easterly, E.
1991   Is Mesha's *QRḤH* Mentioned in Isaiah xv 2. *VT* 41:215–19.

Eichrodt, W.
1967   *Der Herr der Geschichte: Jesaja 13–23, 28–39.* Stuttgart: Calwer.

Eissfeldt, O.
1966   *The Old Testament: An Introduction.* Oxford: Blackwell.

Eitan, I.
1937–38   A Contribution to Isaian Exegesis. *HUCA* 12–13:55–75.

Elat, M.
1978   The Economic Relations of the Neo-Assyrian Empire with Egypt. *JAOS* 98:20–34.

Emerton, J. A.
1977   A Textual Problem in Isaiah 25 2. *ZAW* 89:64–73.
1980a   Notes on the Text and Translation of Isaiah xxii8–11 and lxv 5. *VT* 30:437–51.
1980b   Notes on Two Verses in Isaiah (26:16 and 66:17). Pages 12–25 in *Prophecy: Essays Presented to Georg Fohrer on His Sixty-Fifth Birthday, 6. September 1980.* BZAW 150. Berlin: de Gruyter.

Ephʿal, I.
1982   *The Ancient Arabs: Nomads on the Borders of the Fertile Crescent 9th–5th Centuries* B.C. Leiden: Brill.

Erlandsson, S.
1970   *The Burden of Babylon: A Study of Isaiah 13,2–14,23.* Lund: Gleerup.

Fackenheim, E. L.
1990   *The Jewish Bible after the Holocaust.* Bloomington: Indiana University Press.

Feuillet, A.
1978   Un sommet religieux de l'Ancien Testament: L'Oracle d'Isa 19:19–25 sur la conversion de l'Egypte. *JAOS* 98:20–34.

Fichtner, J.
1951   Jahwes Plan in der Botschaft des Jesaja. *ZAW* 63:16–33 = Pages 27–43 in *Gottes Weisheit: Gesammelte Studien zum Altes Testament.* Stuttgart: Calwer, 1965.

Fischer, T., and U. Rütersworden
1982   Aufruf zur Volksklage in Kanaan (Jesaja 23). *WO* 13:36–49.

Flint, P. W.
1988   The Septuagint Version of Isaiah 23:1–14 and the Massoretic Text. *BIOSCS* 21:35–54.

Fohrer, G.
1963   Der Aufbau der Apokalypse des Jesajabuches (Is. 24–27). *CBQ* 25:34–45
            = Pages 170–81 in *Studien zur alttestamentlichen Prophetie (1949–1965)*.
            Berlin: de Gruyter, 1967.
1968a   *Die symbolischen Handlungen der Propheten*. 2d ed. Zurich: Zwingli.
1968b   *Introduction to the Old Testament*. Nashville and New York: Abingdon.
1982   Der Tag JHWHS. *Eretz-Israel* 16 (Orlinsky Volume):43*–50*.

Fouts, D. M.
1991   A Suggestion for Isaiah xxvi 16. *VT* 41:472–75.

Franke, C. A.
1996   Reversals of Fortune in the Ancient Near East: A Study of the Babylon
            Oracles in the Book of Isaiah. Pages 104–23 in *New Visions of Isaiah*.
            Edited by R. F. Melugin and M. A. Sweeney. Sheffield: Sheffield Aca-
            demic Press.

Fullerton, K.
1905   A New Chapter out of the Life of Isaiah. *AJT* 9:621–42.
1907   Shebna and Eliakim: A Reply. *AJT* 11:503–9.
1925–26   Isaiah 14:28–32. *AJSL* 42:86–109.

Gallagher, W.
1994   On the Identity of Hêlēl Ben Šahar in Is. 14:12–15. *UF* 26:131–46.

Galling, K.
1962   Incense Altars. Pages 699–700 in vol. 2 of *IDB*.
1963   Jes. 21 im Lichte der neuen Nabonidtexte. Pages 49–62 in *Tradition
            und Situation: Studien zur alttestamentlichen Prophetie—Fst. A. Weiser*.
            Edited by E. Würthwein and O. Kaiser. Göttingen: Vandenhoeck &
            Ruprecht.

Geyer, J. B.
1986   Mythology and Culture in the Oracles against the Nations. *VT* 36:129–
            45.
1992   The Night of Dumah (Isaiah XXI 11–12). *VT* 42:317–39.

Ginsberg, H. L.
1950   Some Emendations in Isaiah. *JBL* 69:51–60.
1953   Gleanings in First Isaiah, VI: The Shebna-Eliakim Pericope, 22:15–25.
            Pages 252–57 in M. M. *Kaplan Jubilee Volume*.
1968   Reflexes of Sargon in Isaiah after 715 B.C.E. *JAOS* 88:47–53.

Görg, M.
1992   "Dämonen" statt "Eulen" in Jes. 13,21. *BN* 62:16–17.

Gonçalvez, F. J.
1986   *L'Expédition de Sennachérib en Palestine dans la littérature hébraïque
            ancienne*. Paris: Gabalda.

Gordon, C. H.
1966   Leviathan, Symbol of Evil. Pages 1–9 in *Biblical Motifs*. Edited by A. Alt-
            mann. Cambridge: Harvard University Press.

Gosse, B
1986   Le "moi" prophetique de l'oracle contre Babylone d'Isaïe XXI, 1–10. *RB*
            93:70–84.
1988   *Isaïe 13,1–14,23 dans la tradition* littéraire du livre d'Isaïe et dans la tra-
            dition des oracles contre les nations. Freiburg: Universitätsverlag.

1990   Isaïe 21,11–12 et Isaïe 60–62. *BN* 53:21–22.
1991a   Isaïe 14,24–27 et les oracles contre les nations du livre d'Isaïe. *BN* 56:17–21.
1991b   Isaïe 14,28–32 et les traditions sur Isaïe d'Isaïe 36–39 et Isaïe 20,1–6. *BZ* n.s. 35:97–98.
1991c   Isaïe 17,12–14 dans la rédaction du livre d'Isaïe. *BN* 58:20–23.
Graf, D. F.
1992   Dedan. Pages 121–23 in vol. 2 of *ABD*.
Gray, B.
1911   Critical Discussions: Isaiah 26; 25 1–5; 34:12–14. *ZAW* 31:111–27.
Grelot, P.
1956   Isaïe XIV 12–15 et son arrière- plan mythologique. *RHR* 149:18–48.
Gryson, R.
1996   "Enfanter un esprit de salut" Histoire du texte d'Isaïe 26,17–18. *RTL* 27:25–46.
Hamborg, G. R.
1981   Reasons for Judgement in the Oracles against the Nations of the Prophet Isaiah. *VT* 31:145–59.
Harden, D. M.
1962   *The Phoenicians.* London: Thames and Hudson.
Hayes, J. H.
1968   The Usage of Oracles against Foreign Nations in Ancient Israel. *JBL* 87:81–92.
Hayward, R.
1982   The Jewish Temple at Leontopolis: A Reconsideration. *JJS* 33:429–43.
Helfmeyer, F. J.
1977   "Deine Toten . . . meine Leichen": Heilzusage und Annahme in Jes 26,19. Pages 245–58 in *Bausteine biblischer Theologie: Fst. G. Johannes Botterweck.* Edited by H.-J. Fabry. Cologne and Bonn: Hanstein.
Henry, M.-L.
1966   *Glaubenskrise und Glaubensbewährung in den Dichtungen der Jesaja-apokalypse.* Stuttgart: Kohlhammer.
Hillers, D. R.
1965   Convention in Hebrew Literature: The Reaction to Bad News. *ZAW* 77:86–90.
Hoffman, Y.
1977   *The Prophecies against Foreign Nations in the Bible.* Tel Aviv: Tel Aviv University Press. [Heb.]
Irwin, W. A.
1927–28   The Exposition of Isaiah 14:28–32. *AJSL* 44:73–87.
Irwin, W. H.
1984   The Punctuation of Isaiah 24:14–16a and 25:4–5. *CBQ* 46:215–22.
1994   The City of Chaos in Isaiah 24,10 and the Genitive of Result. *Bib* 75:401–3.
Jacob, E.
1970   Du premier au deuxième chant de la vigne du prophète Esaïe: Réflexions sur Esaïe 27,2–5. Pages 325–30 in *Wort-Gebot-Glaube: Beiträge zur Theologie des Alten Testaments—W. Eichrodt zum 80. Geburtstag.* Edited by H.-J. Stoebe. Zurich: Zwingli.

James, T. G. H.
1991 The Twenty-Fifth and Twenty-Sixth Dynasties. Pages 677–747 in *The Assyrian and Babylonian Empires and Other States of the Near East, from the Eighth to the Sixth Centuries* B.C. Vol. 3, part 2 of CAH. Cambridge: Cambridge University Press.

Janzen, W.
1972 *Mourning Cry and Woe Oracle*. Berlin: de Gruyter.

Jenkins, A. K.
1980 Isaiah 14:28–32: An Issue of Life and Death. *FO* 21:47–63.
1989 The Development of the Isaiah Tradition in Isaiah 13–23. Pages 237–51 in *The Book of Isaiah — Le Livre de Isaïe: Les oracles et leurs relecture. Unité et complexité de l'ouvrage*. Edited by J. Vermeylen. Leuven: Peeters / Leuven University Press..

Jenni, E.
1956 *Die politische Voraussagen der Propheten*. Zurich: Zwingli.

Jensen, J.
1986 Yahweh's Plan in Isaiah and in the Rest of the Old Testament. *CBQ* 48:443–55.
1997 Helel ben Shahar (Isaiah 14:12–15) in Bible and Tradition. Pages 339–56 in vol. 1 of *Writing and Reading the Scroll of Isaiah*. 2 vols. Edited by C. C. Broyles and C. A. Evans. Leiden: Brill.

Jeppesen, K.
1985 The *massaʾ Babel* in Isaiah 13–14. *PIBA* 9:63–80.

Johnson, D. G.
1988 *An Integrative Reading of Isaiah 24–27* Sheffield: JSOT Press.

Jones, B. C.
1996 *Howling over Moab: Irony and Rhetoric in Isaiah 15–16*. Atlanta: Scholars Press.

Kaiser, O.
1962 *Die mythische Bedeutung des Meeres*. 2d ed. Berlin: de Gruyter.

Kamphausen, A.
1901 Isaiah's Prophecy concerning the Major-Domo of King Hezekiah. *AJT* 5:43–74.

Katzenstein, H. J.
1960 The Royal Steward (Asher ʿal ha-Bayith). *IEJ* 10:149–54.
1973 *The History of Tyre from the* Beginning of the Second Millenium B.C.E. until the Fall of the Neo-Babylonian Empire in 538 B.C.E. Jerusalem: Schocken Institute.

Kedar-Kopfstein, B. A.
1962 A Note on Isaiah 14:31. *Textus* 2:143–45.

Kessler, W.
1960 *Gott geht es um das Ganze: Jes. 56–66 und Jes. 24–27*. Stuttgart: Calwer.

Knauf, E. A.
1989 *Ismael: Untersuchungen zur Geschichte Palästinas und Nordarabiens im I. Jahrtausend v. Chr*. Wiesbaden: Harrassowitz.
1992a Jeremia XLIX 1–5: Ein zweites Moab-Orakel im Jeremia-Buch. *VT* 42: 124–28.
1992b Kedar. Pages 9–10 in vol. 4 of *ABD*.
1992c Tema (Place). Pages 346–47 in vol. 6 of *ABD*.

Koenig, E.
1906   Shebna and Eliakim. *AJT* 10:675–86.
Köszegby, M.
1994   Erwägungen zum Hintergrund von Jesaja XIV 12–15. *VT* 44:549–54.
Kooij, A. van der
1982   A Short Commentary on Some Verses of the Old Greek of Isaiah 23. *BIOSCS* 15:36–50.
1986   The Old Greek of Isaiah 19:16–25: Translation and Interpretation. Pages 127–66 in *VI Congress of the International Organization for Septuagint and Cognate Studies: Jerusalem, 1986*. Edited by E. Cox. Atlanta: Scholars Press.
Lagrange, M.-J.
1894   L'Apocalypse d'Isaïe (24–27): À propos des derniers commentaires. *RB* 3:200–231.
Lang, B.
1983   Prophecy, Symbolic Acts, and Politics: A Review of Recent Studies. Pages 83–91 in *Monotheism and the Prophetic Minority*. Sheffield: Almond Press.
Levenson, J. D.
1988   *Creation and the Persistence of Evil*. San Francisco: Harper & Row.
Lindblom, J.
1938   *Die Jesaja-Apokalypse: Jes. 24–27*. Lund: Gleerup.
1965   Der Ausspruch über Tyrus in Jes. 23. *ASTI* 4:56–73.
Linder, J.
1941   Weissagung über Tyrus, Isaias Kap. 23. *ZKT* 65:217–21.
Lindsay, J.
1976   The Babylonian Kings and Edom 605–550 B.C. *PEQ* 108:23–29.
Lipiński, E.
1978   The Elegy on the Fall of Sidon in Isaiah 23. *Eretz-Israel* 14 (Ginsberg Volume):79*– 88*.
Lohmann, P.
1913a   Zu Text und Metrum einiger Stellen aus Jesaja, II: Das Lied Jes 25 1–5. *ZAW* 33:256–62.
1913b   Das Wachterlied Jes 21,11–12. *ZAW* 33:262–64.
1917–18   Die selbstständigen lyrischen Abschnitte in Jes 24–27. *ZAW* 37:1–58.
Loretz, O.
1976   Der Kanaanäisch-biblische Mythos vom Sturz des Sahar-Sohnes Helel (Jes 14,12–15). *UF* 8:133–36.
1987   Der ugaritische Topos *bʿl rkb* und die "Sprache Kanaans" in Jes 19,1–25. *UF* 19:101–12.
Macintosh, A. A.
1980   *Isaiah XXI: A Palimpsest*. Cambridge: Cambridge University Press.
Martin-Achard, R.
1956   *De la Mort à la résurrection d'après l'Ancien Testament*. Neuchâtel: Delachaux & Niestlé. English Translation, *From Death to Life*. Edinburgh and London, 1960.
McKay, J. W.
1970   Helel and the Dawn-Goddess: A Re-examination of the Myth of Isaiah XIV 12–15. *VT* 20:451–64.

Mettinger, T. N. D.
    1971   *Solomonic State Officials: A Study of the Civil Government Officials of the Israelite Monarchy*. Lund: Gleerup.
Millar, W. R.
    1976   *Isaiah 24–27 and the Origin of Apocalyptic*. Missoula, Montana: Scholars Press.
Miller, J. M.
    1989   Moab and the Moabites. Pages 1–40 in *Studies in the Mesha Inscription and Moab*. Edited by J. A. Dearman. Atlanta: Scholars Press.
Mowinckel, S.
    1967   *The Psalms in Israel's Worship*. New York and Nashville: Abingdon.
Na'aman, N.
    1979   The Brook of Egypt and Assyrian Policy on the Border of Egypt. *Tel Aviv* 6:78–90.
Niehaus, J.
    1981   Raz-p^{e}šar in Isaiah xxiv. *VT* 31:376–78.
Noegel, S. B.
    1994   Dialect and Politics in Isaiah 24–27. *AcOr* 12:177–92.
Oldenburg, U.
    1970   Above the Stars of El: El in Ancient South Arabic Religion. *ZAW* 82: 187–208.
Olyan, S. M.
    1988   *Asherah and the Cult of Yahweh in Israel*. Missoula, Montana: Scholars Press.
Otzen, B.
    1974   Traditions and Structures of Isaiah XXIV–XXVII. *VT* 24:196–206.
Pagán, S.
    1992   Apocalyptic Poetry: Isaiah 24–27. *BT* 43:314–25.
Pitard, W. T.
    1987   *Ancient Damascus: A Historical Study of the Syrian City-State from Earliest Times until its Fall to the Assyrians in 732* B.C.E. Winona Lake, Indiana: Eisenbrauns.
Ploeg, R. P. J. van der
    1954   L'espérance dans l'Ancien Testament. *RB* 61:481–507.
Plöger, O.
    1968   *Theocracy and Eschatology*. Richmond: John Knox.
Pope, M. H.
    1955   *El in the Ugaritic Texts*. Leiden: Brill.
Porten, B.
    1968   *Archives from Elephantine*. Berkeley: University of California Press.
    1984   The Jews in Egypt. Pages 372–400 in vol. 1 of *The Cambridge History of Judaism*. Edited by W. D. Davies and L. Finkelstein. Cambridge: Cambridge University Press.
Prinsloo, W. S.
    1981   Isaiah 14:12–15: Humiliation, Hubris, Humiliation. *ZAW* 93:432–28.
Quell, G.
    1959   Jesaja 14:1–23. Pages 131–57 in *Fst. für Friedrich Baumgärtel*. Erlangen: Universitätsbund.

Rabin, C.
1946   Bāriah. *JTS* 47:38–41.
1973   Hebrew *BADDĪM* "Power." *JSS* 18:57–58.
Rad, G. von
1959   The Origin of the Concept of the Day of Yahweh. *JSS* 4:97–108.
Redditt, P. L.
1986   Once Again, the City in Isaiah 24–27. *HAR* 10:317–35.
Reyes, A. T.
1994   *Archaic Cyprus: A Study of the Textual and Archaeological Evidence*. Oxford: Clarendon.
Ringgren, H.
1973   Some Observations on Style and Structure in the Isaiah Apocalypse. *ASTI* 9:107–15.
Robertson, E.
1929   Isaiah XXVII 2–6 an Arabic Poem? *ZAW* 47:197–206.
Rudolph, W.
1933   *Jesaja 24–27*. 4th ed. Stuttgart: Kohlhammer.
1959   Jesaja 23:1–14. Pages 166–74 in *Fst. für Friedrich Baumgärtel*. Erlangen: Universitätsbund.
1963   Jesaja XV–XVI. Pages 130–43 in *Hebrew and Semitic Studies Presented to Godfrey Rolles Driver*. Edited by D. Winton Thomas and W. D. McHardy. Oxford: Oxford University Press.
Sawyer, J. F. A.
1973   Hebrew Words for the Resurrection of the Dead. *VT* 13:218–34.
1986   Blessed Be My People Egypt (Isaiah 19:25): The Context and Meaning of a Remarkable Passage. Pages 57–71 in *A Word in Season: Essays in Honour of William McKane*. Edited by J. D. Martin and P. R. Davies. Sheffield: JSOT Press.
1993   "My Secret Is with Me" (Isaiah 24:16): Some Semantic Links between Isaiah 24:27 and Daniel. Pages 307–17 in *Essays in Honour of George Wishart Anderson*. Edited by G. Auld. Sheffield: JSOT Press.
Scheiber, A.
1961   Zwei Bemerkungen zu Jesaja. *VT* 11:455–56.
Schenker, A.
1995   La fine della storia d'Israele ricapitolerà il suo inizio: Esegesi di Is 19,16–25. *RB* 43:321–30.
Schlossberg, E.
1997   Who Is the Subject of the "Burden of Duma" Prophecy? Pages 237–47 in vol. 4 of *Studies in Bible and Exegesis*. Edited by B. Kasher et al. Ramat Gan: Bar-Ilan University Press.
Schmidt, B. B.
1994   *Israel's Beneficent Dead: Ancestor Cult and Necromancy in Ancient Israelite Religion and Tradition*. Tübingen: Mohr. Repr., Winona Lake, Indiana: Eisenbrauns, 1996.
Schürer, E.
1986   Vol. 3, part 1 of *The History of the Jewish People in the Age of Jesus Christ: A New English Version Revised and Edited by Geza Vermes, Fergus Millar and Martin Goodman*. Edinburgh: T. & T. Clark.

Scott, R. B. Y.
    1952   Isaiah XXI 1–10: The Inside of a Prophet's Mind. *VT* 11:278–82.
Seitz, C. R.
    1993   *Isaiah 1–39*. Interpretation. Louisville: Westminster/John Knox.
Skjoldal, N. O.
    1993   The Function of Isaiah 24–27. *JETS* 36:163–72.
Smend, R.
    1884   Anmerkungen zu Jes. 24–27. *ZAW* 4:161–224.
Smith, M. S.
    1992   Rephaim. Pages 675–76 in vol. 5 of *ABD*.
Smothers, T. G.
    1996   Isaiah 15–16. Pages 70–84 in *Forming Prophetic Literature: Essays on Isa-
                iah and the Twelve in Honor of John D. W. Watts*. Edited by J. W. Watts
                and P. R. House. Sheffield: JSOT Press.
Snaith, N. H.
    1975   The Meaning of *s*ᵉ*ʿirim*. *VT* 25:115–18.
Sweeney, M. A.
    1987   New Gleanings from an Old Vineyard: Isaiah 27 Reconsidered. Pp. 51–
                66 in *Early Jewish and Christian Exegesis: Studies in Memory of William
                Hugh Brownlee*. Edited by C. A. Evans and W. Stinespring. Atlanta:
                Scholars Press.
    1988   Textual Citations in Isaiah 24–27: Towards an Understanding of the Redac-
                tional Function of Chapters 24–27 in the Book of Isaiah. *JBL* 107:39–52.
    1996   *Isaiah 1–39, with an Introduction to Prophetic Literature*. Forms of the
                Old Testament Literature. Grand Rapids: Eerdmans.
Tadmor, H.
    1958   The Campaigns of Sargon II of Assur: A Chronological-Historical Study.
                JCS 12:22–40, 77–100.
    1966   Philistia under Assyrian Rule. *BA* 29:86–102.
    1994   *The Inscriptions of Tiglath-pileser III, King of Assyria: Critical Edition
                with Introduction, Translations and Commentary*. Jerusalem: Israel Acad-
                emy of Sciences and Humanities.
Talmon, S.
    1983   Biblical *repaʾim* and Ugaritic *rpu/i(m)*. *HAR* 7:235–49. Repr. as Biblical
                רְפָאִים and Ugaritic *RPU/I(M)*. Pages 76–90 in *Literary Studies in the He-
                brew Bible: Form and Content*. Jerusalem: Magnes/Leiden: Brill, 1993.
Thacker, T. W.
    1933   A Note on ʿārôt (Is. xix 7). *JTS* 34:163–65.
Tromp, N. J.
    1969   *Primitive Conceptions of Death and the Nether World in the Old Testa-
                ment*. Rome: Pontifical Biblical Institute.
Tuplin, C.
    1996   *Achaemenid Studies*. Stuttgart: Franz Steiner.
Uffenheimer, B.
    1995   "The Desert of the Sea" Pronouncement (Isaiah 21:1–10). Pages 677–88
                in *Pomegranates and Golden Bells: Studies in Biblical, Jewish, and Near
                Eastern Ritual, Law, and Literature in Honor of Jacob Milgrom*. Edited
                by D. P. Wright, D. N. Freedman, and A. Hurvitz. Winona Lake, Indi-
                ana: Eisenbrauns.

Ussishkin, D.
1970   The Nekropolis from the Time of the Kingdom of Judah at Silwan,
            Jerusalem. *BA* 33:34–46.

Vallat, F.
1992   Elam (Place). Pages 424–29 in vol. 2 of *ABD*.

Vaux, R. de
1939   Titres et fonctionnaires égyptiens à la cour de David et Salomon. *RB*
            48:394–405.
1970   The Cults of Adonis and Osiris. Pages 210–37 in *The Bible and the An-
            cient Near East*. London & New York: Darton, Longman & Todd.

Vermeylen, J.
1974   La composition littéraire de l'apocalypse d'Isaïe (Is. XXIV–XXVII). *ETL*
            50:5–38.
1977   Volume 1 of *Du prophète Isaïe à l'apocalyptique*. Paris: Gabalda.

Vermeylen, J., ed.
1989   *The Book of Isaiah — Le Livre d'Isaïe: Les oracles et leur relecture. Unité et
            complexité de l'ouvrage*. Leuven: Peeters/Leuven University Press.

Virgulin, S.
1972   La risurrezione dei morti in Is. 26 14–19. *BO* 14:273–90.

Vogels, W.
1976   L'Égypte mon peuple: L'Universalisme d'Is 19,16–25. *Bib* 57:494–514.

Wakeman, M. K.
1973   *God's Battle with the Monster*. Leiden: Brill.

Watson, W. G. E.
1976   Tribute to Tyre (Isa XXIII 7). *VT* 26:371–74.

Weippert, M.
1961   Zum text von Ps 19 5 und Jes 22 5. *ZAW* 73:97–99.

Welsby, D. A.
1996   *The Kingdom of Kush: The Napatan and Meroitic Empires*. London: Brit-
            ish Museum Press.

Welten, P.
1982   Die Vernichtung des Todes und ihr traditionsgeschichtliche Ort: Studie
            zu Jes 25,6–8, 21–22 und Exod 24,9–11. *TZ* 38:129–46.

Wildberger, H.
1977   Das Freudenmahl auf dem Zion: Erwägungen zu Jes. 25,6–8. *TZ* 33:
            373–83.

Wilkinson, J.
1974   Ancient Jerusalem: Its Water Supply and Population. *PEQ* 106:33–51.

Williamson, H. G. M.
1994   *The Book Called Isaiah: Deutero-Isaiah's Role in Composition and Redac-
            tion*. Oxford: Clarendon.

Willis, J. T.
1993a   Textual and Linguistic Issues in Isaiah 22:15–25. *ZAW* 105:377–99.
1993b   Historical Issues in Isaiah 22,15–25. *Bib* 74:60–70.

Willis, T. M.
1991   Yahweh's Elders (Isa 24:23): Senior Officials of the Divine Court. *ZAW*
            103:375–85.

Wodecki, B.
1992   The Religious Universalism of the Pericope Is 25:6–9. Pages 35–47 in
        *Goldene Äpfel in silbernen Schalen: Collected Communications to the
        XIIIth Congress of the International Organization for the Study of the Old
        Testament—Leuven 1989.* Edited by K.-D. Schunk and M. Augustin.
        Frankfurt am Main: Lang.
Wyk, W. C. van
1979–80 Isaiah 14:4b-21: a Poem of Contrast and Irony. *OTWSA* 22/23:240–47.
Yee, G. A.
1988   The Anatomy of Biblical Parody: The Dirge Form in 2 Samuel 1 and
        Isaiah 14. *CBQ* 50:39–52.
Zyl, A. H. van
1960   *The Moabites.* Leiden: Brill.
1962   Isaiah 24–27: Their Date of Origin. *OTWSA* 5:44–57.

ISAIAH 28–35

◆

Aitken, K. T.
    1993   Hearing and Seeing: Metamorphoses of a Motif in Isaiah 1–39. Pages 12–41 in *Among the Prophets: Language, Image and Structure in the Prophetic Writings*. Edited by P. R. Davies and D. J. A. Clines. Sheffield: JSOT Press.

Albright, W. F.
    1920   The Babylonian Temple-Tower and the Altar of Burnt-Offering. *JBL* 39: 137–42.

Amsler, S.
    1973   Les Prophètes et la politique. *RTP* 23:14–31.

Asen, B. A.
    1996   The Garlands of Ephraim: Isaiah 28:1–6 and the *Marzeah. JSOT* 71:73–87.

Barré, M. L.
    1993   Of Lions and Birds: A Note on Isaiah 31,4–5. Pages 55–59 in *Among the Prophets: Language, Image and Structure in the Prophetic Writings*. Edited by P. R. Davies and D. J. A. Clines. Sheffield: JSOT Press.
    1995   Restoring the "Lost" Prayer in the Psalm of Hezekiah (Isaiah 38:16–17b). *JBL* 114:385–99.

Bartlett, J. R.
    1979   From Edomites to Nabataeans: A Study in Continuity. *PEQ* 111:53–66.
    1989   *Edom and the Edomites*. Sheffield: JSOT Press.

Ben Zvi, E.
    1996   *A Historical-Critical Study of the Book of Obadiah*. Berlin and New York: de Gruyter.

Betz, O.
    1968   Zungenreden und süsser Wein: Zur eschatologischen Exegese von Jesaja 28 in Qumran und im Neuen Testament. Pages 20–36 in *Bibel und Qumran: Fst. H. Bardtke*. Edited by S. Wagner. Berlin: de Gruyter.

Beuken, W. A. M.
    1991   Jesaja 33 als Spiegeltext im Jesajabuch. *ETL* 67:5–35.
    1992a   Isa 29,15–24: Perversion Reverted. Pages 43–64 in *The Scriptures and the Scrolls: Studies in Honour of A. S. van der Woude on the Occasion of His 65th Birthday*. Edited by F. García Martínez et al. Leiden: Brill.
    1992b   Isaiah 34: Lament in Isaianic Context. *OTE* 5:78–102.
    1995a   Is It Only Schismatics That Drink Heavily? Beyond the Synchronic versus Diachronic Controversy. Pages 15–38 in *Synchronic or Diachronic? A Debate in Old Testament Exegesis*. Edited by J. C. de Moor. OtSt 34. Leiden: Brill.
    1995b   What Does the Vision Hold? Teachers or One Teacher? Punning Repetition in Isaiah 30:20. *HeyJ* 36:451–66.

1997 A Prophetic Oracle Transmitted in Two Successive Paradigms. Pages 369–97 in vol. 1 of *Writing and Reading the Scroll of Isaiah*. Edited by C. C. Broyles and C. A. Evans. 2 vols. Leiden: Brill.

Bronznick, N. M.
1981 The Semantics of the Biblical Stem *yqr. HS* 22:9–12.

Carroll, R. P.
1997 Blindsight and the Vision Thing. Pages 79–93 in vol. 1 of *Writing and Reading the Scroll of Isaiah*. Edited by C. C. Broyles and C. A. Evans. 2 vols. Leiden: Brill.

Caspari, W.
1931 Jesaja 34 und 35. *ZAW* 49:67–86.

Childs, B. S.
1967 *Isaiah and the Assyrian Crisis*. London: S.C.M.

Clements, R. E.
1977 Patterns in the Prophetic Canon. Pages 42–55 in *Canon and Authority*. Edited by G. W. Coats and B. O. Long. Philadelphia: Fortress.

Conrad, E. W.
1988 The Royal Narratives and the Structure of the Book of Isaiah. *JSOT* 41: 67–81.

Cresson, B. C.
1972 The Condemnation of Edom in Post- Exilic Judaism. Pages 125–48 in *The Use of the Old Testament in the New and Other Essays*. Edited by J. M. Efrid. Durham, North Carolina: Duke University Press.

Dahood, M.
1969 Accusative *ʿēṣāh*, "wood," in Isaiah 30,16. *Bib* 50:57–58.

Day, J.
1985 *God's Conflict with the Dragon and the Sea: Echoes of a Canaanite Myth in the Old Testament*. Cambridge: Cambridge University Press.
1992 Rahab (Dragon). Pages 610–11 in vol. 5 of *ABD*.

Delekat, L.
1967 *Asylie und Schutzorakel am Zionheiligtum: Eine Untersuchung zu den privaten Feindpsalmen mit zwei Exkursen*. Leiden: Brill.

Dicon, B.
1991 Literary Function and Literary History of Isaiah 34. *BN* 58:30–45.

Dietrich, W.
1976 *Jesaja und die Politik*. Munich: Kaiser.

Donner, H.
1964 *Israel unter den Völkern*. Leiden: Brill.
1990 "Forscht in der Schrift Jahwes und lest!" Ein Beitrag zum Verständnis der israelitischen Prophetie. *ZTK* 87:285–98.

Driver, G. R.
1959 Lilith, Heb. LILIT "Goat-Sucker, Night-Jar" (Is. XXXIV,14). *PEQ* 91: 55–58.
1968a Isaiah 1–39: Textual and Linguistic Problems. *JSS* 13:36–57.
1968b Another Little Drink: Isaiah 28:1–22. Pages 47–67 in *Words and Meanings: Fst. D. Winton Thomas*. Edited by P. R. Ackroyd and B. Lindars. Cambridge: Cambridge University Press.

Eichrodt, W.
1967 *Der Herr der Geschichte: Jesaja 13–23, 28–39*. Stuttgart: Calwer.

Eidevall, G.
1993   Lions and Birds as Literature: Some Notes on Isaiah 31 and Hosea 11. *SJOT* 7:78–87.

Emerton, J. A.
1981   A Textual Problem in Isaiah xxx.5. *JTS* 32:125–28.
1982   A Further Note on Isaiah xxx.5. *JTS* 33:161.

Exum, J. C.
1979   Isaiah 28–32: A Literary Approach. Pages 123–51 in vol. 2 of *SBL 1979: Seminar Papers*. Edited by P. J. Achtemeier. 2 vols. SBLSP 18. Missoula, Montana: Scholars Press.
1981   Of Broken Pots, Fluttering Birds, and Visions in the Night: Extended Simile and Poetic Technique in Isaiah. *CBQ* 43:331–52.
1982   "Whom Will He Teach Knowledge?" A Literary Approach to Isaiah 28. Pages 108–39 in *Art and Meaning: Rhetoric in Biblical Literature*. Edited by D. J. A. Clines et al. Sheffield: JSOT Press: 108–39.

Feigin, S.
1920   The Meaning of Ariel. *JBL* 39:131–37.

Fichtner, J.
1949   Jesaja unter den Weisen. *TLZ* 74:75–80.
1951   Jahwes Plan in der Botschaft des Jesaja. *ZAW* 63:16–33 = Pages 27–43 in K. D. Fricke, ed., *Gottes Weisheit: Gesammelte Studien zum Alten Testament*. Stuttgart: Calwer.

Fohrer, G.
1967b   Entstehung, Komposition und Überlieferung von Jesaja 1–39. Pages 113–47 in *Studien zur alttestamentlichen Prophetie (1949–1965)*. Berlin: de Gruyter.

Fullerton, K.
1920   The Stone of the Foundation. *AJSL* 37:1–50.
1925–26   Isaiah's Attitude in the Sennacherib Campaign. *AJSL* 42:1–25.

Galling, K.
1929   Der Beichtspiegel. Eine gattungsgeschichtliche Studie. *ZAW* 47:125–30.
1971   Tafel, Buch und Blatt. Pages 207–33 in *Near Eastern Studies in Honor of William Foxwell Albright*. Edited by H. Goedicke. Baltimore: Johns Hopkins University Press.

Gerleman, G.
1974   Der Nicht-Mensch: Erwägungen zur hebräischen Wurzel NBL. *VT* 24: 147–58.

Gerstenberger, E.
1962   The Woe Oracles of the Prophets. *JBL* 81:249–63.

Gese, H.
1970   Der strömende Geissel des Hadad und Jes. 28,15 und 18. Pages 127–34 in *Archäologie und Altes Testament: Fst. K. Galling*. Edited by A. Kuschke and E. Kutsch. Tübingen: Mohr.

Godbey, A. H.
1924–25   Ariel, or David Cultus. *AJSL* 41:253–66.

Görg, M.
1985   Jesaja als "Kinderlehrer"? Beobachtungen zur Sprache und Semantik in Jes 28,10(13). *BN* 29:12–16.

Gonçalves, F. J.
  1986   *L'Expédition de Sennachérib en Palestine dans la littérature hébraïque ancienne.* Paris: Gabalda.
  1995   Isaïe, Jérémie et la politique internationale de Juda. *Bib* 76:282–98.
Gosse, B.
  1990   Isaïe 34–35: Le Chatiment d'Edom et des nations, salut pour Sion. *ZAW* 102:396–404.
  1995   Isaïe 28–32 et la rédaction d'ensemble du livre d'Isaïe. *SJOT* 9:75–82.
Graetz, H.
  1891–92   Isaiah xxiv and xxv. *JQR* 4:1–8.
Gunkel, H.
  1924   Jesaja 33, eine prophetische Liturgie. *ZAW* 42:177–208.
Hallo, W. W.
  1958   Isaiah 28:9–13 and the Ugaritic Abecedaries. *JBL* 77:324–38.
Halpern, B.
  1986   "The Excremental Vision": The Doomed Priests of Doom in Isaiah 28. *HAR* 10:109–21.
Handy, L. K.
  1992   Lilith. Pages 324–25 in vol. 4 of *ABD*.
Harrelson, W.
  1994   Isaiah 35 in Recent Research and Translation. Pages 247–60 in *Language, Theology, and the Bible: Essays in Honour of James Barr*. Edited by S. E. Balentine and J. Barton. Oxford: Clarendon.
Heider, G. C.
  1985   Pages 319–32 in *The Cult of Molek: A Reassessment*. Sheffield: JSOT Press.
Hillers, D. R.
  1971   A Hebrew Cognate of *unussu/unt* in Is. 33:8. *HTR* 64:257–59.
Høgenhaven, J.
  1990   The Prophet Isaiah and Judean Foreign Policy under Ahaz and Hezekiah. *JNES* 49:351–54.
Holmyard, H. R. III
  1995   Does Isaiah 33:23 Address Israel or Israel's Enemy? *BSac* 152:273–78.
Huber, F.
  1976   Pages 50–54 in *Jahwe, Juda und die anderen Völker beim Propheten Jesaja*. Berlin: de Gruyter.
Hutter, M.
  1995   Lilith LYLYT. Pages 973–74 in *Dictionary of Deities and Demons in the Bible*. Edited by K. van der Toorn et al. Leiden: Brill.
Irwin, W. H.
  1977   *Isaiah 28–33: Translation with Philological Notes.* Rome: Pontifical Biblical Institute.
Jackson, J. J.
  1974   Style in Isaiah 28 and a Drinking Bout of the Gods (RS 24.258). Pages 85–98 in *Rhetorical Criticism: Fst. J. Muilenburg*. Edited by J. J. Jackson and M. Kessler. Pittsburgh: Pickwick.
James, F. D.
  1959   *A Critical Examination of the Text of Isaiah.* Ph.D. dissertation, Boston University.

Jamieson-Drake, D. W.
1991   *Scribes and Schools in Monarchic Judah*. Sheffield: Almond Press.

Jensen, J.
1973   *The Use of* tora *by Isaiah: His Debate with the Wisdom Tradition*. Washington, D.C.: Catholic Biblical Association of America.
1986   Yahweh's Plan in Isaiah and in the Rest of the Old Testament. *CBQ* 48: 443–55.

Jeppesen, K.
1984   The Cornerstone (Isa. 28:16) in Deutero-Isaianic Rereading of the Message of Isaiah. *ST* 38:93–99.

Jeremias, J.
1965   *Theophanie: Die Geschichte einer alttestamentliche Gattung*. Neukirchen-Vluyn: Neukirchener Verlag.

Johnson, A. R.
1979   *The Cultic Prophet in Israel's Psalmody*. Cardiff: University of Wales Press.

Kaiser, O.
1969   Die Verkündigung des Propheten Jesaja im Jahre 701. *ZAW* 81:304–15.

Koch, K.
1961   Tempeleinlassliturgien und Dekaloge. Pages 45–60 in *Studien zur Theologie der alttestamentlichen Überlieferungen: Gerhardt von Rad Fst. zum 60. Geburtstag*. Edited by R. Rendtorff and K. Koch. Neukirchen-Vluyn: Neukirchener Verlag.

Kuschke, A.
1952   Zu Jes 30,1–5. *ZAW* 64:194–95.

Laberge, L.
1971   Is 30,19–26: A Deuteronomic Text? *Église et Théologie* 2:35–54.

Landy, F.
1993   Tracing the Voice of the Other: Isaiah 28 and the Covenant with Death. Pages 140–62 in *The New Literary Criticism and the Hebrew Bible*. Edited by J. C. Exum and D. J. A. Clines. Sheffield: JSOT Press.

Lewis, T. J.
1989   *Cults of the Dead in Ancient Israel and Ugarit*. Cambridge: Harvard University Press.

Lindblom, J.
1955   Der Eckstein in Jes 28,16. Pages 123–32 in *Interpretationes ad Vetus Testamentum pertinentes Sigmundo Mowinckel septuagenario missae*. Oslo: Forlayet Land og Kirke = *NTT* 56 (1955).

Lindsay, J.
1976   The Babylonian Kings and Edom 605–550 B.C. *PEQ* 108:23–39.

Loretz, O.
1976   Der kanaanäisch-biblische Mythos vom Sturtz des Šaḥar Sohnes Hêlēl (Jes 14:12–15). *UF* 8:133–36.
1977   Das Prophetenwort über das Ende der Königsstadt Samaria (Jes 28,1–4). *UF* 9:361–63.

Lust, J.
1975   A Gentle Breeze or a Roaring Thunderous Sound? *VT* 25:110–15.

1989   Isaiah 34 and the *herem*. Pages 275–86 in *The Book of Isaiah—Le Livre d'Isaïe: Les oracles et leur relecture. Unité et complexité de l'ouvrage*. Edited by J. Vermeylen. Leuven: Peeters/Leuven University Press.

Machinist, P.
1983   Assyria and its Image in the First Isaiah. *JAOS* 103:719–37.

Mare, W. H.
1992   Ariel (Place). Pages 377–78 in vol. 1 of *ABD*.

Mathews, C. R.
1995   *Defending Zion: Edom's Desolation and Jacob's Restoration (Isaiah 34–35) in Context*. Berlin and New York: de Gruyter.

Mattingly, G. L.
1992   Ariel (Person). Page 377 in vol. 1 of *ABD*.

May, H. G.
1939   Ephod and Ariel. *AJSL* 56:44–56.

Mazar, B.
1963   The Military Elite of King David. *VT* 13:316.

Melugin, R. F.
1974   Isa 30:15–17. *CBQ* 36:303–4.

Mosca, P. G.
1984   Isaiah 28:12e: A Response to J. J. M. Roberts. *HTR* 77:113–17.

Mowinckel, S.
1932–33   Die Komposition des Jesajabuches Kap. 1–39. *AcOr* 11:267–92.

Muilenburg, J.
1940   The Literary Character of Isaiah 34. *JBL* 59:339–65.

Murray, R.
1982   Prophecy and the Cult. Pages 200–216 in *Israel's Prophetic Heritage: Essays in Honour of Peter Ackroyd*. Edited by R. Coggins et al. Cambridge: Cambridge University Press.

Mury, O., and S. Amsler
1973   Yahveh et la sagesse du paysan: Quelques remarques sur Esaïe 28,23–29. *RHPR* 53:1–5.

New, D. S.
1992   The Confusion of *Taw* with *Waw-nun* in Reading 1QIsa^a 29,13. *RevQ* 15:609–10.

North, C. R.
1962   Ariel. Page 218 in vol. 1 of *IDB*.

Olley, J. W.
1983   Notes on Isaiah XXXII 1, XLV 19, 23 and LXIII 1. *VT* 33:446–53.

Olmstead, A. T.
1936–37   II Isaiah and Isaiah, Chapter 35. *AJSL* 53:251–53.

Pope, M. H.
1952   Isaiah 34 in Relation to Isaiah 35,40–66. *JBL* 71:235–44.

Poynder, A.
1901–2   "Be Thou Their Arm Every Morning": Isaiah XXXIII.2. *ExpTim* 13:94.

Rad, G. von
1965   Volume 2 of *Old Testament Theology*. New York and Evanston: Harper & Row.

Reymond, P.
1957   Un tesson pour "ramasser" de l'eau à la mer (Esaïe xxx,14). *VT* 7:203–7.

Ringgren, H.
1974   Behold Your King Comes. *VT* 24:207–11.

Roberts, J. J. M.
1980   A Note on Isaiah 28:12. *HTR* 73:49–51.
1983   Isaiah 33: An Isaianic Elaboration of the Zion Tradition. Pages 15–25 in
          *The Word of the Lord Shall Go Forth: Essays in Honor of David Noel
          Freedman in Celebration of His Sixtieth Birthday*. Edited by C. L. Mey-
          ers and M. O'Connor. Winona Lake, Indiana: Eisenbrauns.
1987   Yahweh's Foundation in Zion (Isa 28:16). *JBL* 106:27–45.

Robinson, T. H.
1931   Note on the Text of Isaiah 29 16. *ZAW* 49:322–23.

Routledge, R. L.
1992   The Siege and Deliverance of the City of David in Isaiah 29:1–8. *TB*
          43:181–90.

Sabottka, L.
1968   Is 30,27–33: Ein Übersetzungsvorschlag. *BZ* 12:241–45.

Sasson, V.
1983   An Unrecognized "Smoke Signal" in Isaiah xxx 27. *VT* 33:90–95.

Schoeps, H. J.
1948   Ein neuer Engelname in der Bibel? Zur Übersetzung des Symmachus
          von Jes 33,3. *ZRGG* 1:86–87.

Schreiner, J.
1963   *Sion-Jerusalem—Jahwes Königssitz: Die Theologie der Heiligen Stadt im
          Alten Testament*. Munich: Kosel.

Schunk, K. D.
1966   Jes 30,6–8 und die Deutung der Rahab im Alten Testament. *ZAW* 78:
          48–56.

Schwantes, S.
1965   A Historical Approach to the 'r'lm of Isa.33. *AUSS* 3:158–66.

Scott, R. B. Y.
1935   The Relation of Isaiah, Chapter 35, to Deutero-Isaiah. *AJSL* 52:178–91.

Sheppard, G.
1985   The Anti-Assyrian Redaction and the Canonical Context of Isaiah 1–39.
          JBL 104:202–4.

Smart, J. D.
1965   Pages 292–94 in *History and Theology in Second Isaiah: A Commentary
          on Isaiah 35, 40–66*. Philadelphia: Westminster.

Stansell, G.
1996   Isaiah 28–33: Blest be the Tie That Binds (Isaiah Together). Pages 68–
          103 in *New Visions of Isaiah*. Edited by R. F. Melugin and M. A.
          Sweeney. Sheffield: JSOT Press.

Steck, O. H.
1985   *Bereitete Heimkehr: Jesaja 35 als redaktionelle Brücke zwischen dem Ersten
          und dem Zweiten Jesaja*. Stuttgart: Katholisches Bibelwerk.

Steingrimsson, S. Ö.
1984   *Tor der Gerechtigkeit: Eine literaturwissenschaftliche Untersuchung der
          sogennanten Einzugsliturgien im AT—Ps 15; 24,3–4 und Jes. 33,14–16*.
          St. Ottilien: EOS.

Stewart, A.
1989   The Covenant with Death in Isaiah 28. *ExpTim* 100:375–77.
Sweeney, M. A.
1994   Paranetic Intent in Isaiah 31. Pages 99–106 in *Proceedings of the Eleventh World Congress of Jewish Studies, Division A: The Bible and Its World*. Edited by D. Assaf. Jerusalem: World Union of Jewish Studies.
Tanghe, V.
1991   Der Schriftgelehrte in Jes 34,16–17. *ETL* 67:338–45.
1993a   Dichtung und Ekel in Jesaja xxviii 7–13. *VT* 43:235–60.
1993b   Lilit in Edom (Jes 34,5–15). *ETL* 59:125–33.
Thexton, S. C.
1952   A Note on Isaiah xxviii 25 and 28. *VT* 2:81–83.
Thompson, M. E. W.
1982   Isaiah's Ideal King. *JSOT* 24:79–88.
Toorn, K. van der
1988   Echoes of Judaean Necromancy in Isaiah 28,7–22. *ZAW* 100:199–217.
Torrey, C. C.
1928   *The Second Isaiah: A New Interpretation*. Edinburgh: T. & T. Clark.
Vattioni, F.
1958   I precedenti letterari di Isaia 32,17: Et erit opus iustitiae pax. *RivB* 6:23–32.
Virgulin, S.
1959   Il significato della pietra di fondazione in Is 28,16. *RivBib* 7:208–20.
Vogt, E.
1975   Das Prophetenwort Jes 28,1–4 und das Ende der Königsstadt Samaria. Pages 109–30 in *Homenaje a Juan Prado: Miscelanea de estudios bíblicos y hebraicos*. Edited by L. Alvarez Verdes and E. J. Alonso Hernandez. Madrid: Consejo Superior de Investigaciones Científicos.
Wegner, P. D.
1992   *An Examination of Kingship and Messianic Expectation in Isaiah 1–35*. Lewiston, N.Y.: Mellen.
Weinfeld, M.
1972   The Worship of MOLECH and the Queen of Heaven and its Background. *UF* 4:133–54.
Weis, R. D.
1991   Angels, Altars and Angles of Vision: The Case of 'R'LM in Isaiah 33:7. Pages 285–92 in *Tradition of the Text: Studies Offered to Dominique Barthélemy in Celebration of His 70th Birthday*. Edited by G. J. Norton and S. Pisano. Freiburg: Universitätsverlag.
Werlitz, J.
1992   *Studien zur literarkritischen Methode: Gericht und Heil in Jesaja 7,1–17 und 29,1–8*. Berlin: de Gruyter.
Werner, W.
1988   *Studien zur alttestamentlichen Vorstellung vom Plan Jahwes*. Berlin: de Gruyter.
Whedbee, J. W.
1971   *Isaiah and Wisdom*. Nashville: Abingdon.

Williamson, H. G. M.
1994   *The Book Called Isaiah: Deutero-Isaiah's Role in Composition and Redaction*. Oxford: Clarendon.
1995   Isaiah and the Wise. Pages 133–41 in *Wisdom in Ancient Israel: Essays in Honour of J. A. Emerton*. Edited by J. Day. Cambridge: Cambridge University Press.
1998   The Messianic Texts in Isaiah 1–39. Pages 238–70 in *King and Messiah in Israel and the Ancient Near East*. Edited by J. Day. Sheffield: JSOT Press.
Wong, G. C. I.
1996   Isaiah's Opposition to Egypt in Isaiah XXXI 1–3. *VT* 46:392–401.
Young, E. J.
1964–65 Isaiah 34 and its Position in the Prophecy. *WTJ* 27:93–114.
Ziegler, J.
1933   Das Heuschreckengleichnis Is. 33,4. *Bib* 14:460–64.
1950   Die Hilfe Gottes "am Morgen." Pages 281–88 in *Alttestamentliche Studien Friedrich Nötscher zum 60. Geburtstag 19 Juli 1950 gewidmet*. Edited by H. Junker and J. Botterweck. Bonn: Hanstein.

ISAIAH 36–39

◆

Ackroyd, P. R.
1974   An Interpretation of the Babylonian Exile: 2 Kgs 20, Isaiah 38–39. *SJT* 27:329–52. Repr., pages 152–71 in *Studies in the Religious Tradition of the Old Testament*. London: SCM, 1987.

1979   The Death of Hezekiah: A Pointer to the Future? Pages 219–26 in *De la Tôrah au Messie: Mélanges Henri Cazelles*. Edited by M. Carrez et al. Paris: Desclée. Repr., pages 172–80 in *Studies in the Relgious Tradition of the Old Testament*. London: SCM, 1987.

1982   Isaiah 36–39: Structure and Function. Pages 3–21 in *Von Kanaan bis Kerala: Fst. für J. P. M. van der Ploeg, O. P.* Edited by W. C. Delsman et al. Neukirchen-Vluyn: Neukirchener Verlag. Repr., pages 478–94 in *"The Place Is Too Small for Us": The Israelite Prophets in Recent Scholarship*. Edited by R. P. Gordon. Winona Lake, Indiana: Eisenbrauns, 1995.

1987   The Biblical Interpretation of the Reigns of Ahaz and Hezekiah. Pages 181–92 in *Studies in the Religious Tradition of the Old Testament*. London: SCM.

Barré, M. L.
1995   Restoring the "Lost" Prayer in the Psalm of Hezekiah (Isaiah 38:16–17b). *JBL* 114:385–99.

Begg, C. T.
1986   2 Kings 20:12–19 as an Element of the Deuteronomistic History. *CBQ* 48:27–38.

1987   The Deuteronomistic Retouching of the Portrait of Hezekiah in 2 Kings 20:12–19. *BN* 38–39:7–13.

Begrich, J.
1926   *Der Psalm des Hiskia: Ein Beitrag zum Verständnis von Jesaja 38,10–20.* Göttingen: Vandenhoeck & Ruprecht.

Ben Zvi, E.
1990   Who Wrote the Speech of Rabshakeh and When? *JBL* 109:79–90.

Boer, P. A. H. de
1951   Notes on the Text and Meaning of Isaiah XXXVIII 9–20. *OtSt* 9:170–86.

Brinkman, J. A.
1964   Merodach-Baladan II. Pages 6–53 in *Studies Presented to A. Leo Oppenheim, June 7, 1964*. Edited by R. D. Biggs and J. A. Brinkman. Chicago: The Oriental Institute.

Camp, L.
1990   *Hiskija und Hiskijabild: Analyse und Interpretation von 2 Kön 18–20.* Altenberg: Telos.

Catastani, A.
1983   Osservazioni filologiche sulla cosidetta "Meridiana di Achaz" (Isaia 38:8/ II Re 20:11). *Henoch* 5:161–78.

1989   *Isaia ed Ezechia: Studio di storia della tradizione di II Re 18–20/Is 36–39.*
         Rome: Pontifical Biblical Institute.
Childs, B. S.
1967   *Isaiah and the Assyrian Crisis.* London: SCM.
Clements, R. E.
1980b   *Isaiah and the Deliverance of Jerusalem: A Study of the Interpretation of
         Prophecy in the Old Testament.* Sheffield: JSOT Press.
1983   The Isaiah Narrative of 2 Kings 20:12–19 and the Date of the Deutero-
         nomic History. Pages 209–20 in vol. 3 of *Essays on the Bible and the An-
         cient World: Isaac Leo Seeligmann.* Edited by A. Rofé and Y. Yakovitch.
         Jerusalem: Magnes.
1991   The Prophecies of Isaiah to Hezekiah concerning Sennacherib: 2 Kings
         19.21–34/Isaiah 37.22–35. Pages 65–78 in *Prophetie und geschichtliche
         Wirklichkeit im alten Israel: Fst. S. Herrmann.* Edited by R. Liwak and
         S. Wagner. Stuttgart: Kohlhammer.
Cogan, M., and H. Tadmor.
1988   Pages 240–52 in *II Kings: A New Translation with Introduction and Com-
         mentary.* AB 11. New York: Doubleday.
Cohen, C.
1979   Neo-Assyrian Elements in the First Speech of the Biblical Rab-Shaqe.
         Israel Oriental Studies 9:32–48.
Conrad, E. W.
1988   The Royal Narratives and the Structure of the Book of Isaiah. *JSOT*
         41:67–81.
Dahood, M.
1959   The Value of Ugaritic for Textual Criticism. *Bib* 40:160–64.
Darr, K. P.
1996   No Strength to Deliver: A Contextual Analysis of Hezekiah's Proverb
         in Isaiah 37.3b. Pages 218–56 in *New Visions of Isaiah.* Edited by R. F.
         Melugin and M. A. Sweeney. Sheffield: Sheffield Academic Press.
Deutsch, R.
1969   *Die Hiskiaerzählungen: Eine formgeschichtliche Untersuchung der Texte
         Js. 36–39 und 2 R 18–20.* Basel: Basileia.
Dietrich, W.
1976   *Jesaja und die Politik.* Munich: Kaiser.
Dion, P. E.
1989   Sennacherib's Expedition to Palestine. *Église et Théologie* 20:5–25.
Driver, G. R.
1968   Isaiah 1–39: Textual and Linguistic Problems. *JSS* 13:36–57.
Fullerton, K.
1925–26 Isaiah's Attitude in the Sennacherib Campaign. *AJSL* 42:1–25.
Geyer, J. B.
1971   2 Kings XVIII 14–16 and the Annals of Sennacherib. *VT* 21:604–6.
Gonçalves, F. J.
1986   *L'Expédition de Sennachérib en Palestine dans la littérature hébraïque
         ancienne.* Paris: Gabalda.
Gryson, R., and J.-M. Auwers.
1993   L'Histoire du texte latin d'Isaïe au miroir du cantique d'Ezechias. *RTL*
         24:325–44; 455–77.

Hardmeier, C.
   1991   Die Propheten Micha und Jesaja im Spiegel von Jeremia XXVI und
               2 Regum XVIII–XX: Zur Prophetie-Rezeption in der nachjoshianische
               Zeit. Pages 172–89 in *Congress Volume: Leuven, 1989*. VTSup 43. Leiden:
               Brill.
Høgenhaven, J.
   1990   The Prophet Isaiah and Judean Foreign Policy under Ahaz and Heze-
               kiah. *JNES* 49:351–54.
Honor, L. L.
   1926   *Sennacherib's Invasion of Palestine: A Critical Source Study*. New York:
               Columbia University Press.
Hurwitz, M. S.
   1957   The Septuagint of Isaiah 36–39 in Relation to That of 1–35 and 40–66.
               HUCA 28:75–83.
Jenkins, A. K.
   1976   Hezekiah's Fourteenth Year: A New Interpretation of 2 Kings XVIII 13–
               XIX 37. *VT* 26:284–98.
Jeremias, C.
   1971   Zu Jes. XXXVIII 21 f. *VT* 21:104–11.
Kaiser, O.
   1969   Die Verkündigung des Propheten Jesaja im Jahre 701. *ZAW* 81:304–15.
Konkel, A. H.
   1993   The Sources of the Story of Hezekiah in the Book of Isaiah. *VT* 43:462–
               82.
Kooij, A. van der
   1986   Das Assyrische Heer vor den Mauern Jerusalems im Jahr 701 v.Chr.
               ZDPV 102:93–109.
Laato, A.
   1987   Hezekiah and the Assyrian Crisis in 701 BC. *SJOT* 2:49–68.
Liwak, R.
   1986   Die Rettung Jerusalems im Jahr 701 v.Chr.: Zum Verhältnis und Ver-
               ständnis historischer und theologischer Aussagen. *ZTK* 83:137–66.
Machinist, P.
   1983   Assyria and Its Image in the First Isaiah. *JAOS* 103:719–37.
Millard, A. R.
   1985   Sennacherib's Attack on Hezekiah. *TynBul* 36:61–77.
Nyberg, H. S.
   1974   Hiskias Danklied Jes.38,9–20. *ASTI* 9:85–97.
Ognibene, B.
   1992   Achaz o non Achaz: a proposito del testo di Is 38,8. *RivB* 40:77–86.
Orlinsky, M.
   1939–40   The Kings-Isaiah Recensions of the Hezekiah Story. *JQR* 30:33–49.
Provan, I. W.
   1988   *Hezekiah and the Books of Kings: A Contribution to the Debate about the
               Composition of the Deuteronomistic History*. Berlin and New York: de
               Gruyter.
Rowley, H. H.
   1961–62   Hezekiah's Reform and Rebellion. *BJRL* 44:395–461.

Ruprecht, E.
1990   Die ursprüngliche Komposition der Hiskia-Jesaja Erzählungen und ihre
         Umstrukierung durch den Verfasser des deuteronomistischen Ge-
         schichtswerkes. *ZTK* 87:33–66.
Seitz, C. R.
1991   *Zion's Final Destiny—The Development of the Book of Isaiah: A Reassess-
         ment of Isaiah 36–39.* Minneapolis: Fortress.
1993   Account A and the Annals of Sennacherib: A Reassessment. *JSOT* 58:47–
         57.
Shea, W. H.
1985   Sennacherib's Second Palestinian Campaign. *JBL* 104:401–18.
Sheppard, G.
1985   The Anti-Assyrian Redaction and the Canonical Context of Isaiah 1–39.
         JBL 104:202–4.
Smelik, K. A. D.
1986   Distortion of Old Testament Prophecy: The Purpose of Isaiah xxxvi and
         xxxvii. *OtSt* 24:70–93.
1992   King Hezekiah Advocates True Prophecy: Remarks on Isaiah xxxvi and
         xxxvii. Pages 93–128 in *Converting the Past: Studies in Ancient Israelite
         and Moabite Historiography.* Leiden: Brill.
Sweeney, M. A.
1996   *Isaiah 1–39, with an Introduction to the Prophetic Literature.* The Forms
         of Old Testament Literature. Grand Rapids: Eerdmans.
Tadmor, H.
1985   Sennacherib's Campaign against Judah: Historical and Historiographi-
         cal Considerations. *Zion* 50:65–80. [Heb.]
Ullendorf, E.
1962   Knowledge of Languages in the Old Testament. *BJRL* 44:455–65.
Wildberger, H.
1979   Die Rede des Rabsake vor Jerusalem. *TZ* 35:35–47.
Williamson, H. G. M.
1994   *The Book Called Isaiah: Deutero-Isaiah's Role in Composition and Redac-
         tion.* Oxford: Clarendon.
1996   Hezekiah and the Temple. Pages 47–52 in *Texts, Temples, and Traditions:
         A Tribute to Menahem Haran.* Edited by M. V. Fox et al. Winona Lake:
         Eisenbrauns.
Yadin, Y.
1958   ma^{ca}lot ᵓahaz. *Eretz-Israel* 5 (Mazar Volume):91–95.
Zimmerli, W.
1973   Jesaja und Hiskia. Pages 199–208 *Wort und Geschichte: Fst. für Karl Elliger
         zum 70. Geburtstag.* Kevelaer: Butzon & Bercker.

TRANSLATION, NOTES AND COMMENTS

◆

INTRODUCTION TO
ISAIAH 1–12

◆

The book of Isaiah is a good example of the need to combine a diachronic with a synchronic reading of texts, especially ancient texts. The conventional divisions of the book, beginning with chs. 1–12, are useful as a starting point but inadequate to account for the complex of successive restructurings that the book has undergone in the course of a long history. These restructurings and their interconnections and continuities belong not just to the history of the book but to its total meaning. They are theologically as well as historically significant and therefore cannot be neglected in favor of the final form or the surface structure.

Chapters 1–12, for example, comprise a distinct section beginning with a superscription attributing the book to Isaiah and rounded out with a psalm that plays on his name (12:1–6) and invokes "the Holy One of Israel," a title recurring at regular intervals throughout these twelve chapters and recalling the seer's vision at their midpoint (6:3). While the section gives the impression of having been planned as a distinct unit, it is also connected thematically and linguistically with other parts of the book. Its narrative nucleus, the account in the first and third person of Isaiah's encounter with Ahaz at the time of Tiglath-pileser III around 734 B.C.E. (chs. 6–8), was put together to form a pair of matching panels together with the account of the seer's relations with Hezekiah at the time of Sennacherib three decades later (chs. 36–37). Beginning with the first chapter (1:7–9), the interpretation of the earlier incident in light of the later one and of both in terms of moral causality is never overlooked. In this way the often fragmentary poems, discourses and narratives in chs. 1–12 achieve a kind of unity by coalescing into an overview of the triumph and eventual collapse of the Assyrian imperial power (most clearly in 10:1–34; 11:12–16), a theme that dominates the entire first section of the book (chs. 1–39).

The prophetic theory of moral causality, according to which the vicissitudes of the nation vis-à-vis successive imperial powers are explained with reference to internal societal attitudes and behavior, anchors these first twelve chapters of the book in the first wave of prophetic protest in the eighth century B.C.E.; hence the many points of contact with Amos that will be discussed in the commentary. The critique of imperialism in the person of each successive Assyrian ruler follows a trajectory from the time of Ahaz to that of Hezekiah and, less clearly, but plausibly, to the reign of Josiah, when the Assyrian Empire entered a phase of irreversible decline.

But much of this critique was seen to apply with equal force to the Babylonians, who filled the vacuum created by the collapse of Assyria and brought the Kingdom of Judah to an end. It is not surprising, therefore, that at several points in chs. 1–12 commentators ancient and modern have found allusions to the devastation of Judah and destruction of Jerusalem by the Babylonians in the campaign of 589–586 B.C.E. Also, this opening section (chs. 1–12) is followed immediately by the first of the many anti-Babylonian poems and sayings in the book (13:1–22; 14:3–23; 21:1–10), implying that reflection on the experience of threat and oppression at the hands of the Assyrians provides the interpretative key for understanding the terminal threat posed by their imperial successors.

As we proceed it will become clear that the persistent reorientation towards the future evident throughout chs. 1–12 did not grind to a halt with the massive political and military disasters of 597–586. Sayings spaced at intervals throughout the section or bracketing pronouncements of judgment predict a positive diagnosis for Judah and Jerusalem on the other side of judgment (1:27–31; 2:2–5; 4:2–4; 10:20–23; 11:10–16). It is easy to grasp how concern with the destiny of Judah and Jerusalem, firmly embedded in the Isaian tradition as it is, would be appropriated at a time, reflected in the last section of the book (56–66), when the Jerusalem temple was the focus and center of the religious, political, and social life of the province of Judah under Persian rule. It is therefore relatively easy to explain why these last chapters have been included in a book attributed to Isaiah. The connection with the so-called Second Isaiah is rather more problematic, as we saw above.

An examination of the internal organization of chs. 1–12 confirms the point about successive, superimposed structures. The first and most obvious indication is the repetition of a superscription in 2:1. This duplication confirms the impression of several recent scholars that the first chapter stands by itself in recapitulating themes found throughout the book. It is also significant that the denunciations, indictments, and descriptions of social *anomie* in chs. 2–4 are bracketed within visionary glimpses of the purified and peaceful Jerusalem of the latter days (2:1–4; 4:2–6). The implication is that the word of judgment retains its validity and is not discarded with the passage of time but that it is not the last word to be spoken and heard. The basic idea seems to be that the prophetic word spoken in the past retains its validity but that the past must be continually revisioned and reassimilated in the light of each successive present. By being recontextualized or viewed from a different vantage point or plane of observation it can take on different forms and meanings with the changing circumstances of the present. On this view, the past is not an unassimilable entity but a component of personal and communal self-understanding in the present. We cannot make sense of the formation of the book without keeping in mind this constant assimilation and reinterpretation of the past.

Other indications of structure and order in this first section may be noted. The vineyard song (5:1–7), reinterpreted later in the book (27:2–5), serves as a transition to the narrative core of chs. 1–12, dealing with the Syrian-Samarian attack on Judah. It also prepares for it by explaining in advance why the prophet's intervention failed. On one level of internal organization the narrative core is located between the death of Uzziah, king of Judah (6:1), and the death of his successor, Ahaz (14:28). Since the notice of the death of Ahaz *follows* the first anti-Babylonian poems (13:1–14:23), Assyrians and Babylonians are juxtaposed without concern for chronology as imperial powers subject to the same interpretation and the same judgment. At another level one would be tempted to read 8:18 ("(all this) is from Yahveh of hosts who dwells on Mount Zion") as a *finale* closing out the episode that begins with the vision of YHVH *ṣĕbā'ôt* (6:1–13). Or, again, one might read the "new ruler, new age" poem (8:23–9:6[9:1–7]), with its vision of light, joy, and peace, as a response to the dark scenario of defeat and destruction set out in the first poem in the book (1:5–9). But the clearest of these structural markers is the final psalm, which encodes the names of the principal protagonists—namely, the Holy One of Israel and Isaiah himself (see commentary on 12:1–6).

The narrative core of chs. 1–12 can be summarized as follows. Isaiah attempts to persuade Ahaz that he has nothing to fear from the Syrian-Samarian alliance and to dissuade him from taking ill-advised countermeasures; the attempt fails, and Isaiah subsequently withdraws from involvement in public affairs (chs. 7–8 with considerable editorial elaboration). The commissioning for this task (6:1–13) is couched in the first person, the body of the narrative in the third person (7:1–17), and the last part (8:1–18) again in the first person, an arrangement somewhat reminiscent of the contrasting accounts of Hosea's marital vicissitudes, real or allegorical (Hos 1:1–9; 3:1–3). Since the Isaian core narrative with its many editorial accretions is not a transcript of eyewitnesses but a *literary construct*, it is not impossible that in both Hos 1 and 3 and Isa 7 and 8 we have alternative versions of one and the same episode, the children with the improbable names (Shear-yashub, Maher-shalal-hash-baz) serving a function similar to that of Hosea's children (see the commentary on 8:1–10). As noted above, the story of Isaiah's dealings with Ahaz also links with chs. 36–39, narrating how Isaiah reassured Hezekiah three decades later, faced with an even greater military threat. In the context of this entire section the vision of the heavenly court with its injunction to harden the hearts of his listeners (6:1–13), whatever the date assigned to it, would then function not just to legitimate Isaiah's mission to Ahaz but to account for its failure.

The core narrative is bracketed by sections of what may have been one poem or a poem sequence describing Assyrian military intervention in response to Ahaz's plea and the punishment of the aggressors for going beyond their commission (5:26–30; 10:5–34 with editorial interpolations). While this poetic material is clearly relevant to the situation during the reign of Ahaz, as described in the core narrative, it would be surprising if it had not been expanded at the time of Sennacherib's campaign in Judah three decades later. Also straddling the core narrative is a poem on the divine anger, in five stanzas as the text now stands, each stanza ending with the refrain "yet his anger did not abate; still was his hand outstretched" (5:25; 9:11, 18, 22; 10:4). Its location suggests that it serves to comment on the spiritual obtuseness manifested, according to Isaiah, in the failed mission of 734 B.C.E. But it is also possible that the first stanza (5:25) became separated from the others and accidentally attached to the preceding series of five or six woe-sayings (5:8–24). These sayings of unequal length direct specific indictments against the political, religious, and intellectual leadership. The two poems describing in exalted language the ideal Davidic dynast (9:1–6; 11:1–9) precede the notice about the death of Ahaz (14:28) and therefore express the hope of a better future occasioned (as we shall see) by the birth rather than the accession of Hezekiah.

These are the principal components of this section, but the numerous editorial expansions and adjustments, which will be pointed out as the commentary proceeds, testify to its perceived relevance to later situations—the critical times of Hezekiah and Josiah, Judah under Babylonian rule, the establishment of a new commonwealth under Persian rule, and its further vicissitudes after the conquests of Alexander.

ISAIAH 1–12

◆

TITLE (1:1)

(Anderson; Avigad; Diringer; Fichtner 1949; Gevaryahu; Sweeney 1988; Tucker; Vermeylen 1977, 1:37–42; Hayes and Hooker)

TRANSLATION

1 ¹The vision of Isaiah ben Amoz which he saw concerning Judah and Jerusalem in the days of Uzziah, Jotham, Ahaz, and Hezekiah, kings of Judah.

COMMENTS

As it stands, and in spite of the limitation to Judah and Jerusalem, this first superscription introduces the entire book of Isaiah. The poem in the first chapter was prefixed at some point to the passage predicting the restoration of Jerusalem with its own superscription (2:2–5). Recent scholarship has therefore tended to read this first chapter as recapitulating the message of the book as a whole. With the exception of 38:9, which ascribes a psalm to King Hezekiah, other titles in the book are attached to oracles (generally *maśśā'ôt*) against foreigners (13:1; 14:28; 15:1; 17:1; 19:1; 21:1, 11, 13; 22:1; 23:1; 30:6). The book as a whole is characterized in the title as a vision (*ḥāzôn*), as are also Obadiah and Nahum, which is surprising at first sight since the book reports only two visions (6:1–13; 21:1–10). But this is late usage, consonant with the Chronicler's allusion to one of his sources for the history of Hezekiah's reign as "the vision of the prophet Isaiah ben Amoz" (2 Chr 32:32; see also Sir 48:22, who also speaks of Isaiah's visions). The term "vision" could therefore have the more general connotation of revelation (Duhm 1892, 23) in keeping with the understanding of historiography in the later period as a prophetic activity, for example in Chronicles and Josephus. The term *nābî'* has undergone a similar semantic expansion. A Second Temple date for the superscription is also suggested by the phrase "Judah and Jerusalem," in which the words occur in the same order as in Chronicles-Ezra-Nehemiah (e.g. 2 Chr 11:14; 20:17; 24:6, 8; Ezra 9:9; 10:7) but the reverse of the order in Isian sayings generally taken to be of early date (3:1, 8; 5:3; 22:21).

The dating by reigns is similar to what we find in the superscription to Hosea, except that in the latter the two kingdoms are synchronized. These names of rulers could have been deduced from chronological indications elsewhere in the book, covering as they do the time span from the year of Uzziah's death (somewhere between 742 and 734 but closer to the latter than to the former date) to the fourteenth year of Hezekiah (701). Isaiah's public career, therefore, is presented as spanning four decades, not unlike the superscription to Jeremiah that assigns him forty years, thus aligning his career with the life and mission of the Deuteronomic Moses (Jer 1:1–3 cf. Deut 18:15–18). The idea seems to be that Jeremiah is the last in the series of "his servants the prophets," a series that begins with Moses the protoprophet.

The name *yĕša'yāhû* (shorter form: *yĕša'yâ*, as in later biblical texts, 4QIsa[b], and 3QpIsa) is attached to six other individuals in the Hebrew Bible, all in Second Temple texts, at least three of whom were associated with the Jerusalem temple (1 Chr 3:21; 25:3, 15; 26:25; Ezra 8:7, 19; Neh 11:7). The name also occurs among the Elephantine Jews (AP 5:16; 8:33; 9:21; Cowley 1967, pp. 11, 23, 26) and on two seals, both of uncertain origin and date (Avigad). Like the name of another prophet, Hosea, Isaiah is formed with the verbal stem *yš'*, "save" ("may Yahveh save," or perhaps "Yahveh will save"). Word play on personal names is as prominent in these opening chapters as it is in Hosea, and Isaiah's own name provides the psalm which rounds off chs. 1–12 with its dominant motif of salvation (12:1–3). The father's name, attested only here and on a seal of unknown origin (Diringer 1934, 235), is a hypocoristic form of Amaziah (Amaṣyahu), a name belonging to a Judean king (2 Kgs 14:1–22) and two other individuals (1 Chr 4:34; 6:45). According to a rabbinic tradition (*b. Meg.* 10b; *Lev. Rab.* 6:6), also reported by Rashi, Amoz was the brother of king Amaziah and himself a prophet. Isaiah was therefore held to be a member of the royal family (see Ibn Ezra ad loc.). More recent attempts to assign him the specific role of scribe (Anderson; Fichtner) are only slightly less speculative. For the Isaian *legendum*, see the Introduction to Isaiah 36–39, p. 460 and the commentary on chs. 36–39.

THE GREAT ARRAIGNMENT (1:2–31)

(Abramski; Ben Zvi; Bjørndalen; Claassen; Conrad 1991; Culver; Emerton 1993; Fohrer; Gosse 1992b; Harvey; Hillers; Huffmon; Jensen 1973; Jones 1964; Lack; Liebreich 1955, 1956; Loewenclau; Loewenstamm; Mattioli; Niditch; Nielsen 1979; Rignell 1957b; Robertson; Schoneveld; Tomasino; Tsevat; van Uchelen; Vermeylen 1978, 1.42–111; Williamson 1997; Willis 1985; 1986)

TRANSLATION

i

1   ²Hear, heaven, earth, give heed,
    for Yahveh speaks!
    "Children I have raised and reared,
    but they have rebelled against me.
    ³An ox will recognize its owner,
    a donkey its master's stall;

Israel has no such knowledge,
my people no comprehension."

ii

⁴Woe, sinful nation,
people burdened with crime,
wicked offspring,
depraved children!
They have abandoned Yahveh,
despising the Holy One of Israel
[They have fallen away]ᵃ

iii

⁵Why be forever beaten,
rebelling time out of mind?
The whole head is sick,
the whole heart faint.
⁶From the sole of the foot to the head
there is no soundness in him—
bruises, sores, and open wounds,
not drained, not bandaged, not treated with oil.

iv

⁷Your land is a desolation,
your cities burned to the ground;
before your very eyes
foreigners devour your land.
[a desolation as if overthrown by foreigners]ᵇ
⁸Daughter Zion is left
like a lean-to in a vineyard,
like a shack in a cucumber patch,
like a city besieged.
⁹Had not Yahveh of the hosts
left us a fewᶜ survivors,
we would have shared Sodom's fate,
resembled Gomorrah.

v

¹⁰Hear the word of Yahveh,
you rulers of Sodom!
Give heed to the teaching of our God,
you people of Gomorrah!
¹¹"What are your many sacrifices to me?"
[It is Yahveh who speaks]
"I have had enough of burnt offerings of rams,
and the suet of fatted animals;

I take no pleasure in the blood of bulls,
or of lambs and goats.
[12]When you come to appear in my presence,
who is asking this of you,
this trampling of my precincts?
[13]Bring no more useless offerings,
incense disgusts me.
New moon, sabbath, holy convocation—
I cannot stand wickedness combined with solemn assembly.
[14]I hate your new moons and festivals,
they have become a burden to me,
I am tired of putting up with them.
[15]When you stretch out your hands in prayer
I will hide my eyes from you;
even though you keep on praying,
I will not be listening;
you have blood all over your hands.[d]
[16]Wash yourselves, make yourselves clean;
remove the evil you are doing from my sight;
stop doing evil,
[17]learn to do good;
seek after justice, rescue the oppressed;[e]
defend the rights of the orphan,
plead the widow's cause."

vi

[18]"Come now, let us reason together,"
[It is Yahveh who speaks.]
"If your sins are colored scarlet,
can they become white like snow?
If dyed crimson red,
can they become like pure wool?
[19]If you are willing to obey,
you shall feed off the goodness of the land;
[20]but if you refuse and rebel,
you shall be consumed by the sword[f]
The mouth of Yahveh has spoken."

vii

[21]See how the town once loyal
has become like a whore!
Once she was full of justice,
righteousness lodged in her
[but now assassins].[g]
[22]Your silver has turned into slag,
your beer is watered down;

²³your princes are rebels,
associates of thieves;
each one of them loves a bribe,
runs after gifts.
They do not defend the orphan,
the widow's cause does not reach them.
²⁴"Therefore"—oracle of Yahveh, Lord of hosts,
Strong One of Israel:
"I will assuage my anger on my foes,
I will be avenged on my enemies;
²⁵I will turn my hand against you,^h
burn off your dregs in the furnace,ⁱ
removing all your dross.
²⁶I will restore your judges as of yore,
your counselors as at the beginning;
then your name will be City of Righteousness,
Loyal Town."

viii

²⁷Zion will be saved in the judgment,
her penitents in the retribution,
²⁸but rebels and sinners will be destroyed together,
those forsaking Yahveh will be consumed.
²⁹You will feel shame for the terebinths
in which you took delight;
you will blush for the gardens
that you chose for yourselves;
³⁰you will be like a terebinth
whose foliage is withered,
or like a garden
without any water.
³¹The strong^j will become like tow,
and his deeds like a spark;
both will be burned together,
with no one to put out the fire.

NOTES

^a MT *nāzōrû ʾāḥôr*: absent from LXX and awkwardly translated in Vulg.: *ab-alienati sunt retrorsum* → *zûr* Niphal only here and Ezek 14:5, the latter also in the context of idolatry; in similar contexts *ʾāḥôr* is used frequently with *sûg* (Niphal) in late texts (Isa 42:17; 59:13–14; Jer 38:22; 46:5; Ps 35:4; 40:15; 44:19; 70:3; 129:5); Holladay (1983, 235–37) proposes *nizzĕrû lĕʾaḥēr*, "they dedicated themselves to another [deity]," which seems a bit drastic; in either case, it looks like the hand of a Second Temple glossator not particularly concerned with

either literary elegance or prosody;   [b] Some early commentators (Duhm; Marti) as well as several more recent ones suspect that MT *ûšĕmāmâ kĕmahpēkat zārîm* is a lemma + gloss on the previous stich (1QIsa[a] adds *ʿalêhā*, "upon it [i.e. the land]," after *ûšĕmāmâ*); but, as it stands, this would add nothing at all to the sense and therefore would be rather pointless, unless one reads *sĕdôm* for *zārîm* on the grounds that *mahpēkâ* ("overthrow") always occurs elsewhere with Sodom (Deut 29:22; Isa 13:19; Jer 49:18; 50:40; Amos 4:11). Ibn Ezra proposed *zerem* for *zārîm*, reading "desolate like land overturned by a flood"; [c] *kimʿāt* absent from LXX, Syr., Vulg., leading several commentators either to omit it *metri causa* or move it to the next stich (*kimʿāt kisĕdōm hāyînû*); [d] 1QIsa[a] adds *ʾeṣbĕʿôtêkem beʿāvôn*, "your fingers [are full of] iniquity"—borrowed from Isa 59:3 which, however, is absent from 4QIsa[f];   [e] *ʾaššĕrû hāmôṣ* My translation follows LXX (*rusasthe*, rescue) and other ancient versions (Targ, Syr), assigning a broader range to *ʾšr* (Piel), "make or declare happy," and reading *hāmûṣ*, "oppressed" cf. Ps 71:4 *hômēṣ*, "oppressor"; see Wildberger 1991, 36 and an alternative in Gray 1912, 25–26 ("keep the oppressor within bounds"); [f] *bĕḥāreb* with Syr., Tg., 1QIsa[a]; [g] *vĕʿattâ mĕraṣṣĕhîm* ("but now assassins")— a gloss; the poet would not have introduced such a serious accusation in so casual a manner;   [h] the defective meter suggests that the second hemistich has fallen out;   [i] read *bakkûr* ("in the furnace or smelting oven") for *kabbōr* ("like lye");   [j] 1QIsa[a] reads *hĕḥāsōnēkem*, "your strong one," but 4QIsa[f] agrees with MT; LXX has *hai ergasiai auton* ("their works") cf. Vulg.: *opus vestrum*. I suspect that *ḥāsōn* refers to an idol and *pôʿălô* to the one who made it.

COMMENTS

The title I have assigned to the poem is taken from Heinrich Ewald's *Propheten des Alten Bundes* (*Prophets of the Old Covenant*) published in 1840. This first chapter is made up of a sequence of fairly short stanzas loosely linked thematically or by one of the familiar forms of prophetic incipit or catchword. Thus, 2–3 and 10–17 are introduced with the vocative, the call to hear and give heed, 4 is a short woe-oracle, 18–20 begins and ends with a formulaic designation of Yahveh as speaker, the initial "see how" (*ʾêkâ*) makes 21–23 a kind of lament, and 24–26 is explicitly an oracle (*nĕʾūm*). Mention of Sodom and Gomorrah serves to link 7–9 with 10–17, and there is no compelling reason to demote mention of the Cities of the Plain in 9 to a gloss (as does Barth, 1977, 190–91). But beyond these explicit verbal markers a certain thematic or rhetorical continuity is detectable, though certainly not to the point of complete coherence. (Note, in particular, the frequent switching among first, second, and third person address and between singular and plural). The familial imagery of 2–3 (Yahveh as *paterfamilias*, Israelites as children) is continued in 4, and the figure of the bruised and battered body is applied by a natural and well-attested metaphoric shift to the body politic and the devastated land. The last three stanzas (21–31) shift the focus from people to Zion/Jerusalem, but continuity is still maintained by repeating the injunction about orphans and widows (23 cf. 17). Verses 21–23 and 24–26 are bracketed together by means of the inclusive reference to Loyal Town, City of Righteousness. The concluding stanza introduces a quite different criterion of moral judgment: not neglect of social justice but addiction to syncretic cults of the kind excoriated in somewhat similar terms in the last section of the book (57:1–13; 65:1–12; 66:17). This gives the terms "justice" and "righteousness" in 27 a meaning quite different from the usual prophetic connotation of the hendiadys "justice and righteousness."

The proposal that this first chapter recapitulates themes found throughout Isaiah, and that it runs parallel thematically and linguistically with the final chapters of the book, has been put forward with increasing frequency over the last two or three decades (e.g. Liebreich; Fohrer; Becker; Lack 1973, 139–41; Sweeney 1988, 21–24; Tomasino). The concern to recontextualize, re-edit, and recycle older prophecies to make them serviceable to a later readership is of course apparent in this first chapter as it is throughout the book. But much of this material, most clearly the diatribe against the sacrificial cult (10–17), carries forward a tradition of protest anchored in the eighth century B.C.E. and finding its most striking expression in Amos. But in any case significant thematic and linguistic parallels with the final chapters of Isaiah seem to be limited to the last stanza in our poem (27–31). Both of these points will be more fully expounded as the commentary proceeds.

Setting aside the last stanza (27–31), then, which appears to derive from the same quasi-apocalyptic mentality as is represented in the final chapters of the book, certain Deuteronomistic allusions and echoes noted here and there (especially in vv 18–20) have suggested to some commentators (e.g. Kaiser; Rignell; Vermeylen) the idea that the poem was either composed by a Deuteronomistic author of the sixth century B.C.E. as a prologue to the Isaian compilation or at least directly influenced by Deuteronomistic theology in the post-disaster era. There are indeed some striking parallels with the Song of Moses (Deut 32) noted even by such early commentators as Ibn Ezra and Calvin, which the reader can easily verify: the appeal to heaven and earth (Deut 32:1), Yahveh as the father of degenerate children (5–6, 20), eating the produce of the land (13), the hiding of God's face (20), judgment by fire and destruction by the sword (22, 25, 42a), divine vengeance (35–36, 41b, 43) and, in general, the strongly forensic language in which the indictment is cast. But much of this language is conventional and by no means confined to Deuteronom(ist)ic writings, so a verdict of not proven seems appropriate (see most recently Brekelmans).

Like much of the Isaianic material printed as verse in MT and modern translations, this composition approximates more closely a kind of heavily accented *recitative* or high rhetorical prose than poetry as generally understood, though we will with some licence nevertheless call it a poem. This "high style" will unavoidably fall into sound units arranged in alternating patterns of two or three stresses. In 10–17 the pattern is mostly 3–2, which is also the form of the lament, "limping" measure or *qînâ*, as in 21–23.

2–3. The poem opens with a complaint of Yahveh about the perfidy of Israel, a complaint addressed to heaven and earth, i.e., the entire creation. Since Yahveh is referred to in the third person in 4, it seems that this discourse is limited to the first stanza. The combination "hear/give heed" (*šimʿû, haʾăzînû*) is of frequent occurrence in poetic contexts in Isaiah (1:10; 28:23; 32:9; 42:23; 51:4; 64:3) and elsewhere (e.g. Gen 4:23; Num 23:18; Judg 5:3; Jer 13:15; Ps 5:1–2). The rhetorical call for attention is one of the most characteristic stylistic features of prophetic diatribe and protreptic. Addressed to heaven and earth, it has a certain Deuteronomic resonance (Deut 32:1 cf. 4:26; 30:19; 31:28) suggestive of the indictment or arraignment following covenant violation, which in its turn has taken over a familiar pattern in treaties between the great powers and their vassals (Harvey). We come across a similar cluster of topoi in the Deuteronomic Ps 50: appeal to heaven and earth as witnesses against faithless Israel, covenant linked with sacrifice, and denunciation of worship divorced from moral conduct. The familial imagery is also reminiscent of Deuteronomy, including the death penalty on the rebellious son (*bēn-sôrēr* Deut 21:18–21 cf. Isa 30:1), though the verb used here in the first verse, as in the last verse of the book (66:24), is *pšʿ* not *srr*.

An entire historical tradition is summarized in Yahveh as the one who reared and cared for Israel in its formative period, cf. Hos 9:10–15 also with the verb *gdl* (Piel). The description of Israel's response in political rather than familial terms, i.e., as rebellion (*pšʿ*), is a prophetic commonplace (cf. Hos 7:13; Jer 2:8, 29; 33:8; Ezek 2:3; Isa 43:27; 48:8) and will recur at the very end of the book (66:24). The unflattering contrast with ox and donkey implies a *qal vahomer* (a fortiori) type of argument and sets up the Hosean theme of Israel's failure to recognize the God who is the true donor (Hos 2:10[8] cf. Deut 32:15). It is also in keeping with the didacticism of the sages to draw on the observation of nature, including animal behavior, for guidelines to human conduct. None of this is necessarily inconsistent with Isaian authorship.

The allusion to ox and ass has also suggested the familiar scenario of the Christmas crib that made its debut in Assisi in 1223, one of many ways in which Christian culture, art, and piety are indebted to Isaiah (Sawyer 1996). Parenthetically, the pious and harmless belief that the ox and ass worshiped Christ in the manger provided Calvin with another occasion for anti-Papist polemic: "they have falsely alleged that the oxen and asses in the stall worshiped Christ when he was born; by which they show themselves to be egregious asses" (*Commentary on the Prophet Isaiah*, 1.41).

4. As it stands, this stanza is a separate woe-oracle, though the poet's main point may have been to open with the alliterative and staccato *hôy gôy ḥōṭēʾ*, "woe sinful nation." (As suggested by Ibn Ezra, *hôy* may have simply served as a vocative, as in Zech 2:10–11.) The gloss is limited to the last two words of the verse (*nāzōrû ʾāḥôr*). The stanza develops the situation set up in 2–3 with a step-by-step description of Israelites: first, as a nation like any other (*gôy*); then, a large-scale kinship group (*ʿam*); then a familial unit (*zeraʿ*); finally coming back to the "children" (*bānîm*) of Yahveh's household castigated in the first

stanza. The title "Holy One of Israel" (*qĕdôš yiśrā'ēl*) is characteristic of Isaiah but occurs with greatest frequency in chs. 40–66 and passages in 1–39 of Second Temple origin. It is also found in apposition to "Yahveh [leader] of the hosts [of heaven]" (*YHVH ṣĕbā'ôt*, 5:24; 47:4; 54:5; hereafter simply "Yahveh of the hosts"). Isaiah's vision of the seraphim proclaiming the holiness of Yahveh (6:1–13) does not oblige us to conclude that this title originated with Isaiah. In fact, it more probably derives from the liturgy of the Jerusalem temple (cf. Ps 71:22; 78:41; 89:19) and, further back, from the war prophecy of Israel's beginnings in association with the ark (1 Sam 1:3, 11; 3:3; 4:4).

5–6. The opening rhetorical question is addressed to a plurality, but the description is that of a bruised and battered individual. If we assume a carry-over from the familial metaphor of 2–4, the corporal punishment inflicted on this rebellious son would be severe, not to say dangerously abusive, even by the draconian standards enunciated in the pedagogical aphorisms and instructions of the ancient Near East including Israel (e.g. Prov 10:13; 13:24; 19:18; 22:15; 29:15). Some recent commentators have suggested comparison with the last of Duhm's "servant songs" (ch. 53). Both passages use some of the same terms for medical conditions and procedures, but the language is really not very close. Following targumic tradition Rashi understood this section as a metaphoric expression of the effect of sin on the entire people from the leadership (the head) to the least (the sole of the foot). The key to this image of the abused and untreated body he found in the following stanza: "what has been said hitherto in figurative expressions is now repeated in plain language" (Ibn Ezra).

7–9. The image presented here describes the result of hostile military action rather than earthquake (pace Hayes and Irvine, 1987, 69–73), though there may be echoes of the great earthquake during Uzziah's reign elsewhere in the book (5:25; 9:7–9, 18 [9:8–10, 19] cf. Amos 1:1; Zech 14:5). The situation—devastation, provincial cities burned to the ground, invasion or occupation by hostile forces living off the land, Jerusalem barely surviving—could conceivably refer to more than one historical juncture in the history of Judah. Since we do not know the extent of the damage inflicted during the invasion of the Syrian-Israelite army in 734–733, most commentators have sensibly concluded that Sennacherib's campaign during the reign of Hezekiah (701 B.C.E.) makes the best fit (see Emerton 1993 and the commentary below on 7:1–2). This would not of course rule out a rereading of the stanza in the light of later circumstances, though no event known to us, neither the Babylonian conquest nor the disaster reported to Nehemiah in Susa in 445 B.C.E. (Neh 1:1–3), quite fits this description. But even if taken to refer to the aftermath of Sennacherib's devastation of Judah in 701 (cf. 37:31–32), the allusion to a few survivors (*śārîd kim'āt*, 9) would have had poignant resonance for readers in the immediate post-disaster period, whether in Judah or elsewhere.

A notable feature of this stanza is the distinction between Judah and Jerusalem. The latter is called "daughter Zion" (*bat-ṣiyyôn*, appositional genitive), a title occurring in most sections of the book (10:32; 16:1; 37:22; 52:2; 62:11). Jerusalem is the only thing left standing, but only just. With the metaphors of "lean-to" and "shack," both impermanent and precarious structures, we may compare Sennacherib's reference to Hezekiah shut up in the city "like a bird in a cage" (*ANET*, 288).

It makes little difference whether we read *nĕṣûrâ* (→ *nsr*, "guard") or *nĕṣôrâ* (→ *ṣûr*, besiege) at 8b (the consonantal text allows for either), since the reference is clearly to a besieged or defended city.

10–17. We detect some thematic connection with the preceding stanza in that the ritual appeasement of the deity would tend to be intensified in times of crisis, which remains true even if some of the religious observances mentioned here are more or less routine. Critique of worship continues another protest theme common to the first generation of classical prophecy (cf. Hos 4:6; Amos 5:21–24; Mic 6:6–8). The poem is couched in the form of divine instruction (*tôrâ*) or response to a question, perhaps in sarcastic imitation of a priestly *tôrâ* (cf. Amos 4:4–5), perhaps during or shortly after a sacrificial liturgy. It is addressed to the rulers (*qĕṣînîm*, as 3:6–7; 22:3) of Sodom and the people of Gomorrah. By the time of writing, the Cities of the Plain had come to exemplify egregious social disorder and injustice (as also 3:9; Jer 23:14 and Ezekiel's caricature of Jerusalem as "sister Sodom," 16:46–56) as well as annihilating divine judgment, which such conduct warranted (Isa 13:19; Jer 49:18; 50:40; Amos 4:11; Zeph 2:9). For emphasis on homosexual conduct we have to wait until the Hellenistic period. Primary targets of these attacks in the eighth century prophets are state cults in both kingdoms (Bethel, Dan, Samaria, Jerusalem) that not only provided religious legitimation for an expansive and oppressive state apparatus but also imposed heavy economic burdens of their own. Temple personnel in the service of the state were tax-exempt, economic support of the cult was not optional, and the sacrificial system represented a significant drain on livestock. Perhaps the most remarkable aspect of this diatribe is the questioning of the requirement, written into the so-called Covenant Code in much the same terms as here (Exod 23:15, 17 with *lērā'ôt*, "to appear," cf. the version in Deut 16:16), that adult males present themselves at the state sanctuary three times a year. In the name of Yahveh Amos also rejects festival (*ḥag*) and cultic assembly (*ʿăṣārâ*) celebrated with liturgical music (5:21, 23), to which perhaps the rejection of liturgical prayer (*tepillâ*) in our passage corresponds. New moon and sabbath, with their stipulated animal and cereal offerings (cf. Ezek 45:17; 46:1–8; Num 29:6; 2 Chr 2:3; 8:13; 31:3; Neh 10:34), are also rejected. In Isaiah, as in his near-contemporaries Amos and Micah, animal sacrifice seems to have aroused the strongest negative reaction (cf. Amos 5:22; Mic 6:6–7), more than the cereal and incense offerings, and continued to do so long after this time (e.g. Isa 66:1–4), no doubt because it could be so easily exploited to the advantage of temple personnel. The suet (*ḥēleb*) was the portion reserved for the deity and therefore burned (for "suet" rather than "fat" see Milgrom, 1991, 205–7). There is no reason why this critique of the state cult, which has nothing in common with Deuteronomic or Asaphite theology (pace Kaiser 1972, 27–28), could not have originated in eighth century B.C.E. Judah.

As in the passages in Amos 5:24 and Mic 6:8, our poem closes with the contrast between liturgical religiosity on the one hand and justice and righteousness on the other. The prejudicial interpretation of these texts by liberal Protestant scholars in the nineteenth and early twentieth centuries, in the sense of the contrast between a materialistic, *opus operatum* religion and the religion of the heart, something like their idea of theology and praxis in Roman Catholicism and, more remotely, Judaism, should not lead us to overcompensate by gainsaying the force and passion with which the contrast is expressed. In this instance the first requirement is purification. The washing of bloodstained hands is symbolic of moral cleansing, for the second of the two verbs (*hizzakkû*, "purify yourselves") pre-eminently carries the meaning of moral and inner purification (e.g. Ps 73:13; Job 15:14; Prov 20:9). We recall Hector's plea (*Iliad* 6.268) that he cannot pray imbued with blood and dust. But inner change must be certified by action in the sphere of social and political relations, especially by action on behalf of the marginal—the oppressed and, among those, the orphans and widows, who were charter members of the underprivileged class in eighth century B.C.E. Palestine. We might compare the formulation of the requirements of social morality required for participating in temple cult listed—in the form of a decalogue—in Ps 15. At this point of the poem the wording suggests that ceasing to do evil deeds is a punctual affair, simply a matter of stopping, but to lead a morally positive life implies a *process*, something that must be practiced and learned, which is surely the case.

18–20. The prospect of washing out scarlet and crimson dye creates a catchword link with the washing of bloodstained hands in the previous stanza. In the present section of the poem four conditional sentences are introduced with the kind of forensic language with which the poem begins (2–3). The precise meaning of the verb (*ykḥ* Niphal v 18) is uncertain. If it is taken in the context of an arraignment or indictment—perhaps in the sense of NRSV "let us argue it out"—we should probably read the rest of the verse as if asking, rhetorically and perhaps sarcastically, how Israel can claim to be sinless (Duhm 1892, 32). I have taken it more in the sense of settling out of court, and therefore the questions are not really rhetorical; they are answered in the second pair of conditionals that state the options in the contractual terms of Deuteronomic morality. The ensuing prospect is clearly inconsistent with the scene describing devastation by the sword as a *fait accompli* (7–9). It is also discontinuous with the quite different agenda of the following stanza, to which we now turn.

21–26. The inclusio of Loyal Town, Righteous City (21, 26) marks this off as a distinct stanza composed of indictment (21–23) and verdict, the latter introduced with the customary *lākēn* ("therefore") and identified as a distinct oracle (*nĕ'ûm* 24). The stanza begins as a lament (*'êkâ*, "see how . . .") in a modified *qînâ* (lament) meter, "echoing rhythm," or "limping measure" (3:2 + 2:2), but very soon disintegrates into the customary recitative pattern. Since sound is also part of sense we offer this one example of the Hebrew with accented syllables marked (21–24; glosses in square brackets):

'êkâ hayetá lĕzônâ
qiryá ne'ĕmāná
mĕlé'ătî mišpāṭ
ṣedeq yālín bâ
[vĕ'attâ mĕraṣṣĕḥîm]
kaspék hayá lĕsîgîm
sob'ék māhûl [bammáyîm]
śārayik sôrĕrîm
vĕḥabrê gannābîm
kūllô 'ōhéb šōḥad
vĕrōdép šalmōnîm
yātôm lo' yišpôṭû
vĕríb 'almāná lō'-yabô' 'ălêhém

There is a decisive shift of focus here from the people as a whole to Jerusalem, with only an echo of 16–17 in the allusion to the city's justice and righteousness, now long gone, and the neglect of orphans and widows. The metaphors descriptive of the state of Jerusalem are somewhat scattershot—prostitution, tarnished silver, watered down beer (*sobé'* cf. Hos 4:18; Nah 1:10). Here as elsewhere (3:1–5; 5:18–23; 30:1–5) the target is the ruling class, and more particularly the princes or courtiers (*śarîm*) who served in an administrative, military, and judicial capacity. Subversion of the judicial process, especially by bribery, was a major target of eighth century prophetic protest against the abusive power of the state and its functionaries (cf. Amos 5:10, 12; Mic 3:9, 11; Isa 5:23; 33:15), and can be compared with the situation in Greece reflected in the writings of Hesiod about the same time (e.g. *Works and Days* 263) and in the legislation of Solon some two centuries later designed to limit the arbitrary power of the *aristoi*.

The verdict is announced as an oracle of Yahveh, who is characterized by three epithets: the "lord" (*'ādôn*), "Yahveh of the hosts" (YHVH *ṣĕbā'ôt*), and the "Strong One of Israel" (*'ăbîr yiśrā'ēl*). All occur elsewhere in the book. The first (also combined with YHVH *ṣĕbā'ôt* in 19:4) occurs as a divine title in Phoenician texts and may have passed into Jerusalemite usage (cf. the names Adonibezek, Adonizedek, Adonijah) and the Jerusalem cult from that source. The second (elsewhere in 3:15; 10:23–24; 19:4; 22:5, 12, 14–15; 28:22) is also derived from the official Jerusalemite liturgy. In the more usual form *'ăbîr ya'ăqōb*, the third title is found in the latter part of the book (49:26; 60:16), in a pilgrimage psalm (Ps 132:2, 5), and in the oracle of Jacob on Joseph (Gen 49:24). It seems to have originated in the territory of the Northern Kingdom, perhaps as a demythologized aspect of the Bethel cult of Yahveh symbolized as bull (*'ăbîr* for *'abbîr*; Duhm 1892, 34, wondered whether Isaiah would have been as solicitous as the Masoretes about the spelling of the word). The verdict pronounced by Yahveh opens with a typically Isaianic play on words (*'ennāḥēm, 'innāqĕmâ*), the morphologically related stems *nḥm* and *nqm* (Niphal) meaning, respectively, "to get and feel satisfaction at another party's expense" (*Schadenfreude*) and "to avenge oneself." This poet is clearly not afraid to use strongly anthropopathic language. The enemies in question are the state officials castigated in the previous stanza, even though the city of Jerusalem is addressed in what follows.

It seems that a hemistich is missing after *vě'ašîbâ yadî 'āláyîk* ("I will turn my hand against you" 25a) which, however, is the last note of pure threat in this poem (cf. Amos 1:8b; Zech 13:7; Ps 81:15). Thereafter the image is that of refining precious metal in the smelting oven (*kûr*) by removing the base alloy. The same image, using the same relatively rare terms (*sîg, bědîl*, here "slag" and "dross," respectively, though *bědîl* also means "alloy" and, more specifically, "tin"), is used in Ezek 22:18–22 to describe besieged Jerusalem as a smelting oven. Purification is to be followed by restoration, and in the first place the restoration of a just and sound *political* order represented by upright judges (*šōpěṭîm*) and high-level state officials (*yō'āṣîm*, "counselors"). Since this prospect for the future is still addressed to Jerusalem, the idealized past is presumably that of the city under Davidic rule. The final stich (26b), which does not scan, reads like an additional comment that develops the prospect of restoration in 26a by referring back to 21.

27–31. Unlike 24–26, this last stanza is not oracular. It is a comment by a seer that gathers together and brings the preceding stanzas to a resolution. Several commentators take it to be a fragment appended to the poem (Clements 1980, 37, Wildberger 1991, 70 et al.), but if so it is a deliberate addition with a definite and very different perspective, and it comes from a time when the book was in the final stages of its formation. I take it to be the first of several indications, to be noted in due course, of a remodeling and reshaping of the received Isaianic material in the post-destruction period in keeping with a specific, pietistic, even sectarian point of view. The crucial point is the distinction within the Israel addressed by the seer between the "penitents" and the obdurate. It presents the prospect of a final act of judgment in which this distinction, now obscure, will be made manifest, and the invisible line dividing the elect and the reprobate will be clearly drawn. This is a very familiar feature of apocalyptic. One indication is the semantic shift in the use of the key terms *mišpāṭ* and *ṣĕdāqâ*. In Isaiah and the prophetic tradition in which he functioned, indeed earlier on in the same poem (17, 21), these terms (usually translated "justice" and "righteousness") encapsulate the idea of a social order solicitous for the rights of individuals, especially of the most vulnerable and marginal (e.g. Amos 5:24; 6:12; Mic 3:1, 8–9; 6:8; Isa 5:7, 16; 10:2). In later usage, here and elsewhere in Isaiah, the same terms, either singly or in combination as a hendiadys, connote judgment rather than justice, an intervention in the affairs of Israel and the nations that spells both punishment and vindication depending on criteria laid down by the seer in question (e.g. Isa 3:14; 4:4; 28:6; 34:5; 41:1). The shift towards a decidedly future-oriented perspective is particularly apparent in contexts in which *ṣĕdāqâ* by itself connotes vindication and salvation (e.g. 51:6, 8; 56:1; 59:9, 16–17; 61:10–11; 63:1).

The criteria for distinguishing between the elect and the reprobate are also quite different in this final stanza. We hear no more of violations of the social contract with the economically disadvantaged but only of aberrations in matters of worship condemned in much the same terms as in the last eleven chapters of the book (57:1–13; 65:1–16; 66:17, 24). That this final stanza of the poem derives from the same intellectual and religious milieu as these passages in the last section of the book is also clear from the language: the elect are "penitents" (*šābîm* cf. 59:20); the reprobate are rebels (*pōšĕ'îm* cf. 66:24) who forsake Yahveh ('*ōzĕbê YHVH* cf. 65:11) and positively choose (stem *bḥr*) non-Yahvistic cults (cf. 65:12; 66:3–4). There is a hint in this last stanza of eschatological shame (cf. 65:13; 66:5) consequent on addiction to dubious cults carried out under terebinths (cf. 57:5; 61:3) and in gardens (65:3; 66:17). There is also the prospect of final judgment presented in the nightmare image of unquenchable fire (cf. 66:24). All of this places the reader of the poem on a new plane of observation, providing a different and more disconcerting vantage point which brings the entire first chapter into sharper and clearer focus.

Read continuously, this first literary unit in the book delivers a fairly coherent message even though stitched together out of brief discourses and poems. In dramatically figurative and hyperbolic language typical of much prophetic discourse it denounces first the people of Israel as a whole (2–9), then the civil and religious leadership (10–20), and finally Jerusalem (21–26). God is spoken of as *paterfamilias*, reflecting a situation in which the discretionary judicial power of the (male) head of the household had not yet been curtailed by state encroachment. The uncompromising tone, the anger and hostility evident throughout, are in reaction to the violence that denies justice to those deprived of power and uses conventional religious practices as a means to legitimate and perpetuate the denial. The disasters of military defeat, foreign occupation, death, and destruction are related to social injustices by a theory of moral causality that, though not free of ambiguities, is also not without explanatory power. In the final stanza (27–31) the implications of this situation are drawn out in terms of the radical dichotomies and discontinuities of apocalyptic.

A SECOND TITLE (2:1)

(Ackroyd 1963; Sweeney 1988, 30–32)

TRANSLATION

2 [1]The word that Isaiah ben Amoz saw in vision concerning Judah and Jerusalem.

COMMENTS

This verse is one of several titles that employ the verb "see in vision" (*ḥāzâ*) together with "word" (*dābār*) or "words" (*děbārîm*) or "oracle" (*maśśāʾ*) and are therefore different from the first title, which uses the term "vision" (*ḥāzôn*) for the book as a whole in keeping with later usage. Since there is no further superscription until 13:1, which introduces sayings against foreign nations, we suspect that 2:1 was introduced at a considerably earlier stage than 1:1 as the title to chs. 2–12 (Gray 1912, 40 and others) rather than to chs. 2–4 (Sweeney) or 2:2–4 (Ackroyd; Kaiser 1972, 48).

THE PILGRIMAGE OF THE NATIONS TO ZION (2:2–5)

(Barth 1977, 191–92; Budde 1927; Cannawurf; Cazelles 1980; Clifford; Jensen 1973; Kselman; Lipiński; Loretz 1984; Magonet; von Rad 1966; Sweeney 1988, 134–39; Wildberger 1957, 81–96; Willis 1997; Wolff 1984)

TRANSLATION

2 ²It will come to pass in days to come
 that the mountain, Yahveh's house, shall be established
 at the top of the mountains,
 raised high over the hills.
 Then all nations shall stream towards it,
 ³many peoples shall come and say,[a]
 "Up, let us go to Yahveh's mountain,[b]
 to the house of Jacob's God,
 that he may instruct us[c] in his ways
 that we may walk in his paths."
 For from Zion instruction will proceed,
 the word of Yahveh from Jerusalem.
 ⁴He will adjudicate among nations,
 arbitrate for many peoples.[d]
 They shall beat their swords into plowshares,
 their spears into pruning hooks.
 No nation shall take up[e] the sword against another,
 no more shall they learn to make war.
 ⁵O household of Jacob, come, let us walk in the light of Yahveh!

NOTES

Fragments of text from this passage in 4QIsa[b,e,f] show only slight orthographic variations;   [a] cf. Mic 4:1 *yihyeh . . . nākôn; věniśśāʾ hûʾ miggěbāʿôt; ʿammîm, gôyîm* reversed;   [b] QIsa[a] omits *'el-har-* YHVH;   [c] 1QIsa[a] *vyrvnv* for MT *vyrnv*;   [d] cf. Mic 4:3a *věšāpaṭ bên ʿammîm rabbîm věhôkîaḥ lěgôyîm ʿăṣū-mîm ʿad-rāḥôq*;   [e] cf. Mic 4:3c *yiśʾû* (pl.).

COMMENTS

That chs. 2–4 constitute a distinct unit is indicated by the prediction of a restored and exalted Jerusalem at the beginning (2:1–5) and a similarly future-oriented passage, about the same length, at the end (4:2–6), both in recitative or rhythmic prose. This literary technique of bracketing implies that the judgment threatened in 2:6–4:1 now, after the catastrophe of 586, lies in the past, making space for a different perspective on the future. Both bracketing passages are introduced with formulae indicative of a future-oriented but not necessarily eschatological perspective. "On that day" (*bayyôm hahûʾ* 4:2) is one of the more common prophetic-predictive incipits in the book, whereas *běʾaḥărît hayyāmîm*, literally, "at the end of the days," does occur elsewhere but not in Isaiah, sometimes as a vague indication of the future (Deut 4:30; Jer 23:20; Ezek 38:16; Hos 3:5) but also introducing an oracular saying (Gen 49:1; Num 24:14; Ezek 38:16). These and similar formulas contribute to this thrust towards the future that is one of the most impressive features of the prophetic books.

The passage occurs with variations, for the most part a matter of word order except for the ending, in Mic 4:1–5. (See notes on the text.) After the prediction of universal disarmament, the latter adds the prospect of the eschatological abolition of fear, with everyone sitting under the proverbial vine and fig tree, "for the mouth of Yahveh of the hosts has spoken" (4:4b). The scenario reflects one of the rare occasions for euphoria in the post-disaster period, perhaps following on the accession of Cyrus (Sweeney 1996, 99). The Micah version then adds "for all the peoples walk each one in the name of its God, but we walk in the name of Yahveh our God for ever and ever" (4:5), a statement echoed in our passage with "O house of Jacob, come let us walk in the light of Yahveh." Every possible explanation of this duplication has been given at one time or another—Isaiah borrowed from Micah, Micah from Isaiah (Duhm; Gray; Wildberger)—it entered both books from an earlier, Korahite liturgical composition from the late fifth or early fourth century (Kaiser), or from some other source (Sweeney 1988, 165–69). That variants of the same textual tradition appear in different places is neither strange nor of rare occurrence—compare Obad 1–7 with Jer 49:9–10, 14–16 and Ps 14 with Ps 53. In this instance certainty is unattainable, but it seems that the complex of topoi represented in the passage (see the next paragraph) is more at home in Isaiah than in Micah. Besides, Jerusalem as the place from which moral instruction irradiates is very much a Second Temple *Isaian* theme ("instruction [*tôrâ*] will go out from me, and my justice as a light for the peoples," 51:4), perhaps not unconnected with the origins of proselytism. The idea of final disarmament and the abolition of war is also distinctively though not exclusively Isaian (9:4[5]; 11:6–9 cf. 60:18; 65:25). It appears, moreover, that Mic 5:9–14[10–15]) has borrowed motifs and turns of phrase from the poem about judgment on faithless Israel in Isa 2:6–22. Joel 4:9–12 also borrows from Isa 2:2 but turns it upside down—plowshares are to be beaten into swords, pruning hooks into spears. There is also a strong possibility that the conclusion to Mic 4:1–4—"for the mouth of Yahveh of the hosts has spoken" (*kî-pî YHVH ṣĕbā'ôt dibbēr*)—refers back to the Isaian parallel, especially since this is the only occurrence of the Isaian title *YHVH ṣĕbā'ôt* in Micah.

Isaiah 2:2–5 is a collage of Zion themes that we encounter in all sections of the book: Jerusalem as cosmic mountain at the center of the world (10:12, 32; 11:9; 16:1; 25:6, 7, 10; 29:8; 30:29; 31:4; 37:32; 40:9; 57:13; 65:26), with the temple as its epicenter (4:5; 8:18; 18:7; 24:23; 27:13; 56:7; 65:11; 66:20); the convergence of Gentiles on Jerusalem in different capacities: as pilgrims (45:14–23; 60:1–18), as participants in or observers of the final showdown or singularity in Jerusalem (25:6–8; 55:5; 56:6–8; 60:1–7; 62:2; 66:18–19, 21, 23), as escorts for Judean repatriates (49:22; 60:8–9; 66:20), bearers of tribute, or *Gastarbeiter*, and slaves (14:1–2; 18:7; 49:23; 60:6–18; 61:5–7; 66:12). Similar passages in early Second Temple texts (e.g. Hag 2:7–9; Zech 2:14–16; 8:20–23) help us to locate this kind of exalted "Zionist" mythopoesis, which seems to have crystallized in the prophetic propaganda and cult of Judeo-Babylonian repatriates in the first half-century of Persian rule, though by no means confined to that time. In the last section of the book we will have more than one occasion to note how quite different and often incompatible views on relations with Gentiles coexisted throughout the entire period of the Second Commonwealth.

Notwithstanding the Masoretic *petuḥa* divider (ס), indicating the beginning of a new paragraph, the final v 5 is an exhortation to "the household of Jacob" to take up the invitation addressed to Gentiles immediately preceding. In addition, it serves to link up with the following poem, which opens with the same designation. Like *'ĕlōhê ya'ăqōb* ("the God of Jacob"), the phrase *bêt ya'ăqōb* ("the household of Jacob") became popular in the Second Temple period and is well represented in Isaiah (e.g. 46:3; 48:1; 58:1), even more so in liturgical hymns (Psalms 20, 46, 75, 76, 81, 84, 94). (In Isa 2:3 "the house of the God of Jacob" refers to the temple.) In this respect it is hardly coincidental that the story of the patriarch Jacob's exile in Mesopotamia and return (Gen 25–35) mirrors the experience of deported and repatriated Judeans beginning in the sixth century B.C.E. The invitation to walk in the light of Yahveh also reflects a prominent motif in the later chapters of Isaiah. Unlike the Zoroastrian deity Ahuramazda, Yahveh creates both light and darkness (45:7) and turns darkness into light (42:16); and this light will eventually be available not to the household of Jacob alone but to the nations of the world as well, though not unconditionally (42:6–7; 49:6; 51:4; 60:3). In view of our own sad and guilty knowledge of the violence we continue to visit on each other, on other creatures, and on the environment in general, the eschatological horizon of the abolition of war, and even of violence in the animal world (11:6–9), is one of the most poignant motifs in the book.

THE FINAL JUDGMENT (2:6–22)

(Baker; Blenkinsopp; Cathcart; Davidson; Everson; Jamieson-Drake; Jenni; Milgrom; Sweeney 1988, 139–46, 174–77)

TRANSLATION

2   [6]For[a] you have rejected your people,
the household of Jacob,
for they are full (of sorcerers)[b] from the east
and soothsayers like the Philistines.
They teem[c] with the children of foreigners.
[7]Their land is full of silver and gold,
and there is no end to their treasures;
their land is full of horses,
and there is no end to their chariots;
[8]their land is full of idols
(and there is no end to their idolatry).[d]
To the work of their hands they bow down,
to that which their fingers have made.[e]

[9]*Humanity is humbled, all people are brought low;*
Do not forgive them![f]
[10]Go into the rock,
hide in the dusty earth
from the terror of Yahveh,
from the splendor of his majesty![g]

[11]The proud regard of humanity is brought low,
the pride of all people shall be humbled,
and Yahveh alone shall be exalted
on that day.[h]

[12]For Yahveh of the hosts has a day
against all that is haughty and high,
all that is lifted up and lofty,[i]
[13]against all the cedars of Lebanon [high and lofty],[j]
all the oaks of Bashan,
[14]against all the high mountains,
all the lofty hills,
[15]against every high tower,
every impregnable[k] wall,
[16]against all the Tarshish ships,
all the splendid vessels.

¹⁷The pride of humanity will be humbled,
the haughtiness of the people will be brought low,
and Yahveh alone shall be exalted
on that day.
¹⁸[The idols will utterly pass away.] ¹
¹⁹They will go into caves in the rock,
into caverns in the dusty earth,
from the terror of Yahveh,
from the splendor of his majesty,
when he begins to strike fear on the earth.
²⁰*On that day people will throw out their silver and gold idols that they made
as their own objects of worship to the shrews and the bats,*ᵐ
²¹to go into the crevices of the rocks,
the clefts of the cliffs,
from the terror of Yahveh,
from the splendor of his majesty,
when he begins to strike fear on the earth.
²²*Leave the rest of humanity alone; doomed to perish as
they are, of what value are they?*

NOTES

Probable editorial additions are printed in italics, glosses in square brackets, and words supplied in parentheses. The textual notes of George Buchanan Gray (1912, 57–60) on this difficult passage, though of course pre-Qumranic, are still interesting and valuable.　　ᵃ Here and at v12 *kî* is a connective particle (cf. 3:1, 6, 8; 8:11) rather than asseverative ("surely");　　ᵇ parallelism suggests adding *qôsĕmîm* or *kĕšāpîm* (cf. Mic 5:11) before *miqqedem*, cf. Tg. 1QIsaᵃ and 4QIsaᵇ, which are identical with MT;　　ᶜ *śāpaq* (Hiphil) is hapax; for this meaning see 1 Kgs 20:10; Job 20:22 *śepeq*, "abundance," and MH *śapaq*, "to be sufficient"; the meaning "shake, clap or slap hands," connoting trade relations, would practically require emending *ûbĕyaldê* to *ûbĕyādê* "with the hands [of foreigners]"; LXX "and many foreign children are born to them" (cf. Hos 5:7) is hardly an improvement;　　ᵈ the parallel stich seems to have fallen out; perhaps *vĕʾên qēṣeh lĕʾaṣĕbōtâv*, "and there is no end to their idolatrous images" (cf. Duhm 41);　　ᵉ added in place of the missing stich; ᶠ missing from 1QIsaᵃ but not from 4QIsaᵃ and 4QIsaᵇ, both of which have *vĕlōʾ* for *vĕʾal*;　　ᵍ v 10 missing from 1QIsaᵃ but not from 4QIsaᵃ and 4QIsaᵇ; ʰ the variants 2:17 and 5:15 suggest that the order of vv 10 and 11 may have been reversed to connect with 12 by means of *bayyôm hahûʾ*;　　ⁱ MT has *vĕšāpēl*, "and it will be brought low";　　ʲ *hārāmîm vĕhanniśśāʾîm*, which overloads the line, has been added;　　ᵏ reading *bĕṣûrâ* as Qal passive participle → *bṣr* cf. 22:10 also with *ḥômâ*;　　ˡ pl. with LXX and 1QIsaᵃ;　　ᵐ for MT *laḥpōr pērôt* read *laḥăparpārôt* with LXX and 1QIsaᵃ; the conjecture of an original *laḥpor be'ērôt*, "to dig wells," i.e., to study Torah, a cryptic insertion of the Karaite Masoretes, is ingenious but unconvincing, pace Marx, 1990, 232–37.

COMMENTS

Picking our way through the editorial debris that has gradually accumulated in this passage, the worst preserved in the entire book according to Duhm (1892, 39), we discern the outline of a poem on Judgment Day composed, typically, of indictment (6–8) and verdict (12–16). One of the most obvious additions to this poetic core occurs at the end of the indictment ("to the work of their hands they bow down, to that which their fingers have made," 8b), being an example of standard anti-idolatry polemic of a kind frequently encountered in the second part of the book (40:18–20; 41:6–7; 44:9–20; 45:20), probably therefore from the late Neo-Babylonian or early Persian period. Prosodically even more obtrusive are vv 18 and 20. Together with other passages in Isaiah (30:19–22; 31:6–7), the latter predicts the final purging of the world of idols which, in this case, will be rendered ritually inaccessible by contact with unclean animals (the bat is certainly unclean, Lev 11:18 and Deut 14:18, the shrew probably so). The form in which v 20 is presented, a prose comment on a verse oracle beginning "on that day" (*bayyôm hahû'*), is also of frequent occurrence throughout the book.

A much later addition, and one absent from the parallel 5:15, as also from 1QIsa[a], is v 9b, the prayer or imprecation "do not forgive them" (the verb *nś'* also means "raise up," which allows for a punning connection with "all people are brought low" in the preceding line). Such harsh sentiments excluding the possibility of intercession or pardon on judgment day are characteristic of a certain strand of apocalyptic thinking (cf. 2 Esd 7:102–15). (Jerome translates 22b *quia excelsus reputatus est iste*, "for he is reckoned to be exalted" with reference to Christ.) A mind set similar to 2 Esdras also informs the final v 22, an admonition addressed not to God but to the purified remnant in Israel or, more specifically, to the seer's discipleship. Understood as an injunction to segregate themselves from the rest of humanity, it is quoted in the *Rule of the Qumran Community* (1QS V 17). This reading is more in keeping with the context than an expression of the transitory nature of human life in the manner of Qoheleth (as Kaiser 1959, 63).

The threefold repetition of variants of two stanzas, whole or fragmentary (10, 19, 21, taking refuge in caves and under rocks; 9a, 11, 17, the humbling of pride, also 5:15) raises the question whether these sentences can be read as refrains, such as feature in other Isaian poems (e.g. 5:25; 9:11, 16, 20; 10:4), or whether they simply constitute editorial accretions imperfectly assimilated to the original composition. Pace several of the commentators (e.g. Duhm 1892, 39–40; Gray 1912, 48; Auvray 1972, 55), the repeated injunction to take cover at the prospect of the imminent day of judgment (10, 19, 21 cf. also 26:20–21) is not well placed to serve as a refrain. Its last occurrence (21) looks rather like a variant of 19 separated from it by a brief *bayyôm hahû'* oracle in prose. We are therefore left with either an admonition to hide placed at the end of both indictment and verdict or one such injunction serving as a link between the two parts of the poem (10). In either case the effect is to give a note of immediacy, a sharper edge, to the message of the poetic core. The assertion that the high and mighty will be humbled and Yahveh exalted on that day also follows both sections of the poem (11, 17) and occurs somewhat later in a series of woe sayings (5:11–17). The way in which it is stated in this poem develops the theme of the verdict—the humiliation of power structures in the Syro-Palestinian region—in the direction of judgment on human pretensions in general.

We come now to what I have identified as the core of the passage, namely, the indictment and verdict: the former (vv 6–8) opens with direct address to Yahveh, though the OG translation has third person discourse ("he has rejected his people") and the Targum second person plural ("you have forsaken the fear of the Strong One . . . you of the house of Jacob"). Though some commentators have opted for OG (e.g. Gray 1912, 57; Duhm 1892, 39), there seems insufficient reason to prefer it to MT, and even less to read *bêt ya'ăqōb* ("household of Jacob") as vocative, as if the household of Jacob was abandoning its people, whatever that might mean. I suspect that "household of Jacob," a designation popular in the post-destruction period, is an editorial adaptation linking the poem with the preceding v 5 (see also "God of Jacob," v 3). The roughly parallel passage in Mic 5:9–14[10–15], which foresees the destruction of horses and chariots, cities and strongholds, sorcerers, soothsayers and idolatrous objects, represents a somewhat eschatologized version of the Isaian passage, one introduced with the standard *bayyôm hahû'* formula. The indictment explains why Yahveh has given up on his people: they are accused of sorcery and necromancy, consorting with foreigners, accumulating wealth and—a frequent concomitant of wealth in biblical texts—idolatry. The connection between the first two of these articles of indictment is apparent in the listing of forbidden means of mediation in Deut 18:9–14, forbidden precisely because foreign. Since necromancy was practiced at all times early and late in Israel during the biblical period (cf. Isa 57:3–10 for a late example), especially in times of crisis, it cannot be used to fix the date of this passage. These foreign influences come from east and west, the former not further specified, the latter identified as the Philistine cities. A parallel is at hand in Zeph 1–2 in which foreign presence and influence are attacked and the Philistines threatened with destruction (Zeph 1:8–9; 2:4–7). If the phrase "the children of foreigners" is taken literally, it would recall Nehemiah's distress at coming upon the children of Philistine and Moabite women who could no longer speak Hebrew (Neh 13:23–24), but that is not the most natural reading and, in any case, *yeled, yĕlādîm* is not confined to subadults.

The triadic and climactic denunciation of horses, chariots, and idols that follows is reminiscent of the kind of enumerative saying found in Proverbs (30:15–31) and Amos (1:3–2:8). Silver, gold, and treasures suggest a time of relative prosperity. In the prophetic tradition horses and chariots were symbolic of pride and power (e.g. Isa 30:15; 31:1; 43:17; Mic 5:9) and were also very expensive import items (cf. 1 Kgs 10:29—a horse cost seventy-five times as much as a sheep, and a chariot four times as much as a horse). Bullion and essential war equipment came with foreign trade, and foreign trade brought with it foreign cults. As to the specific time frame, if any, referred to here we can only speculate. Some (e.g. Whitehouse 1905, 102–4) have opted for the reign of Uzziah (ca. 783–742) who captured Elat (2 Kgs 14:22 cf. the Tarshish ships of Isa 2:16), built fortifications, and conquered the Philistine cities (2 Chr 26:6–15). Others (e.g. Clements 1980a, 43) prefer the reign of Ahaz (ca. 735–715), after the defeat of the Syrian-Samarian coalition, acceptance of Assyrian vassal status, and the construction of an Assyrian altar in Jerusalem (2 Kgs 16:10–16). The language is not precise enough to allow for a decision.

The verdict (vv 12–16) presents another variation on the much discussed theme of the Day of Yahveh (bibliography in Cathcart; Everson; Jenni) that, whatever its origins and prehistory, first comes to clear expression in eighth century prophecy, perhaps in Amos 5:18–20. The opening v 12, which presents the key to what follows with four epithets expressive of prideful eminence, is followed by eight features listed in pairs that are destined for destruction on the Day. The first and second of these are natural phenomena, and the third and fourth human constructions. Judgment is pronounced on human pretensions with special reference to the Syro-Palestinian and Levantine regions. The language suggests a life-threatening storm rather than the earthquake during Uzziah's reign (Amos 1:1 and Zech 14:5). As in Ps 29, the storm cuts a swathe from north to south, from the cedars of Lebanon and the oaks of Bashan east of the Jordan and the Sea of Galilee (cf. Ps 29:5,9; 68:15), through the Transjordanian highlands to the Gulf of Aqaba or, in Ps 29:8, the wilderness of Kadesh, but in any case not sparing the Kingdom of Judah. Tarshish ships, whatever the precise meaning of the designation may be (see most recently Baker and Wildberger 97), operated out of Elat (Aqaba) and their mention at this point hints once again at the ambiguities of trade relations seen from the prophetic point of view.

SOCIAL AND MORAL CHAOS (3:1–15)

(Holladay; Oded; Weil; Wildberger 1991, 123–61)

TRANSLATION

3   [1]For now the sovereign Lord of hosts
     will remove from Jerusalem and Judah
     every kind of support,[a]
     all supply of food,
     all supply of water;[b]

²mercenary and warrior,
magistrate and prophet,
diviner and elder,
³captain of fifty,
nobleman and counselor,
skilled magician[c] and expert in charms.
⁴"I will make striplings their princes;
infants will rule over them.
⁵The people will oppress one another,
each one his fellow;
the young will be insolent to the old,
the one of mean estate to the honorable."

⁶If a man were to grab hold of his kinsman in his paternal household and say to him, "You are the one with the cloak, so you shall be our leader, you must take control of this heap of ruins," ⁷he would answer on that day, "I will not be in charge;[d] there is neither food nor clothing in my house; you shall not appoint me leader of the people."

⁸Ah, Jerusalem has stumbled,
Judah has fallen[e]
for in word and in deed they oppose Yahveh,
defying his majestic presence.[f]
⁹Their very looks testify against them,[g]
they vaunt their sin openly like Sodom,
they do not conceal it.
Woe to them!
They have brought evil on themselves.
¹⁰A blessing on the righteous,[h] for it will go well with them,
they will eat the fruit of their labors;
¹¹a woe on the wicked, it will go badly with them,[i]
what they have done will be done to them.[j]
¹²As for my people, their oppressors plunder them,[k]
usurers[l] lord it over them;
O my people, your leaders mislead you,
confusing the course you should take.[m]

¹³Yahveh takes his stand to argue his case,
he rises to judge the peoples;[n]
¹⁴Yahveh enters into judgment
with the elders of his people and their princes:
"It is you who have ravaged the vineyard,
the plunder of the poor is in your houses.
¹⁵How dare you crush my people,
and stamp on the face of the poor?"
—An oracle of the sovereign Lord of hosts.

NOTES

[a] *Maš'ēn ûmaš'ēnâ*, repetition signifying totality (cf. Lev 15:2; Ezek 6:14) as noted by Ibn Ezra;   [b] "all supply of food, all supply of water" is often deleted as a gloss on the grounds that it deals with a different kind of deprivation (e.g. Gray 1912, 63; Duhm 1892, 44; Kaiser 1959, 66, 68; Wildberger 1991, 124) and could be taken for an explanatory of *maš'ēn ûmaš'ēnâ*, but the suggestion has no support either from the versions or from 1QIsaᵃ and there is no obvious metrical reason for its deletion;   [c] *ḥărāšîm* can also be translated "craftsmen," and is so understood in LXX and Vulg.;   [d] the primary meaning of *ḥōbēš* is a bandager of wounds, therefore a physician, but Tg. followed by Ibn Ezra and LXX (*archegos*) translate "ruler," which I follow here;   [e] 1QIsaᵃ corrects *nāpal* to *nāpĕlâ* since *yĕhûdâ* is feminine, but it can be masculine when referring to the population, e.g. Hos 5:13;   [f] literally, "the eyes of his majesty"; the defective writing of *'ênê* is corrected in 1QIsaᵃ;   [g] following LXX's rendering of *hakkārat pĕnêhem* and in keeping with the context; others translate "partiality," "bias" cf. Deut 1:17; 16:19;   [h] MT *'imrû ṣaddîq kî-ṭôb*, "say, how good is the righteous!" does not make good sense; 1QIsaᵃ *'mvrv lṣdyq*, "say to the righteous," is an improvement; others read *'āmĕrû*, "they say," followed by a proverbial saying, but in view of *'ôy* in the following colon it seems better to emend to *'ašrê*, "blessed . . ."; 9b–11 is often explained, speculatively, as an interpolation from a sapiential source;   [i] MT has simply *ra'*, "bad";   [j] literally, "for the retribution of his hands will be done to him"; 1QIsaᵃ reads *yāšûb lô*, "will return to him," for MT *yē'āśeh lô*, "will be done to him";   [k] following LXX (*kalamontai*), Tg., and Vulg. (*spoliaverunt*) as a verbal form (*'ōlĕlû*, "devastate") rather than reading *mĕ'ôlēl*, "infant"; G. R. Driver (1937, 38) reads it as a Polel form of a verb *'ll*, "oppress";   [l] LXX, Aquila, Theodotion, Tg. read *nōšîm*, "creditors, distrainers," for MT *nāšîm*, "women"; *nōšîm* may have been changed to *nāšîm* to align with *mĕ'ôlēl* = "infant";   [m] since it would be natural to end the passage with a blessing and woe, and since v 12 repeats the point made in vv 4–5, this verse may have been tagged on at a later date;   [n] reading *'ammô*, "his people," for MT *'ammîm*, "peoples," with LXX (*ton laon autou*) and Syr.; not therefore a reference to the Israelite tribes (as Duhm 47–48).

COMMENTS

Like ch. 1, this section consists of a number of loosely connected passages. The first (1–5) is verse only in the broad sense of rhythmic utterance, beginning quite prosaically but picking up the beat (alternating two and three stress units) with alliteration in v 1b, a prominent stylistic feature throughout the first part of the book (cf. *hôy gôy ḥōṭē'* 1:4, also 1:13b, 24b; 5:7b). In general, the rhythm picks up as the emotional level rises. This first passage begins as a statement of the seer but slips into *oratio recta* of the deity in 4–5. There follows a brief and vivid cameo scene (6–7) that serves as a kind of narrative illustration of the preceding saying (for similar "cameos" see 4:1 and Amos 3:12; 6:9–10). The state of civil disorder is then explained as a manifestation of moral disorder with particular reference to the arrogant and irreligious attitude of the leadership (8–12). The perspective on the fate of Jerusalem and Judah (for the order in which they are mentioned see the commentary on 1:1) may be anticipatory or retrospective, but the distinction between stumbling and falling fits the situation of 701 and not at all that of 586 B.C.E. (pace Kaiser 72). The blessing and woe amount to a universalizing comment characteristic of the didactic tradition which redirects the reader's attention from the political and social sphere to that of the destiny of the individual. As I suggested in the notes on the text, the final verse 12, in the form of a complaint against the ruling class in divine *oratio recta*, seems to have been tagged on after the sapiential finale of 10–11, no doubt at a late stage in the history of the book. It may have served originally as an editorial comment on 4 dealing with lack of effective government, and then by a slight adjustment reapplied to economic exploitation, the kind of situation envisaged in Nehemiah 5.

The situation foreseen as imminent in 1–7 is the collapse of the political, social and economic superstructure and infrastructure of the country. The protection of the military will be withdrawn, including the professional, largely mercenary force (*gibbôrîm*), conscripts (*'îš milḥāmâ*), and "captains of fifty" (*śar-ḥămiššîm* cf. Akkadian *rab ḫanša*). Swept away also will be the nobility, royal counselors, judicial authorities—magistrates and elders—and religious intermediaries. It is worth noting that the diviner (*qōsēm*) is mentioned without comment or criticism alongside the prophet (*nābî'*), and that the priest is conspicuously and somewhat unexpectedly absent from the enumeration. Order is subverted, roles are reversed, traditional values, including family values, are abandoned. Chaos, in short, with no one in charge and the situation so bad that no one will want to be in charge either (cf. Mic 7:5–6). Since the classes of people who are to be removed are precisely those likely to be uprooted and deported during on a typical punitive campaign (see 2 Kgs 24:14–16; Jer 52:15 and other examples in Oded 1979, 33–40), the situation more likely reflects the anticipated or experienced effects of Sennacherib's Judean campaign in 701 B.C.E (see *ANET*, 288) than unrest earlier on in the reign of Ahaz (as Wildberger 1991, 127–28; Clements 1980a, 47).

The indictment (*rîb*) (13–15) is quite distinctive both in its metrical regularity (3–3) and in the concluding formula that identifies it as an oracle (*nĕ'ūm*). Using standard forensic terminology and the language of judicial procedure and judgment (respectively *rîb*, *dîn*) and the familiar courtroom scenario (cf. Mic 6:1–5; Pss 50; 82), it turns from the situation of social disorder and *anomie* described in 1–12 to accusations of gross social injustice. The indictment of oppressing and plundering the poor, directed against the elite in Yahveh's own words, carries forward the social program of other dissidents of that century, especially Amos (2:6–8; 3:9–11; 6:4–7; 8:4–6) and Micah (2:1–3; 3:1–4, 9–12). The terms in which the indictment is couched are also strongly reminiscent of the instructional writings of the sages. Take, for example:

Do not rob a poor person because he is poor,
or crush the afflicted at the city gate. (Prov 22:22)

It even seems as though Isaiah is quoting back to the ruling class the norms of
social justice that were part of their own education (Wildberger 1991, 143).
The ravaged vineyard mentioned here is often taken to be a metaphor for Israel, anticipating the Song of the Vineyard in 5:1–7. This may be so, but it is
consonant with the physical and concrete imagery in the passage as a whole to
take it realistically as well.

THE FATE OF THE COURT LADIES (3:16–4:1)

(Compston; Edwards; Kaiser 1959, 78–81; Myers; Platt)

TRANSLATION

3   [16]Yahveh declares:
"Because the daughters of Zion have become so proud,
going around with necks thrust out,
and with ogling[a] eyes,
walking with mincing gait,
making a tinkling noise with their feet . . ."
[17]the Sovereign Lord will uncover the heads of the daughters of Zion,
he will lay bare their private parts . . .[b]
[18]On that day Yahveh will remove the finery of anklets, headbands,[c] and
crescents; [19]earrings, bracelets, and veils; [20]head-dresses, armlets, sashes, talismans, and amulets; [21](Yahveh will remove) signet rings and nose rings;
[22]gowns, wraps, shawls, and handbags; [23]mirrors, linen garments, head scarves,
and capes.
[24]Then, instead of perfume there shall be rot,
instead of a sash, a rope,[d]
a shaved head instead of hair well groomed,
a loincloth of burlap instead of expensive robes,
yes, shame where beauty once was.[e]
[25]Zion's men shall fall by the sword,
her warrior class in battle;
[26]her gates shall lament and mourn,
ravaged, she shall sit on the ground.

4   [1]Seven women will grab hold of one man on that day. They will say, "We
will eat our own food and wear our own clothing; just let us take your name;
please take away our shame."

NOTES

[a] *Měśaqqěrôt*, the first of more than a dozen hapax legomena in 16–23, was understood by some Jewish commentators as "painted" (*b. Shabb.* 62b; Rashi) with reference to the use of kohl corresponding to eyeliner, eye shadow, mascara, etc; cf. MH *śqr* (Piel), "to paint the eyes"; but Ibn Ezra translates "ogling" and refers to *Gen. Rabba* 18: "God did not make Eve out of Adam's eye so she would not become a flirt (*śāqranît*)";   [b] *pot* is sometimes translated "forehead" (cf. Akk. *putu*) but in the only other biblical occurrence (1 Kgs 7:50) it is an architectural term translated "socket" in RSV; neither Isaiah nor Ezekiel shrinks from using blunt and coarse language on occasion (Isa 7:20; Ezek 23:26; and Deut 21:12–13 for the treatment of male and female prisoners of war); the meaning of the hapax legomenon *śippah* in the same verse is also unclear, and is sometimes translated "cover with scabs," cf. *mispahat* ("scab") at Lev 13:6;   [c] for MT *haššěbîsîm* 1QIsa[a] and 4QIsa[b] have *hšbšym*, perhaps related to *špš/šmš*, referring to ornaments shaped like little suns (Wildberger 1991, 146);   [d] *niqpâ* is uncertain, but "rope" fits the context better than a reference to illness, pace Zeron 1981, 95–97;   [e] *kî tahat yōpî* absent from LXX; 1QIsa[a] adds *bšt*, "shame."

COMMENTS

The tirade against the court ladies is a distinct saying that sustains *oratio recta* of the deity only for the first verse. The standard sequence of charge and verdict (16–17, 24–26) has been expanded with the notorious catalogue of female attire and adornment from a well-informed but obsessive interpolator (18–23). It is then rounded off with a brief cameo of the same type as 6–7.

It is not immediately obvious why Isaiah (if it is he) turns at this point on the Jerusalemite women, presumably those associated with the court. While ogling and walking with mincing gait hardly represent serious infractions of the social order, any more than lounging on couches and singing idle songs (Amos 6:4–5), the idea is presumably the same as that of Amos (4:1–3), namely, that ostentatious display of this kind as practiced at the court is purchased one way or another with the skin off the back of an oppressed peasantry. Denunciation of ostentatious wealth and conspicuous consumption is, at any rate, a standard topos of moral teaching and preaching in the ancient Near East and Levant, inclusive of Israel (cf. Prov 23:4–5; Amos 6:4–7). It cannot therefore be explained exclusively in terms of a general cultural hostility characteristic of Israelite prophecy, a point made by Max Weber. At all events, the passage does not make for pleasant or edifying reading, quite apart from the record number of hapax legomena it contains (thirteen in the eight verses, 16–24, and ten other words occurring only twice). Yahveh is represented as acting out the role of a victorious army in its routinely savage treatment of female prisoners of war. The final cameo dramatizes the sad situation of the womenfolk after a war, with its heavy drain on manpower. Marrying seven women was not in itself contrary either to law or social mores, but very few men outside of the royal family, even among the upper class, would have been able to support so many wives. In this dramatic little scene seven women, probably acting in unison rather than in competition with one another, are offering to support themselves (one wonders how), thus foregoing the husband's legal duty to provide for them what is prescribed by law—food, clothing, marital rights (Exod 21:10). The only condition is that one of the surviving males will take them on as primary or secondary wives so that they can get rid of the social stigma of childlessness (cf. the shame and misery of the initially childless Rachel, Gen 30:23, and Hannah, 1 Sam 1:4–8). If the male so urgently solicited had turned them down, as he might well have done, we would have had a very close parallel with the earlier cameo (3:6–7) also featuring a desperate attempt to remedy a situation of social and economic chaos.

AFTER JUDGMENT, PEACE AND SECURITY (4:2–6)

(Baldwin; Buda; Cazelles 1982; Herrmann)

TRANSLATION

4 ²On that day, the shoot that Yahveh has planted will be an object of magnificence and glory, and the fruit of the land an object of pride and splendor for the survivors of Israel.[a]
³Those who are left in Zion and who remain in Jerusalem will be called holy, all those who are recorded for life in Jerusalem.
⁴Once the sovereign Lord[b] has washed away the filth of the daughters of Zion[c] and cleansed the bloodstains from Jerusalem with a fiery wind in the judgment,[d] ⁵Yahveh will create[e] over the entire site of Mount Zion and over its liturgical assemblies a cloud by day[f] and smoke together with a brightly burning fire by night. Yes, over all the glorious scene there will be a canopy, ⁶and a booth will serve as a shade from the heat by day and a shelter and refuge from the rainstorm.

NOTES

[a] 1QIsaᵃ adds *vyhvdh*, "and Judah," no doubt to facilitate transition to the next verse;   [b] Tg. has YHVH for *'ădōnāy*;   [c] LXX, more inclusively and politically correctly, *tōn huiōn kai tōn thugaterōn* ("the filth of the sons and daughters");   [d] literally, "with a wind [spirit] of judgment and with a wind [spirit] of burning." 1QIsaᵃ has *sʿr* (whirlwind) for *bʿr*, and this last is sometimes read *bʿr* (Piel) = "cleanse," though this meaning seems to be possible only in the sense of completely burning away impurity; see *DCH* 2:242–3;   [e] LXX *kai*

hexei, "and he will come," reads *ûbā'* for *ûbārā'*; 1QIsaᵃ has *vybr'*;   ᶠ 1QIsaᵃ omits from *v'šn* to *yvmm* in v 6 by homoeoteleuton, but the missing section is in 4QIsaᵃ.

COMMENTS

Together with 2:2–4(5), this description of a people, land, and city that have passed over to the other side of judgment brackets the unrelenting sequence of threat and disaster in 2:6–4:1. It may be noted once again how these bracketing passages recontextualize this dark scenario without erasing it. The worst has happened and now a different future opens up, though the shadow of the past still hangs over the present. Isaiah 2:2–4 envisages Jerusalem as preeminent among the nations, the religious capital of the world to which Gentiles will come attracted by the high ethical ideals embodied in the Jewish law. The God of Israel will be accepted as the arbiter of international disputes, with the result that war will finally become obsolete. Our present passage also features the future Jerusalem, but its author is interested more in the condition of its native inhabitants and the land that will sustain them. Concentrating on the final destiny of Israel, it brings together the intimately connected themes of people, land, and temple.

After the introductory "on that day," the first time in the book this formula has not announced bad news, the seer proclaims the future splendor of "the shoot" planted by Yahveh. After the collapse of the Judean state, this term (Hebrew *ṣemaḥ*) was used as a code name for the scion of the Davidic line, encapsulating the hopes for an eventual restoration (Jer 23:5; 33:15–16; Ezek 29:21). As such it is applied explicitly to Zerubbabel, grandson of the exiled Jehoiachin, in the troubled early years of the reign of Darius I (Zech 3:8; 6:12). But the present context, and especially the parallel "fruit of the land" (*pĕrî hā'āreṣ* cf. Deut 1:25), does not favor this meaning, and the only other occurrence of the term *ṣemaḥ* in Isaiah, a passage very close thematically and linguistically to the present verse, refers to the restored community living on its own land (Isa 61:11). Late Isaian use of the related verb (*ṣmḥ*) also supports this broader connotation (42:9; 43:19; 44:4; 45:8; 55:10; 58:8; 61:11).

Early interpretations of this verse in both Jewish and Christian circles found a messianic allusion here, notwithstanding. The Tg. renders *ṣemaḥ* with *mĕšîaḥ* ("messiah"), and the LXX takes the meaning of shining forth rather than springing forth from the ground, hence *epilampsei ho theos* (from *epilampo*, "shine forth," cf. Syr. *ṣemḥa'*, "brightness"). Other early Greek translations make the same transition, rendering *ṣemaḥ* as *anatolē* (the east, the rising of the sun, or another heavenly body in its ascendancy, as LXX at Zech 3:8 and 6:12 and cf. Num 24:17 *anatelei*). This semantic shift will lead eventually to *anatolē* as a code name for the Christian Messiah in the infancy gospels (Matt 2:2; Luke 1:78).

The three terms characterizing the community as survivors create a further link with and comment on the repeated threats of disaster in 2:6–4:1. The holiness of those living in the Jerusalem of the future reminds us of the *syn-oikismos* (transfer of population) to the "holy city" carried out by Nehemiah, governor of the province (Neh 11:1–24), a process that may not have been as voluntary as the biblical text wishes us to understand (Neh 11:2). Also typical of that period is the careful recording of names, including no doubt those of the new inhabitants of the city (e.g. Ezra 2:62; 8:1, 3; Neh 12:22–23). Such a register of names is easily transferable to the realm of theological abstraction, a "book of the living" (Ps 69:29[28]) or "book of remembrance" (Mal 3:16–18), an idea with a long history in the ancient Near East. We are therefore justified in suspecting that this kind of language is presenting an idealization of the specific form of temple community existing in the province of Judah under Iranian rule (sixth to fourth century B.C.E.).

The passing allusion to the purification of Jerusalem probably does not refer to the tirade against women in 3:16–26 but rather takes menstrual blood as a type of anything that renders unclean (cf. Lev 12:1–2; 15:19–30). "Filth" (*ṣōʾâ*, usually "excrement," Isa 28:3; 36:12 = 2 Kgs 18:28) therefore forms a kind of hendiadys with "blood" (*dāmmîm*), matching "washing" (*rāḥaṣ*) and "rinsing" (*yādîaḥ*), this last used elsewhere in cultic contexts (Ezek 40:38; 2 Chr 4:6). Depicting the judgment to come by means of "wind" (*rûaḥ*) and fire corresponds closely with descriptions in the last chapter of the book—"Yahveh will come with fire, his chariots like the windstorm . . . by fire Yahveh will execute judgment" (66:15–16).

All of this highly charged language projecting a future very different from the unsatisfactory present is in keeping with the perspective of the last few chapters of the book. It finds its central and emblematic point of reference in the temple, which was also the real political and socioeconomic center from the end of the sixth century B.C.E. onwards. The seer evokes the numinous epiphenomena associated with the wilderness sanctuary—cloud by day, column of fire by night, both together expressions of the divine effulgence or glory (Exod 13:21–22; 33:9; 40:34–38). These will cover the entire *mākôn* ("site"), a term used for the dwelling of the deity either in the sky (1 Kgs 8:39–49; Ps 33:14) or in the sanctuary (Exod 15:17; 1 Kgs 8:18; Ezra 2:68). Similar connotations attach to the term "booth" (*sūkkâ*, 2 Sam 22:12 = Ps 18:12; 31:21), a dwelling that will provide protection from the elements. Also covered are Jerusalem's *miqrāʾôt*, an interesting term occurring earlier in the book (1:13), generally taken to refer to ceremonies of the assembled congregation (Lev 23; Num 28–29), or a summons to such a ceremony (Num 10:2) or, in one late text, the liturgical reading of Scripture (Neh 8:8). Unless we are to risk a very late reference to synagogues in Jerusalem we would assume that, in this instance, the expression alludes to ceremonies carried out in the temple, and carried out with very different dispositions and results from those condemned earlier in the book (1:10–17). The passage bringing closure to this first section of the book combines, then, the themes of political disaster survived, purification, and Jerusalem temple liturgy in a scenario of restoration that we will encounter again in the final chapters of the book.

THE VINEYARD SONG (5:1–7)

(Emerton 1992; Graffy; Höffken; Junker; Loretz 1975; Niehr; Ross; Sanmartin-Ascaso; Schottroff; Sheppard; Williams; Willis; Yee; Zobel)

TRANSLATION

5 [1]Let me sing for my friend
my love song about his vineyard.[a]
My friend had a vineyard
on a hillside[b] rich in soil;
[2]he dug it up,[c] cleared it of stones,
and planted it with choicest vines;
he built a watchtower inside it,
hewed out a wine vat in it;
then he looked for it to yield good grapes
but the grapes it produced were rotten.[d]
[3]So now, you who live in Jerusalem,
and you, people of Judah:
judge between me and my vineyard!

[4]What more could be done for my vineyard
that I have failed to do?
Why did I look for it to yield good grapes,
when the grapes it produced were rotten?[d]

[5]So now, I give you notice
as to what I will do with my vineyard:
deprived of its hedge, it will be open for grazing,
its fence breached and broken, it will be trampled down;
[6]I will turn it into a wasteland,[e]
it will be neither pruned nor hoed,
thorns and weeds will spring up,
I will give command to the clouds
to send down no rain upon it.

[7]For the vineyard of Yahveh of hosts
is the house of Israel,
and the people of Judah
the plantation in which he delighted.
He looked for justice,
and instead there was bloodshed,
for righteousness,
and instead a cry of distress.[f]

NOTES

The passage provides little scope for the text critic. 1QIsa[a] shows orthographic variations but little else (*běkarmî* for *lěkarmî* 4a; *ʾāsîr* for *hāsēr*, 5b), and among the fragments, 4QIsa[a] has one indistinct letter from v 1a (*l*[*ydydy*]).   [a] Emerton's proposal to translate *širat dôdî*, "a song about my friend," is syntactically anomalous and the resulting "I will sing about my friend a song about my friend concerning his vineyard" decidedly odd;   [b] "hillside" (*qeren*, usually "horn"), based on an Arabic cognate (and cf. names of mountains like the Horns of Hattin, Matterhorn), is uncertain; Ibn Ezra suggests Keren Ben Shamen, a place-name near Jerusalem;   [c] *ʿzq* is hapax; "dug" depends on the Arabic cognate and MH *ʿăzîqâ*, "ploughed land";   [d] *běʾūšîm* from *bʾš*, "stink," "be odious," cf. the manna (Exod 16:24), oil (Eccl 10:1), and fruit from trees (1QH VIII 25), all of which have gone bad; suggesting, therefore, disease (cf. Amos 4:9) rather than bitter berries (the usual explanation);   [e] the suggested emendation of *vaʾăšîtēhû bātâ* to *věʾašbîtēhû*, "I will make an end of it" (BHS) is unnecessary; as Ibn Ezra, Rashi, and other medieval commentators recognized, *bātâ*, "destruction," occurs in MH, and cf. Akk. *batu*, "destroy" (G. R. Driver 1937, 38).   [f] another striking use of assonance that I have not attempted to reproduce in translation; literally: "he looked for *mišpāṭ*, and behold *mišpāḥ*; for *ṣědāqâ*, and behold *ṣěʿāqâ*" cf. the attempt of the Zurich Bible: "Er hoffte auf Guttat, und siehe da Bluttat, auf Rechtsspruch, und siehe da Rechtsbruch."

COMMENTS

By any reckoning this is a strange composition, beginning with deliberate incongruity as a love song addressed to a vineyard and revealing itself at the end as a kind of parable complete with its explanation. There are other incongruities and problems for the modern reader, e.g., squaring the very mundane language of the poem with love poetry; imagining how a vineyard can be responsible for a poor crop; why the same people represented by the failed vineyard are asked to take sides; or, finally, why the decision to destroy it is taken before those solicited have a chance to respond by making some useful suggestions, e.g., consult an experienced vintner, add compost, try a different kind of grape.

The song itself, which is very brief (1b–2), is introduced by the author, in the guise of composer of the song, who also renders it on behalf of his friend (1a). It is followed by a kind of forensic complaint addressed to Jerusalemites and Judeans (note, once again, the order) and a verdict passed immediately, without due process, on the ungrateful vineyard (3–6). The final verse (7) provides the key to the poem as a parable by stating explicit equivalents for the vineyard and the vine and this in a manner analogous to the parable of Nathan (2 Sam 12:1–14) and some of the gospel parables (e.g. Mark 4:2–9, 14–20). The representation of Israel as vineyard is not peculiar to and did not originate with

Isaiah (cf. Jer 2:21; 12:10–11; Ps 80:9–17; Ezek 15:1–8), though it is unlikely that the detailed allegorical reading of Ibn Ezra and other medieval exegetes (e.g. removing stones = extirpating the Canaanites, the watchtower = the temple) was intended by the author.

Neither the song nor its introduction gives away the identity either of the composer-performer or of the one on whose behalf the song was written and performed. In the introduction and the song itself, however, the latter is referred to as *yĕdîd* ("friend, beloved"), a term closely related to *dôd*, as in the description of the composition as *šîrat dôdî* ("my lovesong" not "the song of my beloved/friend" since it is clear that the beloved or friend neither composed nor sang it). Use of these terms, however, provides quite a deliberate clue to the identity of the disappointed vintner. The word *yĕdîd*, from a verbal form *ydd* attested in Ugaritic but not in Hebrew, occurs with the theophoric element Ya(hu) (Yahveh) in Solomon's personal name, Jedidiah (2 Sam 12:25), and in the name of Josiah's mother, Jedidah (2 Kgs 22:1). It probably also is a divine epithet at Deut 33:12, comparable to Mot's name *ydd 'l*, "beloved of El," in the Ugaritic texts (Zobel 1986, 444–48). The Israelite onomasticon also attests to *dôd* as a divine epithet (Dodai, Dodo, Dodihu, Medad), similar to its equivalent in West Semitic, Old Arabic, and Akkadian (Sanmartin-Ascaso 1978, 143–48). The association of these terms with vegetation deities led orthodox Yahvists to avoid their use—conspicuously in Hosea—but their appropriateness in the context of vineyards, vintners, and vintage would not have been lost on Isaiah's public. These associations carry beyond the otherwise appropriate translation "benevolent patron" (Olivier 1996, 59–65).

It is no easy matter for the modern reader to think of a vineyard or any other plot of land, for that matter, as inspiring not just poetry but *love* poetry. The author's stratagem led him at this point to draw on the ancient literary convention of field, vineyard, or the like as a euphemism for the female body, as in one of the Ugaritic texts (*CTA* 24:23): "I will make her field (*šd*) a vineyard, the field of her love (*šd ddh*) an orchard." Something of the same, but with a more chastened vocabulary, can be found in Hosea's explication of the prophet's transgressive bride with reference to the land (*'ereṣ*, a feminine noun), namely, the physical soil; and it is quite possible that the author is at this point drawing on Hosea, as he may be somewhat later in the use of symbolic names. Much further along the same trajectory, the author of the Canticle will adopt the literary conceit of referring to the young woman in love as a vineyard (Cant 2:15; 4:16; 8:11–12). In the Isaian poem, however, the convention serves only to move the vineyard metaphor, used earlier in the book (1:8; 3:14), into the center, and at the same time endow the composition with a gnomic, riddle-like quality. But the conceit is not sustained, so it does not seem helpful to speculate on the poet as "friend of the bridegroom" or to discover erotic innuendo in the language of digging, planting, and similar agricultural or vinicultural imagery in the poem. The technical side of vine cultivation need concern us even less (see Ross).

That the song was in reality a disguised indictment of Israel becomes apparent with the appeal to Jerusalemites and Judeans to pass judgment (against

themselves!) followed by the pronouncing of the verdict (3–6). With this last
we are in the language field, familiar to Isaiah, of the curse, including curses
appended to treaties, e.g., you shall plant vineyards and not eat their fruit (Isa
5:10; 65:21; Deut 28:30, 39; Amos 5:11; Zeph 1:13). Similar language, probably
influenced by the Vineyard Song, is found in Jeremiah (12:10), and a later
brief commentary on the Song announces the reversal of the cursed condition
(Isa 27:2–5[6]). In the context of this first part of the collection, therefore, the
Song does not in its basic theme of religious unresponsiveness, its social critique (absence of justice and righteousness), or even its dominant motif (see allusions to the vineyard in 1:8 and 3:14) represent a new departure. But since
the previous segment is firmly bracketed by 2:1–4 and 4:2–6, we would prefer
to read it as a prologue rather than an epilogue. The loss of its hedge and fence,
leaving it open to animal and human predators, points in fact unmistakably to
Assyrian invasion, which is a basic concern in chs. 6–12. More specifically, the
thorns and weeds (*šāmîr vāšāyit* v 6), expressive of the subsequent condition of
the "vineyard," recur as a motif throughout the section (7:23–25; 9:17[18];
10:17), as also in latter allusions to the Song (27:2–5; 32:12–13).

For convenience of commentary, the isolated strophe of the woe series (10:1–4)
will be commented on in connection with the other units in the series (5:8–24),
and the isolated strophe of the poem on the divine anger (5:25) will be dealt
with together with the other stanzas of the poem (9:8–21).

A SERIES OF WOES (10:1–4; 5:8–24)

(Bardtke; Blum 1992–93; Brown; Chisholm; Crenshaw; Emerton 1967; Fey; Fichtner; Gerstenberger; Janzen; Kellermann; Korpel; Premnath; Speier; van der Horst; Wright; Zobel)

TRANSLATION

i

10   ¹Woe to those who issue wicked decrees,
      who draft oppressive regulations,[a]
      ²to turn away the needy from judgment,
      to rob of their rights the poor of my people,
      that widows may be their prey,
      that they may plunder the fatherless.
      ³What will you do on the day of punishment,
      in the disaster that comes from afar?
      To whom will you flee for help?
      Where will you leave your belongings?[b]
      ⁴Nothing to do but cower among the prisoners,[c]
      down among those already killed. . . .

Yet his anger did not abate,
still is his hand stretched out.

ii

5 [8]Woe to those who add house to house,
who join one plot of land to another,
until there is no space left
for any but you to be settled[d] on the land!
[9]Yahveh of the hosts has sworn in my hearing:[e]
"many houses will be turned into ruins,
houses splendid and spacious left without occupants;
[10]a vineyard of ten hectares will yield but one barrel of wine,
a homer of seed will produce but one bushel.

iii

[11]Woe to them who rise early in the morning
in pursuit of strong drink,
who stay up late in the evening
that wine may inflame them;
[12]Lyre and harp, timbrel and flute,
and wine are not lacking at their feasts.[f]
They pay no heed to the work of Yahveh,[g]
they regard not the operation of his hands.
[13]Therefore:
bereft of understanding, my people is exiled,
their nobles[h] are famished,[i]
their commoners parched with thirst.
[14]Therefore:
Sheol stretches wide its gullet,
its mouth opens wide beyond measure,
Down go her nobles and commoners,
her throng in the midst of their revels.[j]
[15]*Humanity is humbled, all people are brought low,*
the haughty looks are humbled,
[16]*Yahveh of the hosts shall be exalted in the judgment,*
in the vindication the Holy God will reveal himself as holy.[k]
[17]Lambs will graze in their pasture,[l]
sheep will feed among the ruins.[m]

iv

[18]Woe to those who drag along iniquity like a sheep with cords,[n]
and sin like a heifer with ropes!
[19]Who are saying, "Let Yahveh[o] make haste,
let him speed his work that we may see it,
let the plan of Israel's Holy One soon come to pass
that we may acknowledge it!

v

²⁰Woe to those who call evil good.
and good evil,
who put darkness in the place of light,
light in the place of darkness,
who make the bitter sweet and the sweet bitter!

vi

²¹Woe to those who are wise in their own eyes,
shrewd in their own understanding!

vii

²²Woe to those heroic guzzlers of wine,
those redoubtable mixers of strong drink!
²³who acquit the guilty on payment of a bribe,
while depriving the innocent of their rights.
Therefore:
²⁴As the tongue of fire consumes the stubble,
and chaff shrivels up in the flame,ᵖ
their root will be all rottenness,
their flower disappear like dust;
for they have rejected the instruction of Yahveh of the hosts
and despised the word of Israel's Holy God.

NOTES

ᵃ *Ûmĕkattĕbîm ʿāmāl kittēbû*: Piel participle of *ktb* is unattested and in any case impossible here; the finite verb *kittēbû* (hapax Piel, perhaps with iterative sense) in the second stich follows the participle in the first, as in 5:8, 11; perhaps read *miktābîm*, "things written down," sometimes used of legal material (cf. Exod 32:16; Deut 10:4; 2 Chr 35:4; 36:22 = Ezra 1:1);   ᵇ *kābôd*, "riches," "belongings" (cf. Gen 31:1; 45:13; Isa 66:12), is better attested than "children"; ᶜ *biltî kāraʿ taḥat ʾassîr* absent from LXXᴮ but present in 1QIsaᵃ and, partially, in 4QIsaᵉ, but the text was corrupt at an early stage of transmission; the late nineteenth century reading *bēltî kōraʿat ḥat ʾōsîr*, "Beltis (the goddess Baalat) crouches, Osiris is shattered," is ingenious but foreign to the context; *biltî* is read as an existential qualifier (cf. Job 14:12);   ᵈ no need to change *vĕhûšab-tem* Hophal to Qal in spite of LXX, Syr., Tg.; 1QIsaᵃ *vyštm* may be a scribal error for *vyšbtm*;   ᵉ MT *bĕʾoznáy YHVH ṣĕbāʾôt* ("in my hearing YHVH of the hosts . . ." is defective, but *ʾim-lōʾ*, following, presupposes the taking of an oath; ᶠ reading *vāyáyin bĕmištêhem*, supplying a preposition;   ᵍ 1QIsaᵃ has *pʿlt* for MT *pōʿal*;   ʰ *kābôd*, literally, "glory" cf. Isa.16:14 also with *hāmôn*, "commoners";   ⁱ *mĕtê rāʿāb*, literally "men of hunger," i.e., famished, rather than "dead of hunger," with which the parallel phrase fits less well;   ʲ the fem. suffix (*hădārâ, hămônâ, šĕʾônâ*) refers not to Jerusalem, which is not mentioned here, but to Sheol, a fem. noun; *vĕʿālēz bāh*, literally, "the one exulting in her," has defied explanation: witness the rather extreme solution of Emerton (1967), who transposes consonants to read *vĕʿoz libbâ*, "and the strength of her (Zion's) heart"; it may after all be a syntactically inappropriate gloss. If the reading suggested renders an approximately acceptable meaning it would strengthen the suspicion that v 14 should follow v 12, and v 17 follow v 13; curiously, Ibn Ezra refers it to the kind of laughter sometimes noticed in people at the moment of death;   [k] I take vv 15–16 to be an amplifaction drawing on 2:9a, 11a, 17b; most of it is in 4QIsa[b];   [l] reading *bĕdobrām*;   [m] the four words of v 17b read literally: "swords, fat sheep, residing, will eat," which makes even less sense than Wildberger's literal "and commoners who are standing guard eat small scraps from fatted sheep" (1991, 191); the proposed translation reads *vaḥorābôt*, "ruins," for *vĕḥorĕbôt*, "swords," changes the order, and takes its cue from LXX "sheep graze the deserted places of those taken away";   [n] another crux: literally, referring to dragging iniquity with worthless cords and sin like wagon ropes; parallelism suggests emending *šāvĕʾ* to *śeh*, "sheep," to match *ʿeglâ*, "heifer" (rather than *ʿăgālâ*, "cart"), but this is admittedly speculative; [o] supplyng YHVH as subject of *yĕmahēr*; 4QIsa[b] has *yḥyš*, "it will come about speedily," rather than MT jussive "let him speed . . . ," perhaps a pious *tiqqûn*; [p] 1QIsa[a] has *vʾš lvhbt yrph*, "and flaming fire dies down," for MT *vaḥăšaš lehābâ yirpeh*, "and chaff shrivels up in the flame."

COMMENTS

An initial problem is the connection between the series 5:8–24 and the isolated woe-saying in 10:1–4. Most likely 10:1–4a is a displaced unit of the woe-series that has been subsequently accommodated to the poem on the divine anger by the addition of the refrain at 10:4b. A fairly decisive indication is that the indictments in 5:8–24 and 10:1–4a are directed against the leadership whereas the poem about the divine anger threatens the people as a whole. While its position in the series is not so important, most of those who hold that 10:1–4a for whatever reason has been moved from its original position place it at the beginning rather than the end of the series, i.e., immediately following the vineyard song (5:1–7). Isaiah 5:24b sounds like a final recapitulation, and 10:1–4a leads on naturally into 5:8–10, the theme of which is the manipulation of the legal system in order to confiscate houses and land. (The case is argued by Barth 1977, 110–11.) Furthermore, a stanza (or, more precisely, the end of a stanza beginning "therefore") of the poem on the divine anger has been displaced from its original connection with the other stanzas in 9:7–20[8–21] and tacked onto the woe-series at 5:25. We thus have three distinct series arranged deliberately so as to provide a framework for the autobiographical and biographical centerpiece concerning Isaiah and Ahaz during the Syrian-Samarian crisis: the woe-series (5:8–24 + 10:1–4a), the poem on the divine anger (5:25 + 9:7–20), and the Assyrian pericope (5:26–30 + 10:5–19 or even 10:5–34). While it is important to resist the temptation either to impose more order on the book than was ever intended by its redactors or to privilege unduly putative original arrangements, these restructurings help to explain the failure of the prophet's intervention during the reign of Ahaz by redirecting attention to the moral failure of the people and especially the political leadership targeted in most of the accusations in 5:8–24 and 10:1–4a. In all three series, events are explained in terms of moral causality and the unfolding of a divine plan or agenda to be worked out in the arena of international politics. This way of looking at events would have been particularly apposite during the brief Josian renaissance, as also for the reader or hearer of "the former prophets" (Zech 1:4; 7:7) in the post-disaster epoch. That historical events are intelligible only with reference to such a "plan" ('ēṣâ), and one that is accessible only through prophetic communication, is a central issue in the woe-series (see especially 5:19) and recurs as a theme throughout the Isaian corpus (14:24–27; 19:17; 28:29; 46:10–11).

Having accorded due significance to the present order of the text, I propose to discuss together the seven units in the woe-series and the four stanzas of the poem on the divine anger.

First, then, the woe-series. By dint of including 10:1–4a, or adding a hôy at v 23, or shuffling lines around (e.g. Budde, Hayes, Kaiser, Wildberger), one can come up with a series of seven sayings. Three of the six woes in 5:8–24 include a verdict, with (ii, vi) or without (i) the usual introductory "therefore" (lākēn). Since the addition of the verdict brings the woe-saying into line with the standard prophetic judgment-saying consisting in indictment followed by verdict, the woe-saying probably originated as a simple, brief exclamation with no significant emotional charge or moral content (as in Isa 1:4, 24; 10:5; 17:12; 18:1; 29:1) which was co-opted by prophetic rhetoric. (Whatever its ultimate origin, the use of hôy in funerary contexts is quite limited, 1 Kgs 13:30; Jer 22:18; 34:5.) Like most other sections in the book, this series has been the object of considerable editorial attention, apparent in the uneven length of the units, the unexpected repetition of "therefore" (lākēn) in ii, and the reuse of material from 2:9, 11, 17 in 5:15–16 from the same unit. Far from being a purely arbitrary editorial procedure, this last (for example) served to express the general, human significance of a particular historical experience.

In all probability the first unit takes aim at the practice of manipulating the legal system by those in a position to do so, namely, royal officialdom, in order to facilitate the sequestration of property and the enclosure of peasant holdings. From the prophetic perspective legality is not the same as justice, and the legal transfer of property can be tantamount to robbery (cf. 3:14 where the same verbal stem gzl, "rob," occurs). It is therefore no surprise that tension existed between law scribes in the service of the state and prophets (cf. Jer 2:8; 8:8–9). Prophetic protest in the eighth century was on behalf of the poor (dal, 'onî, 'ebyôn cf. Amos 2:7; 4:1; 5:11; 8:6), not the destitute so much as members of peasant households eking out a precarious subsistence on the ancestral plot of land. In a society organized along patrilineal lines the lot of any woman or child deprived of male protection could be hard, and in Israel the situation was not improved by the relative absence of legal protection for these charter members of the disadvantaged. In the Deuteronomic law widows were commended to public charity and the "social security system" of the triennial tithe precisely because of the absence of provisions in law for them to inherit the property of the deceased husband (Deut 14:29; 26:12–13). The outcome of this officially and legally sanctioned robbery of the poor is described by means of a series of rhetorical questions, doubtless with reference to an imminent Assyrian invasion, the "disaster that comes from afar" (the term *šō'â*, adopted for the Holocaust, occurs here, perhaps for the first time). Rather than representing a proto-apocalyptic strand from the time of Nehemiah (Kaiser 1972, 104, 108), this muted allusion prepares for the resumption of the Assyrian pericope that follows.

In smooth succession unit ii, consisting of a woe and a corresponding verdict, attacks the practice of enclosing peasant holdings on the pretext of insolvency or by application of eminent domain (as with Naboth's vineyard, 1 Kgs 21) or by some form of legal legerdemain. We therefore have a situation similar to that of Greece at the time of Solon or Rome in the days of the Gracchi, one also lamented by Seneca, who actually speaks of the avaricious joining together of field to field (*licet agros agros adiiciat*, see van der Horst). This was a situation in which the system of patrimonial domain was being undermined both by the emerging state apparatus, hungry as always for land, and members of powerful families, a process eventuating in vast social changes including the formation of latifundia and the prevalence of rent capitalism. At this point Isaiah represents an emerging prophetic tradition of protest against exploitation of an immemorial peasant way of life for which ownership of the patrimonial plot (*naḥălâ*) by the household (*bēt 'āb*) was the indispensable basis for subsistence. This tradition of protest is shared with Amos and Micah (see especially Mic 2:1–5), and its existence comes to even clearer expression in the verdict based on a standard curse formula—"you have built houses but shall not live in them, you have planted vineyards but shall not drink their wine" (cf. Amos 5:11; Zeph 1:13; Deut 28:30 and its reversal in Amos 9:14; Isa 65:21–22)—perhaps deriving ultimately from vassal treaty curses. The point about vineyards has been modified, perhaps with the "song of the vineyard" in mind: a vineyard that it would take a yoke of oxen ten days to plough (the *ṣemed*, here translated "hectare," means literally "yoke of oxen") will produce only one paltry *bath* of wine (a liquid measure of about 30 liters here translated "barrel"); a *ḥomer* ("donkey load") of corn seed will yield only an *ephah* (here translated "bushel") i.e., a tenth of a *ḥomer* rather than the traditional tenfold or a hundredfold—the hyperbole is obvious.

The third unit has been expanded out of all proportion though not in an arbitrary way since the addition of 15–16 may have been suggested by the descent of nobles and commoners into the underworld in the previous verse. We also suspect that v 17, in which in spite of the textual obscurity we descry a typical *sic transit gloria mundi* scenario rather like a Poussin landscape, fits after either v 13 or v 10 but not v 14, and that v 14 may have originally followed v 12. The section, in other words, has had a troubled history. The accusation of addiction to strong drink is a common topos in the prophetic tradition of protest directed against state bureaucrats and an *urban* elite (cf. Amos 2:8; 4:1; 6:1; Hos 4:11; 7:5; Mic 2:11 and the realistic scenario at Isa 28:7–8), reflecting the anxiety induced by the rise in urbanization in eighth century B.C.E. Israel. Heavy drinking is also a frequent subject of moralistic preaching in the didacticism of self-styled sages then as now (see, for example, Prov 21:17; 23:19–21, 29–35; Sir 10:16). The condemnation of musical entertainment as symptomatic of a life of leisure and insouciance is also a familiar motif (cf. Amos 6:1, 4–7) and even worse than that is a cynical refusal to grapple with the meaning of international events viewed from a religious (meaning, prophetic) perspective. The threatened outcome of exile is also a common feature of this kind of polemic (cf. Amos 1–2; 4:2–3; 6:7). And not far beyond exile is the prospect of a diminished postmortem existence in Sheol, the underworld described more fully in satirical poems on the death of the Babylonian king (14:4–11; 14:12–20). There is nothing specific enough in this allusion to the descent into the underworld to oblige us to date it after 586 B.C.E. (pace Kaiser 1972, 107, Clements 1980a, 64). We shall hear again, but more cryptically, of people passing into Sheol towards the end of the *Denkschrift* (8:21).

The figure with which the fourth woe-saying opens is notoriously obscure (see Notes) but seems to present the burden of sin under the image of dragging along a large and recalcitrant animal. It is the opposite of the image in Hos 11:4 ("I drew them with human ties, with cords of love" JPS translation), which uses the same vocabulary and may have been in the Isaian author's mind. The nature of the burden is expressed by means of the technique, popular in prophetic rhetoric, of direct quotation (e.g. Amos 4:1; 6:13; 8:5–6; Hos 10:3; 12:8; 13:10; Mic 2:6, 11). Throughout Isaiah quoting the opposition is frequently employed as a direct witness to arrogant self-sufficiency (9:10[9]; 10:8–11, 13–14; 14:13–14) and, as here, to religious skepticism (28:15; 29:15–16; 30:10–11 cf. Mic 3:11; Zeph 1:12; Ezek 8:12). The quotation suggests that the skeptics, presumably the movers and shakers on the political scene in Jerusalem, were expressing themselves by sardonic use of Isaiah's own language—about the Holy One of Israel who has a "plan" (*'ēṣâ*), an "agenda" (*ma'ăśeh*) that will soon come to pass, an obviously unverifiable self-justification of the prophet. We are reminded again of the failure of the prophet's mission to Ahaz and the suggestion to seek an alternative resource by appeal to necromantic practices that seem never to have been too far below the surface in eighth and seventh century B.C.E. Judah (8:19; 19:3; 28:14–15; 29:4).

There follows in strophe v a denunciation of moral sophistry expressed in what seems to be a claim on the part of those addressed to advertise a private morality of their own in defiance of traditional norms. However, juxtaposition with the previous unit, in which Judean bureaucrats manifest skepticism about applying prophetic solutions in the political sphere, strengthens the suspicion that the denunciation in unit v is directed against the religious neutrality of the didactic tradition in which these public officials were educated, a tradition in stark contrast with the radical religious commitment of the prophet (McKane 1965, 65–68). The same point is expressed more clearly in the next and shortest of the woe-sayings (vi), in which the wording implies a counterfeit wisdom and shrewdness, a wisdom over against the "instruction" (*tôrâ*) and "word" (*'imrâ*) of Yahveh (24b). We find the same contrast in a saying attributed to Jeremiah: "How can you say, 'We are wise and the law of Yahveh is with us'? . . . The wise shall be shamed, they shall be dismayed and trapped; see, they have rejected the word of Yahveh so what wisdom can be in them?" (Jer 8:8–9). The accusation of manipulating the legal system, corresponding to the denunciation of the first unit (Isa 10:1–2), strengthens the impression of the woe-series as essentially *political* polemic from a very well-defined viewpoint. Another aspect comes into view in the final unit, which focuses on subversion of the judicial system by bribery (23). Bribery was a major target of protest in eighth century prophecy (Isa 1:23; Mic 3:11; perhaps Amos 2:6). The law prohibiting bribery in the so-called "book of the covenant" (Exod 23:8) adds that a bribe blinds the eyes of officials (*piqĕḥîm*). That this motivation clause is reformulated in Deut 16:19 to apply to "the wise" (*ḥăkāmîm*) confirms the political connotations of this wisdom language in the woe-series. The final verdict (v 24a) is couched in familiar but telling agrarian terms, drawn from the practice of blanching or scorching the stubble after the harvest and the unpleasant experience of finding plants gone rotten. After this point another generalized accusation would not be expected. The statement in 24b was therefore probably added by an assiduous editor who wished to bring the preceding specific accusations under the rubric of violation of the law and rejection of the prophetic message. The statement looks Deuteronomic (in Clements 1980, and others), but neither the designation *qĕdôš yiśra'ēl* ("the Holy One of Israel") nor the term *'imrâ* ("word") belongs to the Deuteronomic vocabulary.

A POEM ABOUT THE ANGRY GOD
(9:7–20[8–21] + 5:25)

(Blum 1992–93; Brown; Crenshaw 1970; Fey; Honeyman; Knierim; Kruger; L'Heureux; Parpola and Watanabe; Soggin 1970; Wallenstein; Yadin)

TRANSLATION

i

9 [7]The Lord sent a message[a] against Jacob,
   and it will fall on Israel;
   [8]the entire people will experience it
   —Ephraim and the people of Samaria.
   In pride and highmindedness they said,
   [9]"So the bricks have collapsed,
   we will rebuild with dressed stone;
   so the sycamores have been cut down,
   we will replace them with cedars."

¹⁰But Yahveh supported[b] their adversaries,[c]
and incited their enemies against them:
¹¹Arameans from the east, Philistines from their rear,
they devoured Israel with mouth open wide.
Yet his anger did not abate,
still was his hand outstretched.

ii

¹²The people did not return to the one who struck them,
they did not seek out Yahveh of the hosts,
¹³so Yahveh cut off from Israel both head and tail.
¹⁴[Elder and dignitary are the head;
the prophet, the teacher of falsehood, the tail.][d]
¹⁵Those who led the people led them astray,
those who were led were left in disarray,
¹⁶so the Sovereign Lord had no mercy[e] on their youths,
no compassion on their orphans and widows,
for they are all ungodly and wicked,
every mouth utters impiety.
Yet his anger did not abate,
still was his hand outstretched.

iii

¹⁷Wickedness burns like a fire,
consuming thorns and weeds,
it has kindled the thickets of the forest,
they go up in the swirling smoke.[f]
¹⁸Through the fury of Yahveh of the hosts
the land is shaken,[g]
the people are fuel for the fire.
No one spares a companion,
all eat the flesh of their children.[h]
¹⁹Here one gorges and is still famished,
there one devours and is not sated.[i]
²⁰Manasseh devours Ephraim and Ephraim Manasseh,
and both of them together against Judah.
Yet his anger did not abate,
still was his hand outstretched.

iv

5   ²⁵So the anger of Yahveh was roused against his people,
he stretched out his hand against them and struck them down.
The mountains quaked, their corpses lay like refuse in the streets.
Yet his anger did not abate,
still was his hand outstretched.

NOTES

[a] Lxx has *thanaton*, "death," as a translation of *deber*, "pestilence," but the stanza does not describe a pestilence;   [b] the only meaning attested for *śgb* Piel, as Ps 20:2; 59:2; 69:30; 91:14; 107:41, and fitting the context;   [c] MT has *ṣārê rĕṣîn*, the "adversaries of Rezin," and *rṣyn* is also attested in 4QIsa[b] and *rṣy'n* (*sic*) in 1QIsa[a], but both sense and meter support an editorial insertion here; emending to *śārê rĕṣîn* does not help much, since why mention his princes rather than Rezin himself? Read *ṣārāv*, "his adversaries";   [d] has the appearance of a Second Temple gloss, cf. Zech 13:2–6, which also speaks of the *nābî'* who speaks *šeqer*, "falsehood";   [e] MT has *lō' yiśmaḥ*, "did not rejoice," but 1QIsa[a] *lv' yḥmvl*, is a closer parallel to *lō' yĕraḥēm*;   [f] *'bk* Hithpael is hapax, perhaps related to *hpk*, "turn around," "swirl"; the meaning of the odd phrase *gē'ût 'āšān*, literally, "a pride of smoke," depends on the meaning assigned to the verb *'bk*;   [g] *ne'tam*, Niphal, is hapax; 1QIsa[a] *nt'm* is probably a slip; LXX *sugkekautai*, "is burned up," is possible, but Syr. and Vulg. suggest the image of earthquake;   [h] 19b is transposed here *metri causa*; *bĕśar-zar'ô*, the "flesh of his arm," is unlikely even though attested in 1QIsa[a] and 4QIsa[e]; read *zĕra'ô*, "his offspring," rather than *rē'ô*, "his companion," as a well-attested topos for times of extreme stress;   [i] for "here" and "there" MT has "to the right" and "to the left," respectively.

COMMENTS

The poem is identified by the refrain "yet his anger did not abate/still was his arm outstretched," repeated five times including 10:4b which, as we have seen, assimilates one of the woe-sayings to the poem on the divine anger. In the present arrangement, therefore, the poem consists of five stanzas. Isaiah 5:25, which is either defective or has been accommodated to the woe-sayings context, contains the clearest allusion to earthquake and encapsulates the essence of the refrain, which is the anger of God and the hand outstretched to punish. As such, it would seem to have belonged to the end of the poem before being moved to its present location before the core narrative, just as 10:1–4 was moved in the opposite direction to the end of the divine anger poem (pace Brown). In its present location 5:25 is followed by the threat of foreign invasion (5:26) that verifies the point of the refrain, i.e., that more punishment is in store. An interesting parallel is the fifth and last vision of Amos (9:1–4), which combines the language of earthquake with that of an invading army. Isaiah 5:25 also parallels the five reproaches listing five "visitations" in Amos 4:6–11, the last of which speaks of the earthquake with reference to which Amos's activity is dated (1:2).

If this is correct, the poem begins with the word of doom sent against Jacob/Israel, i.e., the Kingdom of Samaria (9:7), which I take to be a covert allusion to the preaching of Amos. That the poem is directly dependent on whatever edition of Amos's sayings circulated at that time could be more clearly indicated

only by naming him, but prophets never refer to each other by name. It recalls
Amos both in theme and language: the quaking of the mountains (*rgz* 5:25 cf.
Amos 8:8), corpses awaiting burial or cremation (5:25 cf. Amos 6:9–10; 8:3),
buildings collapsing (9:9 cf. Amos 3:15; 6:11), the whole land on fire (9:18 cf.
Amos 4:11). The key phrase in the refrain, *lō' šāb 'appô* (literally, "his anger
did not return"; for the idiom cf. Gen 27:44) recalls the refrain in Amos's oracles against foreign nations, *lō' 'ăšîbennû* (literally, "I will not cause it to return,"
1:3, 6, 9, 11, 13; 2:1, 4, 6), with reference to anger and punishment (Knierim),
and the reproach *lō' šabtem 'āday* ("you did not return to me," Amos 4:6, 8, 9,
10, 11). This can hardly be a coincidence.

The first stanza emphasizes that the message is addressed to the entire
Northern Kingdom, described as Jacob, Israel or Ephraim (as frequently in
Hosea), and the people of Samaria. The situation is that the population of that
kingdom has survived one disaster only to encounter another, which will not
be the last. In all probability the initial disaster was the major earthquake,
which devastated large parts of the country during the reigns of Uzziah in
Judah (ca. 783–742) and Jeroboam II in Israel (ca. 786–746), and which has left
its mark on the archaeological record (Yadin; Soggin; see Amos 1:1; Zech 14:5
and perhaps obliquely 2 Kgs 14:26). The need to rebuild, and the allusion to
bricks and sycamores and to dressed stone and cedars, respectively, the cheap-
est and most expensive building materials (cf. 1 Kgs 6:36; 7:11; 10:27), point in
this direction and would permit us to read 5:25, in which reference to earthquake is even clearer, as forming an inclusio with 9:7–9. The confidence with
which the survivors set about rebuilding, which to us would appear positively
meritorious, is interpreted as prideful self-sufficiency—a major theme in Isa 1–
12—and an indication that the lesson had not been learned and that therefore
more punishment is in store. Similar sentiments are expressed in Amos 6:1–8.
The next "visitation" was to be in the shape of damaging attacks from Syria and
the Philistine cities, and therefore refers more likely to military activity during
and shortly after the reign of Jeroboam II than to the period 733–722 about a
generation later when the Syrians at any rate, incorporated into the Assyrian
Empire in 732, were in no position to devour anyone with open mouth (pace
Clements 1980a, 67). The earlier period is obscure, but Syrian inroads into the
Galilee, the Golan, and Transjordan and Israelite counteraction are hinted at
in Amos (1:3–5; 6:13–14) and in Dtr (2 Kgs 14:22–29).

The act of "turning" (Buber's translation of *těšûbâ*) implies a reorientation
of mind and action in light of what one perceives to be the will of God. "Seeking" God (verbal stem *drš*) has much the same meaning, but involves a turning
away from the intimately related alternative attractions of false cults and the
unjust pursuit of power and wealth—a point made very clearly in the (probably
Deuteronomistic) "seek" passages in Amos (5:4–7, 14–15) and in later strands
of the Deuteronom(ist)ic corpus (e.g. Deut 4:29; Jer 29:13). Persuading people
to see the errors of their ways by progressively more severe punishment will
seem for the liberal reader today too close to the methods of a penal institution.
We can only observe that the prophet is looking back over a disastrous chapter

of history from some time shortly before the end of the Kingdom of Samaria and trying to make sense of it in terms of his own vivid convictions about God's agenda and concerns.

The cutting off of head and tail is often referred to the violent end of the Jehu dynasty (supported initially by Elisha and condemned by both Amos and Hosea; see Amos 7:10–17 and Hos 1:4–5), which came about with the assassination of Zechariah son of Jeroboam II after a reign of six months (2 Kgs 15:8–10). The death of Zechariah, one of seven rulers of the Kingdom of Samaria to die by the assassin's hand, was probably not unconnected with the accession of the usurper Tiglath-pileser III to the Assyrian throne in 744 B.C.E. But since this leaves the tail unexplained (for which a busy glossator found his own explanation) it will be advisable to allow for a topographical reference, namely, the loss of territory on both sides of the Jordan following the western campaigns of Tiglath-pileser from 738 to 732. These ended with the Assyrian occupation of Gilead and a good part of the Galilee, the usual deportations, and the confirmation of the last Israelite king, Hoshea, on the throne as an Assyrian client (2 Kgs 15:29–31). It would not be surprising if these events, so briefly and laconically recorded in the biblical text, resulted in misery and suffering not just for the combatants (the *baḥûrîm* of v 16) but the ordinary folk, including orphans and widows, who happened to be in the wrong place at the wrong time.

Stanza III moves towards a climax with the image of a brush fire or forest fire burning up a land already devastated, the devastation expressed by the already familiar motif of thorns and weeds (cf. 5:6; 7:23–25). From this burning landscape the author moves abruptly to a condition of turmoil and *anomie*, a society *in extremis*, for the description of which the metaphor of cannibalism was deemed the most appropriate. In reading these lines the remark of Albany in *King Lear*, that "man will become a universal appetite and so eat up himself," comes to mind. The language is that of the covenant curse (e.g. Deut 28:53–57; Lev 26:29), which reproduces the themes and even the wording of the vassal treaties. Esarhaddon's succession treaty, for example, stipulates that in the event of violation "in want and famine may one man eat the flesh of another" (line 449; Parpola and Watanabe 1988, 46). At this point, therefore, the poet sees the Northern Kingdom's descent into chaos as the outcome of a broken religious bond. The description corresponds to the period from the extinction of the Jehu dynasty with the assassination of Zechariah (746/745) to some time during the reign of the last ruler of Samaria, Hoshea (732–722), and is reflected at several points in contemporaneous discourses of that ruler's namesake, Hosea (Hos 4:2; 6:8–10; 7:1–3; 8:4; 13:10). During those two decades four out of six rulers were assassinated, and the last was either executed or deported by the Assyrians. Any attempt to fill in the details of this situation of civil strife (e.g. Hayes and Irvine 1987, 188–90) has to depend on isolated snippets of information in the biblical record, e.g., atrocities and oppressive measures perpetrated by Menahem (2 Kgs 15:16, 20) and military intervention against Judah by Pekah (2 Kgs 15:37). The chronological line stops short of the fall of Samaria, to return, in the final stanza (5:25), to the great earthquake with which the panorama opened.

ASSYRIA IS SUMMONED
TO THE ATTACK (5:26–30)

(Barth 1977, 192–94; Childs 1959; Troxel 1993)

TRANSLATION

5 ^{26}He will raise an ensign for a nation from afar,^{a}
and whistle for it from the ends of the earth.
Swiftly, speedily, it comes!
^{27}None among them^b grows weary, none of them stumbles,
they neither drowse nor sleep;^{c}
no belt is unloosed round the waist,
no sandal laces untied;
^{28}their arrows are sharpened,
all their bows are strung and taut;^{d}
the hooves of their horses are reckoned like flint,^{e}
their chariot wheels like the whirlwind;
^{29}their roaring is like a lion,
they roar^f like lion cubs;
snarling, they seize their prey;
when they carry it off, none can rescue it.
^{30}*He will growl over it on that day like the growling of the sea.*
If one looks to the earth there is only darkness and distress,
the light is obscured by the clouds.^{g}

NOTES

Apart from 1QIsa^a, we have from Qumran only a few letters of vv 26–28 from 4QIsa^b and part of vv 28–30 from pap4QIsa^p, which reads *vhbyṭ* for MT *věnib-baṭ*; ^{a} read *lěgôy mimmerḥāq* as Jer 5:15; MT *laggôyim mērāḥôq* (cf. Deut 28:49) may have been influenced by 11:12 *věnāśā' nēs laggôyim*; ^{b} *bô*, "among them," is missing from 1QIsa^a; ^{c} since *lō' yānûm vělō' yîšān* also occurs at Ps 121:4, with reference to Yahveh's unceasing care for Israel, several commentators take it to be a gloss; however, it fits the present context well and either the dependence could be in the reverse direction or, more likely, it was simply a popular turn of phrase; ^{d} *děrūkôt → drk* can refer to a bow drawn and ready to shoot (cf. Isa 21:15; Jer 46:9), but obviously this would be in battle and not on the march; *drk* suggests using the foot to bend a bow in order to string it; ^{e} read *kāṣōr* (1QIsa^a *kṣvr*) for MT *kaṣṣar*; ^{f} read *věyiš'ag*, "and it lets out a roar," but we would not expect *š'g* to be repeated in the same stich; ^{g} *'ărîpâ* is hapax and the feminine suffix unexplained; perhaps read *ba'ărî-piyyâ*, "in the cloud cover."

COMMENTS

This prediction of an imminent Assyrian *Blitzkrieg* is well situated after the description of the earthquake as the first of two phases of punishment; the same sequence occurs in 9:18–10:4 and in the vision reports of Amos (9:1–4). It also serves as the immediate preface to the core narrative, a circumstance that helps to explain the similar editorial additions with which it and the core narrative conclude (5:30b cf. 8:22). As such, it aligns with 7:18–19 and 8:5–8 in anticipating nothing but trouble from Ahaz's having recourse to Assyria for assistance. A more reflective and hopeful note will be sounded later in a poem about the Assyrians as an instrument in the hand of Yahveh (10:5–19). Later still, certainly in the post-disaster period, the antithesis between punishing events in the past and the expectation of a different future is highlighted by the raising of an ensign with a quite different purpose, to prepare for the return of dispersed Judeans to the homeland (11:12). Comparison with the topographically specific account of the approach of a hostile army in 10:27b–32 suggests that 5:26–29 may have been written somewhat earlier. In keeping with his overall reading of Isa 1–12, Kaiser (1972, 110–13) attributes the passage to a "theologian of history" writing in the fifth century B.C.E. and refers the description of the approaching army to the Babylonians' advancing on Jerusalem.

Commentators have been accustomed to finding mythological motifs in biblical descriptions of invading armies, generally approaching from the north (the so-called *Völkerkampf* motif, cf. Jer 4:5–8, 13; Joel 2:4–9), but in contrast to the agglutinated v 30, the poem 26–29 does not even indulge much in metaphor beyond the familiar image of the lion. True, the Assyrians are not named, but from the perspective of southern Palestine at that time Assyria, 350 miles or so distant, would seem like the ends of the earth. None of the elements of this description is unfamiliar. Like regimental colors, the "ensign" (*nēs*) is for rallying the troops for the march or for battle (e.g. Jer 4:6, 21; 50:2). In the developing Isaian literary tradition it will transmute into a rallying point for the return of dispersed Israelites (11:10, 12; 49:22; 62:10). In the post-destruction period the same will happen to the vivid figure of Yahveh "sicking" the Assyrians on Israel by whistling (cf. 7:18–19); instead, Yahveh will whistle to call the dispersed back to the homeland (Zech 10:8). Military equipment is known in some detail from the Assyrian practice of covering walls with plaques illustrating successful campaigns and the often gruesome fate of their victims. At this point only the elements that contributed most to Assyrian success in war are alluded to, i.e., archers, cavalry, and chariots.

As biblical records and Assyrian records and iconography attest, lions lived in close proximity to human settlements on both sides of the Euphrates during the Iron Age; in fact, lions are attested in Palestine up to the Middle Ages and in Iraq into the early years of the twentieth century. The real and dangerous proximity of these splendid animals combined with their symbolic potential will explain why they occur so frequently in the literature, including the book of Isaiah which has five terms for the lion, two of which occur in our passage.

Since the lion with its fearsome roar is a prominent theme in Amos (1:2; 3:4, 8; 5:19), this is another link between Amos and the Isaian tradition.

The final verse makes a smooth transition from the snarling and growling of lions at feeding time to the similar sound of the sea breaking on the shore (cf. 17:12). That the verse is editorial is evident from the "on that day" (*bayyôm hahû'*) formula indicating what we might call a future-oriented cameo of frequent occurrence throughout the book (in chs. 1–12 see 2:20; 3:18; 4:2; 7:18, 20, 21, 23; 10:20; 11:10, 11). It may have been added in the post-destruction period (as Clements 1980a, 70), but there is no compelling reason to exclude earlier editorial activity at this point. No attempt at deciphering this obscure verse, which has much in common with 8:22, has been entirely successful. As sometimes happens in *bayyôm hahû'* passages, it may express the common theme of eschatological reversal: those who are growling at and feeding on Israel now will be growled over "from another quarter" then (*věyinhom ʿalaw*) and will moreover be surrounded by darkness and misery.

THE THRONE ROOM VISION (6:1–13)

(Baltzer; Budde 1928; Cazelles 1975; Clements 1985; G. R. Driver 1971; Emerton 1982; Engnell; Evans 1982; 1989; Görg; Gosse 1991; 1992a; Habel; Hardmeier; Hesse; Hurowitz; Irvine 1992; Joines; Knierim; Lescow; Liebreich 1954; Lind; Long; Metzger; Milgrom; Niehr; Nobile; Rendtorff 1989; de Savignac; Sawyer 1964; J. M. Schmidt; Schoors 1977; Sonnet; Steck 1972; Whitley 1959; Williamson 1994, 30–56)

TRANSLATION

6 ¹In the year King Uzziah died I saw the Sovereign Lord seated on a throne raised up on high, with his train filling the palace. ²Seraphs were stationed round about him, each with six wings.[a] With two they covered their faces, with two their bodies,[b] and with two they hovered. ³Each cried out to the other saying, "Holy, holy, holy[c] is Yahveh of the heavenly hosts; all the earth is full of his glory." ⁴As each cried out[d] the uprights attached to the threshhold[e] shook and the house began to fill with smoke. ⁵"Alas, I am lost,"[f] I cried, "for I am a man of unclean lips living among a people with unclean lips. My eyes have looked on the king, Yahveh of the hosts!" ⁶One of the seraphs flew to me with a hot coal in his hand he had taken from the altar with a pair of tongs. ⁷He touched me on the mouth with it, saying, "Now this has touched your lips your iniquity has been removed, your sin purged away."[g]

⁸I then heard the voice of the Sovereign Lord saying, "Whom shall I send, and who will go for us?" I replied, "Here I am, send me!" ⁹"Go then to this people," he said, "and say to them, 'Keep on hearing without understanding, keep on seeing without perceiving.' ¹⁰ Make this people dull of perception, hard of hearing, sight impaired,[h] lest they see with their eyes, hear with their ears, and grasp with their mind, and then change their ways and be healed."

[11]Then I asked, "How long, O Lord?" He replied, "Until cities lie deserted without inhabitants, houses without occupants, and the land left a desolation." [12][Yahveh will carry off the people to a distant place, and desolation will be great in the land.][i] [13]If but a tenth of the land[j] is left it will revert to pasture. It will be like the oak and the terebinth which, when felled, have only a stump left.[k] [Its stump is the holy seed.][l]

NOTES

[a] *Šēš kĕnāpáyim*, dual: six wings in pairs;   [b] *raglāv*, "feet," a euphemism for the genitals (cf. Exod 4:25; Isa 7:20);   [c] 1QIsa[a] has *qādôš* twice only, perhaps influenced by the twofold repetition of the acclamation *qādôš hû'*, "holy is He!" in Ps 99; but threefold repetition is liturgically more common and MT is supported by all the ancient versions, cf. the expanded form in the Tg.; [d] *miqqôl haqqôrē'*, literally, "at the sound (voice) of the one crying out";   [e] a guess at the meaning of *'ammôt hassippîm*: *'ammâ* = "forearm," "cubit," but not attested elsewhere as an architectural term;   [f] *nidmêtî* by some taken to be Niphal → *dmh*, "be silent," following Aquila, Symm., Theod., and Vulg., e.g., Wildberger 1991, 248–50, "I must be silent," though this is a problematic translation of the perfect tense; I take it to derive from *dmh* = "destroy," as in Isa 15:1 *nidmâ* parallel with *šuddad*, "destroyed," "ruined," cf. also Jer 47:5; Hos 10:7; Ps 49:13, 21;   [g] lit., "your iniquity has withdrawn" (*sār*), "your sin has been covered up" (*tĕkuppār*);   [h] literally, "glue their eyes shut" → verbal stem *š''* cf. Isa 29:9;   [i] a logical development from 11, but reference to Yahveh in third person suggests a later insertion;   [j] "the land" supplied for *bāh* (*vĕ'ôd bāh 'ăśiriyyâ*, "if a tenth is still in it, i.e., the land"; [k] with the exception of the last three words, v 13 is probably damaged beyond repair; the attempts at reconstructive surgery (see Wildberger 1991, 251) do not improve on MT, which is followed here in spite of the obscure terms *šalleket* (1QIsa[a] *mšlkt*) and *maṣṣebet*, both hapax;   [l] a Second Commonwealth gloss cf. 4:3; see commentary.

COMMENTS

This vision narrative is often referred to as the call of Isaiah to a prophetic ministry, but from its position in the book it is clear that this was at least not the view of the editors who arranged the material. Its location at this point, together with the acknowledgment of failure implicit in the conversation during the visionary experience, suggests rather that it functions in a more limited way as Isaiah's commissioning for a specific political mission in connection with the threat of a Syrian-Samarian invasion in or about the year 734. It is therefore structurally a part of chs. 6–8 known at least since Budde as the Isaian Memoir (*Denkschrift*; though the use of this term has been questioned by Reventlow, Irvine, and others). This section is set out in the sequence autobiographical-biographical-autobiographical, similar to the arrangement of Hos 1–3. We could therefore read the statement towards the end of chs. 6–8 that "[all of this is] from Yahveh of the hosts who dwells on Mount Zion" (8:18) as an inclusio referring back to the commissioning by Yahveh of the hosts in the present passage. The location of 6:1–13 does not, however, necessarily imply that chs. 1–5 date to a time prior to Uzziah's death (contra Milgrom), since the editorial arrangement is not exclusively and not even primarily chronological, and we have seen that some of the paragraphs are certainly later. We cannot establish the precise date of Uzziah's death following on abdication after contracting a serious skin disease (2 Kgs 15:1–7), but 6:1 suggests that it coincided with the beginning of the Syro-Ephraimite crisis, and therefore not earlier than 736 B.C.E.

While there are no compelling reasons to date the passage to the Second Temple period (pace Whitley; Kaiser 1972, 118–21; Gosse), if the account of the commissioning served both to legitimate Isaiah's mission and to explain its failure it must have been written some time after the death of Uzziah (the date is uncertain but probably 736–734). It has been put together as a carefully crafted dramatization of the claim that Isaiah has been admitted to the divine council, that he is therefore privy to the divine agenda, and that he has been charged to implement that agenda in the world of Judean and international politics. The "message," then, is that the mission was God's doing and that its failure was foreseen and foreordained and therefore cannot be laid at Isaiah's door. The seer's question about how long this situation would last also hints at the issue of delay in fulfillment that will come to the fore towards the end of the section (8:16–18). Commentators have been much exercised to explain the incomprehension, the spiritual and moral obtuseness, of the seer's audience as something foreordained—as in fact the whole point and purpose of the mission. The same question arises in connection with another and similar vision, that of Micaiah ben Imlah (1 Kgs 22:19–23), in which one of those surrounding Yahveh on his heavenly throne, referred to simply as "the Spirit" (*harûaḥ*), volunteers to bring about Ahab's death by deceiving him through false prophets and is commissioned to do so. It is no doubt correct to read this disconcerting aspect of Isaiah's commissioning as a post factum justification of failure or, better, to suggest that the mission, which was precisely to harden hearts, in fact succeeded; but to relocate the theological problem in Isaiah's later reflection on the event is not the same as solving it (cf. the reference to the "alien work" of the deity in Isa 28:21). The Old Greek version solved it by the time-honored method of retranslation ("for the heart of this people has exalted itself, they have listened with heavy ears, and have shut their eyes") and, beginning with early Christianity (Matt 13:14–15 and parallels; John 12:40; Acts 28:26–27), abusive appeal to this text throughout Christian history has served to highlight what was perceived to be the obduracy of the Jewish people in not accepting Jesus as messiah and savior (Sawyer; Evans 1989).

As the vision narrative opens, the scenario appears to be that of a throne room. The throne is at a high elevation presumably approached by steps, and the description of the One Enthroned is restricted to his royal robe and its train which—hyperbolically—filled the entire room. Perhaps the author had in

mind something similar to the depiction of Assyrian kings of gigantic proportions compared to those of pygmy size who attended them or the prisoners
paraded before them (e.g. Esarhaddon, *ANEP*, #447). A similar scenario confronts us in Micaiah's vision, referred to above, and in the opening narrative of
Job (1–2). Isaiah often uses the title "Yahveh of the [heavenly] hosts" (*YHVH
ṣĕbā'ōt*), intimately associated with the ark and its sanctuary (it occurs 57 times
in 1–39, 6 times in 40–66), but he never speaks of Yahveh "seated on the cherubim" (*yošēb 'al hakkĕrûbîm*), i.e., on a throne the armrests of which represent
winged mythological creatures (the only occurrence of the expression in the
book, 37:16, is parallel with 2 Kgs 19:15). In the present scene Yahveh is, instead, attended and guarded by an unspecified number of seraphs (*ṣĕrapîm*).

Etymologically the term *ṣĕrapîm* would mean "burning ones," and the ser-
aph is elsewhere a poisonous snake whose bite stings and burns (Num 21:6, 8;
Deut 8:15) and who, like the guardians of the throne, is equipped for flight
(*śārāp mĕ'ôpēp* Isa 14:29; 30:6). It is tempting to associate this aspect of the vision scenario with the cult object in the Jerusalem temple known as Nehush-
tan, a bronze serpent with healing powers of Mosaic origin to which incense
was offered (2 Kgs 18:4 cf. Num 21:6, 8–9). This would at any rate explain the
altar and the hot coals, hardly consistent with the primary image of a throne
room or audience hall. We are perhaps meant to imagine the seraphim hovering in place around but not above the Enthroned One, ready at a moment's notice to do his behest.

The seraphic acclamation, from which derive the liturgical forms of the
Trisagion, Sanctus, and *qĕdûšâ*, proclaims the holiness of the One Enthroned.
The title "the Holy One of Israel" (*qĕdôš yiśrā'ēl*) is one of several features that
confer a certain impression of unity on the book, being found in all its sections;
this, however, does not imply that the title was suggested by the seraphic acclamation (pace Williamson 1994, 41). Holiness implies otherness, removal from
profane reality, the *mysterium tremendum* of Rudolph Otto's once very influen-
tial book *Das Heilige* (*The Holy*, 1917), but it is a quality that can permeate and
serve to define aspects of space and time, a situation amply illustrated in the
Priestly material in the Pentateuch and in Ezek 40–48. Another way of expressing the manifestation of the divine essence is encapsulated in the term *kābōd*,
translated "glory" or "effulgence." Associated with the ark in the account of the
Philistine wars (1 Sam 4:21–22), it is likewise a richly developed topos in P and
in Ezekiel, a theologoumenon that purports to present simultaneously both
the transcendence and the immanence of Godhead. The point can be made
by referring to the strange incident in which Moses asks to see the *kābōd* and is
shown the back rather than the face of Yahveh (Exod 33:18–23). We can read
it as an attempt to solve the theoretical problem of how the transcendent God
can be present among people and under what conditions the divine presence
may be experienced this side of death.

The tectonic phenomena induced by the seraphic acclamation belong to
the standard description of theophanies (cf. the Sinai theophany, Exod 19:18)

and perhaps provide some idea of how the earthquake during Uzziah's reign would have been understood (note the effect on nature of Yahveh's roaring from Zion in Amos 1:1–2). Isaiah's reaction is also understandable in the present context (cf. Exod 3:6; Judg 6:22; 13:22), as he laments that his unclean lips make it impossible for him to participate in the seraphic liturgy. Purification of the lips (rather than, for example, the hands) indicates preparation for a specifically prophetic mission and was a necessary prelude to the conversation and commissioning to follow. It has been compared with the rinsing of the mouth by Mesopotamian cultic functionaries as a preparation for public speaking (Hurowitz). The question about an emissary to be sent "on our behalf" (cf. Gen 1:26; 3:22; 11:7) implies that Yahveh is surrounded by his entourage—here seraphs, elsewhere spirits (1 Kgs 22:20–21) or "sons of God," i.e., lesser deities (Job 1–2)—with whom he may at times confer, as monarchs are wont to do. In the Micaiah vision-narrative the question of the Enthroned One is followed by a discussion, but in this case discussion is preempted by Isaiah's immediately volunteering to serve. In this respect both visions diverge from the more common form of commissioning (e.g. Jeremiah, Moses) in which the emissary expostulates and has to be reassured and practically coerced to undertake the mission. Instead of expostulating, Isaiah asks a question necessitated by the sheer negativity of the language in which the commissioning is couched. The answer to the plaintive question "how long?" (ʿad-matay?), heard often in liturgical laments (e.g. Ps 74:10; 79:5; 94:3), must refer to the future devastation of Judah, rather than the Assyrian conquest of Syria and Israel, since it is Judeans who are to be rendered obdurate as a result of the mission. It is generally recognized that v 12, with its allusion to deportation, was added after 586 B.C.E. Several commentators argue that all of the section vv 12–13 derives from a post-disaster editor. This may be so, but the devastation and decimation would also match the effects of Sennacherib's campaign in 701, the maṣṣebet ("tree stump") referring to the bare survival of Jerusalem. The final phrase—"its stump is the holy seed"—however, reapplies the figure to the Judean community under Persian rule or, more precisely, the Babylonian immigrant community (bĕnê haggôlâ) anxious to remain apart from the native population of the province (cf. Ezra 9:2, the only other occurrence of the phrase zeraʿ qōdeš). Other linguistic and thematic indications of later interest in the passage have been pointed out in recent commentary—for example, the throne raised up on high (rām vĕnissāʾ) and the theme of spiritual blindness and deafness. It has also been argued that the narrative provided the model for the call of the Second Isaiah in 40:1–8 (e.g. Williamson 1994, 30–56). It seems rather that most instances can be explained more readily by the persistence within the Isaian tradition of certain themes and turns of phrase rather than by direct dependence on 6:1–13. Moreover, 40:1–8 has really little in common with the present passage, is not addressed to an individual, and does not look anything like a call to a prophetic ministry.

ISAIAH'S FIRST INTERVENTION IN JUDEAN POLITICS (734 B.C.E.; 7:1–17)

(Ackroyd 1984; Albright 1955; Alt 1964b; Bartelmus; Berg; Bickert; Budde 1933; Clements 1990; Dearman; Dequeker; Dietrich; Fensham; Gelin; Görg 1983; Haag; Hammershaimb 1966, 11–28; Höffken 1980; 1989; Høgenhaven 1990; Irsigler; Irvine 1993; Jensen 1979; Kamesar; Kilian; Laato; Lindblom; Machinist; Mazar; McKane 1967; Mitchell; Oded 1972; Oswalt 1993; Pitard 1987, 145–89; Rice; Roberts 1985b; Saebø 1960; Stamm 1960; 1974; Steck 1982, 171–203; Thompson; Vanel; Werlitz; Wolf; Wolff 1962; Würthwein)

TRANSLATION

7 ¹In the days of Ahaz son of Jotham son of Uzziah, king of Judah, Rezin king of Syria and Pekah son of Remaliah, king of Israel, went up to fight against Jerusalem but were unable[a] to win a decisive victory against it. ²When the house of David was told that Syria had prevailed on Ephraim to join them,[b] its resolve,[c] and the resolve[c] of its people, was shaken as the trees of the forest shake in the wind. ³Then Yahveh said to Isaiah: "Go out to meet Ahaz together with Shear-yashub your son at the end of the conduit of the Upper Pool on the way to Bleacher's Meadow.⁴Say to him, 'See that you remain calm; don't be afraid or fainthearted on account of these two stumps of smoldering firebrands and the fury of Rezin, Syria, and the son of Remaliah.⁵Together with[d] Ephraim and the son of Remaliah Syria has planned to do you harm. ⁶"Let us invade Judah," they are saying, "and terrify it; let us conquer it for ourselves.[e] We will then put the son of Tabeel[f] on the throne of Judah."'"

⁷Thus says the Lord Yahveh:
"It shall not hold up, it shall not continue to be
⁸that Damascus is the head of Syria,
and Rezin the head of Damascus;
⁹that Samaria is the head of Ephraim,
and the son of Remaliah the head of Samaria.
[In sixty-five years' time Ephraim will be broken to pieces and will no longer be a nation.][g]
If you do not hold fast in faith
you will surely fail to stand firm."[h]

¹⁰Yahveh[i] spoke once again to Ahaz: ¹¹"Ask for a sign from Yahveh your God, from as deep as Sheol[j] or as high as the sky," ¹²but Ahaz replied, "I will not put Yahveh to the test by asking for a sign." ¹³Then Isaiah[k] said, "Listen, you house of David: not content with testing the patience of people, will you also test the patience of my God? ¹⁴Wherefore, the Lord God himself will give you a sign: See, the young woman is pregnant and about to give birth to a son; she will give him the name[l] Immanuel. ¹⁵By the time he knows how to reject what is bad and choose what is good he will be feeding on buttermilk and honey. ¹⁶For before the child knows how to reject what is bad and choose what

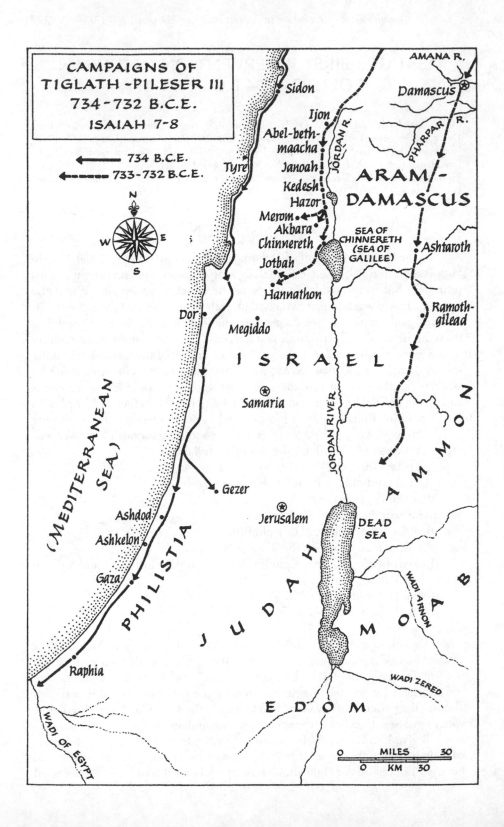

CAMPAIGNS OF
TIGLATH-PILESER III
734-732 B.C.E.
ISAIAH 7-8

→ 734 B.C.E.
⇢ 733-732 B.C.E.

is good, the land whose two kings now fill you with fear will be deserted.[17]Yahveh will bring on you, your people, and your ancestral house a time such has not been witnessed[m] since Ephraim broke away from Judah [namely, the king of Assyria]."

NOTES

[a] Plural with 2 Kgs. 16:5; also 1QIsa[a], LXX[A], Syr., Vulg.; MT has singular; [b] the verbal form *nāḥāh* is difficult and often emended; I follow G. R. Driver (1933, 377) in assigning to it the meaning "ally with," the preposition *'al* suggesting an element of coercion; [c] literally, "heart"; [d] supplied since a preposition is lacking; alternatively *'epráyim ûben-rĕmalyāhû* could have been inserted at a later time; [e] *vĕnabqi'ennâ 'ēlênû: bq'* Hiphil = "break through, invade, break open," therefore "conquer"; [f] with LXX, Syr., Vulg. and cf. Ezra 4:7. The MT *tābĕ'al* is an apparent dysphemism meaning "good for nothing" (Dearman); [g] An evident addition inserted before 9a that gives us a date (669) long after the collapse of the Northern Kingdom (722). It coincides with the death of Esarhaddon and the accession of Ashurbanipal, who may have carried out further deportations subsequent to rebellion in the western provinces (Ezra 4:2, 9–10); [h] the typically Isaian assonance (*ta'ămînû . . . tē'āmēnû*) cannot easily be reproduced in translation; [i] Since Yahveh speaks through the prophet there is no need to replace "Yahveh" with "Isaiah"; [j] *šĕ'ōlâ* for *šĕ'ālâ*; [k] MT *vayyō'mer*, "he said"; [l] reading *vĕqārā't* as a 3d person fem. sing. (GKC §74g); [m] literally, "days that have not come."

COMMENTS

The lineaments of an event can be disengaged from the many elaborations and editorial accretions in this passage. Rezin of Syria (Damascus) persuaded or coerced Pekah, ruler of the Kingdom of Samaria, to ally with him in an attack on Jerusalem with the purpose of forcing Ahaz to join their anti-Assyrian coalition. The overlap between 7:1 and 2 Kgs 16:5 suggests that the narrative core of the passage may have drawn on an alternative version of the account in the History in a manner somewhat analogous to Isa 36–39 (cf. 2 Kgs 18:13–20:19) and Amos 7:10–17 (cf. 2 Kgs 14:23–27). 2 Kings 15–16 provides a broader perspective on the sequence of events, one that covers the reigns of Pekah (ca. 737–732) and Hoshea (ca. 732–722) in Samaria and Uzziah (ca. 783–742), Jotham (ca. 742–735) and Ahaz (ca. 735–715) in Jerusalem. It does so by placing them in the context of Tiglath-pileser III's campaigns in Syria–Palestine, which resulted in the loss of Dor, Galilee, and Gilead to Israel and the fall of Damascus and subsequent deportation of its inhabitants to Kir either in Mesopotamia or the far north of Syria. The Historian also assigns a role at this juncture to Edomites (2 Kgs 16:6 emended text), as does the parallel version in 2 Chr 28:16–19. Hosea 5:8–6:6 may allude to the same sequence of events (following Alt 1964 [3rd edition] [1919]), though this is less certain.

With the help of the annals of Tiglath-pileser III (745–727), unfortunately fragmentary and out of sequence but admirably recomposed by Tadmor, we can contextualize and reconstruct the events of 734–732 as recorded in the biblical texts with a reasonable degree of assurance. After initially submitting to Assyria, Rezin (*ra-qi-a-nu* in Assyrian texts, perhaps originally Radyan), ruler of Damascus from around the mid–eighth century, profited by Assyrian military operations in Urartu and Media (738–734) to put together an anti-Assyrian alliance involving Tyre and the Kingdom of Samaria, the latter ruled by the usurper, Pekah, perhaps as a vassal of the Syrian king. The allies were bringing military pressure to bear on Judah even before the accession of Ahaz (2 Kgs 15:37–38), certainly with the aim of bringing Judah into the coalition, but probably with the additional object of regaining control over the Transjordanian region and the incense route. The invasion of Judah and siege of Jerusalem (the latter mentioned explicitly only in the History) must have followed shortly after the Assyrian campaign in 734 against Tyre and the Philistine cities, a campaign in which the Assyrian army reached as far as the Wadi el-ʿArish, where Tiglath-pileser set up a commemorative stele. Assyrian penetration so far south, following shortly after the conquest of Hamath and other states in northern and central Syria, would have made it seem to Radyan all the more necessary to bring Judah into the alliance, especially in view of the possibility of Egyptian participation. Hence the plan to replace Ahaz with a Syrian puppet ruler, the designated individual being "the son of Tabeel," of uncertain provenance but possibly an Ammonite prince (see Mazar; Oded; Albright; less probable is Vanel's argument for Tubail of Tyre).

The biblical texts are generally interpreted with the sense that, after rejecting Isaiah's advice, Ahaz appealed to Assyria against the Syrian-Samarian axis with the result that Judah became an Assyrian vassal and the allies were defeated and eventually incorporated into the Assyrian Empire. The annals of Tiglath-pileser record tribute paid by Ahaz or Jehoahaz of Judah (*ia-ú-ḫa-zi* [kur]*ia-ú-da-a-a*) together with other western rulers (Tadmor 1994, 170–71), and the statement in 2 Kgs 16:8–9 that the Assyrian king was motivated by a substantial bribe to relieve pressure on Judah may simply refer to this event. In any case, Tiglath-pileser's plans for extending the western reaches of his empire were independent of any decisions reached in Jerusalem. In other words, the campaigns in Syria, Gilead, and the Galilee in 734 and 733, leading to the extinction of Syria's independence and the drastic territorial reduction of the Kingdom of Samaria under the Assyrian-appointed puppet Hoshea, would have happened whatever the course of action taken by Ahaz. It would not be surprising, in fact, if Isaiah had foreseen that this would happen and advised the Judean king accordingly. In fairness to this ruler, we should add that it is also possible that Ahaz's submission afforded Judah an additional century or so of more or less independent existence.

This, then, is the situation in which we first hear of Isaiah playing a political role. The passage refers to him as protagonist in the third person, and this biographical account is bracketed by first person narrative in chs. 6 and 8. It consists of two verbal exchanges between Isaiah and Ahaz (3–9, 10–17) with a brief historical preface (1–2). The first of these describes the situation, prescribes what is to be done, and states what is to happen; in the second a sign reinforcing the prophetic word is offered, declined, but given anyway. This type of salvation oracle, with its characteristic assurance "don't be afraid" (4), is one of the most frequently attested forms of prophetic utterance, in Israel as elsewhere, especially in the context of warfare; parallels may be found among the Mari oracles and in the Zakir Stele. The latter records how, a generation or two before Ahaz, the ruler of Hamath in northern Syria, under siege by an enemy coalition, is assured by his deity speaking through seers as follows: "don't be afraid; I have made you king and will stand by you and save you" (*ANET*, 501). The formula cannot therefore serve to demonstrate the dependence of this narrative on Deuteronomistic war theology, thereby assigning to it a Second Temple origin (contra Kaiser 1972, 138).

The parallelism between Isaiah's encounter with Ahaz and his intervention under Hezekiah thirty-three years later raises the crucial question of the date of composition of 7:1–17 and the question whether the former incident was presented with the critical juncture of Sennacherib's campaign and the siege of Jerusalem in 701 B.C.E. in mind. The injunction not to be afraid occurs in 37:6, also as an oracular utterance to which a sign is attached (37:22–35). As we shall see, the four appendices that follow our passage (7:18–25) fit the disastrous situation in Judah created by the invasion of the Assyrian army in 701, and there are other indications in chs. 1–12 pointing to the events of 703–701 as providing a perspective dictating the interpretation of past events. If the parallelism between the two passages is conscious and deliberate, as seems probable, it might also help to explain some puzzling features of the narrative in 7:1–17. One of these is the role assigned to the prophet's son with the symbolic name Shear-yashub (= "a remnant will return"), a name that understandably lent itself readily to reinterpretation at different historical junctures (Isa 10:20–22; 11:11–16). In the present context the name is clearly one of good omen, but only in the sense of a few people barely surviving a major devastation. While this would fit very well the situation created in Judah by Sennacherib, who claims to have driven more than 200,000 Judeans from their cities but did not take Jerusalem, the point of Isaiah's message to Ahaz is that if he "holds fast in faith" all will turn out well, or at least there will not occur a deportation or displacement from which a remnant might eventually hope to return. The political import of Isaiah's advice to the king, reinforced by the presence of Shear-yashub, is therefore not entirely clear. Ahaz must not be panicked into surrendering to the allies—so much is clear—but there is no indication that he was about to do so. He must also resist the temptation to submit to Assyria, advice that is less clear since, given that he was faced with the inexorable Assyrian advance, just doing nothing was not an option: one submitted and became a tributary to Assyria, as Tyre did in the same year, or one resisted and accepted the consequences, the option taken up with predictable consequences by Damascus and the Kingdom of Israel.

We find a clue to solving these problems in the finale of the narrative, in which we hear of God's hiding his face and of the need to live in hope, in consequence of which the prophecy is written down and consigned to disciples in the expectation of a future fulfillment (8:16–22). Perhaps this may serve as an illustration of the theory of cognitive dissonance in that the fulfillment of the prophecy, unrealized in the present moment, is postponed to a future in which, given the appropriate circumstances, it could be reactivated. That the onslaught of Sennacherib was seen to be such a moment is clear from the allusion to a written prophecy in connection with events at that time (30:8–10). Here, too, in the context of the later crisis, the need for trustful reliance on the truth of the prophetic message is emphasized, with distinct echoes of the prophet's encounter with Ahaz (see commentary on 30:15). It is also possible that the same situation lies behind the allusion to an unfulfilled revelation and the need for faith in the prophetic word in a familiar passage in Habakkuk (2:1–4). Habakkuk's activity is usually dated shortly after the death of Josiah, and it was during his reign that the prophecies of Isaiah must have achieved a new resonance and relevance.

In the first segment, therefore, Isaiah is given a specific mission to reassure Ahaz that the attack of the Syrian-Samarian coalition will fail and, by implication, to dissuade him from responding to the threat by submitting to Assyria. The message concludes by making the future of the Davidic dynasty (the "house of David," v 2), and therefore of the nation, contingent on accepting the truth of the prophetic word (9b). The second segment of the narrative dealing with the sign (10–17) is not necessarily presented as immediately consecutive to the first or as taking place in the same location, i.e., somewhere in the Kidron Valley (3). As a way of encouraging him to accept the proferred advice, Ahaz is invited to ask for a sign and is given the greatest latitude in making his request. A sign could be miraculous and arbitrary (e.g. the sign of the sun's shadow on the stairs in 38:7–8) or merely extraordinary but overtly symbolic (e.g. Isaiah walking naked through Jerusalem, 20:3). Personal and place-names may also have sign value, either hopeful or threatening (e.g. the names of Isaiah himself and those of his children or disciples, 8:18). The ability to perform signs of a miraculous or extraordinary nature was an acknowledged aspect of prophetic role performance (cf. Deut 13:1–2), passing in due course into the annals of hagiography in both Judaism and Christianity (e.g. Hanina ben Dosa, Jesus).

The terseness of the narrative does not permit a clear sense as to why the refusal of Ahaz to put Yahveh to the test elicited such a testy reply. The explanation is no doubt to be sought in the deliberate contrast between Ahaz and Hezekiah, who were faced with similarly critical situations, rather than in the logic of the narrative itself. The sign is presented in a manner reminiscent of birth annunciation scenes familiar from both testaments (e.g. Judg 13:3–5; Luke 1:31–33). Neither the context nor biblical usage in general provides much help in establishing the identity of either the prospective mother or her child, with the result that by now the scholarly debate on the designation of the woman and the name of the child practically defies documentation (see, nevertheless, additional bibliographies in Kaiser 1972, 156–57; Wildberger 1991, 280–82; and Sweeney 1996, 163–64). The term *ʿalmâ* ("young woman") occurs only three times in the singular in Biblical Hebrew, with reference to Rebekah (Gen 24:43) and Moses' sister (Exod 2:8), both unmarried at the time, and in Prov 30:19, "the way of a man with a maiden" (*derek geber bĕʿalmâ*). Use of the article (*the* young woman) has led to speculations about a *hieros gamos* ("sacred marriage") involving a goddess figure (cf. Ugaritic *ǵlmt*), but what this might mean in the context is somewhat opaque. The later allusion to Isaiah's union with the female prophet (*hannĕbîʾâ* 8:3) has suggested a parallelism with *hāʿalmâ*, and therefore reference to a female cult prophet, but it is unclear why, if a female cult prophet was intended, she would be referred to simply as the young woman. We can also discount the idea that the meaning is collective, in the sense that young women in Judah will continue to bear children, will be in a position to nourish them, and will in gratitude give them the name Immanuel (as in Kaiser 1972, 103–4, in the first edition of his commentary). The language, and especially the names, suggest something more specific than that.

We note in passing the position advanced by Otto Kaiser in the second edition of his contribution to the Biblischer Kommentar series (*Isaiah: A Commentary*, 114–72), to the effect that the nucleus of the *Denkschrift* was addressed to the exilic communities with a view to explaining why the Davidic dynasty ended and under what conditions hope might be entertained for the future. This hypothesis does not persuade for several reasons, not least the expedients to which Kaiser has to have recourse in order to account for what is in the text. These include interpreting the references to historical events and persons as a late historicizing strand inserted by a muddled editor who failed to understand that the passage was meant to apply to the catastrophe of 586 B.C.E. Other problems with this hypothesis will be noted in due course.

Ibn Ezra, followed by Rashi, identified the young woman as Isaiah's wife and Immanuel as his son. The sign cannot refer to Jesus, argued Ibn Ezra, since it calls for verification in the near future and, as Jewish participants in debates with Christians in the Middle Ages never tired of pointing out, the correct Hebrew term for *virgo intacta* is *bĕtûlâ* not *ʿalmâ*. Rashi also rejected, on the basis of chronology, the identification of the child with Hezekiah. That the young woman is the wife of the prophet and Immanuel his son at least has the advantage of giving the prophet three children (Shear-yashub, Immanuel, Maher-shalal-hash-baz), symmetrical with the situation of Hosea, with whose discourses Isaiah seems to have been familiar. Isaiah's paternity might also be argued on the supposition that 7:1–17 and 8:1–4 are parallel versions comparable to the two accounts of Hosea's marital vicissitudes (1:2–9; 3:1–5). On the other hand, the sign is addressed to Ahaz as representative of the royal Davidic house (v 13), which suggests very strongly the sense of a reassurance that the royal Judean house will not be supplanted by Tabeel or anyone else and that in a very short time the crisis will be over. The chronological problems involved in identifying Immanuel with Hezekiah, son of Ahaz, and the young woman with Abi or Abijah, daughter of Zechariah (2 Kgs 18:2; 2 Chr 29:1), have generated an enormous amount of commentary since the time of Ibn Ezra. Without reviewing the issue once again in detail, it can be said that the entire biblical chronology for this period is confused and internally inconsistent (e.g. 2 Kgs 15:30 cf. 16:5; 2 Kgs 18:10 cf. 18:13; 2 Kgs 16:2 cf. 18:2), with the result that a conclusion cannot be reached on chronological grounds alone either permitting or excluding identification of Immanuel with Hezekiah. What *can* be said is that the earliest extant interpretation speaks of Immanuel's land being overrun by the Assyrians, a fairly transparent allusion to Hezekiah (8:8, 10) who, as the Historian recalled, lived up to his symbolic name (*vĕhāyāh YHVH ʿimmô*, "and Yahveh was with him," 2 Kgs 18:7). If, as suggested earlier, the prophet's encounter with Ahaz was written up with the Sennacherib campaign and its sequel in mind, this is no more than we would expect.

In excluding identification of Immanuel with Jesus, or by implication with any other figure more than two or three years into the future, Ibn Ezra was pursuing his goal of establishing the literal sense, the *pĕšāt*, of the text in question and doing so centuries before the emergence of the historical-critical method. By pursuing the same inquiry even further, however, we have come to see that the biblical texts themselves testify to a process of generating new and multiple meanings and appropriations in the course of the life cycle of the same texts. Most critical readers of the Bible have also come to accept the possibility of a plurality of meanings, what Buber called the "infinite interpretability" of biblical texts, as they are "recycled" in different interpretative communities. The identification of Immanuel with Jesus and the young woman with the Virgin Mary in one such early Christian community (Matt 1:23), facilitated by the LXX *hē parthenos* (understood as "the virgin") and perpetuated through the Vulgate translation word *virgo*, came to have great significance in Christian theology and iconography (see Sawyer 1996, 66–70 and passim). As we come to the end of our commentary we shall see that this is only one aspect, and perhaps not the most significant, of the process by which the interpretation of the book of Isaiah shaped the self-understanding, identity, and mission of early Christian communities.

DISASTERS OF WAR: FOUR CAMEOS (7:18–25)

(McKane 1967)

TRANSLATION

7 [18]On that day Yahveh will whistle for the flies along the edges of Egypt's streams and for the bees in the land of Assyria, [19] and they will all come and

settle in the steep wadis[a] and the clefts of the cliffs, on all the thornbushes[b] and watering holes.[c]

[20]On that day the Sovereign Lord will shave with a razor borrowed from the king of Assyria[d] across the Euphrates the head and the pubic hair,[e] and he will sweep away the beard as well.

[21]On that day a person will raise a young cow and a couple of sheep, [22]and they will give so much milk that the owner will feed on buttermilk;[f] for everyone left in the land will feed on buttermilk and honey.

[23]On that day every place where there are a thousand vines worth a thousand shekels of silver will be turned into a place of thorns and weeds. [24]People will come there with bow and arrows, for the entire land will be turned into a place of thorns and weeds. [25]For fear of thorns and weeds you will not venture on to any of the hills which used to be worked with the hoe. There oxen will roam free and sheep and goats wander about.

NOTES

[a] *Naḥălê habbattôt* cf. note on 5:6; an Arabic cognate suggests the meaning "cut off," therefore wadis of the cut-off places, i.e., ravines or canyons; probably chosen as much for sound as for meaning (alternating labials and nasals); [b] *naʿăṣûṣ* in MH "thornbush" → verb *nʿṣ* "prick," "pierce"; according to Saadya *spina Christi*; [c] *nahălōl*, hapax, but cf. the place-names Nahalol (Judg 1:30) and Nahalal (Josh 19:15; 21:35), perhaps places where animals were led (verb *nhl*) to be watered, rather than *nahălōlîm* = "thornbushes" (Saadya); [d] *běmelek ʾaššûr* is syntactically awkward and probably added, cf. 7:17b; [e] literally, "the hair of the feet"; *raglăyim*, "feet," a euphemism for the genitals (cf. Exod 4:25; Isa 6:2); [f] *yōʾkal ḥemʾâ kî* not translated in LXX, perhaps MT is expansionary; 1QIsaᵃ as MT.

COMMENTS

The four addenda introduced by the familiar redactional formula "on that day" (*bayyôm hahûʾ*) follow naturally from the allusion immediately preceding to "days that have not [yet] come," which looks like a prediction of disaster at the hands of the Assyrians (17). The first two play on the theme of Assyria as Yahveh's instrument or surrogate for punishing his own people (cf. Assyria as a club, axe, saw, 10:5–19), though whether the prospective victim is the Kingdom of Samaria with its ally or Judah is not explicitly stated. The third and fourth are editorial variations on existing Isaian motifs—buttermilk and honey (cf. 7:15), the vine (cf. 5:1–7), thorns and weeds, hoeing, and the trampling of animals (cf. 5:5–6)—which taken together point unmistakably to a future critical situation in Judah consequent on the decision of Ahaz to accept the Assyrian yoke. The intent is to create a moral nexus between events during the reign of Ahaz and the devastation caused by Sennacherib's invasion, though in fact the latter actually came about as a result of Hezekiah's refusal to pay tribute. Somewhat later, the Assyrian invasion under Hezekiah will be explained quite unambiguously with reference to Ahaz's infidelity (8:5–8).

The representation of the Assyrian army as a plague of killer bees is unexceptional (cf. Deut 1:44; Ps 118:12), and it would be consonant with the drift of the section as a whole to refer the metaphor to Sennacherib's campaign in southern Palestine in 701, culminating in the siege of Jerusalem. Mention of the Egyptians is more problematic. Unlike bees (see Wildberger 1991 for details of apiary lore, 322–23), flies do not respond to whistling or nest among rocks and in bushes; hence the tendency in the commentary tradition to assign this allusion to a later glossator. The editor may have been thinking of the pro-Assyrian policy of Shabako of the twenty-fifth Nubian dynasty (ca. 716–702) rather than that of his successor Shebitku (ca. 702–690), the "broken reed" on whom Hezekiah was advised by the Assyrian generalissimo not to rely (36:6). Elsewhere in Isaiah (e.g. 19:18–25) "Assyria" and "Egypt" serve as code-names for Seleucids and Ptolemies, as we shall see, but 7:18–19 provides no clue that this is the case here. The second cameo presents the brutal but realistic image of shaming captives by shaving off their hair, including facial and body hair (cf. 2 Sam 10:1–5).

The reuse of the buttermilk and honey motif (7:15) in the third editorial addition looks at first sight like an exception to the litany of disasters, and this could indeed be the case if part or all of 22 were added at an even later time (see note on the text), perhaps as indicating an eschatological, messianic scenario (Kaiser 1972, 174, 177). But it is possible to interpret it otherwise: either in the sense that one cow and two sheep represent the minimum for a household to survive or that the loss of cultivated land will have left ample space for grazing or, finally, that the survivors of military disaster will have to live off the natural products of the land rather than meat and cereal products, including bread. The final cameo hyperbolically develops the image of the ravaged vineyard (5:1–7). A shekel (about half an ounce of silver) would be a steep price indeed to pay for a single vine, but soon there will be nothing left of the vineyard but grazing for animals and a hunting ground for the survivors of the disaster.

The child with the name of ill omen (8:1–4)

(Humbert; Jepsen; Morenz; Rignell; Roberts 1985b; Steck 1973; Talmage; Williamson 1994, 95–97)

TRANSLATION

8 ¹Yahveh said to me, "Take a large tablet; write on it with a common stylus[a] 'belonging to Maher-shalal-hash-baz.'" ²So I had it notarized[b] by reliable

witnesses, Uriah the priest and Zechariah son of Jeberechiah. [3]I then approached the prophetess; she became pregnant and gave birth to a son. "Call him Maher-shalal-hash-baz," Yahveh said to me, [4]"for before the child is able to say 'my father' or 'my mother,' the wealth of Damascus and the spoil of Samaria will be brought into the presence of the king of Assyria."

NOTES

[a] *Ḥeret ʾĕnôš,* literally, "a stylus of a man"; *ḥeret* is an engraving instrument (e.g. used by Aaron to make the Golden Calf, Exod 32:4), therefore a scribe's stylus (cf. 1QM XII 3; 1QH I 24); the meaning of this technical term is no longer apparent ("ordinary," "official," "hieratic," and "indelible," are some of the suggestions), but the context suggests easy legibility (cf. Hab 2:2); the least likely reading is *ḥeret ʾānûš,* "disaster stylus" (Wildberger 1991, 331–32; Kaiser 1972, 178), which makes no sense in the context; [b] there is no need to emend *vĕʾāʿîdâ* to the imperative *vĕhāʿîdâ* as LXX (*kai marturas . . . poiēson*) on account of *lî* following, a dative of advantage like *lĕkâ* in 1, also untranslated.

COMMENTS

This strange episode is the first of three locutions of Yahveh to Isaiah recorded in first person narration, each with its appropriate introduction (1–4, 5–10, 11–15), and all three rounded off with a reflective comment (16–22). Our interpretation of this sequence starts out from the postulate that, in spite of the first person narrative mode, this is a *literary construct* not a stenographic report of an episode in the life of Isaiah. The same is true of the entire section artfully presented as it is in the narrative sequence of autobiographical (6), biographical (7), and autobiographical mode (8). A further and by now familiar complication is that this section, in common with most sections of the book, has reached its present state by a process of editorial accretion and recycling—expansions, adjustments, *relectures*, perhaps also omissions, all with the purpose of making the word spoken in the past serviceable in the present. We have seen how reaction to the political crises of 734 and 701 has resulted in a *layered* literary complex of narrative and prophetic address in this first part of the book. And so in the present chapter the treatment of Judah at the hands of Sennacherib is linked causally, once again, with fateful decisions made at the Judean court more than thirty years earlier (see 8:5–10).

An initial problem is to grasp the connection between the sequence of events in this first passage: Isaiah is told to write something on a tablet; he has sexual relations with a woman referred to as the prophetess; a child is born with a name symbolic of the imminent (within about two years) defeat of Syria and Samaria by the Assyrians. The tablet (*gillāyôn*), not a scroll but a writing surface or placard made of stone or wood (cf. *lûaḥ,* 30:8, *lûaḥ rab,* Tg. at 8:1, and *gillāyôn* translated "mirror" at 3:23), was intended for public display since

Isaiah is no longer dealing with the ruler alone but with the people at large. Whatever the precise meaning of the technical term for the writing instrument (see notes on the text) it connotes easy legibility and is reminiscent of the tablets on which Habakkuk was told to write his vision so that it could be read on the run (Hab 2:2). But of course the important point is to know what was written on the tablet. Some have argued that "hasten to seize booty, hurry to gather spoil," a pedestrian rendering of the more succinct and sonorous Hebrew phrase, cannot be the name of the child since Isaiah would not have known of the child's begetting in advance—unless miraculously, of course—so that it must be a kind of slogan or war cry (Morenz and others). But apart from the point made earlier about the section being a *literary construct*, this view neglects the ascriptional or inscriptional *lamed* ("belonging to . . ."), which either denotes possession, like the *lammelek* stamped jar handles or, if translated "concerning . . . ," requires that something further be communicated in the document in question. Isaiah 30:8–11 provides an instructive parallel in that the one addressed is told to write a prophecy on a tablet that will serve as a witness, and this also in view of a situation in which the prophet is being rejected, silenced, or disregarded.

I therefore take it that the tablet contained a prediction encapsulated in the symbolic name of the child to be born, a prediction requiring for its future verification official authentication by two reliable witnesses in accord with normal judicial practice (Deut 17:6; 19:15). One of these, Uriah, is probably the chief priest of the Jerusalem temple during that reign (he is mentioned at 2 Kgs 16:10–16), and the other, Zechariah ben Jeberechiah, may be the father-in-law of Ahaz (2 Kgs 18:2). If so, their agreeing to vouch for Isaiah would testify to Isaiah's being well-connected among the Jerusalemite upper crust. The next act in this small drama is the pregnancy and birth of the child. The prospective mother is referred to as "the prophetess" (*hannĕbî'â*), reminiscent of "the young woman" (*hā'almâ*) of 7:14. We have no reason to believe prophets referred to their wives, whatever their endowments, as prophetesses, and in any case we are not told that this anonymous woman was Isaiah's wife or even that Isaiah himself was a *nābî'* (outside of the titles and the narrative *legenda*, use of the term in chs. 1–39 is rare, invariably hostile, and never applied to Isaiah). We therefore assume that she is, or is represented as being, an officially recognized member of the *nābî'* class, such as Huldah during the reign of Josiah (2 Kgs 22:14), perhaps also a member of the Jerusalem temple staff. Her role may have signified, even more clearly than Isaiah's, the ominously predictive character of the inscription. Once the child is born and the name assigned, the significance of the entire sign-act is at last clearly displayed.

We have still not considered the relation of this sign-act to the one preceding it (7:10–17). The problem is to fit two successive pregnancies, births, and early childhood developments—those of Immanuel and Maher-shalal-hash-baz—into the brief period between the initial Syro-Ephraimite attack and the annihilation of the coalition by the Assyrians. If this is admitted to be problematic, which it certainly seems to be, the very close structural parallel between 7:10–

17 and 8:1–4 would suggest the hypothesis mentioned earlier of *alternative accounts of one sign-act*, the first addressed to the dynasty, the second to the Judean public. The parallelism may be set out as follows:

• Immanuel	• Maher-shalal-hash-baz (8:1, 3)
• The Young Woman	• The Prophetess (8:3)
• "the Young Woman is pregnant and about to give birth to a son"	• "she became pregnant and bore a son"
• "she will give him the name Immanuel"	• "call him Maher-shalal-hash baz"
• "before the child knows how to reject what is bad and choose what is . . . good	• "before the child is able to say 'my father' or 'my mother' . . ."
• "the king of Assyria" (7:17)	• "the king of Assyria" (8:4)

To round it off, the declaration of the meaning of the sign-act is followed in both cases by a threat of punishment for Judah to be administered by the Assyrians as agents of Yahveh (7:18–25; 8:5–10). I conclude, then, that within the prophetic world view, Immanuel and Maher-shalal-hash-baz represent different aspects of the divine intervention in human affairs at that critical juncture. They are, so to speak, the recto and verso of the same coin.

JUDAH WILL BE SUBMERGED (8:5–10)

(Auret; Budde 1926; 1930; Fullerton 1924; Kaiser 1959; Klein; May; Saebø 1964; Sweeney 1993)

TRANSLATION

8 [5]Once again Yahveh addressed me, [6]"Since this people has rejected the waters of Shiloah that flow so softly, rejoicing with Rezin and the son of Remaliah,[a] [7]therefore the Sovereign Lord is about to bring up against them the waters of the River, mighty and abundant [the king of Assyria in all his spendor].[b] It will crest over all its channels and overflow all its banks, [8]sweeping on into Judah in a flood, reaching up to the neck. Its branches[c] will be spread far and wide, filling the breadth of your land, Immanuel.
[9]Acknowledge[d] it, you peoples, and be dismayed,
Give heed, remote places of the earth,
Gird yourselves for war and be shattered!
Gird yourselves for war and be shattered!
[10]Propose a plan—it shall be thwarted,
devise a scheme[e]—it shall not take place,
for God is with us.

NOTES

[a] *Ûmĕśôś 'et . . .* is a *crux interpretum* to which no entirely satisfactory answer has yet been proposed; see Sweeney 1993 for a survey of ancient versions and modern opinions. Perhaps the favorite option (e.g. Duhm 1892, 80) is to emend to *ûmĕsôs*, a verbal form from *mss*, in Qal "faint away" (only in Isa 10:18), in Niphal "melt," but this requires the further emendation of *'et* to *lipnê, millipnê* or (Wildberger 1991, 340–41) *miśś'ēt*, none of which is supported by the ancient versions (note that 4QIsa[f] line 19, is identical with MT: *hhlkym l't vmśvś 'et rṣyn vbn r[*). The reading adopted here, which goes back to Redak (R. David Kimhi), has support from LXX, Vulg., and Syr. 1QIsa[a] offers an alternative that makes little difference to the sense by reading *mśyś* (Hiphil), "causing Rezin and the son of Remaliah to rejoice." I find Sweeney's solution unsatisfactory since the parallelism with Isa 66:10–14 is not very striking and the sexual imagery in 8:5–10 not at all obvious;   [b] *'et-melek 'aśśûr vĕ'et-kol-kĕbôdô*, probably a gloss cf. 7:17b, 20;   [c] literally, "wings" (*kĕnāpâv*), metaphorical usage as in 2 Sam 22:11; Hos 4:19; Ps 18:11; 104:3; Mal 3:20[4:2] and, in the context, not to be taken as a metaphor for divine protection;   [d] read *dĕ'û* for *rō'û*;   [e] literally, "speak a word" (*dabbĕrû dābār*).

COMMENTS

As are the paragraphs preceding and following it, 5–10 is presented editorially as discourse of Yahveh, though divine *oratio recta* is not maintained throughout. How this section fits into the total picture presented in chs. 6–8 depends on how one translates v 6. If the translation offered above is correct, the prediction of disaster would be addressed to the faction, doubtless well represented, in favor of joining the anti-Assyrian coalition. Isaiah would therefore have been caught in the crossfire of the pro-Assyrian and anti-Assyrian factions, the former including Ahaz himself, the latter addressed in this passage. The contrast between Shiloah, a channel flowing from the Gihon spring to the pool of Siloam, and the river Tigris, or possibly the Euphrates, may have been suggested by proximity to the place of encounter between Ahaz and Isaiah nearby in the Kidron Valley. There is also a hint of the mythological topos of the waters of Tehom, the Deep, a powerful figure of Chaos-come-again (May; Kaiser). Whether the description of military invasion under the figure of an inundation corresponds to experience or is a (not unreasonable) prediction of a future event after "Immanuel" had succeeded to the throne cannot very well be determined, but referring it to the king of Assyria and his splendor (cf. the *melammu* or effulgence of the imperial deity Ashur and his weapons in Assyrian royal inscriptions) was in any case appropriate. The hymnic conclusion (9–10) is addressed to the nations at large at a much later time, inviting them to draw the appropriate conclusion from this old story of plotting at the Judean court. It echoes sentiments expressed in such "Zionist" hymns as Ps 46, which contains the Immanuel theme, speaks of a river and its streams' bringing joy to the city, and announces the thwarting of warlike plans opposed to those of Yahveh. In all probability the hymnic conclusion to this paragraph comes from the same fervent Jerusalemite circles that have left their mark on the last eleven chapters of the book (with Kaiser 1972, 188–89 and pace Saebø, who defends its attribution to Isaiah).

ISAIAH AND HIS CO-CONSPIRATORS (8:11–15)

(G. R. Driver 1955; Evans 1985; Irvine 1990; Jones; Lohfink)

TRANSLATION

8 [11]For thus Yahveh addressed me, with his hand strong upon me,[a] warning me[b] against following the lead of this people. [12]"Do not call conspiracy whatever this people calls conspiracy," he said, "neither fear what they fear nor be terrified. [13]But Yahveh of the hosts, with him you shall conspire,[c] he shall be the one you fear and hold in dread. [14]He will be your co-conspirator,[d] a stone, a rock on which both houses of Israel will strike their feet and stumble, a trap and snare for the inhabitants[e] of Jerusalem. [15]Many among them shall stumble, fall, and be broken; they shall be snared and taken captive."

NOTES

[a] *Kĕhezqat hayyād* could be construed as "when he took me by the hand" (NEB[2], JPS[2], and cf. Isa 42:6; 51:18) but we would then expect *yādî* ("my hand") or *kĕhezqatî bĕyād* ("while taking me by the hand"); for the hand of Yahveh as indicating a state of transformed prophetic consciousness see 1 Kgs 18:46; 2 Kgs 3:15; Ezek 1:3; 3:22; 8:1; 33:22 etc and especially Ezek. 3:14 (*yād YHVH ʿalay hāzāqâ*); [b] reading *vĕyissranî* → *ysr* rather than *vayĕsirēnî* → *sûr*, literally, "he made me turn aside," in spite of the support in 1QIsa[a] for the latter; unfortunately none of the fragments contains this part of v 11; [c] MT has *taqdîšû*, "you shall regard as holy," "hold in awe," but in view of the problem with *miqdāš* in v 14 (see below), it seems more consonant with the context to read verbal forms → *qšr* in both places, the scribal *tiqqûn* perhaps due to distaste for the idea of Yahveh involved in a conspiracy; hence *taqšîrû*, "you will take to be your co-conspirator," or (a theologically more acceptable reading) "the one with whom you bond"; [d] *mĕqaššer* rather than *môqēš*, "snare," as in v 14b, for *miqdāš*, "sanctuary," which makes no sense in the context; [e] *yôšēb*, singular for collective; not therefore referring to the king.

COMMENTS

Unlike the previous paragraph, which concerns the pro-coalition party, vv 11–15 provide reassurance addressed to Isaiah and his supporters (the verbs in vv 12–13 are plural) accused of conspiracy, more likely by the pro-coalition and anti-Assyrian party ("this people" cf. 8:6) than by the royalists. The injunction may therefore be read as religious instruction carried out in the circle of Isaian disciples (*limmūdîm* 8:16). The view that Isaiah is urging Ahaz, accused of conspiring against his suzerain the king of Samaria, to stand firm (Hayes and Irvine 1987, 152–59) is too speculative to be convincing. The position of Isaiah and his support group is therefore one of three quite different options entertained in Judah faced with the threat of a Syrian-Samarian takeover. We sense a growing feeling of distress and isolation, which would have helped to generate the intensity expressed through the motif of "the hand of Yahveh" (meaning an ecstatic or trance-like state), rare in Isaiah but a defining characteristic of Ezekiel's prophetic consciousness.

The assurance that Yahveh is Isaiah's co-conspirator, his partner, is really another variation on the Immanuel theme. Yahveh is still the God of the others, but his alienation from them is expressed in an accumulation of negative images. He will be for them a stone on which one strikes one's foot (*'eben negep*), the Hebrew term *negep* also signifying pestilence (Exod 12:13; 30:12; Num 8:19 etc.). The "rock of stumbling" (*ṣûr mikšôl*) figure combines a poetic image of the strong God of Israel, of frequent occurrence in heroic poetry (e.g. Deut 32; 2 Sam 22), with that of a stumbling block, used elsewhere with reference to idols (Ezek 7:19; 14:3, 4, 7; 44:12). "Snare" (*môqēš*) also has the same referent, and "trap" (*paḥ*) carries equally ominous associations, illustrated at a later point in the book—*paḥad vāpaḥat vāpāḥ*—"terror," "the pit," and "the snare" (Isa 24:17; also Jer 48:43).

A CLOSING REFLECTION (8:16–22)

(Carroll 1980; G. R. Driver 1940; Hoffner; Jeppesen; Lewis 1989, 128–32; Lust; Mowinckel 1946; Müller 1975; Reventlow; B. B. Schmidt 1994, 147–54; Sweeney 1994a; Whitley 1978; Williamson 1994, 97–103)

TRANSLATION

8 [16]Secure[a] the message, seal[b] the instruction among my disciples. [17]I will wait for Yahveh who is hiding his face from the house of Jacob. I will wait in hope for him. [18]Here I am with the children Yahveh has given me as signs and portents in Israel. All this[c] is from Yahveh of the hosts who dwells on Mount Zion.

[19]They will surely say to you,[d] "Consult the spirits of the dead and the ghosts that chirp and mutter, for should not a people consult their divine ancestors,[e] the dead, [20]for instruction and a message on behalf of the living?" They will assuredly speak in this way,[f] but what they say will have no magical power.[g] [21]They will pass on into the underworld,[h] wretched and hungry; and when they are famished they will be enraged and will curse their king and their

gods. [22]And if they turn upwards or look down into the underworld[i] all they will see is distress and darkness, gloom and misery; then they themselves will be thrust down into deep darkness.

NOTES

[a] Either *ṣôr* imperative → *ṣrr*, written *plene* (GKC §67n) or infinitive absolute as emphatic imperative → *ṣôr* (GKC §113bb), but in any case with the meaning "wrap up," "put in a container," "secure" e.g. Deut 14:25; 2 Kgs 5:23; 12:11 with reference to money; [b] read either imperative *ḥătôm* or infinitive absolute *ḥātôm* depending on *ṣôr/ṣôr* in previous note; [c] "all this" added; MT reads "from . . . Zion"; [d] *kî* asseverative; [e] *'ĕlōhâv*; see commentary; [f] *'im-lō'*, literally "if not . . . ," a formula of asseveration by taking an oath (GKC §149); [g] an admittedly speculative rendering of a very problematic phrase, following Driver 1940, 162 in interpreting *šāḥar* (usually "dawn") as "magical power," "sorcery" cf. Isa 47:11a and Akkadian cognate *šaḥiru*; [h] literally, "he will pass on into it"; reading *bā'āreṣ*, "underworld," for *bâ* (cf. Isa. 29:4); [i] *'ereṣ* = "underworld."

COMMENTS

In the final and somber act of the drama Isaiah has his utterances delivered during the crisis sealed, secured in a receptacle of some kind, and committed to his disciples. It is possible that the verbs are used metaphorically (as Wildberger 1991, 366), or at least in the sense that Isaiah's discourses are committed to memory by disciples. However, the parallel with 29:11–12, referring to the words of a sealed book (*dibrê hasseper hĕḥātûm*), and with 30:8–11, which speaks of a tablet and a book serving as witness, both in the context of prophecy as problematic, suggests that we take them literally. In that case the message and instruction indicate a text written on papyrus, wrapped in cloth, and put for safekeeping in a jar or other container. They cannot be identical with the large, notarized tablet of Isa 8:1–4, though they would presumably have contained a prediction against the Syrian-Samarian coalition. The Hebrew term translated "message," *tĕ'ûdâ*, signifies a text validated by witnesses (cf. Ruth 4:7); hence, the role of disciples analogous to that of Uriah and Zechariah (8:2) but not identical with them (pace Clements 1980a, 100). The document also contains *tôrâ*, a term for prophetic teaching in the first major section of the book of Isaiah (1:10; 2:3; 5:24; 30:9). Various attempts have been made to emend or get rid of the allusion to "disciples" (*limmûdîm*). The word connotes possession of a particular skill and therefore implies association with a teacher (cf. 50:4; 54:13). It would hardly be surprising if Isaiah had a following; indeed we have already learned so much (8:11–13), though it is going too far to speak of an Isaian school or to identify the disciples as Levitical musicians employed in the temple rebuilt by Zerubbabel (Kaiser 1972, 198). The issue of discipleship, of an Isaian party, sect, or *ecclesiola*, will, however, emerge unavoidably in our reading of the last chapters of the book. At this juncture it will suffice to make the point that the existence of a following or support group provides as good an explanation as any for the first stage in the preservation and transmission of Isaiah's sayings.

The verbs used to describe the attitude of Isaiah and his followers express a patient expectation that the predictions committed to disciples for safekeeping will be validated in a future fulfillment (ḥkh Piel cf. Hab 2:3; Zeph 3:8) and the confidence that this fulfillment will prove to be in some way redemptive or salvific (qvh Piel cf. Gen 49:18; Isa 25:9; and often in psalms of individual lamentation that conclude with an expression of confidence and trust). In this respect there is little difference between "waiting in hope" and "standing firm in faith" (7:9b). Both express the appropriate attitude faced with delay in the fulfillment of prophecy, an attitude that can, in a certain sense, itself open up a future for the word that remains inactive in the present. Nonfulfillment can also be expressed in the idiom of God's hiding his face, sometimes used in tandem with the motif of God's forgetting (Ps 10:11; 13:2). Similar expressions, e.g., lifting up the face (Num 6:26), letting the face shine on the petitioner (Num 6:25; Ps 80:3), seeking the face (Ps 27:8), derive from the immemorial protocol of imperial and regal courts in the ancient Near East (cf. the Amarna letters from the early fourteenth century B.C.E.) and have influenced the language of prayer in Judaism and Christianity down to the present. The reference is not, however, exclusively to unfulfilled prophecy but includes also the failure of Isaiah's attempt to persuade the king and his followers to follow a particular policy. Hence the apparently abrupt transition from disciples to children (Shear-yashub and Maher-shalal-hash-baz) who, together with Isaiah himself, prefigure onomastically the predicted course of the future.

It is tempting to identify the children with the disciples (as Budde 1928, 85), but the context suggests that it is the two children with the ominous names who serve as signs and portents, namely, prefigurations of imminent crisis (cf. 20:3–4). Furthermore, prophetic disciples are referred to as "sons" (bānîm), as in frequent allusions to "sons of the prophets" (běnê hannĕbî'îm), but never as "children" (yĕlādîm).

The final phrase of vv 16–18 (v 18b), liturgical in character (cf. Ps 74:2; 135:21), does not necessarily or even probably refer to the children (18a) since it has just been stated that they were given by Yahveh, which is to say that they were as much the result of a divine imperative as the children of Hosea. I take it to refer to the passage as a whole or, in other words, to the outcome of Isaiah's intervention in Judean politics at that juncture of the history.

Since the final paragraph of this section (19–22) is only very loosely connected with the preceding verses, which have no antecedent for the verb yō'měrû ("they will say"), most commentators take it to be entirely or in part a post-disaster editorial appendix (Budde 1928, 86–87; Wildberger 1991, 371; Clements 1980a, 101–3; Barth 1977, 152–56). Neither the repetition of tě'ûdâ and tôrâ (in inverted order) nor the technical term šāḥar in 47:11 (see note on 20) nor the allusion to necromancy, which was practiced in Israel throughout its history (cf. 19:3; 26:13–19; 28:14–22; 29:4), obliges us to assign a Second Temple date to this appendix. But it is certainly of later date; witness the fact that 18b serves as a finale to the entire Memoir forming an inclusio with the vision of Yahveh of the hosts in 6:1–13, and the dark scenario as described would certainly fit the period immediately after the Babylonian conquest. Recourse to necromancy, common in times of acute economic, political, or military crisis (e.g. in the Weimar Republic after World War I), would be natural at the time of the Syrian-Samarian attack, as in any situation of military crisis, and the editor may have concluded that it would have appealed to Ahaz as an alternative to unacceptable prophetic revelations (cf. 2 Kgs 16:3–4). Presumably it is he, Ahaz, who will be vituperated in the underworld when it will be obvious that his stratagem has led to disaster. The practice of consulting *'ōbôt* and *yiddĕ'ōnîm* (here translated "spirits of the dead" and "ghosts") was proscribed in Levitical and Deuteronomic law (Lev 19:31; 20:6, 27; Deut 18:11), which means that it was going on, generally in connection with the cult of ancestors referred to here and elsewhere as divine beings (*'ĕlōhîm*) or simply the dead (*mētîm*) (Lewis; B. Schmidt). The point of the addition is that such recourse will not be effective and that the practitioners themselves will not escape death and the grim prospect of passing into the underworld (a secondary meaning of *'ereṣ*, "earth," as in Exod 15:12; 1 Sam 28:13; Jonah 2:7[6]; Ps 71:20). The description of this location is reminiscent of the ominous dream of Enkidu (*Gilgamesh* 7:31–54) or *Ishtar's Descent to the Underworld* (obverse 4–10): its denizens inhabit the "house of darkness," they are clothed in feathers, chirp like birds, and are nourished on dust and clay; on the whole, therefore, a decidedly unpleasant prospect for post-mortem existence.

NEW RULER, NEW AGE (8:23–9:6[9:1–7])

(Alt 1964b; Barth 1977, 141–77; Brandscheidt; Carlson; Crook; Emerton 1969; Eshel; Høgenhaven 1987; Kennett; Leskow; Lindblom 1958; Mowinckel 1959, 102–10; Müller 1961; von Rad 1958; Renaud; Reventlow 1971; Schunck; Staub; Sweeney 1994a; Thompson 1982; Vermeylen 1978, 1.232–49; Vieweger; Vollmer; Wegner 1992b; Wildberger 1960)

TRANSLATION

8 ²³[9:1] There is no gloom for her who is oppressed.[a] At that time the earlier ruler[b] treated with contempt[c] the territory of Zebulon and Naphthali, and the later one[b] oppressed the way of the sea, the land across the Jordan, Galilee of the nations.

¹[2] The people that walk in the dark
have seen a great light,
on the dwellers in the land of gloom
light has shone forth.

²⁽³⁾You have increased their joy,ᵈ
and brought them great gladness;
they are glad in your presence
with a gladness like that of the harvest,
as those rejoice who divide the spoil.
³⁽⁴⁾For the yoke with which they were burdened,
the bar across their shoulders,
the rod of their oppressors,
you have smashed as on the day of Midian.
⁴⁽⁵⁾Every boot of troops on the march,ᵉ
every garment cakedᶠ in blood
is destined to be burned, to be fuel for the fire.
⁵⁽⁶⁾For a child has been born for us,
a son has been given to us,
the emblems of sovereigntyᵍ rest on his shoulders.
His titles will be:ʰ Marvelous Counselor,ⁱ
Hero Warrior, Eternal Father,
Prince of Peace.
⁶⁽⁷⁾Sovereignty will be great,ʲ peace will be endless
for David's throne and his kingdom,
to establish and sustain it
in justice and righteousness
from this time forth and ever more.
[The zeal of Yahveh of the hosts will accomplish this.]

NOTES

ᵃ *Kî lōʾ mûʿāp laʾăšer mûṣāq lâ*, the link verse between 8:19–22 and 8:23b–9:6
[9:1b–7], takes off from *mĕʿûp* and *ṣûqâ* in the previous verse and, as an editorial link verse, would logically reverse the dark scenario that precedes the glad tidings cf. the allusion to "the land of gloom" 9:1; numerous attempts have been made to emend it so as to render a meaning acceptable in the context (Wildberger 1991, 377–78); the translation offered takes *mûʿāp* as a substantive → *ʿōp*, "to be dark" not the more common *ʿōp*, "fly" (as 1QIsaᵃ *klv mʿvpp* and Vulg. *avolare*); *mûṣāq* is either Hophal participle or substantive;   ᵇ *hāriʾšôn*,
hāʾaḥărôn cannot qualify *ʿet*, "time," which is feminine (Isa 39:1 is only apparently an exception since in the parallel 2 Kgs 20:12 it is feminine); *kāʿēt* can stand by itself meaning "at the present time" (Num 23:23; Judg 13:23) or "at a certain time" (in the past);   ᶜ *hēqal*, literally, "make light" the precise antithesis of *hikbîd*, literally, "made heavy," which should therefore not be referred to the future;   ᵈ reading *haggîlâ* for MT (and 1QIsaᵃ) *haggôy lōʾ* ("the people not . . ."); ᵉ *kol-sĕʾôn sōʾēn bĕraʿaš* both substantive and verb (participle) are hapax; for the former cf. Akk. *šenu*, "shoe, boot";   ᶠ literally, "rolled" (*mĕgôlālâ*);   ᵍ *miśrâ* hapax, LXX *archē* → *śrr*, "rule";   ʰ reading Niphal *vĕyiqqarēʾ* with LXX, Syr., Vulg. for MT *vayyiqrāʾ* since presumably the

child/son does not name himself; ⁱ it is not clear how *pele'* ("wonder, miracle") and *yô'ēṣ* ("counselor") relate syntactically, since *pele'* is a substantive not an adjective; the uncertainty is reflected in the versions; ⁱ *lĕmarbēh* Kĕtib has final mēm (ם) within the word, possibly → *lām* (*lahem*) *rabbâ . . .* , "for them sovereignty will be great . . ."; some midrashim refer it to the mēm of *ma'ălôt* ("degrees"), which occurs five times in Isa 38:8, the sundial miracle.

COMMENTS

The initial v 23a ("there is no gloom for her who is oppressed") links with the end of the Memoir and prepares for a reversal of fortune after the dark scenario of 8:21–22, in which respect it duplicates the editorial procedure of juxtaposing a promise of redemption with disaster, as in 4:2–6 following 2:6–4:1. The feminine suffix is not explained. It may anticipate the poem, with reference to Judah or Jerusalem at a critical period of its history, not necessarily the immediate post-586 B.C.E. period (pace Clements, 1980a 105), or it could refer to the mother of the son whose birth is celebrated. To understand the sudden reversal back to diatribe at the end of the poem (9:7[8]–10:4) would require us to unravel the complicated editorial history of this section, no easy task. One possibility is that, since 10:24–27a uses the language and themes of the "new ruler, new age" poem (yoke, bar, rod, burden placed on the shoulders, defeat of Midian), it may at one time have followed directly after it. With regard to background and date, it would be prudent to consider the poem independently of its prose introduction (8:23b). The latter refers to two phases of military disaster for parts of the Kingdom of Samaria. The second of these phases almost certainly alludes to the annexation of Israelite territory during Tiglath-pileser's campaign of 732 B.C.E. resulting in the formation of the Assyrian provinces of Duru (Dor, "the way of the sea"), Gal'azu (Gilead, "the land across the Jordan") and Magidu (Megiddo, "Galilee of the nations"). If this is so, the "later one" would be Tiglath-pileser III himself (2 Kgs 15:29). The earlier phase affected the tribal territory of Zebulon and Naphthali, i.e., Upper Galilee and the Golan, the arena of Syrian-Israelite struggle throughout the ninth and a good part of the eighth century, which would suggest identifying "the earlier ruler" with a Syrian, either Hazael or Ben-Hadad (Bir-Hadad III) (as also Eshel). This would seem to be preferable to a more traditional line of interpretation identifying the oppressors as Tiglath-pileser III and Shalmaneser V (as Calvin and, implicitly, Ibn Ezra), since there is no allusion here to the fall of the Northern Kingdom in 722 B.C.E. At any rate, the choice of verbs suggests foreign oppression of these regions rather than an identification with native rulers, either Jeroboam II and Menahem (Hayes and Irvine 1987, 176–79) or Pekah and Hoshea (Ginsberg; Emerton).

On the assumption that the poem begins at 9:1[2] (pace Alt 1964b, 211–12), we must first ask whether the poem and the introductory historical note belong together, either as originally one composition or in the sense that the poem, whenever composed, was written to announce the reversal of the condition described in the note, either as an event that has already taken place or as an aspiration for the future. To answer this question we have to address the issue of the time and circumstances of the composition of the poem. Several exegetes have argued for a postexilic date (e.g. Gray, Fohrer, Lescow) and, in keeping with his overall treatment of these chapters, Kaiser (1972, 203–18) associates it with messianic movements during the Persian period and more specifically with the Levitical musicians' guilds, which he believes were the custodians of the traditional royal liturgy. If we compare it with texts known to be postexilic that focus on the Davidic dynasty we certainly note some duplication of themes, e.g, the throne of David (Isa 16:5; Jer 17:25; 22:2, 4; 33:17, 21), the giving of a name (Jer 23:6), the breaking of a foreign yoke (Jer 30:8–9), the establishment of justice and righteousness (Isa 16:5; Jer 23:5; 33:15), reunification of the two kingdoms (Jer 33:24; Hos 2:1–3; 3:5), but nonetheless the differences are more in evidence than the similarities. Furthermore, the poem says nothing about a future *restoration* of the dynasty and does not fit well with what we know about the religious and intellectual life of the Judean community in the sixth and fifth centuries B.C.E. (Mowinckel 1959, 102–10; Clements 1980a, 104; Wildberger 1991, 389–93).

On the assumption, then, that the one who is given those auspicious names is an actual historical ruler rather than a projection of hopes for the future after the monarchy had passed from the scene, it remains to be asked to whom the poem refers and whether it celebrates a birth or accession to the throne. Many have followed Alt and von Rad in explaining the language of the poem against the background of Egyptian rituals accompanying the accession of a new pharaoh and including the conferring of throne names, generally five in number. There is, however, a problem of *form*, in that in such rituals the deity addresses the ruler-designate directly (as in 2 Sam 7:14 and Ps 2:7) and does so in terms of divine, adoptive sonship, neither of which is the case in the poem (pace von Rad 1958, 230–31). Moreover, only four names are conferred on the son in the poem, and none of the numerous attempts to conjure a fifth name out of v 6[7] has been especially persuasive. It may also be relevant to recall that the death of Ahaz is noted only at a later point in the book (14:28). If, then, we take the poem at face value as speaking of a royal birth, which in the ancient as in the modern world is a natural occasion for celebration and renewal, we would like to know whose birth it is celebrating. Though full of vivid imagery, the language is unspecific enough to have permitted the poem to be recycled on successive occasions, a point generally overlooked by the proponents of this or that ruler. It may well have been used or reused at the time of Josiah (Barth 1977, 141–77 especially 176–77; Vermeylen 1989, 232–49), but aspirations for reunion probably did not originate during that reign, and we have to ask why a poet writing in the second half of the seventh century would limit the geographical perspective to territory annexed by the Assyrians in 733 rather than taking in the entire Kingdom of Samaria. Nothing can be deduced from the description of a victory of epic proportions (vv 3–4[4–5]) either, since nothing of that nature happened at either the birth or the accession of Josiah (648 and

640 B.C.E., respectively). The language imitates the oratorical and declamatory style of the court and corresponds to aspiration rather than political and military reality. Since, after what has been said about him to date we can scarcely suppose the poet is referring to Ahaz (as argued by Hayes and Irvine 1987, 176–84), the only remaining candidate would be Hezekiah. If this is so, Hezekiah would have been born ca. 734–732, his accession to the throne would have been ca. 715, therefore in his late teens rather than at twenty-five years old (as 2 Kgs 18:2), and the fourteenth year of his reign, 701 B.C.E. Needless to say, this does not determine the date of composition. Duhm (1892, 88–89), for example, proposed a date subsequent to the invasion of Sennacherib, adding the excellent suggestion that it may have served as a counterpart to the scenario of defeat and devastation in 1:5–9 corresponding to the disaster of 701 B.C.E. An original reference to Hezekiah seems, then, to be the most likely hypothesis and has the advantage of aligning the poem more closely with the preceding material, including the birth of the child called Immanuel (7:14).

The poem is often compared with the thanksgiving psalms (e.g. Pss 18; 23; 107), but in reality has little in common with them. These psalms address God directly, but in the poem direct address of this kind occurs only in vv 2–3[3–4]. Commentators divide it into strophes (Duhm, 1892, 88, has four) and spell out its meter, but no two solutions are identical. Perhaps all we can say for sure is that it is in an irregularly distributed 3–3, 2–2 pattern, normal for Isaian rhetoric. It opens with the sudden transition from the land of gloom, figurative language for the underworld (cf. Job 10:21–22 *'ereṣ ḥōšek věṣalmāvet*, the "land of darkness and gloom") to a place of brilliant light. "Light" (*'ôr*), and the passage from darkness to light, are dominant images in all sections of Isaiah (see especially 60:1–2); the rest of the poem serves to explicate what this means, but the explication is delayed while the poet describes public rejoicing under the familiar images of harvesting and sharing the spoil after victory. This last suggests a further delay, while oppressive foreign rule is presented under all-too-familiar and related images of servitude: the yoke placed on the neck (*'ōl* cf. 10:27; 14:25), the bar used either to strike or pinion the shoulders (*maṭṭēh* cf. 10:24), the rod for beating prisoners into subjection (*šēbeṭ* cf. 10:24) and as a symbol of dominance in general (cf. Gen 49:10; Isa 14:5). All of these are to be done away with, and the scene closes with the image of the stripping of the dead and incinerating of their bloodstained belongings.

Allusion to the defeat of the Midianites was no doubt suggested by the divine intervention that decided the issue, especially miraculous in view of the disparity in numbers once Gideon's army was reduced from 32,000 to 300 (Judg 6–7). It serves to remind us how seldom the Isaiah tradition, especially in its earlier stages, appeals to what became the normative historical traditions of Israel. No casual allusion to the ancestors (Abraham is referred to only in postexilic passages, 29:22; 41:8; 51:2) or to the exodus, wilderness, and occupation of Canaan appears; nothing except the Cities of the Plain (1:9–10; 3:9; 13:19), a tradition that we know to have arisen independently of its context in the Abraham story.

The eschatological horizon of the abolition of war is a major theme in the tradition of which Isaiah is the chief representative. We heard earlier of the beating of swords into plowshares, a now familiar image of the transfer of resources from military-industrial to domestic-civic use (2:4), and the theme of disarmament will be expressed more clearly in the related messianic poem in 11:6–9. This leads directly to the *peripateia*, the hinge on which the poem turns, the birth of the marvelous child. We now have the key to understanding what has been said so far and realize that it was said in the prophetic perfect tense—i.e., these results that have not yet come about are assured now that the child is born; the birth of the heir to the throne is the necessary condition for these great events to unfold. Whether the sequel to the birth corresponds to ceremonies carried out in the palace on this occasion—a ritual of investiture and the conferring of throne names—we do not know but may consider quite likely. "Emblems of sovereignty," an attempt to render *miśrâ*, which occurs only here, may point to investiture with a robe or other symbol of authority, cf. the "key of the house of David" placed on the shoulder of Eliakim when appointed majordomo of the palace (22:22). The names *may* carry an echo of Egyptian practice, though we have seen that these names differ from the pharaonic throne names both in type and number. What is certain is that they continue the practice in the Memoir of conferring symbolic names or titles on the protagonists, another indication that the poem is more fully integrated into this first section of the book than is commonly acknowledged.

A brief note on the four throne names will suffice. They express important aspects of an ideal polity and government, which was certainly never realized in ancient Israel and, at the same time, intimate a certain transcendental aura attaching to royalty in the ancient Near East. The designation *pele' yô'ēṣ* ("Marvelous Counselor"), a juxtaposition of two words syntactically unrelated, indicates the capacity to elaborate good plans and stratagems, an attribute of Yahveh according to Isaiah (cf. 5:19 and 25:1 *pele' 'ēṣôt*, "miraculous plans"). The title *'ēl gibbôr*, literally, "God warrior," is not an example of the superlative formed with *'ēl*, which would require the reverse order of words (as in 14:13 *kôkĕbê-'ēl*, "mighty stars"), but is a divine title applied to the ruler, as can be seen from its reuse by a later interpreter in 10:21 "a remnant will return (Shear-yashub), the remnant (*šĕ'ār*) of Jacob to *'ēl gibbôr*"; a parallel therefore to the same theophoric element in the name Immanu-el, "El is with us" (7:14; 8:8, 10). Finally, *'ăbî'ad*, "Eternal Father," is a rare but not unattested formation (cf. Hab 3:6 *harĕrê-'ad*, "eternal mountains"). It would be too literal-minded to suppose that the title is incongruous when assigned to a newborn child; the child will one day be ruler, and the ruler's task is to foster or "father" his people; there is also the conventional attribution of "eternal life" to the ruler (e.g. Ps 72:5, 17). The most familiar of these titles is the last, *śar šālôm*, "Prince of Peace," used as a messianic designation by both Christians and Jews (the Targum paraphrases "Messiah in whose days peace will be great for us"). The term *šālôm* signifies more than the absence of hostilities, though that is its essential precondition, for it is also associated with public order founded on justice and righteousness. Peace is what happens when a righteous order prevails (*maʿăśēh haṣṣĕdāqâ*, Isa 32:17), and it is the task of governments royal or otherwise to establish it.

This point linking up the exercise of political power, the preservation of peace, and the establishment of a just order is made in the final three verses (v 6a[7a]) from which, as noted earlier, we should probably not try to extract a fifth title (as, for example, *marbēh hammiśrâ*, "Increaser of Sovereignty," Alt 1964b, 219). The final line, attributing this reversal of fortune to the zeal or passion (*qînʾâ*) of Yahveh of the hosts, occurs in another anti-Assyrian context in the Isaian "legend" (37:32) and has been added to the poem, perhaps, after all the exalted language about the ruler-designate, to dispel any doubt about the ultimate source of these great happenings.

(ISAIAH 9:7[8]–10:4, see pp. 208–19)

"ASSYRIA, ROD OF MY ANGER" (10:5–14)

(Childs 1967, 39–44; Dietrich; Fullerton 1917–18; Huber 1976, 35–76; Machinist; Mittmann; Tadmor 1958)

TRANSLATION

10 [5] Woe to Assyria, rod of my anger,
the stick in their hands is my fury! [a]
[6] Against an impious nation I send him, [b]
against a people that stir me to wrath I commission him
to seize spoil, to pillage and plunder,
to trample them down [c] like mud in the streets.
[7] But he did not reckon it so,
his mind did not see it that way,
destroying was all he intended,
cutting off nation after nation. [d]
[8] He thinks: [e] "Are not my commanders kings every one?
[9] Did Calno fare better than Carchemish?
Did Hamath fare better than Arpad?
Did not Samaria share the fate of Damascus? [f]
[10] Since my hand has grasped worthless kingdoms, [g]
with more images than those of Jerusalem and Samaria,
[11] what I have done to Samaria and its idols
shall I not do to Jerusalem and its images?"
[12] *When the Sovereign Lord will have completed all that he will do on Mount Zion and in Jerusalem, he* [h] *will bring punishment on the high-minded arrogance of the king of Assyria, on the splendor of his lofty regard.*

[13]He thought: "It is by the strength of my own hand I have done it,
by my wisdom, for I have understanding.
I have swept away[i] the boundaries of peoples,
I have plundered their riches,
like a bull I have laid low[i] their inhabitants;[j]
[14]my hand has plundered the wealth of the nations like a nest,
I have scooped up all the earth
as one scoops up abandoned birds' eggs;
no one moved a wing,
or opened his mouth to let out a single chirp.

NOTES

From the 4Q fragments we have only a few letters of 10:5–10 from 4QIsa[e]; the
few variants of 1QIsa[a] will be noted;   [a] the line is overloaded, *hû' běyādām*
is often taken to be lemma + gloss, or *za'mî* is transposed before *hû'* as in LXX;
I have simply omitted *hû'*;   [b] the singular suffix here and in the following
verses refers either to Assyrians collectively or the king as representing them;
[c] read *lěśîmô* with Ketib cf. 1QIsa[a] *vlśvm*;   [d] *gôyim lō' mě'āṭ*, literally, "nations not a few";   [e] *kî yō'mar*, literally, "for he says"; *'mr* covers also internal
dialogue;   [f] literally, "is not (or, surely) Samaria is like Damascus?"
[g] 1QIsa[a] has plural and others emend to *lěmamlěkōt ha'ělleh*, "to these kingdoms", but *'ělîl* singular always means "worthless," never "idol" (Jer 14:14;
Zech 11:17; Job 13:4);   [h] reading 3d person *yipqōd* for 1st person *'epqōd*;
[i] reading *va'āsîr* vav consecutive for MT *vě'āsîr* future, and similarly *va'ôrîd* for
vě'ôrîd in the last line of the verse;   [j] among the ancient versions only Vulg.
(*et detraxi quasi potens in sublimi residentes*) is close to MT; the line is therefore
probably corrupt, but MT as translated here makes sense.

COMMENTS

Though made up of a series of short passages, not all composed at the same
time, the entire section 10:1–34 centers on the Assyrian threat to Jerusalem and
its eventual liquidation. The principal components are as follows: Assyria in the
person of its king is designated by Yahveh as an instrument for the punishment
of his people Israel (5–7); the hubris that leads Assyria to go beyond its commission is expressed in a soliloquy spoken by the Assyrian king (8–11, 13–14); there
follows the prophetic response to the imperial ambitions expressed in the soliloquy (15–19, 33–34); the itinerary of an army approaching Jerusalem from the
north is described (27b–32). This sequence has been expanded with editorial
comment that elaborates themes and motifs already present and produces new
applications of old prophecies by a process of recontextualization (12, 20, 23,
24–27a). The first of the addenda (v 12) was suggested by the disturbing allusion to Jerusalem's idolatrous images immediately preceding. These must be

destroyed before defeat can turn into victory. The work (*ma'ăśeh*) that still remains to be done in Jerusalem is therefore the abolition of idolatry, referring back to an earlier comment probably from the same source (4:2–6). The insertion of an oracle of reassurance with the theme "a remnant will return" (20–23) was prompted by "the remnant of the trees" in the previous verse, which in its turn led to a comment on the new age–new ruler poem (24–27a). The itinerary of the army approaching Jerusalem (27b–32), in the context clearly the Assyrian army, looks out of place and in fact its insertion has helped to isolate vv 33–34 from vv 15–19, to which they belong, as may be seen in the continuation of the metaphor of the destroyed forest. In the context of the chapter as a whole, however, the itinerary continues, at a quickened and more dramatic pace, the so-far victorious advance from north to south of the Assyrian army that began at Carchemish on the Euphrates (10:9–11).

That the passage as a whole represents the perspective of military threat aimed at Jerusalem *after* the fall of Samaria (722) is explicitly stated in the king of Assyria's final rhetorical question, which should not be dismissed as an editorial appendage (10:11). Confirmation is at hand in the parallelism with the Isaian legend of chs. 36–37. There too the Assyrian threat is expressed by direct quotation from an Assyrian source (36:4–20 and 37:24–25) in which rhetorical questions are prominent. Local deities are defeated together with the peoples they sponsor (Hamath, Arpad, and Samaria are mentioned in both places), a circumstance that can also serve to persuade Jerusalem of the futility of resistance (36:18–20 and 37:12–13 cf. 10:8–11). The Rabshakeh also states, somewhat inconsistently and with less rhetorical flourish, that the Assyrian attack on Jerusalem had been commissioned by Yahveh himself (36:10 cf. 10:5–6, also 5:26–30; 7:18–20). Other repetitions—the remnant (37:4 cf. 10:20–23), the injunction not to fear (37:6 cf. 10:24), and the assurance of survival for Jerusalem (37:7 cf. 10:25–27)—confirm our suspicion that parallelism between chs. 7–12 and 36–37 is an important and quite deliberate structuring device in the book. It also complicates the much-discussed issue of the relation between chs. 36–37 and the corresponding passage in the History by suggesting that the latter has borrowed liberally from the present chapter.

The commissioning of Assyria (5–7) is couched somewhat incongruously in the form of a woe-saying, perhaps simply because of the previous saying that also begins with *hôy* (10:1–4). These opening verses may at one time have been attached to the similar passage 5:26–30 which describes the Assyrians without naming them. It may then have been cut off from it, as were sections of the woe series and the divine anger poem, to end up forming a framework for the core narrative. Beginning with this opening charge we come across numerous verbal and thematic elements already familiar to the reader, including the rod and stick used to punish (10:5, 15, 24, 26 cf. 9:3[4]), the anger of Yahveh (10:4, 25 cf. 5:25; 9:11[12], 16[17], 20[21]), Israel as polluted (*ḥānēp* 10:6 cf. 9:16[17]), trampled down earth (*mirmās* 10:6 cf. 5:5; 7:25), and the elite population described as "glory" (*kābôd* 10:16 cf. 5:13). The most obvious of these borrowings is the echo of the children's names, Maher-shalal-hash-baz (10:6 cf. 8:1–4) and Shear-yashub (10:21–22 cf. 7:3). The editorial comments 20–23 and 24–27a also recall the new ruler–new age poem almost to the point of paraphrase: the royal title El Gibbor ("Hero Warrior"), the defeat of the Midianites, an end to being clubbed and beaten up, the throwing off of the foreign yoke. The second of the two editorial notes contains an interesting and, in Isaiah, rare kind of exegetical development by introducing the rod (*maṭṭeh*) that Moses stretched out over the Red Sea to save Israel from the Egyptian army (Exod 14:16). This contrasts not only with the oppressor's rod but with Yahveh's hand outstretched to punish (5:25 etc.).

The Assyrian monologue (8–14) leads up to a threat addressed directly to Jerusalem. The three rhetorical questions alluding to the fate of cities in the path of the Assyrian advance to the west and the south comes to a topographical but not necessarily chronological terminus with the fall of Samaria, 722. The key to this literary procedure is to be found in Amos 6:2: "Go over to Calneh and see/ from there go to Hamath the Great/ then down to Gath of the Philistines;/ are you better than these kingdoms?/ Is your territory larger than theirs?" The Rabshakeh used the same kind of persuasive rhetoric when calling for the surrender of Jerusalem in 701 (Isa 36:18–20; 17:13). This means that all six cities mentioned in Isa 10:9 had fallen to the Assyrians by the time of writing, which must therefore have been sometime between 722 and 701. Since all six, with the possible exception of Calno (Calneh in Amos 6:2), perhaps the Kullani of Assyrian inscriptions but not certainly identified, are targeted by Assyrian armies in the annals of the first five years of Sargon II (721–705) (*ANET*, 284–87), we are led to the period of the accession of Hezekiah in 715, his rebellion against the Assyrian overlord (2 Kgs 18:7), and the consequent threat hanging over Judah. It is of course possible that 10 and 11 were added after the fall of Samaria, but this is an unprovable and unnecessary hypothesis. It is certainly not required by the contemptuous allusion in these verses to native deities, since both here and in the corresponding narrative material (36:18–20 and 37:12) the authors have reproduced an aspect of Assyrian propaganda attested in the annals.

PROPHETIC RESPONSE TO ASSYRIAN HUBRIS (10:15–19)

(Barth 1977, 28–34; Schwartz; Weinfeld)

TRANSLATION

10   [15]Should the axe vaunt itself over the one wielding it?
Should the saw flaunt itself over the one handling it?
As if a rod should brandish the one wielding it!
As if a wooden stick should wield one not made of wood!

[16]Therefore the Sovereign Lord,[a] Yahveh of the hosts,
will send wasting disease[b] among the most prosperous of his people,[c]
under his most distinguished folk[d] a fire will be kindled.
[17]The Light of Israel will become a fire,
the Holy One of Israel will become a flame;
it will burn up and consume in a single day
his land choked with thorns and weeds.
[18]The best[e] of his woodlands and orchards will be destroyed[f] root
    and branch[g]
as a sick person faints and falls;[h]
[19]the remnant of the trees of his forest will be so few
that a child can count them and write them down.

NOTES

[a] Absent from some MSS and LXX; present in 1QIsa[a];   [b] *rāzôn* can refer to a
pathological condition (Ps 106:15) or be used metaphorically as, e.g., "scant
measure" (Mic 6:10);   [c] *mišman* → verbal root *šmn*, "fat," "prosperous," refers to people (Ps 78:31) but also by extension to land (Gen 27:28, 39; Dan
11:24); here the context would permit either;   [d] *kābôd* collectively for
people of high estate cf. 5:13;   [e] also *kābôd*;   [f] pointing *yĕkulleh* (Pual)
for MT *yĕkalleh*;   [g] the curious phrase *minnepeš vĕ'ad bāsār*, literally, "from
soul to flesh," is often simply omitted (as BHS suggests), but it may be a merism
elsewhere unattested, and is so translated here;   [h] *vĕhāyāh kimsōs nōsēs*: mss
Niphal = "melt" but is hapax in Qal, perhaps "faint," "pine away," or something of the sort; that no two ancient versions are alike suggests that this phrase
is damaged beyond repair.

COMMENTS

We now hear a response to the boastful soliloquy of an unnamed Assyrian king.
Most commentators divide at "therefore . . ." (*lākēn* 16), but the soliloquy ends
at 14 and the use of the rhetorical question, often followed by comment, is a
common feature of prophetic rhetoric (Amos 3:3–8; 6:12; Hos 13:10, 14; Mic
1:5; 2:7; Isa 29:16; Jer 2:11, 14; 13:23). The device of putting quotes into the
mouths of self-confident and boastful individuals and following up with a de-
flating response part of the prophetic stock-in-trade (e.g. Hos 12:8; Mic 3:11–
12). Continuity of theme (deforestation) suggests furthermore that at some
point the pericope may have ended with 33–34. The somewhat confused and
forced images and metaphors make it hard to disagree with Gray (1912, 199),
who describes the passage as a muddle, or with Duhm (1892, 101), who finds
it stylistically inept. The author draws on familiar Isaian topoi as rod and stick,
thorns and weeds, and the association of Yahveh with light and fire (cf. 2:5;
9:1), though the divine title "Light of Israel" occurs only here. The author also
appears to be familiar with a saying comparing the Kingdom of Samaria to an

individual wasting away with sickness (17:4–6), one that uses the same language as 10:16 (*kĕbôd yaʿăqōb* = "the glory of Jacob"; *mišman bĕśārô*, literally, "the fat of his flesh").

These rather obvious literary features suggest that the passage was not composed during the Syro-Samarian crisis, quite apart from the fact that it does not fit the international situation of that time (contra Hayes and Irvine 1987, 200–201). Most commentators agree, but the estimates cover a broad spectrum from the time of Josiah (Barth 1977, 28–34; Clements 1985, 113) to the late Persian (Wildberger 1991, 431) or the Seleucid period (Duhm 1892, 101). No doubt the imperial pretensions castigated in this passage were seen to apply to several imperial successors of the Assyrians, including the Seleucids. But the metaphor of wasting sickness recalls the destruction of Sennacherib's army and the tradition recorded in Josephus that this came about by bubonic plague (*Ant.* 10.21–23 cf. Herodotus 2.141 on the incapacitation of the Assyrian army in Egypt by a plague of mice). Isaiah 10:15–19 is not one of the more memorable passages in the book, but it illustrates an important aspect of the message of Israel's prophets, i.e., the critique of imperialism and the refusal to take nationalistic and imperialistic pretensions seriously on their own terms. And, as Weinfeld points out, the language of imperium in Isaiah and other prophetic figures will give rise in due course to the mirror-image metaphor of a spiritual kingdom, the Kingdom of God.

THREE EDITORIAL COMMENTS (10:20–27A)

(Carroll 1978; Cogan; Soggin)

TRANSLATION

10   [20]On that day the residue of Israel and the survivors of the household of Jacob will no longer rely on the one who struck them, but they will rely in truth on Yahveh the Holy One of Israel. [21] A residue will return, the residue of Jacob, to the God of Might,[a] [22] for even if your people Israel were as numerous as the sand of the sea, only a residue of them[b] will return. Destruction is decreed, with vindication abounding;[c] [23] for the Sovereign Lord, Yahveh of the hosts will bring about the destruction that is decreed in the midst of the earth.

[24]Therefore, thus says the Sovereign Lord, Yahveh of the hosts: "O my people who dwell in Zion, do not be afraid of the Assyrians when they beat you with a rod and wield their stick over you as the Egyptians did. [25] In a very short while the time of wrath[d] will be over and my anger will be directed at their destruction.[e] [26] Yahveh of the hosts will wield a whip against them as when he struck Midian at the rock of Oreb. His staff will be extended [over the sea,][f] and he will wield it as the Egyptians did. [27]On that day his burden will be removed from your shoulder, and his yoke broken off from your neck."

NOTES

[a] *'Ēl gibbôr* cf. 9:5[6] where it is translated "Hero Warrior" referring to the ideal ruler;   [b] *bô* partitive;   [c] on *ṣĕdāqâ* = "vindication" rather than "righteousness" see note to 1:27;   [d] for this rendering of *kālâ zaʿam* cf. Dan 11:36 *ʿad kālâ zaʿam*, "until the time of wrath is completed";   [e] *vĕʾappî ʿal-tablîtām*: since *tablît* is hapax and the phrase is syntactically difficult, several commentators accept the emendation of David Luzzato (1867), *vĕʾappî ʿal tebel yittōm*, "and my anger will be consummated on (against) the world," which is brilliant but does not fit the context; for other proposals see Gray 1912, 206; Wildberger 1991, 439–40;   [f] it looks as if *ʿal hayyām*, "over the sea," has been inserted rather incongruously by a pious glossator for whom mention of the Egyptians brought to mind Exod 14:16, Moses extending his staff over the Red Sea to save the Israelites and destroy the Egyptians.

COMMENTS

It is hardly surprising that the critical situation of Judah's first encounter with Assyria should continue to serve as a paradigm for understanding and articulating the nation's attitude towards successive imperial powers. The first and last of these three addenda are introduced with the "on that day" formula indicating an event, juncture, or situation in a future not necessarily remote. The middle passage introduces an oracle with the standard prophetic incipit (24–25) followed by an exegetical comment explaining how the punishment in store for Assyria referred to in the oracle will be administered (26). A feature common to all three is the deployment of familiar Isaian motifs. The "residue of Israel" takes up and develops redundantly the name of Isaiah's child Shear-yashub (7:3); we have already heard a lot about smiting and being smitten (5:25; 9:12[13]), and the poem on the ideal ruler has supplied the topoi of the rod and bar (9:3[4] cf. 10:5, 15), the yoke of servitude (9:3[4]), and the title *'ēl gibbôr*, here translated "the God of Might" (9:5[6]). These motifs tend to recur (e.g. "the residue of Israel" 4:3; 11:11, 16; 28:5; 37:4, 31–32; 46:3), sometimes in a sense quite different from the original occurrence. An obvious example is "the one who struck them," no longer Yahveh (as in 9:12[13]) but Assyria, whose instruments of punishment are now used against them. Then also El Gibbor is used literally of the God of Israel rather than hyperbolically of the ruler, and we may suspect that the verbal element in the name Shear-yashub ("a residue will return") is now used in the sense of conversion or, to use Buber's language, "turning," a change of heart and of life, as in 1:27.

None of the many attempts to relate the first of the three paragraphs to the Assyrian crisis under Ahaz has been convincing, since dating it to the reign of Ahaz can explain reliance on Assyria but not the smiting (Wildberger 1991, 435–36; and Hayes and Irvine 1987, 201–3 for whom the striker is Syria). Similar wording in the section of the book dealing with Isaiah and Hezekiah during the Sennacherib campaign reinforces the impression that has been gaining on us since the beginning of the core narrative that the Ahaz incident has been written up from the perspective of the later crisis. At that time Isaiah gave Hezekiah a sign having to do with vegetation and food and designed to assure him that the crisis would be over by the third year (37:30 cf. 7:15–16). There was to be a residue and there were to be survivors (37:31–32 cf. 10:20), and this outcome is attributed to the zeal of Yahveh of the hosts (37:32b cf. 9:6b[7b]). The predicted fate of the Assyrian king and his army that follows (37:33–38) could also be read as a parallel to 10:16–19.

It is equally probable that the experience of *successive* threats to national existence has left its mark on the book in the form of a cumulative and incremental editorial process reaching deep into the period of the Second Commonwealth. The point may be illustrated by comparing 10:20–23 with 28:14–22, a passage addressed to the ruling elite in Jerusalem, assuring them that the measures they are taking to avoid "the overwhelming flood" will not be successful. The allusion is almost certainly to events connected with Hezekiah's refusal of tribute to Assyria in 704 B.C.E. and the predictable Assyrian response. The language of 10:20–23 indicates dependence on 28:14–22, but the predetermined destruction is now projected into the future: it will affect not just the land of Judah but the whole earth, and from it only a residue will emerge as a new and purified Israel. The different perspective of the two paragraphs is indicated by the eschatologizing "on that day" that opens 10:20–23, the mosaic of Isaian themes that it contains, and such terms as *bēt yaʿăqōb* ("household of Jacob") and *ṣĕdāqâ* with the meaning "vindication" (cf. 1:27) characteristic of late Second Temple usage.

The second paragraph is associated thematically with the first through the reference to physical abuse at the hands of Assyrians. The oracle ostensibly proclaims the imminent end of oppression for Israel and the beginning of retribution to be visited on Assyria—which is entirely in keeping with the poem to which these comments have been appended (10:5–19 + 33–34). The rod and staff and the miraculous defeat of the Midianites also remain within the same perspective. The instruments of punishment wielded against the Assyrians (26) imply application of the *lex talionis*, and the use of a whip may have been suggested by the "overwhelming flood" of 28:15, 18 since the same word (*šôt*) can stand for both whip and flood.

These associations with 10:20–23 and 28:14–22 suggest the possibility of an equally late or even later date for this paragraph. The only other form of address similar to "my people who dwell in Zion" occurs in 30:19–22, manifestly a Second Temple passage, and Dan 11:36 anticipates the end of "the time of wrath" (*ʿad-kālâ zaʿam*), i.e., the persecution of Antiochus IV, since "what is decreed shall be accomplished" (*kî nehĕrāṣâ neʿĕṣātâ* cf. Isa 10:22–23). It is therefore not out of the question that the passage was reread, perhaps even composed, to inspire faith and hope during the troubled history of Judah under the rule successively of Ptolemies (here Egypt) and Seleucids (here Assyria).

THE ENEMY APPROACHES (10:27B–34)

(Aharoni 1979, 387–94; Albright 1924; Arnold; Childs 1959, 187–98; 1967, 61–63; Christensen 1976; Donner 1964, 30–38; 1968; Grayson 1991, 86–102; 762–64; Grelot 1983; Irvine 1990; Sweeney 1994b; Tadmor 1958; Whitehouse 1905, 171–73)

TRANSLATION

10 [27b]They have gone up from . . .[a]
[28]they have come upon Ayyath,[b]
passed by Migron,
left their baggage at Michmash;
[29]they have crossed the ravine,
bivouacked at Geba.[c]
Ramah is racked with fear,
Gibeah of Saul has fled;
[30]cry aloud, Bath-Gallim,
hear it, Laish!
answer her, Anathoth!
[31]Madmenah is in flight,
the people of Gebim take cover.
[32]This very day they halt at Nob,
they shake their fist[d] at the mount of the daughter of Zion,[e]
the hill of Jerusalem.

[33]See, the Sovereign Lord, Yahveh of the hosts,
will lop off the branches with frightening force,[f]
the tallest of them will be hewn down,
the lofty ones laid low;
[34]the thickets of the forest will be cut down with an axe,
Lebanon in its majesty[g] will fall.

NOTES

[a] *ʿōl mippnê-šāmen*, "a yoke [is broken off] because of oil," may have resulted from reading a corrupt text as a (scarcely intelligible) gloss on the preceding *ʿūlô*, perhaps with the anointing of the ideal ruler in mind; commentators agree that the three words belonged originally to the poem following, reading *ʿlh* ("he went up") for *ʿl*. None of the attempts to find a place-name behind *mippnê-šāmen* (Samaria, Rimmon, Bethel, Yeshimon [the desert], Saphon [the north]?) goes beyond a guess, so it seemed best simply to leave it blank. Verbs referring to the invader are in the singular except *ʿābĕrû* (29) which, however, should be singular with 1QIsa[a], LXX, Syr.; I have rendered them in the plural with reference to the invading army as a whole;   [b] 4QIsa[c] reads *ʾl* but MT *ʿal* is supported by 1QIsa[a];   [c] *gebaʿ mālôn lānû*, literally, "Geba is (will be) our

quarters for the night," is possible but the shift to first person seems out of place; read *mālôn lô*;   [d] 1QIsa[a] reads *ynvp ydyv*, "he waves his hands to and fro," but MT Polel and singular give better sense; Bahar (1993, 403–5) suggests a wordplay between this form of *nvp* and Nob;   [e] reading *bat* for *bēt* with 1QIsa[a], 4QIsa[c], LXX, Syr., Vulg.;   [f] some commentators accept Tg. *ma'ăṣādâ*, "axe," for *ma'ărāṣâ → 'rṣ*, "terrify," but emendation is unnecessary; the last three words of 33a are all hapax legomena;   [g] *'addîr* not elsewhere attested as substantive, but "in its majesty" makes a better fit with the context than "by means of a mighty one," i.e., Yahveh.

COMMENTS

This poem about the advance of a hostile, unnamed army on Jerusalem takes up once again the theme of the Assyrian threat (5:26–30; 7:18–20; 8:7–8 cf. 28:2–4) but in more dramatic form. However, its connections with what precedes and follows are tenuous, and we have seen that 10:33–34 has at some point been separated from 10:15–19. We can almost always find some justification for these textual dislocations (e.g. by reading 33–34 as the answer to the threat of 27b–32) but they could also have happened quite accidentally. This kind of highly dramatic and greatly accelerated *Reisebericht* has a parallel in Mic 1:10–16, also with about a dozen place-names that provide occasion for assonance. (There are four examples of this feature in our passage, but only one of them—"Ramah is racked with fear"—could be reproduced even approximately in translation).

Somewhat similar evocations of the approach of danger in the form of an invading army, e.g., Jer 4:5–31, have suggested the mythological topos of "the foe from the north" (Childs 1967, 61–63), or a dramatization of the threat of judgment on Jerusalem with no specific historical referent (Gray 1912, 206–7; Barth 1977, 65–66), but the description of the march on Jerusalem and its effects seems to be too specific for that, though not specific enough to identify the occasion beyond reasonable doubt. The Damascus-Samaria axis attacked Jerusalem in 734, but the location of 10:27b–32 points unmistakably to an Assyrian attack threatened time and again in this section (contra Donner; Hayes and Irvine 1987, 207–10; Irvine 1990, 274–79). This being the case, one would be inclined to think of Sennacherib's campaign in 701, which reached the walls of Jerusalem but did not take the city (Whitehouse 1905, 171, 173; Fohrer 1966, 162–63; Auvray 1972, 138–41; Aharoni 1979, 387–94). But the obvious objection to this opinion is that Sennacherib advanced on Jerusalem from the southwest not from the north, as is clear from the Taylor prism, the account in 2 Kgs 18–19, and perhaps also Mic 1:10–16. Sargon II (721–705) describes himself on an inscription from Nimrud as "the subduer of the land *ia-u-du* which is far away" (*ANET*, 287). The toponym is generally taken to refer to Judah, but since it is linked with Hamath in the same brief statement it is more likely Ya'udi (Sam'al) in northern Syria rather than the southern Palestinian kingdom, and in any case it does not necessarily imply a campaign of conquest. But Sargon conducted campaigns against Philistine city-states in 720 and 713–711, on both of which occasions the participation of Judah in an anti-Assyrian coalition would have been solicited (for the revolt of Ashdod in 711, this is explicitly stated in Prism A, *ANET*, 287, and strongly suggested in Isa 20). Several recent commentators have therefore opted for 713–711 (Wildberger 1991, 450–58; Clements 1980, 117–21). But the defeat of the northern rebels in 720 led by Hamath and including Samaria, followed by a rapid march south to subdue Hannun of Gaza, seems to provide a more fitting context for a show of strength against Jerusalem with the purpose of discouraging Judean participation in the revolt (Sweeney).

On the itinerary itself little need be said (see maps in Kaiser 1972, 249; Wildberger 1991, 454). If the situation is that of Sargon's first western campaign the departure point would probably have been Samaria. Few of the toponyms have been identified securely, though the general direction is fairly clear: the Assyrian army is described as leaving the main north–south highway somewhere near Bethel and taking to the hills to the east in order to approach Jerusalem along the central ridge. The detour would have been dictated by the decision to bypass the fortified point of Mizpah (Tell en-Naṣbeh) on the main road. Ayyath is generally identified with Ai (et-Tell Josh 7:2), Migron was somewhere near Gibeah (1 Sam 14:2), Michmash would be at or near the village of Muhmas where the baggage train was left while the infantry crossed the ravine, none other than the steep and stony Wadi es-Suweinit. Geba (Jeba) and Ramah (er-Ram) are well-attested Benjamnite sites, but the location of Gibeah of Saul, formerly identified with Tell el-Full, remains uncertain. The location of none of the six place-names closer to Jerusalem is known though Anathoth is probably situated at Ras el-Kharrube near the village of ʿAnata. It is assumed that the troops ended their march on the Mount of Olives (*har ṣôpîm*), from which location their intimidating gestures could be seen from within the city wall.

The final two verses (33–34) take up the metaphor of deforestation in 10:18–19 and conclude the poem dealing with the anticipated punishment of Assyria. They are also entirely consonant with the image of axe and saw and the theme of humbled pride in 10:15–19. Textual dislocations of this kind can happen quite accidentally as noted earlier, but in this instance the relocation sets up a contrast with the image of new growth with which 11:1–9 opens. The juxtaposition is appropriate since the collapse of the evil empires of Assyria and Babylonia, signified by the destruction of the forest, would have created a situation in which the possibility of re-establishing the Davidic dynasty could at least be contemplated. The demonstration of divine power, destructive but also salvific, is timed appositely as the enemy is posing a direct threat to Jerusalem (32). Referring the deforestation metaphor to Assyria (Vermeylen 1977, 1.266–68; Clements 1980a, 120–21) rather than to Judah (Kaiser 1972, 251; Wildberger 1991, 427) also calls to mind the Assyrian addiction to scorched earth tactics and cutting down and hauling away cedars from Lebanon (*ANET*, 275–76 cf. Isa 37:24). Far from being ecologically sensitive (but who was at that time?), the Assyrians proudly recorded their indiscriminate devastation of local flora and fauna during their military campaigns and hunting expeditions. By the seventh century B.C.E. they had, for example, hunted the Syrian elephant to extinction. If they had been more technologically advanced they would doubtless have inflicted even more damage on the environment.

THE PEACEFUL KINGDOM (11:1–9)

(Conrad 1988; Crook; Deist; Hermisson; Mowinckel 1959, 17–20, 65–69; Ringgren 1956, 30–33; Roberts 1973; van Ruiten; Steck 1992; Sweeney 1996; Vermeylen 1977, 1.269–80)

TRANSLATION

11 ¹A branch will grow from Jesse's stock,
     a shoot will spring[a] from its roots.
     ²Yahveh's spirit will rest on him,
     a spirit of wisdom and understanding,
     a spirit of counsel and strength,
     a spirit of knowledge and the fear of Yahveh.
     ³[His delight will be in the fear of Yahveh.][b]
     He will not judge by appearances,
     he will not decide by hearsay,
     ⁴but with righteous judgment he will judge the poor,
     and with equity defend the lowly[c] of the earth.
     He will strike the violent[d] with the rod of his mouth,
     with the breath of his lips he will kill the wicked.
     ⁵Justice will be the belt around his waist,
     truth will be the band[e] around his middle.
     ⁶The wolf will share its lodging with the lamb,
     the leopard will lie down beside the goat,
     the calf and the lion cub will feed together,[f]
     even a small child will lead them;
     ⁷the cow and the bear will share their pasture,
     their young lying down side by side,
     the lion will eat hay like the ox,
     ⁸the infant will play at the cobra's hole,
     the child barely weaned will put its hand[g] over the viper's lair.[h]
     ⁹No longer will they hurt or destroy
     in all my holy mountain;
     for the earth will be full of the knowledge of Yahveh
     as the waters cover the sea.

NOTES

[a] Reading *yiprāḥ*, with Tg., LXX, and Vulg. for MT *yipreḥ*;   [b] literally, "and his smell . . ." (*vaḥărîḥô*), a copyist's dittographic error prompted by *rûaḥ . . . vĕyir'at* YHVH in the previous verse (on which see Unterman 1992, 17–23); [c] reading *la'ăniyê-* (→ *'ănî*, "poor") for MT *lĕ'anvê-* (→ *'ānāv*, "humble"), more fitting with *dallîm* (cf. 10:2);   [d] MT *'ereṣ*, "earth," is certainly possible and is supported by 1QIsa[a], but *'āriṣ* in parallelism with *rāšā'* is to be preferred; [e] since it is unlikely that *'ēzôr*, "belt," would be repeated in the same stich, read instead the similar *'asûr*, "band";   [f] MT *vĕ'ēgel ûkĕpîr ûmĕrî' yaḥdāv*, "and calf and lion cub and fatted cow together," which, though supported by 1QIsa[a] and 4QIsa[c], is unlikely since only two animals are juxtaposed in this part of the poem; read *yir'û* or more speculatively *yimrĕ'û* (→ *mr'*, "fatten," MH);   [g] in *yādô hādāh* (as in 1QIsa[a] and 4QIsa[b]; 4QIsa[c] has *ydv yḥdh*) "has stretched out his hand," the perfect is unusual but *yĕdahdeh*, "throw or roll stones," based on an Arab. cognate, is too speculative (see Reider 1952, 115);   [h] *mĕ'ûrâ* (1QIsa[a] *m'vrvt*) often related to Akk. *muru*, "young," but hapax; the safer option is to read *mĕ'ārâ*, "cave," "hole in the ground".

COMMENTS

This splendid poem announces the emergence from David's family line of a ruler divinely endowed with all charismatic attributes required to fulfill the ideal, often proclaimed but rarely if ever realized, of bringing about a just order in which the poor and powerless can enjoy equal rights with the wealthy and powerful. At his coming, war and all manifestations of violence will be abolished (cf. 9:7) not only in human society but in the animal world as well. Within the tradition of a future golden age, often in the form of an *apokatastasis* or restoration of the first creation, the political order and the order of creation as a whole can be and sometimes are connected and interdependent (cf., for example, the text "a ruler will arise" from ancient Mesopotamia, *ANET*[3], 606–7; and Virgil's famous Fourth *Eclogue* ushering in the Augustan age as a renewal of creation). It is therefore by no means necessary to follow those exegetes who argue for a conflation of two distinct poems (1–5, 6–9), a hypothesis that has little to commend it (the thesis is argued by Barth 1977, 60–63; and Vermeylen [ed.] 1989, 275–76; among others). It is also reasonably clear that 11:1–9 is not of a piece with 10:32–33, though its location at this point may have been suggested by the contrast between the destruction of the (Assyrian) forest and the emergence of new (Judean, Davidic) growth.

It will come as no surprise to hear that the date of the poem has been the subject of a long-standing and inconclusive debate, one with little prospect of closure. Duhm assigned it somewhat tentatively to Isaiah as the product of his old age, his swan song (*Schwanengesang*; 1892, 36) and, leaving aside the swan song, several recent commentators are in agreement. Von Rad (1965, 2.169–70), for example, simply assumed Isaian authorship for Isa 11:1–9, which he took to be contemporaneous with Mic 5:1–3[2–4], and Wildberger read the poem as a reaction to Isaiah's disappointment with Hezekiah when the latter failed to heed his warning during Sargon II's Philistine campaign (1991, 467–69). Vermeylen (1989, 271) assigned it to the time of Josiah. For Steck, 11:6–8 is an early postexilic theme taken up again in 65:25 in the Hellenistic period. It is tolerably clear by now that such matters are rarely resolved by simply assigning early or late dates on the basis of themes, including eschatological themes.

Some of the more distinctive vocabulary in the poem (e.g. *ḥōṭer*, "branch"; *gezaʿ*, "stock"; *nēṣer*, "shoot") does, however, seem to point to a later rather than earlier date, as a glance at the concordance will show. This is most clearly the case with the expression "my holy mountain" (*har qodšî*) in the last verse, frequently heard in the last section of the book, the so-called Third Isaiah (cf. 56:7; 57:13; 65:11, 25; 66:20), and, in general, the sentiments expressed in this verse are those of this last section (56–66). Here too we should probably resist the temptation to read this last verse as a later appendage to the poem (as Barth 1977, 60–61; Kaiser 1972, 253). The abolition of war and violence in Jerusalem, where Jesse's descendent will rule, is not at all dissonant with the preceding scenario in the poem, and the knowledge of the true God spreading over the earth from that place circles back to the endowment of the ideal ruler mentioned at the beginning of the poem, especially if Yahveh is *nomen rectum* for both *daʿat* ("knowledge") and *yirʾat* ("fear").

While the restoration of the house of David is far from being a prominent feature of the aspirations expressed in Isa 40–66, the anticipation of a new growth from the old stock of Jesse, ancestor of the Davidic dynasty (1 Sam 16:1), aligns with dynastic aspirations that come to expression in other texts from the post-destruction period (Jer 23:5–6; 33:14–22; Ezek 37:24–28; Amos 9:11–15; Mic 5:1–3[2–4]). While some of these are of quite limited scope, others envisage the advent of a peaceful kingdom including peace with the animal world as here (Ezek 34:23–31; 37:26). Emphasis on spirit-endowment reaffirms the charismatic principle with which the hereditary, dynastic principle would normally be in contradiction. While it no doubt draws on representations of deeds of preternatural power attributed to bandit chieftains and warlords in the early history of the people, including David, in the developed form in which we find it here it aligns with usage in the later sections of the book (42:1; 44:3; 48:16; 59:21; 61:1). Later still it will provide the textual basis for the seven gifts of the Holy Spirit (*sacrum septenarium*) developed in the West by Augustine, Gregory the Great, and Thomas Aquinas on the basis of LXX, which adds piety (*eusebeia* cf. Vulg. *spiritus pietatis*) to make seven.

Wisdom (*ḥokmâ*) and understanding (*bînâ*), key terms in the aphoristic literature, together express an attribute essential for successful living and, as such, they are brought into contact with religious observance in Deuteronomy ("this [law observance] will be your wisdom and understanding in the sight of the peoples" 4:6). The next pair, counsel and strength, indicate both the skill to elaborate sensible plans and the ability to carry them through, attributes essential for successful rule. Knowledge and fear of Yahveh take up themes prominent in

Hosea and Deuteronomistic writings. The subordination of the acquisition of wisdom and learning to godly fear is one of the seminal insights of the emergent Jewish religious-intellectual tradition. It comes to lapidary expression in a saying attributed to Hanina ben Dosa (first century C.E.): "those whose fear of sin takes precedence over their wisdom, their wisdom will endure; those whose wisdom takes precedence over their fear of sin, their wisdom will not endure" (*m. ʾAbot* 3:11).

It seems that all the charismatic endowments listed converge on the task of the equitable administration of justice (3–5). That this was viewed throughout the Near East and beyond as the primary responsibility of the ruler is abundantly in evidence. In promulgating his laws Ur-Nammu ruler of Ur in the late third millennium boasts that in his kingdom "the orphan was not delivered up to the rich man, the widow was not delivered up to the mighty man" (*ANET,* 524), and in the prologue to his laws Hammurapi states that he has been commissioned by the gods Anum and Enlil "to cause justice to prevail in the land, to destroy the wicked and the evil, that the strong might not oppress the weak" (*ANET,* 164). The same ideal is expressed in psalms (e.g. Ps 72:1–4,12–14) and in the aphoristic literature (e.g. Prov 16:10; 20:8), and no abuse receives as much attention in eighth century B.C.E. prophetic protest as the corruption of the judicial system (Amos 2:7; 5:10; Mic 3:9–12; Isa 3:1–3; 5:18–23).

The transition to peaceful coexistence in the animal world is not so abrupt; indeed those commentators who insist on making the following verses into a separate poem may be missing a subtle parallel between 3–5 and 6–8 consisting in the contrast between the strong and the weak in both the human and zoological realms. Powerful, predatory animals like the wolf can also stand for the arbitrary and unjust exercise of power (e.g. Ezek 22:27; Zeph 3:3). The occurrence of 9a in Isa 65:25 and 9b in Hab 2:14 does not justify us in demoting this last verse to the status of a later and inappropriate addition to the poem. The fact that Isa 65:25 combines phrases from vv 6–7 and 9 of our poem and that Hab 2:12–14 alludes to Mic 3:10 in addition to Isa 11:9b points to the originality of 11:9 rather than the opposite, and we have seen that the sentiments it expresses are in any case not out of place in the poem.

A REUNITED PEOPLE (11:10–16)

(Luria; Wegner 1992a; Widengren; Williamson 1995)

TRANSLATION

11 [10]On that day the root of Jesse will stand as a signal for the peoples of the world; him will the nations seek out; glory will rest on him.[a]

[11]On that day the Sovereign Lord will raise[b] his hand to recover the residue of his people that is left from Assyria, from Egypt, from Pathros, Nubia, Elam, Shinar, Hamath, and the islands of the sea.

¹²He will raise a signal for the nations,
and gather the dispersed men of Israel;
he will assemble the scattered women of Judah
from the four corners of the earth.
¹³Ephraim's jealousy will cease,
Judah's opponents[c] will be destroyed;
Ephraim will not be jealous of Judah,
Judah will not be hostile to Ephraim.
¹⁴They will swoop on the flank of the Philistines to the west,
together they will plunder peoples to the east;
Edom and Moab will be in their power,[d]
Ammonites will be subject to them.
¹⁵Yahveh will dry up[e] the tongue of the Egyptian sea,
will wave his hand over the Euphrates River[f]
together with a violent wind.[g]
He will split it into seven channels
so that it may be crossed dry-shod.[h]
¹⁶There will be a highway for the residue of his people,
those left over from Assyria,
just as there was for Israel
at the time they went up from the land of Egypt.

NOTES

[a] *Vĕhāyĕtāh mĕnūḥātô kābôd*, "his resting place will be glory," is exceptional enough to allow for a deliberate play on the spirit-endowment resting (verb *nûaḥ*) on the ideal ruler (2);   [b] for *šēnît*, "a second time," read *šannôt* cf. Arab. *saniya*, "to be high," since *yôsîp* requires a verb in the infinitive;   [c] it seems better to keep the normal meaning of *ṣōrĕrîm* rather than taking it as abstract plural parallel with *qîn'â*;   [d] read *mišlôaḥ* for MT *mišlôḥ*;   [e] reading *vĕheḥĕrîb* (cf. Isa 50:2; 51:10) for MT *vĕheḥĕrîm*, "and he will vow to destruction," following LXX;   [f] MT *hannāhār*, "the River";   [g] MT *ba'yām rûḥô* has not been successfully explained; for the main attempts see Wildberger 1991, 488; LXX, Syr., and Vulg. suggest the meaning "strength," "violence," for *'ăyām* (1QIsa[a] *'yym*), which is hapax; Tg. has "through the word of his prophets"; [h] literally "with sandals."

COMMENTS

Isaiah 11:10–16 consists formally of two appendices to the preceding poem (10, 11–16) both introduced with the customary *bayyôm hahû'* formula. The second is also circumscribed by inclusion—"the residue that is left of his people"—impressed more clearly in the Hebrew by play on the sibilants: *šĕ'ār 'ammô 'ăšer yiššā'ēr mē'aššûr* (11), *lišĕ'ār 'ammô 'ăšer yiššā'ēr mē'aššûr ... ka'ăšer ...* (16). The first of the two is an editorial comment expanding the scope of the poem. This is apparent in the reference to "the root of Jesse" and perhaps also in a more oblique allusion to the spirit-endowment resting (verbal stem *nûaḥ* cf. *měnûḥâ*) on the messianic ruler. The appendices are related to each other by the motif of the "signal" (*nēs*), though used in quite different ways. If the preceding poem dates from the exilic or early Second Temple period as suggested, the two editorial additions would of course represent a still later stage in the development of the Isaian tradition. While this tradition in its later development does not seem to have a strong stake in the restoration of the Judean royal house, Isa 55:3 does speak of David as a witness to the peoples (*ʿēd lěʾummîm*) comparable to the description in our passage of "the root of Jesse" as a "signal for the peoples (of the world)."

That the author of the first comment chose to use the more familiar term *šōreš* ("root") rather than *gēzaʿ* ("stock") is hardly surprising and does not justify interpreting it as an allusion to the community rather than an individual (as Barth 1977, 59; Vermeylen 1989, 277; Clements 1980a, 125). "The root of Jesse" would be a decidedly odd and unprecedented way of referring to a Judean or expatriate community at any point in time. The enigmatic *věhāyětāh měnūḥātô kābôd*, literally, "and his resting place will be glory," could refer to the land ruled over by the descendent of Jesse (*měnūḥâ* in the Deuteronomic sense of the promised land), but the wording is strange enough to allow for the possibility that the writer may have wished to refer back, with some editorial and linguistic license, to the spirit-endowment that rested (*nûaḥ*) on the ideal ruler (11:2). At any rate, this first passage seems to suggest that in a future age the nations of the world will voluntarily submit to the Davidic dynast ruling in Jerusalem. This fantasy of a worldwide empire on which the sun never sets, with Jerusalem as its epicenter, occurs frequently in the later sections of the book, though it is far from clear that the submission of foreign nationals will be voluntary (Isa 45:15; 49:7, 22–23; 54:3; 55:3–5; 60:1–22; 61:5–7).

Noticeable in both passages is the reversal in the metaphoric language vis-à-vis earlier allusions: Yahveh no longer hoists a signal to call in the Assyrians (5:26) or raises his hand to strike in anger (5:25). The second passage begins and ends with the repatriation theme encapsulated in the name of the prophet's son Shear-yashub (7:3; 10:20–23), a theme that recurs as a major leitmotiv through the book. The hoisting of a signal is to alert foreigners charged with responsibility for repatriating exiled Jews that the time has come (also 49:22–23; 62:10; 66:18–21 speaks of a "sign" [*ʾôt*] rather than a "signal" [*nēs*] but the difference is minimal). Since only Assyria and Egypt are mentioned at the end of the second passage (16), most commentators assume that the rest of the locations from Pathros to the islands of the sea have been added; Clements (1980a, 125) in fact thinks that this list could be one of the last additions made to the book. This may be correct, and it is true that Assyria and Egypt are linked in one or two late occurrences with probable reference to Seleucids and Ptolemies respectively (7:18; 10:24; 19:23–25; 27:12–13; 52:4). However, Egypt, Pathros, and Nubia on the one hand and Elam, Shinar, and Hamath on the other are aligned topographically, the first triad from north to south, the second from southeast to northwest. Pathros ("the south land" in Egyptian, *paturisi* in Assyrian records) is Upper Egypt as a distinct administrative region (cf. Jer 44:1, 15; Ezek 29:14; 30:14), and Cush (Akk. *kusu*), ancient Nubia, corresponds to present-day Sudan. Shinar is the alluvial plain of southern Mesopotamia (Gen 10:10; 11:2; 14:1, 9; Josh 7:21; Zech 5:11; Dan 1:2), Hamath is in northern Syria, and the "islands of the sea," i.e., the Mediterranean, would stand for either the Phoenician coastal area or the Aegean islands (the Hebrew *'î* can mean either "island" or "coastal region").

The anticipated reconciliation between south and north, Judah and Ephraim, reverses the situation described earlier (9:21) and reminds us that reunion remained an ideal long after the ten tribes had disappeared from the scene (e.g. Ezek 37:15–28). In the context of the passage as a whole the bad feeling referred to would be between the authorities in Samaria and Jerusalem amply documented in Ezra–Nehemiah. Ezra 4:1–3 reports that opponents of Judah and Benjamin (*ṣārê yĕhûdâ ûbinyāmîn* cf. *ṣorĕrê yĕhûdâ* here) who claimed descent from people settled in Samaria during the Assyrian period offered assistance in building the Jerusalem temple and were repulsed. During Nehemiah's tenure of office opposition came not only from the Sanballats in Samaria but from the Kedarite Arabs under their ruler Geshem (Gashmu) and the Tobiad family (Ammon). Moab, Ammon, and the Philistine city of Ashdod are also potential sources of danger to be kept at arm's length (Neh 13:1–3, 23–27). Thus the background of the poem is Judah of the early to middle Achaemenid period. The poem provides no grounds for attribution to the exilic Isaiah (pace Williamson): chs. 40–54 (or 40–55) evince no interest in the unification of or reconciliation between Ephraim and Judah; it is simply not an issue, nor do they mention the Philistines or the Egyptian diaspora, and the closest parallel to the "dispersed of Israel" (*nidḥê yiśrā'ēl*) is towards the beginning of third section of the book (56:8).

The "tongue of the Egyptian sea" may refer to the tongue-shaped Red Sea (cf. the lower extremity of the Dead Sea known as the Lashon or Tongue), which the repatriates are to cross dry-shod as their forbears did in the exodus (Exod 13:18; 15:4; Num 14:25). By rendering the Euphrates equally fordable, Yahveh will create the right conditions for another exodus from the principal centers of the diaspora mentioned at the beginning of the passage (11). The highway along which the repatriates will return (*mĕsillâ* 19:23; 40:3–5; 62:10–12 cf. *maslûl* 35:8–10), from Babylon mainly but also from Egypt (cf. Zech 10:10), is a major motif in the later stages of the Isaian tradition.

CONCLUDING HYMN
OF THANKSGIVING (12:1–6)

(Ackroyd 1978; Alonso-Schökel 1956; Crüsemann 1969, 50–56; Prinsloo; Vermeylen 1977, 1.280–82; Williamson 1994, 118–25)

TRANSLATION

12 ¹You will say on that day:
Yahveh, I thank you,
for though you were angry with me
your anger has abated,ᵃ
and you have consoled me.
²See, God is my salvation,ᵇ
I will trust and feel no dread
for Yahveh is my strength and my power,ᶜ
God has been my salvation.

³You will draw water with joy
from the wells of salvation.

⁴You will sayᵈ on that day:
Give thanks to Yahveh, call on his name,
make known his deeds among the peoples,
proclaim that his name is exalted.
⁵Sing hymns to Yahveh for he has wrought splendidly,
let this be known over all the earth,
⁶Shout aloud, exult, you who dwell in Zion,ᵉ
for great in your midst is the Holy One of Israel.

NOTES

ᵃ Read *vayyāšob* with LXX, Syr., Vulg. for MT jussive *yāšōb*;   ᵇ the repetition of *ʾēl* in 1QIsaᵃ is probably due to dittography;   ᶜ read *zimrātî* for MT *zimrāt*; a secondary meaning of *zmr* verbal and substantival ("be strong," "strength") is rendered probably by Northwest Semitic personal names (e.g. *bʿlzmr*, Zimri) and Arab. cognate *dimr*, "strong";   ᵈ *vaʾămartem*, plural, in MT, Syr., Vulg. but singular in 1QIsaᵃ, 4QIsaᵉ, and LXX; in the context slight preference should be given MT (see commentary);   ᵉ *yôšebet* fem. participle for collective (GKC §122s); 1QIsaᵃ has *bt syvn* with *yvšbt* written in above the line.

COMMENTS

Two brief psalms (1–2, 4–6), both introduced by "you will say on that day," the first directed to an individual, the second addressing a collectivity at least in MT (see notes on the text), are linked by the injunction to draw water with festive joy, reminiscent of the water-drawing during Sukkoth. They provide an appropriate conclusion to chs. 1–12 by ending the threats, imprecations, predictions of disaster, and less prominent assurances of ultimate well-being on a high note. The repetition of *yĕšûʿâ*, "salvation," in the first of the two mini-psalms plays on the name *yĕšaʿyāhû*, "Isaiah," thereby forming an inclusio with the prophet's name at the beginning of the book. It encapsulates a message in the last analysis more basic than the message expressed in the names of the three children who are featured in the course of these chapters. This circumstance suggests that the first poem is addressed to the prophet himself as the principal actor in the events narrated and the representative of the people. The second psalm would then summon the saved community and the inhabitants of Jerusalem in particular to offer thanks and praise now that the judgments announced in 1–11 are in the past.

Even a cursory reading will reveal that this two-part composition is a patchwork of biblical citations and allusions, especially from the book of Psalms (in order of occurrence Pss 118:21; 88:22; 25:5; 118:14; 105:1; 148:13; 9:12; 30:5). Of particular interest is the verbatim citation from the "Song at the Sea" (Exod 15:2) in 2b. Following on the theme of the new exodus in 11:12–16, this finale to the first section of the book can then be read as thanksgiving for the defeat of another imperial power, Assyria in the historical context of 1–12, Babylonia in the perspective of the time of composition and that of a later readership. In this respect it fits the pattern of those descriptions of a new exodus followed by hymns of praise and thanksgiving in later chapters of the book (42:10–13; 44:23; 49:13).

If 12:1–6 recapitulates the first segment of the book, it could not have been composed as an introduction to the sayings directed against foreign nations, especially Babylon, in 13–23 (pace Vermeylen 1977, 280–82). Furthermore, MT 12:1–6 is followed by a pĕtûḥâ (פ) and both 1QIsaᵃ and 4QIsaᵃ have a blank space two-thirds of a line long before 13:1. Isaiah 12:1–6 does, notwithstanding, make a fitting linkage between chs. 1–11 and the anti-Babylonian poems that follow (13:1–22; 14:3–23; 21:1–10), and the linkage serves to emphasize once again how reflection on the experience of Judah faced with direct and potentially terminal threat from the Assyrians informed the interpretation of events during the rise, heyday, and decline of the Neo-Babylonian Empire. It is also noteworthy that the mention of consolation after anger and punishment (1) anticipates the opening theme of the exilic section of the book (40:1).

The link verse (3) addresses a plurality and introduces the water-drawing motif perhaps, as suggested, with reference to the ceremony of śimḥat bēt ha-shō'evâ ("the rejoicing of the place of water-drawing") during Sukkoth (m. Sukkah 4:9–5:1), even though on that occasion water was drawn from Siloam not from wells. (This liturgical occasion provided the context for Jesus' saying about living water in John 7:37–39.) There may also be a fainter echo of the water from the rock incident in the wilderness (Exod 17:1–7 cf. Isa 48:21), again following an allusion to the new exodus. At any rate 12:3 does not belong to the first brief psalm for the reason stated, and in fact it is thematically closer to the second, which ends on an emphatic note of rejoicing. A recapitulatory intent is also apparent in repeating at the very end of 1–12 the designation qĕdôš yiśrā'ēl, "the Holy One of Israel" (cf. 1:4, 24; 5:19, 24; 6:3; 10:20), in whose name and with whose authority the prophet has been speaking.

INTRODUCTION TO
ISAIAH 13–27

◆

We saw that the psalm in 12:1–6 rounds off and recapitulates the first major section of the book rather than introducing this second section. The opening poem of the second section carries the superscription "an oracle (*maśśāʾ*) about Babylon that Isaiah ben Amoz saw in vision," the third and last of the titles that attribute sayings to Isaiah. The end of this long second section of the book is less clear, though the image of a final harvesting among the nations from Mesopotamia to Egypt resulting in the return of dispersed Israelites (27:12–13) corresponds to the repatriation theme in 14:1–2 near the beginning. The major segments of the book preceding and following this section (i.e. chs. 1–12 and 18–35) contain a sustained critique of the political and religious leadership in Judah during the period of Assyrian ascendancy, the former for the most part during the reign of Ahaz, the latter during that of Hezekiah a generation later. Needless to say, both segments contain much extraneous material and numerous editorial expansions, but the main thrust is clear. Chapters 13–27 also contain denunciations directed against those in power in Jerusalem (22:1–25), but they consist mainly of sayings against foreign countries and peoples—Babylon (13:1–22; 14:3–23; 21:1–10), Philistia (14:29–31), Moab (15:1–16:14), Damascus (17:1–3), Ethiopia (18:1–7), Egypt (19:1–17), Edom (21:11–12), the Kedarite Arabs (21:13–17), and Phoenician cities (23:1–18). Nine of these carry the title *maśśāʾ* ("oracular utterance"), a word that also has the punning undertone of burden, the burden of divine judgment (13:1; 15:1; 17:1; 19:1; 21:1, 11, 13; 22:1; 23:1). Only the first of these, however, is attributed to Isaiah. Isaiah 20:1–6 describes an extraordinary piece of street theater, with the prophet parading naked through Jerusalem as a proleptic sign of the defeat and humiliation of Egyptians and Ethiopians. There are also numerous brief passages, mostly in prose, introduced with the familiar "on that day" formula or, in one instance (18:7), "at that time."

The last four chapters of this segment of the book (chs. 24–27) are generally taken to comprise a distinct literary unit of late date to which, since Duhm, the title "the Isaian Apocalypse" has been given. But these chapters are without introductory formula or structural markers setting them apart from what precedes. Furthermore, much of their content is not at all apocalyptic on any showing (the psalm in 25:1–5, the prayer in 26:7–19, the commentary on the vineyard song 27:2–5, the Moab oracle 25:10b–12), and the passages that may be so described are no more apocalyptic than the opening poem in 13:2–22. It therefore seems advisable to explore the relation of chs. 24–27 to the preceding chapters without prejudicing the discussion by using this designation. I will suggest instead that we read these chapters as an amplification or extension of the anti-Babylonian poems at the beginning and towards the end of the preceding chapters, 13–23 (i.e. 13:1–14:23 and 21:1–10), with emphasis on the contrast between the fate of the city of Babylon and the restoration of Jerusalem, a contrast that will be restated with reference to Edom and Jerusalem in chs. 34 and 35. In this case the contrast is most clearly in evidence in 26:1–6, celebrating Jerusalem at peace behind its strong walls and gates as opposed to the alien city now razed to the ground.

An intriguing problem is posed by the chronological note in 14:28 referring to the year of the death of King Ahaz. As it stands, it could be no more than a formal superscription to the anti-Philistine oracle following (14:29–31). But if it is taken in conjunction with the vision report in ch. 6, dated to the year of Uzziah's death, it could mark off the main stages in Isaiah's career under Ahaz (6:1–14:27) and Hezekiah (14:28 onward), leaving open the question whether he was active during the reign of Uzziah and, if so, whether the record of his activity at that time is reflected in the first 5 chapters of the book. But if this was ever the reason for including the date at this point it is no longer apparent, for there is no straightforward chronological sequencing of the material in chs. 1–39. Isaiah 17:1–6, for example, refers indirectly to events during the reign of Ahaz, whose death is reported in 14:28. It seems more likely that the Babylonian poems 13:1–14:23 were at some stage of the editorial process placed where they are to make the point that the prophetic history about Judah and Assyria recorded in chs. 1–12 provides the essential clues to interpreting the course of events during the time, much closer to the reader, of Neo-Babylonian ascendancy.

The position of the Babylonian poems between the Assyrian material in chs. 1–12 and the concluding segment about Assyria in 14:24–27 has been variously explained, usually as evidence of "an earlier redactional structure" (Clements 1980a, 129). The suggestion offered here is that a first series of untitled sayings directed against Assyria (14:24–27), Philistia (14:28–31), Moab (15:1–16:11), Damascus (17:1–3), Israel (17:4–6), and Egypt (18:1–6; 19:1–15) carried forward the historical perspective of the Neo-Assyrian period in chs. 1–12 down to the definitive collapse of the Assyrian Empire either experienced or foreseen as imminent. Then some time no earlier than the sixth century B.C.E. this series was enclosed within the anti-Babylonian poems in 13–14 and 21:1–10 to form a new literary unit ending appropriately and climactically with the prophetic announcement of the definite collapse of the Babylonian Empire, the fall of the city of Babylon ("fallen, fallen is Babylon," 21:9). At yet a later stage this material was reconfigured into a series of nine *maśśā'ôt* ("oracular pronouncements") omitting Assyria, Philistia, and Israel as of less contemporaneous relevance and incorporating a few additional sayings—Duma (21:11–12), the Kedarite Arabs (21:13–15), the Valley of Vision (22:1–8), and Tyre (23:1–16)— as of greater current interest. The accommodation of existing prophetic pronouncements on international affairs to changing situations and the rise and fall of empires is no more than we would expect. The two series would then have been combined producing the somewhat confusing sequence in the text before us.

Four of the nine oracles against foreign countries (21:1, 11, 13; 22:1) are very brief and their titles, no doubt added by an editor long after the passages were composed, have been suggested by a word or turn of phrase in the poems themselves. Also, one of these four (the Valley of Vision, 22:1–14) is not about a foreign people at all. The series has therefore certainly had a checkered history, and it has also been expanded editorially, often with additions introduced with the familiar "on that day" formula (17:4–6, 7–8, 9; 18:7; 19:16–17, 18, 19–22, 23, 24–25; 22:8b–11, 12–14; 17:4–6; 22:12–14). A close reading of these addenda brings more clearly into view the phenomenon of *serial editing*, the creation of new prophecy out of old, which is a central feature of the editorial history of the book. It also illustrates the point that the earliest stages in this history must be recovered from the texts themselves. Examples in the present section would be the five editorial attachments to the Egyptian saying (19:16–25), the passage chronicling the rise and fall of successive Judean royal officials (22:15–25), and the final addition to the Moab oracle ("This is the saying Yahveh addressed to Moab a long time ago, but now Yahveh says . . . ," 16:13). As in the corresponding series in Jeremiah, some of these prophetic codicils serve to mitigate the harshness of the original pronouncement (19:18–25; 23:17–18 cf. Jer 46:26b; 49:6, 39). It goes without saying that no reconstruction of the editorial history of the book can claim more than plausibility, but a theory of incremental and cumulative exegetical development seems more plausible than a simple conflation of an Isaian core with a post-Isaianic *maśśā'* series (as Fohrer; Wildberger).

Oracular utterances against foreign lands have a long history closely associated with warfare. In their origins they may have accompanied homeopathic magical acts. During the Middle Kingdom, for example, the Egyptians wrote the names of enemies on pots, then smashed the pots ritually while uttering an execration (*ANET*, 328–29). Our concern is not, however, with the origins of the genre but with the way in which these very distinctive texts function in the book. In the modern period the tendency has been to assign them an intermediate position in the pattern: judgment on Israel, judgment on hostile nations, salvation on Israel. We may leave to others the task of deciding whether this is the case with Jeremiah (chs. 46–51 in MT but displaced from the middle of the book, ch. 25) and Ezekiel (chs. 25–32); it certainly does not do justice to the complexities of the book of Isaiah.

We begin with the anti-Babylonian poems (13:1–14:23), which shift the historical focus without any change in the theopolitical perspective, suggesting to the reader of the book in the post-destruction period that events during the period of Assyrian ascendancy, now in the distant past, provide essential clues for interpreting the course of events during the Neo-Babylonian period. The other and less important *maśśā'ôt* could then be read as providing for the same reader additional instantiations of a prophetic theopolitics based on ideas of divine agency and moral causality.

ISAIAH 13–27

◆

THE FALL OF BABYLON PRESAGES UNIVERSAL JUDGMENT (13:1–22)

(Begg; Bentzen; de Boer; Bourke; Budde; Christensen 1975, 55–70; Couroyer; Diakonoff; Erlands-son; Görg; Gosse 1988 *passim*; Hayes; Hillers; Jeppesen; von Rad 1959; Snaith; Williamson 1994:156–83)

TRANSLATION

13 ¹An oracle about Babylon that Isaiah ben Amoz saw in vision.

i

²On a bare hill raise the standard,
shout aloud to them,
wave your hand for them to enter[a]
the princely gates.[b]
³I have issued the command to those sworn to my service;[c]
I have summoned my warriors eager and proud,
to serve as instruments of my anger.[d]
⁴The sound of a rumbling on the mountains
as of a vast horde;
the sound of the clamor of kingdoms,
of nations assembled for battle.
It is Yahveh of the hosts who musters
an army for war.
⁵They come from a distant land,
from the far horizon,
Yahveh and the weapons of his wrath
to destroy all the earth.[e]

ii

⁶Lament, for the day of Yahveh is near,
it approaches like destruction from Shaddai![f]
⁷All hands will then fall limp,
all hearts dissolve in fear,
⁸[they will be terrified].[g]
Convulsions and pains will seize them,
they will writhe like a woman in labor,

they will look aghast at each other,
their faces aflame.

iii

⁹Yes, the day of Yahveh approaches,
cruel, with unbridled fury,
to reduce the earth to rubble,
rooting out its sinners from its midst.
¹⁰For the stars and constellations in the sky
will no longer give their light,ʰ
the sun will be dark at sunrise,
the moon will not shed its light.
¹¹I will visit disaster on the world
and punish the wicked for their crimes,
put an end to the pride of the insolent,
lay low the arrogance of tyrants.
¹²I will make mortals more scarce than pure gold,
human beings than gold of Ophir.
¹³Then will I rattle the heavens,ⁱ
the earth will be shaken from its base
at the fury of Yahveh of the hosts,
on the day of his burning anger.
¹⁴Then, like hunted gazelles,
like sheep with no one to herd them,
all will turn back to their kin,
flee to their native land;
¹⁵any found lagging will be skewered,
any that are caught will fall by the sword;
¹⁶their infants dashed to death in their sight,
their houses plundered, their wives ravished.

iv

¹⁷Observe, I am inciting the Medes against them,
they have no regard for silver,
no great desire for gold,
¹⁸[bows will dismember young men]ʲ
no pity for the fruit of the womb,
their eye will not spare the children.
¹⁹Babylon, most glorious of kingdoms,
the proud splendor of the Chaldeans
will be like Sodom and Gomorrah
when overthrown by God.
²⁰Never will it be inhabited
nor settled for ages to come,
no Arab will bivouac there,
no shepherd tend his flock,

²¹but wildcats will have their lairs there,
owls^k make their nests in the houses;
ostriches will live there,
there satyrs will dance;
²²hyenas will howl in its forts,^l
jackals in its pleasant palaces.
Its appointed time is close at hand
with not many days to wait.^m

NOTES

^a 1QIsa^a has *ybv'*, singular, for MT *wybv'v*;   ^b *pithē nĕdîbîm*, literally, "the gates of the nobles." NEB reads *pithû nĕdîbîm*, "draw your swords, you nobles," consistent with LXX *anoizate* and the structure of the verse, but this meaning is unattested for the verb *pth*;   ^c *limqudāššāy*, literally, "to my consecrated ones" cf. use of the verb *qiddēš* in Jer 51:27,28 in a similar context;   ^d 3a is metrically defective, but transposing *lĕ'appî* from 3b to 3a leaves 3b defective, i.e., with only two accented syllables in the first hemistich; in any case the meaning is unaffected;   ^e *'ereṣ*, "earth," more consonant with the drift of the poem than "land" with reference to Babylonia cf. Jer 50:18; 51:5;   ^f the alliteration in *kĕšod miššaday*, also in Joel 1:15, cannot easily be reproduced in translation; "like destruction from the Destroyer" comes near to the sense; ^g *vĕnibhālû* is metrically anomalous; either the residue of a lost stich or, more likely, a rather superfluous gloss;   ^h 1QIsa^a has *y'yrv* for MT *yāhĕllû*;   ^i most commentators prefer to emend *'argîz* to *yirgāzû* following LXX *thumōthēsetai*, "(the heavens) will tremble," but there is nothing wrong with MT;   ^i the verse is evidently corrupt since the verb *rṭš* cannot be predicated of *qaštôt*, "bows," and *nĕʿārîm* cannot be the subject; comparison with the similar language in Jer 51:1–3 suggests a confused scribal transcription; for a more ambitious emendation see Schwarz 1979, 20–21;   ^k Görg (1992, 16–17) suggests "demons" instead of "owls" for *'ohîm*, but the context favors an animal species; ^l MT *bĕʿalmĕnôtāv*, "in its widows," could conceivably refer to widowed, i.e., abandoned buildings, but better emend to *'armĕnôtāv*, "in its forts";   ^m literally, "its days will not be prolonged."

COMMENTS

Only the last stanza of the poem makes explicit allusion to the fall of Babylon. For the most part the author is working with the larger canvas of a projected cataclysm or singularity, a "Day of Yahveh," affecting the entire cosmos, somewhat in the manner of the poem in 2:6–22 but inspired by the prospect of the destruction of the evil empire of Babylon. In the poem, as Skinner colorfully put it (*The Book of the Prophet Isaiah I–XXXIX*, 114), the air is alive with the demon cries of havoc and war. The apparent disjunction between the first three stanzas and the fourth has encouraged a range of theories of serial composition, all of them conjectural (e.g. Clements 1980a, 132–38). Comparison with the very similar anti-Babylonian poems in Jer 50–51, which surround description of the fall of the city of Babylon with cosmic reverberations, suggests that chopping up the poem in this way is unnecessary and inadvisable. Both the Jeremian and the Isaian poems were composed by an author or authors of an apocalyptic mind set and familiar with the conventional language used in condemning hostile nations.

The date of composition cannot be fixed for certain. That it is not directed against the Assyrians as rulers of Babylon and therefore does not come from the lifetime of Isaiah can be deduced from the prominence given to the Medes, who filled the role assigned to them by the poet only after the rise of the Neo-Babylonian Empire in the sixth century (pace Erlandsson). The final verses have led several commentators to conclude that the poem is predictive of an event to take place in the near future, and must therefore have been composed shortly before the fall of Babylon in 539 B.C.E. (e.g. Sweeney 1996, 231).

Commentators who read it as a *vaticinium ex eventu* are, on the other hand, left with the problem of squaring the poet's description with known historical events and circumstances. The Cyrus Cylinder talks about the Persian army strolling into the city with their weapons tucked away (*ANET*, 315), a description that admittedly does not make a good fit with the scenario of violence and bloodshed described here. But the extent to which autocratic rulers were (and are) prepared to dissimulate in the interests of self-aggrandizement can be illustrated by comparing this propagandistic statement with Herodotus's description of the siege and eventual capture of the city by the Persians after lowering the level of the Euphrates (1.188–191). Darius I also besieged and captured the city, destroyed the walls and gates, and executed several thousand of its inhabitants after putting down the revolt of the Babylonian pretender Arakha in 521. The city was treated even more harshly by Xerxes after suppressing the revolt of Shamash-eriba in 482, the worst blow of all being the carrying off and melting down of the great gold statue of Marduk. But the language of the poem is too stereotypical and lacking in specificity to allow for any definite conclusion along these lines.

The only historically specific item is that the city is being attacked by the Medes, which suggests strongly that the poem is referring to the situation in the decade preceding the fall of Babylon to Cyrus II in 539 B.C.E., more or less contemporaneous therefore with the anti-Babylonian diatribe in Isa 40–48. The structural correspondence between the Babylonian poems in 13:1–22 at the beginning and 21:1–10 near the end of the *maśśā'ôt* series, the latter ending with the fall of the city as seen in a visionary experience, would be consistent with this dating of 13:1–22.

The collection of brief and highly charged anonymous fragments of anti-Babylonian poetry preserved in Jer 50–51 seems to have provided the author of Isa 13 with his raw material to which he imparted a more universalizing and apocalypticizing thrust as well as a certain unity. The thematic and even the linguistic elements coincide at numerous points. Many nations are involved in the attack masterminded and coordinated by Israel's God (13:4–5; Jer 50:9, 15, 22; 51:14, 27–28), among them preeminently the Medes (13:17; Jer 51:11, 28); the attackers serve as the instruments of Yahveh's anger (kĕlē za'ămô 13:5; Jer 50:25) and are "consecrated" to serve his purpose (stem qdš 13:3; Jer 51:27–28); they gather under a standard at a rallying point (nēs 13:2; Jer 50:2; 51:12, 27) with a great tumult and clash of arms (13:4; Jer 50:22; 51:42, 55); the flight of those terrified by the manifestations of divine anger is described in identical terms (13:14; Jer 50:16), as is the devastated city now returned to nature; even the animals that haunt the site are described identically in the two books (13:20–22; Jer 50:39; 51:37). What is significant, viewed against this close relationship of rhetorical expression and theme, is the stronger universalizing tendency of ch. 13 evident in reference to the earth and the world ('ereṣ, tēbēl), including the heavenly bodies (13:10, 13), and to humanity as a whole ('ādām 13:12). In this respect the chapter bears comparison with the poem standing at the beginning of the first major section of the book ("the great arraignment"), which also takes up the theme of the Day of Yahveh (2:6–22).

The title (13:1) marks a new section established at a rather late editorial stage, and therefore can be taken as corresponding functionally to the title in 2:1 introducing the first long section of the book. (Both 1QIsa[a] and 4QIsa[a] confirm this by leaving two-thirds of a line blank before 13:1.) It will be obvious by now that this repeated restructuring in evidence throughout the book leaves many loose ends. Here, for example, as we saw earlier, the anti-Assyrian saying of 14:24–27 is cut off from the similar material in chs. 1–12, especially 10:5–34. The title categorizes the piece as a maśśā', literally, "a lifting up" (of the voice in oracular speech cf. 2 Kgs 9:25), a designation that, with the exception of 30:6, is confined to the section chs. 13–27, where it occurs nine times. This maśśā', however, is the only one attributed to Isaiah. In these and other instances (e.g. Jer 23:33; Ezek 12:10; Nah 1:1; Hab 1:1) such oracles are directed against a nation or, more rarely, an individual though, as usually happens with the passing of time, the designation tends to lose its specific features and is used in a quite generic and vague sense for prophetic speech in general (e.g. 2 Chr 24:27).

The title applies to 13:1–14:32 even though the following poem is introduced as a maśāl rather than a maśśā'. Both compositions are followed by brief passages in prose (14:1–2, 22–23), part of an ongoing commentary or series of commentaries in evidence throughout the entire book.

The first of the four stanzas into which I have divided the poem opens with a command given to muster an army with orders to take an unnamed city, the one issuing the order being none other than Yahveh himself. The army in question is not Babylonian and the city is not Nineveh (pace Clements 1980a, 133). The Babylonian revolts against Assyria in 722 and 705 were unsuccessful, and there was never any question of the rebels taking the Assyrian capital city. And, as we have seen, both this poem and the anti-Babylonian poems in Jer 50–51 allude to *many* nations involved in the destruction of the unnamed city. Affinity with the Jeremian poems is especially in evidence in the description of the lead-up to the sack and subsequent mayhem: the raising of a standard as a rallying point (Jer 50:2; 51:12, 27) taking up a theme occurring earlier in the book (Isa 5:26; 11:10–12), the noise of a vast multinational throng (Jer 50:9, 15, 22; 51:14, 27–28), and the fact that these nations serve as instruments of the anger of Yahveh (Isa 13:5; Jer 50:25).

In the second stanza this scenario leads by association to the traditional prophetic-eschatological topos of the "Day of Yahveh" (*yôm YHVH* cf. Amos 5:18–20) with its attendant imagery, allowing the poet to present the event as presaging a cosmic catastrophe, not unlike Joel who also announces destruction from Shaddai (Joel 1:15). According to the Priestly source (P) the designation Shaddai, of uncertain derivation, was the original pre-Yahvistic name for the national deity (Exod 6:3). That it appears here, the only occurrence in the prophetic books, may not simply be for the sake of assonance (*kĕšod miššaday*), for the author of the poem may have intended to indicate the destructive aspects of divine agency with reference to the verbal stem *šdd*, "destroy" ("like destruction from the Destroyer"); which may incidentally also explain why the designation Shaddai occurs so frequently in the book of Job. The allusion to limp hands, fearful hearts, convulsions like a woman in labor pains (cf. 26:17–18; Jer 50:43), faces flushed with excitement and terror (Ezek 21:7 adds loss of sphincter control) corresponds to a conventional and obviously hyperbolic way of describing reaction to receiving really bad news (Hillers).

In the third stanza the poem picks up the tempo with images of worldwide devastation evocative of projections of the planet in the aftermath of a thermonuclear war. The prophetic literature is of course lavish in presenting such worst-case scenarios. The emphasis is on darkness, like the darkness of a nuclear winter (Amos 5:18–20), specifically the darkening of the sun (Amos 8:9, though this text may refer to a total solar eclipse). Joel 2:30–31 also associates the darkening of sun and moon with the Day of Yahveh, and Isa 24:1–13 adds pollution. The term translated "constellations" (*kĕsîlîm*) is usually taken to refer in the singular to Orion (Amos 5:8; Job 9:9; 38:31) but the present context suggests the more general connotation. In keeping with prophetic ideas of causation, these catastrophic events are presented as punishment for the morally reprobate. The fact that very few, wicked or otherwise, will survive is indeed noted (v 12) but nothing much is made of it. The theme of depopulation, taken up again in the final stanza, occurs at this point with the metaphor of rare gold from Ophir, perhaps referring to a location somewhere in the Yemen or the Horn of Africa (cf. Gen 10:29; 1 Kgs 9:28; 10:11; Ps 45:10; Job 28:16). By closing with the scene, not unfamiliar in our day, of refugees trying to escape a victorious army bent on murder and mayhem, the stanza provides an appropriate transition to the capture and sack of the city of Babylon.

The final stanza, then, explicitly addresses the fall of Babylon, assigning the leading role in the destruction of the city to the Medes, described as more than usually ruthless and impossible to buy off. This Indo-Iranian people inhabiting the northern highlands of Iran and the foothills of the Caucasus begin to appear in Assyrian inscriptions in the ninth century B.C.E. Under their king

Cyaxares they were allies of the Babylonians in the overthrow of the Assyrian Empire (614–612 B.C.E.), and by the time of the fall of Babylon had themselves been conquered by Cyrus II. They also feature in another anti-Babylonian poem (21:2) and are assigned the same role and described in much the same way in the corresponding Jeremian poems, as we have seen (Jer 50:41–42; 51:11, 28). Use of the verb "incite" (*'ûr* Hiphil) also connects with Jer 50–51 (50:41; 51:11) and recalls Yahveh's inciting a conqueror from the north against Babylon, none other than Cyrus, in the second part of Isaiah (41:25 cf. 2 Chr 36:22; Ezra 1:1).

The poet goes on to speak directly about Babylon and its people known as Chaldeans (*kaśdîm*), the term that is standard in the second part of Isaiah (43:14; 47:1, 5; 48:14, 20). The confederation of Chaldean tribes begins to show up in Assyrian annals in the ninth century B.C.E., usually as causing trouble. Their homeland was in southern Mesopotamia, the marshy area near the Persian Gulf called the Sealand, from which they waged an intermittently successful guerilla warfare against the Assyrian superpower. All of the expressions used at this point to characterize Babylon as an imperial power — "glory" (*ṣĕbî*), "pride" (*gā'ôn*), "splendor" (*tip'eret*) — occur elsewhere in the book as attributes both of divine reality (2:10; 4:2; 24:14, 16; 28:5) and of individuals and institutions (13:11; 14:11; 16:6; 23:9; 28:1, 4), in the case of the latter the qualities being more illusory than real. One of the most consistent features of Isaiah is the refusal to accept any institutions, political or religious, with absolute and unconditional seriousness. Comparison with the fate of Sodom and Gomorrah (cf. Amos 4:22; Isa 1:7; Jer 49:18; 50:40) introduces the theme of depopulation, going back to nature, to wilderness, cityscape to landscape, becoming a "No Kingdom" like Edom (cf. 34:8–17). However, this is not the ideal wilderness of which Hosea spoke but nature polluted and poisoned. The soil will not even be good for grazing and will be shunned by the Beduin who can survive in the most inhospitable of environments. It will be the home of satyrs, goat-like creatures of corrupt intelligence and malevolent will who haunt the wild places of the earth, sometimes in the company of the female demon Lilith (34:14 cf. Lev 17:7; 2 Chr 11:15). The topos of a human population displaced by wild animals is conventionally part of this scenario (cf. 27:10–11; 34:11–15; Jer 50:39; 51:37). The precise taxonomy need not detain us, especially with respect to the obscure *ṣiyyim* and *'oḥim*. (RSV plays it safe with "wild animals" and "howling creatures," respectively; Gray 1912, 237 more colorfully with "yelpers" and "shriekers," here more soberly "wildcats" and "owls.") The poem ends with a final admonition that all this will come about in the near future (cf. Jer 51:33). This takes the reader back to the earlier warning about an imminent Day of Yahveh (v 6), and reinforces the idea, fundamental throughout Isaiah, that nothing happens apart from the intention and design of God.

AN EDITORIAL COMMENT (14:1–2)

(Blenkinsopp 1988; Jeppesen; Williamson 1994, 165–68)

TRANSLATION

14 ¹But Yahveh will take pity on Jacob and will once again choose Israel. He will settle them on their own land, and proselytes will attach themselves to them and will be incorporated into the household of Jacob. ²The nations will take them and bring them to their place, and the household of Israel will possess the nations as male and female slaves. They will make captives of those who had captured them and lord it over those who had oppressed them.

COMMENTS

Editorial comments of this kind scattered throughout the book serve to confer a degree of thematic unity on the compilation by viewing historical events from the perspective of the restored post-disaster community. It was suggested earlier that at some point 14:1–2 together with 27:12–13, which also expresses the theme of repatriation, may have served to bracket the entire section. Brief passages of this type were probably not recited liturgically (pace Kaiser 1974, 24); we know too little about Second Temple liturgical history to speculate, and in any case they do not look very liturgical. Most of them are introduced by the familiar *bayyôm hahû'* formula (4:2–6; 10:20–27; 17:7–9; 18:7; 19:16–25; 22:8b–11; 27:1, 12–13), in which respect 14:1–2 is an exception. It may lack an incipit on account of its being more directly a comment on the preceding poem, in the sense that the salvation of Judah is intimately tied in with the fall of Babylon. The more immediate link is with the final verse of the preceding poem anticipating a fulfillment of its predictions in a not too distant future (*qārôb lābô' 'ittāh*, "its appointed time is near at hand," cf. *qĕrôbâ yĕšû'ātî lābô'*, "my salvation will soon come," 56:1). The anticipated fall of Babylon will mean the end of exile and subjection, a reversal of fortune to be brought about by the direct intervention of the God of Israel. The opening phrase also suggests a contrast between those victimized by the Medes, who got what they deserved, and Jacob/Israel as the object of Yahweh's compassion (the same verb *rḥm* [Piel] connoting pity or compassion occurs in 13:18 and 14:1). To this extent the comment anticipates the main theme of chs. 24–27 which, as I will argue, is the contrast between the fate of Babylon (the unnamed city) and restored Jerusalem.

The coming reversal of fortune is expressed here and throughout the following chapters in terms of an act of divine compassion (30:18; 49:10, 13, 15; 54:8, 10; 55:7; 60:10) manifested in a new act of election (41:8–9; 43:10; 44:1–2; 49:7) leading to the foundation of a new commonwealth on the soil of Judah following on the conquests of Cyrus II and the collapse of the Babylonian

Empire. Implicit in this way of speaking is a rather drastic view of discontinuity in the religious affairs of the community with the fall of Jerusalem and subsequent deportations. One expression of this second election can be seen in the way the Ezra–Nehemiah narrative of the founding of the Second Temple community is modeled on traditions of national origins—a new exodus and the celebration of Passover as the official inauguration of a new epoch in which those who had attached themselves to the restored community could participate; note how new beginnings—the *hejira* of Islam, *vendémiaire* during the French Revolution—are often indicated by new calendars (Ezra 6:19–22 cf. Exod 12:1 "this month will be for you the beginning of months; it will be for you the first of the months of the year"). Many of the themes and much of the language in this brief paragraph occur elsewhere in early postexilic compositions (e.g. the comfort and compassion of Yahveh in Isa 49:13b), including the designation Jacob, perhaps the most common title for the Jewish community in the early post-disaster period, but it is going beyond the evidence to conclude authorship by Second Isaiah (pace Williamson 1994, 165–67). Whoever the author was, he has said much in small compass. The compassion of Yahveh and the second election of Jacob/Israel will be manifested in four ways. The people will be resettled in Judah (cf. Jer 50:19), the repatriation will be the responsibility of Gentile nations (cf. 43:5–7; 49:22–23; 60:4, 8–9; 66:20), once they return foreigners will serve them as slaves or at least as *Gastarbeiter* (45:14; 49:7; 60:10–16; 61:5–7), and others will attach themselves to them as proselytes (56:3, 6 cf. Zech 2:15). The conditions under which *gērîm* (now "proselytes" rather than "resident aliens") may be admitted are not specified. Ezra 6:21 requires the abjuration of "pollution," i.e., idolatry, and the Priestly Passover law (Exod 12:48–49) stipulates circumcision. Qualifications for membership in the Jewish community will continue to be debated throughout the entire period of the Second Commonwealth, inclusive of early Christianity, along a broad band from ritual segregation to active recruiting of proselytes.

THE KING OF BABYLON IN THE UNDERWORLD (14:3–23)

(G. A. Anderson 1991, 60–82; Begg; Begrich; Bost; Burns; Clements 1989; Clifford; Craigie; Dupont-Sommer; Erlandsson 1970, 161–65; Franke; Gallagher; Ginsberg 1968; Gosse 1988, 200–78; Grelot 1956; Jensen 1997; Köszegby; Loretz 1976; McKay; Oldenburg; Pope; Prinsloo; Quell; M. S. Smith; Talmon; Tromp; Yee)

TRANSLATION

14 [3]After Yahveh has given you respite from your pain and turmoil, and the hard labor laid on you, [4a]you will intone this oracular poem about the king of Babylon. This is what you will say:

i

⁴ᵇSee how the tyrant has come to nothing,
how the persecutorᵃ has come to an end!
⁵Yahveh has broken the staff of the reprobate,
the scepter of dominion;ᵇ
⁶he who in his fury struck down peoples,
striking again and again,
he who in his rage lorded it over nations
relentlessly hunting them down.
⁷But now the whole earth rests and relaxes,
breaks out into joyful song;
⁸the cypress too rejoices over you,ᶜ
and the cedar of Lebanon:
"Since you were laid low," they say,
"none comes to cut us down."ᵈ
Sheol below is astir,
preparing to greet your arrival,
⁹rousing the shades to meet you,
all the princes of the earth;
raising up from their thrones
all that were rulers of nations.
¹⁰Allᵉ will address you, saying,
"You too have become weak as we are,
you have become like us.
¹¹Your pride is brought down to Sheol
together with the throng of your dead,ᶠ
maggots are the bed you lie on,
worms will be your blanket."

ii

¹²How you have fallen from the sky,
Star of the dawning day!
how felled and fallen to the ground,
you who laid low all the nations.
¹³You thought in your heart:
"I will ascend to the sky,
I will set up my throne
higher than the highest stars,ᵍ
I will take my seat on the Mount of Assembly,
in the furthest reaches of the north.
¹⁴I will ascend on the highest clouds,
become like the Most High God."ʰ
¹⁵Yet here you are, brought down to Sheol,
to the furthest reaches of the Pit.

[16]Those who see you will stare at you,
they will ponder over you, saying:
"Is this the man who shook the earth,
who caused kingdoms to quake with fear?
[17]who turned the whole world into a wilderness,
destroying its cities?
who would not set his prisoners free
to go back to their homes?"[i]
[18]All the rulers of the nations
are one and all laid to rest with honor,
each in his resting place,
[19]but you have been cast out of your grave
like loathsome carrion,[j]
like a corpse trampled underfoot,[k]
covered over by[l] the slain, those pierced by the sword,
gone down to the foundations[m] of the Pit.
[20]You will not be united with them in burial,
for you ruined your land
and slew your own people.
Never more will the name be recalled
of such evil seed.
[21]So get ready the slaughterhouse for his sons
to be butchered for their father's guilt,
let them not undertake to possess the earth,
covering the world's surface with cities.

[22]I will rise up against them (a saying of Yahveh of the hosts) to cut off
Babylon's name and remnant, offspring and progeny (a saying of Yahveh). [23]I
will turn Babylon into the haunt of bitterns,[n] a watery wasteland, and I will
sweep it with the broom of destruction (a saying of Yahveh of the hosts).

NOTES

[a] MT *madhēbâ* is hapax and of unknown meaning; 1QIsa[a] together with several
early witnesses (Symm., Theod., Syr., and Tg.) seem to have read *marhēbâ* →
stem *rhb* cf. 3:5b meaning "oppress," "distress," quite possible in view of frequent daleth-resh confusion; LXX *epispoudastēs* = "overbearing," reading *šābat
hammarhēb*;   [b] reading *šēbet mošēlîm*, literally, "scepter of rulers," as appositional genitive;   [c] sing. collective for MT pl.;   [d] 4QIsa[e] *'lyhm*, 3d person for MT 1st person;   [e] the half-verse is metrically defective; *kullām*, "all
of them," absent from 4QIsa[e];   [f] as it stands, MT *hemyat nĕbālēkâ* would
mean "the noise of your harps," or something of the kind, though *hemyâ* is hapax; this is possible, but not entirely appropriate in the context, hence the alternative *nĕbēlâ*, "corpse," for *nēbel*, "harp," cf. the alternative reading in NEB;

g reading *'el* in *lĕkôkĕbē-'ēl* as superlative;   h *'elyôn*;   i a half-verse is added to accommodate *bĕbētô*, "to his house," untranslated in LXX; the metrical structure is unclear at this point of the poem;   j LXX *nekros* perhaps translating *nēpel* ("a dead fetus," Ps 58:9; Job 3:16; Eccl 6:3), a reading that seems to be preferable to MT "like a loathsome branch" (*nēṣer*) and is widely accepted;   k *kĕpeger mûbās* moved here from the end of 19;   l literally, "clothed (*lĕbûš*) with the slain";   m MT has *'abnē-bôr*, "the stones of the Pit," but more likely *'adnē-bôr*, "the foundations of the Pit" cf. Job 38:6 and Symm. *themēlious* and Vulg. *ad fundamenta laci*;   n *qippod*, often translated "hedgehog" but hedgehogs do not haunt watery wastelands if they can help it; other guesses: "bustard" or "ruffed bustard" in Zeph 2:14 (NEB), "screech owl" (RSV at Zeph 2:14), "porcupine" (Bishop Lowth and the Revised Version).

COMMENTS

Although some commentators have divided 4b–21 into several strophes—five according to Duhm (1892, 117)—the only clear division is marked by the repetition of *'êk* ("see how . . .") in 12. It seems, then, that there are two poems (4b–11; 12–21). The introductory note presents the first of the two under the rubric *māšāl* (also Mic 2:4; Hab 2:6 and cf. Num 21:27), a term that usually denotes a proverbial saying, sometimes enigmatic in character, and that perhaps is intended in this instance to indicate the ironic use to which the conventions of the "dirge" (*qînâ*) are being put. That both poems belong to this genre is apparent from the opening *'êk*, "see how . . . ," and from comparison with other examples, the closest being the equally ironic *qînôt* in Ezek 28–32 against unnamed Phoenician and Egyptian rulers. Both poems are in the 3:2 "limping rhythm" proper to the *qînâ*, though the meter stumbles at times no doubt due in part to faulty textual transmission (vv 9c, 10a, 12b, 19b–20, 21b). One feature of this genre is quotation. Most of the protagonists get to speak—the tyrant himself (13–14), the denizens of the underworld (10–11, 16–17), even the cypresses and cedars of Lebanon (8). The high literary quality of these poems has often been praised. We can acknowledge that the language is forceful and the scenes vividly imagined, even if the unsubtle note of *Schadenfreude* that gathers strength as the poems proceed may not be to our liking. We can also be thankful that there is little evidence of editorial manipulation and expansion, perhaps limited to 5 in which recur the motifs of the "staff" (*maṭṭēh*) and "scepter" or "rod" (*šēbeṭ*), by now familiar to readers of the book, especially in the contrasting portrait of the ideal ruler to come (9:3[4]; 10:5, 15, 24, 26–27; 11:4). This verse is also the only place in the poems in which Yahveh is mentioned.

The main function of the introductory and concluding notes (14:3, 22–23) is to identify the unnamed tyrant as the king of Babylon and, by so doing, to insert the poems into the book as a whole. In itself, the poem could refer to any number of tyrants known or unknown to history. The link is by catchword— Yahveh gives Israel rest on its land (*hinnîḥām* 14:1); Yahveh gives you respite from your troubles (*ḥānîaḥ* 14:3). The same for the concluding comment: the sons are not to rise up (*yaqûmû*) to take possession of the earth; Yahveh will rise up (*wĕqamtî*) against them. The larger context in which the poems are framed invites us to share the perspective and the plane of observation with the reader or hearer in the post-destruction period who is invited to draw meaning for the present, and interpret contemporary events, in the light of the record of God's dealings with Israel in the past. Respite from pain, turmoil, and hard labor (this last, a phrase associated with the sojourn in Egypt, Exod 1:14; 6:9; Deut 26:6) is reminiscent of the language of hope in Isa 40–48 (e.g. 40:1–2), a hope the realization of which is contingent on the judgment about to fall on Babylon. With the help of alliteration (*šēm ûšĕ'ār, nîn vāneked, ṭĕ'ṭe'tîha bĕmaṭ'ăṭē'*), the concluding comment emphasizes the complete undoing of the Babylonian royal house and the city, in contrast to the survival of the Israelite remnant and its enduring posterity and name.

The brief preface to the poems puts them in the category of *māšāl*, a term that must have a broader connotation than a proverbial saying. In Num 21:29, for example, it introduces an ironic lament over the fate of Moab, beginning *'ôy lĕkā mô'āb!* ("woe to you, Moab!") that was to be performed by *mōšĕlîm*, "professional bards" (cf. Mic 2:4; Hab 2:6). The traditional form of the real lament can be deduced from David's lament over Saul and Jonathan (2 Sam 1:17–27): the death of the hero is announced but not revealed to enemies, to prevent their gloating; nature is invoked to fall in with the mood of the lament (a kind of pathetic fallacy); the great deeds of the hero are recounted, where possible over the catafalque. (For further details see Yee.) The form has remained fairly constant for centuries in different cultures—compare the lamenting over the godlike Caesar as reported by Appian and the panegyrics of the great tenth century Islamic poet al-Mutanabbi. The weeping and keening of the women would accompany the recital of the *qînâ*, as a way of sending the deceased on their one way journey to the underearth (Ezek 32:16).

The failure of the poems to name the tyrant in question has left the field open to speculation that continues apace. It may be assumed that poems originally composed subsequent to, or in anticipation of, the death of one of the great Assyrian kings could have been "recycled" for a different occasion during the Neo-Babylonian era or later. We are told that this anonymous tyrant ruled a worldwide empire and did so with unbridled arrogance and tyranny, that he destroyed cities including his own, that he fought against his own people, cut down cypresses and cedars of Lebanon, refused to release captives, died an ignominious death after which his corpse remaining unburied, and finally that his sons could be expected to succeed him. Some of these particulars would fit practically any prominent Mesopotamian ruler, others fit one or other of the candidates proposed, but there is no perfect fit with any one individual. Tiglath-pileser III (+ 727) ruled over a vast area, was certainly oppressive, and assumed direct rule over Babylon, but there is no evidence of internecine warfare or of an ignominious death and non-burial (pace Hayes and Irvine 1987, 227–28).

We hear that Sargon II (+ 705) was not buried in his own house (*ina bitišu*) but that does not mean he remained unburied, and there is no evidence that he warred against his own people (pace Barth 1977, 136; Erlandsson 1970, 161).

Sennacherib (+ 682) looks more promising since we know he was murdered by members of his own family, and the biblical text elsewhere confirms his overbearing attitude (Isa 37:23–29). He also destroyed many cities, including Babylon, but we do not know that his corpse was dishonored. Nebuchadrezzar II (+ 562) and Nabonidus (+ 538) are the only Neo-Babylonian dynasts of sufficient distinction to be considered. The former claimed (in the Wadi Brissa rock relief in Lebanon) to have torn down cedars of Lebanon with his bare hands, which however is a standard kind of hyperbolic claim with a long history. Nabonidus may be thought to have warred against his own people after retiring from Babylon into the Tema oasis; he was at any rate not the most popular of rulers. Duhm (1892, 117) opted for Nabonidus but had to assume that the prediction of the manner of his death in the poem turned out to be wide of the mark. But the allusion to the earth's being at rest and in a state of euphoria (14:7) suggests rather strongly that the tyrant was already dead.

The problem of identification is complicated by the poet's use of a wide range of familiar traditional motifs and topics. One of the most prominent of these is the *mors persecutoris* theme, which will be much in evidence in early Jewish and Christian writing. Death, generally of an extremely painful and messy kind, is presented as divine punishment for overweening pride and hostility towards God's elect (e.g. the death of Antiochus IV, 2 Macc 9:1–29; the death of Herod Agrippa, Acts 12:20–23; both featuring worms). Death and postmortem existence are presented as a fall from the highest to the lowest point, there being no worse fate than to be denied proper burial (cf. Isa 34:3; Jer 14:16; 36:30; 1 Kgs 14:10–11 etc.). In both poems this theme blends into the descent of the recently dead into the underworld and their reception by its denizens (8–11, 16–19). A familiar topic from the time of the Sumerians (e.g. the anticipatory dream of Enkidu on the seventh tablet of *Gilgamesh*), it identifies the recently deceased, describes the reception in the nether world by its denizens, usually adding a description of the diminished and wraith-like existence in that place known to the Greeks as Hades and in Israel as Sheol, the "Pit" or "Cistern" (*bôr, šaḥat*), or simply the "earth" (*'ereṣ*) or "underearth" (*'ereṣ taḥtît* Ezek 31:14, 16, 18; 32:18). The inmates of this spooky region of the dead are the *rĕpā'îm*, here translated "shades" (v 9).

The ongoing discussion about the precise meaning and etymology of the Hebrew term and its Ugaritic counterpart (*rp'm*) need not long detain us. The term is used of the prehistoric inhabitants of the land (Gen 14:5; Deut 3:11), but much more frequently of the dead, including dead ancestors (Isa 26:14, 19; Job 26:5; Prov 2:18; 9:18; 21:16; Ps 88:11). These *rĕpā'îm* are still apparently able to communicate among themselves and, under certain circumstances, with the living. To judge by Samuel's discourse with Saul (1 Sam 28) and the welcome extended to the dead tyrant in these poems, transiting from the world above to the world below does not appear to result in any significant change of disposition or attitude. It seems, moreover, that social distinctions also remained unaffected by the transition. In one variation (Ezek 32:20–32) there is even a distinction between the circumcised and uncircumcised.

The second elegy introduces the ancient myth of the fall from grace of rebellious deities (cf. Ezek 28:11–19; Ps 82:6–7). The closest parallel is that of Phaeton son of Helios (the sun) or of Eos (the dawn) who came to grief when, attempting to drive the chariot of the sun, he lost control of the vehicle and was struck by one of Zeus's thunderbolts. Like several of the ancient Greek myths, this one may derive from a Phoenician-Canaanite source inspired by the rise of Venus the morning star and its rapid disappearance at sunrise. The Hebrew name for the "Star of the dawning day," *Hêlēl ben šaḥar*, corresponds to two deities known from the Ras Shamra texts. About *hll* nothing much is known, but the corresponding verb means "to shine brightly" (cf. Isa 13:10; Job 29:3; 31:26; 41:10). The word *šḥr* is twinned with *šlm* as artificer deity, the first corresponding to the "dawn" (*šaḥar* in Hebrew), the second to twilight. (For further details see Kaiser 1962, 38–40.) Whatever its precise origins, the myth would live on in the doctrine of the fall of Lucifer (the Vulgate translation of *Hêlēl*) and his followers (cf. Luke 10:18; 2 Pet 2:4) and the descent of Christ into the underworld (1 Pet 3:19–20; 4:6) later to be transformed into great poetry by Dante and Milton.

Other motifs familiar from the Late Bronze Age Ugaritic texts are associated with this core myth. The tyrant aspires to take his place among the gods who meet in deliberative council on the Mount of Assembly (cf. the mountain of Elohim, Ezek 28:16), known here and elsewhere (Ezek 38:6, 15; 39:2; Ps 48:3) as Zaphon (the North), and in the Ugaritic texts as the mountain of Baal. It was understandable that Judean savants, familiar with this mythological topos of the seat of godhead, should have applied it to Jerusalem, an accomodation amply attested in the book of Isaiah. The actual location of this Canaanite Olympus seems to have been on Mt. Casius (Jebel el-Aqraʿ) in Lebanon. The tyrant even aspires to replace the high god and president of the divine assembly, here given the name Elyon, either an appellative of El or a distinct deity (cf. Gen 14:18–20; Num 24:16; Deut 32:8). In spite of the distinctive poetic idiom adopted in this second composition, we recognize affinity with the discourses or sermons in chs. 40–48, in which personified Babylon claims ascendancy— "I am, and there is no one beside me" (47:8, 10)—a claim echoed in practically the same terms by the seer speaking on behalf of the incomparable and unique God of Israel (43:10–13; 44:6, 8; 45:5–6, 18, 21; 46:9).

THE END OF IMPERIAL ASSYRIA (14:24–27)

(Bailey; Barth 1977, 103–19; Brueggemann; Childs 1967, 128–36; Clements 1989; Cogan; Fichtner 1951, 16–33; Gonçalvez 1986, 307–9; Gosse 1991a, 17–21; Huber 1976, 41–50)

TRANSLATION

14 ^{24}Yahveh of the hosts has sworn an oath:
Surely^a as I have purposed, so will it be,^{b}
as I have planned, so will it come to pass:
^{25}to shatter the Assyrians^c in my land,
to trample them down on my mountains;
their yoke will be removed from the people,^{d}
their burden lifted from their shoulder.^{e}
^{26}This is the plan devised for the whole earth,
this is the hand outstretched over all the nations;
^{27}for Yahveh of the hosts has planned, who will frustrate it?
it is his hand that is outstretched, who will turn it back?

NOTES

^{a} *'Im-lo'*, the standard asseverative introduction to the oath formula; ^{b} MT
has *hāyātāh*, past tense, which is possible but parallelism requires future, as
1QIsa^a *thyh* and cf. LXX, Vulg.,Tg.; ^{c} for MT *'aššûr*, "Assyria"; ^{d} literally,
"from them"; ^{e} with MT as in 10:27 rather than plural in several of the ancient versions.

COMMENTS

This sudden shift back to Assyria after the Babylonian poems demands an explanation, especially since it is without title or heading; in fact this kind of oath
formula usually follows an indictment or prediction of some kind (e.g. 5:9–10
following 5:8; 22:14 following 22:12–13). While it is possible that the present
arrangement came about by accident or as a result of sloppy editing, it is more
likely that it was deliberate and designed to make the point that the destruction
of Babylon represents the final fulfillment of the anti-Assyrian prophecies. The
reader is also being told once again that the prophetic message about Assyria
provides the key for interpreting the course of events during the rise and fall of
the Babylonian Empire. Babylonians replaced Assyrians, but from the point of
view of the prophetic interpretation of history there is no difference; all imperial pretensions fall under the same judgment.

The language of 14:24–27 is very similar to that of 10:12–27, which concludes with the same assurance that the yoke and burden of the Assyrians will
soon be removed. At some point in the editorial history of the book the passage
may have been detached from the Assyrian material in ch. 10 and relocated, together with sayings about countries in the path of the Assyrian advance at the
time of Sargon II and Sennacherib. But 14:24–27 is also recapitulatory of the
prophecies about Assyria in chs. 5–12 in a more general sense. The idea of a divine plan or agenda has already been mentioned more than once (5:12, 19),

and even where not referred to explicitly it underlies the entire section, indeed the entire book. The burden and yoke of imperial oppression has also loomed large (9:3[4]; 10:27), and the hand of Yahveh outstretched to save or punish provides the refrain for one of the longer poems in the first part of the book (5:25; 9:7–10:4[5:24–10:4]). The recapitulatory intent is also suggested by the superscription immediately following ("in the year king Ahaz died" 14:28). While serving as the title to the oracle about Philistines in 14:29–31, its correspondence with the chronological indication of the death of Uzziah (6:1) suggests closure on the reign of Ahaz as a distinct period of the prophet's activity and the inauguration of a new epoch with Hezekiah.

This brief passage consists of an asseveration of Yahveh confirmed by oath (24–25) followed by a prophetic comment (26–27) that, while rounding it off inclusively with reference to the plan or agenda, restates it in universalistic terms: the agenda of the God of Israel concerns all nations and the entire earth. The oath formula, often employed in Isaiah (5:9; 22:14; 45:23; 54:9; 62:8), perhaps in dependence on Amos (4:2; 6:8; 8:7), indicates the assurance and ineluctability of the predicted event. Comparison with the Isaian prediction issued during the campaign of Sennacherib, which also highlights the plan of Yahveh and the assurance that it will be carried out (37:26–29), suggests that the present passage is meant to refer to the same situation, namely, an Assyrian defeat "in my land, on my mountains." It therefore does not seem helpful to describe the language used here as proto-apocalyptic, nor does it seem necessary to assume an allusion to the defeat of the Syrian armies of Antiochus IV in the second century B.C.E., though "Assyria" does function elsewhere in the book as a code name for the Seleucids, just as Egypt stands for the Ptolemies. It is nevertheless entirely possible that the present passage was read by the pious at that time to refer to the events through which they were living.

It would be easy to miss the broader implications of the seer's comment about the plan or agenda of Yahveh and the outstretched hand. In summarizing the "message" of the first part of the book, mostly about Assyria, he is making a statement about *all* attempts at political dominion whenever or wherever they occur. According to the theopolitical view of the author, all such attempts have a strictly provisional character and, in spite of appearances, fall under a judgment. This is political theory from a specific religious angle, a theory that in due course will be distilled in the symbolism of beasts rising from the primeval deep and the Kingdom of the Saints in Daniel and the book of Revelation. To quote Bernhard Duhm, a commentator of many insights, "Assyria's striving for world dominion was the occasion, not the cause, for prophetic religion daring to take in the whole world. . . . We should be glad to acknowledge one who, for the first time, entertained such a thought, if without full consciousness of its incalculable consequences" (1892, 123).

AN ORACULAR PRONOUNCEMENT ABOUT THE PHILISTINES (14:28–32)

(Begrich; Donner 1964, 110–13; Fullerton 1925–26; Gosse 1991b; Jenkins; Tadmor 1958, 1966; Vermeylen 1977, 297–303)

TRANSLATION

14   [28]In the year King Ahaz died there came this oracle:
[29]Do not rejoice, you people of Philistia,[a]
that the rod that struck you is broken;
for from a serpent's root an adder will come forth,
its offspring[b] will be a flying serpent.
[30]The poor will graze their flocks in my pastures,[c]
the needy will lie down and rest securely,
but your seed he will kill[d] by starvation,
he will slay your remnant.
[31]Wail, O gate, cry aloud, O city!
dissolve in fear, all you people of Philistia,[a]
for the smoke of an army[e] comes from the north,
no one of them strays from his station.[f]
[32]What answer will one give the envoys of the nation?[g]
"Yahweh has established Zion,
the afflicted among his people will find refuge there."

NOTES

[a] MT *pĕlešet kullēk*, "all (you) Philistia";   [b] *piryô*, literally, "its fruit";   [c] MT has *wĕrā'û bĕkôrê dallîm*, "the firstborn of the poor will graze," which sounds suspicious and does not make for good parallelism; read *bĕkarāy*, "in my pastures"; for *kar* = "pasture" see Pss 37:20; 65:14 and especially Isa 30:23; Isa 30:23–26 and 37:30–32 convey the same idea as we find here; "their flocks" added to bring out the transitive usage of the verb;   [d] reading *zar'ēk* with LXX for MT *šorĕšēk*; and the 3d person of the verb for the 1st with 1QIsa[a] and the parallel verb in the stich;   [e] MT has only *'āšān*, "a smoke";   [f] a very speculative translation of a difficult half-verse cf. NEB; 1QIsa[a] has *mvdd* for MT *bôdēd* cf. 4QIsa° which is identical with MT but reads *bmyd'yv* for MT *bĕmô 'ādāv*; the verb *bdd* means "to be by oneself," "to be separated from the group" (cf. Hos 8:9 of the wild donkey and Ps 102:8 of a bird sitting by itself on the roof) and *mô'ād* hapax would presumably be a place of assembly—in this case for the approaching army (cf. *mô'ēd*);   [g] retaining MT in spite of the plural in LXX, Syr., Tg.

COMMENTS

The pronouncement is directed against the Philistines who are rejoicing at the defeat or death of an aggressor but who face worse punishment in the future. It is tempting to relate the saying to the death of the Mesopotamian tyrant in 13:1–14:21, but the editorial history of this part of the book is quite uncertain, as is the identity of the ruler in question. The superscription to the saying appears to solve the problem by dating it to the year of the death of Ahaz of Judah, but at this point we come up against the well-known problems of chronology noted earlier. If one accepts Begrich's date of 727/726 B.C.E. for the death of Ahaz we have a coincidence or near-coincidence with the death of Tiglath-pileser III who would then be the serpent and (incongruously) the one who wielded the rod. According to the Eponym Chronicle, Tiglath-pileser III (745–727) did conduct a campaign against Philistia (*pi-liš-ta*) resulting in the reduction of Gaza and Ashkelon to tributary status. The Chronicler, not generally held in high esteem as a historical source, records Philistine inroads into Judean territory during the reign of Ahaz (2 Chr 28:18). If the topographical detail provided in this notice can tip the balance in its favor, with the help of an allusion to Philistine attacks on Judah in Isa 9:11[12]), it would explain the alternation of threat directed against the Philistines (29, 30b–31) and reassurance for Judah (30a, 32) in the oracle.

Against this reading of the text it can be objected that the superscription has no historical value since it is modeled on 6:1 ("in the year King Uzziah died") and does not fit the kind of title used in the foreign nation sayings in 13–23. While these are not in themselves adequate grounds for rejecting it, the title is nevertheless part of an editorial arrangement and is perhaps more closely related to what precedes than to what follows, in the sense of indicating the conclusion of the Ahaz phase, as 6:1 marked its beginning. (This would not, of course, settle the issue of the historical reference in 14:24–27.) Let us add that there are no grounds for identifying the aggressor as Judah. Apart from the problem of finding a historical fit, it is unlikely that the author would refer to Judean rulers as snakes, adders, and flying serpents.

While some proposals can be excluded, there is little chance of nailing down the historical allusions in this poem to the general satisfaction. All four Assyrian rulers from Tiglath-pileser III to Sennacherib, inclusive, carried out military operations against Philistine cities and arguments have been presented on behalf of all of them at one time or another. In view of Sargon II's punitive campaigns against the Philistine cities and their continued involvement in insurrection under his successor Sennacherib, Sargon's death in battle in distant Anatolia in 705 would certainly be an arguable option. However, attacks on the Philistine cities continued during the Neo-Babylonian period, including the sack of Ashkelon by Nebuchadrezzar II in 604 B.C.E., and it is worth keeping in mind that even if the historical situation could be pinpointed this would not necessarily decide the date of composition. Allusion to three generations of serpentine creatures, even if not taken too literally, suggests that the author is taking the long view, retrospectively and prospectively, on the contrasting destinies of Philistines and Judeans.

The rather sudden shift in 30a from the unpleasant future in store for the Philistines to the pastoral scene of the Judean poor grazing their flocks has persuaded many commentators that an early anti-Philistine poem has been interpolated and expanded sometime in the Persian or even Hellenistic period (Duhm; Marti; Dietrich; Vermeylen). Successive reworkings are also indicated by motifs, not confined to 30a, which suggest the hand of Isaian *epigoni*: the rod signifying both authority and oppression (*šēbeṭ*, 9:3; 10:5, 24; 14:5), the root (*šoreš*, 5:24; 11:1), and the pastoral image of animals or people resting and eating (5:17; 13:20–21). A date considerably later than the time of the historical Isaiah for the contrasting image of the Judean "poor," that is, the devout, is also supported by similar passages in the prophetic corpus. These include Isa 30:23–26 and Jer 47:1–7, the latter featuring danger from the north as the occasion for wailing in the Philistine cities.

Zephaniah 2:4–7 also predicts a Judean conquest of the Philistine region that will provide *Lebensraum* for grazing and pasture land. The perspective of the restoration, the return to Zion (*šibat ṣiyyôn*), is especially in evidence in the concluding verse, which provides a later answer to an earlier question. That Yahveh has established Zion as his residence is a basic postulate of the developed Zion theology familiar from Second Temple hymnography (e.g. Pss 46, 48, 76, 87). That his presence there provides refuge for the poor, needy and afflicted, synonyms for the God-fearers in the later sections of the book, points in the same direction. This final verse therefore functions in the same way as the interpolated Zion passages noted in the commentary up to this point (2:2–4; 4:2–6; 10:12, 20–27a; 11:10; 14:1–2), namely, to establish a common perspective on the events recorded and therefore a vantage point from which they can be viewed and interpreted.

ORACLES AND PRONOUNCEMENTS ABOUT MOAB (15:1–16:14)

(Barrick; Bartlett; Carroll 1986, 778–97; Jones; Knauf 1992a; J. M. Miller; Rudolph 1963; Smothers; van Zyl 1960, 20–23)

TRANSLATION

15 ¹An oracle about Moab

i

Destroyed in the nighttime,[a]
Ar Moab[b] is silenced;
destroyed in the nighttime,[a]
Kir Moab[b] is silenced.

2 The people of Dibon go up to the temple,[c]
to the hill-shrines to weep.
Over Nebo and over Medeba
Moab is wailing;
the hair of all heads[d] is cut back,
all beards are shaved off;
3 in their[e] streets they put on sackcloth,
on the roofs of her houses,
in her open spaces everyone is wailing,
the tears rolling down.[f]
4 Heshbon and Elealah cry out,
their clamor is heard as far as Jahaz,
Moab's warriors cry out,
each one trembling with fear.[g]
5 My heart cries out for Moab,
for those who have fled[h] as far as Zoar.
[Eglath, Shelishiyah].[i]
By the Ascent of Luhith[j]
they go up weeping,
on the road to Horonaim
there are cries of "disaster!"
6 The waters of Nimrim
are a place of desolation,
the grass dried up, the vegetation withered,
no green in sight.
7 They carry their possessions, whatever they can salvage,[k]
over the Wadi Arabim.[l]
8 The cry echoes around the borders of Moab,
her wailing as far as Eglaim,
her wailing as far as Beer-elim.
9 The waters of Dibon[m] run with blood,
yet for Dibon[m] I have worse news in store,
a vision[n] for Moab's survivors,
for the remnant of the land.[o]

ii

16 1 The ruler of the land has sent lambs[p]
from Sela in the wilderness[q]
to the mount of the daughter of Zion.
2 [Like fluttering birds thrown out of the nest
are the Moabite women at the Arnon fords.][r]
3 Take counsel, decide in our favor.
Make your protecting shadow like night in the noonday;
shelter the outcast,
do not hand over the fugitive,

⁴let the Moabite refugees settle among you,
conceal them against the one who would destroy them.

iii

When the oppression^s has come to an end,
when destruction has ceased
and marauders have been cleared from the land,
⁵a throne will be established in loyalty in David's tent;
on it will sit one who judges rightly,
who seeks justice and is swift to do right.

iv

⁶We have heard tell of the pride of Moab,
so very proud!
its haughtiness, pride, and arrogance,
its talk that is full of lies.^t
⁷For this Moab will wail,
the whole country will wail for Moab,
utterly stricken, they will mourn
for the raisin-cakes^u of Kir-hareseth.
⁸The fields of Heshbon languish,
the vineyards of Sibmah,
though their red grapes used to lay low
the lords of foreign lands,
though they spread out as far as Jazer,
ranging out into the wilderness,
though their cuttings were spread abroad,
and crossed the sea.
⁹Therefore I join with the weeping at Jazer,
weeping for the vineyards of Sibmah;
I drown you in my tears,
Heshbon and Elealeh,
for the glad shouts at harvesting
of summer fruit and grain have ceased.
¹⁰Gladness and rejoicing are banished from the fertile land,
no singing or shouting in the vineyards,
no one treads grapes in the wine press,
I have silenced your shouts of joy.
¹¹My innards^v throb like a harp for Moab,
my very being for Kir-heres.

v

¹²When Moab wears himself out presenting himself ^w at the hill-shrine,
when he comes to his sanctuary^x to pray, he will not succeed.

vi

¹³This is the saying Yahveh addressed to Moab a long time ago, ¹⁴but now Yahveh says: "Within three years, the length of employment for a hired laborer, the pomp of Moab will be humbled in spite of its great population. Those who are left will be few indeed and of no account."

NOTES

^a Any solution to the many textual problems in this verse must be tentative. The initial *kî*, the first of eleven in these poems, is a *vox vacua* and need not be translated; MT *bĕlêl* is altered to the more usual *bĕlaylâ* in 1QIsa^a and 4QIsa^o, but if retained it could be read as construct and *šuddad* repointed as *šōdēd*, therefore "in the night of the destroyer," a possible but not obligatory change; for *nidmāh*, Niphal → *dmh* read *nadammāh*, Niphal → *dmm*; ^b following most of the ancient versions which read *ʿar* and *qîr* as common nouns (both = "city," *qîr* also = "wall," therefore city by metonymy), and 1QIsa^a, which reads *ʿyr*, "city," for MT *ʿar*; I take both Ar Moab and Kir Moab to refer to the capital city Dibon or possibly Ar Moab to refer to the country (as Deut 2:9) and Kir Moab to the city; ^c MT "the house and Dibon went up the hill-shrines for weeping" is unintelligible; my translation follows the lead of Tg. and Syr. "they go up to the house (i.e. temple) of Dibon"; ^d literally, "baldness (*qorqâ*) is on all heads" which is ambiguous; 1QIsa^a has singular, but there is no need to alter the text, cf. Jer 48:37 and other texts that mention this routine feature of mourning rites (e.g. Isa 22:12; Ezek 7:18); Easterly (1991, 215–19) finds here a reference to the *qrḥḥ* of the Mesha inscription and reads: *bkl rʾšy qrḥḥ kl zrʿ gdwʿ*, "among all the leaders of qrḥḥ every descendant is cut off"—but the alteration of *zqn* to *zrʿ* in order to avoid the obvious parallelism is arbitrary; ^e MT has masc. sing. suffix, 1QIsa^a has fem. sing.; there is considerable confusion in gender and number in this part of the poem; ^f *yōrēd babekî*, literally, "going down in weeping"; alternatively "weeping as they go [down]"; ^g for MT *ḥălusē* LXX reads *ḥalsē*, "loins," therefore "the loins of Moab tremble" but MT makes good sense; the second half of the verse reverts to the sing., literally, "his soul trembles"; ^h for MT *bĕrîhehâ* 1QIsa^a has *brḥvh*, "they will flee from her"; ⁱ a suspicious-looking toponym (literally, "a three-year-old heifer"), but in any case added from Jer 48:34b; ^j 1QIsa^a *lûḥôt*; ^k again, a switch from singular (*yitrâ ʿāśāh*) to plural (*pĕqudātām*, "what they have laid up"); ^l or "the wadi of the willows"; 1QIsa^a has *ʿrby*, "Arabian?"; another possibility: "the wadi of the Arabah" (cf. 2 Kgs 14:25; Amos 6:14) requiring only a slight change; ^m with 1QIsa^a and Vulg., replacing MT *Dimon*, perhaps due to assonance with *dām*, "blood"; ⁿ "worse news in store" renders MT *nôsāpôt*, literally, "additional things"; MT continues "for Moab's survivors a lion" (*ʾaryēh*), which admittedly could also be bad news, but read *ʾrʾeh*, "I see," referring to a further visionary experience; ^o LXX for the proper name Admah for MT *ʾădāmâ*, "land," but the bad news, announced in 16:6–11, deals

with the devastation of the land; ᴾ an attempt to make sense of MT "send (pl.) a lamb, ruler of the land," with the help of Tg.; Wildberger (1978, 593) suggests *lmšl*, "to the ruler"; �q MT has *midbārâ*, "to the wilderness," but following LXX and Syr. *missela' hammidbār* with reference to a place-name (probably Petra) is more likely correct; 1QIsaᵃ has *mslh* for MT *msl'*, reading "by the wilderness route"; ʳ most commentators agree that this verse is intrusive, perhaps suggested by the weak link between *bat-ṣiyyôn* and *bănôt mô'āb*; ˢ reading *ḥamûs* with 1QIsaᵃ; ᵗ *baddâv*, "his lying, boastful talk," or (with Rabin 1973, 57–58), "his strength"; ᵘ LXX and Tg. read *'anšē*, "men" (cf. also Jer 48:31, *anšē qîr-ḥeres*) for MT *'ăšišē (qîr ḥărešet)*, but MT is acceptable and fits the context well; ᵛ *mē'ay*, "my bowels"; ʷ an original *nr'h*, "presents himself," was probably altered polemically to the similar *nl'h*, "wearies himself," and both happened to be retained; 1QIsaᵃ has *vhyh ky nr'h ky b'*, "when he presents himself, when he comes . . ."; ˣ 1QIsaᵃ adds a supralinear *yod* to turn *miqdāšô*, "his sanctuary," into *miqdāšâv*, "their sanctuaries," perhaps for theological reasons.

COMMENTS

Most commentators agree on the divisioning of these chapters according to sense, even in the absence of clear dividers (15:1–9; 16:1–5, 6–11, 12, 13), needless to say with numerous differences in detail (for a recent survey of opinion see Jones 1996, 1–52). There are also significant variations on how the different parts cohere together or relate to each other. We will work with the assumption that this section comprises a poetic pronouncement (*maśśā'*) about Moab (15:1–9) that introduces a second poem (16:6–11). The connection between these two compositions has been severed by an appeal to Judah to accept Moabite refugees (16:1–4a) and a further addition, suggested by the language of the Moabite appeal but having nothing to do with Moab, that anticipates the reestablishment of the Judean native dynasty (16:4b–5). These compositions are rounded off with a rather laconic appendix referring back to Moabite frequenting of cult places (16:12 cf. 15:2). A final note, probably from the scribe who made the final copy, brings to bear on the entire complex the perspective of a considerably later date. Since it refers a new, contemporaneous saying explicitly to the one preceding it, it provides an excellent illustration of the process of the serial and cumulative editing that the book has undergone (16:13). It is only here that Yahveh is identified as the first mover behind the disasters affecting Moab.

From early days commentators have noted the rough, unpolished style of the two oracular poems, their metric irregularity (the basic *qînâ* is not always easy to pick out), and lack of proportion—we observe, for example, how the second poem goes off at a tangent about the famous red wines of Sibmah (16:8). The impression shared by practically all commentators that the poems lack originality, that they are a work of *bricolage* put together out of bits of traditional prophetic material (the word *mosaikartig* keeps on recurring among German-language commentators), is reinforced by frequent parallels with the Moabite poems or fragments of poems in Jer 48:1–47; 49:1–5; and Obad 5, this last with similar language but referring to Edom. Comparison with the sequence of a dozen or so short poetic pieces on Moab in Jer 48 is particularly instructive.

Of the twenty-three place-names in the Isaian poems fifteen occur in Jeremiah. Both texts begin with a mock lament for the destruction of Moab (verbal stem *šdd*), both lament (ironically) the destruction of its famous wine industry (Jer 48:11–12, 26, 32–33 cf. Isa 16:8–11), and Isa 16:6–12 is a closely parallel version of Jer 48:29–36. While both could conceivably be drawing on older material (see especially the anti-Moabite taunt in Num 21:27–30) the more fragmentary state of Jer 48 suggests that this small collection of anti-Moabite propaganda has provided the raw material for the Isaian poet. The situation parallels closely Isa 13–14 (Babylon) in relation to Jer 50–51. A close study of these interconnected bits of (perhaps originally anonymous) prophetic diatribe permits a tantalizing glimpse into the process by which the prophetic compilations were put together.

The intrusion of the author's own real or, more likely, simulated emotional response to the situation comes in the course of the first poem (15:5) and, if we accept the proposed emendation of 15:9, at its conclusion where he announces a second revelation with even worse punishment in store for the hapless Moabites. I take this announcement to refer to the disastrous situation described in 16:6–11, which states towards the end that this second oracle has indeed been delivered and implemented ("I have silenced your shouts of joy" 16:10). The natural conclusion would be that the two poems come from one and the same author, which would then lead us to re-read the first poem in the sobering light of the second. We may not much like the tone and the sentiments expressed, but we can at least admire how in the first stanza the author keeps in bounds the sarcasm, hyperbole, and simulated grief, only to give them full expression in the second.

The first stanza is, on the surface, a lament following a disaster that has been visited on Moab, the actual circumstances of which are obscure. If we read Ar Moab and Kir Moab (or Kir Moab alone) in the opening verse as referring to Dibon the capital city of that country (see textual note), it seems to have suffered a devasting nocturnal attack, and this reading would be confirmed if the final verse (9a) also refers to Dibon, thus forming an inclusion. But elsewhere in the two poems the author seems to have a natural disaster in mind, probably drought, leading to, at minimum, a temporary depopulation (15:5–7; 16:8–10). While few of the place-names listed in Isa 15–16 and Jer 48 have been identified with a reasonable degree of probability, the disaster in question seems most seriously to have affected the more densely populated part of the country north of the Arnon (Wadi Mujib) where most of the major settlements were situated—Nebo, Medeba, Heshbon, Elealeh, Jazer, Jahaz, and Dibon the capital city.

Whatever the nature of the disaster, it led to the flight of refugees southward in the direction of Edom (Zoar at the southern end of the Dead Sea and presumably the other places mentioned in 15:5). The intercalatory 16:1–4a suggests that the Cisjordanian region was the preferred destination for refugees whenever the political situation permitted it (cf. Jer 40:11 Judeans returning after the appointment of Gedaliah; Ruth in the reverse direction). But our knowledge of the history of Moab is too fragmentary, and the language of the poem itself too vague and stereotypical to permit further specification. The reaction to the disaster is described in the same kind of language: the standard behavior associated with funerary rites—ritual lamenting often of a vociferous nature, shaving off hair and beard, wearing sackcloth (Jer 49:3 adds lacerations)—and appropriate rituals carried out at hill-shrines and the state sanctuary, perhaps including the sanctuary Mesha claimed to have built for his god, Chemosh (*ANET*, 320).

Most exegetes read the last half-verse of the first poem (15:9b) as an editorial addition (e.g. Duhm 1892, 128; Kaiser 1974, 69), but if the proposed emendation can stand it could function as an introduction to the worse things in store, i.e., the bad news announced in the second stanza (6:6–11) corresponding to the concluding personal statement near the end (16:10b). This second stanza is often described as ironic, but the ironic element is restricted to the hyperbolic description of sham grief in 16:9, unless we find an unsubtle and vulgar allusion to the poet's bowels (innards) making a harp-like noise in 16:11.

For the rest, it describes the devastation of the Moabite countryside with special reference to the vineyards of Sibmah, apparently the Napa Valley of Moab, and the loss of the valuable export trade in wine. This is for the most part a standard account of the effects of divine anger (cf. Amos 8:1–3; Hos 2:13–15[11–13]), but unlike the first stanza, this one relates the disastrous scenario to moral delinquency as effect to cause. As in most other oracular poems about foreign nations, self-sufficiency is the basic moral flaw, and self-sufficiency generally comes to expression in what for Isaian authors are degenerate forms of cultic activity. This Isaian author does not, however, enlarge on these points. The allusion to mourning for the raisin-cakes of Kir-hareseth may have a cultic connotation as in Hos 3:1, and perhaps also Jer 44:19, which refers to the goddess cult, but raisin-cakes are also ordinary if apparently particularly prized delicacies (2 Sam 6:19; Cant 2:5). They may therefore in this instance be simply a by-product of the wine trade no longer in existence.

Much of the brief intercalatory poem 16:1–4a has suffered extensive damage in transmission (see textual notes). In particular, most commentators agree that 16:2 makes little sense in the present context and has probably dropped out of the preceding poem, probably after 15:4 or 15:8. We may notwithstanding read it as reflecting the vulnerable situation of women detached from the patrilineal household and the protection of a male relative. The passage seems to be describing a Moabite mission to Jerusalem requesting asylum for refugees. It is therefore thematically connected with the preceding poem (see especially 15:5, 7) but is not from the same author if, as suggested, 16:6–11 is the direct sequel to 15:1–9. It describes very well the *ideal* situation of the *gēr*, the foreigner who has been granted a secure if subordinate place in a foreign land.

Similar language is used of the Moabite woman Ruth, who finds "rest" (*měnûḥâ*) and protection under the wings of Yahveh in Judah (Ruth 1:9; 2:12).

Several exegetes read 16:4b–5 as a direct continuation of 16:1–4a in the sense that when the present crisis is past, the "Greater Israel" of the United Monarchy will be reestablished and law, order, and justice will also prevail in Moab, which was considered to be ideally and theoretically part of that empire (cf. 2 Sam 8:2; Amos 2:1–3). But it is highly unlikely that the fulfillment of a messianic prediction of this kind would be presented as contingent on the conclusion of a critical period in Moab's history. There is moreover no mention of vassal status, and in any case a Moabite vassal ruler would hardly be in David's tent. However inappropriate the placing of the passage may seem to the modern reader, it should be read as one more statement of faith in eventual survival and restoration with special emphasis on the dynastic theme. As such it may be compared with 2:4–6, which establishes an equally fortuitous connection between the preceding diatribe against court ladies (3:16–4:1) and the setting up of a canopy, booth, and shelter in Jerusalem. The "tent" (*'ohēl*) of David is identical with the "booth" (*sukkâ*) of David mentioned in Amos 9:11, terms apparently in use among those in the post-disaster period who entertained hope for the eventual restoration of the native dynasty.

The suggestion advanced by Ewald that the editorial note added at 16:12 is a protasis lacking its apodosis, in the sense that the wearisome and unsuccessful prayer of the Moabites would lead them to be ashamed of Chemosh their deity and embrace the cult of Yahveh (cf. Jer 48:13), is ingenious but unconvincing. As it stands, the comment refers back to the frequenting of temple and hill-shrine near the beginning of the poem (15:2), thus rounding off the series on a firm note of religious condemnation. Representing foreign cults as profitless toil is a familiar staple of Second Temple polemic, especially in the later chapters of Isaiah (e.g. 48:13).

The last addition to the Moab poems (16:13–14) comes from the final stage of redacting the foreign nations material, and should be compared with the same prediction about the Kedarite Arabs in 21:16–17. It provides a valuable indication of the care with which the ancient prophecies were read and the need that was felt to appropriate, justify, and make sense of them in the light of contemporaneous situations and events. It also provides a valuable clue to the emergence of a new kind of prophecy consisting in inspired interpretation of earlier prophecy. While the phrase translated "a long time ago" (*mē'az*) may refer to the fairly recent past (e.g. 2 Sam 15:34), it more commonly alludes to the distant past (e.g. Ps 93:2; Prov 8:22) especially in connection with prophecy (Isa 44:8). The saying comes from a time during the Second Commonwealth when Moab was prospering—a situation predicted for them in Jer 48:47—and when Judean-Moabite relations were at a low ebb. The author of this saying could, for example, have belonged to the integrationist party during Nehemiah's tenure of office when anti-Moabite legislation was being enforced (Neh 13:1–3 cf. Deut 23:4–8[3–7]). At any rate, encouraged by the condemnation of Moab in the old prophecies that lay before him, the editor-seer risked the short-term prediction that, after three years, the length of time for which day laborers were usually hired, the current Moabite prosperity would come to an end.

ONCE AGAIN, THE FATE OF SYRIA AND ISRAEL (17:1–11)

(Delcor; Dietrich; Donner 1964, 38–42; Olyan; Pitard; Tadmor 1994, 273–78; de Vaux; Vermeylen 1977, 308–12; 1989, 49–51)

TRANSLATION

17 [1]An oracle about Damascus

i

See, Damascus has ceased[a] to be a city,
it has become a heap of ruins;
[2]the cities of Aroer are deserted,
they will serve as pasture for herds
that will lie there undisturbed.[b]
[3]There will be no more fortified cities in Ephraim,
nor sovereignty in Damascus;
what remains of Aram will resemble
what the glory of Israel has become.[c]
A word of Yahveh of the hosts.

ii

[4]On that day
Jacob's weight[d] will diminish,
the fat waste away from his body;
[5]It will be as when a reaper[e] gathers in the standing corn,
harvesting the ears in armfuls;
as when one gleans the ears of corn
in the Valley of Rephaim;
[6]as when one beats an olive tree
and only gleanings are left in it—
two or three berries at the top of a bough,
four or five on the branches of the fruit tree.
This is the word of Yahveh, God of Israel.

iii

[7]On that day:
People will look to their Maker, their eyes will turn towards the Holy One of Israel. [8]They will not look to the altars, the work of their hands; they will not turn their gaze to that which their fingers have made [the Asherah steles and the incense altars].[f]

iv

⁹On that day:
Their fortified cities will be like the deserted sites[g] of the Hivites and
Amorites[h] which they abandoned when attacked by the Israelites. There will
be a scene of desolation.

v

¹⁰You[i] have forgotten your God who saves,
the Rock, your fortress, you have not kept in mind;
therefore plant your shoots of Adonis,[j]
sow the slip of an alien god.
¹¹Even if you got them to sprout[k] the day you planted them,
or got them to blossom the morning you sowed them,
the crop will be gone when disease comes along with incurable pain.

NOTES

[a] *Mûsār mēʿîr*; the verbal form is → *sûr* rather than *ysr* ("punish, chastise"), and
the feminine *mûsārāh* would be expected (cf. *hāyĕtāh*); for the tense see commentary;   [b] the common emendation to *ʿārehā ʿădē ʿad*, "her towns are destroyed forever," still leaves this perfectly intelligible phrase unexplained; it
should therefore be left as it is (as Hayes and Irvine 1987, 248–49); nor need it
be bracketed as an accidental misplacement from the Moab poems (for Moabite Aroer see Deut 2:36 and 2 Sam 24:5); for the Masoretes this verse marked
the halfway mark by word count in *Nĕbiʾîm*;   [c] 1QIsaᵃ has singular verb
yhyh; literally, therefore, "the remnant of Aram will be like the glory of the children of Israel";   [d] the meaning of *kābôd* in keeping with the context;
[e] reading *kōṣēr* for MT *qāṣîr*, "harvest";   [f] the copula before *hāʾăšērîm* requires us to read *hāʾăšērîm wĕhāhammānîm*, "the Asherah steles and the incense altars," as an editorial expansion to the list of cult objects;   [g] MT
punctuates as singular, 1QIsaᵃ correctly as plural;   [h] MT *haḥoreš wĕhāʾāmîr*,
"woodland and upland," but the context requires the names of indigenous populations cf. LXX *hoi Amorraioi kai hoi Euaioi*;   [i] *kî* omitted; see note on
15:1;   [j] *niṭʿē naʿămānîm* (1QIsaᵃ *nʿmvnym*) is read as a double plural (GKC
§124q) with reference to Adonis = Naʿaman, the Pleasant God; Duhm (135)
explains the plural with reference to multiple local manifestations of the god
(cf. the *baʿalîm*);   [k] MT *tĕśagśēnî* caused problems in transmission, cf.
1QIsaᵃ *tśgśgśy* (cf. 1QH VIII 9 *ytśgśgv*) and 4QIsaᵃ *tśtgśny*.

COMMENTS

This section provides another example of serial or cumulative composition in
which it is generally possible to detect the often slender thematic or lexical
thread connecting one passage to the next. The motif of harvesting and glean-

ing is certainly present in 17:1–18:7, as it is elsewhere in the book, but the incidence of such motifs does not by itself suffice to determine the demarcation of units (pace Sweeney 1996, 252–61). Formally, we have here a very brief oracular poem about the fall of Damascus, capital of Syria (17:1b–3), to which three "on that day" comments have been attached. (Let us bear in mind that throughout the commentary the term "poem" has a broad and unspecific connotation; note, for example, that sections i, ii, and v could have been set out in continuous prose.) The first of these "on that day" comments (4–6) plays on the word *kābôd*, meaning "glory" (3) and also "weight" (4), with the implication that Israel will share the same fate as Syria now conquered by the Assyrians. The second addition (7–8) replicates a familiar pattern of explaining disaster in terms of cultic aberration, and the third (9) takes off from and enlarges on 17:3, the destruction of the fortified cities of the Kingdom of Samaria. The final passage (10–11), which returns to the theme of cultic irregularity, comes from a time when the fate of the kingdoms of Syria and Israel lay in the distant past.

The trajectory reflected in this editorial history begins with the paradigmatic moment of the Syrian-Samarian crisis (734–732 B.C.E.), the occasion for the subjection of Judah to the Assyrian superpower. We are not allowed to forget that this incident provides the essential paradigm according to which the prophetic-Isaian view of politics and political history is to be understood. The different countries paraded before the reader (most recently Babylonia, Philistia and Moab) present what are in effect different instantiations of that prophetic theology of history. Later, as these nations and their triumphs and disasters recede in the slipstream of history, the nations as a whole begin to be viewed in a unified field of vision but always from the same perspective of divine agency and moral causality.

Since editorial activity presupposes an ongoing reappropriation and reapplication of older texts to new situations, it will more often than not be impossible to assign firm dates to passages. It is, for example, quite likely that what the present text says about Syria was read in the second century B.C.E. as a coded message about Seleucid rule (Kaiser 1974, 76–78), and that what 17:2 says about herds quietly grazing was applied by the devout "servants of Yahweh" in Second Commonwealth Judah to themselves (Vermeylen 1977, 309). But whether the texts in question were *composed* at that time is another and perhaps less important matter.

We owe the title of the Damascus saying (*maśśā'*, "oracle") to the editor who arranged the series against foreign nations (13–23). Units i and ii take us back once again to the crisis of 734–732 (chs. 6–8), the first dealing primarily with Damascus, the second exclusively with the Kingdom of Samaria. If we accept the final, awkwardly worded statement of the Damascus oracle (3b) without emendation, its allusion to the glory (weight) of Israel would establish a connection by catchword to the following unit, in the sense that Damascus and Israel will share the same fate, which in fact was the case. Dating this first saying depends on the tenses of the verbs occurring in it.

It seems that, contrary to most modern translations and commentators, we should read *mûsār* as past tense ("has ceased") and the *wĕhāyĕtāh* following as also past and not vav consecutive; hence, "it has become" a heap of ruins. This reading of the verse is not excluded on the grounds that the Assyrians did not devastate Syria since much of this language is stereotypical, and in any case the annals of Tiglath-pileser III do testify to bloodshed and destruction during the conquest of the Syrian city-state (Tadmor 1994, 78–81; Pitard 1987, 187–88). Only in the final verse (3) does the author look towards the future—the complete incorporation of Syria into the Assyrian Empire and the suppression of later revolts in which Damascus participated. The intermediate verse (2) need not be elided since Aroer marks the southern limit of Syrian control of the Transjordanian region in the ninth and eighth centuries (cf. Mesha inscription and 2 Kgs 10:33). There is therefore nothing to discourage a date during the decade between the fall of Damascus to the army of Tiglath-pileser III (732) and the fall of Samaria. If this fragment of a poem was not written by Isaiah himself, it is certainly close to the linguistic and thematic world of Isa 7–8, for example, in speaking once again of a remnant (*šĕ'ar* cf. 7:2–9). The saying also contains the stereotypical mention of towns and villages depopulated and given over to grazing, a topos of frequent occurrence in the prophetic corpus (e.g. Isa 5:17; 7:25; 13:20–22; 14:23, 30a), sometimes with identical wording (e.g. *'ên maḥărîd*, "with none to disturb," Jer 30:10 = 46:27; Ezek 34:28; 39:26; Zeph 3:13b; cf. Job 11:19).

The second stanza uses the rather disjunctive metaphors of weight loss and harvesting corn and olives to describe the straits to which the Kingdom of Samaria would be reduced as a result of its association with the anti-Assyrian activity of Damascus. We have already encountered language evocative of the diseased or wounded body applied to the body politic (1:5–6; 10:18). Gleaning grain and olives (the latter also in 24:13), the subject of legislation in the Pentateuch worded in much the same way as here (Deut 24:19–22; Lev 19:9–10; 23:22), is readily applicable to the idea of a faithful remnant, one of the central motifs of the Isaian corpus (1:8–9; 6:13; 7:3; 10:19, 20–23). There may have been something distinctive about the Valley of Rephaim southwest of Jerusalem, perhaps poor soil and poor pickings for gleaners. The historical situation alluded to is fairly transparent. As a result of Pekah's participation in the anti-Assyrian alliance of the Syrian ruler Radyan (Rezin in Isa 7), Israel was reduced to a rump state around Samaria, the rest of the country on both sides of the Jordan was incorporated into the Assyrian Empire, and Pekah was replaced on the throne by the pro-Assyrian Hoshea whose rebellion a decade later sealed the fate of the Samarian city-state.

The editorial addendum at 7–8 breaks the connection between the prediction about the fortress or fortified city (*mibṣār*) in Ephraim (17:3) and those alluded to in 17:9 (*'ārē mā'uzzô*). We assume it was placed here to serve as an explanation of the collapse of the Northern Kingdom, along the same lines as the explanation offered by the historian of the kingdoms (2 Kgs 17:7–18) who also alludes to cultic representations of a goddess (17:10, 16). But the field of vision here is broader and doubtless reflective of a later age than that of the historian, envisaging as it does the eschatological horizon of the abolition of idolatry. It speaks of people in general, humanity (*'ādām* cf. 2:9, 11, 17, 20, 22; 45:12), and uses what came to be conventional ways of referring to idolatrous objects (cf. 2:8; 31:7). The cult of the goddess Asherah, a normal part of religious practice in both kingdoms, continued in spite of official proscription (e.g. 2 Kgs 23:4, 6–7) up to the fall of Jerusalem and beyond (Ezek 8:3; Jer 44:15–19; Zech 5:5–11). Hence the condemnation of steles or tree trunks (*'ăšērîm*) consecrated to her cult, perhaps with smooth stones on which incense could be offered (cf. 27:9; 57:3–10).

The brief note about the fate of Israel's fortified cities (iv) enlarges on the statement in 3a about their destruction. It may also have been juxtaposed with 7–8 on account of the traditional reason for the expulsion of the autochthonous Palestinian populations, namely, their unacceptable cults. The prehistorical dolmens and ruins scattered around Palestine gave rise to sometimes picturesque folklore (e.g. Deut 2:10–12, 20–23; 3:11) but also generated a theological message. Hivites (sometimes confused with Horites) and Amorites appear on the standard list of autochthonous peoples (e.g. Deut 7:1; Josh 9:1) and the historical traditions mention them at several points (e.g. Gen 15:16,21; 34:2; Josh 9:7). The message to the population of the Northern Kingdom is rather direct: you will go the same way as they did, and there will remain nothing but a wasteland (*šĕmāmâ* cf.1:7; 6:11).

Isaiah 17:10–11 is certainly a distinct unit since it is addressed to the devotees of non-Yahvistic cults represented collectively as a female, as indicated by the suffixes. At the same time it continues along the same lines as 7–8 with updated examples of cultic aberration. Comparison with the condemnation of the "sorceress" (*'onĕnâ*) in 57:3–13, a personification of the idolaters seen through the eyes of the devout in Judah of the Persian or early Hellenistic period, is particularly instructive. Like the "outsider woman" (*'iššâ zārâ/'iššâ nokriyyâ*) of Prov 1–9 with whom the *'onĕnâ* has much in common, the latter draws on perceptions of a goddess whose cult includes a combination of sexual and mortuary rites proscribed by normative Yahvism (Isa 57:3–13; 65:3–7; 66:17). That some of these rites were practised in gardens (65:3; 66:17 cf. 1:29) may provide a link with 17:10–11. The god Tammuz, whose cult was being carried on in the Jerusalem temple precincts shortly before its destruction (Ezek 8:14–15), is identical with Adonis/Naaman worshiped in Syria and the Phoenician cities.

While this cult is known to us chiefly from authors of the Greco-Roman period, its greater antiquity is confirmed by the biblical texts that refer to it (perhaps including allusion to the one beloved of women in Dan 11:37) and by onomastics (Naaman, Abinoam, Ahinoam, perhaps also Naamah and Naomi). The "shoots of Adonis," the "foreigner" (*zār*) of the parallel half-verse, may refer to quickly growing and quickly withering flowers set out in pots in front of houses and temples to represent the recurring life-and-death cycle of Adonis as a vegetation deity (see, e.g., Plato, *Phaedrus* 276). This would more readily explain the outcome as described in 11. The author contrasts these ephemeral plants with Yahveh, the one who alone brings fertility, life, and salvation (cf. 12:1–6), the Rock (*sûr*), a term much used in Israelite (Ps 18:3; 19:15; 31:3) as in modern hymnography (e.g. Rock of Ages).

A SUDDEN END TO POLITICAL OPPRESSION (17:12–14)

(Childs 1967, 50–53; Clements 1980a, 46–47; Gosse 1991c; Kaiser 1962; Kilian 1994, 49–51)

TRANSLATION

17   [12]Hear[a] the thunder of many peoples,
  they thunder like the thunder of the sea!
  Hear the roaring of the nations,
  they roar like the roaring of mighty[b] waters!
  [13][the nations roar like the roaring of many waters].[c]
  When he rebukes[d] them they flee far away,
  blown away by the wind like chaff on the hills,
  like specks of dust[e] by the whirlwind.
  [14]As night approaches there is terror,
  but before the day dawns they are no more.
  This is the fate of those who despoil us,
  the lot of those who plunder us.

NOTES

[a] MT *hôy*, usually "woe" but here a simple call to attention;   [b] 1QIsa[a] has *kbdym* ("heavy") for MT *kabbîrîm*;   [c] this verse is absent from Syr. but present in 4QIsa[a] and 4QIsa[b]; it looks like an alternative version substituting the more usual *mayim rabbîm* for *mayim kabbîrîm*;   [d] 1QIsa[a] has *vyg'r* perhaps due to misreading the vav consecutive of MT *věga'ar*;   [e] *galgal* lightweight, ball-shaped objects cf. Ps 83:14 parallel with *qaš*, "chaff"; either dust particles (RV) or thistledown (NEB); for the metaphor in general cf. Isa 41:15–16; Ps 1:4; 35:5; Job 21:18.

COMMENTS

Commentators can always be relied on to find connections of some kind between juxtaposed passages in Isaiah but this brief passage beginning with the apostrophe *hôy*—not in this case an expression of lament or introducing a woe-saying—is clearly marked off from 1–11 and even more clearly from 18:1–7 about the Ethiopians. This kind of language describing overwhelming threat directed at Israel (Judah) by foreign powers—deafening noise like the crashing of ocean waves (cf. 51:15; Jer 5:22; 6:23; 31:35; 50:42; 51:55; Ps 46:4), elsewhere animal noises no less threatening (e.g. bears 59:11; dogs Ps 59:7,15)—will be familiar to the reader who has got this far and will recall especially the opening poem about Babylon (13:4–5). The language is strongly reminiscent of those psalms that express the triumph of Israel's God, and therefore of Israel, over political enemies with the cosmogonic battle in which Yahveh wards off the forces of chaos (e.g. Ps 46:4–7; 76:4–9; 104:5–9), the so-called "battle of the nations" (*Völkerkampf*) motif. Echoes of the Late Bronze Age Ugaritic myth of Baal's conflict with Yam, the personified Sea, can also be heard. Yahweh rebukes the sea (Ps 104:7; 106:9; Nah 1:4 and cf. the same topos in the gospel miracle of the stilling of the tempest, Mark 4:39), and the nations that seemed so invincible are seen to be as insubstantial as chaff or dust driven by the wind. The occurrence of this complex of motifs in cultic hymns confirms their origin in the official Jerusalem cult.

Since the early modern period the *opinio communis* has held that 17:12–14 refers to the sudden and unanticipated destruction or retirement of Sennacherib's army besieging Jerusalem in the campaign of 701 B.C.E. The event, on which the relevant Assyrian annals (the Chicago and Taylor prisms) are silent, is attributed to an avenging angel (*mal'āk*), elsewhere known as the Destroyer (*hammašḥît*), in 37:36–37 (= 2 Kgs 19:35). That it is recorded as happening at night would seem also to make a good fit with 17:14. Allusion to the traumatic events of 701 B.C.E. is certainly possible, but the following observations suggest caution: (1) the nighttime is generally the time of danger and terror either real or imaginary (e.g. 15:1; 29:7–8) and the morning pre-eminently the time of salvation (e.g. Pss 30:5; 46:6[5]); (2) the Assyrians are not named either in this passage or in some others assigned by H. Barth to his *Assur-Redaktion* (e.g. 8:9–10); (3) the passage and others of a similar kind speak not of one nation, that is, the Assyrians, but of many (e.g. 8:9–10; 10:33–34 under the figure of trees; 13:4; 29:5–8 cf. Mic 4:11, 13).

So, while there is nothing in the passage that would exclude reference to Sennacherib's reign (as Duhm 1892, 136), a date no earlier than the last decades of Assyria's existence at the time of Josiah is also possible (as Barth 1997, 182; Clements 1980a, 161). This more generalized idea of the nations as globally hostile and globally futile in their opposition to Israel's God serves as a kind of counterpoint to the sayings directed at specific nations throughout chs. 13–23 (14:1–2, 26–27; 17:12–14; 18:3–6) and is heard more insistently in chs. 24–27. It occurs often as a liturgical theme in psalms, beginning with the futile raging of the nations in Ps 2.

AGAINST AN ALLIANCE
WITH EGYPT (18:1–7)

(Donner 1964, 122–24; James 1991, 677–747; Janzen 1972, 60–61; Welsby)

TRANSLATION

18 ¹Woe to a land full of buzzing insect wings[a]
   beyond the rivers of Kush,
   which sends its envoys by sea,
   in reed vessels over the water!
   ²Go, swift messengers,
   to a nation[b] tall and smooth-skinned,
   to a people feared far and near,
   a nation strong and conquering[c]
   whose land rivers divide.[d]

   ³All you denizens of the world,
   you who live on the earth,
   when the signal is raised in the hills you will see it,
   when the trumpet sounds you will hear it.
   ⁴This is what Yahveh said to me:
   "I will calmly look down[e] from my dwelling
   while the heat is bright[f] in the sunlight,
   while the dew covers the ground[g] at the time of the vintage."
   ⁵For before the vintage, when the blossoms are gone,
   and the seed-berry is ripening into a grape,
   he will cut off the shoots with pruning shears,
   lop off and remove the branches.
   ⁶They will all be abandoned to birds of prey on the hills[h]
   and to the beasts of the earth.
   Birds of prey will live off them[i] in the summer,
   all the beasts of the earth in the winter.

   ⁷At that time:
   Tribute will be brought to Yahveh of the hosts from a people[j] tall and
smooth-skinned, a people feared far and near,[k] a nation strong and conquering, whose land is divided by rivers. Their tribute will be brought to Mount
Zion, the place where the name of Yahveh of the hosts is invoked.

NOTES

[a] *'Ereṣ ṣilṣal kěnāpāym*: the verb *ṣll* has several connotations including a whir-
ring or buzzing sound (cf. *ṣělāṣal*, "cricket," Deut 28:42); here it refers to in-
sects, safer than NEB "there is a land of sailing ships" based on Arabic and
Aramaic cognates (perhaps also Targum) and requiring *kěnāpîm*, plural rather
than MT dual, and *kānāp* = "sail" by extension rather than "wing" (G. R. Driver
1968, 45);   [b] 1QIsaᵃ has *lgvy* for MT *'el-gôy*;   [c] MT *gôy qav-qav ûměbûsâ*
here and in vs 7 Qere Or and 1QIsaᵃ have *qavqav* hapax, meaning perhaps
"strength," "power"; if *qav qav* is read, the reference could be to unintelligible

babble, a vulgar but quite common view of foreign languages cf. 28:10, 13; 33:19; *měbûsâ* → *bûs* (14:19, 25; 63:6, 18) "trample," therefore oppression (cf. 22:5); ᵈ *bz'*, hapax, meaning uncertain cf. NEB "whose land is scoured by rivers"; ᵉ zeugma—literally, "I will be calm (→ *šqt*) and I will look down"; for Ketib *'ešqātāh* Qere = *'ešqôtāh*; ᶠ *sah*, "bright" → *shh* cf. 32:4; Jer 4:11 cf. *sahîah* Ezek 24:7–8; 26:4, 14; or "like the heat of Zach," with reference to the name of a summer month on a sixth century Arad ostracon (see Aharoni 1963, 3–4); ᵍ MT *kě'āb tal*, "like a cloud of dew," but *'āb* can also connote a covering or canopy, as in Exod 4:25, 26; 1 Kgs 7:6; ʰ 4QIsaᵇ adds the article *hhrym*; ⁱ an attempt to make sense of MT *věqāš 'ālāv hā'ayit*, literally, "the bird of prey will 'summer' on it"; ʲ *m'm* 1QIsaᵃ for MT *'am* which would suggest that the tribute consists in the people, a not impossible supposition (cf. 14:2; 45:14; 66:20); but to avoid this, Duhm (1892, 140) suggested reading *yôbîl* Hiphil for MT *yûbal* Hophal; ᵏ 4QIsaᵇ reads *mn vhl'h* omitting *hû'* of MT.

COMMENTS

Only the beginning and the end of this unit (1–2, 7) deal with Ethiopia (Kush, Nubia); the middle section (3–6) is addressed to all and sundry, humanity in general, alerting them to wait for a communication from Yahveh, which we assume to be the one that follows immediately afterwards accompanied by the seer's comment. We come across the practice of juxtaposing reference to specific historical situations with more generalizing statements throughout this entire section of the book (13:2, 11–12; 17:12–14; 24:1–6; 26:6, 18), sometimes with mythological undertones that become more explicit with the passage of time (e.g. 51:9–11; Ps 74). In this instance the point may be to contrast the public announcement of the seer—made on the mountaintops and accompanied by a blast on the trumpet—with the secret negotiations and scheming between Judean and Egyptian representatives, which will come to no good.

An initial *hôy* can be a simple exclamation demanding attention (as 17:12) but in this instance it introduces a woe-saying directed against Nubia (Kush). The writer is not well disposed towards this country. Not only is it insect-infested, a characteristic also noted by Herodotus (2.95), and its people hairless and anomalously elongated in height (a more precise translation of *měmuššāk* than "tall"; curiously, the author does not comment on their color as does Jer 13:23), but it engages in profitless political scheming with Judah and other powers.

The reed dhows referred to were not confined to Nile navigation, but could have reached the Palestinian-Syrian coast by hugging the shore without too much difficulty. The injunction to envoys to go on a mission has given rise to considerable discussion. It has been suggested that the envoys are being sent to Assyria in order to divulge details of the anti-Assyrian plot being hatched or that they are being sent from the heavenly court for the same purpose or, finally, that the Nubian envoys arriving at Hezekiah's court are being told to go back

where they came from. The most natural assumption, however, is that Judean
envoys are on their way to the court of the Nubian royal house at distant Napata
near the fourth cataract of the Nile. The tone would be sarcastic. Far from be-
lieving the Nubians to be "a people feared far and near, a nation strong and
conquering," the author would have shared the opinion of the Assyrian generalissimo that they were a broken reed providing no support (36:6). This first brief
passage, therefore, rejects the negotiations going on between Jerusalem and
Napata with a view to opposing Assyrian imperial expansion in southwest Asia
(cf. 30:1–5; 31:1–3).

The kingdom of Nubia (Hebrew: Kush) occupied a vast area between the
first and the fourth cataracts of the Nile comprising much of modern Ethiopia,
Sudan, and Somalia. The Nubian kingdom with its capital city at Napata between the third and fourth cataract, to date unidentified, is first heard of in the
ninth century. During the reign of Py (Piankhy; ca. 747–716 B.C.E.), founder of
the twenty-fifth Nubian dynasty, Egypt seems for the most part to have avoided
hostile contact with Assyria. His successor Shabako (ca. 716–702), who consolidated Nubian power in Lower Egypt, appears to have followed the same non-
interventionist policy; he placated the Assyrians on one occasion at least by
surrendering to them Yamani, ruler of Ashdod, who had fled to Egypt (ca. 712).

Negotiations between Egypt and states subject to Assyria in southwest Asia,
including Judah, intensified after the death of Sargon II (705). The result is well
known. The army of the new Pharaoh Shebitku, commanded by his son Taharqa, was defeated at the battle of Eltekeh south of Yafo, Judah was devastated,
Jerusalem besieged, and the siege was abandoned under rather mysterious circumstances. (Incidentally, the biblical account anticipates by several years the
accession of this Taharqa/Tiharqa to the pharaonic throne, 2 Kgs 19:9; the
event took place in 690 B.C.E., after the death of Hezekiah.) The most likely
setting for the exchange of envoys between Jerusalem and Napata or Thebes
would then be the anti-Assyrian alliance that provoked Sennacherib's campaign
of 701 B.C.E. rather than the revolt among the Philistine cities several years earlier (713–711) in which, as far as we know, Egypt was not an active participant.

The abruptly introduced summons addressed to the entire world has inevitably suggested to several exegetes an editorial insertion in 3 (e.g. Marti 1900,
148–49; Vermeylen 1977, 319; Clements 1980a, 165). Decisions of this kind are
always problematic and often arbitrary since it is not difficult for commentators
to find some degree of coherence with or without an alleged insertion. A "signal" (nēs) and trumpet blast suggest imminent military action (5:26; 13:2–3),
but signals can be set up and trumpets blown for other purposes, for example,
to assemble diaspora Jews prior to repatriation (11:10–12; 27:13; 49:22; 62:10).
In the present context the purpose is to get the attention of the hearers and
readers for a prophetic communication that states, in effect, that Yahveh knows
what is going on but will not intervene. The implications for the seer's audience are spelled out in another oracle presented, it seems, in the same context
of plotting with Egypt: "in quietness and trust shall be your strength" (30:15);
the same message, therefore, as Isaiah delivered at an earlier critical juncture:

If you do not hold fast in faith,
you will surely fail to stand firm (7:9)

As is often the case, the oracular communication is followed by a comment of the seer himself (5–6). If we have correctly identified the historical context, the judgment delayed but inevitable will fall on the Assyrians. The harvest, in this instance the grape harvest, is one of the most persistent images of judgment in biblical literature. With it is associated at this point other figures of frequent occurrence in Isaiah: environmental devastation (5:5–6, 10, 24; 6:11–13; 7:23–25; 10:18–19, 33–34; 15:6; 16:8–10; 17:5–6, 10–1) and the ecologically more friendly image of animals taking over a devastated human habitat (5:17; 13:21–22; 14:23; 17:2).

The final prose statement (18:7), introduced by a variation on the usual *lead-in* to a future-oriented scholium ("at that time"), has a Nubian delegation coming to Jerusalem not to plan military operations but to bring tribute to the temple. The scholiast provides no clue as to whether he understood these Nubians to be Gentiles, proselytes, or diaspora Jews. We have already encountered the broad theme of the centripetal force exercised by Jerusalem on the Gentile world (2:2–4; 14:1), and at several points in the book Gentiles are charged with the task of repatriating diaspora Jews (14:2; 49:22–23; 66:20). Throughout the period of the Second Commonwealth Jewish presence was growing in Lower and Upper Egypt and beyond the first cataract of the Nile, and this important part of the diaspora comes increasingly into view in later biblical texts including Isaiah (Isa 19:18–25; 27:12–13; 45:14; Zeph 3:9–10; Ps 68:30–31; 87:4). The demographic expansion of the Jewish ethnos between the Persian and Roman periods cannot be explained without taking a strong proselyting movement into account, and this too is attested in the biblical record.

Some commentators find a particularly close parallel between 18:7 and 45:14 ("the wealth of Egypt and merchandise of Kush, together with the Sabeans of great stature, will cross over to you and belong to you . . .") and take it as indicating that chs. 1–39 had not reached their final form before chs. 40–66 were added to it (Clements 1980a, 166). The conclusion may be correct anyway, but apart from the mention of Nubians in both passages the similarity is not very striking. Isaiah 45:14 seems to be saying that Nubians and Sabean Arabs (only the latter are described as being remarkably tall) will acknowledge Yahveh as the true God but will be brought to Jerusalem as slaves (cf. 14:2)— an understandable reaction to colonial status but a dangerous "fantasy of the oppressed" nevertheless. Rather closer to our text than Isa 45:14 is Zeph 3:10 in which those who bring tribute from Nubia are members of the Jewish diaspora ("my scattered ones"). Since this text reproduces fairly closely the language not just of Isa 18:7 but also 18:1 ("beyond the rivers of Kush"), it has probably drawn on the Isaian text rather than the reverse.

The fate of Egypt (19:1–15)

(Cheyne 1893; Elat; Naʾaman; Loretz 1987)

TRANSLATION

19 [1]An oracle about Egypt

i

See how Yahveh comes riding on a swift cloud,
on his way[a] to Egypt.
The idols of Egypt tremble at his approach,
the hearts of the Egyptians[b] melt within them.
[2]"I will incite Egyptians against Egyptians,
kin will contend against kin,[c] neighbor against neighbor,
city against city, kingdom against kingdom.
[3]Egypt's spirit will be poured out[d] and voided,
I will confound[e] their plans.
They will consult the idols, the spirits of the dead,
the shades and the ghosts,
[4]but I will hand Egypt over to a hard taskmaster,[f]
a powerful king will lord it over them."
This is a saying of the Sovereign Lord,[g] Yahveh of the hosts.

ii

[5]The water will be dried up from the Nile,[h]
the river will be parched and run dry,
[6]the canals will be foul,[i]
Egypt's[j] watercourses drained and dried up,
the rushes and reeds will wither,
[7]the plants by the Nile, at the edge of the Nile,[k]
with all that is sown beside the Nile
will wither, blow away, and be no more.[l]
[8]Fishermen[m] also will lament,
all who cast hook in the Nile will mourn,
those who spread nets over the water will pine away.
[9]The workers in flax will be troubled,
carders and weavers grow pale,[n]
[10]the weavers[o] of Egypt will be crushed,
all the brewers[p] sad at heart.

iii

[11]The princes of Zoan are nothing but fools,
Pharaoh's counselors have counseled him folly.
How can you say to Pharaoh,

"I am descended from a line of sages,
from kings of ancient times?"
¹²Where then are your sages
to tell you and make it known^q
what Yahveh of the hosts has planned for Egypt?
¹³The princes of Zoan have become fools,
the princes of Noph are deluded,
her tribal leaders^r have led Egypt astray;
¹⁴Yahveh has poured^s into them a spirit of confusion,
they have led Egypt astray in all its operations
like a drunkard reeling in his own vomit.
¹⁵There will be nothing anyone can do for Egypt,
neither head nor tail, palm branch nor reed.

NOTES

^a Literally, "and will come";   ^b literally, "Egypt," masc. here and 3, 14b, fem. 10, 13, 14a;   ^c literally, "a man against his brother";   ^d for MT *věnā-běqāh* read *něbāqqāh* Niphal → *bqq*, "to be empty";   ^e *blʿ* Piel as 3:12; ^f *ʾădonîm* pl. but sing. adjective suggests plural of excellence, GKC §§124g, 124i, 132k;   ^g *hāʾādôn* often omitted as dittographic with LXX and Syr., but it is in 1QIsa^a and may be a deliberate contrast with *ʾădonîm* in the previous verse;   ^h *yām*, the "sea," but referring to the Nile in flood as at 18:2; cf. Arab. *el-bahr*, the "sea," referring to the Nile;   ^i 1QIsa^a *věhiznîḥû* Hiphil → *znḥ* gives the correct reading;   ^j *māṣôr* a variant of *miṣrāyim*, also in 37:25; 2 Kgs 19:24; Mic 7:12 cf. Akk. *muṣur*;   ^k "by the Nile" omitted in LXX but read MT; *ʿārôt* hapax is quite uncertain; usually translated "bare places" which, however, is not well adapted to the context; for "lotus" see Thacker 1933, 163–65; ^l for MT *věʾēnennû* 1QIsa^a has *vʾyn bv*, "there is not in it";   ^m 1QIsa^a has *hdgym*, "the fish," perhaps with Exod 7:21, the death of the Nile fish due to plague, in mind;   ^n read *ḥāvērû* with 1QIsa^a and 4QIsa^b for MT *ḥôrāy*, in LXX *tēn bysson*, "byssus";   ^o literally, "her textile workers" cf. Tg. which has in mind the Aram. verb *šth*, "weave";   ^p reading *šēkār* for MT *šeker* with LXX and Syr.; it is not clear why Skinner (1915, 157) accuses LXX of "dragging in the liquor trade";   ^q read *věyodiʿû* Hiphil for MT *věyēdʿû*;   ^r *pinnat šěbātehâ*, "the cornerstone of her tribes," either collective or read plural *pinnôt*; for the metaphor see Judg 20:2; 1 Sam 14:38; Zech 10:4;   ^s MT *māsak* = "mix," "mingle"; we would expect *nāsak* as in 29:10, a reading proposed here by Duhm (1892, 144) that has now turned up in 4QIsa^b.

COMMENTS

In view of the way Egypt is represented in traditional accounts of national origins as the oppressor par excellence it would be surprising if it did not loom large in any series of sayings directed against hostile nations. Isaiah 18–20, Jer 46 and Ezek 29–32 contain such sayings that develop related themes and motifs, e.g., the drying up of the Nile (Isa 19:5 = Ezek 30:12). A brief narrative about Isaiah, unmistakably Deuteronomic in character (20:1–6), was attached at a fairly early date to the original anti-Egyptian saying, the fourth in the *maśśāʾ* series (19:1–15). The passage was eventually augmented with five addenda each opening with the now familiar "on that day" formula (19:16–25). The *maśśāʾ* itself falls readily into the three strophes as set out above, though only the first has a concluding formula. Since the middle stanza (5–10) is quite distinctive in concentrating on ecological rather than political and military disaster it has generally been thought to have been spliced in between 1–4 and 11–15, though the devastation of the environment in the wake of military disaster is as common a literary topos (e.g. Ezek 32:13–15) as it is an experienced reality. In any case the title applies to the entire poem, which is therefore part of the distinctive series of nine oracular pronouncements in chs. 13–23.

This series has been superimposed on or interspersed with a string of passages, now disconnected, which continue the theme of Judah's vicissitudes faced with the Syrian-Samarian attack and the much greater threat from the Assyrians (14:24–31; 17:1–3, 12–14; 22:15–19) until the theme is taken up again in ch. 28. It has also been expanded and updated with numerous editorial scholia beginning "on that day" or, in one case (18:7), "at that time."

Though the author seems to be well informed on Egyptian affairs, the only specific historical allusion is to conquest by a foreign nation (4). The taskmaster and powerful king in question has been identified with such an extremely wide range of individuals, from Sargon II or Py (Piankhy) in the eighth to Antiochus III in the second century B.C.E., that a consensus is unlikely to emerge. Nebuchadrezzar's name keeps cropping up in anti-Egyptian sayings in other prophetic books (Jer 46:2, 13, 26; Ezek 29:18; 30:10; 24, 25; 32:11), but Nebuchadrezzar did not occupy Egypt. But even when the range is narrowed to rulers who not only inflicted defeat on the Egyptians but conquered and occupied the country it is still difficult to decide among several possible candidates—the Ethiopian Py (Piankhy), the Assyrian Esarhaddon, the Persians Cambyses and Artaxerxes III, and the Macedonian Alexander. As is so often the case, there is no well-marked path for the interpreter to follow from text to historical realia. Perhaps the most telling clue is the reference to civil disorder, which suggests the situation leading up to the establishment of the Napatan regime (the twenty-fifth Nubian dynasty) in the last quarter of the eighth century B.C.E.

The first stanza is presented as an oracular utterance in the name of Yahveh (2–4) and is couched in the traditional, mythic language of theophany or epiphany. The figure of Yahveh as charioteer on the storm cloud draws on the poetic image of Baal the charioteer of the clouds (*rkb ʿrpt*) in the Ugaritic poems, an image taken over into Israelite hymns (*rōkēb bāʿărāpôt* emended text Ps 68:5; see also Pss 18:10; 104:3; Deut 33:26). The consequent demoralization of the spiritual powers of Egypt—characterized as *ʾĕlîlîm*, "nonentities" (2:8, 18, 20; 10:10, 11; 31:7)—prepares the way for the collapse of the political and civic order and ecological disaster, reminiscent of the contest between the representatives of the Israelite deity and the Egyptian magi in the plagues narrative (Exod 7:8–11:10). The result is civic disorder with perhaps an allusion to conflict between Upper and Lower Egypt. (LXX contemporizes "kingdom against kingdom" as "nomes against nomes.") As often happens in this situation of disorder and *anomie*, and especially under foreign occupation, people turn to the dubious spiritual resources of necromancy—dubious, we should add, from the prophetic viewpoint (cf. 8:19) since the cult of the dead was a prominent aspect of Egyptian religion. Deuteronomy 18:9–14 provides a fairly exhaustive list of divinatory and necromantic specializations represented as foreign imports but quite familiar in Israel and early Judaism.

One of these is *šō'ēl 'ôb vĕyiddĕ'onî*, "one who consults a shade or a ghost," suggesting that the *'ôb* and *yiddĕ'onî* mentioned here (19:3b) refer to the spirits of the dead rather than to their human manipulators. It goes without saying that this attack on the immemorial religious traditions of Egypt is no less tendentious than the prophetic onslaught on the religious and intellectual traditions of Babylon in the second section of the book (Isa 44:25; 46:1–2; 47:9, 12–13).

The second stanza presents an impressionistic but also detailed and realistic description of ecological disaster precipitated by the failure of the annual flooding of the Nile basin. This phenomenon, occurring between mid-June and mid-October as a result of heavy rainfall in equatorial Africa, was well known in Palestine (Amos 8:8; 9:5; Jer 45:7–8). Its nonoccurrence led to the drying up of irrigation canals (mentioned by Herodotus, 2.108), loss of the alluvial soil brought down by the floodwaters, and consequent serious ecological stress. The poem mentions specifically its effect on the livelihood of those engaged in fishing by line or net, textile workers and brewers, all well represented in ancient Egyptian iconography. A similar scenario is depicted in the anti-Egyptian poems in Ezekiel with the drying up and fouling of the waters of the Nile (30:12; 32:2, 6), in addition to bloodshed and darkness over the land (32:6, 8)—perhaps providing raw material for the narrator of the plagues inflicted on the Egyptians in Exod 7–11.

The tirade against the internationally famous political wisdom of the Egyptian court that follows connects more readily with the first stanza in which Yahveh reveals his design to deliver Egypt over to a foreign conqueror. It is this plan that the Pharaoh's counselors in Zoan (also known as Tanis) in the northeast Delta region and Noph (also known as Memphis, capital of Lower Egypt) failed to detect. As a literary art form, the diatribe follows along familiar lines: rhetorical questions (cf. 10:3–4, 15; 14:16–17), allowing the opposition to condemn themselves in their own words (cf. 5:19; 9:10; 10:8–11, 13–14; 14:13–14; Jer 8:8), and the use of striking and sometimes repellent images, as that of the drunkard reeling in his own vomit (cf. 28:7). In keeping with the deep suspicion of secular political wisdom in the Isaian tradition, an example of what Max Weber referred to as prophetic culture hostility, this state of affairs is attributed directly to a spirit of confusion originating with Yahveh, comparable to the spirit of whoredom infused in Ephraim (Hos 5:4) or the spirit of deep sleep poured out on imperceptive prophets (29:10).

The final verse is often said to be an editorial summing up (e.g. Clements 1980a, 166), but the use it makes of the same proverbial saying as in 9:13[14] by itself hardly justifies this conclusion.

"BLESSED BE MY PEOPLE EGYPT" (19:16–25)

(Causse; Cowley; Delcor 1968; Feuillet 1978; Hayward; van der Kooij; Porten; Sawyer 1986; Schenker; Schürer 1986, 38–60; Sweeney 1996, 270–72; Vogels)

TRANSLATION

i

19 [16]On that day the Egyptians[a] will be as weak as women. They will tremble with fear on account of the raised hand of Yahveh of the hosts when he raises his hand to strike them.[b] [17]The land of Judah will strike terror[c] into Egypt. Anyone who so much as hears it mentioned will be filled with fear on account of the plan[d] of Yahveh of the hosts which he has devised against Egypt.

ii

[18]On that day there will be five cities in the land of Egypt speaking the language of Canaan and swearing their oaths in the name of Yahveh of the hosts. One of them will be called the City of the Sun.[e]

iii

[19]On that day there will be an altar to Yahveh in the middle of the land of Egypt and a monument dedicated to him at its frontier. [20]It will serve as a sign and testimony to Yahveh of the hosts in the land of Egypt. When they appeal to Yahveh on account of those who are oppressing them he will send them a savior who will come to their defense[f] and rescue them. [21]Yahveh will make himself known to the Egyptians, and the Egyptians will acknowledge him on that day and will worship him with animal sacrifice and cereal offering. They will make vows to Yahveh and perform them. [22]Yahveh will strike Egypt, but with a blow that heals; then they will turn to Yahveh, he will hear their prayers and heal them.

iv

[23]On that day there will be a highway from Egypt to Assyria. Assyrians will come to Egypt and Egyptians to Assyria. Egyptians will worship together with Assyrians.[g]

v

[24]On that day Israel will make up one-third of a whole together with Egypt and Assyria, a blessing in the middle of the world. [25]Yahveh of the hosts will pronounce this blessing over them: "Blessed be my people Egypt,[h] Assyria the work of my hands, Israel my possession."

NOTES

[a] Literally, "Egypt" (*miṣrayim*) but 1QIsa[a] has verbs in plural; [b] literally, "against him" (*'ālâv*); [c] *ḥāggā'* (1QIsa[a] *ḥvgh*) hapax but probably cognate with the verb *ḥgg* e.g. Ps 107:27; [d] 4QIsa[b] has *mpny tnvpt yd YHVH ṣb'vt*, probably haplography cf. v 16; [e] MT *heres* hapax as substantive but the corresponding verb = "destroy," therefore "destruction," impossible in the context; Tg., Symm., Vulg. read *heres* = "sun" (Job 9:7; Judg 1:35 cf. Josh 19:41) supported by 1QIsa[a] and 4QIsa[b] though Tg. adds tendentiously "which is about to be desolate" (cf. *m. Menaḥ.* 13:10); LXX presupposes *'ir haṣṣedeq*, perhaps a correction by the Egyptian translator to legitimate this cult center (cf. Ps 51:21 *zibḥē ṣedeq*, "legitimate sacrifices"); less likely is the option of Duhm (1892, 145) for *heres* = "lion" (cf. Arab. *haris*) with reference to Leontopolis, "Lion City"; [f] *vĕrāb* → *rîb* for MT *vārāb*; 1QIsa[a] has *vyrd*, "he will come down," perhaps with the idea of a heavenly savior in mind or (Hayward 1982, 441) with reference to Onias, who "went down" to Egypt; [g] "Egyptians will serve Assyrians as slaves" is possible and has support from LXX and Tg. but is inconsistent with the context; [h] LXX reads *en aigyptō*, strengthening the claim of the Egyptian diaspora to be Yahweh's real people cf. Tg. "Blessed are my people whom I brought forth from Egypt."

COMMENTS

These five editorial addenda have been attached *serially* to 19:1–15 in much the same way that 17:7–8 and 17:9 have been attached to 17:1–6 and 18:7 to 18:1–6. The first (16–17) is distinctive in being directly related to the preceding anti-Egyptian saying (e.g. mention of fear inspired by Yahveh's approach in 19:1 and 3) and in its adoption of the Isaian themes of the hand raised to strike (11:15) and the political agenda or plan of Yahveh (cf. 19:3, 11–13). It therefore must have been the original conclusion to 19:1–15.

The remaining four "on that day" additions have nothing in common with 19:1–17 apart from speaking about Egypt, though 19:22 could be read as a reinterpretation of the anti-Egyptian poem. What they have in common among themselves is a strong interest in the Judeo-Egyptian diaspora and its religious significance for the country as a whole. With the possible but by no means certain exception of the first, these addenda are of late date (pace Sweeney 1996, 270, 272, who puts them in the reign of Manasseh) but how late is difficult to determine. Duhm's dating of ii (1892, 18) to shortly after 160 B.C.E. has generally been ruled out on the basis of the textual evidence of LXX and Qumran. The date of the LXX translation of Isaiah is not known with any precision, that of 1QIsa[a] is not free of difficulty but in any case is no earlier than 160, and the fragments of 4QIsa[a] and 4QIsa[b] relevant to the passage have been assigned a date towards the end of the first century B.C.E. Duhm's dating is, nevertheless, almost certainly too late, a fortiori Kaiser's suggestion (1974, 110) that the fourth addition could be alluding to the Treaty of Apamea in 118 B.C.E.

The first addition probably derives from a scribe convinced that the weak condition of Egypt at the time of writing fulfilled the prediction of 19:1–15 and specifically the threat implicit in Yahveh's plan for Egypt (19:12); one more example, therefore, of the cumulative process of appropriation and reinterpretation of earlier prophecy in evidence throughout the book. We can construct more or less plausible scenarios in which it could have made sense to say that the land of Judah inspires terror in Egypt—for example, when Palestine served as the staging ground for Cambyses' conquest of Egypt in 525, or after the defeat of the Ptolemies at the battle of Panias in 198—but these would be no more than guesses. It was enough that Egypt was going through a phase of political weakness for this Isaian epigone to discern in the contemporary political situation the fulfillment of prophecy.

The second addition alludes to the spread of the Jewish diaspora in Egypt and with it the Yahveh cult involving the use, at least for liturgical purposes, of Hebrew and of the name of Yahveh in forensic affairs and in sealing contracts—a situation amply illustrated in the Elephantine papyri (Cowley; Porten). If five is not a round number—for which the evidence is not unambiguous (cf. for example, 30:17)—these "cities" or settlements may have formed a kind of federation or network of Jewish communities, and it may be purely coincidental that we can recover the names of five Egyptian centers of Jewish population from Jeremiah. Tahpanes or Baal Zaphon, later Daphne (Tell Defneh), was a border fortress in the Delta (Jer 2:16; 43:7; 44:1), east of which, near Pelusium, was situated Migdol (Jer 44:1; 46:14; Ezek 29:10; 30:6). At the southern end of the Delta lay Memphis (Jer 44:1) and Heliopolis (On Jer 43:13), ancient center of the cult of the solar deity Re. Pathros, the fifth named in Jeremiah (44:1, 15; also Isa 11:11), was the designation for Upper Egypt in general.

If the emendation proposed above is correct, the one named location in this second addition would be Heliopolis, the nome in which Onias IV, the high priest ousted from his post in Jerusalem around 170 B.C.E., built a temple to rival the one in Jerusalem. As Josephus tells it (J.W. 7.420–36; Ant. 12.387–88; 13:62–73, 283–87), Onias received permission from Ptolemy Philometor to build a temple on the site of an ancient, ruined cult center (probably dedicated to the lion-headed goddess Bast) at Leontopolis (Tell el-Yehudieh), and he did so inspired by the ancient prophecy in Isa 19:19 about an altar of Yahveh in the land of Egypt. That 19:19 is a *vaticinium ex eventu* alluding to this event cannot be absolutely excluded on chronological and text-historical grounds, but it is not the only possibility. Jeremiah (44:1; 46:14) attests that exile centers existed in Egypt beginning in the sixth century B.C.E., the Jewish military colony on the island of Elephantine at the first cataract was established, and its temple built before the Persian occupation of Egypt in 525 B.C.E., and Jewish mercenaries served in Egypt and received fiefs there, from as early as the Saitic period (*Letter of Aristeas* 13). The Jewish diaspora in Egypt has a long history of which we obtain only glimpses through references and names in papyri (conspicuously the Aramaic papyri discovered at Elephantine and Saqqara) and authors of the Greco-Roman period.

It is therefore possible that cult centers could have existed at anytime during the period of the Second Commonwealth. The prohibition of regional sanctuaries in Deuteronomy may not have been thought to apply outside the land of Israel, or it may simply have been disregarded. In any case, it did not prevent the establishment of cult centers at Elephantine, ʿAraq el-Emir east of the Jordan, Leontopolis, and Gerizim.

That the altar is in the middle of Egypt rules out an identification with the temple of the Jewish military colony on the island of Jeb (Elephantine) at the first cataract. The monument (*maṣṣēbâ*) on the border was not a boundary marker (as, for example, Gen 31:45) but a symbolic representation of Yahveh, as the context makes clear. These cultic monoliths were proscribed by Deuteronomic orthodoxy (Deut 7:5; 12:3; 16:22) and the proscription is reflected in Jeremiah (43:13), but the reaction of Egyptian settlers to Jeremiah's preaching (44:15–19) is only one indication of somewhat different religious attitudes in the diaspora. The *maṣṣēbâ*, perhaps set up in a border post assigned to a Jewish military unit like Elephantine, served as a sign of divine assistance during times of local persecution such as led to the destruction of the Elephantine temple in 411 B.C.E.

At this point the language is reminiscent of the pattern of oppression, supplication, and the sending of saviors in the Book of Judges (e.g. Judg 3:9, 18) and of Yahveh's intervention on behalf of his oppressed people in Egypt (Exod 3:7–9). The Exodus association is apparent also in Yahveh's making himself known to the Egyptians (cf. Exod 2:25 reading *vayyivvādaʿ ʾălēhem*, "he made himself known to them"), which opens up the prospect of significant numbers of Egyptians attaching themselves to the Yahveh cult. What the writer meant by the final comment, about a blow that heals, is unknown, but once again we hear echoes of the traditional story of the sojourn in Egypt—in this instance the plagues inflicted on the Egyptians (the verb *ngp*, "strike," occurs here and in Exod 12:23, 27).

The same association of ideas and motifs carries over into the fourth comment, since the highway (*mĕsillâ*) inevitably recalls the road along which the exiles are to return from Babylon in the latter part of the book (Isa 40:3 and 60:10–12 also *mĕsillâ* cf. 35:8 *maslûl*). By the time of writing, however, the motif had to be adapted to accommodate the repatriation of exiled Jews from two great diaspora centers, Babylon and Egypt. Babylon is referred to here and in other late texts as "Assyria" (Isa 11:16; Zech 10:10), and when linked with Egypt we may suspect a coded allusion to the Seleucid and Ptolemaic Empires respectively.

Perhaps the author was inspired by the alliance between Antiochus II and Ptolemy II—"the king of the north" and "the king of the south" in Dan 11—to think of widespread conversion to Judaism or at least of a situation in which diaspora Jews could move freely from one end of the Fertile Crescent to the other and take part in common worship. In the final passage this imagining of the future opens up into the vision of a tripartite axis in the middle of the known world (as set out in the "Table of the Nations" in Gen 10) bound together in the common worship of the God of Israel, a central zone in which the Abrahamic promise (Gen 12:1–3) attains its fullest instantiation. Israel (Judah) still occupies the central position both geographically and symbolically as uniquely the possession of Yahveh, but Egypt is also God's people and Assyria (Syria, Babylon) owes its existence to the same source.

We see here, and will see at later points in our reading (e.g. 45:22–23; 49:6), how the Isaian tradition served as one of the most powerful vectors of the broader and more inclusive way of thinking about God's saving purpose for the world throughout the period of the Second Commonwealth. What the commentator-editor has to say about Assyria, the most oppressive of imperial powers, bears comparison with the divine compassion for the inhabitants of Nineveh, "who do not know their right hand from their left" at the conclusion of Jonah (4:11). At no point, not even within that tradition, was this more open attitude free of challenge from more integralist understandings of the relation between Israel and other nations; indeed, the history of the interpretation of 19:16–25 provides illustrations of this tension.

It is—perhaps needless to say—simplistic and extremely misleading to speak of the tension between these two tendencies as finally resolved in early Christianity's rejection of Jewish particularism; the tension was a feature of Jewish life and thought throughout the entire period of the Second Commonwealth and has left its mark on the book of Isaiah at numerous points.

An Ominous Sign-Act (20:1–6)

(Fohrer 1968a; Lang; Tadmor 1958; 1966)

TRANSLATION

20   [1]In the course of the year during which the commander in chief, having been dispatched by Sargon, king of Assyria, came to Ashdod, fought against it, and took it—[2]at that time Yahveh sent this message to Isaiah ben Amoz: "Go, untie the sackcloth from around your waist and take your sandals[a] off your feet." He did so and went around naked and barefoot. [3]Yahveh then said, "Just as my servant Isaiah walked around over a period of three years naked and barefoot as a sign of ill omen[b] to Egypt and Ethiopia, [4]so shall the king of Assyria lead away Egyptians into captivity and Ethiopians into exile, both young and old, naked, barefoot, their buttocks exposed[c] [the nakedness of Egypt].[d] [5]They will be aggrieved and ashamed on account of Ethiopia the source of their confidence[e] and Egypt the source of their pride. [6]At that time, the inhabitants of this coastal region will think, "So that is what happened to those to whom we looked for help and to whom we fled[f] looking for assistance and rescue from the king of Assyria. How then shall we escape?"

NOTES

^a MT has *vĕna'alkâ* sing.; read pl. with 1QIsa^a and other ancient versions; ^b zeugma; MT *'ôt ûmôpēt*, "a sign and a portent," cf. 8:18; ^c read *ḥăśûpē* for MT *ḥăśûpay*; ^d *'ervat miṣrāyim* since it is not linked by conjunction with *śēt* it may be a gloss with the purpose of replacing dorsal with frontal nudity (*'ervâ* = "genitals" or "nakedness") which has slipped into the text, though the phrase is in 1QIsa^a and apparently also 4QIsa^b (*'[rw]t*); ^e reading *mibtāḥām* for MT *mabbāṭām* with 1QIsa^a; MT was perhaps influenced by *mabbātēnû* v 6; ^f 1QIsa^a has *'šr nsmk*, "on whom we relied."

COMMENTS

This concluding passage in the Egypt–Ethiopia series (18:1–20:6) is distinctive in character in that it is narrative about Isaiah, and a quite different Isaiah from the person to whom the sayings have so far been attributed. Up to this point the narrative character of the book has been limited to the headings or superscriptions recording visionary and auditory experiences represented as real events (1:1; 2:1; 13:1) and the third-person account of Isaiah's involvement in politics under Ahaz (7:1–17). The account of his activities during the reign of Hezekiah (36–39) duplicates the chronicle of the reign in Dtr (2 Kgs 18:13–20:19), and does so in a way consistent with the presentation of prophetic figures throughout the history. Several indications suggest that Isa 20:1–6 belongs to the same narrative complex and is in the same historiographical mode. It opens with a precise chronological marker (cf. 36:1), gives the prophet's full name (1:1; 2:1; 13:1; 37:2, 21; 38:1), and refers to him as Yahweh's servant (*'ebed*) in keeping with a standard way of referring to prophetic figures in Dtr (1 Kgs 15:29; 2 Kgs 9:36; 10:10; 14:25).

This last is the most telling indication of Deuteronomistic origin, but it is not the only one. The passage opens in the formulaic way of describing military campaigns characteristic of Dtr (1 Kgs 14:25–26; 2 Kgs 12:18; 15:29; 16:5; 18:9, 13; 24:10; 25:1): a temporal indication, the name of the aggressor, the attack (with *'lh, bô'*), and its result in the capture or failure to capture the place in question (with *lkd, lqḥ, tpś*). That the passage has been excerpted from the same annalistic source is also suggested by the fact that Sargon is the only Assyrian ruler during the second half of the eighth century whose name is absent from Dtr. Turns of phrase characteristic of the Deuteronomistic corpus also occur. The simple temporal phrase *bā'ēt hahî'* ("at that time") occurs elsewhere in Isaiah only in 18:7 and 39:1 but is exceedingly common in Deuteronom(ist)ic writings. Also characteristic of the Historian's style is the reference to the prophetic communication—*dibbēr YHVH bĕyad*, followed by the name of the prophet ("Yahveh spoke by means of prophet X," e.g. 1 Kgs 8:53, 56; 12:15; 16:7, 34; 17:16; 2 Kgs 14:25; 17:13, 23). Isaiah is to be a sign and portent (*'ôt ûmôpēt*), and signs and portents are what can be expected of prophets according to the Deuteronomistic view of the matter (Deut 13:1–2; 34:11). The theme also makes a good fit with the xenophobic tendencies of the Deuteronomists and more specifically with the discouragement of foreign alliances, especially with Egypt (cf. Deut 17:16 and 2 Kgs 18:21, 24). It therefore seems that 20:1–6 has either been excerpted from Dtr by an editor to complete the Egyptian section of the *maśśā'ôt* series or that, together with chs. 7 and 36–39, it is part of a Deuteronomistic redaction of chs. 1–39 similar to, but on a much smaller scale than the Deuteronomistic rewriting and overwriting in Jeremiah.

The historical context of this remarkable demonstration is well known from Sargon II's annals (*ANET*, 286–87). Briefly: in 714, Azuri ruler of the city-state of Ashdod tried to put together an anti-Assyrian alliance but was deposed by the Assyrians and replaced by his brother Ahimiti. He in his turn was deposed by the anti-Assyrian faction in Ashdod that put Yamani—a Greek or an Arab to judge by his name but in any case an outsider—on the throne. Yamani's anti-Assyrian allies included Tyre, one or other of the Syrian ("Hittite") states, Edom, Moab, and Judah. It was the threat posed by this alliance that led to the campaign under the commander in chief (*turtanu* in Akkadian, *tartan* in 20:1 and 2 Kgs 18:17) in 711. The Assyrian army reduced Ashdod and took over the entire coastal region, Yamani fled to Egypt but was handed over to Sargon by Shabako (716–702) in keeping with his non-interventionist policy vis-à-vis the Assyrians, and the rebellion collapsed.

If we take the sequence of events in 20:1–6 at face value Isaiah received the command to carry out this extraordinary demonstration in the year of the Assyrian campaign against Ashdod (711). He did so over a period of three years with the purpose of prefiguring the fate not of Ashdodites but of Egyptians and Ethiopians (Nubians) at the hands of the conquering Assyrians. This creates a problem since Egypt was not involved in hostilities with Assyria in 714–711, much less invaded by an Assyrian army. Of course, the fate of Egyptians and Ethiopians may not have happened as predicted, but a demonstration against an Egyptian alliance would on the whole make a better fit with the circumstances of the rebellion leading to the punitive campaign of Sennacherib against Judah and Egypt a few years later (705–701).

Mimetic and symbolic acts of the kind described here are otherwise unattested in Isaiah but are closely related to the symbolic use of names (7:3, 14; 8:1) and symbolizations narrated in the form of parable or allegory, for example, planting a vineyard (5:1–10) or offering a book to a person who could not read (29:12). (The prophet's recourse to the *něbî'â*, 8:3, is not significative in its own right, as is Hosea's relation with Gomer.) There is, however, a ready interchangeability between parabolic sign-making in other parts of the Bible and such acted out signs as Isaiah is said to perform here; suffice it to recall figs and the fig tree as metaphor (e.g. Jer 24:2–6), the parable of the barren fig tree (Luke 13:6–9), and the acted out parable of the cursing of the fig tree (Matt 21:18–22 and parallels). Acted out signs, many of which in the prophetic books are in effect a kind of street theater (e.g. Jer 27:1–28:17; Ezek 4:1–17; 5:1–4; 12:1–7), can be understood as a form of communication further along the spectrum of language. While it is no doubt true that they originated as mimetic or homeopathic magic (e.g. shooting arrows to simulate and enhance the likelihood of victory, 2 Kgs 13:14–19), they serve eventually to draw the consciousness of the actor more fully into identification with the prophetic role.

On the details of Isaiah's demonstration little need be added. Its purpose was to simulate the shaming of prisoners of war as illustrated in Assyrian reliefs and here and there in biblical texts (e.g. 2 Sam 10:4). Assuming some historical basis to the description, Isaiah would have paraded *at intervals* over a period of three years in the guise of a prisoner of war. Sackcloth, a kind of burlap cloak or wrap, has been interpreted (e.g. by Marti 1900, 160) as distinctive prophetic garb (cf. Zech 13:4; 2 Kgs 13:4; Matt 3:4) or as a simple rough outer garment. But it is preferable to take it as indicating mourning (cf. 3:24; 2 Sam 21:10), especially in view of Mic 1:8–9 in which, like Isaiah, the prophet Micah goes barefoot and naked but also in mourning. The Micah parallel may also suggest that the public demonstration was rendered more effective and visible by the participation of Isaiah's followers as well.

"FALLEN, FALLEN IS BABYLON" (21:1–10)

(Ackroyd 1968, 223; Bach; Barnes; Bosshard-Nepustil 1977, 23–42; Cobb; Dhorme; Erlandsson 1970, 81–92; Galling 1963, 49–62; Gosse 1986; 1990; Macintosh; Scott; Uffenheimer)

TRANSLATION

21 [1] The oracle "the wasteland by the sea"[a]

As whirlwinds in the Negev advance,
coming from the wilderness, from a land of terror,[b]
[2] a grim vision is announced to me:
"The treacherous one is betrayed,
the despoiler is despoiled.[c]
Attack, then, Elam!
Lay siege, Media![d]
I have brought all sighing to an end." [e]

[3] At this my loins are filled with anguish,
pangs have seized me
like the pangs of a woman in labor;
I am so bent double I cannot hear;
I am so dumbfounded I cannot see.
[4] My mind reels.[f]
Shuddering, I am filled with dread;
the cool of the evening[g] I longed for
has been turned for me into trembling.

⁵Set the table,
lay its covering,^h
eat and drink!
Then arise, you princes,
rub your shields with oil,
⁶for thus the Lord has addressed me:
"Go, post a lookout,
let him announce what he sees;
⁷when he sees chariots drawn by two horses,ⁱ
riders on donkeys, riders on camels,
let him listen hard, very hard."

⁸Then the seer^j cried out,
"On the watchtower, O Lord, I stand
all the day long;
at my post I take my station
night after night."
⁹Now, look, there approaches
a man riding^k in a chariot drawn by two horses,
when addressed, he replies,^l
"Fallen, fallen is Babylon,
and all the statues of her gods
lie smashed on the ground!"

¹⁰O my people, once threshed and winnowed,^m
what I have heard from Yahveh of the hosts,
from the God of Israel I have announced to you.

NOTES

^a *Midbar-yām*, literally, "the wilderness of the sea," is problematic; proposed emendations include *yehĕmeh*, "groaning" (BHS), *midbar dĕbārîm* cf. 1QIsa^a *mś' dbr ym* (Scott), *yôm* for *yām* (G. R. Driver 1968, 46–47); it is tempting to follow LXX *to horama tēs erēmou* and assume that the title is taken from the poem (v 1b cf. 21:11, 13; 22:1a, 5a), but MT may be retained as the equivalent of Akkadian *mat tam-tim* or *kur tam*, "the sealand," referring to the marshy delta of the Tigris and Euphrates in southern Mesopotamia (cf. *ARAB*, vol. 2, #66), and Jerome justified his version *onus deserti maris* with reference to Jer 51:36 "I will dry up her (Babylon's) sea";   ^b the 1QIsa^a scribe first wrote *mē'ereṣ rĕhôqâ* (as in 39:3 and often elsewhere), then deleted *rhvqh* and wrote *nvr'h* above it;   ^c reading *habbôgēd bugad, haššôdēd šudad* Qal passive rather than Pual participle, with Syr. and Tg.;   ^d the verbs *'ălî, sûrî* are feminine for countries;   ^e *hišbatî* need not be emended to *hašbitî* imperative, especially if the phrase is part of the "grim vision" announced at the beginning of the verse;   ^f 1QIsa^a has *tv'h vlbby* for MT *tā'āh lĕbābî*;   ^g to bring out the

sense of *nešep*, "twilight";   [h] *ṣāpît*, hapax, but *ṣāpāh* Piel = "to lay," "over-lay," hence "rugs" (RSV, NEB), but the idea of a tablecloth seems more suited to the context; Vulg. *contemplare in specula*, suggested by *ṣph*, "watch," is some-what arcane (cf. Ewald's "observe the horoscope");   [i] *rekeb* collective; 1QIsa[a] and 4QIsa[a] *smd (smyd) 'yš pršym* perhaps influenced by *rkb 'yš smd pršym* 9a;   [j] reading *hārō'eh* with 1QIsa[a] for MT *'aryēh*, "lion" cf. Tg. "the standard of a lion," a Sassanid emblem;   [k] *rōkēb* participle for MT *rekeb*; [l] rendering *vayya'an vayyo'mer*, literally, "he replied and said";   [m] literally, "my threshed one and the son of my threshing floor."

COMMENTS

This poem with the obscure title is the fifth and therefore central unit in the *maśśā'ôt* series corresponding to the Babylonian poems in chs. 13–14. As in the Moab poems, the seer speaks in his (less probably her) own name. Its interpre-tation is beset by numerous problems beginning with the title, and it seems to have no clearly defined structure. The opening verse has been understood to describe the approach of a great army, either Elamites and Medes or Assyrians (cf. 5:28; Jer 4:13), in which case the injunction to have a meal and prepare for battle in 5 would more likely refer to the besieged Babylonians and would re-call the tradition that the king and court were feasting while the city was being besieged (Herodotus, 1.191; Dan 5:1–31). The other option, adopted here, is to read the first part of the poem (1–4) as an account of the onset of prophetic ec-stasy, but it then remains unclear whether the "grim vision" includes the state-ment about the treacherous and despoiling people and the injunction to Elamites and Medes to go into action, or whether the vision begins only with the banquet and preparations for battle. There also appear to be two quite different descriptions of the visionary experience itself. On one reading, the turmoil inseparable from the state of mental dissociation is compared to a whirlwind and is accompanied by acute bodily discomfort like the labor pains of a woman about to give birth (Jer 4:19 adds convulsive movement and rapid heartbeat, while Hab 3:16 speaks of trembling lips, reeling, and a sensation of rottenness in the bones). But this *spontaneous* onset of ecstasy is quite different from the description of the seer as *soliciting* a visionary experience (here *ḥāzût* as in 29:11) in the guise of a lookout or sentinel on a watchtower, a representa-tion well represented in the prophetic literature (e.g. Ezek 3:16–21; 33:1–9; Isa 62:6–7). The aspect of patient and attentive waiting for a revelation is expressed in such similar language in Habakkuk (2:1)—"I will take my stand on the watchtower and station myself on the rampart; I will keep watch to see what he will say to me"—that it suggests that the seer named Habakkuk had in mind the prediction, unfulfilled at the time of writing, of the fall of Babylon in the present poem. But if this is so, the combination of such diverse evocations of the reception of a revelation also suggests that 21:1–10 has undergone some editorial elaboration.

Reaching a decision on the historical referent of the poem comes up against the by now familiar problem of the re-application or "recycling" of the same political saying with reference to successive historical situations—at least two, corresponding to the Neo-Assyrian and Neo-Babylonian periods, according to Macintosh's reading of the text as a palimpsest. If the Negev whirlwinds are taken to refer metaphorically to the onset of ecstasy, there is really nothing to recommend an original reference to an Assyrian or Babylonian attack on Jerusalem, re-edited to apply to the fall of Babylon (pace Bosshard-Nepustil 1977, 41–42). Furthermore, Babylon fell many times before becoming, for a while, the center of the world empire of Alexander the Great. It was captured by Sargon II in 710 B.C.E., twice by Sennacherib in his struggle to suppress Merodach-baladan, in 700 and 689, it was occupied briefly by Elamites under their king, Urtak, in 667 and by Ashurbanipal in 648. Its capture by Cyrus II in 539 B.C.E. is recorded on his famous cylinder, Darius crushed a Babylonian rebellion under Arakha (alias Nebuchadrezzar IV) in 521, and the city was sacked by Xerxes after his suppression of the revolt of Belshimani in 482. As the text now stands, participation of the Medes in the campaign rules out the Neo-Assyrian period since they were allies of Babylon at that time. Moreover, the combination of the verbs ʿlh ("go up, attack") and sûr ("besiege") rules out a reference to defensive warfare in 2b, in the sense that Elamites and Medes are being urged to rebel against the attackers (pace Sweeney 1996, 281). We can also dismiss the suggestion that the poet is alluding to Elamite and Medan conscripts in the Assyrian army (Hayes and Irvine 1987, 274), since it is unclear why he should mention them and not the Assyrians themselves. Elam and its principal city Susa were rather thoroughly devastated by Ashurbanipal in 647, but the Persepolis and Susa reliefs show Elamites serving in the armies of Cyrus a century later, so there is nothing implausible in the idea of Elamites and Medes taking part in the siege of Babylon. Whatever its prehistory, therefore, the poem could be more or less contemporaneous with the anti-Babylonian diatribe in Isa 47 written in the years immediately preceding the occupation of Babylon by Cyrus II. We also hear echoes of our poem in the anti-Babylonian discourses in Jeremiah: the announcement of the fall of the city together with its gods (50:2; 51:8), the role of the Medes in the attack (51:11, 28), and the summons to the armies of several nations to the siege (50:14–16, 29–30; 51:11–12). All of these compositions make much of the destruction of the images of Babylonian deities, though Cyrus in his propagandistic cylinder—probably composed for him by sympathetic Babylonian priests—claims to have restored the cult of Marduk after its neglect by Nabonidus (ANET, 315–16). This may serve as a reminder that a date in the years immediately prior to 539 B.C.E. would not exclude the discovery of new relevance in the poem later in the Persian period (Vermeylen 1977, 327–28), for example, after the ideologically inspired destruction of the esagila sanctuary and its statue of Marduk by Xerxes in 482. The somewhat similar language employed in some of the night visions of Zechariah (horsemen and charioteers, 1:8–11 and 6:1–8; prediction of trouble for Babylon, 2:10–13[6–9]) might be taken to point in the same direction.

The ambiguities of the poem continue into the final verse, for though the seer assures his hearers and readers that he has faithfully passed on the revelation announced at the beginning, we are not told who the threshed and winnowed ones are. That the Babylonians are so described in the Jeremian poems (51:2, 33) and that elsewhere Israel is spoken of as Yahweh's threshing sledge (Isa 41:15), might lead us to suspect that the frightful vision of anticipated slaughter and mayhem evoking the poet's horror also induced a degree of pity and empathy, as is also the case, to some extent, in the oracular poems about Moab. But it seems more likely that the announcement of the conclusion of the vision would be addressed by the seer to his own people, who had suffered so much at the hands of Babylon. The agrarian image is no longer immediately recognizable to most of us, but it is a violent image of crushing, flailing, and pulverizing. There is so much violence in Isaiah and other prophetic books because there was so much violence in the world in which they lived—as there still is in our world—and we with our experience so many years later cannot afford to be too critical if it was only slowly, painfully, and partially that the authors of these poems found a way to come to terms with what Hegel called *der Schlachtbank der Geschichte*, "the slaughterhouse of history."

ORACLES ABOUT ARAB PEOPLES (21:11–17)

(Bartlett 1979; 1992; Ephʿal; Galling 1963; Geyer; Gosse 1990; Graf; Knauf 1989; 1992a; 1992b; 1992c; Lindsay; Lohmann 1913b; Schlossberg; Vallat)

TRANSLATION

i

21 ¹¹An oracle about Dumah

> Someone is calling me from Seir,
> "Sentinel, how much of the night is left?ᵃ
> Sentinel, how much of the night is left?"
> ¹²The sentinel replied,
> "The morning is coming, though it is still nighttime;ᵇ
> if you wish to ask you may do so,
> come back once again."

ii

¹³"In Arabia": an oracle

> In the scrubland, in Arabia where you lodge,ᶜ
> you caravans of Dedan,
> ¹⁴go to meet the thirsty, bring them water;
> you dwellers in the land of Tema,

meet the refugees with the food they need;[d]
[15]for they are fleeing from the sword,[e]
from the drawn sword,
from the bent bow and the stress of battle.

iii

[16]This is what Yahveh[f] said to me:
"Within three[g] years, the length of employment for a hired laborer, all the pomp of Kedar will come to an end, [17]and the remaining archers[h] among the Kedarite warriors will be few in number, for Yahveh, Israel's God, has spoken."

NOTES

[a] *Mlyl* in 1QIsa[a] for MT *millaylâ* with mem partitive;   [b] rather than "the night is finished," *wĕgam* assumed to derive from verb *gāmam*, attested however only in MH, see Scheiber 1961, 455–56;   [c] LXX "in the evening" (*hesperas*) for *bā'ereb* cf. also Syr., Tg., Vulg. in keeping with *tālînû*, but the context suggests that their stay was not limited to the evening, and in any case *bĕlaylâ* would be more fitting; for *'ărab* = Arabia see also 2 Chr 9:14; Jer 25:24; Ezek 27:21;   [d] an attempt to render the suffix in *bĕlaḥmô* cf. 1QIsa[a] *blḥm*;   [e] MT: *hărābôt* pl.;   [f] YHVH in 1QIsa[a] but *'dny* in 4QIsa[a];   [g] supplying the numeral with 1QIsa[a] *šlš* as 16:14;   [h] either *qešet*, "bow," stands for "bowmen" or, more likely, reverse the order of words to *gibbōrē qešet*.

COMMENTS

Two brief and enigmatic sayings continuing the series of *maśśā'ôt* are rounded off with an addition similar enough to the addition to the Moab poem (16:13–14) to suggest identity of authorship. The first of the poems (11–12) is linked with the preceding through the motif of the seer as lookout or sentinel (*šōmēr* 21:7–8 cf. 62:6, on the wall of Jerusalem; also *ṣōpēh* 52:8; 56:10; Ezek 3:17; 33:1–9), a kind of antenna or early warning system. Mention of Seir (southeast of the Dead Sea, Gen 33:14; Num 24:18; Judg 5:4) also recalls the Judean Negev at the beginning of the previous section (21:1). Everything about this first *maśśā'* is problematic. The overt sense of the question addressed to the sentinel seems to be obvious enough, but who is asking such a question in the middle of the night, and why would anyone need a sentinel to tell him the time? We can only surmise that it has something to do with the changing of the night watch, but the surface meaning remains opaque enough to suggest very strongly a symbolic interpretation, perhaps not so different from Rom 13:12, "the night is far gone, the day is at hand," with reference to the dawning of salvation. The sentinel is the prophet—so much is clear; but how does his reply to the query qualify as an oracular pronouncement? If the translation offered above is permissible, rather than "the morning is coming and also the nighttime" or "is

there any news on the night watch?" (Sweeney 1996, 284–85), the seer is holding out the hope of eventual deliverance, light at the end of the tunnel, for
the nighttime is the time of defeat and danger (8:29; 21:8), just as the morning is the time for redemption (9:1). This is as far as the speaker can peer into
the future, though he leaves open the possibility of a more precise prophetic
communication at a later point in time and therefore invites further consulta-
tion. The occurrence of the verb *šûb* ("return") in the last verse led the Targumist to read the answer as an invitation to repentance or "turning" (*těšûbâ*).
Though clearly unsuited to the context (apropos of which Duhm 1892, 156
notes dryly that the author was not writing as a theologian), this reading merits
our consideration as part of the *latent* content or potential range of meaning of
the text (see e.g. Vermeylen 1977, 331).

It will be obvious to anyone familiar with the range of opinion in the commentary tradition that there is little hope of assigning a definite historical context to this first oracular poem. That the title was almost certainly prefixed to
the passage long after it was composed implies that the editor who added it
may have had nothing to guide him except the passage itself, in which the only
fixed point is the reference to Seir (= Edom). On the reading proposed above,
an inhabitant of Edom is therefore represented as consulting a prophet during
a period of hardship and distress. The situation may be connected with pressure on Edom from Arab tribes farther east beginning around the middle of the
seventh century and leading to infiltration into the Judean Negev but not yet to
the point of provoking a hostile reaction from the local inhabitants. In that case
we might discern here a parallel with the plight of the Moabites as described in
15:5 and 16:1–4. At any rate, mention of Seir in this poem makes it unlikely
that the Dumah of the title refers to the oasis in north-central Arabia (Dumat
al-Jandal in Wadi Sirhan) often identified as the most likely candidate by commentators (e.g. Eph'al 1982, 119–21). The consonantal form of the apparent
toponym Dumah (*dvmh*) is close to that of Edom ('*dvm* cf. LXX *idoumaia*), and
would be even closer if we were to assume that the initial 'aleph was lost
through haplography. *Dûmâ* also means "silence" and occurs as a synonym for
Sheol, the realm of the dead (Pss 94:17; 115:17), a circumstance which may
have suggested to the editor who arranged the titles a suitable pun on Edom
whose name became, like Babylon, a symbol of hostility, oppression, and mal-
ice (e.g. in the Mekhilta of R. Ishmael).

The title of the second poem was also suggested by something in the poem
itself, the equally obscure *ba'ĕrāb* (see notes). The sentence can be parsed in
more than one way, but it seems most natural to align "caravans of Dedan" and
"dwellers in the land of Tema" in parallelism, the one to supply drink, the
other food. In that case, all we are told about those to be assisted is that they are
refugees, therefore not unlike the Moabites of whom we heard in a previous
poem (15:5; 16:1–4a). The juxtaposition of poems i and ii might suggest
Edomites as the ones in flight from the sword and the bow, and since Edom
was overrun by the Kedarite Arabs this is how the editor who added the final

note (16–17) would have understood it. Biblical texts confirm the existence of a close association between Dedan, Tema, and Edom (Jer 49:7–8; Ezek 25:13). Dedan and Tema (Taima) were the principal commercial centers in Northern Arabia from the Neo-Assyrian period to the Nabatean conquest in the first century B.C.E. The oasis of Dedan was situated near al-ʿUla in the Hijaz on the major trade route from the Mediterranean to the Persian Gulf. Something of its history has emerged from several hundred inscriptions in Dedanite and Lihyanite recovered from the region, and its prosperity depended on trade in blankets, incense and other commodities (Gen 25:3; Ezek 27:20; 38:13). The caravan oasis of Tema lay north of Dedan on the incense route and an important stopover on the way east to the Persian Gulf and north-northeast to the cities along the Euphrates. Both Dedan and Tema were attacked by Nabonidus during the years following his transfer of the court to Tema (552–542). After the fall of Babylon they came eventually under Kedarite control. One of the Lihyanite inscriptions from Dedan refers to Gashmu, a Kedarite ruler of the region, perhaps identical with Geshem, ally of Sanballat of Samaria and opponent of Nehemiah (Neh 2:19; 6:1–2, 6). The Kedarite kingdom grew out of the most powerful and warlike of the Bedu tribes of northern Arabia. The anti-Kedarite oracle (16–17) may have been added in the belief that the Kedarites are the aggressors referred to in 15, and mention of the bow reminds us that the Kedarite Arabs were known to be expert archers (cf. Gen 21:20). Their prosperity rested on trade in cattle, camels, and the manufacture of woven goods (Jer 49:29; Ezek 27:21; Isa 60:7), and after surviving hostile contact with Assyrians and Babylonians they secured control over a vast area from the northern Arabian and Syrian desert region to the Sinai.

As noted earlier, the addition (16–17) has much in common with the addition to the poems on Moab (16:13–14). Both issue short-term predictions of misfortune on a foreign people at a high point of its history and do so using the same kind of language. Somewhat similar editorial addenda occur throughout this section of the book—aimed at Babylon (14:22–23), an unnamed people (17:9), Egypt (19:16–17), and Tyre (23:13–18). With these we may associate the prospect of foreign peoples' bringing tribute to Jerusalem (14:1–2; 18:7), a major theme in Isa 60–62, which also mentions tribute from Kedar (60:7). These interpolations represent a stage in reflection on and interpretation of international affairs inspired by the Isaian compilation then existing and therefore incorporated directly in the book. The Kedarite addendum may have been inspired by Nehemiah's struggle against Sanballat, Tobiah, and Geshem (Gashmu) the Kedarite Arab, but in any case it is much later than the brief poems to which it is appended.

THE VALLEY OF VISION (22:1–14)

(Amiram; Avigad; Bosshard-Nepustil 1997, 42–67; Broshi; Childs 1967, 22–27; Clements 1980a, 33–34; Dietrich 1976, 193–95; Donner 1964, 126–28; Emerton 1980a; Wilkinson)

TRANSLATION

22 ¹"The Valley of Vision": an oracle

What is wrong with you that you go up,
all of you, to the rooftops,
²inhabitants of a cityᵃ in tumult, full of clamor,
of a town in an uproar?
Your slain were not slain by the sword,
they did not perish in battle;
³your leaders have fled, one and all,
withdrawnᵇ out of range of the bow;
your strongest warriorsᶜ
have fled far away.

⁴Therefore I said: "Turn your gaze away from me,ᵈ
leave me to weep bitter tears,
do not attempt to console me
for the ruin of the daughter of my people!"

⁵The Sovereign Lord Yahveh of the hosts has a day of tumult, trampling, and turmoil in the Valley of Vision, with crying out for help to his holy place on the mountain.ᵉ

⁶Elam has picked up the quiver,
with chariots of Aramᶠ and horsemen;
Kir has uncovered the shield.
⁷The best of your valleys teemed with chariots;
horsemen were stationed at the city gate,
⁸leaving Judah naked and defenseless.ᵍ

You looked [on that day] to the weapons stored in the "House of the Forest." ⁹You observed that there were many breachesʰ in the defenses of the City of David, and you brought together the waters of the Lower Cistern. ¹⁰You made a census of the houses in Jerusalem, and demolished some houses to strengthen the city wall. ¹¹You made a reservoir between the two walls for the water of the Old Cistern, but you did not look to the One who made it all, or take account of the One who fashioned it ages ago.

¹²The Sovereign Lord Yahveh of the hosts called [on that day] for weeping
    and mourning,
for heads shaved bare and the wearing of sackcloth;
¹³but instead there was gladness and joy,
killing of oxen, slaughtering of sheep,
eating meat, drinkingⁱ wine.
"Eat and drink," you said, "for tomorrow we die."

[14]This message has been revealed in my hearing
[Yahveh of the hosts]:[j]
"Such iniquity will not be pardoned you until you die."
[This is the message of the Sovereign Lord Yahveh of the hosts.]

NOTES

[a] For MT *ʿîr*, "city";   [b] 1QIsa[a] has *ʾsvrh* for MT *ʾussārû* → *ʾsr*, "bind," "capture," in which case *miqqešet* would be translated "without a bow (being used against them)"; the present translation presupposes *husārû* → *sûr* Hophal; [c] reading *ʾammiṣayik* for MT *nimṣāʾayik*, "those of you who are found," and omitting *ʾussĕrû* on account of dittography;   [d] 1QIsa[a] has *švʿv mmny* for MT *šĕʿû minnî*;   [e] 5b defies translation and has probably been seriously damaged in transmission; the present translation depends on 1QIsa[a] (*mqrqr qdšv ʿl hhr*), which makes better though by no means perfect sense and of which MT (*mqrqr qr všvʿ ʾl hhr*) may represent a damaged version; following Weippert (1961, 98–99) and G. R. Driver (1968, 47–48), *mĕqarqar* represents either a participle or substantive related to an Arabic and Ugaritic cognate meaning "tumultuous sound";   [f] cf. MT "with chariots of a man" (*bĕrekeb ʾādām*), which may be a technical term elsewhere unattested cf. *rekeb ʾîš* 21:9a, but the connection between Kir and Aram (Amos 1:5; 9:7; 2 Kgs 16:9) supports the reading adopted here;   [g] literally, "denuding Judah of its cover"; *māsak* refers elsewhere to the curtain of the temple (Exod 26:36–37 etc.) and a roof (2 Sam 17:19);   [h] rather than emending to "you filled with water the many pools" (*bĕqiʿê*) with NEB and Clements (1980a, 186);   [i] 4QIsa[c] has *vštv* 3d person pl.;   [j] an addition; inconsistent with syntax and meter.

COMMENTS

In spite of its general lack of coherence this passage forms an independent unit, marked off from the preceding *maśśāʾ* by the concluding formula of the latter (21:17b) and by its own title and from the prose passage about court officials that follows, introduced by the customary prophetic incipit in 22:15. Juxtaposition of the present passage with the condemnation of Shebna may, however, have been suggested by the location of the Shebna's tomb in the Kidron Valley and his probable involvement in politics during the critical period 705–701.

This next to the last oracular pronouncemens is problematic, not least because it is the only one in the series not directed against a foreign people. The title resembles the two preceding it in being taken from a phrase within the passage, i.e., the mention of the Valley of Vision in 22:5, but its meaning has given rise to much discussion. Following G. R. Driver (1968, 47), NEB proposes "Valley of Calamity" as an alternative translation, but this option has not been accepted due to the fact that *ḥizzāyôn* never has this meaning in the Hebrew Bible; it refers exclusively to a visionary experience, often parallel with a dream, and with one possible exception (2 Sam 7:17) appears exclusively in late texts (Job 4:13; 7:14; 20:8; 33:15; Joel 3:1; Zech 13:4). Others take it to refer to Babylon where Ezekiel had his visionary experiences (Vermeylen 1977, 338) but, apart from other problems, the texts in question (Ezek 1:1; 3:22; 8:4; 37:1) use different terms for both valley (*biq‘â* not *gē’*) and vision (*mar’eh* not *ḥizzā-yôn*). Taking it to allude to Jerusalem as the object of prophetic revelation (as does Wildberger 1977, 821), leaves unanswered the question why Jerusalem, situated on a hill, should be referred to *tout court* as a valley. The question is not unanswerable if we bear in mind that the title, added long after the composition of the original nucleus of the passage in 1b–4 + 6–7 + 12–14, is taken from the apocalyptic addendum in 5 using the familiar language of the Day of Yahveh as the day of final judgment. The location is the Valley of Jehoshaphat of Joel 4:2, 12[3:2, 12], later given the sobriquet "the Valley of Decision" (*‘ēmeq heḥārûs*, 4:14[3:14]), perhaps identified with *gē’ hinnôm*, the Valley of Hinnom, later Gehenna, of which we will hear again in the final verse of Isaiah. Not unlike the present passage, this eschatological event features the noise and tumult of military action (Joel 4:9–12[3:9–12]). On this reading, the *maśśā’* redactor chose the title from this final addition to the present unit at a time when its original specific concerns had receded into the distant past.

The first segment (1–3) rather cunningly sets up a contrast between the *qînâ* or lament meter (3:2) in which it is cast and the theme of misplaced rejoicing, a theme that will be repeated towards the end (13). The speaker addresses the city (Jerusalem, referred to more explicitly as we read on) in the second person feminine singular. Her inhabitants are rejoicing after surviving an attack but one in which the army and its leaders seem to have chosen discretion as the better part of valor—a point interestingly confirmed by Sennacherib's account of the campaign, which speaks of troops brought into the city deserting Hezekiah's cause (*ANET*, 288). The language is specific enough to suggest events in the not too distant past. The situation following Sargon II's Philistine campaign (711) has been proposed (e.g. Vermeylen 1977, 334; Hayes and Irvine 1987, 277). According to Sargon's annals Judah was associated with this uprising (*ANET*, 287), apparently against the advice of Isaiah (20:1–6), but withdrew in time to avoid the punishment meted out to the Philistines. But, on the whole, Hezekiah's rebellion against Sargon's successor Sennacherib makes a better fit. Judah was ravaged during the punitive campaign of 701: Sennacherib claims to have devastated 46 Judean towns and driven out 200,150 of their inhabitants, and the wall panels depicting the fate of Lachish give some idea of what would have happened to Jerusalem if the siege had not been suddenly and mysteriously lifted (*ANET*, 287–88; 2 Kgs 18:13–16 cf. 19:35–37, the miraculous version).

The prose expansion 8b–11 confirms this reading of the first segment even though it is out of chronological order, dealing as it does with preparations for the siege. It also changes from feminine singular (addressing Jerusalem) to masculine singular (*wĕtabbēṭ*) followed by masculine plural, with reference to Hezekiah and his people. The armory in the "House of the Forest," so named on account of the cedar columns supporting it (1 Kgs 7:2–5; 10:17), had to be checked and the defensive perimeter of the city secured. This involved structural repairs to the existing wall and the construction of a second wall to enclose the western expansion of the city (cf. 2 Chr 32:5), a segment of which has been excavated in the Jewish section of the Old City (Avigad). The stone required for this work of repairing and building was provided by demolishing private houses, an expedient that would be repeated during the Babylonian siege of the city over a century later (Jer 33:4). Securing the water supply was, of course, crucial. The measures taken are detailed in the accounts of the reign and the famous Siloam tunnel inscription (2 Kgs 20:20; 2 Chr 32:3–4,30; *ANET*, 321). They involved filling the Lower Cistern (birket el-hamra, about 200 meters south of Siloam), digging the Siloam tunnel from the Gihon spring to Siloam, and presumably securing the Upper Cistern as well (cf. 7:3; 36:7).

Expression of the seer's own emotional response to stressful situations is not unprecedented (cf. 15:5; 16:9, 11; 21:3–4) and may be a convention of this kind of discourse. In this instance (22:4) it is addressed no longer to the personified city but to a plurality. The cause of the weeping is the ruin of the people (*šôd* from the verbal stem *šdd*, of frequent occurrence in this section; see 13:6; 15:1; 16:4; 21:2). "Ruin" would not be an inappropriate description for the state of Judah following Sennacherib's punitive campaign of 701, which resulted in destruction, loss of life, and the forfeiture of Judean territory to the Philistine city-states. But we are then left with an insurmountable contrast with the prophet's attitude towards the siege and its aftermath as described in chs. 36–39. Since similar expressions of grief are of frequent occurrence in Jeremiah (e.g. 4:19–22; 14:17–18), and since moreover the expression "the ruin of the daughter of my people" (*šeber bat-ʿammî*, using a different word for "ruin") is limited to Jeremiah (8:11) and Lamentations (2:11; 3:48), 22:4 might be taken to refer to the greater catastrophe of the fall of Jerusalem. But since nothing requires this interpretation and the context discourages it, the contrast seems instead to confirm the hypothesis of a deliberately different prophetic profile in the narrative sections of the book emanating from a source of Deuteronomic origin.

Ambiguity of historical reference persists in 6–8a which has troops from Elam, Kir, and Aram (see the notes) taking part in an attack on Judah. There is no justification for excising 6 as part of a later "fall of Babylon" stratum, though 6–8a may refer to a Babylonian rather than Assyrian attack on Jerusalem. All we know about Kir is that it was the destination of Syrian or Aramean deportees, situated perhaps in southern Mesopotamia (Amos 1:5; 9:7; 2 Kgs 16:9). Elam, east of Mesopotamia, was mentioned earlier as taking part in the attack on Babylon in 539 B.C.E. (21:2). During the Neo-Assyrian period, Elam was an ally of Babylon in the constant struggle against Assyria. It was attacked by Sargon II and Sennacherib and eventually the Elamite kingdom was extinguished by Ashurbanipal in 647 B.C.E. While it is possible that Elamite contingents served in the army of Sennacherib in the campaign of 701 in southern Palestine, it is equally possible that Elamites, especially prized for their skill as archers (cf. Jer 49:34–39), took part in Nebuchadnezzar's subjugation of Judah more than a century later. It may be prudent to add that all of this assumes that the writer was at least as familiar with the history of the Neo-Assyrian and Neo-Babylonian periods as we are today.

Translated literally, 22:8a says that he (Yahveh) stripped Judah of its covering. In most contexts the covering (*māsak*) has a theological and symbolic connotation: it is the cloud that covered the tent (Ps 105:39) or the screen or curtain of the temple (Exod 26:36–37; 27:16; 35:12, 15, 17; 39:38 etc.). In an earlier passage we heard about the canopy and pavilion that provided shade and refuge for the inhabitants of Jerusalem (4:5–6). The *māsak* mentioned here may belong to the same semantic field, in which case we are being offered another theological explanation of the destruction of Jerusalem and its temple by the Babylonians.

Most commentators agree that the final section (12–14) takes up again and rounds off the diatribe of 1–3. The situation called for mourning expressed in the traditional ways (cf. 15:2–3; 32:11–12) rather than for rejoicing. But now the rejoicing sounds a bitter, fatalistic note expressed in a proverbial form familiar throughout antiquity, from Siduri's advice to Gilgamesh to Horace's *carpe diem* (examples in Wildberger 1978, 827–28). The concluding word of judgment, introduced by a particularly asseverative kind of oath formula (cf. 5:9), affirms that only in the death anticipated in the proverb just quoted by the revellers will guilt be expiated (verbal stem *kpr*). This means, in effect, that the guilt will never be expiated, that the course on which those addressed have entered is irreversible and their condition terminal. If this is still to be located in the context of the events of 701 B.C.E., namely, the aftermath of the withdrawal of the Assyrian army, the mood is very different from the mood a reading of the Deuteronomic chs. 36–39 would have us believe prevailed at that time. We therefore have not only the same ambivalence as was noted in the description of military disaster and the condemnation of attitudes to it at the beginning of the book (1:4–9) but also a decidedly different reaction to the situation on the part of the prophetic author of this passage from that of the *nābî'* in the prose account in Isa 37.

PALACE OFFICIALS CONDEMNED (22:15–25)

(Albright 1932; Auret; Avigad 1953; 1986; Fullerton 1907; Ginsberg; Jenni; Kamphausen; Katzenstein 1960; Koenig; Mettinger; Ussishkin; de Vaux 1939; J. T. Willis 1993a; 1993b)

TRANSLATION

22 [15]About Shebna superintendent of the palace[a]

This is what the Sovereign Lord Yahveh of the hosts said: "Go, then, to this official and say to him:[b] [16]'What business have you here, and whom do you have here to authorize you[c] to hew out a tomb for yourself, hewing out a tomb on the high ground and carving out a resting place for yourself in the rock? [17]Yahveh will knock you to the ground with great force, my fine fellow,[d] he will grab hold of you firmly,[e] [18]and fling you like a ball[f] into a broad and spacious land. There you will die, and there will your splendid chariots be. You are a disgrace to your master's household.

[19]I will dismiss you from your office,
and banish[g] you from your post.

[20]On that day:
I will summon my servant Eliakim ben Hilkiah[h]; [21]I will invest him with your robe, bind your sash on him, and hand over your authority to him. He will be a father to the inhabitants of Jerusalem and to the household of Judah. [22]I will place on his shoulder the key of the house of David. When he opens no one will close, and when he closes no one will open. [23]I will fasten him firmly in place like a peg. He will be like a throne of honor to his paternal household.

[24]They will hang on him all the weight of his household, their offspring and their issue,[i] all the smallest[j] utensils, from beakers to every kind of bowl.

[25]On that day:
[Oracle of Yahveh of the hosts] The peg fastened firmly in place will give way. It will be cut down and fall, and the load that was on it will be destroyed'"; for Yahveh has spoken.

NOTES

A good part of the text is reproduced in 4QIsa[a,b,c,f] but with no major divergence from MT;   [a] the title has been inserted into the text (15b), awkwardly especially in view of ʿal instead of ʾel;   [b] "and say to him" added with LXX, Vulg., and Tg.;   [c] an attempt to render the sense of ûmî lĕkā poh, literally, "whom do you have here?";   [d] vv 17–18a are obscure and perhaps seriously damaged; mĕṭalṭēl Pilpel participle → ṭûl may mean (1) "hurl," "fling" cf. Jer 22:26 in Hiphil; (2) "shake out," as in MH, leading to emendation of geber to beged, "garment" (metathesis) as in NEB following Ginsberg (1950, 55–56) and G. R. Driver (1968, 48–49); (3) "stretch out," "lay low," as in Arab. cognate; ṭalṭēlā is a substantive, but ṭalṭēl haggeber, infinitive absolute followed by vocative, would fit the rest of the phrase better;   [e] ʿṭh cf. Arab. ʿaṭa, "seize," rather than "delouse" cf. Jer 43:12 also with beged; possible, but why delouse a garment and then throw it away? (Wildberger 1978, 832);   [f] the usual meaning "wrap up" for the verb ṣnp does not fit the context; the similar text Jer 22:26, supported by LXX, suggests a meaning similar to hēṭîl, "throw"; read either kakaddûr, "like a ball," or sĕnēpat kaddûr;   [g] 1st person with Syr., Tg., Vulg. for MT (and 4QIsa[f]) 3d person;   [h] 4QIsa[a] has the longer form *hlqyhv*, 4QIsa^f same as MT; ^{i} *šĕpi'ôt* uncertain, perhaps "leaves," "shoots"; ^{j} *haqqāṭān*, superlative (GKC §133h).

COMMENTS

This self-contained passage with its own title (see the notes), incipit and excipit is a relatively rare case of prophetic invective directed against individuals (see also Amos 7:16–17; Jer 20:1–6; 28:12–17). Since no sustained metrical regularity is detectable, we take it to be a straightforward prose appendix to 22:1–14, similar therefore to 20:1–6, appended to the preceding anti-Egyptian sayings. The connection would suggest an addition dictated by prophetic opposition to the pro-Egyptian and insurrectionist policy pursued by this Shebna prior to the campaign of 701 B.C.E. At the same time, it presents one of the clearest cases of serial composition and editing in the book, apparent in the hostile and sarcastic tone in which the downfall of Eliakim is announced in 25, following the exalted language in which his elevation to high office is proclaimed in 20–23. The lead-in to 25 ("on that day") also suggests an addition in view of the way Eliakim's tenure of office ended. The rather bland statement about Shebna's dismissal from office in 19, following the intemperate language preceding it, has led most commentators to read this verse as marking the transition from Shebna to Eliakim and therefore as an addition, which is possible but by no means certain. It would be better to take 15–23 without a break as prophetic approbation of Eliakim for high office including an explanation of the circumstances under which he came to occupy the office. Note that the beginning of the Eliakim section is still referring back to Shebna (your robe, your sash, your authority).

On the reading of 15 proposed above, the name Shebna occurs only in the title. We know that titles can be attached to texts long after they were written and be mistaken, but they can also be attached at the time of writing and be correct. Shebna, hypocoristic for Shebanyahu (1 Chr 15:24) or Shebaniah (Neh 9:4–5; 10:5, 11, 13; 12:14), is described in the title as superintendent or majordomo of the palace—literally, "the one who is over the house" (*'ăšer 'al habbāyit*). The title corresponds to the Akk. *ša bitāni* and is attested in both Northern and Southern Kingdoms (1 Kgs 4:6; 16:9; 18:3). In the text itself as distinct from the title, the object of the prophet's invective has the title *sōkēn*, a biblical hapax (the fem. *sōkenet*, approximate meaning "attendant," describes Abishag the Shunnamite's function, 1 Kgs 1:2, 4), though the corresponding term is attested in Aramaic, Ugaritic, Phoenician and Punic texts, meaning "governor," "regent," or "deputy." Though the tone in which the speaker refers to him is contemptuous ("this official" cf. "this Sheshbazzar" Ezra 5:16), the office itself is not necessarily incompatible with the title.

The prophet's address to Shebna, therefore, comprises a superscription and introductory formula followed by the customary indictment (16) and verdict (17–19). The prospect of death in a foreign land, no doubt Mesopotamia, constitutes a brutally direct negation of this official's tomb-building in or near Jerusalem. Whether Isaiah is represented as confronting Shebna in situ, i.e., at the tomb-building site (*poh*, "here," is repeated three times in one verse) cannot be decided. It seems that Shebna was what the Assyrian annals call a "son of a nobody," and is consequently being put in his place as a social climber. (Note that while he is the black sheep of his family, Eliakim does his family proud, 18b, 23b.) Curiously, the Shebna who was sent to negotiate with the Assyrian Rabshakeh during the siege of Jerusalem together with Eliakim ben Hilkiah and Joah ben Asaph is the only one of the three without a patronymic (36:3, 22; 37:2), a normal indicator of status and honor. Even so, the punishment threatened seems to be quite disproportionate to the offense, and practically unintelligible except on the assumption that the text is silent about the real reason for the hostility it displays. This may well be Shebna's political agenda, the conviction that he was one of those who were leading Hezekiah astray by advocating a highly dangerous anti-Assyrian alliance (cf. 3:12).

The second section deals with the investiture of Eliakim ben Hilkiah, whose office is described in solemn and exalted terms reminiscent of the "messianic" poems in 9:5–6[6–7] and 11:1–5. The language does not justify the idea that the text is really dealing with the *royal* office, but it is possible that the account belongs to a Josian redaction, with 24–25 added after the tragic death of Josiah (Clements 1980a, 188). This Eliakim is designated Yahveh's servant (*ʿebed*), an honorific designation signifying in biblical texts a privileged relationship with the deity, generally referring to either the prophetic office or royalty (for the latter see 2 Sam 3:18; 1 Kgs 8:24–26; 2 Kgs 19:34 = Isa 37:35). It has also turned up on seals belonging to individuals high up in court administration, including the magnificent Megiddo lion seal of Shema, servant of Jeroboam (*lšmʿ ʿbd yrbʿm*). Eliakim is summoned (*qrʾ* cf. 42:6; 45:3–4; 49:1) to his investiture, which is described is solemn fashion not unlike the anointing of a royal figure. He is invested with the robe of office (*kutonet*, also a sacerdotal vestment: Exod 28:4; Lev 8:13), the sash (*ʾabnēṭ*, a word of Egyptian origin) is put round his waist, and the authority and jurisdiction inhering in the office (*memšālâ* Mic 4:8; Jer 34:1; Zech 3:7) are committed to him, no doubt with a set form of words. The keys of the palace—much larger than modern keys—are draped around his neck, symbolizing his responsibility for the security of the royal palace and the absolute nature of his authority under the ruler. A parallel metaphor is the peg that holds the tent in place, language that inevitably brings to the reader's mind the idea of responsibility for maintaining the tent or pavilion of Zion (4:5–6; 33:20; 54:2) and the booth of David (Amos 9:11).

As a result of his investiture, Eliakim is to be a *father* to the people of Jerusalem and Judah. This designation (*ʾab*) belongs to the traditional language of the pharaonic court and signifies the protection afforded by the just government administered by the Pharaoh, generally by means of his vizier. In his capacity as vizier, for example, the patriarch Joseph acts on behalf of Pharaoh (Gen 45:8), and the same function is attributed to the proverbially wise and ubiquitous Ahiqar.

Inspired by the language of investiture, the insignia of office, the officeholder as father to his people, the tent peg fixed in a *firm* place (*neʾĕmān* cf.

2 Sam 7:16), some commentators have speculated on the messianic character of the passage, or even suspected a conflation of Eliakim son of Hilkiah and Eliakim son of Josiah, renamed Jehoiakim (2 Kgs 23:34), or a replacement of the latter by the former, an idea perhaps first suggested by Fullerton. Such a reading is understandable, but the oracle is clearly about a specific individual named elsewhere, and the editor or editors who added the final two verses seem to have entertained no doubts about his identity. The pericope has, nevertheless, inspired messianic re-readings in early Christian circles. The sixth of the seven letters to the churches in Rev 3:7 begins by invoking the Holy One who holds the key of David, who opens and no one shuts, shuts and no one opens, and the same passage appears among the antiphons of the Advent liturgy (*O clavis David*). As a symbol of authority, possession of keys also features in the incident in which the Jesus of Matthew's gospel confides to Peter the keys of the Kingdom of Heaven (Matt 16:19).

According to Dtr, Eliakim ben Hilkiah superintendent of the palace, Shebna (or Shebnah) the "scribe" (*sōpēr*), and Joah ben Asaph the "herald" (*mazkîr*) were given the unenviable task of parleying with the Assyrian generalissimo during the siege of Jerusalem in 701 B.C.E. (2 Kgs 18:18, 26, 37 = Isa 36:3, 11, 22). Shortly afterwards Eliakim, Shebna, and senior priests were sent to Isaiah to persuade him to intervene in the extreme crisis of that year (2 Kgs 19:2 = Isa 37:2). The occurrence of both names, Eliakim and Shebna, strongly suggests identity with the individuals who feature in Isa 22:15–23. Certain seals and seal impressions (bullae) and one inscription from the period of the late Judean monarchy have also been brought to bear on their identification. Impressions from the seal of a certain Eliakim were discovered at Tell Beth-Mirsim and Tell er-Rumele inscribed *l'lyqm n'r yvkn* referring, according to W. F. Albright's interpretation, to Eliakim, a palace superintendent during the reign of Jehoiachin. It will be obvious, however, that Albright's view rules out identification with Dtr's Eliakim, active almost a century earlier, and thus it seems prudent to conclude that the seal belonged to a different person with the same not uncommon name. Another bulla in the Israel Museum in Jerusalem is inscribed *lyhvzrh bn hlq[y]hv 'bd hzqyhv* ("belonging to Yahuzarah [?] ben Hilkiah servant of Hezekiah"), chronologically compatible with the biblical data, but since Hilkiah is also a common name there is no guarantee that it belonged to a brother of Eliakim. I mention, finally, the inscription associated with a rock-hewn tomb—of the kind Shebna was taken to task for preparing—in the village of Silwan, southeast of Jerusalem (Avigad; Ussishkin). The inscription identifies the tomb as belonging to a palace superintendent (*'šr 'l hbyt*), the ending of whose name, -*yahu*—the only part surviving—is compatible with Shebanyahu, the full form of Shebna, but with many other names as well. So identification with Shebna's tomb remains at best a tantalizing possibility.

It would be tempting to solve the problem of the relation between the biblical texts by assuming that by the year 701 Eliakim had already assumed the office of palace superintendent, that Shebna had been demoted to *sōpēr*, and that none of the dire consequences of his hubris had as yet come about. It is noteworthy, however, that during the final century of the Judean monarchy the highest office under the ruler appears to have been the *sōpēr* (corresponding more or less to Secretary of State or Prime Minister) not the *ʾăšer ʿal habbāyit*. If that is so, Eliakim would be the last to bear this title (omitting the Gedalyahu, so designated on a seal from Lachish), but we can reconstruct from Jeremiah a list of *sōpĕrîm* covering the period from Josiah to Zedekiah—Shaphan, Ahikam (probably), Elishama, Jonathan (2 Kgs 22:3; Jer 26:24; 36:12, 20–21; 37:15–20). It is therefore possible that the Historian has anachronistically combined alternative titles for the highest office under the ruler.

In language that is both vivid and unappealing, a later editor has appended an accusation of nepotism (24) to the investiture of Eliakim. The peg in the ground that held the tent in place is now a peg in the wall on which kitchen utensils are hung—an odd but not entirely inappropriate image for "hangers-on" from Eliakim's "paternal household" (23). The inevitable result is stated in what, to judge by the introductory "on that day," is a further addition to the passage, reflecting the fall of Eliakim (not Shebna, pace Sweeney 1996, 297) from power together with the ruin of his family.

About Phoenicia (23:1–18)

(Ackroyd 1958; Erlandsson 1970, 97–101; Fischer and Rüterswörden; Flint; Harden; Katzenstein; Lindblom 1965; Linder; Lipiński; Reyes 1994, 49–68; Rudolph 1959; Tuplin; Watson)

TRANSLATION

23 ¹An oracle about Tyre

Wail, Tarshish ships,
for your harbor[a] is destroyed!
When they came[b] from Cyprus[c]
they found it out.[d]
²Lament,[e] dwellers on the seacoast,
merchants[f] of Sidon,
whose agents traverse the great waters,[g]
³whose harvest is the grain of Sihor,[h]
whose revenue is the commerce of nations.[i]
⁴Be ashamed and cry out,
Sidon, harbor by the sea,[j]
"I am not in labor,
I do not give birth,
I neither rear young men
nor bring up young women."
⁵[As soon as the Egyptians hear it
they sway in anguish at the news about Tyre.][k]

⁶Cross over to Tarshish,
wail, dwellers on the seacoast!
⁷Is this your bustling city
whose origin was so long ago,
whose people took off and voyaged[l]
to settle in far distant lands?
⁸Who has devised this thing
against Tyre, bestower of crowns,[m]
whose merchants were princes,
whose traders were the most honored in the world?
⁹Yahveh of the hosts has devised it
to puncture all pride and splendor,[n]
to bring the world's most honored into contempt.
¹⁰Till your land, for there is no longer a harbor
for the Tarshish ships.[o]
¹¹He has stretched out his hand over the sea,
he has shaken kingdoms.[p]
Yahveh has given the command
to destroy the harbors of Canaan.[q]
¹²[r]You will no more exult,
oppressed virgin daughter of Sidon.
By all means cross over to Cyprus,
even there you will have no respite.
¹³[This is the land of the Chaldeans,[s] this is the people . . . it was not. . . .]
There the Assyrians established it for their fleet,[t] they erected their siege towers[u] and destroyed their palaces,[v] turning the place into a ruin.
¹⁴So wail, ships of Tarshish,
for your harbor[a] is destroyed!

¹⁵On that day:
Tyre will be forgotten for seventy years, one king's lifetime. At the end of seventy years Tyre will experience what the song says about the harlot:
¹⁶Take up a harp,
go around the town,
poor, forgotten harlot!
Play a sweet tune,
play song after song,
so they may remember you!

¹⁷At the end of seventy years Yahveh will be mindful[w] of Tyre. She will engage once more in commerce, and she will play the harlot with all the kingdoms of the world on the face of the earth. ¹⁸Her trade and commerce will be
dedicated to Yahveh. Her merchandise will not be put in storage: it will not be
hoarded but will serve to feed to satiety and clothe in rich attire those who
dwell in the presence of Yahveh.

NOTES

^a MT *mibbayit* (cf. Vulg. *vastata est domus*) makes no sense in the context; among the principal proposals are: *bētām*, "their residence," i.e. for ships (cf. Tg.); *mābô'* = "entrance," i.e. "harbor"; *mābît* cf. Arab. *mābit*, "shelter for the night" (Eitan 1937–38, 69); since the rest of the poem emphasizes the capture and destruction of the harbor, we take our cue from v 14 *māʿuzzĕken*, understanding it to mean "your fortified harbor";   ^b retaining MT *mibbô'*, "from (the time of their) coming," rather than *mābô'*, "port of entry" (NEB);   ^c MT *'ereṣ kittîm*; see commentary;   ^d literally, "it was revealed to them";   ^e MT *dommû*, "be silent," is not a good parallel to *hêlîlû*, "wail"; some emend to *nidmû* Niphal → *dmh* II, others read as Niphal → *dmm* (Duhm 1892, 166 *vertilgt*, "annihilated"); I have taken the option first proposed by F. Delitzsch in 1884, deriving it from *dmm* = "lament" cf. Akk. *damāmu*;   ^f MT and 4QIsa^a have sing. *sōhēr*, but read pl. parallel to *yōšĕbē 'î* with LXX, Vulg., Tg.;   ^g MT reads "crossing the sea, they replenish you," cf. 1QIsa^a and 4QIsa^a *ʿbrv* pl. but *ʿōbĕrîm* (participle) reads better; for MT *mil'ûk* read *mal'ākāv*;   ^h MT "the grain of Shihor was the harvest of the Nile"; omit *yĕ'ôr*, "Nile," with LXX; ⁱ omit *vatĕhî*;   ^j MT "be ashamed, Sidon, for the sea has said, the fortress (harbor) of the sea, saying," which can hardly be correct; read *'imrî* (cf. 1QIsa^a *'mrh*) and delete *lē'mor*;   ^k read *yiššāmaʿ* or *nišmaʿ* for MT *šēmaʿ*; the verse appears to be a gloss, perhaps with reference to Alexander the Great's conquest and destruction of Tyre;   ^l MT *yobilûhâ raglēhā*, "her feet carried her," a curious phrase when speaking of sea travel;   ^m *hammaʿăṭîrâ*, reading Hiphil participle from *ʿṭr* hapax cf. *ʿăṭārâ*, "crown," perhaps referring to city-states politically dependent on Tyre in Cyprus and points west; differently Vulg. *coronata*;   ⁿ a slight change of order from MT with 1QIsa^a *lhll kvl g'vn šby*; ^o MT is unacceptable: "cross over your land like the Nile [cf. 3b!], daughter-Tarshish . . ."; we follow the lead of LXX, "till your land, for no more ships come from Karchedon," in agreement with 1QIsa^a *ʿbdy* (but 4QIsa^c has *ʿbvry*); another instance of daleth/resh confusion; for *mēzaḥ* read *māḥoz* = "harbor" or *mānoaḥ* = "resting place (for ships)";   ^p 4QIsa^c reads *lhrgyz*, "to shake . . ."; ^q read *ʿal* for *'el* and *maʿuzēhâ* with 1QIsa^a for MT *māʿuznēhâ*;   ^r omit *wayyo'mer* metri causa; also, what follows is not a command;   ^s the first part of the verse is damaged, probably beyond repair; MT reads literally: "Behold the land of the Chaldeans; this is the people; it did not exist"; *hēn 'ereṣ kaśdîm* and *zeh haʿam* appear to be glosses appended at different times; there are no grounds for emending either *kaśdîm* to *kittiyîm* or *ʿaššûr* to *'ăšer* (as does Duhm 1892, 170); *'aššûr* (fem.) is required as the subject of *yĕsādāh* = "found," "establish (the earth, the vault of the sky)," less commonly, "appoint for punishment" (only Hab 1:12, also with reference to Babylon);   ^t *ṣiyyîm* = either a species of wild animals (see commentary on 13:11; 34:14) or more likely ships in view of Dan 11:30 *ṣiyyîm kittîm* and Num 24:24 reading *vĕṣiyyîm* for *vĕsîm* in *vĕsîm miyyad kittîm vĕʿinnû 'aššûr . . .* ;   ^u read *bĕhînāv* Q *bḥvnyv* cf. 1QIsa^a

bhynyh fem. suffix; precise meaning uncertain; [v] with fem. suffix cf. 4QIsa[c] masc.; [w] MT *yipqod*, "attend to," in either a positive or negative sense, depending on the context.

COMMENTS

This last unit in the *maśśā'* series (23:1–14) is in the "limping meter" (3–2) appropriate to lamenting or even ironically exhorting others to lament as here (cf. 13:6–22; 14:4–20; and especially 15–16, the lament over Moab). It has its own title (1a) and develops by way of a series of imperatives addressed to the inhabitants of the Phoenician littoral: they are to wail (1b), lament (2–3), be ashamed and cry out (4–5), cross over to Tarshish and wail (6). These exhortations lead to a rhetorical question (8), which is nevertheless answered: Yahveh is behind the destruction of the harbor and there is nothing to be done about it (9–12). The poem is then rounded off with an inclusio (14). There is no need to assume a conflation of distinct poems about Tyre and Sidon or have recourse to emendation to eliminate one or the other city (e.g. by emending *ṣōr*, "Tyre," to *sidôn* 23:8, with Duhm 1892, 168; and Kaiser 1972, 160). Tyre and Sidon are usually mentioned in tandem (e.g. Jer 25:22; 47:4; Ezek 28:20–23; Joel 4:4–8[3:4–8]). 1 Kgs 16:31 refers to Ittobaal king of Tyre as the king of the Sidonians: Hiram of Tyre, who paid tribute to Tiglath-pileser III, appears to be identical with the Hiram king of the Sidonians named on a bronze Cypriot bowl (Harden 1962, 53–54, 119) and Sennacherib's annals refer to the Tyrian ruler Luli as king of Sidon (*ANET*, 287; cf. Josephus, *Ant.* 9.138, for whom Ithobalos was king of both Tyrians and Sidonians). At any rate, the authors of the additions in 15–18 appear to have read 1–14 as a poem about Tyre, as did the editor who provided the title. Since 5 seems to interrupt the flow rather sharply, it may have been slipped in with reference to Alexander's seven-month siege of Tyre in 332 on his way to Egypt (Wildberger 1978, 873); and if 13 contains the debris of one or more glosses (see the notes), it clearly cannot bear the weight laid on it by the exegetes who give it a pivotal role in the formation of this part of the book (e.g. Seitz 1993, 120, 123). It serves nevertheless to bring the attention of the reader back once again to the Babylonians (*kaśdîm*, "Chaldeans"), the subject of the first poem in the series (13:1–14:23), the evil empire par excellence.

The note of *Schadenfreude* is even more in evidence here than in the Moab poem and is colored by the typical Israelite allergy to the sea, seafaring, and international trade. We hear it in the injunction addressed to the conquered Phoenicians—now till your own land like the rest of us, if that is the correct reading of 10—and in the gratuitous analogy between trade and prostitution, reminiscent of the fierce opposition of Dtr to the alliance between the Omrids and the Tyrian royal house in the ninth century B.C.E. Yet, in contrast to the anti-Phoenician poems in Ezekiel (26–28), the element of moral condemnation is relatively muted and confined to 9 and 11 (which need not on that account be set apart as additions), in which divine intention and agency are expressed in the Isaian leitmotifs of *the plan of Yahweh* and *the outstretched hand* (cf. for the former 14:24, 26–27; 19:12, 17; 22:11, and for the latter 14:26–27 and 19:16). Here, as so often in the compositions surveyed up to this point, the main thrust is against pride and arrogance, which seem to be the cardinal vices throughout the book, inclusive of this segment (cf. 13:11, 19; 15:6; 16:6; 21:2), as they are in the much more elaborate anti-Phoenician series in Ezekiel (28:2–10, 17).

To repeat: the poem is not a lament but rather an ironic injunction to others to lament, and as such it achieves its rhetorical effect by repeated imperatives and rhetorical questions, a very common device in this kind of composition (cf. 14:16–17, 27; 19:11–12; 22:1–2). Direct speech is also used quite freely, and the author of the present poem attributes to the "virgin daughter Sidon" what appears to be a quotation from a lament, a lament within a lament therefore. (The Hebrew of 4b reads: *loʾ ḥaltî/loʾ yāladtî/loʾ giddaltî baḥûrîm/rômamtî bĕtûlôt.*)

The first injunction (1b) is addressed to ships of Tarshish approaching the Phoenician coast from Cyprus (the land of Kittim). It is generally acknowledged that Tarshish (Tartessos in Greek) was located somewhere in the western Mediterranean—either in southern Spain, Sardinia, Malta, or along the North African coast (the *Vetus Latina* version identified it with Carthage), and that the place-name Kittim derives from Kition, a major trading center near Larnaka on Cyprus. While we do not know how extensive the author's knowledge of geography and the history of the Phoenician cities was, he was at least aware of their great antiquity (7) and the amazing extent of their voyages in search of new sources of raw materials and markets for their own goods (of which Ezek 26–28 provides a detailed itemization)—reaching, as we now know, as far as the Cassiterides, "the Islands of Tin," namely, the Cornish coast in southwest England. Particularly important in this respect, given the limited land available for cultivation in Phoenicia, was the import of grain from Lower Egypt, here referred to as Sihor in the second injunction (3).

With respect to chronology, the situation is far less clear. By failing to provide unambiguous clues to the historical events and situations described, the poet has tested the ingenuity of exegetes throughout the modern period. Basically, all we are told is that a major Phoenician harbor had been destroyed (1, 10) at a time when the Phoenicians still controlled Cyprus and had a lively trade with Egypt. The Targumist simplified the task by contemporizing the poem with reference to conquest by the Romans (Kittim). Surveying the historical record in reverse, it would not be surprising if Alexander's siege and conquest of Tyre and the brutal treatment of its inhabitants after the storming of the island fortress (332 B.C.E.) had left their mark on this poem as they apparently have on Zech 9:1–8, which speaks of the downfall of Tyre (Fohrer; Lindblom). The suppression of the Tennes revolt by Artaxerxes III in 343, the sack of Sidon, and subsequent Persian reconquest of Egypt have also been proposed (Duhm 1892, 166; Kaiser 1974, 162), but 8 speaks of a major disaster visited on Tyre, and the Babylonians are mentioned in the text, even if the context is obscure (13). The protracted siege of Tyre by Nebuchadrezzar (585–573), much in view in the Ezekiel poems (26:7–14), is also a possibility, but has the disadvantage that the city and its harbor were not taken and destroyed on that occasion. If a Neo-Assyrian background is assumed, and specifically the campaigns waged against the Phoenician cities by Sennacherib (705–701) and Esarhaddon (678, 671), the obscure and disjointed allusion to the land of Chaldeans, Assyrian ships, and a campaign of destruction in v 13 may refer to Sennacherib's campaign against Merodach-baladan with the help of Phoenician and Cypriot ships and sailors in the Persian Gulf region. But here, too, we cannot exclude a rereading of the text in the Hellenistic period that assigned new referents for *kittîm* and *'aššûr*. There seems little point in attempting greater chronological precision.

The last four verses consist in a later mitigation of the scene of doom reminiscent of the notes appended to the sayings against Moab (16:13–14) and the Kedarite Arabs (21:16–17). All three predict a change in fortune within a specific time period—for the worse with respect to Moab and Kedar; somewhat better with respect to Tyre. Seventy years is, of course, less specific than one year or three, and is well attested as signifying a period of misfortune of considerable duration, about the length of a human lifespan (Ps 90:10; Jer 25:12; 29:10; Zech 1:12; 2 Chr 36:21; Dan 9:2). Moreover, the variation "one king's lifetime" is not so strange in view of the custom of periodizing the history of a city-state like Tyre according to reigns. Repetition of the phrase *miqqēṣ šibʿîm šānâ* ("at the end of seventy years," 15, 17) suggests the possibility of a two-stage addition, in which case the analogy between international trade and prostitution may have inspired a second reader, aware of Tyre's notorious brothels, to add a little local color with the ditty about the aging prostitute.

Since this postscript is ostensibly a projection into the future of what was said about Tyre's past misfortunes in the pronouncement itself, the identification of historical circumstances is even more problematic. If the poem looks back to the struggle for survival of the Phoenician city-states and their dependents during the Neo-Assyrian period, the addenda would perhaps refer to the debilitating effects of the Babylonian siege of Tyre at about the same time as the beginning of Judah's "seventy years." From then until well into the Achaemenid period Sidon remained in the ascendancy along the Phoenician littoral. The partial recovery of Tyre anticipated by the editor was probably underway long before the destruction of Sidon by Artaxerxes III in 343 or, a fortiori, the granting of autonomy to Tyre by Ptolemy II in 274. That the results, in the form of revitalized trade activity, would be in the service of the Jerusalemite temple community is one more expression of a powerful but dangerous envisioning of the future that seems to be especially characteristic of the emergent Judean commonwealth in the Achaemenid period (cf. 14:2; 18:7; 45:14; 49:23; 60:4–16; 61:5–6).

PREFACE TO CHAPTERS 24–27

Before we proceed with the commentary, a few additional remarks on chs. 24–27 are in order. I noted earlier that this section is not set apart from the rest of the book by introductory or concluding formulae. Since the commentary of Bernhard Duhm (1892, 172) and an important contribution by Rudolph Smend (1884, 161–224), the entire passage, or at least its core components, have nevertheless been known as the Isaian Apocalypse. If we take Daniel and the Enoch cycle as standard examples of the apocalyptic genre, some features characteristic of apocalyptic are present here (resurrection of the dead 26:19, the abolition of death 25:8, the imprisonment of the heavenly host 24:22) but others are lacking (periodization of history, heavenly journeys, a systematically dualistic way of thinking), and in any case much of the section (25:1–5, 10b–12; 26:7–19; 27:2–5) has nothing in common with apocalyptic. There is therefore a growing consensus that this designation is misleading and should be abandoned.

The four chapters comprise a number of loosely connected passages of uneven length, the sequence of which manifests no immediately obvious logical order. Apart from sayings introduced with the familiar "on that day" formula (24:20–23; 25:9–10a; 26:1–6; 27:1, 2–5, 12–13), few sayings are clearly and formally delineated. Duhm distinguished between a core of prophetic sayings (24:1–23; 25:6–8; 26:20–27:1, 12–13) that he took to be the original apocalypse, songs or hymns (*Dichtungen*) interspersed with these sayings (25:1–5, 9; 26:7–19) added at a later date, and one or two passages appended even later. The apparent alternation of prophecy and psalm suggested to Lindblom (1938) the original idea of a cantata performed processionally ("throw open the gates that a righteous people may enter!" 26:2), and the idea was taken up by Fohrer (1963), who distinguished three "moments" in the liturgy (24:1–20; 24:21–25:10a; 27:1–6, 12–13). Interesting though it is, his hypothesis has now been abandoned, and with good reason, given our ignorance of liturgical history in the Second Commonwealth period. As noted in numerous points of the commentary above, our urge to identify an overall structure or pattern must be tempered by the awareness that the text has undergone a process of successive restructuring over a significant period of time.

Exegetically of equal importance as the internal arrangement of chs. 24–27 is their place and function in the book, in which respect the decisive point is their relation to the sequence of sayings about foreign peoples in chs. 13–23, especially the anti-Babylon poems (13:1–14:23; 21:1–10). We saw that in these poems historical acts of judgment adumbrate a more universal and cosmic doom. Right from the beginning we are told that on Yahveh's appointed day destruction will be visited not just on Babylon but on the earth (*'ereṣ*) and the entire world (*tēbēl*) (13:5, 11; 18:3). In a catastrophic event involving the sun, moon, and stars, as well as the earth (13:10, 13), the world will be depopulated (13:12, 15–16), sinners destroyed (13:9), and idolatry finally suppressed (17:7–8). Somehow in all of this there will be redemption for Judah and Jerusalem

(14:1–2, 32; 18:7; 21:10). The juxtaposition of these chapters with 24–27 can be taken to imply that what happens to the nations mentioned by name in chs. 13–23 instantiates and prefigures the general doom now being announced. And if this is so, we would be led to suspect that the anonymity of the doomed city often referred to in this section (24:10, 12; 25:2–3; 26:5; 27:10) is deliberate and that it represents a kind of composite of the named cities in the previous section or a symbolic Babylon as the embodiment of opposition and hostility to Yahveh's purposes (as much later in Rev 14:8; 18:2, 10). The entire section, therefore, hinges on the polarity between this city and the city of the righteous nation, the *civitas Dei* mentioned, surely not by coincidence, at the precise mid-point of the section (26:1–2).

While the links of chs. 24–27 with the preceding chapters are stronger than with those that follow, it is worth noting that chs. 28–34 conclude with a prediction of doom on the nations of the world, though now Edom has taken the place of Babylon, real and figurative, as the evil empire *par excellence*. Both nations embody the idea of chaos (*tōhû* 34:11 cf. 24:10); on the appointed day (34:8 cf. 13:6) both will revert to nature, the domain of wild animals and demons (34:11–15 cf. 13:20–22 etc.). Analogously to Babylon, Edom will also serve as a code name for oppressive power in texts from the intertestamental period and in the midrash.

So much, then, for the proximate context of these chapters. The extent to which the authors have drawn on the Isaian literary tradition beyond this immediate context can be gauged by citations, sometimes in the form of reinterpretations, together with less overt intertextual links with several other sections of the book. The most explicit instance is no doubt the reinterpretation of the song of the vineyard in 27:2–5 referring back to 5:1–7, but there are many others. The following list from ch. 24, by no means exhaustive, may serve to illustrate the extent of the borrowing from and remodelling of existing prophetic texts: 24:1 cf. Jer 51:2; 24:2 cf. Hos 4:9; 24:3 perhaps referring to an earlier prophecy, e.g., 13:5; 24:7–9 cf. 16:10–11; 24:13 cf. 17:6; 24:16 cf. 21:2 and 33:1; 24:17–18 cf. Jer 48:43–44; 24:20b cf. Amos 5:2a; 24:23b cf. Mic 4:7. However, this section has little in common with the so-called Deutero-Isaiah (chs. 40–55), and it does not seem at all likely that the Deutero-Isaian author had a hand in inserting it into the book or arranging and editing its contents (pace Williamson, 1994, 156–83). Thus, the motif of Jerusalem-Zion as a mountain occurs at intervals in these chapters (24:23; 25:6, 7; 27:13 (*har haqqodeš*), reappears in the last eleven chapters of the book (56:7; 57:13; 65:11, 26; 66:20, all *har qodšî*), but is absent from 40–55.

The occurrence of the phrase "perpetual covenant" (*běrît 'ôlām*) near the beginning (24:5) is also one of several indications of intertextual links with the Priestly version of the history of early humanity in Gen 1–11. We will take a closer look at these literary borrowings and interconnections at the relevant points in the commentary.

Some final remarks about the date of composition. Study of the language, vocabulary, themes, and tone of these chapters persuaded practically all critical readers as early as the first half of the nineteenth century (e.g. Vatke; Ewald) that they come to us from the time of the Second Temple. Once the designation "apocalypse" came into vogue, it was inevitable to associate them with Daniel, Enoch and the Sibylline texts. Duhm remarked, in fact (1892, 172), that Isaiah could as well have written the book of Daniel as Isa 24–27. According to Duhm, then, 24:7–12 reflects the conditions following the conquest of Jerusalem by Antiochus Sidetes in 135/134 B.C.E.; the city the devastation of which is celebrated (25:1–6; 26:5–6) is Samaria destroyed by Hyrcanus in 107 B.C.E. (Josephus, *Ant.* 13.280), and the gruesome fate of Moab (25:9–11) alludes to its conquest by Alexander Jannaeus some years later. Like the author of Daniel, the author of the core apocalypse was one of the *asidaioi* (*ḥăsîdîm*) and wrote to strengthen the eschatological faith of colleagues in a time of great trials.

For most readers the epigraphy of the Qumran Isaiah material rules out assigning these chapters to the late second century or, a fortiori, the early first century B.C.E. (Needless to say, other considerations would discourage dating them to the second century C.E., as van Gilse 1914, 167–93.) Nevertheless Duhm's approach to the issue of origin and authorship was highly suggestive and provided insights, which were taken up by Otto Plöger (1968, 53–78). Plöger detected a similarly sectarian voice especially in 24:14–16 and 26:20–21, while dating the bulk of chs. 24–26 more plausibly to the century of the Ptolemies. If these chapters were written, as Plöger claims, to serve as "a prayerbook for the eschatological groups" (1968, 66), comparison with the beliefs and sectarian attitudes evidenced in the last chapters of the book (especially 65:13–16; 66:5) would be rewarding.

For most commentators who have struggled with this intractable and uncooperative text, the issue of date has been inseparable from the identification of the anonymous city mentioned at intervals in it (24:10–13; 25:2; 26:5–6; 27:10–11). The commentary tradition exhibits a wide range of options. Since it is the only place referred to by name in chs. 24–27, Moab was an obvious candidate (as in Eissfeldt 1966, 323–27) but hardly more than a guess since the history of that region in the later period is almost a complete blank. Other proposals include Dibon in Moab, ca. 250 B.C.E. (Mulder), the Syrian citadel in Jerusalem, 147 B.C.E. (Ludwig), Carthage in 146 B.C.E. (Procksch), Samaria in 107 B.C.E. (Duhm). But increasingly the argument in favor of Babylon, based on the close association between 13–23 and 24–27, has come to the fore in recent scholarship. Babylon was conquered several times between the collapse of the Neo-Babylonian Empire to the final eclipse of the city in the Seleucid period, and each of these occasions has been identified by one or another commentator as the referent for these chapters: the conquest of the city by Darius in 521 (Ewald), by Xerxes in 482 (Lindblom; Vermeylen), and by Alexander in 331 (Rudolph). While it is possible that all of these events, and others unknown to us, have left their mark on the text, it seems likely that the point of departure was the fall of the city to Cyrus in 539. The first of several drafts of chs. 24–27 could therefore have been written at a time quite close to the composition of Isa 40–48.

A CURSE ON THE EARTH AND ITS INHABITANTS (24:1–13)

(Chisolm; Irwin; see also bibliography pp. 141–54)

TRANSLATION

i

24 [1]Observe, Yahveh is about to lay waste the earth[a] and split it open,[b]
contort its surface and disperse its inhabitants.
[2]Then it will be the same for priest as for people,[c]
for master as for slave,
for mistress as for female slave,
for the one who sells as for the one who buys,
for the lender as for the borrower,
for the creditor as for the debtor.
[3]The earth will be utterly laid waste,
utterly despoiled;
for Yahveh has spoken this word.[d]

ii

[4]The earth dries up and withers away,
the whole world languishes[e] and withers away,
the highest heaven languishes[f] with the earth.[g]
[5]The earth lies polluted beneath those who dwell on it,
for they have transgressed laws,[h]
disobeyed statutes,
violated the perpetual covenant.
[6]Therefore a curse has consumed the earth,
its inhabitants suffer for their guilt.[i]
Therefore the dwellers on earth dwindle,[j]
leaving but a few people.
[7]The new wine dries up,
the vine languishes,[k]
all the revellers[l] moan.
[8]The joyful beat of the tabor is stilled,
the shouting of the merrymakers hushed,
the joyful sound of the harp is stilled.
[9]No longer do they drink wine as they sing;
strong drink now tastes bitter to those who drink it.
[10]Chaos Town is broken down,
all its houses closed so that no one can enter.
[11]They cry out for wine in the streets,
all joy has reached its eventide,

gladness is banished from the earth.
¹²The city is left a shambles,
the gate lies broken in pieces.ᵐ
¹³This is how it will be in all the earth,
among all the peoples—
as when an olive tree is beaten,
and gleanings are leftⁿ when the harvest is over.

NOTES

ᵃ 1QIsaᵃ has *'ădāmâ* for MT *'ereṣ* cf. LXX *oikoumenē(n)* for the more usual *gē(n)*;
ᵇ the precise meaning of the verbs *bqq* and *blq*, chosen for alliteration, is not
entirely clear; see Wildberger (1978, 913) for different opinions;   ᶜ literally,
"it will be like people like priest"; reversal of the order is required by the sense
that social distinctions will lose their significance;   ᵈ though this longer
form is unique in Isaiah, as opposed to *kî YHVH dibbēr* 22:25; 25:8, it is present
in 1QIsaᵃ and 4QIsaᶜ and should be retained;   ᵉ *'umlĕlāh* omitted in LXX
but present in 1QIsaᵃ and 4QIsaᶜ; two verbs in the second semistich balance
the two in the first;   ᶠ read singular with 1QIsaᵃ, Syr., Vulg. for MT pl.;
ᵍ reading *'im hā'āreṣ*, "with the earth," for *'am hā'āreṣ*, "the people of the
land," and *hammārôm* (with the article) for MT *mĕrôm*;   ʰ 4QIsaᶜ has *tôrâ*
sing.;   ⁱ 1QIsaᵃ *vysmv*, "are destroyed," though the omission of *'aleph* is not
uncommon;   ʲ "dwindle" seems to be required by the context, though MT
hārû is obscure cf. 1QIsaᵃ and 4QIsaᶜ *hvrv* → *hrr*, "burn," "glow," usually used
metaphorically for anger. I follow G. R. Driver (1958a, 44), who appeals to Arab.
cognate *hāra*, "to be weak," assuming an otherwise unattested stem *hvr*, which
is admittedly speculative;   ᵏ 4QIsaᶜ adds *yshr* after *gpn*, perhaps influenced
by Joel 1:10, which has much the same vocabulary as our passage;   ˡ *śimhĕ-
lēb*, literally, "glad of heart," cf. 1QIsaᵃ *śvmhy-lb*;   ᵐ MT *šĕ'iyyâ* hapax, but
presumably → stem *š'h*, "to be desolate," cf. 4QIsaᶜ *šv'h*, "shoah";   ⁿ literally, "like gleanings when the harvest is over," an apparent adaptation of 17:6.

COMMENTS

Isaiah 24:1–3 is, formally, a self-contained unit introduced in a typically Isaian
manner (cf. 10:33; 19:1; 22:17; 30:27) and rounded off with an inclusion, a prophetic communication formula identifying the origin of what precedes rather
than what follows—though perhaps we should not exclude the possibility that
the word of Yahveh refers to an earlier prophecy, the fulfillment of which is
now in sight. The alternative reading of 1–6 as introductory to 7–9 with 10–12
and 13 as additions (Wildberger 1978, 915; followed by Clements 1980a, 200) is
less satisfactory since it relies on subject matter rather than on formal features.
To suppose that allusion to the city, its gate, and its streets (10–12) must be a
later addition is too restrictive of authorial licence and assumes, anachronistically, a clear distinction between city and countryside. "Chaos Town" (*kiryat*

tōhû) is not, in any case, a city like the cities addressed in chs. 13–23, for which the more common term *ʿîr* is used. It simply maps the point where one can speak of the breakdown of the distinctions on which social order rests; and in fact the term *tōhû* ("chaos") is often used in contexts suggestive of a breakdown of order and reversal of role performance (Isa 40:23; 41:29; Ps 107:40; Job 12:24). There is also no sudden change from natural to military disaster in 10–12. The place has become a ghost town peopled only by derelicts and drunks, its gate delapidated and rubble blocking access to houses and courtyards.

Throughout this section the meter consists in an irregular combination of bicola and tricola, confirming a suggestion made earlier that much that passes for verse in the book is closer to a kind of recitative or a high rhetorical and cadenced style reflecting declamatory public speech. This particular example of recitative achieves its effect through repetition, climactic parallelism, and alliteration. In 1–3 social upheaval is described in six paired opposites, while 4–13 exhibits five examples of synonymous or progressive parallelism (4, 5b, 7, 8, 11). In several cases, finally, it seems that alliteration or assonance has decided the choice of vocabulary (e.g. *bôqēq, bôlqāh* 1, *ʾābĕlāh, nābĕlāh* 4, cf. *bûqâ ûmĕbûâ ûmĕbullqâ*, Nah 2:11[10]).

In presenting this scenario of destruction and social upheaval the author has drawn on a variety of sources, including *written* prophecy. The phenomenon, which can be seen in all parts of the book, testifies to a new idea of the prophetic function. Its presence at this point is particularly clear if the asseveration with which 1–3 concludes ("for Yahveh has spoken this word") is taken to refer to earlier prophecy (e.g. 13:4–16). Thus the language of the first section (1–3) suggests familiarity with Nahum's vision of the destruction of Nineveh (see especially Nah 2:3[2], 10–11[9–10]), and the social leveling set out in 24:2 seems to have been suggested by a reading of Hos 4:9, identical with the first of the six paired opposites. A somewhat different way of conjuring up a situation of *anomie* comes to expression in 3:4–7 (boys and women will rule the land), a way of putting it that could have been familiar to the author from didactic writings of great antiquity. The Egyptian Teaching of Ipu-Wer, for example, laments that "poor men have become the possessors of treasures . . . all maid servants make free with their tongues . . . noble ladies are now gleaners and nobles are in the workhouse" (*ANET*, 441–42). In this instance the reversal encompasses the subversion of religious, social, and economic but not political order, no doubt reflecting conditions in the province of Judah at some point in the Persian or early Hellenistic period.

We are given a clue to another aspect of intertextuality, and perhaps also to the identity of the city to be referred to obliquely throughout chs. 24–27, in the allusion at the beginning to the dispersal of humanity, reminiscent of the tower of Babel story (verb *hēpîṣ* cf. Gen 11:4, 8, 9). The suspicion that the writer has in mind the early history of humanity as narrated in Genesis (in whatever form it then existed) is confirmed by the reference to the violation of a perpetual covenant (*bĕrît ʿôlām*, v 5 cf. Gen 9:16) as the cause of the earth's condition. The Isaian author appears to have understood the so-called laws of Noah as stated in Gen 9:1–7, especially the prohibition of shedding blood, in a different way from the Priestly author—namely, as stipulations attached to the perpetual covenant, the violation of which cancelled the divine promise not to destroy the earth a second time. Bloodshed pollutes the earth (cf. the Greek concept of *miasma*), bringing a curse on the one responsible, and causing infertility (cf. Num 35:33; Ps 106:38). That at this point the author is incorporating his own reading of the primeval history is also suggested by the title *kiryat tōhû* (Chaos Town, cf. the primordial *tōhû* of Gen 1:2), the diminution of the world's population (6b) signifying the annulment of the creation command to increase and multiply (Gen 9:1, 7), and perhaps also by the rather obtrusive emphasis on wine (7–11), reminiscent of the drunkenness of Noah and consequent curse on Canaan (Gen 9:20–27).

This train of thought will be pursued further in the following passage with the threat of another destructive deluge, an undoing of creation, chaos-come-again (24:18b cf. Jer 4:23–28). It seems permissible to conclude that the author has abstracted from the preceding indictments against nations and cities (13–23) and from other clues within the Isaian literary tradition as it then existed (especially 2:6–22) a somber view of the condition of humanity as a whole, setting them over against the prescriptions governing the new and damaged post-diluvial world in Israelite traditions about human origins. The concern to relate the fate of the earth to human behavior, a somewhat opaque idea for generations of commentators in the early modern period, can now in view of the environmental crisis be seen as an anticipation of one of the truly fundamental moral issues confronting humanity at the dawn of a new millennium.

DIES IRAE, DIES ILLA (24:14–23)

(Irwin; Niehaus; Sawyer 1993; T. M. Willis 1991)

TRANSLATION

i

24 [14] They lift up their voices,
    singing joyfully of Yahveh's majesty;
    they exult[a] more loudly than the sea![b]
    [15] Therefore give glory to Yahveh in the east,[c]
    in the western isles to Yahveh's name,
    Yahveh, Israel's God!
    [16] From the ends of the earth we hear the refrain
    "Glory to the Conquering One!" [d]
    But meanwhile I thought,
    "I have my secret, I have my secret![e]
    Woe to the unfaithful ones[f] who deal faithlessly,
    who deal with an utter lack of faith!"

ii

¹⁷Terror, the trap, the deep pit^g
await you who dwell on the earth!
¹⁸If you flee^h from the sound of the terror
you will fall into the pit;
and if you get out of the pit,
you will be caught in the trap;
for the sluicegatesⁱ of the sky are opened
and the earth's foundations quake;
¹⁹the earth is utterly shattered,^j
the earth^k is tossed about,
the earth^k shudders and shakes;
²⁰the earth^k reels like a drunkard,
swaying like a shelter in the wind;^l
its sins lie heavy upon it,
it falls, to rise no more.

iii

²¹On that day:
Yahveh will punish the hosts of the high heavens in the sky and the kings of the earth on the earth. ²²They will be herded together like prisoners^m in a deep pit and confined in prison. Then, after a long interval, they will be punished. ²³The moon will be put to shame and the sun abashed,ⁿ when Yahveh of the hosts inaugurates his reign on Mount Zion and in Jerusalem, revealing his glory in the presence of his elders.^o

NOTES

^a *Ṣahălû* perfect is unexpected after two imperfects, but the usual expedient of reading *ṣahălû* imperative obliges us to delete *ʿal-kēn*;   ^b dividing into two pairs of bicola: *hēmmāh yiśʾû/qôlām yāronnû//bigʾêôn YHVH/ṣāhălû miyyām* rather than following the Masoretic punctuation (with Athnah), which reads the first line as 3:3; *miyyām* can also mean "from (in) the west," but west would then be mentioned twice;   ^c LXX omits the difficult word *bāʾurîm* and Vulg. translates *in doctrinis* with Urim and Thummim in mind; 4QIsa^c *bvʾrym bʾrm kbvd* seems to derive from scribal error (dittography); rather than emending to *bāʾummîm*, "among the nations," or *bāʾiyyîm*, "in the islands (coastlands)," it seems more suited to the context to relate the word to *ʾûr*, "light," with the meaning "dawn" or "east";   ^d since *ṣaddîq* is never used of Yahveh as an epithet, it seems to fit the context better to take it in relation to *ṣĕdāqâ* = "victory," "vindication," frequent in later parts of the book (59:9, 16–17, 21; 61:10–11); see commentary ad loc.;   ^e *rāzî-lî, rāzî-lî* is a notorious crux, simply omitted by LXX; some assume a verbal stem *rzh*, "pine away" (RSV cf. Zech 2:11; Isa 17:4 Niphal and *rāzeh* = "thin," *rāzôn* = "emaciation"); I have followed several of the early versions (Lucianic, Syr., Symm., Theod., Vulg.) that presuppose the

Aram. *rāz*, "secret," cf. Tg. "the mystery of the reward for the righteous is visible to me, the mystery of the retribution for the wicked is revealed to me!" The repeated phrase, which is absent from LXX, may be a marginal gloss imparting a more explicitly apocalyptic color to the passage; see further the commentary; [f] for MT *'ôy lî bōgĕdîm* read *'ôy labbōgĕdîm*;   [g] *paḥad vāpaḥat vāpāḥ* (cf. Jer 48:43; Lam 3:47) is not easily rendered in translation;   [h] literally, "he who flees . . .";   [i] *'ărubbâ* = "window" gives entirely the wrong, even an absurd, impression: the word is used of openings in the sky through which rain was thought to pass (Gen 7:11; 8:2; 2 Kgs 7:2; Mal 3:10) but also of alcoves for doves, presumably not called upon to open windows (Isa 60:8), and of a hole from which smoke comes (Hos 13:3);   [j] for MT *ro'āh* read *roa'* with 1QIsa[b]; MT stems from dittography;   [k] *hā'āreṣ*, with article, as in 1QIsa[a];   [l] "in the wind" added to make the meaning clear;   [m] *'assîr* is missing from 1QIsa[a], LXX, and Tg., perhaps therefore a gloss on the hapax legomenon *'ăsēpâ*; 4QIsa[c] has *v'sp 'svp 's[yr]*;   [n] LXX reads *lĕbēnâ* = "clay brick" and *ḥômâ* = "wall," which make poor sense in the context (cf. the similar 13:10);   [o] reading *yikkābēd* for *kābôd* with LXX, Syr., Vulg.

COMMENTS

Since it has no introduction of its own, this passage could be read as a continuation of 1–13, though the allusion to joyful singing makes a very abrupt transition after merrymaking has just been brought to an end, and the only noise is that of people wandering about the streets looking for something to drink. That the passage ends at 20 is clear from the finality of the sentence "it falls to rise no more," echoing Amos 5:2, and the "on that day" formula that introduces 21–23. Moreover, the tectonic imagery of 19–20 corresponds to the language in the opening statement of the chapter. The opening stanza of this section (14–16) defies prosodic analysis; the second (17–20) has the usual alternation of tricola and bicola, indistinguishable from rhetorical utterance in prose; and the same is the case with the *bayyôm hahû'* addendum (21–23).

The unidentified participants in a liturgy praising the majesty, glory, and name of the God of Israel are certainly Jewish and are joined by their coreligionists in the eastern and western diaspora, reminiscent of "Assyria" joining with "Egypt" in the worship of Yahweh in a previous editorial scholion (19:23). In view of the prophetic author's inability to join in the liturgical euphoria, we should probably read the exhortation to praise Yahveh in song (15) as the participants addressing each other. Much the same liturgical vocabulary of praise occurs in the psalm with which the first section of the book is rounded off (12:1–6). In Isa 59:15b–20, devotees of Israel's God in the east and the west revere his name and glory, and Yahveh himself is presented as a victorious warrior, as here. This is one of the contexts in which the stem *ṣdq* connotes "victory" or "vindication" rather than "righteousness," and which therefore justifies the translation "glory to the Conquering One!" (*ṣĕbî laṣṣadîq*) in the present passage. We assume that the euphoria in Judah and the diaspora was occasioned by one of the many political crises occurring during the Persian or Hellenistic period from the conquests of Cyrus to those of Alexander and beyond, one that could be interpreted as a striking intervention of Yahveh on behalf of his people subject to foreign rule.

The account of the rejoicing is followed by one of the many occasions in which the seer emerges from the shadows of authorial anonymity and speaks in the first person. Some of these cases are simply aspects of the conventional authorial persona expressing real or simulated emotional responses (e.g. 15:5, 9; 16:9, 11) to situations or describing the reception of a revelation (e.g. 21:1–10; 22:14). But in other instances we may be hearing the voice of an apocalyptic seer addressing a group of disciples. The speaker's invitation to his own people to take refuge in view of the imminent judgment (26:20–21) is a case in point, especially since it follows a psalm praying for vindication for the righteous and punishment for the reprobate (26:7–19). We might also compare the self-referential statement in the present passage (24:16b) with the text referred to above (59:15b–20), since it ends with direct address to the seer promising the permanence of the prophetic spirit among his disciples (59:21). But the apocalyptic tone of the seer's utterance in our text and the woe pronounced on the faithless ones echo with particular clarity the address of the anonymous prophetic leader to those who tremble at Yahveh's word and anticipate the eschatological joy at Yahveh's imminent *parousia* in 66:5 (cf. 65:13–16). Taken together, these voices indicate the uneven progress of the Isaian tradition in the direction of the apocalyptic world view familiar from the book of Daniel and therefore raise the question in an acute form regarding the bearers of that tradition and the social situation in which it came to final expression. These issues will call for further and closer discussion in the commentary on the last eleven chapters of Isaiah.

According to the only other biblical occurrences of *rāz* ("secret"), in the book of Daniel (2:18–19, 27–30, 47; 4:6), this Persian loanword in Aramaic connotes information known only to God but revealed by God to chosen intermediaries, generally in a context of prayer, fasting, visions, and converse with angels. Implicit in this process is a God-endowed interpretative skill, the *interpretandum* being of many different kinds—a dream in the head of a mad king, ghostly writing that appears on a wall, or a prophetic text such as Jeremiah's prediction of seventy years' exile. In the present context, then (perhaps as read and understood by an anonymous glossator with an apocalyptic mindset) the seer would be claiming to know by divine inspiration the true meaning of what is transpiring and that the people celebrating liturgically are also, though unaware of it, under the judgment described in the following stanza, which takes over where 1–13 left off. We are reminded somewhat of the critical attitude to worship in 66:1–4 and the judgment pronounced on the "brethren" who oppose those who tremble at God's word in 66:5. The reason for the seer's refusal to join in the general religious euphoria is that he believes the celebrants to be unfaithful and has therefore presumably concluded that their liturgy is disingenuous or at least misguided. In a manner somewhat reminiscent of incantations or curses, the key verbal stem *bgd*, connoting infidelity, is repeated five times in v 16. It occurs elsewhere predominantly in the context of marital or familial rather than political relations (e.g. Jer 3:8, 11, 20; 12:6; Hos 5:7; Mal 2:10–11, 14–16), and its occurrence here was no doubt suggested by the "grim vision" about the betrayal of the treacherous one in the anti-Babylonian poem, where the same word occurs four times (21:2 cf. also 33:1).

The following stanza (17–20) reads more like the sequel to 1–13 than as the content of the mystery together with its *pešer*, analogously to the writing on the wall incident in Dan 5:25–28 (pace Niehaus). It begins forcefully with a scenario of inescapable perils—an unnamed terror, a pit, and a hunter's snare—one may survive one or another but not all three. The author has taken this topos out of its specific context in Jer 48:43–44 (*paḥad vāpaḥat vāpāḥ*), where it applies to Moab, and given it a general reference. It can perhaps be traced back to the triad of perils in Amos's account of the Day of Yahveh (5:18–20). Here the successive perils are represented by a lion, a bear, and a snake that make up an obstacle race no one can expect to survive. Following on the sequence of images in 1–13—the perpetual covenant, the curse, the depopulation of the earth—the focus then shifts to the great deluge and the opening of the floodgates of the sky (Gen 7:11; 8:2). A comparison between the account of the first creation (Gen 1:1–2:3) and the story of the great deluge (Gen 6:5–8:22) shows that the deluge is an act of uncreation, a return of the world to its watery *materia prima*, a reaffirmation of the chaos that always threatens to flood the narrow beachhead of order on which we live out our lives (cf. Jer 4:23–26). The force of this mythic scenario lies in its power to communicate the overwhelming scale of divine judgment under which humanity lies, combined with the central prophetic idea of a *remnant*; hence the frequent appearance of the deluge and the ark in Jewish and Christian preaching and iconography. The author then reverts to the earthquake imagery with which this section began (20 cf. 24:1).

Not content with the images of terrestrial destruction in 17–20, the author of the editorial addendum (21–23) presents a more comprehensive description of the cosmic end-event. The essential features of this apocalyptic scenario are: the imprisonment of celestial and terrestrial powers hostile to Yahveh's purposes, their punishment after an indeterminate period of time, and the final manifestation of the rule of God in Jerusalem. This scenario can be filled out by a reading of apocalyptic writings from the third century B.C.E., from which the earliest sections of the Enoch cycle probably derive, to the Christian book of Revelation in the late first century C.E. The heavenly hosts are the celestial bodies understood as animate, intelligent, angelic beings whose movements determine human destiny, an idea that persisted into the early modern period and still lives on in the practice of astrology. The idea is, of course, very old. Worship of sun, moon, and other celestial bodies was widespread in antiquity and quite familiar in Iron Age Israel (e.g. Deut 4:19; 17:3; Jer 8:2; 19:3; Zeph 1:5). The idea of hostile and malevolent celestial powers is also rooted in ancient cosmogonies and theogonies that narrate the theme of celestial rebellion (e.g. *Enuma Elish*, Hesiod). The writers of apocalyptic link this motif with prophetic history by assigning such powers as heavenly patrons to the nations of the world (e.g. *En.* 90:22–25; Sir 17:17; Dan 10:13, 20–21 cf. Deut 32:8–9).

The theme of the binding of these malevolent celestial powers, with whom the rulers of the nations are—in the apocalyptic world view—in league, is also well attested in apocalyptic writings (e.g. *En.* 18:11–19:3; 90:24–25; Jude 13; 2 Pet 2:4). The author of the Christian apocalypse, the book of Revelation, follows the Isaian text in presenting the hostile powers under their king, the angel Abaddon, imprisoned in a dark and bottomless pit (Rev 9:2, 11). There will be a lapse of time, estimated by the same apocalyptic writer as 1,000 years (Rev 20:1–3 cf. *En.* 91:12–17), between their imprisonment and the execution of the sentence. This interval allows for different baroque elaborations in apocalyptic circles and continues to provide occasion for speculation among readers of apocalyptic sentiment today. It ends, as our passage makes clear, with the establishment and universal acknowledgment of the rule of God throughout the cosmos.

The way in which this core metaphor of the kingdom of God has been formulated at the end of the passage (23b) provides an interesting example of intertextuality within the Isaian tradition (e.g. 52:7) and beyond. "Yahveh has inaugurated his reign" (*mālak YHVH*) is evocative of the opening acclamation of the enthronement psalms (Pss 93, 95–99), but in the present context it has become the climactic moment in a sequence of apocalyptic events. The author has also superimposed the event on the vision of the royal throne of God, the divine glory or effulgence (*kābôd*), granted to Moses, Aaron, his sons, and seventy elders in the account of the ratification of the covenant on another mountain, Mount Sinai (Exod 24:9–11). Since this vision is followed by a meal, it seems that the same train of thought is continued in the description of the messianic banquet in 25:6, which is therefore perhaps from the same hand. There is also continuity between concern with the great empires of Assyria and Babylon in the earlier stages of the history of the book of Isaiah and the scenario described in this passage, written long afterwards; for, the seminal concept of the kingdom of God, deeply and for many today problematically embedded in Jewish and Christian piety and prayer as it is, is the mirror-image of the great political empires, of political *imperium*, just as the City of God is the mirror-image of the unnamed alien city mentioned from time to time throughout this section.

THE ESCHATOLOGICAL BANQUET (25:6–8)

(Chilton 1987, 49–50; Martin-Achard 1956; Welten; Wodecki)

TRANSLATION

25 ⁶Yahveh of the hosts will prepare
for all peoples on this mountain

a banquet of rich food,
a banquet of wine well aged,
of food rich in marrow,[a]
of well-aged wine strained clear.
[7]Yahveh will destroy on this mountain
the mantle in which all peoples are wrapped,[b]
the covering cast over all the nations;
[8]he will swallow up[c] death for ever.
Then will the Sovereign Lord Yahveh wipe away tears from every face,
and remove the reproach of his people from all the earth;
for Yahveh has spoken.

NOTES

[a] Pual participle → a verbal stem *mḥḥ* related to *moaḥ*, "marrow";   [b] *lôt* hapax related to verbal stem *lvt* (cf. 1 Sam 21:10) followed by passive participle
hallûṭ for MT *hallôṭ*; 1QIsa[a] omits *hallôṭ*;   [c] read *ûbillaʿ* for MT *billaʿ* past
tense rather than Pual *ûbullaʿ*; the rendering in 1 Cor 15:54 reads passive and
lĕneṣaḥ as "in victory" (*eis nikos*) cf. 2 Sam 2:26 LXX.

COMMENTS

The sumptuous banquet described here enlarges on the earlier reference to
the meal of which the elders partook at Sinai (Exod 24:11), but it is also the
conclusion to the ceremony of the accession of Israel's God to the throne on
Mount Zion and in Jerusalem (24:23). Since therefore the passage belongs
quite clearly to the scenario described in 24:21–23, it may be helpful to comment on it before turning to the first of three psalms in 25:1–5.

The attempt to establish the existence of an ancient festival of the enthronement of Yahveh during the time of the kingdoms failed for lack of evidence,
not surprisingly, given the reluctance of ancient authors to describe liturgies,
but the idea of the kingship of Yahveh was certainly familiar and we can hardly
doubt that it was celebrated liturgically in some way, if not necessarily re-
enacted, probably at the Feast of Tabernacles–Sukkoth (Zech 14:16–17). *Enuma
Elish* (3:129–38) and the Ugaritic Baal texts (51 IV 35–59) also speak of ban-
quets following the victory and accession to the throne of Marduk and Baal,
respectively, and there can be no doubt that this association of ideas was quite
familiar.

Sharing a meal has always been one of the most effective means of achieving
and celebrating reconciliation and of bonding in general and one of the great
metaphors for well-being, and as such it has featured prominently in religious
representation and practice throughout the ages. The motif of the eschatological banquet, which makes its first appearance here, came into its own in the
later Second Temple period. In some versions the elect will feast on the flesh
of Leviathan (e.g. *4 Ezra* 6:52 cf. *En.* 60:24 and *b. B. Bat.* 74b), not improbably

an echo of the punishment of Leviathan in Isa 27:1. Groups with a strong eschatological orientation, such as the community for which the Qumran rule books were written, celebrated the banquet proleptically in their community meals (1QS II 17–21), and the theme is well represented in the gospels (Matt 8:11–12; 22:1–14). It is also part of the fuller and richer meaning of the Christian eucharist; we may recall Jesus' anticipation of drinking new wine with his followers in his Father's kingdom (Matt 26:29).

Description of the meal is limited to rich meats served with oil, marrow extracted from bones, and of course choice wine—a menu calculated to alarm the health-conscious today but standard fare for the well-heeled in antiquity. Since apocalyptic prose specializes in combining disparate and sometimes incongruous images, it is no surprise to pass from the banquet to the idea that the time for mourning is now past. Some commentators have taken the mantle or pall as a figure of spiritual blindness, perhaps influenced by Paul's midrash on the veil with which Moses covered his face (2 Cor 3:12–18). But if we read it in the context of the abolition of death and the drying of tears, it would more naturally suggest the end of a period of mourning for the dead, during which, as we know, it was the custom to cover the head and face (2 Sam 15:30; 19:5; Jer 14:13–14; Esth 6:12).

The following verse, announcing the eschatological overcoming of death, is often assumed to be a later addition (e.g. Clements 1980a, 208–9) on the grounds that belief in a spiritually and morally meaningful postmortem existence only emerged clearly in the late biblical and early postbiblical periods—whether in the form of a *selective* resurrection of the dead (Dan 12:2) or some form of astral immortality (Eccl 3:21), or the Orphic-Platonic doctrine of the immortality of the soul (Wis 2:33–34). But it is rather risky to draw conclusions of this kind on the basis of such partial and incomplete attestation, quite apart from the question whether we can claim that such an idea was unknown (e.g. to the authors of Pss 16 and 73) simply because not clearly articulated. Yahveh will *swallow* death: the wording seems to have been chosen to recall the old Canaanite myth of Mot (the Canaanite deity whose name means death) who swallows Baal at the beginning of the arid season and who is himself in due course overcome. The mythological undertow pulls the meaning of the phrase in the direction of death as something more than a punctual event, as a force of disorder, negativity, and aridity, morally and physically, in connection with which the actual dying of the individual is episodic and incidental. We shall have to come back to this theme in our discussion of the long poem at the center of this segment of the book (26:7–21).

The image of God wiping away tears from every face makes up for much but perhaps not all of the ugly violence perpetrated or contemplated in the name of the Deity in this present section (13–27). Here at least Martin Buber's "God of the sufferers" can be recognized, if only by those who have some acquaintance with suffering—for, as Kierkegaard put it, how can the God of heaven wipe away the tears of those who have never wept? It is also consoling, and perhaps remarkable, that *all peoples* are invited to the banquet, the mantle of mourning will be removed from *all nations*, and the tears will be wiped from *every face*, unconditionally, with no restrictions or reservations. Only then do we hear that the reproach of Israel, which in the context we assume to be subjection to foreign rule, will be removed.

THREE THANKSGIVING PSALMS
(25:1–5, 9–12; 26:1–6)

(Coste; Doyle; Emerton 1977; Gray 1911; Lohmann 1913a; 1917–18; Mowinckel; van Zyl 1960, 158–59; Vermeylen 1977, 363–69)

TRANSLATION

i

25 [1]Yahveh, you are my God.
I exalt you, I praise your name,
for you have carried out your wonderful counsels
firm and sure, formed ages since.
[2]You have reduced the city[a] to a heap of rubble,[b]
turned the fortified town into a ruin,
the citadel of the insolent is destroyed,[c]
never will it be rebuilt;
[3]for this will cruel peoples respect you,
ruthless nations[d] fear you.
[4]Truly you have been a refuge to the poor,
a refuge to the needy in their distress,
shelter from the rainstorm, shade from the heat
[5][for the blast of the ruthless is like a winter rainstorm,
like heat in a time of drought].[e]
You suppress the clamor of the insolent,[f]
[heat in the shadow of a cloud][g]
the singing of the ruthless is silenced.[h]

ii

[9]You will say[i] on that day:
"See, this is our God,
we have waited for him to save us.
[this is Yahveh, we have waited for him].[j]
Let us be glad and rejoice in his salvation."

[10a]For Yahveh's hand will rest on this mountain.

[10b]Moab will be trampled in its place[k]
as straw is trampled down in a cesspool.[l]

¹¹Moab spreads out his arms in the cesspool
as a swimmer spreads them out to swim,
but his pride will sink with each stroke that he takes.^m

¹²The lofty defense of your walls he has brought low;
he has thrown it down, brought it downⁿ to the ground,
down into the dust.

iii

26   ¹On that day
this song will be sung^o in the land of Judah:
"A strong city is ours!
He has set up its walls and ramparts^p as our salvation.
²Throw open the gates that a righteous people may enter,
a people that keeps faith!
³Those of trustful mind^q you keep in peace,^r
in peace, since in you they trust.^s
⁴Trust in Yahveh for ever,
for Yahveh^t is the rock of ages!
⁵He has brought low the dwellers on the height,
the lofty town he throws down,
throws it down to the ground,^u
lays it in the dust.
⁶It will be trodden underfoot,^v by the feet of the oppressed
and the tread of the poor.

NOTES

^a *Mēʿîr* is possible only if one reads *gāl* for MT *laggāl* cf. 17:1; read *hāʿîr* since it seems the scribe's eye may have wandered to *mēʿîr* in 2b; LXX reads plural (*poleis*);   ^b read *lĕgal* for M *laggāl*;   ^c reading *zēdîm* for MT *zārîm* cf. 13:11 *zēdîm* parallel with *ʿārîṣîm* and the reading *tōn asebōn* in some LXX MSS; I follow Emerton's proposal to emend *mēʿîr* to *mûʿar* Hophal participle → stem *ʿrr*;   ^d omitting *qiryat* to preserve grammar (pl. verb) and meter;   ^e the verse looks like a gloss since it repeats as if to explain the metaphors of rainstorm and heat, repeating *ʿārîṣîm, zerem, ḥoreb* from 3–4a cf. 4:6; for MT *qîr* ("wall") read *qor* ("cold," "winter"); unsuited to the context is "a storm of Kir," (Irwin 1984, 215–22);   ^f read *zēdîm* for *zārîm* (see note c above);   ^g absent from LXX, probably a gloss;   ^h read *yēʿāneh* Niphal for MT *yāʿăneh* with Syr. and Tg.;   ⁱ for MT *wěʾāmar*, "he will say," 1QIsa^a and Syr. read 2d person sing., the generic "you";   ^j absent from LXX, perhaps a gloss;   ^k *taḥtāv* can also mean "under him" (i.e. Yahveh); our rendering is supported by Tg. and cf. 2 Sam 7:10;   ^l *bĕmô madmēnâ*: *bĕmô* = preposition *bĕ* (cf. Ug. *bm*), but since *madmēnâ* allows a pun on the Moabite city Madmen(ah) (Jer 48:2) perhaps the unusual *bĕmô* is meant to recall Moab;   ^m on the meaning of

'orbôt yādāv one can only speculate; I have followed G. R. Driver (1937, 42–43) and Wildberger (1978, 971), who appeal to Arab. cognate *aruba*, "to be skillful," "crafty," and take it to refer to swimming; ^{n} 1QIsa^a has future *ygyʿ*; perhaps the scribe thought the total destruction of Moab had not yet taken place; ^{o} 1QIsa^a has *yšyr*, "he (one) will sing"; 4QIsa^c *yvšr* (*yûšar*) as MT; ^{p} Vulg. and Tg. read passive *yûšat* but MT *yāšît* is in order; 4QIsa^c has feminine pronominal suffix with *ḥômôt* and *ḥēl*; ^{q} *yēṣer sāmûk*, "a trustful disposition," should not be emended; ^{r} LXX and Syr. do not repeat *šālôm*, but 1QIsa^a and 4QIsa^c do; ^{s} for MT *bāṭûaḥ* LXX read 3d person pl. *elpisan* and Vulg. 1st person pl. *speravimus*; for passive participle meaning "trustful" cf. Ps 112:7 *bāṭûaḥ baYHVH*; ^{t} *bĕyāh*, omitted by LXX, contains the short and probably archaic form of the divine name; the juxtaposition of short and normal form is unattested and improbable; either original *yāh* is glossed with YHVH or *yāh* belonged originally to 3b (*bĕyāh bāṭûaḥ*) or we should reverse the order of *kî* and *bĕyāh* ("trust in Yahweh, forever in Yah . . ."), for which however there is no support in the versions or in 1QIsa^a and 4QIsa^b; ^{u} *yašpîlāh* is omitted by 1QIsa^a, LXX, Syr., but this type of repetition is common throughout the section; ^{v} omission of *regel* has overwhelming support from the ancient versions, but here also repetition is in keeping with the rhetorical style of the section.

COMMENTS

Similarity in form and vocabulary suggests that these three brief compositions may be reciprocally illuminating. They fall into the familiar pattern of psalms of praise, thanksgiving, and confidence, their brevity and editorial history notwithstanding. The first, the only one without an introductory rubric, is addressed to God in the language of praise familiar from the book of Psalms (*rûm* Polel, "exalt"; *ydh* Hiphil, "praise"). The sentiments are uttered by an individual ("my God" cf. Pss 31:15; 86:2; 118:28), but one who speaks for the congregation. The other two psalms express confidence in salvation (*qvh* Piel, *bṭḥ*), and all three go on to state the reasons for praising and having confidence in God which, as is so often the case in the canonical psalms, has to do with the discomfiting of enemies. Common to all three is the identification of the enemy as a city now thoroughly destroyed, one described throughout in similar language—it is walled (25:12) and fortified (25:2,12 cf. 27:10), but has nevertheless been destroyed, brought low, laid in the dust (25:11–12; 26:5). We also find here the familiar contrast between the poor, needy, and oppressed (25:4; 26:6) over against the ruthless and insolent (25:3–5).

The attempt to identify the unnamed city has obsessed commentators in the modern period but to little effect; as Duhm put it, it is a ghost no one can get hold of (Duhm 1892, 179). On this issue two observations are in order. First: the anonymity of the city in question is probably deliberate rather than fortuitous; second: in the course of the transmission of these texts several cities in succession could have qualified both early and late but probably not as late as the destruction of Samaria by John Hyrcanus in 107 B.C.E., as proposed by Duhm. Yet these texts continued to find new applications well into the post-biblical period. In paraphrasing 25:2b, for example, the Targumist asserts that "a temple of the Gentiles (i.e. Romans) never will be built in the city of Jerusalem," an assertion that must be dated prior to 136 C.E., when a temple to Jupiter Capitolinus was in fact erected in the city.

The presence of an anti-Moabite diatribe attached to the second and shortest of the three compositions (25:10b–12) does not provide a definitive solution to the identity of the city. Since as we shall see, and as most commentators agree, the diatribe is later than the psalms, it only implies that a scribe with a strong animus against Moabites identified the city referred to in the psalms with a city in Moab, presumably the capital city Dibon. It is more important to note the function of these short psalms in the section chs. 24–27 as a whole. If, as I suggested earlier, 25:6–8 is the continuation of 24:21–23, it will be seen that prophetic-eschatological discourse at the beginning and end of the section (24:1–23 + 25:6–8; 27:6–13) brackets a series of hymns that, for the most part, express confidence that Israel will survive the terrors of the *eschaton* so vividly described in the surrounding discourse. The effect of this arrangement is to create a balance between the certainty of catastrophic judgment and the possibility of salvation, which also implies a tension, never fully resolved, between the destiny of the nations of the world in general and that of the people of Israel. This does not amount to apocalyptic as generally understood on the basis of *Enoch* and Daniel, but we may find in these features of chs. 24–27 the seeds of apocalyptic.

Use of Isaian language in the first of the three compositions leads us to suspect that it is a psalm composed explicitly for its present context by a scribe familiar with the Isaian literary tradition as it existed at that time. Among the more obvious Isaian motifs are the plan or counsel of Yahveh (*'ēṣâ*, 9:5; 10:5–19; 14:24–27) and the presentation of Yahveh as a refuge and shelter from the storm and heat (4:6 and 32:1–2 using the same language). The forces hostile to the plan are also similarly described as ruthless, tyrannical, insolent, and clamorous (as in 5:14; 13:11) and their cities as destined to become a heap of rubble (*mappēlâ* 17:1; 23:13). One more indication, therefore, that the book of Isaiah is the product not of a haphazard accumulation of editorial accretions but of a consistently transmitted and developed textual and exegetical tradition.

The second psalm is very brief, composed as it is of two tricola distichs, depending on whether one retains "this is Yahveh, we have waited for him" as an original part of the psalm (25:9; see notes). The introductory rubric ("you will say on that day") links it with the fateful day of judgment described in 24:21–23 + 25:6–8, in relation to which it expresses an attitude of hopeful and trustful anticipation, an attitude much emphasized throughout the book (e.g. 7:9b; 30:18). The invitation to be glad and rejoice in the prospect of salvation in counterpoint to the surrounding threat of judgment adumbrates the theme of eschatological reversal heard frequently in the last chapters of the book: you, the elect, will rejoice while they, the reprobates, those who reject the eschatological faith, will be put to shame on judgment day (65:13–14; 66:5).

The following line (Yahveh's hand will rest on this mountain, 10a) belongs to the psalm neither metrically nor thematically. It links directly with the announcement of what will happen "on this mountain" in 25:6–8, a fairly clear indication therefore that the psalms were inserted into the pronouncements rather than the reverse. In general, the hand signifies powerful agency and, as a continuation of the thought in 6–8, Yahveh's hand is here extended over the mountain (Mount Zion) to protect, similar in some respect to the protective canopy and booth over Mount Zion mentioned earlier in the book (cf. 4:4–6). But in Isaiah the hand of Yahveh is more often than not raised in punishment (1:25; 5:25; 9:11; 10:4; 14:26–27), and it is this that may have prompted or justified the addition of the anti-Moabite saying that follows, especially in view of the mountainous nature of that country.

A world of thought and emotion separates the drying of tears and the prayerful and trustful expectation of salvation from the scene that follows (10b–12). We can only record with dismay the grotesque and deeply offensive image of a man being deliberately drowned in a cesspool and pushed back into it while trying to avoid an extremely ugly death. The only image in the book to compare with this for pornographic violence is that of Edomites being trodden into a bloody pulp in the winepress (63:3–6), the passage that proved to be the last straw for Friedrich Delitzsch in his rejection of the Old Testament. While Edom was to become a more prominent symbol of hostile and malign power down into the Greco-Roman period, hostility to Moab seems to have run even deeper. Only slightly less offensive than this version of Moab's end is the ethnic satire in which its incestuous origins are spoofed (Gen 19:30–38). Unlike Edomites, who could be admitted to the "assembly" (qāhāl) in the third generation, Moabites were excluded in perpetuum (Deut 23:4–9[3–8]). Whatever the origins of this law concerning qualifications for membership in the Israelite community, it was appealed to during Nehemiah's tenure of office as justification for excluding Moabites and Ammonites, though the book of Ruth demonstrates that, fortunately, more liberal and inclusive counsels could at times prevail.

We know too little about the history of Judean-Moabite relations in the period of the Second Temple to identify the situation that inspired the sentiments expressed here and in the late anti-Moabite saying in 16:13–14. In keeping with the historical background he assigns to the section in general, Duhm (1892, 182) argued that 25:10b–12 gave expression to Judean Schadenfreude at the conquest of Moab by Alexander Jannaeus, but we have seen that the presence of the passage in the great Qumran Isaiah Scroll would seem to rule out a date this late. More plausible would be the governership of Nehemiah around the mid–fifth century, when the province of Judah was asserting its autonomy against threats from several quarters, including the Transjordanian region.

The third of these brief passages is presented as a song or a hymn (šîr cf. Pss 30:1; 92:1; 137:3) and its "on that day" rubric locates it in the context of the great turning point in history with which the entire section is concerned. It begins rather like the psalms that are expressive of pride in Zion as the dwelling of the deity and a source of unbounded confidence (Pss 48, 76, 84, 87, 122) but proceeds to contrast a well-fortified and divinely blessed Jerusalem with a city defeated and undone together with its inhabitants. This is clearly the city referred to in the first of the three psalms and in 24:10–13. In describing its downfall the author uses similar language (26:5–6 cf. 24:10; 25:11–12), but the only additional information we are given is that it is situated "on the height" and will be trodden by the feet of the oppressed and poor, presumably Judean oppressed and poor. It will be obvious that this brings us no closer to identifying it.

The injunction to open the gates of Jerusalem so that a righteous people may enter is in keeping with the language used in processional psalms (Pss 24:7–10; 100:4; 118:19–20) and connects with the small moral catechisms that specify qualifications for participating in temple worship. The wording used at this point (26:2) is very close to Ps 118:19–20 ("open to me the gates of righteousness that I may enter through them. . . . This is the gate of Yahveh; the righteous will enter by it"). Psalm 24:3–4 is more specific, and Ps 15 contains a decalogue of moral requirements for those who aspire to take part in worship, an echo of which can be heard in Isa 33:15–16. The moral dispositions listed here are less specific. The author speaks of a "righteous people" (*'am ṣaddîq*), one who "keeps faith" (*šōmēr 'ĕmûnîm*). The word *ṣedeq* connotes conformity to the moral order as embodied in the laws and customs of a particular society, while in the context of morality the root *'mn* implies firmness, fidelity, reliabilty; one therefore speaks of a morally reliable witness (*'ēd 'ĕmûnîm* Prov 14:5) or messenger (*sîr 'ĕmûnîm* Prov 13:17). As elsewhere in Isaiah, trust—in God who is the Rock (*ṣûr* Deut 32:4; Ps 62:8)—is not just an attitude of the individual but must be operative in the political sphere. It is therefore noteworthy that in this psalm the gates through which the righteous are to pass are the gates of the city, not of the temple, as in the processional psalms. Whatever the origin of this composition may have been, we are reminded of Nehemiah's rebuilding of the city wall, his *synoikismos* (repopulation of Jerusalem), and the solemn consecration of the wall and the city (Neh 12:27–43) after overcoming opposition from many quarters. Here and throughout the book piety and politics are inseparable.

AN ESCHATOLOGICAL PSALM (26:7–27:1)

(B. W. Anderson; Birkeland; Day 1980; G. R. Driver 1956; Emerton 1980b; Fouts; Gordon; Gryson; Helfmeyer; Kaiser 1962; Levenson; Martin-Achard 1956; van der Ploeg; Rabin; Sawyer 1973; Schwarz; Virgulin; Wakeman)

TRANSLATION

26   [7]For the righteous the path goes straight;
you smooth out the course of the upright;[a]
[8]Yahveh, we look to you

for your just decrees to be manifest.[b]
To invoke your name[c] is the soul's desire.
[9]My soul yearns for you in the nighttime;
my spirit within me[d] seeks you eagerly,
for when your judgments are manifest on the earth
the inhabitants of the world learn righteousness.

[10]But if mercy is shown[e] to the wicked
they do not learn righteousness;
disregarding the majesty of Yahveh,
they pervert what is straight on the earth.[f]
[11]Yahveh, your hand is raised,[g]
but they do not see it;
may they be ashamed when they see your zeal for your people,
may the fire consume them that is destined for your enemies.
[12]Yahveh, decree well-being for us,
for all that we achieve is your doing.[h]
[13]Yahveh our God,
masters other than you have ruled over us,
yet your name, yours alone,[i] we invoke.
[14]The dead will not live,
the shades will not rise from the dead;
to this end you punished and destroyed them,
obliterating[j] their memory entirely.
[15]Yahveh, you enlarged the nation,
you enlarged the nation, won honor for yourself,
extending wide the boundaries of the land.
[16]Yahveh, in distress we sought you,[k]
your chastening has been a burden for us.[l]
[17]As a pregnant woman, when her time is at hand,
writhes and cries out in pain,
so, Yahveh, were we in your presence;
[18]we were with child, we were in labor,
but brought forth nothing but wind;
we do nothing to redeem the earth,
no one is born to people the world.[m]

[19]Your dead will live,
their corpses[n] will rise from the dead;
you that lie in the dust, awake[o] and sing for joy!
For your dew is a radiant dew,[p]
and earth will bring forth the shades of the dead.

[20]Come, my people, enter your rooms,
shut tight the doors behind you,

take cover for a little while
till the wrath has passed;
²¹for Yahveh will proceed from his place
to punish those who dwell on the earth
for their iniquity.
The earth will disclose the blood shed on it;
no longer will it cover up its slain.

27 ¹On that day:
Yahweh will punish with his sword
grim, mighty, and strong,
Leviathan the pursuing serpent,
Leviathan the twisting serpent,
and he will slay the dragon in the primeval sea.

NOTES

ᵃ The line is overloaded; 4QIsaᶜ has *yš*]*rv m'gl ṣdq*[; either omit *yāšār* with LXX, which in any case cannot refer to YHVH (as in RSV), or omit *ṣaddîq* and retain *yāšār* as misplaced parallel with *laṣṣadîq*; ᵇ reading *qivvînû* with 1QIsaᵃ, LXX, Syr., Tg., a reading adopted by Gray (1912, 443) following Bishop Lowth; ᶜ an attempt to render the sense of *zēker* as the divine name invoked in worship (cf. Exod 3:15); 1QIsaᵃ has *ltvrvtk*, reading "your name and your laws"; ᵈ I have resisted emending to *babbōqer*, "in the morning" (as does Wildberger 1978, 983), since it is unsupported by ancient versions and copyists; ᵉ 1QIsaᵃ has *yhvn* active for MT passive: "if he (YHVH) shows mercy to the wicked"; ᶠ *bā'āreṣ* for MT *bĕ'ereṣ*, with LXX, Syr., Tg.; ᵍ 4QIsaᵇ has *rvmh* active, but MT is supported by 1QIsaᵃ and versions (Vulg.: *exaltetur*); ʰ BHS proposes *kig-mūl* for MT *gam-kol* based on Syr., but the emendation is unnecessary; ⁱ *lĕbadkâ* for MT *lĕbad-bĕkâ*; ʲ 1QIsaᵃ has *vt'sr* for MT *vattĕ'abēd*; ᵏ reading 1st person pl. *pĕqadnûkâ* with 2 LXX MSS, Arab., Eth. versions; also therefore *lānû* for MT *lāmô* at the end of the verse; ˡ the translation offered for MT *ṣāqûn laḥaš mûsārkâ lāmô* is tentative: LXX *en thlipsei* cf. Tg. and Vulg. *in tribulatione*, perhaps presupposing a substantive → verb *ṣûq* Hiphil, "oppress"; some exegetes (e.g. Kaiser 1974, 209) emend to *ṣā'aqnû*, "we have called out"; *laḥaš* suggests necromantic practices and snake charming (verb: Ps 58:6; substantive: Isa 3:3, 20; Jer 8:17; Eccl 10:11) or whispering (Hithpael: 2 Sam 12:19; Ps 41:8 cf. Tg. "in their distress they were teaching the teaching of your law in a whisper," a clever allusion to a time of persecution); I have followed G. R. Driver (1937, 43), who proposed "burden" on the basis of Akk. cognate *laḥāšu*, "to be bowed down"; cf. Fouts: "O Lord in distress we paid attention to you; we poured out a whispered prayer while your discipline was upon us"; ᵐ cf. Wildberger "und Erdenbewohner kommen nicht zur Welt" (1978, 982), based on a rare meaning of *npl*, "fall," referring to birth; ⁿ MT *nĕbēlātî*, "my corpse," impossible with *yĕqûmûn*; perhaps a personal statement from the

scribe?;   ° 1QIsaᵃ *yqyṣv* future, as in LXX, Syr., Tg. (". . . will live and sing before you");   ᴾ lit., "a dew of lights"; for *'ôrâ* = "light" cf. Ps 139:12.

COMMENTS

The passage is not clearly delineated as a distinct unit, though in 7–19 an individual speaking in the name of the nation (as can be seen in the reference to
foreign rule in 13) addresses Yahveh in the familiar psalm style, while 20–21
reads like a follow-up to the psalm addressed directly to the congregation.
Isaiah 27:1 ("on that day") elaborates further on the punishment threatened in
26:20–21 (*yipqod*, "punish," 26:21; 27:1). Many exegetes have demoted verses
here and there to "secondary" status, but the reasons adduced are not always
compelling. To assume that allusions to post-mortem existence (14, 19) must
be insertions from a later hand begs several questions—about the date of composition of the unit to begin with and then the issue of belief or non-belief in
a meaningful postmortem existence throughout the biblical period. The bringing forth nothing but wind (18) *could* be read as an expansive comment on the
metaphor of birth pangs in the previous verse—a metaphor that will be much
developed in apocalyptic circles—but it could just as well be a continuation of
the same train of thought by the same author.

The passage is often classified as a psalm of communal lament. The speaker
does indeed do some lamenting for past failures and present unsatisfactory situations (13, 17–18), but there is also a meditative side to it that brings to mind the
so-called wisdom psalms (Pss 49, 62, 73, 91, 112). We are alerted to this aspect of
the composition in the opening verses, with their heavy concentration of language from the didactic and aphoristic literature—*'ōraḥ* ("path"), *ṣaddîq* ("righteous," "innocent"), *yāšār* ("upright"), etc. It is, in any case, a literary imitation
of familiar liturgical genres rather than a psalm in the strict sense of the word.
The initial expression of confidence in God and in divine approval for the righteous (7–11), mixed with anxiety about the congruence of divine with human
ideas of justice, turns to a dominant note of regret (12–18) in which the principal gravamen is foreign domination. In its penitential survey of the nation's
history (all the major verbs are in the past tense) it can be compared with 63:7–
64:11[12], which also laments foreign rule and in which God's deeds of mercy
(*ḥasdē YHVH*) are the counterpart to God's *mišpāṭîm* (deeds that manifest the
divine justice) in our poem. Similar in these respects are Ezra 9:6–15 (especially 7–9) and Neh 9:6–37 (especially 30–31, 36–37), which also lament and
decry subjection to foreign rule; later still, the Qumran *Words of the Heavenly
Luminaries* (4QDibHam = 4Q504). Clearly, this rueful contemplation of a history of infidelity ending in disaster is characteristic of prayer and piety throughout the Second Temple period. Then, following the accepted model, the psalm
concludes with a *Heilsorakel*, an assurance of ultimate well-being (19).

If *apocalyptic* is defined with reference to the book of Daniel as paradigmatic, this composition is lacking some of the essential elements of apocalyptic noted in the introductory remarks on chs. 24–27. Moreover, the perspective

is still that of the righteous nation as a whole over against foreign nations rather than a segment of the nation, the "elect," over against "brethren" who reject the eschatological faith or the version of it adhered to in the group (cf. 66:5). On the other hand, the universalizing note is sounded at least as clearly here as elsewhere in chs. 24–27. The suffering and lamenting people are contrasted with the world (*tēbēl* 9, 18) or the entire earth (*'ereṣ* 21), reminiscent of the "Great Arraignment" of 2:6–22, with its frequent allusions to humanity (*'ādām*) as a whole (2:9, 11, 17, 20, 22). The poem therefore encompasses the destiny of Israel within a broadly universal perspective. Its denial of mercy to the wicked in the final accounting, a frequent theme in apocalyptic, also reflects the request that God *not* forgive in 2:6–22 (26:10; 2:9 cf. 27:11), and the final injunction to take cover during the time of wrathful judgment points in the same direction (cf. 2:10, 19, 21). The image of judgment by fire at the beginning and end of the book (1:31; 66:15–16, 24) is also represented here (11). Perhaps most indicative of a peculiarly Isaian kind of eschatological thinking is the idea of looking to and waiting for God, which means waiting for vindication, for God's righteous acts of judgment (*mišpāṭîm* 8–9 cf. 58:2), God's interventions in human affairs, and especially God's final intervention, to be made manifest. Comparison with 59:9–20, a similar complaint occasioned by the non-appearance of an anticipated divine intervention in Israel's troubled history followed by an assurance of ultimate salvation, places 26:7–21 in the context of the delay in the *parousia*, notoriously problematic for early Christians, and the paramount need for trust and an attitude of positive patience. This attitude has been brought into clearer focus in recent decades by appeal to the theory of cognitive dissonance—namely, in terms of response to the discomfirmation of the sustaining beliefs and expectations of a particular group. We shall have occasion to return to this theory in our reading of the third and final section of the book.

The poem fits the context as an extended reflection on what is implied in the earlier reference to a "righteous nation" (26:2 cf. "the way of the righteous," 26:7). It opens in the manner of the so-called torah-psalms, with more or less alternating three- and two-stress groupings and, as noted above, a heavy concentration of terminology from the didactic and aphoristic literature ("righteous," "wicked," "path," "track," "make straight," "righteous judgments," etc.). The same vocabulary occurs in the torah-psalms, beginning with Ps 1, but it is also of frequent occurrence throughout Isaiah. In these opening verses repetition serves to bind together ideas of justice and righteousness and the expectation of response in the form of vindication. Looking to God to intervene is one of the most characteristically Isaian motifs. Waiting for God implies waiting for vindication, the restoration of a just order, in the first place by punishment on the obdurate through "righteous acts of judgment." It has often been pointed out (e.g. by Fackenheim, 1990) that, while our experience of history no longer permits a naive appropriation of this view of how divine justice works within human history, it must still leave intact the demand for justice as an essential condition for a meaningful faith. But we may readily admit the danger lurking in this claim to be God's righteous people when it is linked with the demand that punishment be visited on "the others."

Literally translated, 8b reads "the desire of the soul is for your 'name' (*šēm*) and your 'memorial' (*zēker*)." The *zēker* is The Name as recited liturgically (cf. the verb *hazkîr* in 26:13 and often elsewhere with reference to the liturgical pronouncing of The Name), evoking the revelation to Moses in the burning thornbush—"this is my name forever, this is my *zēker* for all ages" (Exod 3:15). It seems that the pronouncing of the divine name, the *zēker*, in the context of a solemn act of worship (e.g. Pss 30:5[4]; 97:12; 102:13[12]; 135:13 cf. Hos 12:6) was for many the climax of religious experience in Israel.

The poem continues with the lament proper and the expression of assurance in a better future (12–19). There is, first, an implicit plea for God to intervene in the apparently random and morally chaotic jumble of human affairs. While 9–10 is textually problematic, the point seems to be that the nations of the world, the "others," will only acknowledge the hand of God and therefore the necessity of pursuing a moral line of action, if chastened by disaster, by "acts of God," here also symbolized by the hand raised to strike. The historical theme is then pursued in a somewhat uneven fashion. If the expansion of the nation and its boundaries (15) refers to a Davidic-Solomonic empire viewed through the prism of heroic legend, the foreign rulers might be taken to refer to the Pharaohs of the Egyptian oppression. But a more generalized view of the past with its succession of oppressive colonial powers seems to be preferable, and the expansion of the nation as referring to the ancestral promise with its great nation theme (Gen 12:1–3), a theme that comes increasingly into view within the developing Isaian tradition (e.g. 54:1–3). The consignment of these hostile powers to death and oblivion was exemplified earlier by the shades of the dead (*rĕpā'îm*; see commentary on 14:9) receiving the Babylonian oppressor in Sheol or Hades (14:9–20). Sheol as the land of no return, of oblivion, is also of course a theme that runs through many of the psalms (e.g. 49:10–20), where the impossibility of praising God in the postmortem state is used to motivate the Deity to maintain the supplicant in life (Pss 6:5; 30:10[9]), a naive but touching aspect of biblical prayer.

The promise of life beyond death (19) may be read as the response to the situation described in 16–18, a situation of distress expressed in the symbolic language of labor pains (cf. 13:8). It therefore conforms to the pattern of the lament psalms, which end with an assurance of redress or vindication delivered by a member of the temple personnel, perhaps a cult prophet. That the first part of the verse has suffered in transmission is fairly obvious; literally translated it would read "your (sing.) dead will live, my corpse they will rise . . ."; furthermore the LXX translator and the 1QIsa^a scribe have changed the following injunction addressed to the dead to future tense, presumably as an affirmation of their belief in the resurrection of the dead. That textual corruption seems to be the fate of passages deemed to be religiously controversial is hardly surprising. To take another example, Job 19:25–27 ("I know that my redeemer lives . . ."), no doubt the best-known passage in the book of Job, is also one of the most textually corrupt. That Israelite religion is characterized by the absence of belief in a meaningful postmortem existence, in keeping with Mesopotamian ideas and in contrast to ancient Egyptian religion, is part of the conventional wisdom that hardly needs documenting. This *opinio communis* calls for qualification, however. It is arguable, in the first place, that the frequent denial of a meaningful afterlife, especially in Psalms (e.g. Pss 49:10–20; 88:5, 10–12; 115:17), reflects polemic against ancestor cults and necromantic practices rejected by Deuteronomic and Priestly orthodoxy but practiced at all times during the biblical period. It is also arguable that, while the idea of individual resurrection is not clearly attested before the persecution launched by Antiochus IV (Dan 12:2), a less clearly delineated conviction of survival after death was emerging long before that time. We detect something of this in the experience of worship here and there in Psalms (e.g. Ps 73:17, 21–28), in the conviction that Yahveh is God of the living whose gift is life, and the demand for justice as an absolute precondition for faith.

The assurance that *your* dead will live (19) but that *their* dead will not (14) suggests that the idea of Yahveh's people returning from the dead was also intended metaphorically. But one has the impression that "corpses" (M has "my corpse," *nĕbēlātî*) has displaced "shades" (*rĕpā'îm*) in order to bring out belief in individual, physical resurrection more clearly; and if this is so the text in its final form would express this belief. The language is familiar: death is sleep (Ps 88:11; Jer 51:39 cf. Matt 27:52), the dead are consigned to the dust of the earth (Gen 3:19; Pss 7:6; 22:16, 30; Job 21:26). The second half of the verse shifts to the image of dew revivifying and fructifying the dry earth. Together with rainfall, dew (understood as a kind of precipitation) was an essential feature of the ecology of Mediterranean rim countries. The good people of Ugarit worshiped a goddess of dew (*ṭly*), and no curse more lethal than the withholding of rain and dew could be thought of (2 Sam 1:21; 1 Kgs 17:1). Since the verse is addressed to Israelites (Judeans), there is perhaps in the reference to radiant dew (literally, "a dew of lights") a hint of the ultimate transformation of the natural order.

The psalm is rounded off with an admonition to take cover in preparation for the imminent destructive judgment to be visited on all the (other) inhabitants of the earth (20–21). The theme appears to be taken from the "Great Arraignment" towards the beginning of the book (2:10, 19, 21). If read as strictly continuous with the preceding verse, the injunction to enter their rooms could refer to the period in which the dead wait in their graves for the final resurrection. This idea is expressed in later apocalyptic writings (e.g. 2 Esd 4:35; 7:32, 95) but, unlike *miškāb* ("bed" 57:2), *ḥeder* ("room") nowhere occurs in Biblical Hebrew as a metaphor for *qeber* ("grave," "tomb"), and 20–21 is not part of the psalm. There is also no clear indication that the writer had the closing of Noah's ark (Gen 7:16) or the last of the Egyptian plagues (Exod 12:23) in mind (as Vermeylen 1977, 373). The message is clearly one designed to strengthen the wavering faith of the community in an intervention of God, the final theophany, the "singularity," which is delayed only for a little while but which is imminent; the scribe simply states this without attempting to explain it. When it happens, a just order will be established, sinners will be punished, and the earth will render up the blood of the innocent which it now conceals (cf. Gen 4:10).

The final addition to the composition, another "on that day" scholion (27:1), restates the punishment (verbal stem *pqd*) predicted in 26:20–21 in mythological terms. Exegetes have worried over this brief verse like a dog with a bone: Does it refer to three, two, or one embodiment of evil, disorder, and negativity? Does it allude cryptically to world empires (Assyria, Babylonia, Persia, Macedon) or individuals (following the Targum to this verse, which mentions an unnamed Pharaoh and Sennacherib)? Do the epithets for Leviathan refer perhaps to the Tigris and Euphrates? It does not seem either necessary or advisable to postulate three monsters on the basis of the three attributes of Yahveh's sword (grim, mighty, strong). Furthermore, Leviathan is mentioned twice, and the two epithets used of it occur in the same order in the mythological texts from Late Bronze Age Ras Shamra–Ugarit (*ltn btn brḥ/btn ʿkltn*: Baal cycle 67:I 1–3; ʿAnat III 35–39) with the additional information that, like the Hydra, this creature had seven heads (cf. Ps 74:12–17). It is less clear that the dragon (*tannîn*) in the primeval sea is a distinct entity, since the word seems to have a more generic meaning and occurs in the plural in Ps 74:13. Elsewhere both Tannin and Rahab, but not Leviathan, occur as code names for Egypt (Isa 30:7; Ezek 29:3; 32:2). There can be little doubt that, in the context of 13–27 as a whole, a *political* connotation is present and intended, but the introduction at this point of the ancient motif of the cosmic conflict and victory of the creator-deity suggests that the scribe has in mind the final overcoming of evil as a metahistorical and metaphysical force.

In keeping with the tendency in post-destruction compositions such as Job to "philosophize by means of myth," as Plato claimed to be doing in *The Republic*, 27:1, admirably encapsulates the essence of the "message" conveyed in a variety of ways in chs. 13–27. We recall that even before focusing on specific political entities and situations, this section presented the prospect of destruction and the unraveling of the political and social order on a universal scale (13:5 cf. 24:1–13, 17–20). The scenario was filled out with the old motif of the Day of Yahveh (13:6–13 cf. 22:5; 24:21–23) and with images drawn from the fund of ancient Canaanite myth—Babylon as Helel ben Shahar (14:12–14) and Yahveh swallowing Death, thereby reversing Mot's swallowing of Baal (25:7). The durability of these images will be appreciated by anyone familiar with apocalyptic writings from later Judaism and early Christianity. Like the dragon (*tannîn*) in our text, the monsters of Daniel's great vision and the Beast of Revelation emerge from the primeval sea (Dan 7:2–3; Rev 13:1). The anxiety induced by these unnerving images is assuaged somewhat by the thought of Leviathan as meat on the hoof (4 Esd 6:49, 52; *b. B. Bat.* 74b) or as the plaything of the deity (Ps 104:26)—according to one whimsical rabbinic dictum, God plays with him three hours a day (*b. ʿAbod. Zar.* 3b). But no one can doubt the intense, almost Manichean sense of evil behind these representations. It has long been recognized that the conflict with monsters at the end of time corresponds to the cosmogonic victory of the deity at the beginning (cf. Isa 51:9–10). These creatures therefore stand for embodiments of the primordial chaos, which is restricted by the creative act but is never, in our historical existence, fully overcome and therefore always a recurring threat to the well-being and stability of the created order (Levenson). As we look back on one of the most horrific centuries in human history (at this writing, December 31, 1997), we may find this a not inappropriate way of representing the persistent power of evil in the world.

THE VINEYARD REVISITED (27:2–6)

(Alonso-Schökel; Jacob; Robertson; Sweeney 1987)

TRANSLATION

27 ^{2}On that day:
A lovely^a vineyard, sing about it!^{b}
^{3}I, Yahveh, am its guardian,
I water it all the time
lest any harm come to it;^{c}
^{4}I hold no grudge against it.^{d}
If it gives me thorns and weeds,
I will wage war against it,^{e}
burn it all up;^{e}
^{5}so let it cling to me for protection,
let it make peace with me,
let it make peace with me.

^{6}In days to come^f
Jacob will take root,
Israel will bud forth and blossom,
filling the whole world with fruit.

NOTES

^{a} Reading *ḥemed* with BHS and LXX *kalos* rather than *ḥemer* = "fine wine" (BHK: Leningrad Codex) and cf. 1QIsa^a *ḥvmr*; for the expression see Amos 5:11 *karmê-ḥemed* and Isa 32:12 *sĕdê-ḥemed*; ^{b} feminine suffix is unusual since *kerem* is masculine, as in 5:1–7, though Lev 25:3 may be an exception; perhaps the author was thinking about the land of Israel (*'ereṣ* fem.); ^{c} reading *yippāqēd* Niphal (cf. Num 21:17) for MT *yipqod*, which requires a subject; ^{d} literally, "I have no wrath"; however, at this point the real problems begin: LXX *teichos* = "wall" → *ḥômâ* (cf. Syr.), leading in a direction quite different from MT; NEB "but I get no wine," following G. R. Driver (1958b, 133–35), who emends to *ḥēmâ*, on the assumption that this could be another word for wine cf. *ḥemer* (Deut 32:14); it seems better on the whole to stay with MT;   [e] feminine suffixes; see note b above;   [f] read *bayyāmîm habbā'îm*, "in the days to come," for MT *habbā'îm*.

COMMENTS

"On that day" passages are generally appended to the text immediately preceding as commentary or as extending the horizon of the text into the future. This is not apparent in the present case, however. Duhm (1892, 189) concluded that 27:2–5 must have been in the margin of the scroll and thence introduced accidently into the text, while Day suggested that dependence of 26:17–27:11 on Hos 13:13–14:10 might explain its textual disconnectedness—though in fact the similarity is limited to 27:6 (cf. Hos 14:6–8[5–7]). The verb *pqd*, "punish," of frequent occurrence in this section (13:11; 23:17; 24:21, 22; 26:14, 16, 21; 27:1, 3), provides a catchword link with the prediction of the punishment of Leviathan immediately preceding (7:1), but otherwise there is no overt connection. The passage opens with an invitation to the poet's audience to break into song about Yahweh's vineyard, rather like the invitation to sing about a well in Num 21:17, in which the same verb (*'nh* Piel) appears. Its inclusion could have been suggested by the "song of the city" (26:1), and it does in fact serve in its context as another expression of Yahveh's concern for Israel's ultimate well-being, especially if the thorns and weeds refer metaphorically to prohibited cult practice (cf. 27:7–13). Furthermore, the withdrawal of Yahveh's anger (*ḥēmâ*, here translated "grudge") from his vineyard could *in context* be referred back to the apocalyptic wrath (*za'am*) spoken of in the preceding poem (26:20).

It is hardly surprising that Israel as a whole or either Israel or Judah is often presented under the agricultural image of a vineyard (cf. 1:8; 3:14; Hos 10:1; Jer 2:21; 5:10; 12:10–11; Ezek 15:1–5), but the present passage is clearly meant to be read in relation to the song of the vineyard in 5:1–7. The vineyard is flourishing (cf. the "hillside rich in soil"), Yahveh as vintner waters it sedulously—that is, Yahveh provides the rain denied earlier (perhaps a hint at the Garden of Eden here; Gen 2:5–6), but the metaphor is left behind as he waits for *šālôm*, "a good relationship," rather than *mišpāṭ ûṣĕdāqâ*, "justice and righteousness." "Thorns and briers" is a peculiarly Isaian topos (5:24; 7:23–24; 9:17[18]; 10:17; 32:12–13), one that could easily be taken to refer to foreign invaders or opponents in general, especially in view of the odd image of going out to battle against weeds and such—which Wildberger compares to dropping bombs on ants (1978, 582). Reasonably, therefore, Jacob (1970, 328) suggests a reference to the Samaritan opponents of Nehemiah, and Kaiser (1962, 225) identifies them as Samaritans *tout court*. But in the vineyard song the thorns and weeds stand for the failure of the vineyard itself, an internal process of decay and degeneration, and this would seem to make the best fit here. In any case, 27:2–5, read as a radical revision or eschatological abrogation of 5:1–7, presents a theologically interesting case of development within the Isaian tradition.

Rather than serving as introduction to 27:7–11, with which it has nothing in common (pace the 1QIsa[a] scribe, who left a space after 27:5, and some other commentators), 27:6 should be read as a further comment on 27:2–5, using the same agricultural images of taking root, budding, blossoming, and extending the care of Yahweh for his plot into the distant future.

ONCE AGAIN, AND FINALLY, THE DESTINY OF THE CITY AND OF GOD'S PEOPLE (27:7–13)

(Day 1992; Galling 1962; Kessler 1960, 170–72; Plöger 1968, 71–75)

TRANSLATION

27   [7]Did God[a] strike Israel[b] like those that struck him?[c]
Or is Israel[b] slain, as those that slew him lie slain?[d]
[8]By driving her out, by sending her away,[e]
 God contended[f] with her,[g]
removing her with a fierce blast, as when the east wind blows.
[9]By this, then, is Jacob's iniquity purged,
this it is that removes his sin, and all that comes of it:[h]
when he shall have treated all the stones of his altars
like limestone blocks that have been crushed to powder,
with no Asherah pillar or incense altar left standing.
[10]The fortified city is solitary,
an abode[i] now abandoned, deserted like the wilderness;
there calves will graze,
there they will lie down and strip off[j] the branches;
[11]when the boughs dry out they are broken off;
women come by and light their fires with them.
For this is a people deprived of understanding;[k]
therefore the One who made them will show them no mercy,
the One who formed them will not regard them with favor.

[12]On that day:
Yahveh will thresh out the grain[l] from the basin of the Euphrates to the Wadi of Egypt; and you, people of Israel, will be gathered in one by one.

[13]And on that day:
A great ram's horn will be blown; those who were lost in the land of Assyria, and those dispersed in the land of Egypt will come and worship Yahveh on the holy mountain, in Jerusalem.

NOTES

[a] "God" is supplied for the masculine subject of the verb and masculine suffix to render intelligible the reading proposed;   [b] for the same reason "Israel" is supplied for the suffix of *makkēhû* and the subject of *horāg*;   [c] literally, "did he strike him like the striking of the one who struck him?"; LXX *plēgēsetai kai* . . . presupposes Hophal *hukkāh*, "was he struck down," with the masculine suffix detached from the verb and attached to the next word, *'im*;   [d] in agreement with LXX and Syr., 1QIsa[a] reads *hvrgyv*, active participle for MT *hărugâv*, "his slain," i.e., those slain by him; this reading is accepted by many modern commentators, but it is not required and does not give a better sense, e.g. "or has he been slain by his slayers?" (Kaiser 1974, 226), "or did he murder it as his murderers were murdered?" (*sic*) (Wildberger 1978, 588);   [e] the problems continue in this verse, in the first place the change from masculine to feminine suffixes; BHS takes *běsalḥāh* to be a gloss on the obscure hapax legomenon *běsasě'āh* but without compelling reason on the grounds of sense or meter; *sasě'āh* (pointing dubious) apparently understood by Tg. and other ancient versions in relation to *sē'â*, "a measure" (third of an ephah), giving the meaning "measure by measure," "little by little," which might be taken to refer to successive deportations and is preferable to explaining with reference to an Arab. cognate *sa'sa'*, used of driving pack animals (G. R. Driver 1928, 371–72); context and meter counsel a word with a meaning similar to *šalḥāh*;   [f] reading *yěrîbennāh* for MT 2d person *těrîbennāh*;   [g] the change to feminine suffixes is sudden but not unprecedented; perhaps with reference to Jerusalem/Zion;   [h] an attempt to render *věkol-pěrî*, "and all its fruit," relocated at the end of the verse; it is difficult to see how it could be a gloss on *hāsir* (BHS); [i] *nāveh* (4QIsa[f] *nhvh* but 1QIsa[a] is identical with MT), often with this meaning (e.g. Exod 15:13; 2 Sam 15:25; Ps 79:7; Isa 32:18; 33:20) in addition to "meadow," "pasture";   [j] translating *killāh* (or *kālāh, kālû*), literally, "finish off";   [k] pl. *bînôt* only here;   [l] reading *šibbolet mēhanāhār*; 1QIsa[a] has *mšbl* masc. for MT *miššibbolet* fem.; in view of the verb *ḥbṭ* (cf. Deut 24:20; Judg 6:11; Ruth 2:17) the meaning assigned is to be preferred to "stream of water," as in Ps 69:3, 16.

COMMENTS

This is one of the more obscure pericopes in the book for the text critic and translator, not to mention the reader who is simply looking for a coherent line of thought, argument, or imagery. The translation must therefore be regarded as tentative. The only formal divisions occur with the two "on that day" addenda (12, 13) dealing with return from the diaspora and the eschatological reintegration of scattered Israel. If, with several commentators, we take the fate of the unnamed city to be the main theme, obvious solutions would be either to bracket 9 as interrupting the account of the city's destiny or to rearrange the order of verses (as NEB does in the order 7, 9, 10a, 8, 10b). But obvious solutions are not always the best ones; if we retain the order of MT we can trace a thread of meaning at least through 7–9, to the effect that the historical judgment through which Israel (Judah) has passed differs from God's judgment on the nations, especially Babylon. Moreover, the judgment on Israel has redemptive meaning as an expiation or collective purging of guilt and spiritual failure, comparable therefore to 40:1–2, which represents the exile as "doing time" for past sins. And, finally, the efficacy of the expiatory suffering at the hands of God is contingent on the complete abjuration of alien cults.

The proposal is therefore to read these opening statements as a historical retrospective, another attempt to wrest meaning from the disasters through which the people of Judah have passed. The reference is, first, to the population (masc. suffixes in 7), then to Jerusalem (fem. suffixes in 8), then finally to Jacob explicitly (9). The rhetorical questions require answers in the negative: Israel's punishment, a beating by God, a kind of dying, is not comparable to the punishment inflicted on other nations; it is severe but not terminal. It would be consonant with the section as a whole to refer this metaphorical language to the disaster of 586 B.C.E. and the deportations—being driven out (from their land) by a blast from the east, i.e., from Babylonia. The following verse (9) then insinuates the reason for the disaster in keeping with standard Deuteronomistic thinking (e.g. 2 Kgs 17:7–12), laying down the conditions under which the historical consequences of Israel's guilt could be purged—namely, the removal of all idolatrous cult objects.

There is nevertheless some confusion of images in these opening lines (7–8)—being struck down by an avenging deity, slain but not entirely, driven along like a pack animal, blasted by the scirocco from the desert regions of the east (Hos 13:15). An apt image this last, at least, since the east wind (*qādîm*) can blight crops (Gen 41:6, 23, 27; Ezek 17:10), sweep away houses (Job 1:19; 27:21) and ships (Ezek 27:26; Ps 48:8), or bring on a plague of locusts (Exod 10:13). In the post-Holocaust era we are no doubt more aware of the dangers and ambiguities lurking in this "for our sins we are punished" interpretation of historical events, especially when expressed in the uncompromisingly strong metaphorical language that we encounter here. There is perhaps no satisfactory answer to this issue, but within the trajectory of the Isaian tradition this is not an isolated response, nor is it the only or last word on the subject. But it is clear that for the authors of passages such as this, events, especially catastrophic events, retain a degree of intelligibility only if one accepts some idea of moral causation and agency at work in the historical process. We have to wait for Qoheleth for anyone in Israel to say that things just happen.

The question about what Jacob must do to affect the course of events is posed. Reference to the people of Israel as Jacob has been claimed in support of the identification of the fortified city as Samaria, though there is no consensus to which crisis in its history the poet is referring, either prospectively (Plöger 1968, 71–75) or retrospectively—whether its fall to the Assyrians in 722 (e.g. Auvray 1972, 243) or events shortly after the conquests of Alexander (Kessler 1960, 170–72, Wildberger 1978, 1016–18), or the punitive action of John Hyrcanus in 108 (Duhm 1892, 192)—the last certainly too late. This quest for chronological precision has been pursued unsuccessfully for a long time, and there is no realistic prospect of a decision. It seems reasonable to assume nonetheless that readers in the Hasmonean period could have identified the city with Samaria, and the point about a people deprived of understanding (i.e. religious sensitivity) is echoed in Ben Sira's gibe about the foolish people living in Shechem (Sir 50:26).

It does not seem at all likely that the author is the Josian editor postulated by Barth and Clements and is referring to the destruction of Bethel and the anticipated incorporation of the territory of the former Kingdom of Samaria into Judah (Sweeney 1996, 350–52). The tone is altogether too somber, there is no allusion to the Northern Kingdom, and Bethel does not qualify as a fortified city and, as far as we know, was not destroyed by Josiah. (The archaeological evidence suggests it was destroyed in the late Neo-Babylonian or early Achaemenid period.) It seems more consonant with the section as a whole and with earlier allusions to a foreign, fortified city (*ʿîr běṣûrâ* 27:10 cf. *qiryâ běṣûrâ* 25:2 with *ʿîr* in parallelism with *qiryâ*) that the poet had Babylon in mind as the symbol and epitome of hostility and oppression, and this conclusion would be practically required if the one who struck Israel down and is now itself stricken in the opening verse is Babylon. It was also noted that the line of thought connecting Israel's punishment, the purging of sin and guilt, and idolatry is precisely what we find in chs. 40–48, and the designation Jacob, although applicable to the territory of the Northern Kingdom and Samaria, is the standard term for the Judean community addressed in the second section of the book (40:27; 41:8, 14, 21; 42:24; 43:1, 22, 28; 44:1, 2, 5, 21, 23; 45:4, 19; 46:3; 48:1, 12, 20).

It is of interest to note that the actions to be taken in the matter of cultic practice are precisely those enjoined by the Deuteronomic program (Deut 7:5; 12:13; Exod 32:20, probably of Deuteronomic origin). Altars set up on the "high places" (*bāmôt*), generally made of limestone blocks, are to be ground down or pounded into dust (cf. Exod 34:13; 2 Kgs 23:15; 2 Chr 34:7). Incense stands (*ḥammānîm*), generally associated with the *bāmôt* and their altars (Lev 26:30; Ezek 6:4, 6; 2 Chr 14:4[5]; 34:4, 7), are well attested archaeologically, and it is now generally agreed that they are not connected with a solar cult. The *ʾăšērîm*, symbolizing the great Canaanite goddess, are proscribed so often by the religious elite that they must have been a prominent feature of popular religion at all times of the history, as indeed the historical and prophetic books and surviving inscriptions testify. They also played a significant role in the state cult of both kingdoms at different times. An *ʾăšērâ* was installed in the temple before the Josian reform (2 Kgs 23:6), the statue of the goddess was still there in the last decade of Judah's independence (Ezek 8:3), and the Judeans settled in Egypt in the aftermath of Gedaliah's assassination countered Jeremiah's preaching by attributing the disaster to the official proscription of the Asherah cult (Jer 44:17).

The condemnation of idolatry is one of the strongest lines of continuity in the book. It connects this passage with the comment about idolatry in 17:7–8 ("on that day"), where the same three cultic objects are mentioned, a comment certainly later than the preceding diatribe against the kingdoms of Damascus and Samaria. Both passages move along the same trajectory as the "great arraignment" of 2:6–22, which anticipates the ultimate abolition of idolatry.

The transition to the fate of the fortified city is abrupt but no more so than the introduction of the City of Chaos into a scene of universal desolation in 24:10, followed immediately by rejoicing in the diaspora (24:14–16). The destruction of the city is also juxtaposed with a measure of consolation for the poor and afflicted cf. 25:4. It should not surprise us that at the end of the section we return to its central theme, namely, the polarity between the *civitas Dei*, whose punishment is referred to in 7–8, and the *civitas mundi*, an antithesis most clearly expressed in 26:1–6, the exact midpoint of chs. 24–27. The familiar Isaian topos of cityscape to landscape, going back to nature (5:17; 7:24–25; 13:20–22; 17:2; 32:14), expresses the total obliteration of the city and in fact would be a quite realistic description of what happened to many of the great Assyrian and Babylonian urban centers. The writer seems to get carried away with the image—cattle strip the leaves from the branches, the trees die, the branches snap off, women gather them for fuel, the last vestiges therefore end up in the fire; perhaps with a side glance at the satire on idolatry in 44:14–17, in which the same piece of wood serves both for fuel and for making an idol.

One of the least attractive aspects of the apocalyptic world view is the apparent need to condemn everyone who does not share it, an attitude by no means confined to ancient world views. It is true that the lack of understanding, the stupidity, referred to here (cf. Sir 50:26, with respect to Samaria, and similar condemnations in Isa 2:9b and 26:10) is of the religious kind, but it is fortunate that it can be balanced against other biblical views—that of the author of Jonah, for example, whose God insists on pitying the people of Nineveh (the hostile city par excellence), who do not know their right hand from their left.

The concluding "on that day" passages (12, 13) serve as appendices to 7–11 and provide one more illustration of the way the book of Isaiah results from a continuous, sequential and more or less coherent textual tradition. The image of harvesting that they present is very different from the images at the beginning of the poem (being driven on like a donkey, blasted by the east wind, perhaps also divorce). That the people of Israel will be gathered one by one is a refinement of the metaphor of threshing the wheat, which involves separating wheat from chaff, in the course of which one can expect to lose many grains of wheat. The ingathering in the first appendix from the Euphrates to the river bordering on Egypt (wadi el-ᶜarish, Num 34:5; Josh 15:4, 47) and in the second from Assyria and Egypt repeats a theme recurring at regular intervals (10:21–22; 11:11–12, 15–16; 14:1–2; 19:23–25) and reflecting the main centers of the Jewish diaspora in the Persian and Hellenistic periods, and indeed much later. One may regret the nonappearance here at the end of the section of the universalist theme that emerges throughout it from time to time but, from the rhetorical point of view, the blowing of the ram's horn to summon the people no longer to battle but to the final liturgical assembly (cf. Zech 9:14) forms an appropriate conclusion to chs. 13–27.

INTRODUCTION TO
ISAIAH 28–35

◆

In spite of the absence of a title or superscription, a new section of the book certainly begins with ch. 28. The opening verse introduces the first in a series of six woe-sayings just as the opening verse of the previous major section (chs. 13–27) introduces a series of sayings presented under the title *maśśā'* (oracle). Chapters 13–27 are also rounded out and therefore distinguished from what follows by a prediction of the return of the deportees or their descendants, parallel to a similar passage near the end of chs. 1–12 (27:12–13 cf. 11:11–16). These and similar indications of ordering and sequencing are found throughout the book.

The first of the woe-sayings in this section (28:1–4), directed against the leadership in Samaria, gives the impression that the Kingdom of Samaria is still in existence. It could have been composed specifically for insertion at this point to link up with the subject matter of chs. 1–12 and to make the point that the policies that led to the ruin of Samaria would lead to the same disastrous conclusion for Jerusalem. But it is also possible that it was composed after 722 and includes reference to a situation after the fall of the city. It appears, at any rate, that Samaria continued to give the Assyrians problems after that date. The city joined with Arpad and Hamath in a rebellion against Sargon II in 720, and both Ezra 4:2 and the gloss in Isa 7:8b suggest disturbances leading to deportations as late as the reign of Esarhaddon (680–669). In reading these texts we are continually reminded how incomplete and fragmentary is our knowledge of situations and events in the history of the kingdoms.

The woe-sayings in this section (28:1–4; 29:1–4, 15–16; 30:1–5; 31:1–3; 33:1) have their counterpart in a similar series in chs. 1–12 (5:8–10, 11–17, 18–19, 20, 21, 22–24; 10:1–4, 5–11). But since this type of prophetic utterance is directed against internal targets, the last of the six in chs. 28–35 (33:1), targeting an unnamed foreign tyrant, will be left aside as far as structure is concerned (pace Vermeylen 1977, 429–30). This major section of the book is therefore composed of three subsections: a series of five woe pronouncements in 28–31, a return to the theme of the once and future king in 32–33, and the finale to the entire compilation, in chs. 34–35, with the contrasting panels of the evil empire now symbolized by Edom and the restored City of God, a major theme throughout the book.

The first and second of the three subsections deal, whether by direct reference or indirectly, with the events leading to Hezekiah's rebellion and the rebellion itself, corresponding to the first four years of Sennacherib's reign

(705–701). While it is notoriously difficult to pin down historical allusions in the discourses, explicit reference to negotiations aimed at an alliance with Egypt against Assyria at that time (30:1–7; 31:1–3) justify the hypothesis that the events of those critical years can be discerned behind much of chs. 28–33 in spite of the presence of much later editorial elaboration. Hence, chs. 28–31 may be read as a counterpart to the prophet's intervention in international affairs a generation earlier during the reign of Ahaz when the issue was also foreign alliances. On both occasions the oral communications of the prophet fail to persuade and are therefore committed to writing to confirm their authenticity at the anticipated time of fulfillment (8:16–22; 30:8–14). Both of these passages are of particular importance for the development of the Isaian tradition and the history of prophecy in general.

If the hypothesis proposed above can be sustained, Sennacherib would be the one who is the powerful and strong one (28:2), the treacherous tyrant (33:1), the Akkadian-speaking Assyrians—named in 30:31 and 31:8—would be those jabbering in an unintelligible language (33:19), and the punitive campaign of 701, familiar from the annals of Sennacherib, would be referred to as a hailstorm, a destructive tempest, a raging flood (28:2, 15). As noted above, negotiations with Egypt are more clearly indicated (28:15; 29:15–16; 30:1–7; 31:1–3) and the anticipated siege of Jerusalem, under the code name Ariel, only slightly less clearly (29:3). The ultimate defeat of the rebellion is confidently predicted, with perhaps an allusion to the defection of some of Hezekiah's troops mentioned in the Assyrian annals (29:3–4; 30:15–17 cf. 22:2–3 and *ANET*, 288), even though Jerusalem itself will be rescued (31:4–5). The euphoria in the city after the departure of the Assyrian army (22:1–4) is in sharp contrast to the depopulation, physical destruction, and social breakdown resulting from the Assyrian invasion and temporary occupation (32:9–14; 33:7–9).

There can be no doubt that the attitude to the political and religious leadership is overwhelmingly negative in this section, and since the sense is being conveyed that policies pursued at the court are dangerous, misguided, and foolish, the diatribe must also take in Hezekiah, even though he is not named. Since the ideal government under a righteous king described in chs. 32–33 (32:1–8; 33:17–22) is designed to put an end to the situation described earlier (foolish plotting 32:6, foreign control 33:19), it is also quite likely that the ideal government / righteous king stands in contrast to the situation under Hezekiah's rule as interpreted by the prophetic author. At this point we encounter once again the major problem that the events and personalities in the sayings are interpreted in a way that is radically different from the interpretation in the narrative sections of the book. In chs. 28–33 the direst threats, including the prospect of defeat and death (28:18–19, 22; 29:4), are directed against the political leadership in Jerusalem during the period leading up to the punitive campaign of Sennacherib in 701, all of which makes for a stark contrast with the scene described in chs. 36–39. In the latter, Isaiah plays a supportive role vis-à-vis Hezekiah and his political advisers, and his counsel is actively solicited, not rejected, as in 30:8–14. Hezekiah himself comes through devout, assiduous in prayer, and heedful of the prophetic word, not engaged in a foolish military adventure with no prospect of success in defiance of prophetic advice. The contrast calls for an explanation, but for the moment it will be enough to note the strategy of the Historian of the kingdoms who incorporated an account of events involving Isaiah in the History. Hezekiah is profiled in a positive light to emphasize the contrast with Ahaz who preceded him and Manasseh who followed. Isaiah, too, had to be presented in a way quite different from the announcer of judgment and disaster, as a man of God who heals, works miracles, and gives oracles of assurance in keeping with other prophetic *legenda* in the history. A relevant parallel would be the way in which, in the account of Jeremiah's trial (Jer 26:18–19), Micah's categoric announcement of the destruction of Jerusalem (Mic 3:12) is reinterpreted as a call to repentance addressed to Hezekiah. In something of the same way the Historian, wishing for his own reasons to present Jeroboam II and the Jehu dynasty to which he belonged in a positive way, as postponing the inevitable destruction of the Kingdom of Samaria, highlighted the supportive prophet Jonah ben Amittai and omitted mention of the dire threats and comminations of Amos, who was active during that reign (2 Kgs 14:23–29, with a possible allusion to Amos in 14:27). The problem of the contrasting profiles of Isaiah in the sayings and the narrative sections will call for further discussion in the commentary on chs. 36–39.

To return to chs. 28–31—it is obvious that the woe-sayings make up only a small part of this section. We could read the rest as expansive commentary on these sayings, but in so doing we would have to admit that the section ranges far beyond what we today would consider an acceptable way to do commentary. This additional material is also formally and thematically heterogeneous. There are passages in straightforward prose interspersed with verse or recitative (29:11–12; 30:19–26, 29–33; 31:6–7), an "on that day" addendum (28:5–6), a *māšāl* (28:23–29), a pronouncement with the title *maśśāʾ* ("oracle") that at first sight looks out of place (30:6–7), and a variety of mostly brief passages introduced with rhetorical calls to attention—"listen," "behold," "thus says Yahveh," "hear the word of Yahveh," and the like. Such a compilation can be understood only as the product of *sequential* composition. I have argued that the earliest stage was associated with the crucial juncture of the Assyrian Palestinian campaign of 701 B.C.E. and the events leading up to it. But at each point the comminations and predictions of disaster are followed by words of assurance and promise, a feature also prominent in chs. 1–12 (28:5–6, 16–17; 29:5–8, 17–24; 30:18–33; 31:8–9; 32:15–20).

That the destiny of Jerusalem is a salient theme in the addenda to the woe-series is understandable in view of the mortal danger in which the policies pursued at the Judean court placed the city in 705–701 B.C.E. and the remarkable way in which the tradition represents its survival of that danger. These events clearly made a strong impact that could still be felt much later when the city was in the process of rehabilitation as the political and religious center of the province of Judah (Yehud) during the first century of Persian rule. This checkered history is reflected and refracted in this section of the book, which speaks of the refounding of the city (28:16–17), the defeat of those bent on its destruction (29:5–8; 31:4–5), and the final annihilation of the anti-Jerusalemite forces presented under the code name Assyria (31:8–9)—the first of such designations, at the same time historical and symbolic, used throughout subsequent history (later Babylon, Edom). In these respects the editorial expansions belong thematically with the last part of the book (chs. 56–66), in which the destiny of the city and its temple is a major concern.

The tension, conflict and sometimes violent animus in evidence throughout these chapters comes down to a struggle for the theopolitical agenda of institutionally unattached prophets such as Isaiah against the *Realpolitik* of the Judean state system at that time, late eighth century B.C.E. The archaeological evidence reveals that during the late eighth and early seventh centuries B.C.E., the lifetime of Hezekiah, both the extent and the population of Jerusalem increased considerably, indicating an increasing urbanization, centralization, and a more thorough consolidation of the Judean state apparatus. Pointing in the same direction is a marked increase at that time in trade, imported goods, luxury items, and the consolidation of native industrial activity (Jamieson-Drake). These trends may help to explain the self-confidence castigated in this part of the book. On the other hand, it is hardly surprising that the political elite regarded Isaiah's prescriptions in the field of foreign policy as naive and simplistic and that they attempted to silence him by the time-honored method of ridicule (28:9–10; 30:10–11). For his part, Isaiah expounded what he took to be a transcendental imperative, the divine plan or agenda (*'ēṣâ*, 28:29; 29:15; 30:1), and railed against the willful obtuseness of his hearers; they were drunk (28:7–8; 29:9), blind (29:9, 18), deaf (29:18), and spiritually comatose (29:10). This issue of the nonacceptance of the *oral* message of the prophet is then taken up in the form of reflection on the reception or nonreception of the *written* prophecies of Isaiah—i.e., on the book of Isaiah as it existed at that time. Reference to *written* prophecy in Isaiah (8:16–18; 30:8) and Jeremiah (36:1–32) seems to be a direct reaction to the nonacceptance of the oral message. The short prose passage about the sealed book containing "the vision of all these things," a book that remains unread by the literate and the illiterate (29:11–12), is of quite extraordinary interest since it contains a coded comment on the book of Isaiah as a whole in the form in which it circulated at that time (see commentary on 29:11–12).

In view of what we have seen so far about structure, it is not surprising that chs. 28–31 conclude with the prediction of the final defeat of Assyria, the historical and perhaps also symbolic Assyria, by divine agency (31:8–9). This is the last reference to Assyria and Assyrians in chs. 1–35. Chapters 32–33 contain many echoes of the preceding discourses—the themes of seeing and not seeing, hearing and not hearing (32:3), unintelligible foreign speech (32:4; 33:19), taking refuge from the tempest (32:2), cities going back to nature (32:13–20)— but these two chapters form a distinct and cohesive compilation unified by the theme announced at the beginning and end of (32:1; 33:17). That these two passages parallel the poems about a future ruler in 9:1–6[2–7] and 11:1–9 is hinted at by the studiously vague way in which this savior-figure is referred to: a king will reign (32:1; 33:17); a shoot or branch will spring up (11:1); he will inaugurate an epoch of justice, righteousness (32:1 cf. 9:6[7] and 11:3–4), and freedom from foreign domination (33:18–19 cf. 9:3–5[4–6]); the rights of the poor and socially marginal will be respected (32:7 cf. 11:4); and under his rule as vicegerent of Yahveh, Jerusalem will at last be secure (33:20–21 cf. 11:9).

The final subsection (chs. 34–35) serves as a kind of hinge on which the two major segments of the book, First and Second Isaiah, turn. (The Masoretic dead center of the book calculated by verses is flagged at 33:20.) It rounds off the entire compilation of richly annotated material in chs. 1–33 by contrasting the fate of Edom with the restored Jerusalem of the future, thus introducing the theme of eschatological reversal that will reappear in the final chapters of the book (for example, 65:13–14). The contrast is worked out in such detail as to justify and perhaps require us to read chs. 34–35 as one unit, a kind of diptich that encapsulates the essence of what the book of Isaiah is about. As such, it must derive from a very late stage in the editorial history of the book.

ISAIAH 28–35

◆

THE FATE OF SAMARIA AND
ITS LEADERS (28:1–13)

(Asen; Barthel 1977, 280–303; Betz; Beuken 1995a; G. R. Driver 1968b; Exum 1979; 1982; Görg; Hallo; Halpern; Jackson; Loretz 1977; Mosca; Roberts 1980; Tanghe 1993a; van der Toorn; Vogt)

TRANSLATION

i

28 [1] Woe, proud[a] coronet of the drunkards of Ephraim,
a flower doomed to fade[b] is its splendid beauty
at the head of a fertile valley[c]
[overcome with wine].[d]
[2] Observe, the Sovereign Lord[e] is holding in reserve one who is strong
    and powerful;
Yahveh will bring him down on the land with violence,
like a hailstorm, a destructive tempest,
a downpour of mighty water overflowing.
[3] Then the proud coronet of the drunkards of Ephraim
will be trampled underfoot,
[4] and the flower[f] of its spendid beauty doomed to fade
at the head of a fertile valley
will be like figs that ripen before the summer;
those who see them will swallow them
as soon as they have them in their hand.

ii

[5] On that day:
Yahveh will be a splendid coronet, a beautiful diadem
for the remnant of his people,
[6] a spirit of justice for the one who sits in judgment,
and strength for those who turn back the fighting from the gate.[g]

iii

[7] These too stagger with wine,
lurch about with strong drink;
priest and prophet stagger with strong drink;
they are befuddled with wine;

they lurch about with strong drink,
stagger as they see visions,[h]
go astray in giving judgment;[i]
[8]all tables are covered in vomit,
no place free of filth.

iv

[9]"To whom would he impart knowledge?
To whom would he expound what has been heard?
Those newly weaned from milk?
Those just taken from the breast?
[10]For it is *ṣav lāṣāv, ṣav lāṣāv,*
qav lāqāv, qav lāqāv,
here a little, there a little!"

[11]It will be with stammering speech
and in another language
that God[j] will speak to this people.
[12]To them God[j] once said,
"This is true rest,[k] let them give rest to the weary,
this is true repose"[k]—but they would not listen.
[13]So to them the word of Yahveh will be:
"*ṣav lāṣāv, ṣav lāṣāv,*
qav lāqāv, qav lāqāv,
here a little, there a little,"
so that when they walk
they will stumble and fall backwards,
injured,[l] trapped, and taken.

NOTES

[a] 1QIsa[a] has *gʾvn* for MT *gēʾût* (but *gʾvt* = *gēʾût* at 3); [b] *nōbēl* present participle with imminent future sense; [c] 1QIsa[a] *gʾy* for MT *gêʾ*, "valley," on the basis of which NEB reads "[on the heads of revelers] dripping with perfumes" (see G. R. Driver 1968b, 47–48); [d] *hălûmē yayin*, literally, "struck [down], hammered with wine" (cf. 16:8; and *halmût*, the hammer with which Jael disposed of Sisera, Judg 5:26); the reference must be to the revelers rather than to the city, perhaps from a re-reading of the verse referring it exclusively to the *šikkorē ʾeprayim*; [e] 1QIsa[a] YHVH; [f] for MT *ṣîṣat*, fem. sing. construct; we would expect *ṣîṣ* (masc. as in Exod 28:37; 39:30; Isa 40:6–8), but the verb (*vĕhāyĕtāh*) is fem.; *tērāmasnāh*, "trampled," fem. pl., may have arisen as a result of attraction to *ʿăṭeret*, "coronet" (fem.) when the subject matter of 3–4 was rearranged (see in more detail Barthel 1977, 281–82); [g] *šaʿĕrâ*, literally, "to the gate" (*hē locale*), which does not fit well with *mĕšîbê milḥāmâ*, "those who turn back the fighting" (literally, "battle"); 1QIsa[a] has *šaʿar*; [h] reading

bĕroʾāh infinitive absolute for MT *bāroʾeh*; ⁱ reading *biplîlyyâ*; the word is hapax cf. *pĕlîla* 16:3, *pĕlîl*, "judge (?)," Exod 21:22; Deut 32:31; Job 31:11 and *pĕlîlî*, "judicial," Job 31:28; ʲ "God" absent from MT is supplied; ᵏ MT *hammĕnûḥâ, hammargēʿâ*, "rest," "repose"; ˡ *wĕnišbārû*, literally, "they will be broken."

COMMENTS

This first in the series of woe-sayings (28:1–4) is directed against Samaria and its political leaders. It appears to be chronologically out of synchrony with the four following, which deal with events some two decades after the collapse of the Kingdom of Samaria, but we have seen that in this case appearances may be misleading. To the woe-saying is attached an addendum ("on that day," 5–6) that takes up the language of 1–4 ("beautiful coronet," "splendor"), juxtaposed ironically with the squalid scene of drunkenness and vomit, and applies it to Yahveh in his relations with the restored Israel of the future. The original diatribe then resumes, taking aim at the religious leadership in Judah (7–13) as is apparent from the way it continues (*gam ʾēlleh*, "these too . . ."). If we resist the temptation of wholesale emendation of the opening verse (1), the proud coronet must refer to Samaria situated in the fertile Valley of Jezreel (literally "a valley of fat things," the same idiom as in 5:1b), though it seems that this elaborately figurative allusion to the city was also meant to refer, or was subsequently made to refer, at the risk of compounding confusion, to the ruling elite in their cups. At any rate, the fate of the city at the hands of the Assyrians is alluded to obliquely but no less surely in the expressive metaphor, recurring often in the book (4:6; 8:8; 25:4; 28:17; 30:30; 32:2), of a violent storm. It may be readily admitted that anti-Samarian diatribe originating in eighth century Judah would have been reread with reference to the Samaria of the Sanballat dynasty, opponents of Judah in the Achaemenid period and, later still, in the light of Judean-Samaritan hostility in the Hasmonean period, but the reasons adduced by Kaiser (1974, 237–38) for dating the composition of the passage to the Hasmonean period do not persuade. That the Assyrians are referred to only obliquely does not necessarily indicate a late date (cf. 5:26; 8:7 and Amos 3:11; 6:14), and the wearing of crowns or garlands at a feast does not point exclusively to the Hellenistic symposium, quite apart from metaphoric usage (as in Ps 8:6). By the same token, the powerful individual who is to serve as Yahveh's agent (2), as the "rod of his anger" (10:5), will be one of the Neo-Assyrian rulers, Sargon II if the author had in mind the original capture of the city and deportations; Sennacherib if (as suggested above) the historical background is the participation of the Assyrian province of Samerina in the western revolts during that reign. It goes without saying that the reader of a later day, unburdened with the modern interpreter's concern with original situations and meanings, may well have had in mind Ptolemy I or Demetrius Poliorcetes, to both of whom Samaria fell victim, to the first in 312 and the second in 296 B.C.E. (see Vermeylen 1977, 386–87, who finds evidence of an anti-Samaritan recension here).

The first part of the diatribe (1–4) forms a simple but effective unit with an inclusio, and the reader of the Hebrew text of the entire passage will note verbal subtleties, some of them difficult to express in translation. These include examples of double-entendre: Samaria crown of the kingdom at the head of a valley juxtaposed with crowns on the heads of the drunkards who rule there; a flower doomed to fade, with the verbal stem *nbl* meaning "to fade" or "to be stupid"; *šmn* meaning "oil" or "fat," with reference to both the city and its self-indulgent rulers; priest and prophet confused with wine, with verbal stem *blʿ*, "confuse," more commonly with the meaning "to swallow," "gulp down" (7); stammering or jabbering speech (the exact meaning uncertain), which in Hebrew is also mocking speech (*lʿg* cf. Ps 35:16). To these we may add examples of paranomasia (e.g. *gēʾ/gēʾût*; *ṣîṣ/ṣĕbî*) and—if the interpretation offered is correct—another instance of the device, common in the earlier sections of the book, of quoting the words of the opponents (cf. 5:19; 29:15; 30:10–11, 16) to testify against them (other examples of literary art in Exum).

The accusation of drunken revelry directed against the political and religious leadership is part of the stock-in-trade of prophetic diatribe that seems to go back, like so much else, to Amos (2:8; 6:4–7). It can also serve figuratively to express spiritual stupor, as in 29:9–10, which may be read as an exegetical extension of the present passage. The scene is etched out by repeating the same verbs in staccato fashion and setting up realistic scenarios of the effects of a drunken binge (cf. 19:14 and, in more loving detail, Prov 23:29–35). What often lies behind this kind of language in the prophetic books is a religious festival featuring the consumption of considerable quantities of alcoholic beverages. Amos speaks of the elite drinking wine in the house of their god (their god not mine, understood, 2:8), and in a remarkably crude and explicit manner Hosea associates drinking with sexual rites (4:17–18), "on the day of our king" (7:5). Isaiah himself also speaks of drinking in connection with festivals (5:12) and sacrifice (22:13). The festival in question was probably in most cases the funerary banquet (*marzēaḥ* or *mirzēaḥ*). Though the term occurs only twice in the Hebrew Bible (Amos 6:7 and Jer 16:5), the cultic practice to which it corresponds was remarkably durable, being attested in the Late Bronze Age texts from Ugarit, an Aramaic ostracon from Elephantine, Phoenician and Punic inscriptions from the western Mediterranean, and Nabataean and Palmyrene inscriptions down to the third century C.E. (Lewis 1989, 80–94). As in the Irish wake in more recent times, generous imbibing seems to have been de rigueur. That the diatribe takes aim at cultic personnel—priests and prophets (*nĕbîʾîm*)—alongside state officials (also Hos 4:4–6; Mic 3:11) is understandable in view of the close connections of the state cult with the court and its function of providing religious legitimation for state policies, including military campaigns and the withholding of tribute (cf. Amos 7:10–17; Jer 28:1–17; 29:24–32). Apart from sacrificing, priests were charged with providing religious instruction and handing down binding decisions within their sphere of competence, while the primary responsibility of the *nābîʾ* was to intercede and to serve as a medium of communication between the deity and the people by means of oracles and visions (Hos 4:4–6; 5:1; 12:10; Mic 3:11; Jer 18:18; Ezek 7:26), the understanding being that the deity would as a general rule speak in support of the status quo. As described vividly here, the drunken condition of both priests and prophets left them in no condition to discharge these functions.

The author of the diatribe pulls out all the stops in presenting a truly disgusting cameo of a drunken spree, with these religious specialists staggering around, surrounded by vomit and excrement.

Lack of quotation marks and the mark for the interrogative in ancient Hebrew script leaves it uncertain whether we are still hearing the prophetic-authorial voice in 9–10. If so, we would have to assume that the speaker/writer is asking, rhetorically, whether such priests as he is addressing could teach anyone anything or whether their equally incapacitated prophetic confrères could expound the message that they have received to anyone except an infant who, after weaning at the age of three or thereabouts, might be taking the first steps in learning the alphabet. This is Ibn Ezra's approach: it is like teaching small children one precept (*ṣav*) and one line of text (*qav*) at a time. It seems incongruous, however, to compare drunkards to weaned children or the gibberish spoken by them to clearly enunciated letters of the Hebrew alphabet. Other suggestions in the commentary tradition may be mentioned: that they were making fun of the prophet's speech impediment or his gait—on neither of which, however, we are well informed; that *ṣav* and *qav* encode the idea of commandment and hope through the corresponding verbs *ṣivvāh* and *qivvāh*—which seems too elevated and detached from the context; that they refer to the first letter of *ṣē'â* (*ṣo'â*)("excrement") and *qî'* ("vomit"; Halpern; Tanghe), which would make sense but only if spoken by the prophet; finally, that the priests and prophets were mocking the speaker's ecstatic and unintelligible speech (Wildberger 1978, 1059), which might be characteristic of temple prophets but not of Isaiah, who is presumed to be the speaker. It is interesting, however, that this text was in fact read as referring to glossolalia in some Qumranic and early Christian circles (Betz).

It seems more likely that this is one of many instances in chs. 1–32 of the rhetorical device of quoting the opposition, in which the quotation is generally followed by a response of a threatening nature. For example: the Judean politicians inquire, sarcastically, about Yahveh's political plans and when they will be unveiled (5:19); Assyria brags about its many conquests, only to be silenced (10:8–11); Babylon aspires to ascend above the stars of God, only to go down to the underworld (14:13–14); the political schemers in Jerusalem ask, "Who sees us? who knows us?" (29:15b), and so on. This reading is supported by the repetition of the sing-song *qav lāqāv*, etc, turning their own words against them by presenting these words as spoken *in another language* (11), such as the (to them) unintelligible Akkadian they are destined to hear in due course from their Assyrian conquerors. Since, however, quoting the opposition is a literary and rhetorical way of making a point, what we are to understand the priests and prophets to be saying is not gibberish but a rejection of what they regard as the simplistic solutions offered by the seer and pitched at such a low level (the first steps in literacy, i.e., learning the letters of the alphabet) as to insult their educated intelligence.

The basic pattern of an offer to Judah mediated through the prophet and the serious consequences of its refusal underlies the narration of events under Ahaz, especially in the rejection of the offer of a sign (7:10–12) and the refusal of the waters of Shiloah (8:5–8). The pattern is repeated here and, in similar language in 30:15–17, in connection with diplomatic measures pursued at the court of Hezekiah, which were to lead to the Assyrian punitive expedition of 701 B.C.E. In the Deuteronomic lexicon "rest" (*měnûḥâ*) connotes secure possession of the land together with freedom from external threat (Deut 12:9; 30.15), and this political connotation is clearly intended here. The final verse (13) cites 8:15 verbatim, thus establishing a link between the failure of prophetic intervention under Ahaz and Hezekiah—another example of continuity and intertextuality but one that once again reminds us of the interpretative gap between the chapters we are considering and chs. 36–39. Since, however, the exchange between the prophet and his interlocutors is already complete, some commentators have suspected with reason that 13 is a post-586 B.C.E. comment about disaster consequent on failure to take seriously the message of "his servants the prophets"—precisely the point made repeatedly by the Historian of the kingdoms.

Returning now, finally, to the interpolated verses (5–6): we have the impression that a Second Temple scholiast is using the language of the text before him ("a beautiful coronet," "a splendid diadem") to redefine the situation without losing contact with past realities. The one who sits in judgment is, no doubt, the righteous king reigning in a restored Jerusalem, and those who turn back the fighting from the gate (if this is the correct reading) the defenders of the city. In view of the context of this subsection as a whole, we find in this projection of an ideal polity an implicit criticism of Hezekiah (as also in 32:1–8 and 33:17) and a reflection closer to what really happened during the Assyrian punitive campaign, closer at any rate than the story told in chs. 36–37 (cf. 22:3). As in similar editorial comments, especially 4:2–3 and 10:20–23, the remnant includes descendants of both kingdoms. Far from being lost from sight during the struggle for Judean autonomy from Nehemiah to the Maccabees, the ideal of one Israel comes more and more clearly into the picture with the passing of time, and the importance of the twelve-tribe idea in sources extant from that time and beyond (conspicuously Qumran and early Christianity) hardly needs demonstrating. As described here, the relationship between Yahveh and this twelve-tribe remnant is a dominant theme in the last chapters of the book, the so-called Third Isaiah (e.g. 60:19; 62:3; 63:12, 14–15), though these chapters evince little interest in the kind of nostalgia for the Judean dynasty that seems to be expressed here ("the one who sits in judgment") and in other editorial expansions in this and other prophetic books (e.g. Isa 11:1–5; Amos 9:11–12; Mic 5:1–14 [2–15a].

THE DEAL WITH DEATH UNDONE (28:14–22)

(Barthel 1997, 306–28; Bronznick; Donner 1964, 146–53; Fullerton 1920; Gese; Jeppesen; Landy; Lindblom; Roberts 1987; Stewart; Virgulin)

TRANSLATION

28 [14]Therefore, hear the word of Yahveh, you scoffers
who rule[a] this people in Jerusalem:
[15]You have declared:
"We have cut a deal with Death,
with Sheol we have made a pact,[b]
that when the raging flood[c] passes through
it will not touch us;
for we have made a lie our shelter,
in falsehood we have taken refuge."
[16]Wherefore, thus says the Sovereign Lord Yahveh:
"I will lay[d] in Zion a stone, a foundation stone for a tower,[e]
a precious[f] cornerstone set firmly in place;[g]
the one who is trustful will not act hastily.
[17]I will make justice the measuring line,
righteousness the plummet;
hail will sweep away the shelter of lies,
water will overwhelm the refuge;
[18]then your deal with Death will be annulled,
your pact with Sheol will not stand;
when the raging flood passes through
you will be battered down by it.
[19][Whenever it passes through it will reach you,
it will pass through morning after morning,
by day and by night;
grasping the message will bring nothing but panic]
[20]for the bed is too short to stretch out on,
the blanket too skimpy for a covering.
[21]Yahveh will arise as he arose on Mount Perazim;
he will rage as in the Valley of Gibeon,
to do his deed—strange is his deed!
to perform his work—uncanny is his work!
[22]And now, do not go on scoffing
or your bonds will be tightened even more,
for I have heard destruction decreed
by the sovereign lord Yahveh of the hosts
over all the earth.

NOTES

[a] *Mōšĕlē hā'ām hazzeh*: the direct object requires the alternative meaning of *mšl* = "rule" rather than "who speak in riddles"; [b] *ḥōzeh*, usually "visionary" cf. v 18 *ḥāzût*, usually "vision," but "pact" seems to be required by the context; see commentary; [c] reading *šôt* with Qere and 1QIsa[a] for MT *šît*; *šôt* more commonly = "whip" (1 Kgs 12:11, 14 = 2 Chr 10:11, 14; Isa 10:26; Nah 3:2; Job 5:21; Prov 26:3), but this meaning is ruled out by the context; [d] reading *yōsēd* participle with 1QIsa[b] for MT *yissad* cf. 1QIsa[a] *mysd* Piel participle; past tense as in 14:32, *YHVH yissad Ṣiyyôn*, is here incompatible with *hinĕnî*; [e] *'eben bōḥan* is variously explained: → *bḥn*, "test," therefore a stone that serves as a model for the mason—poorly if at all attested; *buḥan*, Pual participle = "tested"; "a block of granite" (NEB) or some other kind of hard stone, based on an Egyptian loanword; "massive" (Roberts); a tower of some kind cf. 32:14 and perhaps 23:13 and cf. 1QS VIII 7–8; 1QH VI 25–27; VII 8–9; for a fuller discussion of the issue see Wildberger 1982, 1066–67; [f] better attested than *yqr* = "solid" (Bronznick); [g] *mûsād mûssād*: substantive followed by Hophal participle; there is no justification in the versions or *metri causa* for eliminating *mûssād*.

COMMENTS

The initial "therefore" creates a nexus with 1–13, which suggests that we are now to hear the verdict following the indictment. The verdict, however, consists in a pronouncement of Yahveh that contains its own verdict (16). The present passage is nevertheless closely connected with 1–13 and is continuous with it. The diatribe shifts from Samaria to Judah in 28:7 ("these also . . .") and is now addressed to the scoffers in Jerusalem (*'anšē lāṣôn* cf. Prov 29:8, the scoffers who spell disaster for a city). The theme of mocking and rejection of the prophet's message occurs in both, and in both the common tactic of quoting the opposition is employed. The issue throughout is where to find security at a time of extreme and possibly terminal crisis, and the crisis is described in both sections as a storm with hail and a raging flood of water. The strange and uncanny work of God (Luther's *opus alienum*) (21) recalls the reference in the previous section to Yahveh's speaking to "this people" (a pejorative appellation, as elsewhere in Isaiah) in a strange language, and in each part there is interpolated a perspective on a future when justice and righteousness will finally prevail (6, 16–17).

At the same time, we can hardly fail to note the uneven literary character of this passage. It achieves a certain unity by beginning and ending on the theme of scoffing, meaning, concretely, rejection or skepticism vis-à-vis prophetic prescriptions, but the awkwardness and unevenness of the language are much in evidence. The architectural metaphors (laying a foundation stone, etc.) do not sit well with making a deal with death and the underworld and even less with the image of inadequate bedding. It is understandable therefore that commentators have bracketed at least 16–17a ("I will lay . . . plummet") as an editorial expansion, the removal of which allows the metaphorical raging flood to flow freely. The inauguration of a new building in Zion adds another dimension, a new layer of meaning, by contrasting the dysfunctional contemporaneous society with a new social order based on justice and righteousness. Verse 19 represents an editorial note of a different kind, addressed more directly to the reader, a glossator's way of representing the historical crisis in the distant past of Hezekiah's reign as paradigmatic of a recurring threat. The note has been rounded off with a warning about the effect of this somber prediction on the reader. The last statement (22b) recalls 10:22–23: "Destruction is decreed with vindication abounding; for the Sovereign Lord Yahveh will bring about the destruction that is decreed in the midst of the earth." Both reflect the apocalyptic world view of the author of Daniel (Dan 9:27; 11:36) and belong to the final stages in the production of the book of Isaiah.

The indictment is directed against the ruling elite in Jerusalem, the Judean counterparts of the "drunkards of Ephraim." The author uses the device, common in Isaiah, of condemning them out of their mouths, in their own words, which are not their words at all—they would hardly have admitted putting their trust in lies and falsehood. What they are supposed to mean by making a pact with Death and the Underworld is not clear. The allusion is often taken to refer to negotiations with Egypt with a view to a common front against Assyria, a situation that actually obtained in the last years of the eighth century B.C.E. (cf. 30:1–5; 31:1–3). Some commentators have also suspected a covert reference to the well-known Egyptian preoccupation with death and the afterlife. Not incompatible with this suggestion would be allusion to necromancy and the occult, often resorted to in times of crisis (e.g. during pestilence and military disaster) and well represented in Isaiah (2:6; 8:19–22; 29:4; 57:8–9).

The personification of Death (*māvet*) and Sheol as partners in covenant-making also provides the occasion for introducing Mot, known from the Ugaritic texts as son of El, opponent of Baal, and lord of the underworld. Making a deal with Mot would then presumably imply placating this deity, always greedy to swallow the living (cf. 5:14; 25:8; Hos 13:14; Hab 2:5), in order to avoid or postpone entering his realm. The precise meaning of the statement is rendered particularly obscure on account of *ḥōzeh* (15) and *ḥāzût* (18), only here in parallelism with *běrît*, "covenant," "pact." With the help of R. Moshe Hakkohen, Ibn Ezra made a valiant effort to preserve in some way the normal meaning of visionary and vision, the meanings respectively attaching to the terms in question ("we have made a prophet's covenant"). This suggests the following possibility. The covenant (*běrît*) with Mot implies both a repudiation of the Sinai covenant and a parody of the scene on the mountain when Moses and his companions saw God in vision (*ḥzh*) and sealed the covenant with a meal (Exod 24:9–11)—therefore somewhat like a Black Mass. What has taken place is therefore a ritual, probably of an orgiastic kind, involving eating, drinking, and sacrificing to Mot, consonant therefore with the gross inebriation of priests and prophets referred to earlier.

Consistent with this reading of the rulers' confident statement is the claim to have made a lie their shelter. The language of lying (*kzb*) is frequently associated with visions and divination of a dubious nature (Ezek 13:6–7, 9; 21:34; 22:28) and, on one occasion, with unacceptable treaties with foreign powers (Hos 12:2[1]). The true shelter (*maḥseh*) is none other than Yahveh (25:4; Jer 17:17; Joel 4:16; and often in Psalms), who is therefore being deliberately repudiated, at this time of crisis, in favor of Mot. A similar turning back to the old gods and goddesses, whose writ ran in the land long before Yahveh arrived on the scene, is attested following a time of even greater crisis, the fall of Jerusalem more than a century later (Jer 44:15–19).

There is also a mythological subtext in the reference to the raging flood about to pass through the land. We are reminded at once of the dark waters of death (cf. Pss 18:5–6; 124:4–5), but the Hebrew *šôṭ*, here translated "flood" only because of the adjective accompanying it (as in 30:28), usually means "whip," "scourge." The language is reminiscent of the Northwest Semitic Hadad, identified with Baal, god of the storm and rain cloud, destroyer and preserver of life, represented as horned and carrying either a thunderbolt or a whip. Since Mot and Hadad-Baal are enemies, there is a certain consistency in the imagery of making a pact with the former in order to avoid falling victim to the latter.

As in the previous passage, the description of present unpropitious realities alternates with a glimpse into a less threatening future. The architectural imagery connotes a new society, a new polity, based on moral order. The important element is that justice and righteousness are the criteria according to which this or any society is to be judged. The point is made clearly in that the measuring line (*qav*, Jer 31:29; Job 38:5) and lead plummet (*mišqelet* 34:11; 2 Kgs 21:13) are implements employed not just in building from scratch but in determining whether an existing building should be condemned and demolished — a point made very clearly in 34:11. This figurative language of cornerstone or foundation for a house or temple tends to recur wherever it is a question of new beginnings and the formation of community (e.g. Zech 10:4; Ps 118:22). St. Paul (Rom 9:33) found a new use for the text by combining it with Isa 8:14: "Behold, I am laying in Zion a stone that will make people stumble, a rock that will make them fall; and he who believes in him will not be put to shame." A second or third generation Christian homilist identified the stone of Isa 28:16 with Jesus as the foundation of a new community (1 Pet 2:4–6). Whoever the author of our passage may have been, the ideas expressed in it are not inconsistent with the Isaian core: political action is not religiously and morally autonomous; it must be based on trust in God, not on the self-interested assistance of foreign powers (cf. 7:9b; 30:15).

The metaphor of a raging flood has suggested a reference, of a kind rare in Isaiah, to traditional stories about divine interventions in Israel's distant past. The first is Joshua's victory at Gibeon, brought to a successful conclusion with the help of the sun miracle, which also involved the lesser miracle of preternaturally large hailstones (Josh 10:10–15). The second is David's victory over the Philistines at Baal-perazim, when Yahveh broke through their ranks like a raging flood of water (2 Sam 5:17–25). Apart from a passing allusion in 10:24–26, the first part of the book (chs. 1–39) is silent on the sojourn in Egypt and the forty years in the wilderness, in marked contrast to chs. 40–54. The destruction of Sodom and Gomorrah is referred to occasionally (1:9–10; 3:9) but is exceptional since we know that this folk tradition existed independently of the stories about the early ancestors. The conquest account is represented in 1–39 only by a brief allusion to Gideon's victory at the Rock of Oreb (10:26) and to the autochthonous Hivites and Amorites (17:9), a reference that looks suspiciously Deuteronomic (cf. Deut 2:10–12, 20–23; 3:11; 7:1; 20:17). The current explanation, which owes a great debt to von Rad, is that Isaiah and Isaian *epigoni* drew on Zion–Jerusalem traditions of quite different origin and inspiration from the Ephraimite traditions of the Egyptian sojourn, the trek through the wilderness and conquest of Canaan. This is no doubt true as far as it goes, but it is also possible that some of these traditions were consolidated in narrative form at a mature point in the formation of the book. Abraham, in particular, is a latecomer on the scene, to judge by the few and late allusions to him in the prophetic compilations.

The temptation to over-interpret has proved difficult to resist with respect to the description of divine activity as strange (*zār*) and uncanny (*nokrî*) — a counterpart to the strange language (Akkadian) in which, courtesy of the Assyrians, the message was destined to be delivered to the obdurate (28:11). The context suggests that this description applies to the two incidents from Israel's past insofar as divine intervention then came about by quite extraordinary, even miraculous means: a preternaturally destructive hailstorm, the sun standing still, the timing of an attack by the rustling of the wind in the trees. The point is that this element of the unanticipated, the sudden, the astounding, is what happens when God "arises," i.e., chooses to intervene in human affairs. The prophetic view repeatedly sets this sudden and unanticipated divine action over against what the movers and shakers of the world plan. In the two incidents referred to at this point the intervention was salvific, but the God of Israel was also known as a God who, as Luther put it, terrifies in order to save. Whether in salvation or judgment, these interventions cannot be circumscribed by human calculations, even when carried out by the best and brightest of minds (29:14b).

THE PARABLE OF THE GOOD FARMER (28:23–29)

(Auvray 1972, 253–56; Barthel 1997, 329–48; Jensen 1973, 50–51; 1986; Mury and Amsler; Thexton; Whedbee 1971, 51–68)

TRANSLATION

i

28   ²³Listen with attention to my voice.
Take note and hear what I say:
²⁴Does the plowman plow all day long [for the sowing],[a]
breaking up his soil and harrowing it?
²⁵Or rather, when he has leveled its surface,
will he not scatter fennel and sow cummin,
plant wheat in fair measure,[b] barley in its proper place,[c]
and spelt as a border?
²⁶He deals with it in just measure; his God provides the rain.[d]

ii

²⁷Fennel is not crushed[e] with a threshing-sledge,
a cartwheel is not rolled over[f] cummin,
but fennel is beaten with a stick,
cummin with a rod.
²⁸Grain for bread[g] is pounded,
but the thresher doesn't thresh it forever;[h]
he drives[i] the cartwheel over it,
he spreads it out but doesn't crush it.[j]
²⁹This too is a lesson that comes from Yahveh of the hosts;
wonderful[k] is his counsel,
great is his wisdom.

NOTES

[a] *Lizroaʿ* overburdens the 3:3 line and is often omitted *metri causa*, probably correctly (e.g. Duhm 1892, 174);   [b] *śôrâ* hapax: some translate "millet," but the context alludes to the proper way to plant wheat, barley, and spelt, which favors Ibn Ezra's proposal *śûrâ* for *bammĕśûrâ*, "in fair measure" (cf. Lev 19:35);   [c] *nismān* has no correspondent in LXX and Syr., but *gĕbûlātô* supports assigning it an adverbial function rather than Niphal participle → *smn*;
[d] a problematic line: *ysr* Piel = "correct," "discipline"; in the context the subject is the farmer, not Yahveh, and the antecedent for the masculine suffix the plowed and planted land, not the farmer; but the choice of verb is dictated by the analogy with Yahveh's dealings with his people; *lamišpāṭ*, "in just measure" cf. Jer 10:24 in the same context of Yahveh's dealings with Israel; *yôrennû* continues the ambivalence since *yrh* Hiphil = "teach" (cf. 2:3) as well as "irrigate," "provide rainwater" (Hos 6:3; 10:12);   [e] for MT *yûdaš* 1QIsa[a] has *ydš* (Qal) and 4QIsa[k] *ydvš* passive participle; in either case the sense is not affected;
[f] here too 1QIsa[a] has Qal *ysvb* for MT *yûssāb*;   [g] "grain for bread"—literally, just "bread" (*leḥem*); 1QIsa[a] adds the conjunction *vlḥm*;   [h] *kî lōʾ lāneṣaḥ*,

literally, "for not forever," is syntactically awkward and perhaps, as many commentators suggest (e.g. Procksch 1930, 364), out of place; LXX opts for a targumlike translation reminiscent of 57:16, which also features *lo' lānesah*; for MT *'ādôš* 1QIsaᵃ has participle *hdš* (*haddāš*), which is probably correct cf. 1 Chron 21:20; [i] the meaning of *hāmam* hapax is provided by the context; [j] following the proposed reading *ûpĕrāšô* (BHS) for the improbable MT *ûpārāšâv lo'-yĕduq-qennû*, literally, "and/but his horses do not crush it"; ". . . no—he has to crush it" (Thexton) is syntactically anomalous; [k] for MT *hiplî'* 1QIsaᵃ has *hplh* and 4QIsaᵏ *hpyl* ʿ[ṣ'].

COMMENTS

This passage has a distinctly different tone from the one preceding it. Though without a descriptive title, its didactic character is announced in the elaborately formal demand for a hearing containing four imperatives (for the combination *šim'û/ha'ăzînû* see also 1:2, 10; 32:9; 51:4) and is reinforced by the idea of instruction imparted by God (verbal stems *ysr* and *yrh*, the latter deliberately ambiguous, 26) whose counsel (*'ēṣâ*) and wisdom (*tušiyyâ*) are incomparable (29 cf. Prov 8:14, where these terms occur together). A major stylistic feature of this didactic genre is a series of rhetorical questions leading the reader, by means of analogy, to assent to the truth of a proposition (cf. the series in Amos 3:3–8 beginning "do two walk together unless they have made an appointment?"). From one perspective the passage could be described as a parabolic illustration of the dictum that "for everything there is a season" (Eccl 3:1) or the Stoic doctrine of *eukairia* ("timeliness"), and the practice of illustrating the force of this dictum by analogies drawn from husbandry is well attested in antiquity from the Sumerian "Farmer's Almanac" to Virgil's *Georgics*, not excluding the Hebrew Bible (cf. Prov 20:4, about the lazy farmer who does not plow in time for sowing). In the present context the moral is transparent. There is a right and a wrong method and time for growing herbs, legumes, and grain known to the trained and experienced countryman. The method involves violence, the application of force—the soil must be broken up, harrowed, plowed—but if force is exerted excessively or for too long the outcome will not be successful.

The relevance of the analogy to the strange, uncanny, and often destructive ways in which divine activity is said, in statements immediately preceding, to impinge on the human subject and human society (28:21) is unmistakable. The parable is addressed to the reader of a later day who might justifiably be perplexed or offended by such language, and the intent is to justify divine action with respect to its inner consistency, its not infrequent but wisely directed violence, and its duration. It may therefore be read as an *apologia* for the theopolitical understanding of human events according to the prophetic and Isaian tradition. Several of the major commentators (e.g. Dillmann, Duhm, Fohrer, Wildberger) attribute it to Isaiah. We could admit that the language is, broadly speaking, Isaian, and we have encountered motifs such as the stick and the rod (*maṭṭeh*, *šēbeṭ*) more than once in putatively early material (9:3; 10:5, 15, 24; 14:5). Such lexical and thematic features can, however, be as easily explained by familiarity with earlier Isaian material as by common authorship. Barth (1977, 211) and Clements (1980a, 233) assign it in somewhat arbitrary fashion to their Assyrian-Josian redaction. Others read it as a *literary* composition from the period of the Second Temple (e.g. Kaiser 1974, 259). These questions are rarely answerable with assurance. It can at least be said that, if it is an independent literary composition, it was composed specifically for use at this point, as a kind of exegetical reflection in parabolic form on the preceding words of judgment.

The lesson is imparted in two brief discourses, each ending with a reflection on divine activity (24–26, 27–29). The second, the distinct configuration of which is confirmed by the concluding phrase "this too" (*gam-zō't* 29) referring to it, goes beyond the first in stressing the importance of avoiding excessive force in these agrarian procedures. Most of the routine agricultural activities mentioned have a metaphoric application. Given the existence of an agrarian society, the extensive use of such imagery is to be expected. Hos 10:11–12, for example, parallels our passage in speaking of plowing, breaking up the ground, sowing, harrowing, reaping, and the need for rain in metaphoric illustration of the religious life of Samaria and Judah. Plowing can connote physical destruction as a result of military action (Mic 3:12; Jer 26:18) as well as sexual violence (Judg 14:18). The metaphoric potential of harrowing is apparent in English whenever we speak of a harrowing experience (cf. Hos 10:11; Job 39:10; Sir 38:26), and threshing, winnowing, and beating olive trees to detach the olives can describe the violence inseparable from military conquest and occupation by a victorious army (17:13; 21:10; 41:15–16; Amos 1:3; Mic 4:13). It is an interesting attempt to reflect, we suspect somewhat uneasily, on collective suffering and hardship inflicted as a form of divine education. We encounter the same theme in the contribution of Elihu to the debate with Job where its limitations are even more clearly in evidence than they are in the Isaian context.

ARIEL'S REVERSAL OF FORTUNE (29:1–8)

(Albright 1920; Barthel 1997, 349–76; Feigin; Godbey; Jeremias 1965, 123–36; Mare; Mattingley; May; North; Routledge; Schreiner 1963, 255–63; Werlitz; Wong)

TRANSLATION

i

29 [1]Alas[a] for Ariel, Ariel,[b]
town where David encamped!
Let one year follow another,[c]
let the festivals follow their course.

²I will still bring distress on Ariel.
There will be^d moaning and mourning;
she will be^e an Ariel indeed for me!
³I will encamp [like David]^f against you,
besiege you with a siege tower,
erect ramparts against you;
⁴you will be brought down, you will speak from the underworld,
from the dust your words will issue,
your voice will sound like a ghost from the underworld,
your words like a whisper from the dust.

ii

⁵But then the horde of your foes^g will become like fine dust,
the horde of oppressors like chaff blowing by;
then suddenly, in an instant,
⁶punishment will come from Yahveh of the hosts,
with thunder, earthquake, and a fearsome noise,
whirlwind, tempest, a flame of devouring fire.
⁷Then the horde of all the nations that war against Ariel,
all who build siegeworks against her,^h
all who oppress her,
will fade like a dream, like a vision of the night;
⁸like one who is famished and dreams he is eating,
and wakes up as hungry as before,
or like one who is thirsty and dreams he is drinking,
but wakes up as thirsty and parched as before.
So shall be the horde of all nations
that war against Zion.

NOTES

^a *Hôy*, "woe";   ^b 1QIsa^a seems to read *'rv'l* ("Aruel" = city of El?), though the close similarity between vav and yod renders this uncertain;   ^c 1QIsa^a has *svpy* for MT *sĕpû*;   ^d for MT *vĕhāyĕtāh* 4QIsa^k has *v]thyh*, apparently changing the tense from future to past;   ^e literally, "she will be for me like an Ariel"; there is no need to emend MT *vĕhāyĕtāh* to *vĕhāyit*, "you (fem.) will be";   ^f MT *kaddûr* ("ball?") is obscure and its adverbial use ("round about her") is unattested and improbable; frequent confusion between resh and daleth suggests reading *kĕdāvid*, "like David," as do LXX and 4QIsa^k (though the final daleth is not entirely clear), in which case it is probably an inappropriate gloss suggested by *kiryat ḥānāh dāvid* 29a cf. a similar gloss in Amos 6:5;   ^g reading *ṣārāyik*, "your foes," or *zēdāyik*, "those who scorn you," with 1QIsa^a (cf. LXX and Syr.) for MT *zārāyik*, "your foreigners," perhaps a deliberate alteration by a xenophobic scribe;   ^h omitting *ṣobehāh* on account of dittography with *haṣṣob'îm* in the previous line and reading *mĕṣurotehāh* for MT *ûmĕṣodātāh*.

COMMENTS

This is the second in the series of woe-sayings following 28:1–22 and preceding 29:15–21, the connection obscured somewhat by the editorial addition of the agrarian parable (28:23–29) and the reflections on spiritual imperception in 29:9–14). Like the following woe-saying, it announces the judgment of Yahveh manifested in historical events followed by the prospect of eventual redemption. It is addressed to Jerusalem (feminine suffixes throughout), though towards the end (7–8) there is a change to the third person. The change of fortune, the *peripateia*, will come about in a sudden and unanticipated way; hence "suddenly, in an instant" (5) is the pivot on which the passage turns. The discourse immediately following (29:9–12) returns to the theme of imperceptive prophets touched on earlier (28:7), and this is followed by other sayings in which the often strange and incomprehensible plan and *modus agendi* of the deity constitute a dominant theme (29:13–30:7). There is therefore an underlying theme in the entire section 28:1–30:7 that can be stated as follows: while God's presence can be perceived in the apparently random course of events, there is always an element of the incalculable, inscrutable, and strange in the way God's purposes work themselves out.

The final passage in this segment of the book (30:1–7) at last states explicitly the historical circumstance that occasioned this talk about a political agenda that, though supported by priests and prophets, was in opposition to Yahveh's plan. This circumstance was the attempt to form an anti-Assyrian alliance with Egypt in the last years of the eighth century, one which would bring down on the Judah of Hezekiah the full weight of the Assyrian military machine. The situation referred to obliquely in 29:1–8 is Jerusalem under siege, acute distress, then sudden deliverance. This corresponds closely with the description of Hezekiah shut up in Jerusalem—as Sennacherib's account puts it, "like a bird in a cage"—then finding sudden and unanticipated relief with the retirement of the Assyrian army.

The one addressed is referred to five times with the cryptic designation Ariel, literally "lion of El" or perhaps "mighty lion." The reference is certainly to Jerusalem and therefore brings to mind the lion as emblematic of Judah (Gen 49:9). In some late texts Ariel is a personal name (Ezra 8:16 but cf. Iduel in the parallel 1 Esd 8:43), but at an earlier stage it seems to have served to designate a cult object. According to Ezek 43:15–16 the term refers to the surface of the altar. It is square-shaped (12 × 12 cubits) with horns or protruding corners, of the type reconstructed from stone blocks in secondary use at Iron Age Beersheba. The term may have the same or a similar meaning in the Moabite stele (line 12), in which King Mesha claims to have dragged it into the presence of the national deity, Kemosh. (Albright; *ANET*, 320, prefers to read it as the name of an Israelite chieftain captured by the Moabites.) The two Moabite "ariels" killed by David's warrior Benaiah require the quite different connotation of a military champion, though the allusion immediately following to the killing of an *'ărî*, "lion," might suggest some textual disarray (2 Sam 23:20). However, none of this helps us to determine why the same designation is here used of Jerusalem. The meaning in Ezekiel, "altar hearth," seems to be the preferred option, pars pro toto, and is at least consistent with the reference to cult that follows and perhaps also with the threat that Jerusalem will become like an ariel, i.e., a place of sacrifice or slaughter. There is no direct connection with Akkadian *arallu*, which refers to the abode of the dead, the netherworld, gods associated with the netherworld, or the birthplace of demons (*CAD* A/2 226–27), though the allusion to descent into the underworld immediately following might suggest an indirect association of some kind. It is also possible that the designation is deliberately cryptic and polyvalent, perhaps including an allusion by assonance to *har-ʾēl*, "the mountain of God."

The deliberately archaic resonance of the word also fits the tradition of David's siege of Jerusalem (2 Sam 5:6–10). If the anticipated Assyrian siege of the city in 701 B.C.E., which perhaps never got completely underway, lies behind the present passage, the allusion to distress, mourning, and lying in the dust would refer to the hardship occasioned by the presence of the Assyrian army, even though the city did not fall (cf. 37:3). The verb *ḥānāh*, "encamp," "pitch a tent," can refer to a siege (e.g. Josh 10:5, 31, 34; Judg 9:50; 20:19; 1 Sam 11:1; 13:5; 2 Sam 12:28), but also provided an opening to the tradition about the wilderness sanctuary around which the Israelite tribes encamped (Num 1:50–53 etc.). Association between this sanctuary and the Jerusalem temple is well attested in Isaiah (the canopy and pavilion protecting Jerusalem in 4:5–6; Zion as a tent, complete with stakes and ropes in 33:20) and is not inconsistent with the dismissive allusion to the annual round of religious festivals that follows. The same point is made in Jeremiah's temple sermon: "add your burnt offerings to your sacrifices and eat the meat . . ." (Jer 7:21), with the clear implication that it will do you no good.

Jerusalem besieged, by Yahveh's instrument, the Assyrian army, is then described as reduced to the diminished and etiolated existence of wraiths and ghosts, denizens of the underworld (*ʾereṣ*, "earth" parallel with *ʿāpār*, "dust"; see commentary at 8:19–25). What is here described, however, is not the death and extinction of Jerusalem but a near-death experience, a not inappropriate description of what actually must have happened during Sennacherib's 701 campaign.

The most problematic feature of the address to Ariel is the shift from condemnation to assurance, from negation to affirmation, at its midpoint. Several commentators have followed the lead of Cheyne, writing more than a century ago (1880, 188), in taking the punishment referred to in 5–6 as in store for Jerusalem and 7–8 as the work of an editor anxious to mitigate the severity of the condemnation. This is improbable for the following reasons. After the near-death experience of 3–4 it would make no sense to speak of punishment suddenly being visited on the city. We are also left wondering about the identity of Jerusalem's *internal* foes and oppressors. Most importantly, the sudden switch from the prospect of punishment to the preternatural destruction of enemies fits very well the reprieve of the besieged city, which happened, we are told elsewhere, in a single night (37:36). The adverb "suddenly" (*pit'om*) is therefore the hinge or fulcrum of the passage; and though it more often than not refers to the onset of disaster (as in 30:13 and 47:11), disaster for some can be good news for others as, for example, with the sudden fall of Babylon (Jer 51:8).

It is possible that the passage 5–8 was added to the condemnation of the Egyptian alliance in 1–4 after the Assyrian army retired (as Barth 1977, 184–90; Clements 1980a, 234–35; Vermeylen 1977, 401–2), but predictions of a brighter future punctuate the harsh diatribe throughout the entire section, certainly not all from the same hand or from the same time (28:5–6, 16–17a, 23–29; 29:5–8, 17–21, 22–24).

The punishment is therefore to be visited on the enemies of the Judean people, and it is described in the conventional language of theophany: thunder, tectonic movement, whirlwind, tempest, and fire. That it proceeds from Yahveh of the hosts and therefore from the temple, the place where the divine effulgence (*kābôd*) is manifest (6:1–5), is also well attested (e.g. Amos 1:2; Joel 4:16[3:16]). The same theophanic language is transferred from Zion to Sinai (Exod 19:18–20; 20:18) and it can serve to indicate an irruption of power for either salvation or disaster. In this instance the language consolidates into the familiar theme of the defeat of hostile nations, generally but not invariably as they assemble before Jerusalem, the so-called *Völkerkampf* ("battle of the nations") motif well represented in Isaiah (17:12–14; 24:21–23; 30:27–28, 29–33; 31:4–5; 34:1–4). The retirement of the Assyrian army in 701, perhaps following the raising of the siege of the city, would have contributed greatly to the popularity and prestige of this ancient topos.

The final metaphor, in fairly straightforward prose (8), has been much maligned in the commentary tradition as insipid and anticlimactic but not by Augustine, who made effective use of it in his *Confessions* ("the food eaten in sleep is very much like food eaten when awake, except that by it those who are asleep are not nourished," 3.6). Pace these commentators, the quite overpowering sense of substance and reality one can experience in dreaming, followed by the (sudden) realization of insubstantiality and unreality on waking, is a very effective analogy for the prophetic sense of the insubstantiality of the display of military and political power juxtaposed with the abiding reality of the divine.

THE BLIND AND THE OBTUSE (29:9–14)

(Aitken; Carroll; Williamson 1994, 94–115)

TRANSLATION

i

29   [9]Be in a daze,[a] be in a stupor,
       close your eyes fast,[b] be blind,

be drunk,[c] but not with wine,
stagger,[d] but not with strong drink!
[10]For Yahveh has poured out upon you
a spirit of deepest slumber;
he has closed your eyes [the prophets]
he has covered your heads [the seers].[e]

ii

[11]The vision of all these things has become for you like the words of a sealed book. When they hand it to one who knows how to read[f] saying, "Read this," he replies, "I can't, for it is sealed." [12]When they hand the book to one who cannot read saying, "Read this," he replies, "I don't know how to read."

iii

[13]The Lord says:
Because this people approach me with their mouths[g]
and honor me[h] with their lips
while their hearts are far from me,
and their reverence for me is[i] a human commandment learnt by rote,
[14]I will perform yet more[j] strange and wonderful things with this people;
the wisdom of their sages shall vanish,
the discernment of their knowing ones shall disappear.

NOTES

[a] For MT *hitmahmĕhû* Hithpalpel → *mhh* read *hittammĕhû* Hithpael → *tmh* as in Hab 1:5 *hittammĕhû tĕmāhû* cf. LXX *ekluthēte* and Syr., Vulg., Tg.;   [b] MT *hišta'aš'û* Hithpalpel → *š'' =* "paste together," "shut tight" (or possibly *š'h =* "avert the gaze" rather than → *š'' =* "enjoy oneself," as in NEB;   [c] read imperative *šikrû* (cf. LXX *kraipalēsate*) for MT *šakĕrû*;   [d] read imperative *nû'û* for MT *nā'û*; 1QIsa[a] *n'vv vlškr* omits aleph in *lo'* cf. *vlv' myyn*, "but not from wine," preceding, more plausibly than MT, which omits the preposition;   [e] that *'et-hannĕbî'îm* and *haḥozîm* are glosses is suggested by the defective syntax; see commentary;   [f] reading *sēper* with Qere and 1QIsa[a] for MT *hassēper*;   [g] zaqep qaton (: superscript) must be transferred from *hazzeh* to *bĕpîv*; otherwise we must read "when this people approaches me, they honor me with their mouth and lips . . .";   [h] retain 3d person pl. with MT; 1QIsa[a] is unclear but probably not *kbdty* pace BHS (New 1992, 609–10);   [i] LXX *matēn de* presupposes *vĕtōhû* "and their reverence for me is worthless" (cf. Matt 7:7), but MT is unexceptional;   [j] read *yôsēp* participle for MT *yôsip* perfect.

COMMENTS

This passage contains three distinct paragraphs (9–10, 11–12, 13–14). The third is formally identified as an utterance of Yahveh addressed to the seer about "this people." The first and second are linked by the theme of spiritual imperception and hebetude under the metaphors of blindness, drunken stupor, sleep, and illiteracy but are rhetorically quite different from one another. The second is rather similar to the brief, graphic images encountered earlier in the book (3:6–7; 4:1 cf. Amos 3:12; 6:9–10) that I have called cameos. In spite of its extreme brevity, it is also reminiscent of such prophetic sign-acts as Jeremiah's offering wine to the Rechabites (Jer 35:1–11). The three paragraphs seem at first sight to contribute little to the immediate context, but we may take the first as developing the accusation of drunkenness and high living and the description of their effects (28:1, 7–8), a common theme in prophetic and Isaian diatribes (e.g. 5:11–12, 22; 22:13), in the direction of a corresponding spiritual incapacity. Then, towards the end, we are brought back to that other theme of the strange, uncanny ways in which Yahveh impinges on human affairs (29:14 cf. 28:21).

From the time of Eichhorn and Ewald there has been a critical consensus that the closed eyes and covered heads were identified as belonging to prophets and seers, respectively, by a later glossator, who shared the low opinion of prophets that appears to have been widespread in the post-destruction period (cf. the similar gloss in 9:14 that identifies the lying prophet as the tail; Lam 2:14 and especially Zech 13:2–6 also evince a low regard for the *nĕbî'îm*). The change to straightforward prose in 11–12 has also convinced most recent commentators that this figurative allusion to Isaian prophecies as a sealed book is an editorial addition referring the incomprehension of the public vis-à-vis the prophet's *oral* communication—represented figuratively as linguistic incompetence (28:11)—to the *written* prophecies in whatever form they existed at that time. The modal change is understandable in view of the greater prominence of written prophecy at the time when this brief section (11–12) was added.

At intervals throughout the book we hear of people hearing without comprehension and seeing without perception, of the stopping of ears and shutting of eyes, and all of this induced by the very delivery of the prophetic message (6:9–10; 30:10), but the disability will be removed in the last days (32:3–4; 35:5–6). The same point is made here in the reference to a "profound hypnotic slumber" (Skinner 1915, 234), a condition of imperception or inspissation of mind brought on by Yahveh. The state thus induced, *tardēmâ* in Hebrew, recalls the anaesthesis of the first human being (Gen 2:21), the trance-like state into which Abraham fell during the "covenant of the pieces" (Gen 15:12), and the deep, Yahveh-induced sleep that allowed David to approach Saul and his company safely (1 Sam 26:12)—in all of these narratives the same word, *tardēmâ*, occurs. Since according to the glossator this state also affects prophets, it is not surprising that the corresponding verb (*rdm* Niphal) is used to describe Jonah's profound sleep in the hold of the ship that was carrying him, he thought, away from the presence of Yahveh (Jonah 1:5).

Something more is being said in this talk about stupor and slumber than just intellectual ineptitude. The idea seems to be that the publication of the prophetic message confronts the hearer or reader with a new, critical situation, in which it is no longer possible to reach political decisions simply by delibera-tion, by weighing options, or seeking a consensus. The prophetic word is pe-remptory, a challenge to commit to a possible and necessary alternative. Hence the emphasis on the strange and alien nature of these prophetic communica-tions throughout this section of the book (28:11–13, 21; 29:14; 31:2).

The editorial comment about the sealed book is of particular importance in reflecting the reception or non-reception of the Isaian prophecies—that is, of the book of Isaiah in the form in which it then existed, here described as "the vision of all these things" (*ḥazût* cf. *ḥāzôn*, also "vision," for the entire book at 1:1). We hear of the committing to writing and sealing (i.e. notarizing and thus authenticating) of prophecies on two occasions in the book. After the failure of Isaiah's intervention in international politics under Ahaz, the prophetic testi-mony and teaching—referring to prophecies delivered during that crisis—were sealed and committed to disciples for safekeeping. This is at least a defen-sible interpretation of 8:16–18. Much the same happened during the critical period leading up to Sennacherib's punitive expedition some three decades later. The prophet is told to write his words on a tablet and a scroll as a witness to those who were attempting to prohibit him from fulfilling his appointed role (30:8–11). A similar situation confronted Jeremiah, prohibited from addressing the public in the temple precincts, with the result that he committed his words to writing instead (Jer 36:4–6). In the context of this section of Isaiah (28–31) the prophecy would presumably have dealt with the consequences of relying on an Egyptian alliance. In speaking of the book's reception, the glossator of 29:11–12 took in a broader field of vision. He seems to refer to two types of readers: those who will not take the trouble, or who disingenuously do not con-sider themselves qualified to break the seal, that is, to decrypt the prophetic writings; and those whose ignorance and spiritual insensitivity rule out even the attempt to grasp what is written.

The reception of the message of Isaiah *in written form* seems, then, to be a major preoccupation in this section, a point made long ago by the British Old Testament scholar Thomas Cheyne (1880, 171); and in keeping with the point-counterpoint of threat and promise we hear that, notwithstanding, the day will come when the blind will see and the deaf will hear the book read to them even if they themselves cannot read (29:18 cf. 32:3).

Isa 29:13–14 represents a further stage in the uneven progress of the diatribe and is set out in the customary form of indictment (13) and verdict (14). Be-hind this diatribe, which includes accusations of drunkenness, high living, arrogance, the self-assurance of the ruling class, and especially indifference or outright hostility to prophetic interventions, we detect anxiety induced by the encroaching Judean state system. The evidence suggests that this process reached maturity no earlier than the eighth century B.C.E. Hence the constant attack in this section on political wisdom divorced from the traditional re-course to prophetic revelation (28:9–13; 29:15–16; 30:1–5; 31:1–3; add the fact that Jer 8:8–9 denounces the pretensions of legal specialists in the service of the state system even more strongly). The official state cult is represented as driven by convention and routine, and not of a kind that might actually make a difference in the world of social and political realities, a situation not unknown in our own day. This critique of conventional religion was touched on earlier in the diatribe (29:1) and with greater vehemence and in greater detail near the beginning of the book (1:10–17). We note in passing that here and elsewhere in the book the seer distances himself from those addressed by the neutral and often pejorative designation "this people" (*hā'ām hazzeh* 6:9–10; 8:6, 12; 9:15; 28:11, 14).

The verdict finds another way to express the strange, alien, shocking, and unanticipated *modus agendi* of Yahveh in contrast to human wisdom and discernment—a recurring motif in this section (28:11–13, 21; 29:5; 30:13; 31:2). There is here a remarkably consistent refusal to accept the political order as autonomous even when legitimated and reinforced, as it routinely was, by traditional religious ideas and practices.

THE LIMITATIONS OF POLITICAL KNOW-HOW (29:15–24)

(Beuken 1992a; Carroll; Clements 1977; Donner 1964, 155–58; Whedbee 1971, 73–75; Williamson 1994, 58–63)

TRANSLATION

i

29 ^{15} Woe to those who would hide their plans
too deep for Yahveh to see,
and think, since their deeds are done in the dark,
Who sees us? Who knows what we are about?"
^{16}You have things the wrong way round![a]
As if the potter were no different from the clay,[b]
or as if what is made were to say of its maker,
"He did not make me,"
or the product made of clay[c] of the one who fashioned it,
"He has no skill."

ii

^{17}In just a little while
will not Lebanon be turned into a fertile land
and fertile land be as common as scrubland?[d]
^{18}On that day the deaf will hear the words of a book,
and free of all gloom and darkness
the eyes of the sightless will see;
^{19}the lowly will once more have joy in Yahveh,
the needy will rejoice in the Holy One of Israel;

²⁰for the violent will be no more,
the arrogant will cease to be;
all those who are prompt to do evil,
²¹who frustrate those seeking redress,^e
who entrap those bringing a case to judgment,
who pervert by falsehood the cause of the innocent,
—all these will be extirpated.

iii

²²Therefore, thus says Yahveh, the God of the household of Jacob,^f who redeemed Abraham:
This is no time for Jacob to be ashamed,
no time for his face to grow pale;
²³when his children^g see what I do in their midst
they will hallow my name,
they will hallow the Holy One of Jacob,
stand in awe of the God of Israel;
²⁴those who err in their thinking will acquire understanding,
the obstinate will accept instruction.

NOTES

^a MT *hapkĕkem* (1QIsa^a *hpk mkm*) has been variously understood: *hēpek* = "difference," "perversity" (cf. Ezek 16:34), therefore "your perversity!" (Kaiser 1974, 275); *hakĕpakkîm* = "like flasks" (Robinson 1931, 322; and BHS); *hăkakem* = "is he (God) like you?" (Ehrlich, 1912, 4.105); 2d person pl. of verb *hpk* as here;   ^b literally, "(as) if the potter were reckoned (to be) like the clay"; ^c 1QIsa^a has *ḥmr* for MT *'āmar*, reading "or the product of clay about the one who fashioned it . . . ," which is probably correct since we would expect either *yo'mar* as in the previous line or no repetition of the verb;   ^d literally, "and the fertile land (*karmel*) be regarded as scrubland";   ^e *maḥăṭî'ē 'ādām* could be translated "who cause a person to sin" (*ḥṭ'* Hiphil) cf. NEB "those who charge others with a sin," but the context favors the other meaning accepted here;   ^f the syntax of the sentence suggests reading *'ēl* for *'el* preposition; ^g *yĕlādâv* is often taken to be a gloss (Kaiser 1974, 278; BHS) but without support from 1QIsa^a or the ancient versions; *bĕqirbô* has a singular suffix but the verbs are in the plural.

COMMENTS

It will no longer occasion surprise that a woe, this third in the series of woes in chs. 28–33 (29:15–16), is followed by the prospect of a reversal of fortune in the future (17–24). While the general impression conveyed is somewhat disjointed and harsh (Vermeylen [1977, 407] speaks more charitably of the style as being anthological), the theme of reversal provides at least a thin thread of unity,

beginning with the pot's usurping the place of the potter and ending with ecological and social transformation. The woe-saying itself (15–16) is in the familiar
form of a disputation, accusing those addressed with statements from their own
mouths and directing rhetorical questions at them. It exploits the topos of humanity shaped out of clay familiar from the didactic literature (Job 10:9; 33:6)
and developed in different ways in myth and parable (Gen 2:7,19; Jer 18:1–4).
Since it is directed against the political machinations of the Judean leadership,
it does not imply any sustained reflection on creation and Yahveh as creator
such as we encounter later in the book. Since ceramic ware was ubiquitous in
everyday life, the figure of God as potter would have come very naturally. The
most sustained prophetic use of the metaphor is the sign-act of Jeremiah's visit
to the potter's workshop (18:1–11), but it also occurs in Isa 45:9 in somewhat
similar language. Since Isa 45:9–10 is the only example of a woe-saying in Second Isaiah (55:1 begins with *hôy* but is manifestly not a woe-saying), this may
be a rare case of Second Isaiah's borrowing from earlier Isaian material.

The attack on the political maneuvering of the Judean court employs the by-
now familiar strategy of quoting the opposition's words back to them (cf. 28:14–
15; 30:10–11, 16). One of the leading themes of the book is the confrontation
between autonomous political wisdom and prudence on the one hand and the
agenda of the God of Israel, communicated through the prophet, on the other
(5:18–23; 8:9–10; 14:24–27; 19:3, 11–15; 25:1–2; 28:29; 30:1–2). The allusion to
scheming and elaborating plans in the dark may simply refer to the obvious
need for secrecy in negotiating an anti-Assyrian alliance in the early years of
Sennacherib's reign, and Isaiah would understandably have been among those
kept in the dark. It is not difficult to sympathize with the Judeans, who were using their best judgment in the attempt to get out from under the shadow of a
brutal imperial power, an attempt that they knew carried the gravest risks. They
may also, with some reason, have wondered whether the alternative proposed
by Isaiah in the name of Yahveh made any political sense; on at least one occasion they suggested rather clearly that it did not (5:19). To the extent that a
political program capable of implementation can be extracted from the Isaian
discourses, it was one that agreed with the ruling elite in the goal of autonomy
and independence but differed by absolutely excluding alliances as a means to
that end—whether with Assyria at the time of Ahaz (7:4–17) or with Egypt and
Babylon at the time of Hezekiah (18:1–19:15; 28:14–22; 29:15–16; 30:1–7;
31:1–3; 39:5–7). In purely political terms, then, it seems that those addressed by
the prophet were being presented with a quietist option since it is clear that no
action taken by Judah alone with a view to achieving independence from the
imperial superpower had the remotest chance of success.

In vv 17–21, environmental change by which a forested region can be turned
into rich land for grazing or raising crops, or an inhabited area can become a
wilderness (a recurrent theme in Isaiah that we will encounter in more developed form in 32:15–20) leads by analogy to the theme of eschatological reversal, of frequent occurrence in apocalyptic writings. This *bouleversement*, which
is expected to take place within a short space of time (cf. 10:25; 26:20), will in

the first place affect the physical environment, but exactly how is not entirely clear. Lebanon, noted for its cedars, will revert to the condition of fertile land for growing crops and grazing that existed before it was covered with trees, and fertile land (*karmel*, also 10:18; 16:10; 32:15–16; 37:24) will be as common as scrubland or forest (*ya'ar*)—in other words, agriculturally unprofitable land. (This theme of ecological reversal will be discussed further in the commentary on 32:15–20.) Today, few would doubt that the survival of the physical environment calls for profound social adjustments and radical changes in attitudes and policies. In this respect it is striking that here and elsewhere in Isaiah ecological transformation goes in tandem with radical social change.

We do not have to choose between a literal and metaphorical restoration of hearing and vision (18). The lack of comprehension and perception on the part of the movers and shakers in late eighth century Judah is a major theme of this section—the people are unable not just to hear but to understand, not just to see but to perceive (28:11–13; 29:9–10, 11–12; 30:9), and the same was said of the leadership at the time of Ahaz (6:9). This theme will recur often in the later chapters of the book (42:7, 16, 18–20; 43:8; 56:10; 59:10). It is an essential part of the restorationist eschatological view that people are not meant to be deaf, blind, lame, indigent, subject to violence, and deprived of access to judicial process. At the great turning point of history, which the readers are assured is coming soon, these aspects of the damaged second creation will be removed and the created order restored to what it was intended to be at the beginning. The *literal* removal of disabilities is clearly indicated in 35:5–7, which envisages the lame person leaping like a deer and also includes the reversal of environmental degradation. The terms "lowly" and "needy" (*'ănāvîm* and *'ebyônîm*) may be taken to indicate social and economic deprivation, respectively, the two closely related, as always. They come to be used quite naturally with reference to the God-fearers in the pietistic writings from the Second Temple period that emanate from circles deprived of power and influence in the Judean community. The removal of natural disabilities, the restoration and repristination of the life of the individual and of society, are signs that the turning point in history is imminent. It is for this reason that the miracles of healing worked by Jesus can be presented in the gospels as the fulfillment of Isaian texts and signs of a new dispensation (Matt 11:5; Luke 4:18–19).

The fuller meaning of being incapable of hearing with the inner ear and therefore accepting the promise of the fuller life offered in this vision of the future is particularly in evidence in the remarkable prediction that on that day "the deaf will hear the words of a book." We are not told what the book (namely, the scroll) is from that someone will read aloud to the formerly deaf. If, as seems likely, this is a comment on 29:11–12, the book in question will contain the prophecies of Isaiah (as in 34:16), and the implication is that there will eventually be an end to the spiritual dullness and lack of perception with respect to the prophetic message, which is a major theme throughout chs. 1–39.

The final paragraph (22–24) is a later addendum, indicated by a new superscript. The assurance that the household of Jacob will survive and grow in numbers and that this is also part of a future prospect to be brought about by the action of God explains the rare allusion to Abraham and his rescue or redemption from Mesopotamian idolatry. It seems that the narrative and genealogical traditions about Abraham only achieved prominence, and perhaps only came into existence, in the post-disaster period. In texts from this later period, Abraham and Sarah are the parents of the Israelite people (Isa 51:2; 63:16), while the people itself takes by preference the name Jacob, the standard designation in texts from the exilic and postexilic periods, especially in Isaiah. The term *bēt ya'ăqob*, "the household of Jacob," is characteristic of but not exclusive to Isaiah. Some commentators detect here a preview of Abrahamic traditions known from pseudepigraphal writings, especially the statement in the *Apocalypse of Abraham* ch. 8 that the voice calling him to leave his kindred and paternal household saved him from the punishment by fire inflicted on the people of Ur on account of their sins. But a simpler and more accessible explanation would be that Abraham was redeemed out of Ur as Israel was to be redeemed out of Egypt and, in due course, out of Babylon (33:10; 51:11).

THE FOLLY OF AN ALLIANCE
WITH EGYPT (30:1–5)

(Barthel 1977, 391–427; Beuken 1997; Childs 1967, 32–33; Donner 1964, 132–34; Emerton 1981; 1982; Fichtner 1951; Gerstenberger; Gonçalves; Kuschke; Werner 1988, 85–94)

TRANSLATION

30 [1]Woe to the rebellious children
[an oracle of Yahveh]
making plans but not derived from me,
seeking security[a] but not inspired by me,[b]
piling[c] sin upon sin.
[2]They set out on the journey to Egypt
but without consulting me,
to take refuge[d] under Pharaoh's protection,
to shelter in Egypt's shadow;
[3]but Pharaoh's protection will bring you shame,
sheltering in Egypt's shadow will end in humiliation,
[4]for though his[e] nobles are at Zoan,
and his envoys have reached Hanes,
[5]all remain disillusioned[f]
on account of that profitless people;[g]
for them they can offer no help, no advantage,
only shame and disgrace.

NOTES

[a] The phrase *vĕlinsok massēkâ* could refer to pouring a libation (cf. 40:19; 44:10), possibly in connection with a treaty-making ceremony (cf. LXX), but in the absence of evidence for this ceremony as part of sealing an agreement, the alternative sense of seeking cover or protection is preferable (cf. 22:7; 25:7; 28:20); "casting molten images" (Dahood 1969, 57–58) does not fit the context and is implausible on other grounds;   [b] literally, "but not my spirit";   [c] for MT *sĕpôt* read *lāsepet* infinitive → *ysp* rather than *sph* cf. Num 32:14;   [d] for MT *lā'ôz* read *lā'ûz* cf. LXX;   [e] with reference to the Judean king not Pharaoh;   [f] read *hobîš* Hiphil → *bôš* with Qere and 18 MSS;   [g] several commentators take v 5a to have been inserted to link with vv 6–7 by means of *'al-'am lo' yô'îlû*; perhaps, but it could be simple repetition.

COMMENTS

Isa 30:1–17 presents a protracted argument about the wisdom or folly of pursuing the policy of playing off one great power, namely, Egypt, against another, namely, Assyria. As such it is reasonably coherent. Most commentators on chs. 28–31 favor the period 705–701 as the historical background for these arguments and counterarguments rather than a reference to Judean involvement, real or contemplated, in the rebellion of the Philistine city of Ashdod against Assyria a decade or so earlier (defended by Kuschke 1952, 194–95 and Donner 1964, 133–34, amont others). Negotiations among the western states with a view to an anti-Assyrian coalition, for which the participation of Egypt was considered practically essential, were a constant feature of international politics in the region from the ninth to the seventh century B.C.E. Unrest in Assyria following the death of Sargon II (705) and the accession of Sennacherib encouraged a particularly active phase of resistance in the west. According to the biblical record Hezekiah played a supporting role in the revolt of Babylon under Merodach-baladan, together with Elamites, Arameans, Arabs, and some of the Phoenician and Philistine city-states (2 Kgs 20:12–19; Isa 39:1–8; also Josephus, *Ant.* 10.30–31). After the suppression of the Babylonian revolt led by Merodach-baladan II in 702, Sennacherib was free to move against the western states. It was at this point that Judah and Ekron appealed for help to the Nubian Pharaoh Shebitku who had succeeded Shabako on the throne in that year, and it is probably to this appeal that reference is made either directly (30:1–7; 31:1–3) or indirectly (28:14–15, 18–22; 29:15–16) in this section of the book. The defeat of the Egyptian army at Eltekeh shortly afterwards must have dashed any hopes these western states still entertained of any change in the political status quo.

This fourth in the series of five comminations or woes in chs. 28–31, which many commentators are prepared to attribute to Isaiah himself, reveals a strain of anxiety at the secularization of politics manifested in the failure of the Judean bureaucracy to seek "the good word" from a prophet before embarking on political or military initiatives. Addressing them as "rebellious children" sounds outrageously paternalistic to us but should perhaps be read against the background of the *bēn sōrēr* ("rebellious son") law in Deut 21:18–21, which involves the death penalty (cf. Isa 1:2). Piling sin upon sin may also be understood in the context of the violation of oaths taken in the vassal treaty, which would have forbidden alliances with other countries—compare Hezekiah's admission of having sinned addressed to Sennacherib (2 Kgs 18:14).

The prophet's denunciation of making alliances, which is what one expects responsible governments to do, was inspired by a kind of political quietism based on uncompromising and absolute trust in the protection of Yahveh. We can appreciate the fact that for Hezekiah's advisers to follow this policy would seem to call for either heroic faith or heroic folly. But there happened to exist at this juncture grounds for serious misgivings about Egypt, quite apart from atavistic Judean hostility towards that country. The noninterventionist policy pursued by Shabako and the internal problems experienced by the Nubian dynasty might have persuaded the Judean leadership that Egypt would prove to be an unreliable ally—an opinion apparently shared by the Assyrian generalissimo, who described them as a broken reed or unreliable walking stick (36:6), an opinion justified by the course of events. It would therefore not have called for a high level of inspiration for the prophet to predict that the negotiations then underway would come to nothing. Since Judah was the petitioner, these overtures took place in Egypt—at Zoan or Tanis (San ʾel-Hajar) in the eastern Nile delta, where the Nubians had only recently established themselves, and at Hanes or Herakleopolis south of Memphis in Upper Egypt. In the context the allusion to his (that is, Hezekiah's) envoys implies a negative verdict on the actions of Hezekiah himself and therefore highlights once again the difference between the profiles of both prophet and king here and in the annalistic account in chs. 36–39.

ANIMALS OF THE NEGEV:
AN ORACLE (30:6–7)

(Day 1985, 88–101; 1992; Schunk)

TRANSLATION

30 ⁶Animals of the Negev: an oracle:
Through a land of dire distress,
the haunt of lioness and roaring lion,[a]
poisonous snake and flying serpent,
they carry their goods on the backs of donkeys,
their treasures on the humps of camels
to a profitless people.

[7]Vain and worthless is Egypt's[b] help;
therefore, I name it:
"Rahab reduced to silence."[c]

NOTES

[a] *Mēhem* is problematic; 1QIsa[a] reads *v'yn mym*, "and there is no water," but the context requires another animal; *mēhem* = "among them," lacks an antecedent; Hiphil participle → *hmm*, "confuse," "disturb" is attested only in Qal; a better option is *hmh*, also attested only in Qal, but representing a sound emitted by bears (59:11) and dogs (Ps 59:7, 15); [b] *ûmiṣrayim* probably a gloss to clarify the previous verse; the half-verse is overloaded; [c] *rahab hēm šebet* is a famous crux; even allowing for the slogan-like character of these sobriquets in sentence form, this does not make sense as it stands; attempts at a solution have been many and varied, some of them colorful (e.g. "Rahab-la-chômeuse" i.e. "Rahab out of work," Vermeylen 1977, 411), others cumbersome (e.g. "ein Ungeheuer das zu Untätigkeit verurteilt ist," i.e. "A monster condemned to inactivity," Wildberger 1982, 1157); among solutions requiring no consonantal emendation the most plausible are *hammĕšabbēt* (Piel), *hammašbît* (Hiphil), and *hammošbāt* (Hophal), all derived from *šbt*, "cease," rather than *yšb*, "sit."

COMMENTS

This little poem takes the woe-saying further with a vivid cameo of the Judean delegates' making their tortuous way through the Negev to their destination in Egypt. The title may have been added by the editor who arranged the *maśśā'* units in chs. 13–23 and provided them with titles, especially those titles suggested by a phrase in the poem in question (21:1, 11, 13). It is also possible that this title was suggested by the urge to pun on the word *maśśā'*, which can mean "oracle" or "burden"—the burden of tribute carried on animals of the Negev— which could also have suggested the inclusion of the four less accomodating local species mentioned in addition to donkeys and camels. That the envoys took this route rather than the easier and safer coastal road may have been due to the need for secrecy (cf. 29:15) and this in spite of the threatening presence of lions, poisonous snakes (cf. 59:5), and flying serpents (14:29). Deuteronomy 8:15 adds scorpions to the perils of that "great and terrible wilderness."

The idea seems to be to set up a contrast between the futility of the goal and the immense pains and dangers involved in trying to achieve it. It is all summed up in the symbolic and farcical name attached to Egypt. This is a type of designation in sentence form comparable to Maher-shalal-hash-baz (8:1–4) or Sha'on-he'ebir-hammo'ed, applied to Pharaoh, which may with some license be translated "Big Mouth who missed his chance" (Jer 46:17). It will be evident from the brief textual note above (see a fuller listing of variants in Goshen-Gottstein 1995, 121) that these three words are obscure enough to permit a wide range of options. The Targum goes its own way, translating "I will bring the appointed ones upon them," and Ibn Ezra takes *rahab* metaphorically to mean strength and translates "their strength is to sit still," with reference to those who stayed in Jerusalem. More commonly Rahab is one of those personifications of chaos with which the Israelite imagination peopled the dark, circumfluent waters around and under the narrow foothold of land on which they lived. Together with its cohorts (Job 9:13), it is associated with Yamm (Sea), Tannin (Dragon) and, of course, Leviathan (51:9; Pss 74:12–14; 89:11; 104:26; Job 3:8; 7:12; 26:12). In the course of time these dramatis personae of primordial myth were drawn into the heroic narrative of national origins in which the defeat by divine power of Egypt and subduing of the sea, the Papyrus Sea, featured prominently. It was therefore not surprising that the names Rahab (also in Ps 87:4) and Tannin (Ezek 29:3; 32:2) stuck to Egypt as Chaos personified, the evil empire par excellence.

WRITE IT FOR POSTERITY (30:8–14)

(Exum 1981; Galling 1971; Reymond; Williamson 1994, 103–6)

TRANSLATION

i

30 [8] Now come, write it on a tablet,
   inscribe it in a book in their presence[a]
   that it may be there in time to come
   as a witness[b] forever;
   [9] for they are a rebellious people,
   deceitful children,
   children unwilling to obey[c]
   Yahveh's instructions;
   [10] who say to the seers, "Do not see,"
   to the visionaries, "Do not envision what is right for us,
   tell us smooth and soft things,
   see seductive visions,
   [11] turn aside[d] from the way,
   leave the right path,
   stop talking to us about the Holy One of Israel!"

ii

[12] So, this is what the Holy One of Israel says:
   "Since you reject this saying,
   trusting in a perverse oppressor[e]
   and placing your confidence in him,

¹³this iniquitous act will be for you
like a fault in a lofty wall
bulging out and ready to fall;
its collapse will come suddenly, in an instant,
¹⁴it will come apart like the breaking of a potter's vessel
that is smashed without mercy;
among its fragments no sherd will be found
for carrying fire from the hearth
or scooping water from the cistern."

NOTES

^a Since the meter of this section is irregular, *'ittām*, literally, "with them," should not be deleted *metri causa* (as BHS, following Vulg.);   ^b *lĕ'ēd* for MT *lā'ad*;   ^c 1QIsa^a has *lišmoa'* for MT *šĕmoa'*;   ^d 1QIsa^a has *tasîrû* for MT *sûrû*; ^e preferable to RSV "oppression and deceit" on account of *'ālāv* (sing.) following; also cf. the combination of the epithets *ḥāmās* ("violent") and *nālôz* ("perverse") in Prov 3:31–32.

COMMENTS

We are not told what the prophet was commanded to commit to writing. Analogy with the writing of the name Maher-shalal-hash-baz (8:1–4) would suggest what immediately precedes, i.e., the name of the Beast, a name that is of the same symbolic type as the name of the prophet's son. This reading would, however, be feasible only on the assumption that the name was a way of recapitulating the message repeated throughout this section about the folly of relying on an Egyptian alliance. It would not follow that v 8 belongs with vv 6–7 as the conclusion to the *maśśā'* (pace Vermeylen 1977, 410–11), since the following v 9 explains why the writing is necessary. There has been much discussion about how the writing was done, the meaning of the verbs employed and why two different writing surfaces are involved. This curiosity is legitimate, but it is well to recall that this is not a transcription of an order received by Isaiah or some other prophet; it is a *literary construct* similar to Job's request that his case be set down in writing, using the same two verbs as here. It does not in any event seem likely that the prophet is being told to make two copies of what is to be recorded. Terms for recording in writing are not always precise. Several different verbs are used for writing on a tablet (*lûaḥ*), including *ḥrt* (Exod 32:16), *ḥrš* (Jer 17:1), *b'r* (Hab 2:2), *psl* (Exod 34:1; Deut 10:1, 3), in addition to *ktb* (Exod 34:1, 28; Deut 10:2, 4), and if one can inscribe or engrave (*ḥqq*) on the hand (Isa 49:16) one can surely do so on papyrus, as here. The "book" (*sēper*) would be in the form of a scroll (cf. 34:4, the skies rolled up like a book), which would be inscribed on one side and then sealed (cf. 8:16).

The command addressed to the prophet to write is in evident parallelism to the writing and sealing of a text after the failure to influence Ahaz a generation

earlier (8:16). Both texts are said to contain *tôrâ*, which in Isa 1–39 always connotes prophetic instruction, and both are written to *testify* at a future time to
the truth of the prophetic communication (*tĕʿûdâ* 8:16; *ʿēd* 30:8). These two
occasions point to an early period in the transmission of prophetic oral delivery
in writing as a kind of emergency measure. Other references to writing and
reading (29:11–12, 18; 34:16) represent a later editorial stage when there existed a "book" of Isaiah, no doubt in embryonic form.

The command to write is followed by an explanation that is practically a
reprise of 30:1–5 with respect to the severe, paternalistic tone but with the important addition of the attempt to control and redirect prophecy into more
accomodating paths. We are therefore dealing with the issue of the reception
or non-reception of prophecy. What is rejected is the instruction (*tôrâ*) of God
communicated through prophetic intermediaries, in which connection we
note the studious avoidance of the standard term for "prophets," *nĕbîʾîm*, and
the corresponding verbal forms (*nibbāʾ, hitnabbēʾ*) in favor of the less specific
language of seeing, visioning, and speaking. The injunction is therefore to fill
the public role of the official *nābîʾ* and the expectations of the public that create the role—therefore, to engage in a more accommodating and supportive
form of prophesying and, failing that, to just keep quiet.

The attempt to silence, control, or redirect prophetic activity is well attested
for ancient Israel, the classic paradigm being the encounter between Amos and
Amaziah at Bethel (Amos 7:10–17; see also 2:12 and Mic 2:6). At the time of
Jeremiah the leading clergy of the Jerusalem temple are taken to task for not
controlling prophetic activity in the temple precincts (Jer 29:26–28), though
we hear of Jeremiah himself being banned from the temple—not surprisingly,
given his anti-temple tirades (Jer 36:5). Jeremiah's reaction to the interdiction
would suggest that writing prophecies was a response to the non-reception of
their oral delivery, a supposition that also fits the two occasions on which Isaiah
is said to have committed his words to writing (8:16; 30:8).

We have seen how frequently in Isaiah the rhetorical device of quoting the
opposition and thereby condemning them out of their own mouths is employed. Usually the quotations are intended to convey either misplaced political self-confidence (9:10; 28:15; 30:15) or religious skepticism (5:19; 29:15).
The injunction to turn aside from the way and deviate from the path may well
be a sarcastic mimicking of often-repeated prophetic-homiletic platitudes (cf.
28:9–10). It need not be taken as proof of Deuteronomistic editing of the passage (argued by Vermeylen 1977, 412–14), a thesis that relies heavily on parallels with other prophetic texts deemed to be of Deuteronomistic origin (e.g.
Amos 2:11–16) or on such common complaints as Israel's refusal to listen to
Yahveh (e.g. Deut 21:18, 20), or on analogy with the law of the rebellious son
(Deut 21:18–21 cf. Isa 30:9). We would need clearer indications than these in
order to pass safely from literary influence to editorial activity.

The reply to the invitation to stop preaching in the name of the Holy One of
Israel is, argumentatively, made in the name of the Holy One of Israel (12–14).
The prophetic utterance (*dābār* 12), so decisively rejected, refers to the drift of

prophecy in chs. 28–31 as a whole. The reliance of the seer's interlocutors on violent solutions, on the devious maneuverings inseparable from *Realpolitik*, and specifically on the Egyptian Pharaoh will be like leaning for support on a wall about to collapse—rather like the Assyrian commander's comparing Egypt to a reed or walking stick that will gouge the hand of anyone foolish enough to lean on it (36:6). As happens occasionally in these chapters, this is a case of a good metaphor overworked: one metaphor developed at length (a smashed pot) serving to illustrate another (a collapsed wall)—a metaphor within a metaphor, therefore.

IGNOMINIOUS DEFEAT AWAITS YOU (30:15–17)

(Donner 1964, 159–62; Gonçalves 1995; Melugin 1974)

TRANSLATION

30 [15]This is what the Sovereign Lord Yahveh, the Holy One of Israel, has said:
   "In turning back and staying still you will be safe,
   in quiet confidence your strength will lie"
   —but you did not want it.
   [16]"No," you said, "we can always flee on horseback."
   "All right, then, flee you shall!"
   "Swiftly will we ride."
   "Then those who pursue you will swiftly follow."
   [17][A thousand will flee when threatened by one.][a]
   "You will flee when threatened by five,
   until you are left
   like a flagpole on top of a mountain,
   like a lookout post on a hill."

NOTES

[a] MT reads "one thousand faced with the threat of one," which requires us to supply a verb, probably *yanûsu*, "will flee"; but the entire line is probably a gloss.

COMMENTS

This pronouncement of judgment with its own incipit seems to come disguised as a promise (so Melugin), but the allusion seems to be to *past* offers of security and strength accompanied by exhortations to political quietism (7:4, 9;

12:2; 26:2, 8; 28:12), all of which have been declined. The point is made in the form of a lively altercation. Since talk about beating a fast retreat seems somewhat out of keeping with the upbeat attitude of the war party under Hezekiah, Vermeylen (1977, 415–16) reads these verses as a Deuteronomistic *relecture* from the time of the first or second Babylonian invasion more than a century later. But it is difficult to see how the conversation makes better sense in that context, and moreover the language is not strikingly Deuteronomistic. More importantly, relocating this exchange to the Neo-Babylonian period evades the problem alluded to earlier, namely, the lack of congruity between the interpretation of events leading up to and during Hezekiah's revolt as presented in the narrative section (chs. 36–39) with the very negative view of the Judean political and military establishment expressed in this compilation of sayings (chs. 28–31). The Deuteronomists may well have been responsible for the discrepancy between the two versions by presenting the events according to their own very definite views of the prophetic role and their interpretation of the person and activity of Hezekiah, but that is something quite different. There is also some support for the disdainful tone of this passage from Sennacherib's account, which alludes to the desertion of Judean troops brought into Jerusalem by Hezekiah (*ANET*, 288).

The form in which the disputation is couched is somewhat strange, but the point seems clear enough: in the worst scenario we will seek our safety and security not in your promises but by escape on horseback. This too is a literary construct and echoes warnings heard occasionally about excessive confidence in the horse, the symbol of military pride (Deut 17:16; Ps 20:7; 33:17; 147:10–11). Moreover, the depiction of a rout followed by headlong flight is a topos of prophetic diatribe, perhaps drawing on colorful formulations in treaty curses (e.g. Amos 2:13). If we include the glossator's contribution, the proportion between pursuers and pursued (1 to 1000) is much more shameful than 1 to 20 or 1 to 100 (Lev 26:8) and even worse than fleeing the scene of action with no one in pursuit (Lev 26:17).

MERCY WILL EMBRACE YOU ON EVERY SIDE (30:18–26)

(Beuken 1995b; Laberge)

TRANSLATION

i

30 [18]Therefore Yahveh waits to show you favor,
   therefore he bestirs himself [a] to have compassion on you;
   for Yahveh is a God of justice,
   blessed are all those who wait for him!

ii

¹⁹You people in Zion, you who dwell in Jerusalem,ᵇ you shall weep no more. Heᶜ will surely show you favor when you cry for help, and he will answer you when he hears you. ²⁰The Sovereign Lord may give you the bread of adversityᵈ and the water of affliction, yet your teacherᵉ will no longer remain hidden. Your eyes will see your teacher, ²¹and whenever you turn aside either to the right or the left your ears will hear a word spoken behind you: "This is the way, keep to it."ᶠ

²²Then you will reject as unclean your silver-coated images and your molten idols plated with gold. You will refer to them as filth and throw them out like a thing unclean.ᵍ

iii

²³Yahveh will give rain for the seed with which you sow the soil, and grain for bread, the produce of the soil will be rich and abundant. On that day your cattle will graze in broad pastures, ²⁴and the oxen and donkeys that work the land will feed on rich fodder winnowedʰ with shovel and pitchfork. ²⁵On every high mountain and on every lofty hill there will flow channels of running water—on a day of great slaughter when the towers come crashing down. ²⁶Moonlight will be as bright as sunlight, and sunlight will be seven times brighter than now [like the light of seven days].ⁱ All this on the day Yahveh binds up the broken limbs of his people and heals the wounds caused by the blows inflicted on them.

NOTES

ᵃ *Yārûm*, literally, "rise up";   ᵇ there is no justification for eliminating *bĕṣiyôn* as a gloss (Clements 1980a, 250); for *yēšēb* read probably *yōšēb* with BHS; ᶜ 1QIsaᵃ has *YHVH* after *ḥānôn yoḥnĕkâ*;   ᵈ emending *ṣar* to *mēṣar* or *miṣṣār* = ("instead of adversity") and *lāḥaṣ* to *millāḥaṣ* ("instead of affliction") with BHS is unnecessary;   ᵉ 1QIsaᵃ has *mvr'yk* cf. LXX; *môrêkâ* could be either plural or singular but the verb *yikkānēp* is singular; Clements (1980, 250) translates "your early rain will not be withheld" and deletes the second *môrêkâ* as a gloss on *ēnêkâ*, but the translation is incongruous in the context and the deletion arbitrary;   ᶠ *lĕkû bô*, literally, "walk in it";   ᵍ reversing the order of MT; *tizrēm → zrh* = "scatter," with LXX, rather than → *zûr/zôr* = "to be loathsome," elsewhere only in Job 19:17, cf. *yašlîk* 2:20 in a similar context; *kĕmô dāvâ*: *dāvâ* = "menstrual blood" (Lev 15:13; 20:18 and the corresponding verb in Lev 12:2); LXX and Syr. apparently read *kĕmē*, "like the water," for *kĕmô*, "like" (LXX "you shall scatter them as the water of her that sits apart and like ordure you shall remove them"); the second half of the verse, *ṣē' to'mar lô* reads, literally, "'Get out,' you will say to it," an attempt to soften the unpleasant image by substituting *ṣē'* for *ṣē'â* = "feces";   ʰ 1QIsaᵃ has *yzrh* imperfect for MT *zōreh* participle; read *zōrāh* passive;   ⁱ absent from LXX; a somewhat inept statement, often taken to be a gloss on the previous verse.

COMMENTS

Irrespective of the time of composition, the opening statement (beginning "therefore") is connected with the preceding pericope and thus falls into the pattern of alternating threat and promise. The rest of the passage (19–26) can then be read as a prose comment on v 18 with the purpose of explaining how God will show favor and have compassion and why it is worthwhile to wait for God, as God himself waits. It is needless to emphasize that all this talk of waiting for God can ring hollow to those suffering from miseries of various kinds, as the seer's contemporaries no doubt were. That the author was not unaware of this may be indicated by the reminder that "Yahveh is a God of justice," for the demand for justice is an essential postulate for maintaining faith in God at all and therefore for having a reason for waiting. Waiting for God is therefore waiting with God, the justification for which is not subject to verification but can only take the form of a blessing on the one who waits even while not free of doubt. However, waiting for and with the God who waits sooner or later raises the question, "How long?" ('ad-mātay), a question often heard in liturgical prayer, and gives rise to the temptation to provide a precise answer, which is the way of apocalyptic. Hence the injunction, also in the form of a blessing, at the conclusion of the book of Daniel: "Blessed is the one who waits and (then) arrives at the (conclusion of) the 1335 days"—a formulation perhaps modeled on Isa 30:18b. Here as elsewhere (e.g. Hab 2:3) the call for patient waiting is a response to the disconfirmation of expectations about an imminent spectacular reversal of fortune, a decisive intervention of God in human affairs in favor of those who feel that God owes it to them to intervene. Hence the need for reassurance and for the affirmation that justice will prevail in spite of appearances to the contrary.

A footnote: the numerical value of the letters lamed and vav (lô) in the last phrase of 30:18 ('ašrē kol-ḥôkē lô "blessed are all those who wait for him") permitted the reading, by gematria, "blessed are those who wait for the thirty-six" (lamed = 30, vav = 6). According to Jewish lore, these are the thirty-six righteous ones, the lamed-vavniks who, unknown to themselves and to others, maintain the world in existence.

In the first commentary on the promise of favor and compassion (19–22) the Second Temple author moves along the same general line as previous descriptions of a better future (25:1–9; 26:1–15; 28:5–6; 29:17–24), especially the assurance that there will be no more weeping (25:8). The people will be called on to suffer more adversity, in reference to which the language may be taken metaphorically or literally (Ibn Ezra refers it to famine) or both, but they will not be left without guidance. The identity of the teacher is not stated, and the language gives the impression of being deliberately indirect and obscure. God is elsewhere described as a teacher (môreh Job 36:22) and we hear allusions to teachings and instructions emanating from God (e.g. Isa 2:3; 48:17), generally mediated through prophets. We also hear of God's hiding himself (if that is the meaning of the hapax legomenon knp), so that it is no surprise that ancient

Jewish exegesis found a reference to God as teacher here (Targum: "your eyes will see the Shekinah in the sanctuary") and that the same view has prevailed in the commentary tradition (e.g. Duhm 1892, 223; Marti 1900, 225; Fischer 1937, 203–4; Fohrer 1967, 2.103–4). But the explicit mention of Yahveh immediately preceding strongly supports identification with a teacher other than God, and why would God's word be heard *behind* the listeners? One could think of the steps of children being guided by a father (so Skinner 1915, 246) or a mother (so Fohrer 1967, 2.104) walking behind them, but this way of speaking does not fit well with the language about the future in the verse on which the present passage is commenting, and it is without parallel in Isaiah or indeed in the Hebrew Bible. The alternative, then, is that the devout, those who wait for the divine favor to be revealed, are promised guidance from a human teacher, one now hidden, perhaps imprisoned, perhaps deceased. Hence the message that comes to them from behind, that is, from the past, reminding them of the teachings to which they are to adhere. If this much is granted, we are led to think of a prophetic figure comparable to, perhaps identical with, the "Servant" (*'ebed*) of 50:4–11 and 52:13–53:12. This individual is equipped to convey a "word" or "message" (*dābār* 50:4 cf. 30:21a) to the dejected; the language in which his fate is described is overwhelmingly suggestive of persecution and violent death, and he is mourned by those who at one time had turned aside to their own ways (53:6). The walking metaphor for the moral conduct of life (verbal stem *hlk*) and the metaphor of the way (*derek*) for its direction, are drawn from the predominantly moralistic didacticism of the sages (e.g. Prov 1:15; Ps 1:1). But "the way" can also refer to teaching specific to a school or prophetic discipleship. In the period of the Second Temple there is notable emphasis on the teaching function of the prophet, no doubt in dependence on Moses the protoprophet who is the preeminent teacher (e.g. Deut 4:1, 5, 14; 6:1), and in this sense "the way" came into use in early Christianity as a self-designation (*hodos* Acts 9:2; 18:25–26 etc.). The same connotation may provide the clue to the meaning of the present passage.

The eschatological horizon of the abolition of idolatry (30:22) is a theme that recurs regularly in Isaiah in more or less similar form. The idolatrous objects are of silver and gold, and they will be defiled (rendered ritually inaccessible) by association with what is unclean (2:20; 17:7–8; 31:7). These brief notices may represent a distinct redactional phase, perhaps from one and the same source. A further redactional comment (vv 23–26) is suggested by the prediction about the bread of adversity and the water of affliction (v 20) that will be brought to an end by the blessing of abundant rain. The eschatological image is therefore the familiar one of a miraculous and superabundant fertility (e.g. 29:17 cf. Amos 9:13–15). Many commentators regard the prediction of greatly enhanced light, absent from LXX, as a very late addition. It is perhaps understandable that, in his enthusiasm, the author overlooked the inconvenience of a sevenfold increase in temperature, not to mention the ecological impact of doing away with the alternation of day and night. But whenever the final scenario, the "singularity," is the issue, we can expect an accumulation of such hyperbolic expressions, even more noticeably in postbiblical Jewish apocalyptic writings (e.g. *Jub.* 1:29; 19:25; *En.* 91:16). Alternative scenarios envisage the dimming of the sun and moon (24:23; 60:19; Joel 3:4[2:31]) or their being extinguished as no longer necessary (Rev 21:23; 22:5). And we can expect that the day of ultimate salvation will also be "a day of great slaughter," a connection well represented in prophetic writings (Isa 25:1–5; 26:5; Jer 12:3; Ezek 25:15).

ASSYRIA: THE FINAL PHASE (30:27–33)

(Barth 1977, 92–103; Heider 1985, 319–32; Huber 1976, 50–54; Ringgren; Sabottka; Sasson; Weinfeld)

TRANSLATION

i

30 27Observe: the name of Yahveh comes from afar
blazing in anger,
heavy with a sense of doom;[a]
his lips are charged with wrath,
his tongue is a consuming fire,
28his breath is like an overflowing torrent
that reaches up to the neck;
he will place on the nations a yoke[b] that spells their ruin,[c]
a bit on the jaws of the peoples to lead them
where they would not go.[d]

ii

29But for you there will be singing as on a night of sacred pilgrimage; heartfelt rejoicing as when one sets out to the sound of the flute to go to Yahveh's mountain, the rock of Israel. 30Yahveh will make his glorious voice heard and reveal his arm sweeping down in furious anger, together with a flame of devouring fire, with cloudburst, torrents of rain, and hailstones. 31At the sound of Yahveh's voice Assyria will be seized with terror as Yahveh plies the rod.[e] 32Every stroke of the stick that Yahveh lays on them in punishment[f] will be to the sound of tabors, harps, and dancing.[g] [His brandishing arm fights for him.][h] 33For his tophet[i] was set up long ago;[j] [it was also prepared for Molek];[k] his pyre Yahveh has made deep and wide, with fire and wood in abundance. Yahveh's breath inside it will keep it burning like a stream of sulphur.

NOTES

[a] *Věkobed maśśā'ā* should read *věkābēd maśśā'oh*;   [b] the probable meaning of *nāpâ* rather than "sieve," (BDB); *hănāpâ* hapax was chosen for assonance with *nāpat*; if derived from *nôp* (cf. 10:15; 11:15; 13:2; 19:16) it would connote

a swinging to and fro, which does not readily fit the present context; ᶜ *šāv⁾* = "destruction," "ruin," as in Ps 35:17 and cf. *šô⁾â*; ᵈ *mat'eh* → *t'h*, "stray"; ᵉ literally, "with the rod he strikes"; unnecessary to read passive *yukkāh*; ᶠ for MT *mûsādāh* (cf. 1QIsaᵃ *mvsdv* with masculine suffix) read with Syr. *mûsārô*, "his punishment"; the feminine suffixes in 32–33, for the country Assyria, are inconsistent with masculine *⁾aššûr* and with the action here described; ᵍ for MT *ûbĕmilḥămôt*, "and with battles," read *ûbimḥolôt*, "and with dancing"; ʰ this appears to be a somewhat inconsequential gloss commenting on *ûbĕmil-ḥămôt* and therefore added after the latter found its way into the text; for the meaning of *tĕnûpâ* see 19:16 notes; ⁱ read *toptōh* for MT *topteh*; ʲ read *mē⁾etmol* for MT *mē⁾etmûl*; ᵏ transparently a gloss; read *lammolek* for MT *lammelek*, though there is probably a double meaning here (see commentary).

COMMENTS

The prediction or celebration of an Assyrian defeat and the final disappearance of the Assyrians from the scene is unified somewhat by the motif of judgment by fire at the beginning and end and by the breath of Yahveh represented as a flood of water at the beginning and as a stream of fiery sulphur at the end. Rsv sets out 27–28 as verse and the remainder in prose, but the former is hardly more regular prosodically than the latter, and we have had occasion to note that much in chs. 1–35 can be described as *recitatif* rather than verse as generally understood. The metaphors change with bewildering rapidity: features contorted with anger, blows raining down, a flood of water and violent storm, festal liturgies, instrumental music keeping time to a victim being flogged—another unpleasantly sadistic image (cf. 25:10–12; 63:1–6) not adequately justified as a reaction to the notorious cruelty and sadism of Assyrian armies. Suggestions have been made with a view to improving the flow of the narrative by shuffling verses around (30 after 27–28, 31–33 following 29) but without achieving any notable improvement, and in any case the task of the interpreter is to explain what is there not to improve on it.

The debate about whether this pericope was composed by Isaiah (Wildberger 1978, 1210–15) or an anonymous prophet during Josiah's reign (Barth 1977, 92–103; Clements 1980a, 252–54), or a much later apocalyptic writer of the Hellenistic period (Kaiser 1974, 305–10) remains, predictably, without a definite resolution. There is no lack of Isaian motifs and turns of phrase— Assyria as an overwhelming flood now itself flooded (cf. 8:7–8), Assyria as a rod now being punished with a rod (cf. 10:5), recalling the frequent mention in putatively Isaian passages of rods, whips, and yokes (10:1–19, 24–27; 14:24–27)—but these could as well have been adopted by an Isaian epigone of the Second Temple period. The passage also fails the test of Isaian authenticity by reason of its lack of thematic cohesion. Furthermore, the parallelism with the conclusion of the book should be taken into account: Yahveh comes in a flame of devouring fire (66:15), and his enemies are destined to be incinerated in an unquenchable fire outside Jerusalem (66:24).

One of the most difficult questions to answer and one asked more persistently by this generation of Isaian scholars than in the past concerns the interconnections among the pericopes into which commentators divide the book. We cannot assume that the arrangement and sequencing of these passages are entirely fortuitous, but on the other hand there is the temptation to impose more order on the book than it can reasonably be expected to exhibit. It is not just a matter of finding thematic and linguistic links between adjacent passages or different kinds of nexuses between nonadjacent sections or chapters. These are important, but we need also to be alert to exegetical developments within the book, in the belief that the first chapter in the history of the interpretation of Isaiah must be extracted from the book itself. In the present instance, then, we might essay reading 30:27–33 as the last in a series of exegetical expansions on the theme set out briefly in 30:18: "Therefore Yahveh waits to show you favor . . . blessed are all those who wait for him!" These editorial elaborations (30:19–33) address the questions raised by this statement of assurance (30:18): How will God show us favor? Why is it worth our while to wait on God? When will the period of waiting end? What will happen when it does end? The answer in vv 19–21 is about prophetic guidance, v 22 looks forward to the eschatological horizon of the abolition of idolatry, vv 23–25 predict fertility, v 26 cosmic upheaval and renewal, and vv 27–33 final judgment on the forces of evil encapsulated in the name Assyria, as they will be later encapsulated in the names of Edom and Rome. All of these facets can be found elsewhere in the book and, though from different individuals and groups at different points on the historical continuum, all cohere in a very general way in what may be called an Isaian literary tradition.

The theophany in fire and flood is followed by a vividly described scene of a kind of auto-da-fé involving a personified Assyria as victim (29–33). The occasion is a pilgrimage to Jerusalem, for which ritual preparation is made the evening before departure, as was customary for festivals in general (cf. Num 11:18; Josh 7:13). The euphoric mood is sustained by musical instruments and percussion, reminiscent of the band of dervishes worshiping at the high place with similar instrumentation—harp, drum, flute, and lyre (1 Sam 10:5). The background to this scene is provided by the pilgrimage psalms (Pss 120–34) with their characteristic note of joy and the celebration of freedom from oppression ("the scepter of the wicked" Ps 125:3). The goal of the pilgrimage is Jerusalem, and the ceremony concludes with the ritual immolation of Assyria in the Valley of Hinnom, later Gehenna. The *tophet* prepared for this occasion may have originated as a place-name somewhere south of Jerusalem (2 Kgs 23:10; Jer 7:31–33; 19:5–7) but came to designate a cultic site set up for ritual infanticide. Both literary and (for the western Mediterranean) archaeological evidence for this practice is adequate if not abundant. As a solicitous glossator points out, the practice was associated, in Israel as elsewhere, with a chthonic deity whose name usually appears as Molech, perhaps originally Malik or Milk (Lev 18:21; 20:2–5; 2 Kgs 23:10; Jer 32:35; Isa 57:9). In this instance, and in the last sentence of the book (66:24), this cultic setting provides the lurid backdrop for the final overcoming of evil.

THE ALLIANCE WITH EGYPT IS DOOMED (31:1–9)

(Amsler; Barré; Dietrich 1976, 144–52; Donner 1964, 135–39; Eidevall; Exum 1981; Sweeney 1994; 1996, 401–8; Wong)

TRANSLATION

i

[1] Woe to those who go down to Egypt[a] for help,
who rely on horses,
who put their trust in chariots[b] on account of their size
and in horsemen on account of their great strength,[c]
but do not look to the Holy One of Israel
nor seek guidance from Yahveh.
[2] But he too is wise and can bring about[d] disaster;
he does not renege on what he says
but will rise up against a household of evildoers,
against those who help others do wrong.
[3] Egypt is human, it is not superhuman,
its horses are flesh and not spirit;
when Yahveh puts forth his hand
the helper will stumble, the one helped will fall,
and both will perish together.

ii

[4] This is what Yahveh said to me:
As the lion or the lion cub growls over its prey[e]
when a band of shepherds is called out against it,
and is not frightened off by their shouting
nor cowed[f] by their clamor,
so Yahveh of the hosts will descend to do battle
on Mount Zion and on its summit.
[5] Like birds hovering overhead
so will Yahveh of the hosts protect Jerusalem;
he will protect and deliver,
he will spare and rescue.[g]

iii

[6] Return, O Israel, to the One whom you have so profoundly offended, [7] for on that day all of you will reject your gods of silver and gods of gold that your sinful hands made for yourselves.

iv

⁸Assyria will fall by no human sword,
and no mortal sword will consume him;
before that sword he will flee,ʰ
his youths will be put to forced labor,
⁹his leadersⁱ will pass away from terror,
his officers shrink in terror from the enemy's standard.ʲ

¹⁰ This is a saying of Yahveh, whose light burns in Zion, whose furnace is
in Jerusalem.

NOTES

ᵃ 1QIsaᵃ has *lmṣrym* for MT *miṣrayim*;   ᵇ 1QIsaᵃ *hrkb* for MT *rekeb*;   ᶜ LXX
plēthos sphodra, "a great multitude";   ᵈ 1QIsaᵃ *vyby'* simple imperfect (future), predictive, for the MT *vayyābē'* imperfect consecutive, referring to past
action of Yahveh, probably therefore less suitable in the context;   ᵉ 1QIsaᵃ
trpyv pl. for MT *tarpô*;   ᶠ 1QIsaᵃ seems to repeat *yḥt* followed by *y'nh*,
though the script is unclear at this point;   ᵍ 1QIsaᵃ *vpsḥ vhplyt* for MT *pā-
soaḥ věhimlîṭ* but with no essential difference in the sense;   ʰ 1QIsaᵃ *vns
vlv' mpny ḥrb*, "he will flee but not before the sword";   ⁱ *sal'ô*, literally, "his
rock," taken literally in LXX (*petra*), which had a different text in front of it, but
in the context a metaphor for the Assyrian king rather than an Assyrian deity
(Ashur) cf. 32:2 *sela'* referring to the king and his officers or princes; see further
Wildberger 1978, 1245–46; G. R. Driver 1968, 52;   ʲ rather than "his captains too dismayed to flee" (NEB), reading *minnûs* (cf. 1QIsaᵃ *mnys*) for MT
minnēs; also preferable to "his officers desert the standard in panic" (RSV) cf.
the same verb in 31:4.

COMMENTS

The fifth and last of the woe-series in chs. 28–31 (1–3) is followed by an assurance of the survival and flourishing of Jerusalem (4–5 + 8–9), into which an exhortation to put an end to idolatry has been inserted (6–7). This pattern of
threat followed by assurance is maintained throughout the entire section:

threat	*assurance*
28:14–15	28:16–17
29:1–4	29:5–8
29:15–16	29:17–21
30:1–17	30:29–33
31:1–3	31:4–5, 8–9

The threat has the purpose of dissuading the Judean leadership from embarking on an anti-Assyrian rebellion with the support of Egypt (for the historical

circumstances see the commentary on 30:1–5). The programmatic juxtaposition of threat and assurance is a literary construct put together after the events of 705–701, for the most part long after, with the purpose of re-contextualizing the denunciations and comminations to create a message more appropriate for the time of writing. The woe-saying itself may well be authentically Isaian (conceded even by Kaiser 1974, 311–12), but the passage as a whole is later. The period of the decline of Assyria towards the end of the reign of Ashurbanipal, as proposed by Barth (1977, 83–84) and followed by Clements (1980a, 256–57), is possible, but we would require more precise criteria than the texts afford to exclude a date after the fall of Jerusalem (as Vermeylen 1977, 421–24).

The woe follows the same line as the previous one (30:1–5). The basic issue is subsumed in the verbs expressing trust and reliance. The problem is that the Judean leadership refuses to seek guidance or consult (*drš*) Yahveh, understood as obedient attention to prophetic communications. Several commentators read 31:2 as an interpolation or gloss (Donner 1964, 135–36; Jensen 1973, 131), but it fits the context in the sense of a confrontation between Egypt, with its age-old traditions of wisdom and magical power, and Yahveh, whose wisdom is destructive as well as creative (cf. 28:21; 29:15–16; 30:1). That the Egyptians were well known as breeders and exporters of horses (cf. Deut 17:16; 1 Kgs 10:29) suggests another example of prophetic antiequine prejudice (cf. 30:15–16). And the final statement, denying godlike status to Egypt, appears to be a rejection of the claim to divinity made by and on behalf of the Pharaohs. The bottom line is that the projected Egyptian alliance will lead to disaster. The image is of a man coming to the assistance of someone about to fall — into a pit? — who himself stumbles, with the result that both collapse together.

We note again, in passing, that while the Egyptian intervention in the campaign of 701 was turned aside by the Assyrian army at the battle of Eltekeh, and to this extent the warnings delivered here are historically to the point, the attitude to these events and to the Judean participants ("a household of evildoers") in this saying is strikingly different from the sympathetic viewpoint and the description of the prophet-king relationship in evidence throughout the annalistic section chs. 36–39.

Isaiah 31:4–5, continued in 8–9, is the by now expected counter to the word of judgment and threat. The theme is the protection of Jerusalem and discomfiting of the Assyrians. It is introduced with one of those rare allusions to the seer to whom the message is delivered (4). The metaphors of the lion defending its prey and the bird hovering overhead connote protection not destruction (pace Clements 1980a, 256–57 and Barré). The lion is often but not invariably a figure of menace directed against Israel (e.g. Amos 3:2; Hos 5:14 but cf. Amos 1:2), and the birds hovering over the city are just birds (*ṣipporîm*), not birds of prey (*'ayiṭ*). This reading of the text misses the force and poignancy of the image: Israel or Judah or Jerusalem is the prey of God; Jerusalem is wounded, near to death, but will remain God's prey, not the prey of other nations, and as such will be guarded, ferociously if necessary, like a lion or lion cub or a bird whose nest or whose food is threatened. The defeat of the Assyrians by superhuman agency rounds out this scenario by linking thematically with the denial of superhuman status to the Egyptians. Since, as we shall see, the annalistic account betrays knowledge of the sayings, this last reference in chs. 1–35 to the Assyrians may have suggested the slaying of the 185,000 Assyrians by "the destroying angel" (*hammašḥît*) in the historical conclusion (37:36–38).

The interpolated exhortation to put aside idolatry (6–7) is of a piece with similar pleas and predictions throughout chs. 1–39 (2:20; 17:8; 30:22) and probably derives from the same source. It is a plea for "conversion" (*těšûbâ*) heard elsewhere in the book, especially in the later sections (44:22; 55:7; 59:20 cf. 1:27; 10:21–22). The connection in prophetic writings between idol worship and trade or alliance with foreign nations is a matter of record. The Egyptian export trade in horses and chariots is seen, here and elsewhere, as a particularly dangerous example of the connection (2:20 cf. 2:7–8; Mic 5:10–15).

THE RIGHTEOUS KINGDOM (32:1–8)

(Carroll; Fichtner 1949, 75–80; Gerleman; Gosse 1995; Irwin; Olley; Thompson; Wegner 1992, 275–301; Whedbee; Williamson 1995, 133–41; 1998, 264–70)

TRANSLATION

32 ¹When a king reigns with righteousness,
and princes[a] govern with justice,
²each of them will be like a refuge from the wind,
a shelter from the tempest;[b]
or like streams of water on the parched soil,
like the shade of a great rock in an arid[c] land.

³Then the eyes that can see will no longer be closed,[d]
the ears that can hear will listen,
⁴the minds of the rash will understand and know,
the tongues of stammerers[e] will speak freely,
⁵a fool will no longer be called noble,
nor a villain reckoned of high estate;
⁶for fools speak only what is foolish,
their minds devise[f] only what is worthless,
they act in an impious fashion
speaking deviously even to Yahveh.
They do not satisfy the appetite of the hungry;
they leave the thirst of the thirsty unquenched.
⁷The ways of the villain[g] are evil;
he devises infamous plans
to destroy the poor with false discourse,
and the cause of the needy with their speech;[h]

⁸but those who are noble devise only what is noble,
taking their stand on honor.

NOTES

ᵃ Read *vĕśārîm* for MT *ûlĕśārîm* with LXX, Syr., Tg., Vulg.;   ᵇ read *mizzerem* for MT *zerem* cf. 1QIsaᵃ *strm zrm*, apparently a case of misdivision of words; ᶜ *ʿāyēpâ*, literally, "tired" cf. Ps 63:2 parallel with *ṣiyyâ*, "arid" and Ps 143:6; ᵈ read *tušāʿenāh* Hophal for MT *tišʿenāh* → *šᶜᶜ* = "stick or paste together," cf. 6:10 and 29:9;   ᵉ *ʿillogîm* hapax and the verbal stem *ʿlg* unattested but cf. *bĕlaʿăgē śāpâ*, 28:11;   ᶠ *ḥôšēb* with 1QIsaᵃ for MT *yaʿăśeh*;   ᵍ MT *vĕkēlay kēlâv rāʿîm*, "and as for the villain, his vessels are evil"; the choice of *kēlâv* for the sake of alliteration leaves the sense obscure; hence the more generalized translation;   ʰ the second hemistich is problematic; following Delitzsch, Kaiser reads, "even when the plea of the needy is right," which requires *ûbidĕbar* for MT *ûbĕdabbēr*; moreover, *mišpāṭ* cannot function as an adjective; the reading adopted here takes *ûbĕdabbēr* as parallel with *bĕʾimrē-šeqer* and *lĕhabbēl* as applying to what is done to both poor and needy; 1QIsaᵃ reads *ʾebyônîm* for MT *ʾebyôn* and omits *mišpāṭ*.

COMMENTS

Following the woe-series, chs. 32–33 constitute a new, distinct section, one that is given a semblance of unity by beginning and ending with a description of the ideal ruler and polity (32:1–8; 33:17–22). In between these "book ends," however, the logical thread can easily be lost as we move in a disjointed fashion from an injunction to the women to lament a temporary condition of drought and depopulation (32:9–20), to the predicted end of a tyrant (33:1), a short psalm (2–6), a situation of social *anomie* that will call for divine intervention (7–12), and a brief moral catechism (13–16). Whether there is any continuity of theme in this sequence can be determined, if at all, only after a close reading of each unit in turn.

In the first passage (32:1–8) there are many topical and verbal links with the woe-series and other parts of the book: finding shelter from the storm (4:6; 16:4; 25:4; 28:15, 17; 30:2–3) and shade from the sun's heat (4:6; 25:5), streams of water in an arid land (30:25), eyes that finally see and ears that finally hear (6:10; 29:9–10, 18). It makes for fairly straightforward and coherent reading, and there seems no good reason to separate off vv 6–8 as a later sapiential comment on the theme of good government with special reference to what is to be done with fools and villains (Kaiser 1974, 321 and Clements 1980a, 259). On the contrary, the entire passage has a strongly didactic and reflective character. The theme of good government and the maintenance of a just social order is one of the favorite topoi of Near Eastern sages (examples in Wildberger 1982, 1255–56) and is well represented in the didactic and aphoristic writings in the Hebrew Bible (e.g. Prov 20:8, 26, 28). Williamson (1998, 264–70) has pointed to some

proverbial or sapiential features of the language in 32:1: the absence of the article before *melek* ("king"), the use of denominative verbs (*mlk, śrr*), *ṣedeq* ("righteousness") preceding *mišpāṭ* ("justice"), as in the proverbial literature (Prov 1:3
and 2:9) but not in the prophetic books, and the parallel statement about good
government by kings and princes, using some of the same language and the
same verbs, in Prov 8:15–16 (*bî mĕlākîm yimlokû . . . bî śārîm yaśorû*). The parallels are not confined to this opening verse. The metaphor of streams of water
(*palgē mayim*) applied to the ruler is also found in Proverbs (21:1), as is the contrast between the fool (*nābāl*) and the noble or highborn individual (*nādîb*)
(Prov 17:7). Other themes familiar from the didactic and aphoristic literature—
knowing, understanding, foolish talk, impiety—can easily be picked out.

At first sight, these distinctive features seem to strengthen the case of commentators who argue for a sapiential edition of the book, or at least of chs. 1–
35. In the present instance, at least, this hypothesis is complicated by the close
parallels with similar themes expressed in much the same language elsewhere
in the book. The just ruler serves as a shelter and refuge in the same way as
Yahveh at 25:4–5 (*'ebyôn, zerem, ṣēl, ṣāyôn* occur here and in 32:1–2). The
change in the condition of the blind and deaf, the poor and needy, and those
deprived of access to judicial process is also the theme of 29:17–21, which concludes with a prediction of the end of an oppressive ruler, comparable therefore to 33:1. We have heard that Isaiah's mission resulted in the closing of the
eyes of the sighted, the stopping up of ears otherwise capable of hearing, and
the inspissation of minds (6:9–10). We now hear that the situation so described
will be reversed once a just social order is established. This theme of "vision
and blindsight" (Carroll) is an Isaian theme (29:9–12,18; 35:5; 42:18–20; 43:8)
and cannot be derived from the didacticism of the scribes, though it admits of
influence from that quarter. According to 29:17–21, mentioned above, the
blind will see, the deaf will hear, and justice will be available to the poor and
needy only with the passing away of an unjust social order. Only then, too, will
there be true discernment. The mind will be opened to knowledge rather than
illusion, and the emendation of the intellect will make clear speech possible
(32:4 cf. 28:11–13).

These various ways in which the passage is situated within the Isaian tradition practically rule out the possibility, entertained by several exegetes older
(Duhm; Skinner) and more recent (Auvray; Hayes and Irvine; Williamson)
that it was composed by Isaiah himself, and increase the odds against its attribution to an author writing during the reign of Josiah (Barth 1977, 167–68;
Clements 1980a, 259). We could read it as a reflection on good government,
prompted no doubt by the criticism of political leadership in the two kingdoms
that occupies such a prominent place in the Isaian material. A basic postulate
is that the primary duty of rulers and the ruling class is to protect the rights of
the poor and to prevent their exploitation by the powerful and wealthy while at
the same time preserving the social order with its hierarchy of class based on
wealth and property. When the established social order is subverted—the
young showing no respect for the elderly, youngsters and women in control,

slaves on the same footing as their masters (3:4–5, 12; 24:2)—no one benefits, and one way in which the subversion takes place is when fools and villains are no longer recognized for what they are.

The epithet translated "fool" (*nābāl*) carries a sense of moral imbecility, which can go as far as to deny the existence of God (Pss 14:1; 33:2), and the contrast between this category and the honorable person (*nādîb*) is a familiar topos in the aphoristic literature of Israel and surrounding regions (Prov 17:7, 21, 26; 19:6; 25:7; 30:22). There seems to be a progression from the fool to the villain (if this is a correct rendering of *kilay*, which occurs only in 32:5, 7). The fool has nothing to say worth listening to, is uninformed about religious matters, without spiritual discernment, and unconcerned about the disadvantaged in society. The villain, however, acts deliberately in pursuing harmful and destructive ends and, rather than just neglecting the poor, goes out of his way to exploit them by subverting the judicial process.

Our brief study of this pericope raises once again the issue raised by several exegetes, that the book of Isaiah has undergone redaction by professional didacts, members of the so-called "wisdom schools" in ancient Israel. "Wisdom" is a slippery term that has served to characterize many different kinds of writings in the Hebrew Bible, and it is now acknowledged that one should err on the side of rigor rather than generosity in classifying this or that text as sapiential. The relevant vocabulary (wisdom and folly, counsel, knowledge, understanding, learning and teaching, etc.), genres (parable, proverb, instruction), and themes (counsel, folly), as reflected in Isaiah, have been thoroughly worked over (e.g. Whedbee, Jensen, and most recently Williamson in English language scholarship). While several of the examples put forward are impressive (in particular, the parable in 28:23–29 and the moral catechism in 33:15), the incidence of language and theme lacks the degree of overall consistency necessary to sustain the hypothesis and points to contacts and influences rather than a specific sapiential redactional stage in the production of the book.

MOURNING, BUT NOT FOREVER (32:9–20)

(Fohrer 1967, 2.122–28; Vattioni)

TRANSLATION

32 [9]You women at ease,[a] hear my voice;
   complacent young women, attend to what I say:
   [10]Though now without a care, within a year at most[b]
   you will be trembling with fear;
   the vintage will be lost, the harvest will fail.[c]

   [11]So shake with fear, you women at ease;
   tremble, you complacent ones;

strip yourselves bare,
put a cloth around your waists,
¹²beat your breasts^d
for the fields once pleasant, the vine once fruitful.
¹³On the soil of my people
you bring up thorns and briars,^e
in every happy home
and in the bustling town.
¹⁴For the palace is abandoned,
the city once crowded deserted,
the citadel^f and the watchtower have become open fields^g forever,
the joy of wild donkeys
pastureland for flocks . . .

¹⁵. . . until a spirit from on high is poured out on us,
then the wilderness will be turned into fertile land,^h
and fertile land will be reckoned as common as forest;^i
¹⁶justice will make a home in the wilderness,
righteousness will dwell in the fertile land,
¹⁷peace will be the outcome of righteousness,
justice will bring about tranquillity and trust forevermore;
¹⁸my people will reside in a peaceful abode,
in secure dwellings where they can rest at ease.
¹⁹It will hail when the forest goes down,
and in the lowlands the city will be laid low.^j
²⁰Happy will you be as you sow beside every waterway,
leaving ox and ass to roam free.

NOTES

^a MT adds *qomnāh*, "arise," but delete *metri causa* with Duhm, Fohrer, Kaiser, and others;   ^b *yāmîm ʿal-šānâ*, an idiom referring to the end of the agricultural year;   ^c "vintage" and "harvest," respectively, *bāsîr* (24:13b) and *ʾosep* ("gathering in"; 33:4; Mic 7:1), synonyms referring to the harvesting of grapes and olives;   ^d *ʿal-šādayim sōpĕdîm* the masculine plural participle is impossible in the context; *spd* = "strike," "beat" is unattested, but read *sĕpodāh* with that meaning following LXX (*koptesthe*), Syr., and Vulg.;   ^e *qôs vĕšāmîr*; for this familiar Isaian topos see 5:6; 7:23–25; 9:17; 10:17; 27:4;   ^f *ʿōpel*, literally, "mound," not necessarily referring to the Ophel in Jerusalem (2 Chr 27:3; 33:14; Neh 3:26–27; 11:21); there was an Ophel in Samaria (2 Kgs 5:24) and in *qrḥḥ* in Moab (Mesha Stele line 22);   ^g or "dens" (MT *mĕʿārôt*);   ^h MT *karmel*, see note and commentary on 29:17;   ^i *yaʿar* understood broadly to include land unsuitable for grazing or growing crops; see 29:17;   ^j v 19a is obscure, perhaps beyond recovery; NEB "it will be cool on the slopes of the forest then, and cities shall be peaceful in the plain" rests on an Arabic cognate *baruda* = "to be cool," for Hebrew *brd* and assigning the meaning "to lie peace-fully" to *špl*; it avoids the intrusive note of menace (but cf. 30:25b) but must be regarded as a long shot indeed; one suspects that the writer's addiction to asso-nance (*ûbārad-bĕredet, šiplâ-tišpal, hayaʿar-hāʿir*) is partly responsible for the confusion; the translation offered reproduces MT and will be defended in the commentary but is admittedly speculative.

COMMENTS

This fairly long passage seems to drift inconsequentially from one topic to another and has given commentators a great deal of trouble. There is no justi-fication for breaking it up into two distinct compositions (8–14, 15–20), since 15–20 not only is without title but begins in the middle of a sentence. We may therefore read 15–20 as the continuation of the projection in 1–8 of a new political and social order that brings with it fertility and general well-being, though in the meantime great hardships must be endured. The turning point is the pouring out of the transforming spirit, which brings about the reversal of fortune characteristic of eschatological and apocalyptic thinking (e.g. 65:13–14; Ezek 37:5, 9–10; Joel 3:1[2:28]).

The summons to the married (*nāšîm*) and unmarried (*bānôt*) women to la-ment and engage in the (by our jejune standards) extravagant displays of mourning is not another depressing indictment of women as such (as, e.g., 3:16–4:1; Amos 4:1–3), nor is the characterization of the women as at ease and complacent necessarily limited to women of the court. Whatever their station, they are urged to engage in the gender-specific activity of public lamentation. (It is of interest to note that the Targum understands the two classes of women as provinces and cities, respectively.) Lamenting was a professional or quasi-professional skill passed down either within a specialist guild or from mother to daughter (Jer 9:19[20]). Our text mentions trembling, tearing the upper gar-ment, wearing a kind of belt probably of sackcloth or burlap, and beating the breast as a ritualized form of self-laceration. The tomb of Abiram of Byblos rep-resents four women mourners, two of whom appear to be striking their breasts. No doubt a kind of ritualized wailing or keening was called for, perhaps also the composition and rendition of dirges (in 2 Chr 35:25 women mourners are called "singers," *šārôt*).

The immediate cause for lamenting is the failure or destruction of the au-tumn harvest (grapes, olives, figs) and the depopulation of towns—understand-ing v 14 to refer not to a specific site, presumed by many to be Jerusalem, but to towns in Judah in general. Some of this language has already been encoun-tered in chs. 24–27. The connection between failed grape harvest and devastated city is precisely what we find in the threatening language about the unnamed city in these chapters in which the same themes, and sometimes the same language, occur as here, including the themes of depopulation and the return of cities to nature (e.g. 24:4–13). Lamenting for the lost harvest provides an entry point for the theme of reversion to the natural state that keeps on recurring throughout chs. 1–39. In some instances the city or land that reverts to a habitat for sheep, cattle, jackals, hedgehogs, ostriches, and occasionally satyrs and other demons is explicitly hostile—Babylon (13:19–22; 4:22–23), Damascus (17:1–2), and Edom (34:11–15), the last named destined to provide hospitality for an entire menagerie. Elsewhere the city in question is unnamed and not necessarily foreign (5:17; 7:23–25; 27:10–11).

While this continuity of theme is an important factor in the making of the present passage, it does not help to fix the historical occasion, if any, for this public display of grief. In tackling this issue the commentators have ranged far and wide. Duhm (1892, 236) dated it to the earliest period of Isaiah's career. For Fohrer (1967, 2.123–24) it was Isaiah's last prophecy, following Sennacherib's campaign in 701. Barth (1977, 211–13) took the second half of the passage (15–20) as the conclusion to his Assyrian Redaction, and Clements (1980a, 263) adds that it forms "a beautiful and fitting conclusion to the message of Isaiah" composed just after the fall of Jerusalem. Wildberger (1978, 1267), finally, dates 9–14 just before that event. The solution adopted in this commentary has already been noted. The situation that is said to be the occasion for lamenting is precisely what we would expect after the withdrawal of the Assyrian army in the autumn of 701 B.C.E. We recall that Sennacherib claimed to have taken 46 cities, citadels and villages, to have driven out of them 200,150 people (a totally unrealistic figure), and to have taken the livestock as booty. The Assyrian troops would, in the meantime, have been living off the land, and they had a nasty habit of destroying what they could not use. This fit with the situation of 701–700 would not in itself settle the issue, since there were many other occasions of military and natural disaster in the history of Palestine during the biblical period, but in the context of chs. 28–33 it must be a strong contender.

The agent of transformation is the spirit of God, and the process can be either destructive or renovative (cf. 44:3–4). This theme of the transformation of the natural order is prevalent in Second Temple writing (41:18–20; 42:15; 43:19–20; 48:21; 49:9–11; 51:3; 55:12–13) and will be given a cosmic context in the apocalyptic projection of new heavens and new earth (65:17; 66:22). It is a theme somewhat neglected in the history of interpretation but one that deserves close attention in an age of ecological crisis. The author's somewhat curious ideas about ecological transformation, always associated with the creation of a social order based on justice and righteousness, are constructed with the help of three terms that connote symbolically conditions of existence as much as specific regions or environments. They are in ascending order: wilderness (*midbār*); forest, including land unsuitable for growing crops (*ya'ar*); and fertile land (*karmel*), all three juxtaposed with the city. The point of the transformation by the spirit rests on the obscure v 19 (see textual note). In the verses preceding it, we were told that cities, including their palaces and forts, will be destroyed and that nature will take over. In the verses that follow, we hear of a transformation within the natural environment brought about by the spirit of God: *midbār* will be turned into *karmel* (cf. a reversal in the opposite direction in Jer 4:26), and the latter will be as abundant as *ya'ar*, normally much more in evidence than cultivable land (cf. 29:17). This environment will then be the setting for a just and equitable social order where warfare and internecine strife will come to an end. If we now take the MT of v 19 (supported by 1QIsa[a]) on its own terms, we hear that both badlands and city are destined to disappear, leaving only *karmel* as the ideal, rural utopia—rather like the nineteenth century dream of a New Harmony far from the satanic mills of an oppressive and humanly destructive urban society.

A similar scenario is set out in 30:23–25: the towers of the city fall and give way to an idyllic scene of farmers sowing grain, pampered oxen and asses, and abundant water supply. A scenario very different, therefore, from the new Jerusalem as the goal of pilgrimage from the nations of the world and a reminder that prophets and prophetic groups elaborated more than one way of envisioning the future.

A TYRANT CONDEMNED (33:1)

(On ch. 33 in general: Beuken 1991; Childs 1967, 112–17; Gunkel; Irwin; Murray 1982, 200–216; Roberts 1983, 15–25)

TRANSLATION

33 [1]Woe to you, destroyer, not yourself destroyed,
      treacherous one, who has not been betrayed![a]
      When you have finished your destroying[b] you yourself will be destroyed;
      when you have finished[c] acting treacherously you will be dealt
          with treacherously.

NOTES

[a] There is no need to emend *bô* to *bāk* (in pause); literally: "whom they have not betrayed";   [b] *šôdēd* functions as infinitive (GKC §120b);   [c] MT *kannĕlotkâ* Hiphil infinitive → *nlh* or *kĕnil'ôtkâ* → *l'h* cf. Symm. *hotan kopiasēs*; 1QIsa[a] *kkltk* (*kĕkallôtkâ*) as in BHS, probably correctly.

COMMENTS

Ch. 33 presents the reader with a disjointed and uneven sequence of mostly brief passages. In a study published in 1924, Gunkel proposed to read the chapter as a prophetic liturgy composed of three lyrics, two imitations of popular laments and what he called a Torah liturgy. Gunkel's standing in the discipline initially assured a wide acceptance to his hypothesis, but the obvious problem was and is that we have no idea what a prophetic liturgy was like or even whether such a liturgy ever existed. We can identify elements of the standard psalm of lament: petition (2–4), praise (5–6), description of the complaint (7–9), and the response, this last perhaps communicated through a cultic prophet (10–12 cf. Pss 20:6–8; 28:6; 60:6–8), but this hardly amounts to a prophetic liturgy. It is also generally acknowledged that the ethical catalogue in 15–16 has a different liturgical coordinate.

As noted earlier, this saying about an unnamed tyrant does not rightly belong to the woe-series in chs. 28–31, and it has no immediately obvious link with what precedes or follows. In the context of chs. 32–33, considered a more or less integrated and distinct unit, it serves as a contrast to the portrait of the just ruler at the beginning and end by depicting a tyrant who engages in gratuitously oppressive and treacherous behavior. The syntax is somewhat obscure, again due to the author's need to exploit repetition and assonance, cf. 24:16: *bōgĕdîm bāgādû ûbeged bōgĕdîm bāgādû* ("the unfaithful ones deal faithlessly, they deal with an utter lack of faith")—a rather extreme case. Either of the two epithets—*šôdēd*, "destroyer," and *bôgēd*, "treacherous one"—or both together occur with reference to the devastator of Moab (16:4), a Babylonian ruler (21:2), the destroyer of Babylon (Jer 51:53, 56), and the anonymous foe from the north (Jer 6:26). The attempts by the commentators to identify the one so described have been even more diverse: Shalmaneser V (Hayes and Irvine 1987, 361–62), Sennacherib (Vermeylen 1977, 1.430), Nebuchadnezzar II (Clements 1980a, 265), an individual or state in the early Persian period (Wildberger 1982, 1287–88), one of the Diadochoi or one of their revenue agents (Kaiser 1969, 342), Antiochus Eupator who attacked Jerusalem in the year 163 B.C.E. (Marti 1900, 237–39; Duhm 1892, 208–9). The context of chs. 28–33 as a whole would favor an identification with Sennacherib, but the structural relationship noted earlier with the just ruler at the beginning and end of chs. 32–33, a ruler whose government will bring oppression to an end (33:18–19), suggests that, whoever the writer had in mind, both ruler and tyrant are idealized, abstract portrayals. We note the same connection in the Moab saying where the destroyer (*šôdēd*) is juxtaposed with a just Davidic ruler, once oppression and destruction have come to an end (16:4–5, using the same two verbs, *kālāh*, *tāmam*, as here).

A PSALM OF PETITION AND PRAISE (33:2–6)

(Beuken 1991; Gunkel; Murray; Poynder; Schoeps; Ziegler 1933; 1950)

TRANSLATION

33   [2] Yahveh,[a] show us your favor,
     in you we place our trust;[b]
     be our support[c] every morning,
     our salvation in the time of trouble.

³At the sound of a tumult peoples take to flight,
when you rise up in majesty[d] nations are scattered;
⁴then spoil is gathered as the locust gathers it,[e]
like swarming locusts[f] they settle upon it.
⁵Yahveh is exalted, for he dwells on high,
he has filled Zion with justice and righteousness;
⁶he will be the stability of her times;[g]
wisdom[h] and knowledge are riches that lead to salvation;
her treasure[i] is the fear of Yahveh.

NOTES

[a] Written in archaic script in 4QIsaᶜ, which contains fragments of 2–8 and 16 but no significant variants;   [b] *qivvînû*; Isaian usage requires a stronger sense than "wait" cf. 8:17; 25:9;   [c] read *zĕroʿēnû*, "our arm," for MT *zĕroʿām*, "their arm";   [d] MT *mērômĕmutekâ*, "at your lifting up" (hapax legomenon); 1QIsaᵃ *mdvmmtk*, "at your rumbling" → *dmm* cf. 1 Kgs 19:20 *dĕmāmâ*, which Lust (1975, 110–15) translates "a roaring thunderous sound"; others derive from putative *rmm* cf. Akk. *rimmatu*, "thunder"; LXX *apo tou phobou sou*;   [e] reading *šālāl kĕmô ʾosep* for MT *šĕlalĕkem ʾosep*;   [f] *maššaq* and *gēb* are hapax legomena; there are no equivalents for the twelve Hebrew words for types of locust or stages of this insect's development, as in Joel 1:4–7;   [g] reading *ʿittehâ* for MT *ʿittekâ* in keeping with the context referring to Zion (fem.); the sense of the line is obscure; see Wildberger 1978, 1284 for the range of options;   [h] reading *ḥokmâ* or *ḥokmôt* (pl. with sing. meaning cf. Prov 9:1);   [i] *ʿôṣārāh* (fem.) for MT *ʿôṣārô*.

COMMENTS

This composition gives the impression of being a literary imitation of a psalm rather than a psalm in the normal sense. Whether it was ever used liturgically we do not know, but it certainly is not itself a liturgy (pace Fohrer 1967, 2.129), and the thesis that ch. 33 comprises a liturgy, often repeated since Gunkel and Mowinckel, is not well founded. It exhibits the elements of petition, praise, and response but switches from the second to the third person at midpoint. It opens on a psalm-like note with *YHVH ḥonnēnû*, "Yahveh, show us your favor" (cf. Ps 123:2), to which corresponds an attitude of trustful and hopeful expectation on the part of the petitioner (see the commentary on "waiting for God" in 30:18–19). The request for divine assistance in the morning is a commonplace of Israelite hymnography (Pss 5:4; 30:6; 46:4; 59:17; 88:14; 90:14; 143:8). The motif is explained in different ways: it is the time of the morning offering or the successful conclusion of a nocturnal *incubatio* ritual, or it commemorates the completion of the work of salvation during the Passover night (Ziegler). The more mundane and likely explanation, however, is simply the feeling that morning puts an end to night as a time of danger and fear; it is a time for new beginnings.

The requested assistance, the answer to the prayer of petition, comes in the familiar form of the scattering or annihilating of hostile forces by the majesty of Yahveh (cf. 17:12–14; 29:7–8; Ps 48:5–9), a motif usually accompanied by a strong note of *Schadenfreude* as here. Hence the location of the psalm following the commination on the unnamed tyrant (33:1). Following Yahveh's annihilating intervention, Israel will fall on the spoil like a swarm of locusts. (The Targum modifies the picture somewhat by representing the Israelites gathering the riches of the peoples that hate them, as people gather locusts.) The devastating effect of a swarm of locusts on the vegetation makes it an appropriate metaphor for the impact of a conquering army (cf. Judg 6:5; Jer 46:23; Joel 2:20; Nah 3:15).

The poem continues with expressions of confidence in the availability of the salvation prayed for at the beginning. That God's dwelling is above, in the sky, is an ancient representation, but it occurs frequently in Second Temple texts, no doubt in response to the need to emphasize the transcendent and universal character of the deity (40:22; 57:15; 66:1 cf. 1 Kgs 8:27). The endowment of Zion, i.e., its inhabitants, with the fundamental moral virtues of justice and righteousness and the fundamental intellectual qualities of wisdom and knowledge, subsumed under the rubric of "the fear of Yahveh" (cf. 11:2; 29:13), may be regarded another indication of the close contact and interchange between the bearers of the Isaian tradition and the religious didacticism of the sages (cf. Prov 1:4).

A SCENE OF SOCIAL AND PHYSICAL DISASTER (33:7–13)

(Hillers; Johnson; Mazar; Schwantes; Weis)

TRANSLATION

i

33 [7]Hark, Ariel's people[a] cry for help in the streets,
Salem's messengers[b] are weeping bitterly.
[8]The highways are destroyed,
there are no more wayfarers;
he has broken the agreement, despised the witnesses;
people have no thought for others.[c]
[9]The land is mourning,[d] pining;
Lebanon, ashamed,[e] is withering away;
Sharon has become a desert;
Bashan and Carmel are stripped bare.

ii

¹⁰Now, Yahveh declares, "I will rise up,
now I will exalt myself,ᶠ
now I will raise myself up.
¹¹You conceive chaff, you bring forth stubble;
a fiery windᵍ will consume you;
¹²nations will be turned into heaps of burnt-out ash,
like thorns cut down and set on fire.
¹³Hear, you who are far away, what I have done,
acknowledge my power, you who are close at hand."

NOTES

ᵃ MT *'er'ellām* usually emended to *'ări'ēlîm*, "ariels," i.e. "warriors" cf. 2 Sam 23:20; 1QIsaᵃ has *'r' lm*, "I will appear to them," cf. Vulg. *videntes*; LXX reads *yr'* ("fear") rather than *r'h* ("see"): "Behold, in their fear (*en to phobo hūmōn*) they will be terrified," but Codices B and ℵ read *boēsontai*, "they will cry out," as does MT; for attempts to emend see James, 1959, 104–7;   ᵇ *šālēm* for *šālôm* cf. Gen 14:18; Ps 76:3;   ᶜ a difficult verse; read *'ēdîm*, "witnesses," with 1QIsaᵃ for MT *'ārîm*, "cities"; Hillers proposes *'dy'* = "treaty," as in the Sefire inscriptions and in agreement with verb in singular, and "land tax" for *'ĕnôš* on the basis of Akk. *unussu*, an opinion rejected by Loretz 1976, 449;   ᵈ reading *'ābĕlāh* for MT *'ābal* in agreement with *'ereṣ* fem.;   ᵉ NEB "Lebanon is eaten away and crumbling" rests on the suggestion of G. R. Driver 1968, 53 of Arab. cognate *hafara*, "to be eroded," for MT *hehpîr* → *hpr* Hiphil cf. 54:4;   ᶠ 1QIsaᵃ has *'trvmm* Hithpolal for MT *'ērômām*;   ᵍ reading *rûaḥ kĕmô 'ēš*, literally, "a wind like fire" cf. Tg. and Vulg.

COMMENTS

After the annihilation and pillaging of the enemy in the previous poem we are surprised to hear of the desperate situation obtaining in the country. One is tempted to appeal to the repeated alternation between petition and description of the petitioner's miserable condition in the psalms of lamentation, but this passage is neither introduced nor worded in a way that is parallel to these psalms. The first part describes a condition of distress in Jerusalem and the countryside leading to the breakdown of social life (7–9), and the second section records Yahveh's response to this situation, addressed to Judeans but concerning foreign nations as well (10–13, notwithstanding the Masoretic *setuma* separating v 12 from v 13). The language throughout is oblique and enigmatic. The identity of those crying for help in the streets of the city has proved difficult to determine both for ancient (LXX and Targum) and modern readers. The two ariels dispatched by David's captain Benaiah (2 Sam 23:20) and the Israelite ariel dragged before the god Kemosh by the Moabite king Mesha (*ANET*,

320–21) have suggested the idea of champions (Mazar) or valiant warriors (RSV) or members of the royal bodyguard (Schwantes); but as Wildberger (1978, 1294) crisply put it, champions and heroes are not in the habit of crying out for help in the streets. The meaning "messengers" proposed by Kimḥi and Ibn Ezra is justified only by parallelism with *malʾăkē šālôm*. It therefore seems advisable to assume a reference to the symbolic name Ariel for Jerusalem, taking it to be the equivalent of Jerusalemites (see commentary on 29:1), with which the reading Salem would be in agreement (cf. Gen 14:18; Ps 76:3).

Why messengers are singled out among the distressed Jerusalemites is not explained. It may be simply that the condition of the country made it impossible for them to do their job. If the passage is assigned a Second Temple date, one might think of the condition of Judah during the early Persian period, when the country was afflicted with drought (Hag 1:10–11; Zech 8:12) and when, for a time, travel was difficult if not impossible (Zech 7:14; 8:10). But the reuse of the term Ariel and the allusion to a broken covenant suggest a different explanation, namely, that this is a sequel to the description in 32:9–14 of the state of the country following the punitive campaign of 701. The situation is identical: depopulation, social breakdown, and devastation of the environment. Of the four places mentioned, all proverbial for luxuriant vegetation, two (Lebanon and Carmel) have been given a symbolic role in this section (29:17). Ariel is Jerusalem threatened by a besieging army (29:1), and the mission of its messengers or envoys has been condemned as futile (30:2, 4). If this is so, it is difficult to avoid the conclusion that the one who has broken his agreement and despised those who witnessed to it (including Yahveh?), is none other than Hezekiah who, in rebelling, broke his oath as vassal to the Assyrian overlord. The condition of the country would then be interpreted as the outcome of the curses attached to the vassal treaty, including famine and drought (Parpola and Watanabe 1988, 5, 11, 46–47).

Those who adopt the cultic interpretation of the passage take 10–13 as God's response to the community's cry for help. But in these psalms the assurance of assistance is expressed by the psalmist in the first person individual or collective except in cases in which an oracle is quoted (Pss 60; 81; 108), and this is not the case here. Furthermore, the decision of Yahveh to intervene, to rise up, etc., is by no means confined to the "assurance of salvation" component of the lament psalms—not to mention that the statement following is hardly reassuring. This raises the question who is being addressed with this threatening language. We probably owe the curious metaphor of conceiving chaff and bringing forth stubble (a similar metaphor is used at 26:18) to the writer's desire to make a play on the words *ḥăšaš* and *qaš*. The reproach is addressed to Judeans, as is the threat of being burned by a fiery wind, but it will be worse for foreigners who will be burned in the fire so thoroughly that not even bones remain (cf. Amos 2:1b and the similar curse in the treaty of Ashur-nerari V with Matiʾilu of Arpad lines 8–9; Parpola and Watanabe 1998, 8). This is not the first time that this fire imagery, threatening people both within and outside of the Judean community, has been used in this section (see 29:6–7; 30:27–28) to give a broader significance to a historically particular judgment. The final exhortation (13) added, we suspect, at a much later time, is couched in apocalyptic, end-time language and is addressed to readers, either Gentiles and Jews, or Jews in the diaspora and the homeland, urging them to acknowledge the power and majesty of God (cf. Dan 9:7).

A MORAL CATECHISM (33:14–16)

(Delekat; Galling; Gunkel; Koch; Murray; Steingrimsson; Wong)

TRANSLATION

i

33 [14]Sinners shake with fear in Zion;
trembling has seized the impious.
Which of us can abide this devouring fire?
which of us can abide this everlasting burning?

ii

[15]Those whose conduct is righteous,
whose speech is honest,
who scorn what is gained by oppression,
who shake their hands free of a bribe,
who stop their ears from hearing murderous plans
and close their eyes so as not to look on evil.
[16]These are the ones who dwell on the heights,
whose refuge is a fortress among the rocks,
whose bread is at hand, whose supply of water[b] is secure.

NOTES

[a] *mēmâv*, literally, "his water."

COMMENTS

We know we are approaching the end of this major section in chs. 28–33 when the reader, overwhelmed by the threat of divine judgment recurring throughout it, asks how one can avoid the final obliterating judgment represented under the figure of a devouring fire (*'ēš 'okelet* 29:6; 30:27, 30 cf. Deut 4:24; 9:3) and the less familiar metaphor of the altar hearth with its perpetually burning fire (*môqĕdē 'ôlām* cf. Lev 6:2[9]; Ps 102:4). Fear-induced shaking and trembling of sinners and at times even the righteous is a common theme in the hymns (Ps 2:11; 48:7; 55:6; Exod 15:15). All of this has the purpose of introducing the brief ethical catechism that follows. It has long been assumed that this type of recital served to express the moral qualities necessary and appropriate for participation in temple liturgy. It has therefore been described as an entrance liturgy (*Torliturgie*), the prime example of which is Ps 15, though we have no direct evidence that such a recital actually served to admit people to the temple liturgy or exclude them from it. The corresponding "negative confession" or *Beichtspiegel* form has been compared with formulations in the Egyptian Books of the Dead. The formulation is as follows:

> I have not committed sin in the place of truth
> I have not blasphemed a god
> I have not made anyone weep
> I have not killed.   (*ANET,* 34)

It belongs, however, to the forensic rather than the liturgical realm, as may be seen in the one biblical example in Job 31:

> If I have walked with falsehood, and my foot has hastened to deceit. . . .
> If I have seen anyone perish for lack of clothing . . .

The form is the oath of clearance, involving a self-imposed curse to guarantee the truth of the asseveration. Comparison with the ethical decalogue is also in order (Koch), though the relation between the decalogue and Isa 33:15 is complicated by the fact that both draw on traditional ethical formulations passed on within the kinship network and eventually within didactic circles. We can exclude the hypothesis of an origin in the institution of asylum (Delekat), for which such formulations as we find here and in Ps 15 would be totally inappropriate.

Both the lead-up to the list and the conclusion make it clear that, whatever its origin and Sitz im Leben, this ethical paranesis has been adapted to the eschatological context of a final act of judgment and how one may hope to survive it. This will emerge very clearly by comparing the questions to which the list provides the answer with similar hymnic formulations:

> Who may go up to the mountain of Yahveh?
> Who may stand in his holy place? (Ps 24:3)

or

> Who may sojourn in your tent?
> Who may dwell on your holy mountain? (Ps 15:1)

The eschatological character of the questions is brought out more clearly in LXX with the question Who will tell about the eternal place? and in the Targum, which identifies the fire with the everlasting fire of Gehenna. It is interesting, though, and perhaps even consoling, that the passage itself uses the homely image of salvation as security—having a roof over your head and enough to eat and drink.

A close study of these small ethical catechisms would no doubt provide interesting information on moral perceptions in different societies and the ancient Near Eastern moral-didactic tradition. Both the Isaian passage and Ps 15 open with general ethical statements: righteous conduct and honest speaking. In these and the more specific requirements following we note many parallels with the moral didacticism of Israel's sages, as we shall see below. It is also worthy of note that the requirements for worship are ethical rather than ritual, though the latter are sometimes more in evidence; for example, the people are to prepare for the Sinai theophany by washing their clothes, sexual abstention, and keeping their distance from the sacred area, Exod 19:10–15.

The more specific moral requirements that follow have in common with the tenfold list in Ps 15 an exclusive concentration on the practice of social justice. Unlike Job's confession of innocence and the Egyptian negative confessions, examples of sexual transgression are absent. Injunctions against profiting by unjust and exploitative means are of frequent occurrence in the didactic literature (Prov 15:27; 28:16; Job 31:39) and no doubt included injunctions against lending at interest (Ps 15:5), which was forbidden between Israelites but apparently not between Israelites and foreigners (Exod 22:24[25]; Lev 25:35–38). How fundamental to the working of the judicial system the prohibition of bribery was can be seen in legal formulations, moral teaching, and prophetic comminations against accepting a bribe ("a bribe blinds the eyes of the wise and subverts the cause of those who are in the right" Deut 16:19). The last two formulations are less clear. The first of the two, moral teaching, connotes a refusal to be a part of conspiracy to commit murder rather than just refusing to listen to someone boast of having committed a crime. Likewise, the refusal to look on evil very likely corresponds to the avoidance of slander in Ps 15.

The eschatological context that accommodates this list of moral requirements has an interesting parallel in the list of requirements in Ezek 18:5–9, the observation of which gives life. The Ezekiel list is a decalogue that reflects the priestly concerns of Ezekiel by combining the ritual and the ethical. The *imperative* of feeding the hungry and clothing the naked comes closer to the scene in Matt 25:31–46, a scene that is explicitly eschatological and where the final distinction between the saved and the reprobate is made exclusively on the basis of this imperative to care for the hungry and the thirsty, the naked, the sick, the stranger, and the unjustly imprisoned.

A FUTURE WITHOUT FEAR (33:17–24)

(Beuken 1991; Gunkel; Holmyard; Murray; Roberts 1983; Wildberger 1978, 1309–23)

TRANSLATION

33 [17]Your eyes will behold a king in his beauty;[a]
they will look on a land stretching far and wide;
[18]your mind will dwell on what you once dreaded:
"Where is the one who took the census?
Where is the one who assessed the tribute?
Where is the one who counted the towers?"[b]
[19]You will no longer see an insolent[c] people,
a people whose speech is too obscure to understand,
stammering in a language you cannot comprehend.
[20]Look on Zion, city of our festivals;[d]
let your eyes look on Jerusalem,
a secure place to live, a tent that will not be moved,[e]
whose pegs will never be pulled out,[f]
and none of its ropes untied.
[21]There the glorious name of Yahveh will be ours.[g]
[It will be a place of broad rivers and streams,[h]
but there no galley can sail,
no stately ship can pass.][i]
[22]Yahveh is our ruler, Yahveh is our leader,
Yahveh is our king, he will save us!
[23][Your rigging is slack,
it cannot hold steady the mast
nor can they spread the sail.][j]
Then even the blind will have their share of abundant spoil;[k]
even the lame will take part in the pillage.
[24]None of the inhabitants will say, "I am sick";
the people that live there will be quit of all guilt.

NOTES

[a] 1QIsa[a] has *byvpyv* for MT *bĕyopyô*; *yopî*, "beauty," can describe male as well as female subjects (Ezek 27:3; 28:7, 12, 17); the Targum translates: "the glory of the Shekinah of the King of Ages in his beauty shall your eyes see";   [b] Duhm (1892, 245–46) translates: "Wo ist der Präfekt mit den Zollnern?" ("Where is the prefect with the tax collectors?" → *'ayyēh tupšar 'et-hamminzārîm*) cf. Akk. *tupšarru* = "prefect," but this translation is altogether too adventurous; G. R. Driver (1968a, 53) takes *migdālîm* in this context to mean "piles" or "store chests" cf. Cant 5:13; but there is nothing incredible about towers' being counted for tax purposes or for some other reason unknown cf. 22:10;   [c] *nô'āz* → *y'z* Niphal participle hapax or → *'zz* = "overbearing," rather than emend to *lô'ēz* cf. Ps 114:1;   [d] read plural with 1QIsa[a], Aquila, Symm., Theod.;   [e] the verb *ṣ'n* is hapax but cf. Aram. *ṭĕ'an* and Arab. *za'ana* = "depart";   [f] for MT *yissa'* read pl. *yis'û* with BHS rather than Pual *yussa'*;   [g] reading *šēm*,

"name," for *šām*, "there," which has the advantage of restoring the noun governed by the adjective *'addîr*; *'addîr* appears to be a divine epithet cf. the names *'drb'l* (Phoenician), *'drmlk* 2 Kgs 19:37 = Isa 37:38, but not with YHVH; [h] since Jerusalem is evidently not a place of broad rivers and streams, some emend *měqôm* to *měqôr*, "source," or *miqveh*, "reservoir"; *něhārîm* probably a gloss on the less common *yě'orîm*; [i] probably a gloss; [j] v 23a looks like a misplaced gloss on 21; *nēs* = "sail" or "flag" cf. Ezek 27:7; Sweeney (1996, 425–26) translates: "your pains are relieved, they shall not seize the base of the staff, an ensign shall not be unfurled," a rather desperate attempt to get rid of the nautical imagery that does not make good sense; furthermore, *ḥăbālîm*, "ropes," here "rigging," also means "labor pains" but not pains in general; [k] reading *ḥilleq* or *yěḥalleq* for *ḥullaq* and *'ivvēr*, "blind," for *'ad*; 1QIsa[a] has *mrvbh* for MT *marbeh*.

COMMENTS

There follows a particularly recalcitrant passage, which holds out the prospect of a future in which the rule of Yahveh and his human representative are finally manifested, in which the people of Judah are left in secure possession of their land free of foreign domination, and in which the disastrous situation described in 33:7–9 and elsewhere in chs. 28–33 will seem just like a bad dream. Neither this passage nor ch. 33 as a whole constitutes either a prophetic liturgy (Gunkel) or a royal ritual (Murray), though the chapter may use language and themes from different liturgies hypothesized on the basis of the psalms. It is even clearer that it does not report a prophetic vision (pace Sweeney 1996, 424–25, 428) since the relevant indications are lacking and the verb *ḥzh*, in parallelism with *r'h* at 33:17, 20, does not necessarily connote seeing in vision (see, for example, Isa 26:11; 47:13; 48:6; 57:8).

Chapters 32–33 are united by the mention of the righteous king at the beginning and end, which also implies that, contrary to the opinion of the Targumist and many modern commentators, the once and future king of 33:17 is a human figure who will represent the lordship of Yahveh in Jerusalem. This conclusion is supported by the absence of the article at both points (32:1; 33:17). Furthermore, "beauty" (stem *yph*) is attributed to males as well as females (Joseph Gen 39:6, David 1 Sam 17:42, Absalom 2 Sam 14:25), including kings (Ps 45:3; Ezek 28:12, 17), but never Yahveh. The inclusio, therefore, gives a distinctive character to chs. 32–33 as the conclusion to chs. 28–31 and perhaps, at one point of the editorial history, to the entire first half of the book of Isaiah. What is therefore being described in this finale is the reversal of the situation at the critical juncture of Sennacherib's campaign. Zion will be secure, as it certainly was not at that point (v 20 cf. 32:18); the Assyrians speaking their unintelligible language will be long gone (v 19 cf. 28:10–11); tribute will no longer be exacted (v 18 cf. 2 Kgs 18:14–16). The emphasis on *vision* (verbs of seeing occur five times) also recalls the motif of blindness and imperception of frequent occurrence in this section of the book (28:7; 29:9–12, 18; 30:10; 32:3). We may also suspect that to conclude with the image of a good and righteous king who will bring security under the rule of God carries an implicit criticism of Hezekiah, whose policies are repeatedly condemned throughout this section.

The poem, if that is what it is, shows little evidence of coherence or thematic unity—disparate images following one another in bewildering succession. One of the strangest of these is the picture of a land of broad rivers closed to the navigation of hostile vessels (21b), there being no broad rivers in the country and this being one of the few ways in which Israel had never been threatened. (Perhaps this verse inspired the Christmas carol about three ships sailing into Bethlehem.) The idea may have been suggested by 32:2b, reading "streams of water in Zion" (ṣiyyôn for MT ṣāyôn, "parched land"); or the author may be reproducing an imaginary vision of Jerusalem as a place of abundant fresh water, drawing on Ezek 47:1–12 (cf. Joel 4:18[3:18]; Zech 14:8; Ps 46:5); or, finally, it may refer to the land rather than the city, reflecting the fantasy of a Greater Israel, on which the sun never sets, stretching from the River of Egypt to the Euphrates inclusively (Gen 15:18). It is, at any rate, almost certainly a later insertion into the poem, which reads more smoothly without it. The original conclusion was probably the acclamation: "Yahveh is our ruler, Yahveh is our leader, Yahveh is our king, he will save us!" The addition about the unseaworthy ship (23a) would therefore be a further elaboration on the galleys and stately ships mentioned earlier, a rather inconsequential addition to an addition. Isa 33:23b is a further and rather curious elaboration of the end-time scenario, one that contradicts the assumption that at the consummation of history there would be no sightless or lame people (32:3–4; 35:5–6). It therefore called for a final *corrigendum* excluding the persistence of sickness and disability and the inevitable corollary of sin and guilt.

The poem opens with another prediction of a king ruling over a land stretching far into the distance (cf. 32:1–8). This imperial Israelite fantasy of an empire stretching from sea to sea and from the Euphrates to the ends of the earth (Ps 72:8; Zech 9:10), dangerous as well as fantastic in retrospect, has for its subtext the Abrahamic promise (e.g. Gen 15:18). Both here and in 32:1–8, therefore, the decisive turn of events will involve an individual ruler, the instrument of divine rule, though there is not the same sense of immediacy and level of concern for the restoration of the native dynasty as in other texts from the early post-destruction period (Jer 33:14–26; 23:5–6; Ezek 37:24–28). Both 32:1 and 33:17 speak unspecifically of a ruler without mentioning David or the Davidic dynasty. The thing once dreaded, now in the past, is foreign domination, and the three rhetorical questions express the economic burden of foreign occupation or vassal status. Taking a census was essential for tax collection or paying tribute (as Menahem to Tiglat-pileser III 2 Kgs 15:19–20, and Hezekiah to Sennacherib 2 Kgs 18:14–16), which explains why David's census was deemed to be reprehensible (2 Sam 24:10). It will be unnecessary to labor the point that taxation and tribute continued to be a source of grievance throughout the Second Temple period. Nehemiah 5:1–5 records complaints that people had to mortgage their fields or give their children over to indentured service in order to pay the heavy taxes imposed by the Persian imperial authorities, and the Zeno papyri testify that the problem was no less severe in the Hellenistic period. The third question about counting towers, conveniently omitted in the Targum, hardly calls for the flurry of emendation in commentaries recent and not so recent, since assessing the number of dwellings and fortified installations would also be a necessary prelude to collecting tribute (cf. 22:10). So the hated revenue officers and tribute collectors are nowhere to be seen, and the irritant of constantly having to listen to the harsh, unintelligible language of the conquerors will also be removed—a transparent allusion to the *ṣav lāṣāv* of the Assyrians (28:10–11).

At this point the focus shifts to a positive vision of what the future holds in store. Jerusalem, place of festive gatherings, will be a secure *nāveh*, a term originally connoting pastureland (34:13; 35:7; 65:10) and therefore making room for the metaphor of shepherding (32:18 cf. Exod 15:3; Jer 31:23). Jerusalem is frequently presented under the figure of the wilderness tent, protected by a canopy (4:5–6) and complete with ropes and pegs (54:2). Claiming the name of Yahveh for the population of the new Jerusalem (v 21a emended reading) corresponds to the eschatological motif of conferring new names (cf. 65:15–16) and leads to the acclamation of the kingship of Yahveh in Zion (cf. 52:7). The titulary of Yahveh—*šōpēṭ* ("judge," "ruler"), *měhoqēq* ("clan leader"), *melek* ("king")—is deliberately traditional and archaic. The first designation carries the broader connotation of military in addition to judicial functions—as in the book of Judges (cf. the Carthaginian *suffetae*, "war lords," mentioned by Livy); the *měhoqēq* was originally a tribal leader (Judg 5:14), and the representation of Yahveh as chieftain or king is also ancient (Exod 15:18). The poem therefore ends with the assurance of ultimate salvation, expressed in terms designed to recall traditional and primordial Israelite realities and beliefs.

A SWORD OVER EDOM (34:1–17)

(Bartlett 1979; 1989; Ben Zvi; Beuken 1992b; Cresson; Dicon; Donner 1990; G. R. Driver 1959; Emerton 1982; Gosse 1990; Handy; Lindsay; Lust; Mathews; Muilenburg; Pope; Tanghe 1991; 1993b; Torrey 1928, 279–301; Vermeylen 1977, 1.439–46; Williamson 1994, 211–21; Young)

TRANSLATION

i

34 ¹Approach, you nations to listen;
you peoples, give heed!
Let the earth and what fills it hear,
the world and all its issue!
²Yahveh is incensed with all the nations,
his fury is directed against all their hosts,
he has doomed them and destined them for slaughter;

³their slain will be cast out,
the stench of their corpses will arise,
the mountains will flow^a with their blood;
⁴all the hosts of heaven will rot,^b
the sky will be rolled up like a scroll;
all its hosts shall wither away
like the leaf that withers from the vine,
like the fruit that withers from the fig tree.

ii

⁵When my sword is seen^c in the sky
then it will descend upon Edom,
on a people I have destined^d for judgment.
⁶Yahveh has a sword, it is covered in blood,
it is dripping^e with fat,
with the blood of lambs and goats,
with the fat from the kidneys of rams;
for Yahveh has a sacrifice in Bozrah,
a great slaughtering in the land of Edom;
⁷wild oxen will be felled^f with the people,^g
bulls alongside of their strongest;^h
their land will drink deep of blood,
their soil will be soaked in fat.

iii

⁸Yahveh has a day of vengeance,
a year of reckoning for Zion's complaint;^i
⁹the wadis of Edom^j will be turned into pitch,
her soil into brimstone,
her land will be burning pitch;^k
¹⁰night and day it will burn unquenched,
its smoke will go up for ever.
From age to age the land will lie waste,
to all eternity no people will pass through it.
¹¹The hawk and the hedgehog will claim it as their own,
owl and raven will make it their home;
Yahveh has stretched over it the measuring line of chaos,
and the stones^l of turmoil.
¹²Her nobles . . .^m
They shall acclaim no monarchy there;
all her princes will be of no account.
¹³Thorns will spring up in her palaces,
nettles and thistles in her forts;
it will become the haunt of jackals,
the abode of ostriches;

¹⁴wildcats will gather with hyenas,
the satyr will call to his mate,
there too will Lilith[n] alight
and there find a spot for herself;
¹⁵there the owl will nest,
lay her eggs, hatch them, and give them shelter;[o]
there too the kites will gather,
not one without its mate.[p]

iv

¹⁶Consult the book of Yahveh, read it:
none of these will be missing,
[not one of them without its mate][p]
for from his own mouth came the command,[q]
and with his own breath he has assembled them;
¹⁷it is he who has allotted them their place,
his hand has assigned it with the measuring line;
they will claim it as their own forever,
they will dwell there for all ages to come.

NOTES

[a] *Nāmassû*, literally, "melt" cf. Mic 1:4; Ps 97:5;   [b] 1QIsaᵃ: *vh'mqym ytbq'v vkvl ṣb' hšmym ybvlv*, "the depths will be split open and all the host of heaven will wither away"; for the second half of the phrase cf. *věkol-ṣěbā'ām yibbôl* (dittography); no need to emend *ṣěbā' haššāmayim* to *haggěbā'ôt* (BHS);   [c] reading *tērā'eh* with 1QIsaᵃ for MT *rivvětāh*, "is sated";   [d] no need to emend *ḥermî* to *ḥermô* or *ḥarbî* to *ḥarbô* (1st to 3d person); the change between 1st and 3d person in divine discourse is well attested;   [e] literally, "made fat," "gorged" (verb *dšn* Hophal);   [f] *věyārědû*, literally, "will go down";   [g] taking the antecedent of *'immām*, "with them," to be the population of Edom;   [h] I read *'abîrîm* for MT *'abbîrîm*, "bulls," referring to Edomite leaders;   [i] no need to emend to *lěrab ṣiyyôn*, "for the Great One of Zion," or *lěrāb ṣiyyôn* (participle → *rîb*), "the champion of Zion" (NEB);   [j] literally, "her wadis";   [k] 1QIsaᵃ has *vb'rh* for MT *bo'ērâ*, reading "her land will be pitch and it will burn";   [l] MT *'abnē bōhû* is usually taken to mean a plummet, but cf. 28:17 where *mišqelet* with that meaning is parallel with *qav* = "line"; also *'ăbānîm* pl. does not suit this meaning, and why use a plummet for measuring land? The function of the stones is unknown;   [m] the rest of the line is missing;   [n] 1QIsaᵃ *lylyvt* pl. with verbs in pl.; cf. Tg. "night hags," but no need to emend MT (see commentary);   [o] the line is overloaded, and the vocabulary (*těmallēṭ*, *dāgěrāh*) and therefore the translation, is uncertain; *dāgěrāh běṣillāh* perhaps "deposits them in her shade";   [p] *'iššâ rě'ûtāh lo' pāqādû*, "not one without its mate," is out of place in 16b and incomplete in 15b, where it belongs;   [q] reading *kî pîhû* with 1QIsaᵃ cf. Syr., Tg.

COMMENTS

Chapters 34 and 35 belong together, comprising a recapitulation of the message of the book as understood in eschatological terms by a writer of the later Second Temple period. Together they form a diptych in which the final annihilation of Edom is contrasted with the ultimate well-being of Zion. The contrast embodies the theme of eschatological reversal stated more incisively in the last section of the book (e.g. 65:13–14): whereas Edom will be turned into an uninhabited wasteland, the Judean wilderness and arid land will bloom like Lebanon and Carmel. The contrast is worked out in some detail: the wadis of Edom will be turned into pitch; wadis of the Israelite land now barren will have a plentiful water supply (34:9; 35:6). Nettles and thistles are contrasted with reeds and rushes, plants that grow near water (34:13; 35:7b). Jackals and other unpleasant animals will take over in Edom; they will lose their habitat in the transformed Israelite wilderness (34:13; 35:7b, 9). There will be no way of traveling through Edom; there will be a highway for all except the ritually unclean in the transformed land of Zion (34:10b; 35:8). A close reading will confirm the detailed correspondence between the contrasting images. Chs. 34 and 35 therefore form a coherent unit that juxtaposes the fate of hostile powers with the ultimate salvation of Zion, a juxtaposition found elsewhere in the book, especially in the last eleven chapters (e.g. 59:15b–20; 62:1–63:6).

The function of this unit in the book, the reason that it is located at this juncture shortly after the midpoint (the Masoretic midpoint marker calculated by verses is at 33:20), has been much discussed. It is still customary to attribute ch. 35 to the putative Second Isaiah and to read it as closely dependent on chs. 40–48, 40–55, or 40–66. In his commentary on the Second Isaiah (121–26, 279, 295–96) Torrey argued that both chapters make up one unit, which must be assigned to his Second Isaiah, writing in the fifth century B.C.E. More commonly, however, only ch. 35 is aligned with the section of the book beginning with ch. 40. There are some striking parallels between 35 and the chapters commonly designated Second Isaiah (40–55), of which the most impressive occurs in the last paragraph, which speaks of a highway for the redeemed returning to Zion (35:8–10 cf. 40:3–5). The question that will have to be asked in the next section is how they are to be explained. Linguistic and thematic parallels with discourse in the first part of the book (e.g. 13:1–22) are also in evidence (given a broadly encompassing Isaian tradition, this is not surprising), but they can be explained along the same lines as the adaptation of earlier themes in the last chapters of the book, the so-called Third Isaiah. Both 57:14 ("build up, build up, prepare the way") and 35:8–10 could, for example, represent a metaphorical adaptation of 40:3, which speaks of the highway on which the deportees will return from the diaspora. In general, ch. 34 is much closer to material in the Third than in the Second Isaiah (these terms are used purely for convenience). The fundamental issue, the salvation of Zion and annihilation of forces hostile to Zion, is present in both. In 34:1–17 and 63:1–6 Edom is destroyed by Yahveh without the intervention of any human agency. In 63:1–6 the annihilation of Edom—depicted in a horrifying cameo of violence—follows the celebration of the future glory of Zion described in terms similar at several points to 35:1–10: the vision of Yahveh's glory (35:2; 60:1), joyful singing (35:2; 60:5), the glory of Lebanon (35:2; 60:13), the highway through the land (35:8; 62:10), a land no longer desolate (62:4). The Dantesque landscape of decay and corruption that introduces the annihilation of Edom (34:1–4) is also replicated in the dark scenario with which the book ends (66:24).

It also seems that Edom has replaced Assyria and Babylonia as the personified embodiment of the evil empire. It is therefore not surprising to find in the description of Edom's undoing the same motifs that we noted in the judgment on Babylon, also presented in the context of cosmic upheaval (13:1–22). The most distinctive of these are the return to nature and the land ravaged by the divine anger turned into a habitat of wild animals (13:20–22; 34:11–15). Ch. 34 is also reminiscent of the judgment pronounced on Assyria earlier in the book, there too linked with the promise of well-being for Jerusalem (30:23–33). In both there is a great slaughter (30:25; 34:6), a smiting with rod, stick, or sword (30:30–32; 34:5–7), and the smell of brimstone and rotting corpses (30:33; 34:3, 9).

What then is the place of chs. 34–35 in the book? The considerations advanced lead to the conclusion that this unit belongs to a late stage of redaction, certainly later than 40–48. If Edom has taken the place of Assyria and Babylon as personifying forces hostile to God's purposes, a function that it retained into the Roman period, its place in the book is easily grasped—first Assyria, then Babylon, then Edom. Whether these chapters served as a bridge or link between major components of the book is another matter. It is difficult to see how the unit as a whole could serve this function. We have seen that the link with ch. 40 is the last paragraph that speaks of a highway for the return to Zion (35:8–10), and it is possible, though unprovable, that it was added at a late stage in the editorial history of the book precisely for that reason. An instructive parallel can be found in the prose narrative that follows (chs. 36–39), taken with adaptations from the History to complete the information on Isaiah, in which Isaiah's prediction of exile in Babylon (39:1–8) links with the prospect of return from the same place in 40:1–5. Concerning the circumstances under which the two units, 34–35 and 36–39, each with its own nexus with the following chapters, were brought together at this midpoint of the book, we can only speculate.

The anti-Edomite diatribe is prefaced with an appeal to the nations to heed an announcement of doom (1–4). Rhetorical appeal to the earth, the sky, and foreign nations to witness the spectacular intervention of Yahveh in human affairs is common in the prophetic books, and the form in which it is expressed here is not particularly characteristic of Second Isaiah (pace Torrey 1928, 282). The strongly rhetorical character of the entire passage, with its numerous examples of paranomasia, assonance, and dominant sound patterns, favors an oral origin, however reworked scribally (Muilenburg). The grim language in which the devastation is expressed is reminiscent of Assyrian annals describing punitive campaigns in gruesome detail, but the language is also suggestive of the ban or *ḥerem*, a dreadful feature of warfare among the small Cisjordanian and Transjordanian tribal states, according to which all the survivors of a defeat in battle were butchered as an offering to the deity of the winning side. Ample documentation is available in the book of Joshua and in the Mesha Stele, which reads as follows:

> I went by night and fought against it (Nebo) from the break of dawn until noon, taking it and slaying all, seven thousand men, boys, women, girls and maid-servants, for I had devoted them to destruction for (the god or goddess) Ashtar-Chemosh.   (*ANET*, 320)

No reason is given for Yahveh's anger, perhaps because the scene of general devastation on earth and in heaven is simply a prelude to Edom as the focus of the divine fury. (Other examples of this cosmic contextualizing appear in 13:1–13; 24:1–6; 30:27–28.) The scene after the slaughter has ended, including disposal of the putrifying corpses of the victims, is part of this dark scenario often reproduced (cf. Joel 2:20; Nah 3:3 and especially Isa 66:24).

Warfare in the heavens is an old mythological topos that appears from time to time in biblical texts (e.g. Dan 10:12–14) and has survived down into modern times (e.g. the "angel of Mons" in 1914 during the First World War). It is symbolized by the sword of Yahveh, the principal weapon of Yahveh as warrior deity (Deut 32:40–42; Isa 27:1; 66:16; Jer 46:10), with which he has dispatched Assyria (31:8) and which is now transferred to ground level as the instrument of Edom's punishment. It was natural to represent slaughter as sacrifice—exploiting the similarity of sound between *zebaḥ* and *ṭebaḥ*—since animal sacrifice obviously involves slaughtering (cf. 2 Kgs 23:20, Josiah's slaughter of the priests at Bethel where the verb "to sacrifice," *zbḥ*, is used; also Jer 46:10; Ezek 39:17–20). But here people and animals are slaughtered without distinction, and the whole land of Edom, including its principal city Bozrah (Buseirah) south of the Dead Sea, is turned into the kind of shambles that must have existed in the Jerusalem temple during a sacrificial ceremony. (So much for "the sanctuary of silence"!) Naturally, too, nothing is said about the sacrificial meal that was meant to be a joyful occasion.

The intensity of resentment and hatred directed at Edom in the post-disaster period can be gauged by the brutal images displayed here and in 63:1–6, where Yahveh is described pounding a personified Edom into a bloody pulp in the winepress, a passage that finally convinced Friedrich Delitzsch to give up on the Old Testament. Anti-Edomite animus pervades prophetic texts that purport to come from the sixth and fifth centuries B.C.E. (Obad 1–14; Jer 49:7–22; Ezek 25:12–14; 32:29; 35:1–15; Joel 4:19[3:19]; Mal 1:3 cf. Ps 137:7). It can be traced back to the initial Edomite infiltration into Judah in the late seventh century B.C.E. (Iron IIIa) under pressure from Kedarite Arab tribes to the east. Edomite names on the ostraca from Arad, together with evidence of their hostile presence in the region on Ostracon 24, attest to their forward progress during the last century of independent Judah. The Edomites profited by the Babylonian conquest to occupy large areas of the Judean Negev, an occupation now well documented archaeologically (e.g. Aroer, Tel Malhata, Horvat ʾUza, Horvat Qitmit). They may even have taken part in the destruction of Jerusalem and temporarily occupied the city (Jer 49:11, 13, 16; 1 Esd 4:45). Long after the Nabatean conquest of Edom in the fifth century B.C.E., the name Edom continued to stand for a hostile and oppressive power, and it is aligned with Rome in the Targum on the present chapter ("the streams of Rome shall be turned into pitch" 34:9).

Much of the negative emotion and expressive, violent, and confrontational language in evidence here and elsewhere in the book can be correlated with an increasingly sectarian way of looking out at the world beyond the boundaries of the province of Judah or, more likely, beyond the boundaries of religious factions within Judah. While anti-Edomite animosity was real enough, it is possible that both here and in 63:1–6 (Edom trodden down in the winepress) Edom has already come to stand for domestic enemies as deserving of vituperation as the historical Edom. The day of Yahveh's vengeance (*yôm nāqām* cf. 61:2; 63:4; Jer 46:10) is in the function of Zion's legal brief against Edom (8); similarly in 62:10–63:6 the salvation of Jerusalem is proclaimed against the backdrop of the destruction of Edom, and in Mal 1:2–5 Yahveh demonstrates his predilection for Jacob (Judah) by his rejection of Esau (Edom). The judgment is carried out in the form of environmental degradation so thorough that it leaves us wondering how the assorted animals and birds that take over could possibly survive. The fire-and-brimstone imagery directly evokes the destruction of Sodom and Gomorrah (Gen 19:24–25), referred to explicitly in the same connection in Jer 49:17–18, and indirectly evokes volcanic phenomena familiar in the southern Arabian peninsula.

The "back to nature" theme is well developed in the book (5:17; 13:20–22; 14:22–23; 17:2; 27:10; 32:14). The social and political infrastructure of the country is destroyed (12); urban life comes to an end (13); devoid of human inhabitants, the land becomes once again the habitat of wild life. Among the names of twelve species of creatures to which Edom is, so to speak, juridically handed over (by means of the measuring line and stones, whatever purpose the latter served), the meaning of only two (*ʿorēb*, "raven"; *tan*, "jackal") is beyond doubt. At least five of the twelve are ritually unclean (cf. Lev 11:15–18; Deut 14:13–17), which would have been seen as entirely appropriate. It would also be appropriate for demons to move into the devastated landscape, though on this subject the text is less clear. The word *śāʿîr* (14) can mean either he-goat or goat-demon (satyr), a precursor of Pan, the recipient of cult in the Kingdom of Samaria and perhaps Judah also (Lev 17:7; 2 Chr 11:15). Here the *śĕʿîrîm* just call to one another but in 13:21 they dance, an unlikely activity for ordinary goats. Lilith, perhaps originally a minor Assyrian demon (*lilītu*), is well known in Jewish folklore as Adam's first wife, the other persona of the Queen of Sheba, who poses deadly riddles, a winged female incubus, a danger for women in childbirth and especially for men who sleep alone. However, both the Qumran scroll (1QIsaᵃ) and the Targum have the plural (see notes on the text), thus allowing for the more mundane meaning of "nightjar" (as NEB), a bird whose secretive habits might qualify it for inclusion in the list, assuming of course that it was known in the Near East. But on the whole it seems better to accept MT and to read this verse (14) as the installation of Lilith as queen of this spooky realm of death in place of the king and princes who are no more (12).

The poem is rounded off with a note (16–17) that Duhm (253) described as one of the strangest passages in the prophetic writings. Quite out of the blue, the reader is addressed directly and urged to consult a book of Yahveh. From allusions elsewhere to such a book we gather that it contained the names of God's elect (Exod 32:32–33; Ps 69:29; Mal 3:16), including also their life span (Ps 139:16), prayers, and sorrows (Ps 56:8). But the feminine forms and suffixes in these verses and the measuring out of the region to be occupied by the animals (cf. 11) leave no doubt that the note is referring back to the animals in the poem immediately preceding. It is unlikely that it refers back to Isa 13:21–22, a passage listing the animals that will take over the destroyed site of Babylon, for the last named among them are not female and their territory is not marked out. Jer 50:39–40 is similar in some respects and may even be an isolated fragment of anti-Edomite diatribe, but it does not qualify for the same reasons. Prophetic books did, however, contain Yahveh's words (e.g. Jer 36:11), so the "book of Yahveh" (sēper YHVH) referred to here must be a prophetic book containing the preceding passage—therefore, a sacred text that the readers are encouraged to consult to verify that a prophecy had been made about Edom in the past and that it was now fulfilled. Somewhat comparable would be the addition updating an anti-Moabite oracle (see commentary on 16:12–14). Together with the other reference to a book noted earlier (see commentary on 29:11–12), this brief colophon by a scribe and collector of prophetic-eschatological texts provides a rare glimpse through the obscurity surrounding the process by which prophetic books were compiled.

THE FINAL RESTORATION OF JUDAH (35:1–10)

(Graetz; Harrelson; Olmstead; Pope; Scott; Smart 1965, 292–94; Steck 1985; Torrey 1928, 295–301)

TRANSLATION

i

35   ¹Let the desert and parched land be glad,ᵃ
the wilderness rejoice and blossom;
²let it burst into blossom like the asphodel,
rejoicing and shouting for joy.ᵇ
The glory of Lebanon will be given to it,
the splendor of Carmel and Sharon;

they will witness the glory of Yahveh,
the splendor of our God.

ii

³Strengthen the hands that are weak,
steady the knees that are feeble,^c
⁴say to the fearful of heart,
"Courage, don't be afraid;
Behold your God!
Vengeance is at hand,
fearsome retribution;^d
it is he who comes to save you."

iii

⁵Then the eyes of the blind will be opened,
the ears of the deaf unstopped;
⁶then the cripple will leap like the deer,
and the tongue of the dumb shout for joy.
Yes, water will burst forth in the desert,
wadis flow^e in the wilderness;
⁷the mirage^f will turn into a pool,
the parched land into gushing streams;
the haunt where jackals crouched^g
will be a place of reeds and rushes.
⁸There will be a highway there;^h
it will be called The Way of Holiness;
the unclean will not pass by that way,
it will be for the use of pilgrims,ⁱ
fools will not wander along it.
⁹There will be no lions there,
no savage beasts will come up on it,
none shall be found there.^j
The redeemed shall walk there,
¹⁰those ransomed by Yahveh shall return;
shouting for joy, they shall enter Zion
crowned with joy everlasting;
gladness and joy will be theirs,^k
sorrow and sighing will depart.

NOTES

^a Omit final *mem* from *yĕśuśûm*, dittography with initial *mem* of *midbār*;
^b *gilâ* for *gilat*;   ^c *kōšĕlôt*, literally, "stumbling";   ^d *gĕmûl ʾĕlohîm*: *ʾĕlo-
hîm* as superlative;   ^e add *yēlĕkû* with 1QIsa^a cf. LXX;   ^f with NEB; as
Duhm (1892, 256) pointed out, *šārāb* refers to the shimmering heat, hot, dry

weather, and then the mirage or *fata morgana* that it can produce (as in Modern Hebrew), rather than "burning sand" (RSV); ᵍ MT reads "in the haunt of jackals is her resting place" cf. 1QIsaᵃ "in the haunt of jackals he lies (lay) down"; the feminine suffix may be due to an original reference to *běnôt ya'ănâ*, "ostriches" (*binveh*, originally *běnôt?*) cf. 34:13 and 43:20, which has jackals, ostriches, and wadis provided for in the wilderness; ʰ omit *vāderek* with 1QIsaᵃ; LXX adds *kathara* → *ṭāhôr*; ⁱ MT "and it is for them a traveler and fools will not go astray" is unintelligible; it looks like a gloss identifying the *derek haqqōdeš* as a pilgrim route; ʲ *lo' timmāṣē'* is in 1QIsaᵃ and 4QIsaᵇ and should not be elided; ᵏ *yaśśîgû*, literally, "they will attain."

COMMENTS

With this projection into a visionary future of the transformed land and saved people we reach the conclusion of the richly annotated compilation of poems and discourses in chs. 1–35. As was noted earlier, the transformation of the natural environment described in this chapter is in deliberate contrast to the ecological degradation of Edom in the preceding chapter. What is here referred to as the desert and parched land is not the wilderness through which the descendants of the deportees are to return (cf. 43:19–21) but the scarred land in which the poet's contemporaries were living. The contrast between the fate of Edom and that of Judah is worked out in detail. Both chapters announce the coming of the avenging God in judgment (34:1–4; 35:4); thorns, nettles and thistles contrast with reeds and rushes (34:13; 35:7); one will lack fresh water, and the other will abound in it (34:9; 35:6–7); Judah will no longer be, like Edom, the haunt of jackals (34:13; 35:7) or other dangerous animals (34:14; 35:9); in Edom travel will be impossible, but in Judah there will be a paved way where pilgrims can safely travel (34:10; 35:8). That this highway is restricted to people in a state of ritual purity indicates that it is a processional way leading to the sanctuary (cf. Exod 15:17), reminiscent therefore of the procession to the esagila sanctuary in the great *akitu* festival in Babylon. The climax of the poem comes with the triumphant entry into Jerusalem, no doubt followed by the acclamation of the kingship of Yahveh (cf. 52:7–10).

The many linguistic points of contact between chs. 35 and 40–48 or 40–55 have led several commentators to the conclusion that ch. 35 is an integral part of Second Isaiah, which for some reason has been separated from it by the narrative in chs. 36–39. There are indeed many such contacts, together with significant differences, but the similarities are susceptible of more than one explanation. In the first of the three stanzas into which I have divided the poem we hear of the "desert" (*midbār*), the "parched land" (*ṣiyyâ*) and the "wilderness" (*'ărābâ*) rejoicing, and a similar theme occurs in 42:11. But in ch. 35 the promise is addressed to the devastated land of Judah, while 42:11 is exhorting the Arab lands of Kedar and Sela to rejoice; hence, the situation is quite different. The theme of rejoicing is in any case much more in evidence in the last chapters of the book (60–66) than in 40–55, and the occasion for rejoicing is ecological transformation brought about by an abundance of water. Perhaps significantly, also, the expression "the glory of Lebanon" (*kĕbôd hallĕbānôn* occurs only at 35:2 and 60:13. Encouragement is offered to the doubters and those of weak resolve in ch. 35 and in Second Isaiah but, again, using different language (35:3–4a; 40:9, 29–31). Throughout Isaiah the self-manifestation of God spells judgment on the reprobate, but the language in which this topic is expressed here is not the same as in chs. 40–55, and the terms *nāqām* ("vengeance") and *gāmûl* ("recompense") in 35:4b are characteristic of Third rather than Second Isaiah (59:17–18; 61:2; 63:4; 66:6). A final example: the removal of blindness and deafness occurs in Second Isaiah but in a manner quite different from 35:5–6a. In the latter the author is speaking of the *literal* removal of disabilities, as is apparent from the miraculous healing of the lame in addition to the blind and deaf. In Second Isaiah, on the other hand, Cyrus's opening the eyes of the blind is a metaphor for remedying the situation of expatriate Judeans (42:7), while in other passages the blind and the deaf are those who will not or cannot accept the seer's message (42:18–20; 43:8).

These are the most prevalent themes recurring throughout these chapters that have led a majority of exegetes to align ch. 35 with Second Isaiah. But the most explicit link is the theme of the highway or processional route with which ch. 35 ends and ch. 40 begins. The connection was broken by the insertion of the historical material in chs. 36–39, a section that concludes with Isaiah's prediction of exile in Babylon (39:5–8), thus creating a new link with what follows.

The problem with the alignment of ch. 35 with Second Isaiah is that the panorama of ch. 35 is completely different from the historical particularities central to chs. 40–48: the career of Cyrus in the first place, but also the anticipated fall of Babylon and polemic against the Babylonian intellectual and religious tradition. Chapter 35 gives us a completely ahistorical and imaginative projection which, on the basis of the contacts discussed above, draws on themes and turns of phrase in chs. 40–48 but also on chs. 1–33. An example of the latter would be the theme of the removal of disabilities in the coming kingdom (29:18; 30:21; 32:3–4; 33:23). Comparison with 62:10–12 will help to clarify the point. This passage also speaks of the highway (*derek*, *mĕsillâ* cf. *maslûl* 35:8) and the advent of salvation and recompense (cf. 35:4) for the redeemed (*gĕʾulē YHVH* cf. *gĕʾulîm* 35:9) and the holy people (*ʿam haqqōdeš* cf. *derek haqqōdeš* 35:8). The connection with chs. 40–48 is obvious, but the highway along which the descendants of the deportees are to return to Judah is in both ch. 35 and ch. 62 a metaphor for passage to the new age about to dawn. It therefore seems reasonable to conclude that (1) chs. 34 and 35 are one unit; (2) as such, they were composed and placed at this point to conclude chs. 1–33, in whatever form they then existed, and recapitulate their message; (3) the author has drawn on motifs and turns of phrase in both First and Second Isaiah; (4) whether these chapters come to us from the fifth century B.C.E. (Clements 1980a, 277), or the fourth (Vermeylen 1977, 446) or even later (Westermann 1974, 362), they derive from a social and spiritual environment very different from that of the so-called Second Isaiah.

INTRODUCTION TO
ISAIAH 36–39

◆

The long narrative in chs. 36–39 comprises three episodes involving Isaiah as prophet to King Hezekiah, but a very different Isaiah from the remorseless critic of the ruling class in Judah whose portrait emerges from the sayings, especially those in chs. 28–33 which, in the generally accepted opinion, refer to the events with which chs. 36 and 37 are concerned—namely, preparations for the rebellion against Assyria, the campaign of Sennacherib, and its immediate aftermath. In the first episode, Isaiah plays a role in the crisis of Sennacherib's Palestinian campaign of 701 B.C.E. A first intervention is solicited by Hezekiah (37:2–7), and this is followed by an unsolicited intervention (37:21–35) in which he predicts Sennacherib's failure to conquer Jerusalem, his subsequent return to his own country and violent death. In the second episode he heals Hezekiah from a potentially fatal illness (ch. 38), and in the third (ch. 39) his prediction of exile in Babylon is announced following a visit by a Babylonian delegation to the Judean court. The order in which the incidents are presented is ostensibly chronological. Since Isaiah promises both that the king will recover and that the city will be saved from the Assyrians (38:5–6), Hezekiah must have taken ill either before or during Sennacherib's invasion of Judah. It will be noted that the promise of an additional fifteen years of life is based on Hezekiah's age at accession, the length of his reign, and the dating of the campaign to the fourteenth year of the reign as reported in the History (2 Kgs 18:2, 13); a point that, incidentally, supports the priority of the account in the History. The visit of the Babylonian envoys is said to have taken place during the king's convalescence (39:1), but the sequencing of events is dictated by the intent to conclude with a prophecy of exile in Babylon (39:5–8), thereby linking up with the announcement of the return of the expatriates in ch. 40. From the point of view of historical plausibility, however, neither the manner of presentation nor the order in which the events are narrated is free of problems. We would find it odd that envoys would have traveled from Babylon in order to visit Hezekiah during his convalescence (Isa 39:1) or that, impelled by scientific curiosity, they would have made the trip in order to investigate the miracle of the steps (as in 2 Chr 32:31). The fact that the rebellion in Babylon had been decisively crushed in the previous year renders a visit at that time even less likely. It seems historically more plausible that they would have come, if they came at all, to solicit support for Merodach-baladan's anti-Assyrian policy—therefore sometime between 704 and 702 B.C.E.

Before engaging with the narrative at close quarters we need to get some sense of the place and function of chs. 36–39 in the book. We begin with the assumption that this entire section is an insertion taken from the History (2 Kgs 18:13–19:37) and that the two versions of the first episode (see the commentary on chs. 36–37) had already been conflated before the transfer. This hypothesis is much more probable than a transfer in the opposite direction (argued by Smelik; and Vermeylen 1977, 95–118). The last chapter of Jeremiah, identical with 2 Kgs 24:18–25:30, is an instructive parallel, since it does not even mention Jeremiah but serves to take the episodic history of the reign of Zedekiah in the book to its tragic conclusion. (For a recent discussion of the arguments on both sides see Seitz 1991, 66–71, 136–40; Williamson 1994, 189–211.) Major differences between 2 Kgs 18–19 and Isa 36–39 are the omission in Isaiah of the problematic narrative of Hezekiah's surrender (2 Kgs 18:14–16 = version A) and the inclusion of a psalm attributed to Hezekiah in Isa 38:9–20. The several minor divergencies will be noted in the commentary.

It would be natural for the editors and compilers of Isaiah to include in the book any information about the principal protagonist available and, if chs. 34–35 formed, as suggested above, a rounding out of the previous 33 chapters, it would likewise be natural to insert this additional material after that conclusion as a kind of narrative appendix. Following this move, 39:1–8, in which Isaiah predicts exile in Babylon, took over the function of linkage from 35:8–10, providing a smooth passage from the Assyrians to the Babylonians as the focus of prophetic concern and the target of divine action. Attempts are occasionally made to read the entire section as linking First with Second Isaiah, but the evidence is simply not there. Chs. 36–39 form a structural counterpart and counterbalance to the similar type-scene recording Isaiah's intervention in international politics under Ahaz in chs. 7–8, a narrative that is also related to the parallel section in the History (Isa 7:1 cf. 2 Kgs 16:1, 5). By interesting coincidence, if this is what it is, Isaiah confronted Ahaz in precisely the same location where thirty-three years later the Rabshakeh would call for the surrender of the city (7:3; 36:2). Other points of contact ("don't be afraid" 7:4 and 37:6; the giving of a sign 7:11 and 37:30) have often been noted. We shall see that the raison d'être of the parallelism is the contrast between the attitudes of Ahaz and Hezekiah, faced with similar critical situations and vis-à-vis prophetic mediation.

The hypothesis that an editor took narrative involving Isaiah from the History and appended it to the book of Isaiah has the advantages of simplicity but is not without its problems. First, the relation between 2 Kgs 18–20 and Isa 36–39 is complicated by fairly clear indications that the narrative material common to both (the B version) has drawn extensively on sayings in chs. 1–35 and perhaps also, if to a much lesser extent, on discourse in chs. 40–48. The theme of trust in God and his instructions communicated through the prophet recurs throughout the book and also, with different emphases, in the Rabshakeh's harangue (different forms of the verbal stem *bṭh*, "trust," occur nine times in the two speeches). Another major theme that we have noted in the sayings is the plan or agenda of Yahveh contrasted with human machinations, and this too is prominent in these chapters, beginning with the Rabshakeh's sarcastic inquiry about their military plan (*'ēṣâ*, 36:4–5; also 37:26 cf. 29:15–16; 30:1–2). The bragging about previous Assyrian conquests in the same speeches is paralleled in 10:8–14, where some of the same cities are listed (cf. 36:19; 37:12–13). The low opinion of Egypt as a potential ally ("a splintered reed that will gouge the hand of the one who leans on it," 36:6) is consistent with the frequent repudiations of an alliance with Egypt as an unprofitable enterprise (19:1–7; 20:1–6; 30:1–5; 31:1–3). Other parallels and borrowings will be noted as the commentary proceeds. It is fairly clear, then, that whoever put these stories together was acquainted with a compilation of sayings attributed to Isaiah, in whatever form they then circulated.

This leads to the question of the source and authorship of these stories about king and prophet and the miraculous rescue of Jerusalem from capture and destruction. This question resolves itself into the other question of the source on which the Historian drew for inserting the stories into the History. These lively stories are of a kind quite different from the Historian's annalistic report of the reign. Coming immediately after the Historian's account of Hezekiah's surrender and payment of heavy tribute (2 Kgs 18:14–16, designated version A), the mission of the Rabshakeh and his colleagues and the call for the city's surrender make little sense. We are also left wondering how, after paying an enormous indemnity that even obliged him to strip the gold from the doors of the temple, Hezekiah would have had any silver, gold, and other precious items left to display before the admiring Babylonian envoys, as is recorded in version B (2 Kgs 18:16; 20:13). Since we have no grounds for either reading 2 Kgs 18:14–16 as a later insertion into the History (pace Seitz 1991, 51–61) or as omitted from Isaiah (suggested by Childs 1967, 69–73), we are entitled to conclude that one of the several prophetic *legenda* incorporated into the history, in some respects comparable to stories about Elijah, Elisha, and other prophets who healed and worked miracles, had Isaiah as its protagonist in close association with King Hezekiah. Particularly interesting is the parallel with the delegation sent by Josiah to Huldah who, like Ahijah confronting Solomon (1 Kgs 11:31–36), and Isaiah with Hezekiah (Isa 39:5–8), announces good news for the short term and bad news further into the future. *Qua legendum*, the account of the remarkable rescue of the city has an interesting parallel in the story told by Herodotus (2.141) about the Pharaoh whose land was invaded by Sennacherib and who, during a visit to a temple, received a revelation that all would be well. The story ends with mice gnawing through the strings of the Assyrian bows and leaving their owners helpless in battle and is rounded off somewhat anticlimactically, or tongue in cheek, with the erection of a statue of the Pharaoh holding a mouse. The Isaiah *legendum* would represent an early stage in the development of a biographical tradition represented in the work of the Chronicler (2 Chr 32), Ben Sira (48:17–25), Josephus (*Ant.* 10.11–35), and *The Martyrdom of Isaiah*.

If the *proximate* origin of the Isaiah *legenda* is to be located in the History, it would be advisable to take them together with other bits of narrative that have found their way into the book of Isaiah and that can be confidently traced to the same source. The record of Isaiah's dealings with Ahaz in relation to which, as the many parallels between them indicate, chs. 36–39 serve as a kind of mirror image is prefaced with a sentence, only slightly edited, from the history of the reign of Ahaz (Isa 7:1; 2 Kgs 16:5). We therefore have two versions of events during the reign of Ahaz, one more or less favorable to the king in which Isaiah has a role (Isa 7–8), the other decidedly unfavorable from which he is absent (2 Kgs 16:1–20). This situation contrasts with the substantial amount of material on Isaiah incorporated by the Historian into his account of Hezekiah's reign, clearly with a view to reinterpreting Hezekiah, perhaps in defiance of historical realities, and bringing him into sharp contrast with the reprobate Ahaz (see further Ackroyd 1987, 105–51). The clear indications of a Deuteronom(ist)ic hand in the composition of Isa 20:1–6 (see commentary) furthermore suggest the possibility that more biographical or hagiographical material about Isaiah was in circulation than has survived by being incorporated into the History. Its transcription, with editorial adjustments, into the book of Isaiah has resulted in a rather basic disjunction between the prophetic profile of the sayings and the profile of the *legenda*. The contrast comes clearly into focus when we compare the *saeva indignatio* ("savage indignation") of the Isaiah of chs. 28–33 directed against the Judean political leadership during the Assyrian campaign and in its aftermath with the attitude of the Isaiah of the *legenda* during the same period as reported in chs. 37–39.

Since the historical issues behind the quite different accounts designated A and B are the primary responsibility of commentators on 2 Kings, they will not receive exhaustive attention here. Discussion of these issues, which has been going on since the early modern period and shows no signs of abating, is often vitiated by the common mistake of passing too quickly from literary creation to historical realia. One conclusion needs to be stated, however. In the absence of documentation, and since the literary evidence does not compel us to adopt it, the hypothesis of two campaigns, whether occurring in the same year (701) or some years after the other (e.g. Shea 1985, 689, 701), will be left out of this account.

ISAIAH 36–39

◆

JERUSALEM THREATENED AND RESCUED (36:1–37:38)

(Cohen; Darr; Cogan and Tadmor; Fullerton 1925–26; Geyer; Honor; Jenkins; van der Kooij; Machinist; Millard; Rowley; Seitz 1993; Shea; Smelik 1986; 1992; Wildberger 1979)

TRANSLATION

First Version

36 [1]In the fourteenth year of King Hezekiah, Sennacherib king of Assyria attacked and captured all the fortified cities of Judah.[a] [2]The king of Assyria then sent[b] the Rabshakeh from Lachish to Jerusalem to King Hezekiah together with a large force,[c] and the Rabshakeh stationed himself at the conduit of the Upper Pool on the way to Bleacher's Meadow. [3d]There went out to him Eliakim ben Hilkiah superintendent of the palace, Shebna the first minister, and Joah ben Asaph the herald.

[4]The Rabshakeh addressed them: "Give Hezekiah this message: thus says the great king, the king of Assyria, 'What makes you so confident? [5]Do you think[e] mouthing mere words amounts to a plan for waging war and the means to do it? On whom, then, are you relying that you have rebelled against me? [6]So you are relying on Egypt, a support no better than a splintered reed that will pierce and gouge the hand of the one who leans on it. Such is Pharaoh king of Egypt for all those who rely on him. [7]And if you tell me[f] you are relying on Yahveh your God, was it not he whose high places and altars Hezekiah removed, instructing Judah and Jerusalem that they were to worship before this altar?[g] [8]Come now, make a wager with my master the king of Assyria: I will give you two thousand horses if you can put riders on them. [9]How then can you, relying as you do on Egypt for chariots and cavalry, repulse a single one among the least of my master's servants? [10]Furthermore, was it without the consent of Yahveh that I attacked this land[h] to destroy it? No; Yahveh himself told me, "Attack this land and destroy it."'"

[11]Eliakim [Shebna and Joah][i] made this reply to the Rabshakeh: "Please address your servants in Aramaic, since we understand it; do not address us in Hebrew in the hearing of the people who are on the wall." [12]But the Rabshakeh replied: "Did my master send me to deliver this message to you and your master and not also to these people sitting on the wall who together with

you are doomed to eat their own shit and drink their own piss?" [13]So the Rab-shakeh stood up and shouted out loud in Hebrew: "Hear the message of the great king, the king of Assyria! [14]These are the king's words: Do not let Heze-kiah deceive you; he is unable to rescue you.[j] [15]Do not let Hezekiah con you into relying on Yahveh with the message, 'Yahveh will surely rescue us; this city will not be handed over to the king of Assyria.' [16]Do not listen to Hezekiah. This is the message of the king of Assyria: Make your peace with me; come out to me; then each one of you may eat the fruit of his own vine and fig tree and drink the water from his own well, [17]until such time as I take you to a land like your own, a land rich in wheat and wine, grain and vineyards.[k] [18]Do not let Hezekiah mislead you with his claim, 'Yahveh will rescue us.' Did any of the gods of the other nations rescue his land from the king of Assyria? [19]Where now are the gods of Hamath and Arpad? Where are the gods of Sepharvaim?[l] Where are the gods of the land of Samaria? Did they rescue Samaria from me?[m] [20]Did any of the gods of these lands rescue their lands from me? How then will Yahveh rescue Jerusalem from me?"

[21]They[n] remained silent, answering him not a word, for the king had or-dered them not to answer him. [22]So Eliakim ben Hilkiah superintendent of the palace, Shebna the first minister, and Joah ben Asaph the herald went back to Hezekiah with their clothes torn and reported to him what the Rabshakeh had said. 37 [1]When King Hezekiah heard it, he tore his clothes, put on sack-cloth, and went to the house of Yahveh. [2]He sent Eliakim superintendent of the palace, Shebna the first minister, and the senior priests clothed in sack-cloth to the prophet Isaiah ben Amoz. [3]They said to him, "This is Hezekiah's message: Today is a day of trouble, reproach and contempt. We are like women who do not have the strength to bring forth their children as they are about to be born.[o] [4]It may be that Yahveh your God will pay heed to the words of the Rabshakeh whom his master the king of Assyria sent to insult the living God and will refute what Yahveh your God heard said. Offer a prayer, then, for the remnant that is left here."

[5]King Hezekiah's officials then came to Isaiah [6]and Isaiah told them, "This is what you must say to your master: this is the message of Yahveh: 'Do not be alarmed at what you have heard said when the king of Assyria's officials reviled me. [7]I am about to put a spirit in him; he will hear a rumor, return to his own country, and I will cause him to fall by the sword in his own land.'"

[8]Having heard that the king of Assyria had moved on from Lachish, the Rabshakeh returned to find him attacking Libnah.

Second Version

[9]When the king heard that Tirhakah the Nubian king had set out to wage war against him, he [once again] sent envoys to Hezekiah with this message: [10]"This is what you are to say to Hezekiah king of Judah: 'Do not let your God in whom you trust deceive you with the promise that Jerusalem will not be handed over to the king of Assyria. [11]You must have heard what the kings of

Assyria did to all the countries, destroying them completely, and you expect to escape? [12]Did the gods of the lands that my ancestors destroyed rescue them — the gods of Gozan, Haran, Reseph, and the people of Eden living in Telassar? [13]Where now is the king of Hamath, the king of Arpad, the king of the city of Sepharvaim or of Hena or of Ivvah?'"

[14]Hezekiah took the letter from the envoys and read it. He then went up into the house of Yahveh and opened it out in the presence of Yahveh. [15]Hezekiah offered this prayer to Yahveh:

[16]Yahveh of hosts,[p] God of Israel enthroned on the cherubim, you alone are God of all the kingdoms of the earth. It is you who made the heavens and the earth. [17]Yahveh, incline your ear and listen; Yahveh, open your eyes and see; hear all the words that Sennacherib has sent to insult the living God. [18]It is true, O Yahveh, that the kings of Assyria have devastated every land[q] [19]and have consigned the gods of these lands to the fire, for they are no gods but rather objects of wood and stone, the work of human hands, and so they were destroyed. [20]But now, Yahveh our God, rescue us from his grasp, so that all the kingdoms of the earth may acknowledge that you alone, Yahveh, are God.[r]

[21] Isaiah ben Amoz then sent the following message to Hezekiah: This is what Yahveh God of Israel says: Since you have prayed to me concerning Sennacherib king of Assyria,[s] [22]this is the word that Yahveh has spoken concerning him:

The virgin daughter of Zion despises you, she scorns you;
the daughter of Jerusalem tosses her head as you withdraw.
[23]Whom have you mocked and abused?
Against whom have you raised your voice?
You have looked down on the Holy One of Israel!
[24]Through your servants[t] you have mocked the Sovereign Lord;
you have declared: "With my many chariots
I have gone up the highest mountains,
to the inner recesses of Lebanon;
I have felled its tallest cedars,
its finest cypresses;
I have reached its highest point,[u]
the forest of its pasture land;
[25]I have dug wells,
I have drunk the water of foreigners;
with the sole of my foot I have dried up
all the streams of Egypt."

[26]Have you not heard
how I devised it a long time ago,
devised it from days of old?[v]
And now I have brought it about
that fortified cities are turned into heaps of rubble,[w]
[27]their inhabitants devoid of strength,
dismayed, ashamed.

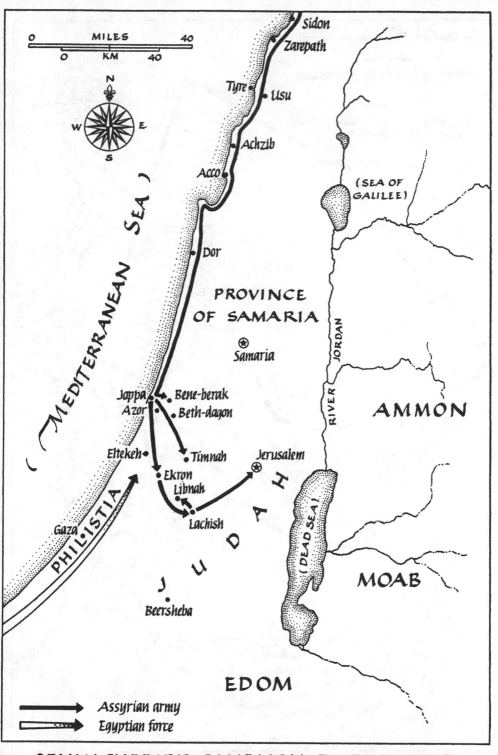

**SENNACHERIB'S CAMPAIGN TO THE WEST
701 B.C.E.
ISAIAH 36-37**

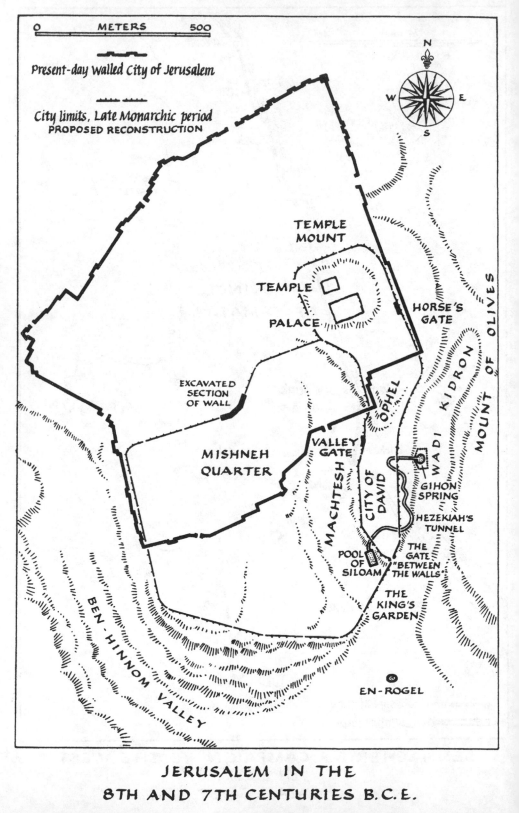

JERUSALEM IN THE
8TH AND 7TH CENTURIES B.C.E.

They have become like wild plants,
like green grass,
like grass on the housetops, blighted by the east wind.[x]
[28]I know your rising up and your sitting down,[y]
your coming and your going;
[29]your fury directed at me and your arrogance[z]
have come to my hearing.
I will put my hook in your nose,
my bit through your lips,
and I will lead you back by the way you came.

[30]This shall be the sign for you: This year eat aftergrowth, in the second year what grows naturally,[aa] but in the third year sow and reap, plant vineyards and eat[bb] their fruit. [31]The remaining survivors of the household of Judah shall once again take root below and bring forth fruit above; [32]for from Jerusalem a remnant shall go forth, survivors from Mount Zion. The zeal of Yahveh of hosts shall bring this about.

[33]This, therefore, is the word of Yahveh concerning the king of Assyria:
He shall not enter this city,
he shall shoot no arrow there,
he shall not advance on it with shield
nor cast up a siege ramp against it.
[34]By the way he came he will return,
but this city he shall not enter!
An oracle of Yahveh.
[35]I will defend this city to rescue it,
for my own sake and for the sake of my servant David.

[36][cc]The angel of Yahveh went out and struck down one hundred and eighty-five thousand people in the Assyrian camp; when morning came they were all lying dead. [37]Then Sennacherib king of Assyria broke camp and left. He returned to Nineveh and stayed there. [38]While he was worshiping in the temple of Nisroch his god, Adrammelek and Sarezer his sons killed him with the sword and escaped to the land of Ararat. Esarhaddon his son reigned in his place.

NOTES

Variations in the parallel 2 Kgs 18–19 will be noted; 4QIsa[b] contains fragments of 36:1–2 but with only orthographic variants.   [a] 2 Kgs 18:14–16 narrates the submission of Hezekiah and payment of tribute;   [b] 2 Kgs 18:17 adds "the Tartan and the Rab saris";   [c] 2 Kgs 18:17 adds: "to Jerusalem; they went up and arrived at Jerusalem, they went up and arrived";   [d] 2 Kgs 18:18 adds: "they called for the king and . . .";   [e] reading *ʾāmartāh* 2d person for MT *ʾāmartî* with 2 Kgs 18:20;   [f] pl. *toʾmĕrûn* with 2 Kgs 18:22 and 1QIsa[a] (cf. LXX) for sing. in MT;   [g] 2 Kgs 18:22 adds "in Jerusalem";   [h] for MT *ʿal-hāʾāreṣ hazzoʾt* 2 Kgs 18:25 has *ʿal-hammāqōm hazzeh*, "[to] this place" i.e. the city and its temple;   ⁱ 2 Kgs 18:26: "Eliakim ben Hilkiah";   ^j 2 Kgs 18:29 adds "from his hand";   ^k 2 Kgs 18:32 adds "a land of olives, oil, and honey, so that you may live and not die; do not listen to Hezekiah . . .";   ^l 2 Kgs 18:34 adds "Hena and Ivvah";   ^m the unintelligible second half of the verse is emended according to 2 Kgs 18:34; read *hăkî* for MT *věkî*;   ⁿ 2 Kgs 18:36: "the people";   ^o literally, "for children came to the birth and there was no strength to bring them forth," a proverbial saying;   ^p 2 Kgs 19:15 omits "of hosts";   ^q 2 Kgs 19:17: "the nations and their lands";   ^r *'ĕlohîm*, "God," absent from MT but added from 1QIsa^a, LXX, and 2 Kgs 19:19;   ^s Kgs 19:20 adds: "I have heard [your prayer]";   ^t 2 Kgs 19:23: "messengers";   ^u 2 Kgs 19:23: *mělôn qiṣṣoh* = "its furthest lodge/retreat" for *měrôm qiṣô*;   ^v read *yěṣartîhâ* with 1QIsa^a;   ^w reading *něṣûrîm* 1QIsa^a for MT *niṣṣîm*;   ^x *qdym* 1QIsa^a for MT *qāmâh*;   ^y reading *quměkâ věšibtěkâ* with 1QIsa^a;   ^z omit *ya'an hitraggezkâ 'ēlay* with 1QIsa^a and read *ûšě'ônkâ*, "your arrogance," for MT *věša'ănankâ*, "your careless ease";   ^{aa} *šāhîs*, 2 Kgs 19:29 has *sāhîš*; 1QIsa^a *š'ys*, hapax;   ^{bb} 1QIsa^a has four infinitives absolute for MT plural imperative;   ^{cc} 2 Kgs 19:35: adds "during that night."

COMMENTS

This first and longest of the three episodes amounts to a fairly coherent narrative that reads as follows: While Sennacherib was still besieging the fortress city of Lachish, one of his staff was sent to call for the surrender of Jerusalem. The incident described is not therefore a siege, as is often assumed, since the army under Sennacherib's command was still in the lowlands southwest of Jerusalem; it was a mission with the clear purpose of inducing surrender without the need to engage in a necessarily protracted siege. With this in view, the Rabshakeh made an intimidating speech in front of the walls of the city while parleying with Judean officials. After the latter reported to Hezekiah, a prophet (Isaiah) was consulted, as was the custom, and gave a good prognosis. The Assyrian official rejoined his king after the fall of Lachish (37:8), and the news about an imminent Egyptian intervention led to a second attempt to intimidate Hezekiah into surrendering the city, an attempt thwarted once again by prophetic intervention, this time unsolicited. In keeping with the prophetic prediction, Sennacherib was forced miraculously to retire and was subsequently murdered by his own sons in Nineveh.

While this narrative sequence is relatively coherent, it is probable, and generally acknowledged, that it was created by conflating two more or less parallel accounts. There are two boastful harangues by the Rabshakeh (36:4–20; 37:10–13), in both of which the same cities destroyed by the Assyrians are mentioned (Hamath, Arpad, Sepharvaim); Isaiah intervenes twice and pronounces two oracles dooming the expedition of Sennacherib to failure (37:2–7; 37:21–35); and Hezekiah visits the temple twice (37:1; 37:14–20). The events are described as taking place in 701, but the account could not have been put together before the death of Sennacherib two decades later and could be even later. Most commentators have agreed to designate chs. 36–37, with the parallel narrative in 2 Kgs 18:1–19:38 (minus 18:14–16), Version B and to divide it into 36:1–37:9a + 37:37–38 (B^1) and 37:9b–36 (B^2). The former concludes with the return to Nineveh and murder of Sennacherib (37:37–38 cf. 37:7), the latter with the destruction of the Assyrian army in Judah (37:36). Version A would be the very different, brief and more annalistic account of Hezekiah's submission to Sennacherib and payment of tribute (2 Kgs 18:14–16) that has so exercised the ingenuity of commentators and historians. Where exactly B^1 breaks off and B^2 begins is unclear. The suggestion advanced here is that 37:7 + 37:37–38 formed the original conclusion to B^1 and that vv 37–38 were moved to their present position when the versions were amalgamated. Isaiah 37:8 is therefore an editorial link-verse removing the Rabshakeh from the scene and preparing for B^2. Needless to say, enough inconcinnities, aporias, and additions remain in both accounts to perplex the modern reader, as the commentary will show. The role of Isaiah is in the fore in B^1, less so in B^2 which is more hagiographical, highlighting the piety and devotion of Hezekiah in connection with the temple and priesthood, and introducing a miraculous element (the Destroying Angel) absent from the other version. Both accounts could be described as narrative theology, encapsulating ideological features and a message about power and violence and how they are to be confronted. The story also brings the reader once more up against the immensely problematic nature of divine intervention in human affairs, whether through human agency as in the first version, or the more spectacular and problematic form of miracle in the second.

36:1–3. This *mise-en-scène* of the monologue before the walls of Jerusalem is practically identical with 2 Kgs 18:13, 17–18. We have just seen that the account of Hezekiah's submission and payment of tribute to Sennacherib in 2 Kgs 18:14–16 (version A) is quite distinct, a conclusion reinforced by the shorter form of the name Hezekiah (i.e. *ḥizqîyâ* rather than *ḥizqîyāhû*) and "Hezekiah king of Judah" rather than "King Hezekiah," as in the B version. We know from the royal Assyrian annals (*ANET*, 287–88) that Sennacherib's western campaign, ending with the submission of Hezekiah and the reduction of Judah to a rump state, took place in 701 B.C.E. If this corresponds to the fourteenth year of Hezekiah as our text states, Samaria would have been incorporated into the Assyrian provincial system and its last king, Hoshea, would have died before Hezekiah came to the throne, and therefore the synchronic data given in 2 Kgs 18:1, 9–10 would be inaccurate. The time-honored alternative is to emend the text, in this case from the fourteenth to the twenty-fourth year, but there is no textual justification for doing so, and it seems more advisable to let the text stand and date Hezekiah's accession to 715 B.C.E., *after* the fall of Samaria. The fifteen additional years allotted to him after 701 in the second episode (Isa 38:5 = 2 Kgs 20:6) were evidently calculated on the basis of data provided in the History (2 Kgs 18:2, 13), thus providing another indication that the narrative as a whole was transcribed from the History to the book of Isaiah rather than in the opposite direction.

The precise location of this hostile encounter is identical with the earlier one between Isaiah, accompanied by Shear-yashub, and Ahaz (see commentary on 7:3). This circumstance draws the reader's attention to the parallelism between the two critical moments of history and the conduct of the two kings, obliged by the course of events to make fateful decisions on behalf of their people. While the parallel Kings account has a team of three on the Assyrian side matching the three Judean officials (2 Kgs 18:17), the Isaian version concentrates on the Rabshakeh. The holder of this office (Akk. *rab šake* = "chief butler") was apparently a civilian with diplomatic and linguistic skills in the service of the king and his generalissimo (the Tartān/*turtanu* of 2 Kgs 18:17). He was sent on ahead with a detachment to negotiate the surrender of Jerusalem. His mission must have occurred during or shortly after the reduction and destruction of Lachish (graphically portrayed on the wall panels now in the British Museum, see *ANEP*[2], 371–73) and the devastation of the 46 locations and their inhabitants mentioned on the Rassam Cylinder (*ANET*, 288).

According to 22:15–25, Eliakim replaced Shebna as superintendent of the palace or grand vizier (*'ăšer 'al-habbāyit*), though he too apparently failed to live up to the demands of this high office. Whether the fall from grace of both of these officials occurred before (followed by reinstatement) or after 701 we do not know. Likewise, the title *sōpēr* (usually translated "scribe"), borne by Shebna, may imply demotion to the level of secretary and scrivener, but since it is also the term used for the highest political office from the time of Josiah (Jer 26:24 etc.), it is possible that the author anachronistically juxtaposed two terms for the same office (see further the commentary on 22:15–25). The function of the *mazkîr*, the office held by Joah, third member of the mission, is not entirely clear—perhaps that of official spokesman or herald.

36:4–10. The speech of the Rabshakeh consists in a blatant attempt to intimidate and bully the people of Jerusalem into submission. The Rabshakeh's insistence on directing his oratory towards the common people as well as the king's emissaries (36:12) is in accordance with the Assyrian practice of holding the entire population of a vassal state responsible for keeping the peace, with the obvious purpose of encouraging them to depose or assassinate their rulers in the event that the rulers rebel. This policy also served to justify atrocities committed against civilians, amply and gruesomely documented by the Assyrians themselves in their annals and iconography. The speech is evidently a free composition of the author of B[1], in keeping with the common practice in ancient historiography of putting speeches into the mouths of leading characters at important points of the narrative (e.g. Herodotus, Thucydides, Acts of the Apostles).

While the author may have had some indirect acquaintance with the bombastic style of Near Eastern royal inscriptions, including titulary (great king, king of the world, etc.), he or, less probably, she has drawn extensively on the Isaian prophetic material available at the time of writing. The speech reaches at once to the center of Isaian theopolitics with the first rhetorical question: what is the source of your confidence? This is a fundamental issue in all parts of the book of Isaiah. The specific instance on which several Isaian sayings converge is illusory confidence in an Egyptian alliance (19:1–15; 28:14–22; 30:1–7) and in the ability and willingness of Egypt to supply the horses and chariots that the Judeans lack and with which the Assyrians are abundantly supplied (30:16; 31:1–3). How misplaced this confidence was is summarized in the dismissal of the Egyptians as a "profitless people" (30:5, 7), and the same opinion is expressed more vividly by the Rabshakeh (cf. Sargon II's description of the Pharaoh as "a king who cannot save," Cogan and Tadmor 1988, 231). There is also an echo of the theme of contrasting and conflicting human and divine plans (as in 29:15–16)—plans for making war (36:5) over against Yahveh's own plan for Assyria devised ages past (37:26).

Since Assyrian campaigns with their attendant slaughter and mayhem were conducted to the greater glory of the imperial deity, Ashur, it is not surprising that the Rabshakeh came up with religious and ideological as well as practical reasons for surrendering. A standard explanation for military disaster, and therefore a standard excuse for inflicting military disaster on others, was the anger of the native deity at his or her devotees. The Israelites were believed to have devastated Moab because Kemosh was angry with his land (*ANET*, 320). That first the Assyrians and then the Babylonians devastated Israel and Judah because of the anger of Yahveh is one of the most recurrent motifs of prophetic preaching, and we can say that the prophetic ethic developed, in good part, out of the attempt to explain the divine anger manifested in the course of international events. A key criterion for the Historian's evaluation of rulers was their attitude about the *bāmôt* ("high places"), and therefore a key element in the positive evaluation of Hezekiah was his abolition of the same (2 Kgs 18:3–7 cf. 2 Chr 31:1). It is not surprising that the author has this spokesman for an evil empire express views at variance with Deuteronomistic orthodoxy and represent Hezekiah's religious reforms as positively sinful—not unlike the vigorous rejection of this Deuteronomic innovation by Jeremiah's male and female audience in Egypt, a rejection that added up to an interesting alternative explanation for the disaster of 586 b.c.e. (Jer 44:15–19).

To this the Rabshakeh adds a more decisive argument by adducing an oracle of Yahveh addressed to Sennacherib commanding him to destroy Judah, one similar in wording to the prediction recorded in Jeremiah's scroll that "the king of Babylon will certainly come and destroy this land" (Jer 36:29). This further example of religion in the service of absolute power was apparently not uncommon in the Near East; for example, both Sargon II and Cyrus claimed that Marduk had called them to conquer Babylon. But destroying a foreign god's land is another matter. The author may therefore have wished us to understand that this was a barefaced lie, since no such oracle existed, or the claim may have drawn on the multiple threats of punishment by military action leveled at Judah in the Isaian material. Another possibility, suggested by the close links in transmission between Isaiah and Micah, is that the author had Mic 3:12 in mind, a very direct threat of the comprehensive destruction of Jerusalem, though one addressed not to Sennacherib but to Hezekiah. Whatever the author had in mind precisely, placing such a claim of divine revelation in the Rabshakeh's mouth, when taken with other indications, intimates strong reservations on the part of the Deuteronom(ist)ic author or editor about prophetic threats of total destruction leveled against their Israelite contemporaries. It was suggested above that this may help to explain the Historian's failure to mention Amos, and the transformation of Micah's prediction of the destruction of Jerusalem (Mic 3:12) from an unconditional to a conditional prediction of doom (Jer 26:17–19).

36:11–20. The composer of the scene has used the issue of linguistic competence to prepare for the Rabshakeh's direct address to the population of the city represented by the bystanders on the wall. Aramaic was the diplomatic lingua franca of the Neo-Assyrian Empire, beginning as early as the seventh century B.C.E., and it continued to be, into the Achaemenid period. The request of the Judean officials implies that Aramaic and the Jerusalem dialect of Hebrew (yĕhûdît, also Neh 13:24) were not mutually intelligible, at least not for the linguistically uneducated (see further Ullendorf 1962). It seems surprising that the Rabshakeh had a fluent command of spoken Hebrew, unless he was one of the Samarian deportees who had risen through the ranks, as has been suggested. At any rate, the Rabshakeh deployed this unusual competence in pursuit of his purpose of driving a wedge between the people and their ruler. In doing so he alternated brutal threats with blandishments and promises, a technique still used by interrogators to break down resistance. The threats, delivered in deliberately crude and offensive terms, are reminiscent of standard descriptions of the horrors of a protracted siege in curses attached to treaties (e.g. the vassal treaties of Esarhaddon, ANET, 534–41) and reproduced in biblical covenant formulations (e.g. Lev 26:29; Deut 28:53–57 cf. Ezek 4:16–17; Lam 2:20; 4:4–5, 10). But then, in describing the charms of the land to which those addressed were to be deported, the Rabshakeh changes his approach and sounds rather like an enthusiastic travel agent (the publicity is more developed in 2 Kgs 18:17), though as often happens with such advance descriptions the reality would turn out to be rather different. In the interval between surrender and deportation, the Assyrians will generously leave the now subject people free to enjoy the fruits of their agricultural labors (cf. Lev 26:10, 16; Deut 11:14; 28:39–40, 51; Amos 5:11). The length of the interval is not stated; presumably not as long as some of the Samarians had to wait to be transported to northern Mesopotamia (Isa 7:8b; Ezra 4:2, 9–10).

In urging the population not to be taken in by Hezekiah's assurances, the Rabshakeh presents an excellent summary of Isaiah's message: Yahveh will save us; Jerusalem will not fall (clearly in 37:35 cf. 29:5–8; 31:4–5, 8–9). But in setting up the confrontation in these terms the author left an enormous question hanging over the heads of the survivors of the catastrophe of 586 B.C.E. The warning is followed by what seems to be a decent offer. The phrase ʿăśû-ʾittî bĕrākâ (16), literally, "make with me a blessing," which occurs only in this place, has been variously interpreted: something like "do me a favor (and surrender the city)" or "let's be good friends" or "let us enter into a covenant with its blessings (and curses)" or, finally, "send me a gift," since *běrākâ* means "gift" elsewhere though not as part of this idiom (see Josh 15:19; 1 Sam 30:26; 2 Kgs 5:15; Cogan and Tadmor 1988, 232). In view of the immediate context, it reads very much like an invitation to surrender. The tone then changes to bluster as the Rabshakeh enumerates earlier Assyrian victories over comparable states and their comparable deities, at which point the author could draw on existing Isaian diatribe couched in much the same terms (10:8–11, 13–14). Hamath (Hama) in central Syria was taken and its population deported by Sargon II in 720; Arpad (Tell Rifaʾat), chief city of Bit-agusi in northern Syria, fell to Tiglath-pileser III twenty years earlier. Both Sepharvaim (unidentified) and Hamath provided transfer population for depopulated Samaria (2 Kgs 17:24), and the new settlers from Sepharvaim offered the cult of child sacrifice to a deity called Adrammelek, curiously the same name as the name of the parricidal son of Sennacherib (Isa 37:38); the one takes the life of his children, the other the life of his father.

Samaria provides the last example of defeated peoples and deities, which was intended to put the erstwhile Northern Kingdom and its later occupants on the same plane religiously as the pagan nation-states of Syria listed with it. This is in keeping with both Isaian polemic and the viewpoint of the History in which the fall of the Northern Kingdom is attributed to aberrant cults. The contrast between South and North, Judah and Samaria, will remain a prominent issue down to the end of the Second Temple period.

36:21–37:8. The silent reception of the Rabshakeh's harangue is at first sight surprising since the Judean officials had been sent to parley. Either they simply refused to continue the dialogue in Hebrew in the hearing of the populace, or silence was considered the only response to blasphemy. The Rabshakeh's mission was therefore unsuccessful, but no one on the Judean side would have harbored any illusions about the consequences. This prospect alone would justify the traditional signs of mourning by the officials and the king, though the author may also have had in mind the blasphemy against Yahveh. (On ceremonial mourning see commentary on 22:12; also 15:2–3 and 32:11–12.) From this point on the story has to accommodate two protagonists, the prophet who serves as intermediary between the deity and the beleagered people and the pious monarch who abases himself and betakes himself at once to the temple. While his prayer is recorded only in the alternative version (37:15–20), we are to understand that he went to the temple to pray and that the result was the sending of a delegation to consult Isaiah.

At this point we are confronted with a particular aspect of the ideology inscribed into the story about king and prophet. Chs. 28–33, much of which has to do with policies pursued at the Judean court leading up to, during, and immediately after the revolt against Sennacherib, record the unrelenting criticism directed against the ruling class in Jerusalem, not least because of their disregard for the prophetic message. While Hezekiah is never mentioned, it is inconceivable that he was exempt from criticism: we hear of *his* officials on a futile mission to solicit assistance from Egypt (30:4); the "house of evildoers" (*bēt mĕrēʿîm* 31:2) could well refer to the royal house; and we noted in the commentary that concluding the section with the prospect of a righteous king and political leaders in the future (32:1; 33:17) could be an implicit criticism of the less-than-righteous situation in the present. To this we may add that in the account of Jeremiah's trial (Jer 26:17–19) Micah's unconditional prediction of the destruction of Jerusalem (3:12) is presented as the occasion for Hezekiah's change of heart, and the threat of destruction itself is the result of bloodshed and wrongdoing in Jerusalem (Mic 3:10). Ackroyd (1979, 12) has, moreover, plausibly suggested that the original form of Isa 39 envisaged condemnation for Hezekiah on account of his involvement with a foreign power, Babylon. In this respect, therefore, he was no different from Ahaz, who guiltily sought assistance from Assyria (2 Kgs 16:7–9). The difficulty of understanding how exile in Babylon could follow from a mere act of political naiveté would be reduced if the text originally referred to overtures towards a Babylonian alliance. The conclusion towards which these misgivings about the present state of the text point is, therefore, that, whatever its origin, the story about king and prophet has served the purposes of the Historian, which included setting up a contrast between the reprobate Ahaz and the pious Hezekiah and pinning responsibility for the destruction of Jerusalem and exile firmly on Manasseh (2 Kgs 21:10–15). In a form apt for fulfilling this function, it was transcribed, with further modifications, into the book of Isaiah.

Consulting a prophetic intermediary at a time of crisis is attested throughout the Near East as early as the reign of Zimrilim of the Kingdom of Mari in the eighteenth century B.C.E., if not earlier. The delegation to Isaiah is composed of Eliakim, Shebna, and the senior priests. Joah is missing, no doubt because a herald would be *de trop* in a private meeting with a prophet. We hear of a similar delegation sent by Josiah to the prophet Huldah (2 Kgs 22:11–20) and by Zedekiah to Jeremiah (Jer 21:1–2), both instances in which priests took part. There is no direct request for miraculous intervention. A proverb expressing a sense of powerlessness is quoted (cf. Hos 13:13), and the group asks whether the living God (cf. 1 Sam 17:26, 36) will refute the Rabshakeh's argument, which evaluates the reality and efficacy of divinity in terms of the manifest exercise of power, a very common procedure in all ages. This is the language heard so often in the psalms of lament: why is God silent and inactive? (e.g. Ps 9:19–20; 10:1–2), and the cry has often been heard since then. The delegates conclude their brief representation by requesting that Isaiah do what prophets were expected to do—that is, intercede for the remnant of Judah (cf. 37:30–32 and 7:3)—in other words, for all that was left after the murderous assault of the Assyrian army.

Isaiah's reply is succinct by contrast with his intervention in the alternative version, the succinctness no doubt due to the restructuring of the narrative line when the two versions were conflated. The basic message is one of reassurance—"don't be afraid" (*ʾal-tîrāʾ*)—corresponding to the message delivered to Ahaz three decades earlier (7:4) and to the consoling word repeated frequently in the discourses of the so-called Second Isaiah (41:10, 13, 14; 43:1, 5; 44:2, 8;

54:4). It is interesting to observe that in this version divine intervention comes about not by way of the Destroying Angel but by a kind of mind control or psychological conditioning. Yahveh will inject a "spirit" (*rûaḥ*) into Sennacherib, like the "evil spirit from Yahveh" that accounted for Saul's abnormal behavior (1 Sam 16:14–16, 23; 18:10; 19:9–10) or the spirit commissioned by Yahveh to make Ahab's prophets deceive him and bring about his death (1 Kgs 22:20–23). Yahveh can therefore also work by bringing about changes of mood or instilling presentiments of disaster and death, even when, as in this instance, they may have no obvious rationale. The rumors no doubt emanated from the court at Nineveh, but we know of no disturbance that may have occasioned them at that time. Sennacherib did in fact fall by the sword, but only two decades after the time in which the story is set. The details are provided at the end of the second version (37:37–38) which, as noted earlier, were probably located originally at the end of the first version.

37:9–20. It is really not very important to decide the precise point of suture between the two versions. Editorial logic required that the Rabshakeh retire and a pretext be supplied for a second challenge. The Rabshakeh therefore rejoined Sennacherib, and the hostile approach of Tirhakah occasioned a second attempt to bully Jerusalem into surrendering. The connection between vv 8 and 9 is weak, since *vayyišmaʿ* ("and he heard") has no antecedent; the point of juncture may therefore be here. If we retain the second *vayyišmaʿ* (*vayyišmaʿ vayišlaḥ*, "when he heard he sent . . ."), it will imply that when Sennacherib heard the bad news of the approach of Tirhakah he sent envoys to Hezekiah; but if we emend to *vayyāšob vayišlaḥ* ("he once again sent"; see notes on the text) the point that this was a second mission would be made explicitly, no doubt by the editor who conflated the two versions.

At this juncture the historical account is somewhat confused since Taharqa of the Nubian or Napatan dynasty only ascended the throne of both Egypts in 690/689, more than a decade after Sennacherib's Palestinian campaign. In 701, Shebitku his father reigned, having followed *his* father Shabako on the throne the year before the Palestinian campaign (see commentary on 18:1–7 and 30:1–5). Perhaps the error arose because Taharqa commanded the army defeated at Eltekeh by the Assyrians.

The second and shorter discourse (10–13) in epistolary form takes aim more directly at Yahveh than at Hezekiah and therefore strikes more closely at the heart of Isaiah's message of confidence in Yahveh as the essential attitude in a time of crisis (7:9b; 8:17; 12:2; 26:3; 30:15, 18b). We cannot help wondering how this would have been read after 586 B.C.E., when no Destroying Angel appeared from heaven. Sennacherib's tone of self-confident braggadocio is the same as in the Rabshakeh's speech: in the encounter with the Assyrian juggernaut nations are utterly destroyed and their gods exposed as worthless. The list of victims is somewhat longer. In addition to Hamath, Arpad, and Sepharvaim we hear of the extinction of the following: Gozan (*guzanu* = Tell Halaf on the Upper Habor, to which Israelites were exiled 2 Kgs 17:6); Haran (*ḥarranu* on the Upper Balik, annexed by Assyria in the ninth century); Reseph (*rasappa*,

Upper Mesopotamia); Eden (*bit-adinu* on the Euphrates cf. Amos 1:5); Telas-sar (perhaps *til-assuri* on the Lower Diyala). Hena and Ivvah are missing from 36:19 and from the corresponding place in LXX; if they are cities their location is unknown. The Targum ("did they not cast them out and exile them?") appears to have read these names as verbal forms from *nv'* (Hiphil) and *'vh* (Piel), respectively.

The repeated challenge leads to another visit to the temple and serves to set the piety and humility of Hezekiah in sharp contrast to the impiety and hubris of his adversary. We have seen that the motif of the temple visit, piety towards the deity, and defeat of the tyrant also occurs in Herodotus' story about Pharaoh Sethos who, when attacked by Sennacherib, prayed to the god Ptah and received assurance of success (2.141). Hezekiah read the letter (or had it read to him cf. 2 Kgs 22:10; Jer 36:21) and displayed it before Yahveh enthroned in the temple, somewhat reminiscent of "letters to the gods" placed in Mesopotamian temples after successful campaigns. The prose prayer follows the classical pattern of invocation, petition, description of the suppliant's situation, and final confession. The titulary *YHVH ṣĕbā'ôt yôšēb hakkĕrubîm* ("Yahveh of the hosts seated on the chrubim") and *'ĕlohê yiśrā'ēl* ("God of Israel") is traditional and well attested in liturgical prayers and in Isaiah. The pervasive influence of Deuteronomistic language and theology is evident throughout the prayer (cf. the prayers of David and Solomon 2 Sam 7:18–29; 1 Kgs 8:23–53), not least in the confession of Yahveh as the only God in heaven and earth (1 Kgs 8:23, 60), sovereign of all the kingdoms of the earth (Deut 28:25), together with the denial of the reality of other gods (2 Sam 8:22). It is not surprising that the account of the Assyrian treatment of other cults lacks nuance (see Cogan 1974, 15–20), but it offered an occasion for anti-idolatry polemic in terms familiar from Deuteronomy (4:28; 28:36, 64; 29:17) and the so-called Second Isaiah (40:18–20; 41:6–7, 21–24, 28–29; 44:6–8, 9–20; 45:16–17). The prayer ends by repeating the petition and the confessional formula (*Bekenntisformel*) of the type "so that X may know (acknowledge) . . . ," of frequent occurrence in Ezekiel and in evidence in other post-disaster texts (e.g. Isa 45:3b).

37:21–38. If we read chs. 36–37 as a seamless narrative, we would have to conclude that Hezekiah was no more convinced by Isaiah's reassuring statement (37:5–7) than his predecessor Ahaz, so that another oracle had to be delivered. At any rate, Isaiah does make a second appearance in the narrative, knows telepathically of Hezekiah's prayer, and delivers a second oracle with a positive prognosis for the immediate future. Since 21 calls for a saying addressed to Hezekiah rather than Sennacherib, and since in that situation of crisis the recital of a fairly long poem would be inappropriate and incongruous, most commentators accept that 22–29 has been inserted, no doubt to give greater prominence to Isaiah and to answer taunt with taunt. The placing of the sign (30–32) at this point is also problematic, since the purpose of a sign is to reinforce the validity of an oracle already delivered (as 7:3–16). It may have been connected with the first oracle of Isaiah at an earlier stage, since the idea of the remnant occurs only here (37:31) and in the B[1] version (37:4); or, alternatively, the editor may have read it as confirming the prediction of Sennacherib's defeat in the previous verse (37:29). However this may be, 33a ("this, therefore, is the word of Yahveh concerning the king of Assyria") should be read as resumptive of 22a ("this is the word that Yahveh has spoken concerning him") and the saying in 33b–35 as the one announced in 22a.

The poetic response to Sennacherib's insulting diatribes (21–29) follows a pattern familiar throughout Isa 1–35 of quoting the boastful words of the enemy (24–25) and then the refutation (26–29 cf. 10:8–11, 13–14 followed by 10:15–19). The counter-taunt is put in the mouth of the woman Zion/Jerusalem, with the implication of the scornful rejection of a clumsy attempt at seduction—one of the earliest examples of this metaphoric use of the language of siege warfare so common in French novels of the early modern period. The tossing of the head therefore indicates not sorrow (Cogan and Tadmor 1988, 237) but contempt (cf. Pss 22:8; 109:25). The heinous nature of the blasphemy is indicated by the use of the designation "the Holy One of Israel" (*qĕdôš yiśrā'ēl*), of particularly frequent occurrence in the exilic section of the book (chs. 40–55) and, interestingly enough, in the sayings dealing with the Assyrian campaign of 701 B.C.E. (30:11, 12, 15; 31:1).

The words put into Sennacherib's mouth (24–25) provide a third opportunity for boasting, this time with respect to Assyrian penetration into the Lebanon range to secure timber (cf. *ANET*, 276, 291), the provision of water, and (with obvious hyperbole) the drying up of the branches of the Nile (cf. 19:5–10; 51:10). (It will be obvious that ecological awareness was not well developed in ancient Assyria.) The reply (26–29) opens with a type of formulaic rhetorical question ("have you not heard?") attested in the so-called Second Isaiah (40:21–24, similar also in content, and 40:28–31) and introducing the theme of the plan or agenda of Yahveh with respect to the nations and Assyria in particular (cf. 10:5–6; 20:15–16; 30:1). The implication is that the rise and fall of Assyria (its "rising up and sitting down") were planned and preordained from the beginning of time and that the prophet's contemporaries are about to witness the consummation of that plan. The concluding image draws on the cruel practice of putting a metal ring through the cheeks or lips of prisoners (see, e.g., the Assyrian relief of Esarhaddon with a Tyrian and Egyptian ruler held on a leash attached to a ring through the lips, *ANEP*, 447), expressive of how the author would like to see the campaign brought to a close.

To judge by the closely parallel 7:14–16, the sign (37:30–32) had the purpose of providing a guarantee of the truth of the prophetic word as well as motivation for acting in accordance with it. The message is that you will be able to resume the normal agricultural processes in the third year, after the loss of two harvests caused by the Assyrian army's living off the land, destroying what they did not eat, and driving the population (200,150 of them, according to the doubtless exaggerated statistics of the Rassam Cylinder) away from their homes. But by that time Sennacherib would have been long gone and the prophetic prediction seen to be fulfilled (37:7, 29, 34). We must therefore take it in a more general sense of a reassurance that Judah will survive just as the good

earth survives devastation and continues to flourish in spite of human exploitation (cf. 27:6; Mic 5:7–8). Isa 37:32a ("from Jerusalem a remnant shall go forth,
and survivors from Mount Zion") reads like a programmatic statement and
may have been added some time in the Second Commonwealth period (cf.
4:2–3; Mic 4:7), though the text does not speak of a remnant *returning* (cf.
10:20–23). The final statement (v 32b) is also found at the conclusion of the
poem on the birth of the future king, perhaps referring to Hezekiah, who is
here being addressed (see commentary on 8:23–9:6[9:1–7]).

As I noted above, the solemnly formulated oracle in vv 33–35 at one time
formed the sequel to 37:22, and in the final state of chs. 36–37 it is the third
prediction of Sennacherib's return to his own country. The colophon *ně'um
YHVH* implies that the following verse (35) is an addendum, perhaps suggested by Yahveh's decision to protect Jerusalem in 31:5. The oracle is peremp-
tory: there will be no attack on the city, no siege ramp of the kind still visible at
Lachish (*tell ed-duweir*), and Sennacherib will not enter the city—this last is
stated at the beginning and repeated at the end for emphasis. The addendum
(35) is explanatory rather than oracular. In God there can be no distinction between disinterestedness and self-interest. When God acts, whether to blot out
sin, to save, or to punish, he always acts for his own sake or for his name's sake
(cf. 43:25; 48:9). The specific point where the self-interest of Yahveh coincides
with Israelite (Judean) self-interest is the Davidic dynasty as the focus of national aspirations. This is a Deuteronomistic topos (1 Kgs 11:13, 34; 15:4; 2 Kgs
8:9), and therefore suggests that v 35 originated among the people in the years
following the disaster of 586 B.C.E. who anticipated the restoration of the Davidic dynasty.

If, as I suggested above, the final scene of the assassination of Sennacherib
served as the original conclusion to B[1], the editor did well to use it for the
grand finale of his story. The intervention of the angel of Yahveh (a nocturnal
intervention according to 2 Kgs 19:35) illustrates the element of the *sudden* in
the way the divine can irrupt into human lives (cf. 29:5), as well as the conviction that this can happen without any detectable human agency (cf. 29:6;
31:8). According to the Passover *sēder* it was "the Destroying Angel" (*hammašḥît*) who spread death throughout the land of Egypt (Exod 12:23), and the
same agent of destruction struck Jerusalem in the form of a plague (2 Sam
24:16–17) because of David's taking a census of the population of his kingdom.
Some commentators have understandably but gratuitously followed Josephus
(*Ant.* 10.19–21) in assuming that it was also a plague that wiped out the Assyrian army. The assassination of Sennacherib is confirmed by the Babylonian
Chronicle (III 34–38) and a tradition recorded in a Nabonidus text (*ANET*,
309), though it took place twenty years later. That he was cut down while at his
devotions before his god Nisroch, a deity otherwise unknown and perhaps fictitious but at any rate helpless to intervene, is the author's final twist of the
knife.

HEZEKIAH'S SICKNESS AND RECOVERY (38:1–22)

(Ackroyd 1974; 1982; Barré; Begrich; Catastani 1983; 1993; Jeremias; Ognibene 1992; Seitz 1991, 149–66, 172–82; Williamson 1994, 202–8; Yadin)

TRANSLATION

38 [1]At that time Hezekiah fell sick and was close to death. The prophet Isaiah ben Amoz came and said to him, "This is what Yahveh has said: 'Put the affairs of your household in order for you are going to die; you will not recover.'" [2]Hezekiah turned his face[a] to the wall and prayed to Yahveh: [3]"Remember, Yahveh, I beseech you, how I have conducted myself in your presence faithfully and wholeheartedly, and how I have done what pleases you." And Hezekiah wept copious tears.

[4]Then the word of Yahveh came to Isaiah:[b] [5]"Go[c] and tell Hezekiah:[d] 'This is what Yahveh, God of David your ancestor, has said: I have heard your prayer, I have seen your tears. I will add[e] fifteen years to your life span. [6]I will also rescue you and this city from the grasp of the king of Assyria, and I will defend this city.[f] [7][g]This is the sign for you from Yahveh that Yahveh will bring about what he has promised.

[8]When the sun sets on the stairway to the upper room of Ahaz,[h] I will turn backwards a distance of ten steps the shadow on the stairs. The light from the setting sun went back ten steps on the stairway.'"[i]

[9]A composition of Hezekiah king of Judah written after he had recovered from his sickness.

[10]I thought, in the prime of life[j]
I must depart,
consigned to the gates of Sheol
for the rest of my days.
[11]I thought, Yahveh[k] no longer will I behold
in the land of the living,
no longer look on mortals
with the people who inhabit the world.[l]
[12]My dwelling is plucked up, removed from over my head[m]
like a shepherd's tent;
I have gathered up[n] my life like a weaver;
he cuts me off from the loom.
All day long, all night long, you consume me.[o]
[13]I cry for help[p] until the morning.
Like a lion he breaks all my bones,[q]

¹⁴like a swallow or a thrush^r I chirp,
I moan like a dove,
my eyes are worn out^s from looking upwards;
O Lord, take up my cause,^t be my surety!
¹⁵What can I say? for he has addressed me,^u
it is he who did it.^v
I toss to and fro^w all the time I am sleeping
because of the bitterness of my soul.
¹⁶Lord, those to whom you give life will live,
all these have the spirit of life;^x
restore me, let me live!

¹⁷Bitterness was my lot instead of peace,^y
but now in love you have preserved my life
from the pit of destruction;^z
for you have cast all my sins
behind your back.
¹⁸Sheol cannot thank you,
death cannot praise you;
those who go down to the abyss
cannot hope for your faithfulness.
¹⁹It is the living, the living that will thank you
as I do this day.
The father makes known to the children
how faithful you are.
²⁰Yahveh is here to save us,^{aa}
let us make music with psalms of praise
all the days of our life in the house of Yahveh.

²¹Then Isaiah said, "Let them take a cake of figs and apply it to the boil."
[They did so] and he recovered.^{bb}

²²Said Hezekiah, "What is the sign assuring me that I will go up to the
house of Yahveh?"^{cc}

NOTES

Variations from the parallel 2 Kgs 20:1–11 are noted.   ^a 2 Kgs 20:2 omits
ḥizqîyahû, which however is in LXX, Syr., Tg.;   ^b 2 Kgs 20:4: "Before Isaiah
had gone out of the inner court the word of Yahveh came to him" (emended
text; see BHS ad loc.);   ^c 2 Kgs 20:5: *šûb* ("go back");   ^d 2 Kgs 20:5 adds:
něgîd 'ammî ("leader of my people");   ^e read *yôsēp* (participle) for MT *yôsîp*
cf. 2 Kgs 20:6 *věhosaptî*; 2 Kgs 20:5 adds: "I am going to heal you; on the third
day you will go up to the house of Yahveh";   ^f 2 Kgs 20:6 and 1QIsa^a add:
"for my own sake and for the sake of my servant David" cf. 19:34. The following

verse 2 Kgs 20:7, as also 1QIsa[a] = Isa 38:21; [g] 2 Kgs 20:8a adds: "Hezekiah said to Isaiah, 'What is the sign that Yahveh will heal me so that I may go up to the house of Yahveh on the third day?' Isaiah replied . . ."; [h] inserting *ʿălîyat* with 1QIsa[a]; [i] 2 Kgs 20:9b–11: "The shadow has progressed along ten steps. Will it go backward ten steps? Hezekiah replied, 'It is easy for the shadow to lengthen ten steps; let the shadow rather go backward ten steps.' The prophet Isaiah cried out to Yahveh and Yahveh turned the shadow backward the ten steps it had progressed down the stairway of Ahaz"; [j] *bidĕmî yāmay*, literally, "at the halfway point of my days" → *dĕmî* = "half, halfway" (hapax) rather than → *dmh* = "to be still, quiet" or → *dmm* = "lament" (Kaiser 1974, 398: "in the misery of my days"), unattested; [k] MT *yâ yâ*, short, poetic form of *YHVH* repeated cf. *yâ YHVH* 12:2 and 26:4; 1QIsa[a] has *yah*; [l] *ḥedel* hapax → verb *ḥdl* = "cease (to exist)" but emend to *ḥeled* = "world" cf. the same textual confusion in Ps 49:2 and 89:48; [m] *dôr* is hapax with this meaning, with possible exception of 53:8a; [n] *qpd* is hapax, perhaps "roll up" cf. *qippod* = "hedgehog," 14:23; 34:11; 1QIsa[a] has *sprty—sippartî* cf. NEB "thou hast cut short my life like a weaver"; [o] an attempt to render *šlm* Hiphil; for NEB "torment" see G. R. Driver 1968, 56; [p] read *šivvaʿtî* for MT *šivvîtî*; 1QIsa[a]: *spvty*; [q] MT adds, by dittography, "all day long, all night long, you consume me"; [r] read *kĕsîs* for MT *kĕsûs*, "like a horse," and for MT *ʿāgûr* read *vĕʿāgûr*, though this word may have slipped in from Jer 8:7; here and elsewhere in Isaiah, animal and bird names are often uncertain; [s] *dallû* → *dll* = "to be weak"; [t] MT *ʿošqâ-lî* = "I am oppressed," but *ʿośqâ-lî* = "take up my cause" (cf. Gen 26:20) fits the context better; [u] MT *vĕʾāmar-lî* cf. 1QIsa[a] *vʾymr-li* cf. Tg.: "but what praise can I speak and say before him?"; [v] 1QIsa[a] adds *lî*, perhaps by dittography with *lî* on the same line; [w] MT *ʾeddaddeh* cf. 1QIsa[a] *ʾdvdh* → *ndd* "wander" cf. Job 7:4 *nĕdudîm* = "restlessness," rather than → *ddh* (Ps 42:5); [x] an unavoidably speculative attempt to make sense of MT "O Lord, to them (masc.) they will live and to all in them (fem.) the life of my spirit," which is unintelligible and the line seriously corrupt; cf. the discussion and very different translation in Duhm 1892, 281–82; [y] either delete the second *mar* or replace with *mĕʾod* cf. 1QIsa[a] *mʾvdh*; [z] for MT *miššaḥat bĕlî* 1QIsa[a] has *miššaḥat kĕlî* = "from the pit of annihilation"; [aa] read *lĕhôšîʿēnû* for MT *lĕhôšîʿēnî*; [bb] "They did so" is added to make it clear that *vĕyeḥî* belongs with the construct chain and should not therefore be translated "that he may live" cf. 2 Kgs 20:7; [cc] 38:21–22 = 2 Kgs 20:7–8.

COMMENTS

According to the basic version in the History (2 Kgs 20:1–11), Hezekiah lay dangerously ill and Isaiah, either spontaneously or summoned by the king, came and advised him that he was about to die and should therefore make his final dispositions. The same expression (*ṣivvāh lābayit*) is used of Ahithophel before his death, 2 Sam 17:23, and what it involved can be seen in David's final instructions on his deathbed, including arrangements to benefit friends and relatives and a moral exhortation to offspring (1 Kgs 2:1–9). Hezekiah prayed that he might recover, and his prayer was answered immediately; Isaiah was inspired to return as he was about to leave the palace, and in the name of Yahveh he promised the king recovery within three days and fifteen additional years of life. To this was attached an assurance that Jerusalem would survive the Assyrian attack. Isaiah instructed attendants to apply a fig poultice (figs were widely believed to have a curative as well as aphrodisiac capacity), and Hezekiah's request for a sign confirming the truth of the predictions was met by a miracle worked by Isaiah after praying to Yahveh. Hezekiah's recovery is not stated but is implied in the episode immediately following (20:12).

Isaiah 38:1–22 comprises a filled-out version of the Historian's account (2 Kgs 20:1–11), with one or two significant differences. In the latter, Hezekiah requests a sign and insists on its miraculous character, but in the Isa 38 version, he does neither. The request for a sign has however been tagged on at the end by an assiduous scribe concerned not to miss anything (38:22), but it is not part of the story. The omission doubtless had the purpose of highlighting the piety of the king by contrast with the faithless Ahaz (7:10–16) and therefore represents a further stage in the religious rehabilitation of Hezekiah. The application of the fig poultice that precedes the sign in the History follows it here, the miraculous sign takes place without the prophet's prayer, and the king's recovery is explicitly noted. The promise of a visit to the temple on the third day is omitted, but it probably suggested the inclusion of a psalm of thanksgiving uttered by the king, presumably in the temple. The Targum tells us that when he was dying Hezekiah turned his face to the wall of the sanctuary, thereby circumventing the promise to visit the temple.

In both versions the assurance of recovery is accompanied by the assurance that the city will be saved (2 Kgs 20:6; Isa 38:6); the king's sickness therefore antedates the events recorded in 2 Kgs 18:13–19:37 = Isa 36–37. The same is true of the visit of the Babylonian delegation, which took place during the king's convalescence. The arrangement of the three accounts is therefore dictated by considerations other than chronological. The vague temporal indications introducing the second and the third ("in those days," "at that time") would in fact suggest that they formed part of a longer *catena* of prophetic *legenda* featuring Isaiah. We come across similarly vague incipits in earlier prophetic stories (e.g. 1 Kgs 14:1) and similar lack of chronological sequencing, for example, in the Elijah narrative cycle. The narrative pattern of the healing story is, however, similar to the narrative pattern of the first of the three episodes in chs. 36–37: there exists a critical situation—the pious monarch goes to the temple and prays—the prophet Isaiah intervenes—a miracle occurs—there is a successful outcome.

Since the Isaian version is organized around the psalm of thanksgiving that occupies most of its length, it is interesting to note that no explicit connection is made between sickness and sin. The normal pattern for this kind of typescene can be inferred from another psalm of thanksgiving, Ps 107: someone is sick and near death on account of having sinned—the sick person prays and is healed by the word of God—there follow thanksgiving and sacrifice with singing and music in the temple. This is what we find in the Isaian version except that Hezekiah makes no confession of sin, and the connection between sickness and sin comes up only in passing in the psalm (38:17b). Even the author of Chronicles, who is quick to detect such connections, does not make it in this instance, though he does attribute disasters that lay in the future to Hezekiah's pride (2 Chr 32:24–26). The author of the Isaian version would presumably not have agreed with the Rabshakeh's accusations of impiety directed at Hezekiah, but the sickness-sin link must surely be lurking in the background. According to Jer 26:17–19 the destruction of Jerusalem predicted by Micah (3:12) was averted, or postponed, after Hezekiah repented and heeded the prophetic warning. Here, too, the king prays—the prophet intervenes—and the result is a postponement of the king's death by 15 years and a postponement of the destruction of the city by 115 years. Reading between the lines of both incidents, the healing and the visit of the Babylonian legates, we detect traces of an earlier and less favorable interpretation of Hezekiah's character and activities.

Concerning the source of the basic story line: the Historian's hagiographical portrayal of Hezekiah, one of his heroes, has incorporated a popular story about a miraculous healing, one of several such prophetic *legenda* that have gone into the History (e.g. 2 Kgs 4:8–37; 5:1–19a; also a refusal to heal in 2 Kgs 1:2–17). The type-scene is well attested and familiar: someone is sick—the wonderworking prophet is asked to intervene—the healing is accompanied by certain acts and the use of certain materials (e.g. flour, water, a fig compress)—the success of the healing is verified in some way (e.g. the beneficiary is able to walk, visit the temple, go home)—and the reaction of witnesses is recorded ("we never saw the like," "how does this man do it?"). In drawing on a cycle of stories about Isaiah the prophet, wonder-worker, and holy man, the Historian launched a biographical tradition that would be taken up by the Chronicler (2 Chr 32), Ben Sira (Sir 48:20–25), Josephus (*Ant.* 10.11–35) and *The Martyrdom of Isaiah*. The parallel between Micah and Isaiah (designated a *nābî'* only in these narratives) also suggests the possibility that stories of healing and miracle-working by an anonymous figure associated with Hezekiah were at some point drawn, like iron filings to a magnet, into a dominant Isaian tradition.

The story of Hezekiah's sickness, near-death experience, recovery, and subsequent liturgical celebration may well have been read in the post-destruction period as foreshadowing the experience of the people, and we saw that the parallelism between the fate of Hezekiah and that of the Judean people was an aspect, if not of the explicit literary strategy that dictated the inclusion of chs. 36–39 in the book (Ackroyd 1987,165–66; 1982, 113; Williamson 1994, 202–3, 206–7), then at least of the implicit content of the incident. Also implicit but nearer the surface is the contrast between the death of the Assyrian king and the recovery from death of the Judean king as foreshadowing the respective destinies of their peoples in a proximate future. This may be seen to support the view of scholars who date the inclusion of this incident, perhaps also the one preceding it, to the reign of Josiah, when the Assyrian Empire entered a phase of irreversible decline. As is usually the case, however, other possibilities can be entertained. It is more important to note that the inclusion of this incident, with Hezekiah's psalm as its centerpiece, places this powerful theme of the prospect of death and the possibility of deliverance from death firmly at the core of this section, chs. 36–39 as a whole.

38:1–8. The account of Hezekiah's sickness and recovery, introduced by a vague temporal indication (bayyāmîm hahēm, "in those days"), should logically precede the survival of Jerusalem (38:6; 39:1) but is placed after it in order to bring Hezekiah's rescue from death into immediate juxtaposition with the violent and untimely death of Sennacherib (37:38). Isaiah is designated a nābî' only in the brief legenda in this section of the book (37:2; 38:1; 39:3) in which, correspondingly, he is depicted as a holy man ('îs 'ĕlohîm) and wonder-worker ('îs ma'ăśeh), a kinder, gentler version of Elijah or Elisha. It seems that the Historian has drawn on narrative material, originally perhaps circulating orally, which profiled an Isaiah very different from the Isaiah of the diatribes and threats of imminent disaster. The prediction of the king's imminent demise and its later abrogation illustrate the theological point that God remains free to act even after the prophetic word has been uttered (cf. 2 Sam 7:3–4; 12:13–14 and of course Jonah). A classic example, and one particularly close to the situation described in the first of these three episodes, is the prediction of the destruction of Jerusalem attributed to Micah and revoked after Hezekiah entreated the favor of Yahveh (Mic 3:12; Jer 26:18–19), one of several indications of close linkage in the transmission of Isaiah and Micah. Here, too, in the three episodes under discussion, Hezekiah is a man of prayer (37:14–20; 38:3, 9–20). The language of his brief prayer when at the point of death is characteristically Deuteronomistic: to be "wholeheartedly," bĕlēb šālēm, true to Yahveh is a criterion by which kings are judged in the History (1 Kgs 8:61; 11:4; 15:3, 14). It therefore suited the Historian's idealized portrait of Hezekiah as a devout and just ruler after the manner of David.

The scribe who adapted the Historian's version intended to set in bolder relief the contrast between Ahaz and Hezekiah and therefore omitted the request for a sign and the choice of the kind of miracle to be performed. (For the sign offered to Ahaz see the commentary on 7:11.) An explanation that is feasible for the shadow miracle is relegated to commentary on Kings, but we may at least exclude correlation with the solar eclipse of January 11, 689 B.C.E., since the date is wrong and it is difficult to see how the phenomenon of an eclipse fits the description of the miracle. Since the text says nothing about the measurement of time, it also seems better to take ma'ălôt in its normal meaning of a stairway (as in 1QIsaᵃ) than as referring to the face of a sundial.

38:9–22. The psalm attributed to Hezekiah belongs to the familiar type of thanksgiving hymn for deliverance from danger and death (e.g. Ps 107) and contains nothing peculiar to Hezekiah's situation. Its secondary attribution to Hezekiah fits the tradition of literary activity during his reign attested in the compilation of aphorisms of the "men of Hezekiah" (Prov 25:1) and in the rabbinic tradition of Hezekiah as author or redactor of several compositions including (surprisingly) the book of Isaiah (*b. B. Bat.* 15a). The economic, demographic, and cultural development in late eighth and early seventh century Judah indicated by recent archaeological discoveries suggests that these hints of increased literary activity at that time may have some historical foundation. This conclusion would stand whether the rubric introducing the psalm is read as *miktāb* ("writing," "composition") as in MT or, with BHS and several commentators, *miktām* (a type of "Davidic" psalm, Pss 16 and 56–60). The insertion of this psalm in the narrative is in keeping with an understandable impulse to dwell on the moment of release from mortal danger by divine intervention. We may compare the psalm of Jonah recited in the inside of the fish, which also ends with praise and thanksgiving according to the temple liturgy.

The transition from lamentation to thanksgiving and praise occurs with the prayer and (implicit) confession of sin in 16–17. Up to this turning point the psalmist dwells on death and the anticipation of death under a variety of metaphors and figures familiar especially from Psalms and Job. To die is, simply, to depart (cf. Ps 39:14 "turn your gaze from me . . . before I depart and am no more") but without the prospect of returning (Job 7:9–10; 10:21). It is to pass through a gate or door (cf. Ps 9:14; 107:18; Job 38:17) into a dark house (Job 30:23), a figure familiar from the Sumerian *Descent of Ishtar* and Dante's *Inferno*. Apart from the standard designation šĕ'ôl (Sheol) for the realm of death, it is also known as the underworld ('ereṣ, e.g. Pss 22:30; 63:10; Jonah 2:7[6]), the pit (šaḥat, bôr e.g. Pss 16:10; 28:1; Job 17:14), the region dark and deep (Ps 88:7). It connotes silence (Ps 115:17), sleep (Ps 13:4; Job 3:13), and darkness (Ps 88:13; Job 10:22). Death may also be personified as Belial (Ps 18:5) and Abaddon (Ps 88:12; Job 26:6; 28:22; 31:12). The author of the Hezekian psalm adds his own variations on the theme. To die is to strike camp or, more likely, to find your tent pulled down over your head. As the rapid movement of the weaver's shuttle can stand for the brevity of life (Job 7:6), so the gathering or rolling up of the woven cloth and cutting the thread attaching it to the loom signifies the end of life. The twittering, chattering, and moaning bird sounds could be an anticipation of the sounds emitted by the ghosts and shades of the dead (as in Isa 8:19), reproducing an ancient topos of the dead as bird-like, e.g., in Enkidu's dark dream of the underworld in *Gilgamesh*.

A recurring theme in liturgical prayers for deliverance from death, and one of the most disconcerting for the contemporary Jewish or Christian believer, is that death means the end of association with the believer's God. Death is the land of forgetfulness. The dead not only lose all memory of their lives (e.g. Ps 6:6) but God forgets them (Ps 88:6). Death is feared not least because it excludes the possibility of praising and thanking God, a consideration that allows the psalmist a certain *captatio benevolentiae* in praying, since the deity is also diminished in a way by the diminution of the sum total of liturgical praise (e.g. Ps 6:6; 30:10; 88:11; 115:17). No longer to be able to look on Yahveh (38:11 cf. Pss 11:7; 17:15; 27:4, 13; 88:5) means no longer to be able to participate in temple worship. Hence the conclusion of the psalm in music and singing in the temple as a form of thanksgiving, certainly, but also as an affirmation of life. The intense experience of divine presence in the act of worship may have contributed to a change in attitude towards post mortem existence (e.g. Ps 73:16–28).

The conclusion to the story records the king's recovery (see textual note) following the application of the fig poultice. That figs were and are thought (perhaps correctly) to have curative properties, e.g., among Arabs and Turks, reminds us that the recovery is not explicitly represented as miraculous even though effected through prophetic intervention. The translation "boil" for šĕḥîn is probably incorrect since people afflicted with a boil are not generally in danger of death, but in the absence of further information speculation on the nature of Hezekiah's illness would be pointless.

A BABYLONIAN DELEGATION
VISITS HEZEKIAH (39:1–8)

(Ackroyd 1974; Begg 1986; 1987; Brinkman; Clements 1983; Seitz 1991, 182–91; Sweeney 1996; 505–11)

TRANSLATION

39 [1]At that time Merodach-Baladan[a] son of Baladan king of Babylon sent envoys[b] with a gift to Hezekiah, for[c] he had heard that he had recovered[d] from his illness. [2]Hezekiah made them welcome.[e] He showed them all[f] his treasury, silver and gold, spices and precious oil, his armory and everything in his storerooms. There was nothing in his palace and in all his realm[g] that Hezekiah did not show them.

[3]Then the prophet Isaiah approached Hezekiah and asked him, "What did these people say, and where did they come from to you?" "They came to me from a distant land, from Babylon," replied Hezekiah. [4]Then Isaiah asked, "And what did they see in your palace?" "They saw everything in my palace," replied Hezekiah. "There was nothing in my store rooms that I did not show them." [5]Isaiah then said to Hezekiah, "Hear the word of Yahveh of the hosts:[h] [6]The time is coming , says Yahveh, when everything in your palace and everything that has been accumulated by your forebears down to the present will be carried off to Babylon.[i] Not a thing will be left. [7]They will also take some of your male descendants who will issue from you,[j] whom you will beget, and they will be made eunuchs in the palace of the king of Babylon." 8 Hezekiah said to Isaiah, "The word of Yahveh that you have spoken is positive." He was thinking: "So long as there is peace and security in my lifetime."[k]

NOTES

Variations from the parallel 2 Kgs 20:12–19 are noted.   [a] 2 Kgs 20:12: bĕrodak for Isaian (also LXX, Syr., Tg., Vulg.) mĕrodak;   [b] 2 Kgs 20:12 also reads *sĕpārîm* = "letters," "dispatches" (cf. LXX *epistolas*, Vulg. *libros*); some MSS read *sôpĕrîm* = "scribes"; perhaps *sĕpîrîm* cf. Akk. *šapîru* = "envoy"; *sarîsîm* = "eunuchs" (Duhm 1892, 284) is unwarranted; LXX adds *kai presbeis*, "and elders"; ᶜ *kî šāmaʿ* 2 Kgs 20:12 for MT *vayyišmaʿ*; ᵈ 2 Kgs 20:12: *ḥizqîyāhû* for Isaian *vayyeḥĕzāq* cf. 1QIsaᵃ *vyḥyh* = "but had lived" (survived); ᵉ 2 Kgs 20:3: *vayyišmaʿ* = "he heard"; a careless scribal error; ᶠ *kol*, absent from MT, is supplied from 2 Kgs 20:13 and 1QIsaᵃ; the second *kol* in this verse, *vĕ'ēt kol-bēt kēlâv*, is missing from 2 Kgs 20:13; ᵍ 1QIsaᵃ: *mmlktv*, "his kingdom"; ʰ *ṣĕbaʾôt* absent from 2 Kgs 20:16; ⁱ 1QIsaᵃ *vnśʾv* (pl.) for *vĕniśśaʾ* and adds another verb, *ybyʾv*, "they will bring"; 4QIsaᵇ: *bb]lh* for *bābel*; ʲ MT, 2 Kgs 20:18 and 4QIsaᵇ: *mimmĕkâ*; 1QIsaᵃ: *mmʿykh* = "from your loins"; ᵏ following 2 Kgs 20:19: *hălô' 'im-šālôm* . . . rather than a literal translation of MT: "he (Hezekiah or Isaiah?) [had] said that there would be peace and security in my days".

COMMENTS

This third and last episode illustrates the boldness of the *nābî'* (Elijah, Micaiah, Elisha, Isaiah) vis-à-vis the ruler, a salient characteristics of the prophetic *legenda* incorporated into the History. The structure is simple. Hezekiah's favorable reception of the delegation together with the display of his wealth is described (1–2); Isaiah the *nābî'* appears on the scene, asks two questions and gets two answers (3–4); the interrogation of the monarch leads to an oracular utterance introduced in the standard way predicting exile for Hezekiah's descendants and his court, and Hezekiah's reaction to it is recorded (5–8). The visit of the Babylonian envoys had to be the last of the three episodes if Isaiah was to predict successfully peace and security for the rest of the reign and if a connection was to be made with the announcement of the end of exile predicted by the prophet. If the purpose of the visit was to console Hezekiah in his convalescence it would also of course have to follow the story of the sickness and healing, though the Masoretic Text of 39:1 assumes that they learned about his condition only after arriving (see notes on the text). That Hezekiah's treasure had recently gone to buy off the Assyrians and would therefore not have been available to impress the Babylonians (2 Kgs 18:14–16) creates an obvious problem for the Historian but not for the author of the B version or the editor of Isaiah chs. 36–39, who simply bypasses this (more historically plausible) version of events.

Before looking more closely at the episode in 39:1–8 and Isaiah's role in it, it will be useful to see how it functions in the History (2 Kgs 20:12–19). There is no connection between the eunuchs who will function at the Babylonian court (39:7) and those threatened with expulsion from the community on the basis of Deuteronomic law (Isa 56:3–5; Deut 23:2[1]), and it is not necessary to place the composition of the episode in the Persian period because of the presence of eunuchs at the Persian court or the absence of a strong sense of sorrow and grieving (Kaiser 1974, 410). There were eunuchs at other courts including

the one in Jerusalem (2 Kgs 24:12, 15). We are also not obliged to date its composition between the first and second Babylonian capture of the city on the
grounds of its failure to mention the fate of the temple (Clements 1980a, 294),
since the temple is either not mentioned at all or mentioned only incidentally
in other predictions of the fall of Jerusalem. The Historian, nevertheless,
clearly indicates that the fulfillment of Isaiah's prediction was the first assault
on Jerusalem in 597 B.C.E. resulting in the deportation of Jehoiachin together
with his *sārîsîm* ("eunuchs," "officials") and the confiscation of his treasures—
all of which happened "as Yahveh had said" (2 Kgs 24:10–17). As the story is
told in both versions, however, Hezekiah is the unwitting occasion of the
prophecy and the prophetically predetermined disaster to follow but not its
efficient cause. The strategy of the Historian is, rather, to put the burden of
responsibility for the disaster on Manasseh and to exonerate Hezekiah and
Josiah, and this is done by means of prophecies in which judgment is postponed, a technique first used to explain the division of the kingdom after Solomon's reign (1 Kgs 11:11–13). The innocent Hezekiah is granted peace and
security for the balance of his reign, but disaster will follow in due course. A
close parallel is recourse to the prophet Huldah after the discovery of the law
book during Josiah's reign. She exonerates Josiah from blame and grants him
(erroneously it seems) a peaceful end because he wept and, presumably,
prayed, as Hezekiah had done before him, but here too the prospect for the
more distant future is bleak (2 Kgs 22:15–20). During Manasseh's reign, prophets held him responsible for the destruction of Jerusalem to follow (2 Kgs
21:10–15), and his guilt is emphasized at later points in the narrative (23:26–27;
24:3–4). We are reminded of the programmatic presentation in Ezek 18:5–18 of
the three generations—good, bad, good (cf. Hezekiah, Manasseh, Josiah)—and
their respective fates.

This is the overt and ostensible meaning assigned to the incident within the
ideological framework imposed by the Historian on the events leading to the
end of Judah's independent existence. Beneath the surface of the narrative,
however, and not far beneath the surface, we can detect indications of a different interpretative framework. The *ostensible* reason for the visit, to console a
convalescing monarch 400 miles away, strains credulity only slightly less than
the reason given by the Chronicler (2 Chr 32:31)—namely, the scientific curiosity of the Babylonian princes about the miracle of the shadow. No reason is
given for Hezekiah's display of his wealth. He may simply have been incredibly
naive, but a more plausible reason is the intent to demonstrate his resources as
a credible ally of Babylon in Merodach-Baladan's long struggle against Assyria.
We know, and the Historian would probably have known, that Merodach-
Baladan (Marduk-apal-iddina II) had revolted against Assyria and that his revolt was over by 703 B.C.E. Hence the delegation to Jerusalem, if it took place,
would have had to take place before that date. We cannot fail to detect a note
of suspicion and hostility in the two questions put to Hezekiah by Isaiah, and
the oracular utterance that follows, though lacking any overt condemnation of
the king, is no less unconditionally negative than other judgment sayings

throughout the book. It seems therefore that an original prophetic condemnation of Hezekiah's planned alliance with Babylon, similar to condemnations of overtures to Egypt in chs. 28–33, has been rewritten in the interest of the Historian's rehabilitation of Hezekiah. One indication of Deuteronomistic editing can be seen when Hezekiah tells Isaiah that the envoys had come "from a distant land" (*mē'ereṣ rĕḥôqâ*); this expression is used exclusively by Deuteronomist writers and in the context either of treaty-making (Josh 9:6, 9) or of foreigners' coming to view the disasters inflicted on Judah (Deut 29:21 [29:22]; 1 Kgs 8:41).

On the historical background, little need be added to the commentary on previous passages dealing with this critical period in the history of Judah (18:1–7; 20:1–6 and 30:1–5). The visit of Babylonian envoys to Jerusalem is set in the context of the struggle of Marduk-apal-iddina for independence from Assyria in southern Mesopotamia, where he ruled from 720 to 709 and again, briefly, in 703. Such a visit is not independently attested but is compatible with Babylonian attempts to draw Syrian, Phoenician, Transjordanian, and southern Palestinian states into an anti-Assyrian alliance. This was the situation during the Babylonian revolt of 703 supported passively by the Nubian Shabako and rather more actively by Judah, a revolt that ended with the complete defeat of Marduk-apal-iddina and his retreat into Elam, which exposed the small western states including Judah to the full weight of the Assyrian military machine. If this is the background to the episode, the diplomatic mission of the Babylonians described here, whether historical or fictitious, would align historically with overtures between Judah and Egypt denounced by Isaiah earlier in the book (18:1–19:17; 30:1–7; 31:1–3).

On matters of detail: Merodach is probably a dysphemism or distortion of Marduk (the imperial Babylonian deity) formed with the vowels of the participle *mĕqullal*, "cursed"; Baladan appears to be a very corrupt version of *apal-iddan*, implying a request for a son. As stated, the real object of the visit and gift-giving was to draw Judah into an anti-Assyrian alliance, and Hezekiah's response was intended as proof of the adequacy of his economic and military resources (not, however, of his wine cellar, pace Dahood 1959, 162–63). Isaiah's prophecy that all these treasures would end up in Babylon was fulfilled and the fulfillment noted, after the first conquest of Jerusalem in 597 B.C.E. (2 Kgs 24:12–16). Hezekiah's reaction to this disconcerting prophecy will seem laconic to a fault. But rather than explaining his attitude psychologically (after all, he had just recovered from a serious illness), we should see it in the context of a disaster delayed but not removed, as in Huldah's prophecy to Josiah's officials (2 Kgs 22:15–20). We may also credit Hezekiah with the awareness that repentance could change this verdict, as his own prayers and tears had reversed the prediction of imminent death, but the Historian knew only too well that this did not happen.

INDEX OF SUBJECTS

◆

INDEX OF BIBILICAL AND OTHER ANCIENT REFERENCES

◆

INDEX OF KEY HEBREW TERMS

◆